Donizetti

A bust of Donizetti by Piero Brolis

Donizetti

WILLIAM ASHBROOK

CASSELL · LONDON

CASSELL & COMPANY LTD
35 RED LION SQUARE, LONDON WCI
MELBOURNE, SYDNEY, TORONTO
JOHANNESBURG, CAPE TOWN, AUCKLAND

Made and Printed in Great Britain
by Jarrold and Sons Ltd, Norwich
F.1264

To
F. diZ. A.
and
H. B. R.

Contents

ACKNOWLEDGEMENTS   *page* xi

PART ONE

1   THE BEGINNINGS   3
2   LAUNCHING A CAREER   46
3   ESTABLISHING A REPUTATION   114
4   TRIUMPH AND BEREAVEMENT   162
5   WIDENING HORIZONS AND
    GATHERING SHADOWS   222
6   DISINTEGRATION   287
    POSTSCRIPT   349

PART TWO

7   FORM IN DONIZETTI'S OPERAS   353
8   SOME ASPECTS OF DONIZETTI'S
    STYLE   368
9   DONIZETTI'S REVISIONS AND
    SELF-BORROWINGS   413
10 THE LIBRETTISTS AND LIBRETTOS
    OF DONIZETTI'S OPERAS   443
    LIST OF DONIZETTI'S COMPOSI-
    TIONS   499
    BIBLIOGRAPHY   521
    INDEX   533

List of Illustrations

frontispiece

A bust of Donizetti by Piero Brolis (*Photograph supplied by Piero Brolis, Bergamo*)

following page 82

A drawing of Donizetti by an unknown artist dated Rome 1827 and dedicated to Mayr (*Bertarelli Collection, Bergamo*)

Donizetti's birthplace in Borgo Canale, Bergamo (*Reproduced by permission of the Museo Donizettiano, Bergamo*)

Andrea and Domenica, Donizetti's parents. A copy by Teodoro Ghezzi of a drawing by Francesco Coghetti (*Reproduced by permission of the Museo Donizettiano, Bergamo*)

The building where Mayr opened his music school (*Picture supplied by Bruno Zavadini*)

Giovanni Simone Mayr. Portrait by Gaetano Barabini, 1827 (*Reproduced by permission of the Museo Donizettiano, Bergamo*)

Four Bergamasc tenors associated with Donizetti: Giacomo David, Giuseppe Viganoni, Giulio Marco Bordogni, and Andrea Nozzari (*Bertarelli Collection, Bergamo*)

following page 242

Virginia Vasselli Donizetti painted by Teodoro Ghezzi in 1829 (*Reproduced with permission of the Museo Donizettiano, Bergamo*)

Elizabeth (Elisabetta) Ferron, the English prima donna; and Carolina Ungher as Antonina in *Belisario*, 1836 (*Bertarelli Collection, Bergamo*)

Giovanni Battista Rubini, the greatest of the Bergamasc tenors; and Guiditto Pasta, the greatest singing-actress of her generation (*Bertarelli Collection, Bergamo*)

Four singers associated with Donizetti's early operas: Fanny Eckerlin, Rosamunda Pisaroni, Maria Ester Mombelli, and Domenico Donzelli (*Bertarelli Collection, Bergamo*)

ix

Four prominent sopranos associated with Donizetti's operas: Henriette (Enrichetta) Méric-Lalande, Anna Thillon, Fanny Tacchinardi-Persiani, and Giuseppina Ronzi di Begnis (*Bertarelli Collection, Bergamo*)

Jacopo Ferretti, who supplied Donizetti with four texts; and Felice Romani, the most famous theatre-poet of his day (*Pictures supplied by Casa Ricordi, Milan*)

Caricature of Donizetti, drawn by himself in 1841; and Antonio Dolci, a lifelong friend of Donizetti (*Reproduced by permission of the Museo Donizettiano, Bergamo*)

Donizetti's piano which he acquired in 1822 and used until his departure from Naples in 1838 (*Reproduced by permission of the Museo Donizettiano, Bergamo*)

following page 370

Manuscript page from the score of *Il Campanello* (*Photograph supplied by Walter Toscanini from the Collection of the late Maestro Arturo Toscanini*)

Antonio Pourcelot, Donizetti's servant who tended his master faithfully until the day of the composer's death; and a daguerrotype of Donizetti and his nephew Andrea, taken on 3 August 1847 at the avenue Chateaubriand No. 6, Paris (*Reproduced with permission of the Museo Donizettiano, Bergamo*)

Giovannina Rota-Basoni Scotti and her children; and the Palazzo Basoni where Donizetti passed the last months of his life (*Pictures kindly supplied by Baronessa Maria Scotti Perego*)

Singers in some famous Donizetti premières: Rosine Stolz and Louis-Gilbert Duprez in Act 4 of *La favorite*, Celestino Salvatori as Belisario, Luigi Lablache as Doge Marino Faliero, and Giorgio Ronconi as Cardenio in *Il furioso* (*Bertarelli Collection, Milan*)

Acknowledgements

This book has grown out of a lifelong interest in opera. Over the years many people have contributed much that has made the writing of this book possible.

I have two basic debts. First, to Max de Schauensee who has taught me much about opera during our friendship of more than twenty years. Second, to that fine mezzo-soprano Bruna Castagna, whose performance of Leonora in *La favorite*[1] opened my eyes to a new and richer side of Donizetti's art. As a result of her performance I promised myself I would write a book about Donizetti one day.

To Herbert van Thal I am deeply indebted for unfailing assistance and encouragement. Dr Marcello Guidi of the Italian Embassy in Washington made it possible for me to travel to Italy to do basic research for this book. Other material assistance to my studies came by way of Dr Raleigh Holmstedt, President of Indiana State College, and the late Richard Thursfield, former Dean of Faculty there.

In Italy I was treated with unforgettable kindness and generously assisted in finding the materials I needed. Bruno and Anna Maria Zavadini, son and daughter of the late Guido Zavadini, have been unstinting in their friendship and help. All students of Donizetti are forever in their father's debt for his editing of Donizetti's letters. Maestro Giuseppe Cesati, the present Curatore of the Museo Donizettiano in Bergamo, was helpful in countless ways. I am also grateful for the help I

[1] Although this performance was sung in Italian as *La favorita* this opera is referred to throughout this book by its original French title because the music as Donizetti originally composed it was a setting of the French text of Royer and Väez. *La fille du régiment* and *Les Martyrs* (to distinguish the four-act version of *Poliuto* Donizetti made for the Opéra) are also referred to by their French titles, but not *Le duc d'Albe* since Donizetti never completed the score and it has never been performed in French; there I speak of *Il duca d'Alba*.

received from the Director and staff of the Biblioteca Civica di Bergamo, and for the hospitality accorded to my wife and myself by the Mayor of Bergamo, Tito Simoncini, and by the Vice-Mayor, Ippolito Pippia. A very special word of thanks must go to Baronessa Maria Scotti Perego for her kindness in showing me the room where Donizetti died and in answering questions about the friendship between Donizetti and her family. Signor Filippini and his daughter Clara, Piero Brolis and his wife, were all most kind.

In Milan, I am particularly indebted to the House of Ricordi for opening their vaults to me, and to Maestro Raffaele Tenaglia, who assisted me there with unfailing help and sympathy. Maestro Natale Gallini supplied much valuable information and allowed me to see a portion of his remarkable collection of musical autographs. For permission to examine the fascinating holograph copy of *La favorite*, I must thank Count Luigi Treccani degli Alfieri.

In Bologna, Professor Napoleone Fanti, Librarian of the Liceo Musicale, assisted me by opening the treasures of that remarkable library to me.

In Naples, the Directress of the Library of the Conservatory, Anna Mondolfi, and all her staff, particularly Signorina Lydia Albano, allowed me to examine the wealth of manuscript materials there. Tony Gambardelli, also of Naples, supplied me with much helpful information.

In the United States I owe an inexpressible debt to Mr Walter Toscanini for his generosity in permitting me to browse through his priceless collections and for his invaluable suggestions and advice. Lillian Moore Maclay always found time from her busy career to answer puzzling questions and to send along helpful information that she turned up in her own researches, thereby offering added proof of a friendship of long standing. Mr Herbert Weinstock has been generous both in sharing information and in his willingness to discuss the many fascinating problems of Donizetti's biography. Edward J. Smith was a great help in tracking down performances of Donizetti's rarely performed works. Mr Thomas Schippers found time to discuss his version of *Il Duca d'Alba* with me. I am deeply grateful to Phillip Miller, Sidney Beck and others of the staff of the Music Department of the New York Public Library for their assistance. The Music Department of the Library of

Congress have helped me both in person and through inter-library loans.

I am particularly obliged to Ross C. Allen of the University of Indiana for his contagious enthusiasm, generosity, and encouragement. I must thank Dean Wilfred C. Bain, of the School of Music, University of Indiana, for his kindness in allowing me the freedom of the Music Library. I am further indebted to Dr Jack G. Weinbaum, pathologist; to Professor Sandford Watts for his advice. I am grateful to David T. Darling for making the preliminary drawings of the musical examples for me; I am much indebted to Malcolm Lipkin for re-drawing the musical examples as they appear in the text.

Miss Dorothy Shinoske and others of her staff at the Library of Indiana State College have been most patient and obliging. I am most grateful to Cynthia N. Wolfe, to Mary Olga Peters, and to Mary B. Royse for their help. With the task of putting this material in shape, Elizabeth C. Ross and Mary R. McMillan were endlessly helpful, patient, and industrious. The assistance of Shirley Jowell has been invaluable; her patience and diligence have been repeatedly tried and never once found wanting.

None of my debts is greater than that to my wife, who has put in a staggering number of hours on every phase of this book, while somehow managing to keep our lives on an even keel.

No matter how hard one declares war on errors, some inevitably sneak by. I take full responsibility for the information and judgements contained in this work. In Chapter 9, my discussion of Donizetti's Revisions and Self-Borrowings is intended to be representative rather than complete. The task of a minute collation of all Donizetti's scores, autograph and non-autograph, and sketches, is staggering, and although I have examined as many as possible, it has been impossible to check each one against all the others. I would be very grateful indeed, therefore, to hear of any revisions and self-borrowings besides those mentioned in Chapter 9.

WILLIAM ASHBROOK
Terre Haute, Indiana

Part One

CHAPTER 1

The Beginnings

Gaetano Donizetti was born in Bergamo, then part of the newly formed Cisalpine Republic, on 29 November 1797. His birth certificate, dated 3 December 1797, is to be found in the parish records of S. Grata inter Vites. It reads:

> *Dominicus Cajetanus Maria filius Andreae Donizetti et Domenicae Nava Legitimum Iugalium natura die 29 9mbris in hoc suburbio, hodie baptizzatus a me Antonio Mauro Bonzi Praeposito —Patrino Dominico Iraina ex Zanica.*

At the time of Gaetano's birth his parents occupied a basement apartment at Borgo Canale, No. 10 (now No. 14 and marked by a plaque). Today the house has been designated a national museum. The dark, cramped quarters eloquently testify to the poverty in which the family lived. Gaetano never forgot the place; he wrote of it a few years before his death:

> . . . I was born underground in Borgo Canale. You went down cellar steps, where no glimmer of light ever penetrated. And like an owl I took flight . . . never encouraged by my poor father, who was always telling me: it's impossible that you will compose, that you will go to Naples, that you will go to Vienna. . . .[1]

For many years local tradition had mistaken the birthplace of

[1] Guido Zavadini, *Donizetti: Vita—Musiche—Epistolario* (Bergamo, 1948), No. 496, p. 679. Ltr. to Mayr, 15 July 1843.

Donizetti until Ciro Caversazzi,[1] after making an exhaustive search of census reports and parish records, established which was the right house.

The confusion is not surprising, because many Donizettis lived on the Borgo Canale, a street that slants down the north-west shoulder of the hill topped by the old town of Bergamo. A higher hill stood to the north; on its summit, against the skyline, rose the old church of S. Vigilio. Next door but one to the house where Gaetano was born, his grandfather, Ambrogio Donizetti, had lived from about 1759 until his death in July 1797. Gaetano's uncle, Giovanni Donizetti, his father's elder brother, occupied that same house off and on, living there with his wife and children. The house directly next door was occupied by his father's half-sister, Angela, who was married to a musician named Giacomo Corini.

About 1786 Gaetano's father, Andrea Donizetti married Domenica Nava and moved two doors up the street to the cellar apartment. Here his six children were born. The eldest, Giuseppe (6 November 1788–12 February 1856), became a musician. After some training by his uncle Corini and some private lessons with Mayr, he joined Napoleon's army, serving sometimes as a rifleman, sometimes as a bandsman; later he directed a band in the Sardinian Army. Giuseppe moved to Constantinople in 1828, where he assumed the responsibilities of Chief of Music to the Ottoman Armies, introducing Western scales, notation, and harmony to Turkey. He prospered at this work and stayed in the Levant until he died. About 1840, he was rewarded with the title of Donizetti Pasha and allowed to enter the harem as singing master, a development that could come straight out of the plot of an opera buffa. The next of Andrea's children was a daughter, Maria Rosalinda (1 May 1790–8 February 1811), of whom little is known save that she was supposed to have died of apoplexy. The third child was Francesco (7 February 1792–20 December 1848). If not down-right mentally deficient, Francesco developed but little intelligence and less initiative. He was content to remain at home and, after his parents' death, let his brothers support him. Francesco's musical ambitions soared no higher than playing the cymbals in the Bergamo Civic Band and strutting around in a gaudy

[1] Ciro Caversazzi, *La casa dove nacque—la famiglia—l'inizio della malattia* (Bergamo, 1924).

4

uniform. Three years later another daughter was born, Maria Antonia (20 September 1795–5 March 1823); she married a local fellow named Tironi. After she died of tuberculosis, her daughter moved in with Andrea and Domenica and kept house for the elderly couple. Next came Gaetano, and after him another daughter, Maria Rachele, who was born in March 1800 and lived barely a month.

Exactly how Andrea supported his family during the early years of his marriage is not known. Many of the families who lived at that time in the Borgo Canale were engaged in the trade of weaving, and some writers have supposed that is how Andrea earned his livelihood. Caversazzi suggests he may have been a tailor for a time, or even a musician. The latter suggestion seems unlikely because his son Giuseppe had his first lessons from his uncle rather than from his father. Further, Andrea's notorious lack of enthusiasm for Gaetano's career, his repeated urging that his son check his ambition and seek regular employment as a village organist or music master, suggests that Andrea lacked any appreciation of Gaetano's unusual talent. It is known, however, that in 1808 Andrea assumed the humble duties of porter to the civic pawnshop, the Monte di Pietà, a position he held until his death.

At one time it was suggested that Donizetti had Scots blood in his veins, that his grandfather was Donald Izett from Perthshire. In the face of Caversazzi's copious evidence, this claim seems preposterous. Apparently it was first put forward by George T. Ferris in his book, *The Great Italian and French Composers* (1878). Here is his tale:

> The young Scot was beguiled by the fascinating tongue of a recruiting-sergeant into his Britannic majesty's service, and was taken prisoner by General La Hoche during the latter's invasion of Ireland. Already tired of a private's life, he accepted the situation, and was induced to become the French general's private secretary. Subsequently he drifted to Italy, and married an Italian lady of some rank, denationalizing his own name into Donizetti.[1]

[1] George T. Ferris, *The Great Italian and French Composers* (New York, 1878), p. 87n. See also the correspondence on this question in *Musical Opinion*, issues of June, July, and August 1948. *Opera News* (27 December 1948) contains an article, 'Was it Izett?'.

But since Hoche's expedition did not sail from Brest until December 1796, when Donizetti's family had been established in Bergamo for more than forty years, and since the French fleet was scattered in a storm off Kerry and never reached Ireland, not only is Ferris's time wrong, but the opportunity for any such romantic adventures was lacking.

Ferris arouses no more confidence by his account of Donizetti's youth. He misdates Donizetti's birth, speaks of his father as a 'man of moderate fortune', and adds that the composer received 'a good classical education'. In all this, it is difficult to recognize Andrea, the porter of the pawnshop, who was able to send Gaetano to a music school only because a free institution for poor boys had just been started in Bergamo. When Ferris tries to bolster his claim to a Scottish ancestry for Donizetti by finding a Highland lilt to the serenade from *Don Pasquale* and a strong flavour of 'Scottish sympathy and minstrelsy' in *Lucia*, he is using an argument that would posit two Orientals in Puccini's family tree: one for *Butterfly* and another for *Turandot*!

It is not to Scotland, then, but to Lombardy, that we must look to appreciate Donizetti's character and heritage.

Bergamo lies at the northern edge of the Lombard plain at the foot of the Bergamasc Alps. In ancient times the site was inhabited by a tribe known as the Orobii; later it became the Roman municipality of Bergamum. Traces of the Roman fortifications are still to be seen. Destroyed by Attila, the city was rebuilt and became a Lombard duchy. In 1264 control of the city passed to the Milanese who ruled it until 1428, when it came under the control of the Venetians, who surrounded the city with sturdy walls that still stand today. Bergamo remained in the hands of Venice for almost four centuries. In 1797, the year of Donizetti's birth, Bergamo was included in Napoleon's Cisalpine Republic. After the Congress of Vienna, the town, along with the rest of Lombardy and Venetia, passed to the Austrians.

The city consists of two parts: the Città Alta on the crest of a hill, and the Città Bassa at its foot. The upper town contained within the Venetian walls preserves, even today, a strong sense of the past; the lower town, much smaller a century and a half ago than it is today, has become a modern city. Undoubtedly Bergamo exerted a strong influence on Donizetti; all his life, even in those years when he saw it but rarely, he retained his fondness for it and his loyalty to it. The Torre di Gombito, an eleventh-century tower, one of the most characteristic landmarks of the old town, held a particular place in Donizetti's affections; in more than one letter he speaks of his longing to see it again.

When Donizetti climbed to the upper end of the Borgo Canale and entered the old town, he was confronted with the city's artistic heritage. Looming largest in Donizetti's perspective was the ornate church of S. Maria Maggiore, whose musical traditions, dating back to the fourteenth century, were the pride of the province. Here Donizetti had some of his earliest musical experiences; here his beloved teacher Mayr was *maestro di cappella*, and here he sang in the choir, first as a contralto and later as a bass. Connected to S. Maria Maggiore is the elaborate Colleoni Chapel with its intricate façade of polychrome marble; inside it are the noble tombs carved by Amadeo and the ceiling painted by Tiepolo. Whatever the darkness and poverty of his home, Donizetti found at hand in Bergamo a living tradition of art and music.

In Donizetti's youth, the most influential musician in Bergamo was Johann Simon Mayr, and the results of Donizetti's association with Mayr remained all his life. Mayr had settled in Bergamo in 1802, at the time of his appointment at S. Maria Maggiore. His impact upon local opinion may be deduced from a decree, dated 12 March 1805, instituting a music school to be known as the Lezioni Caritatevoli,[1] to be administered by the Pio Luogo della Misericordia Maggiore, and to be under the personal direction of Mayr. The primary purpose behind the founding of the school was to train poor boys as choristers and instrumentalists to participate in the services at S. Maria Maggiore. By that time enlightened opinion no longer countenanced the inhuman practice of providing *castrati* for church choirs; this decree, then, bespeaks a humane desire to provide a continuous supply of boy sopranos and contraltos. The school's first students were enrolled on 6 May 1806, and the third name on the rolls is that of nine-year-old

[1] The school still exists today, but now it is named after its famous graduate: L'istituto musicale Gaetano Donizetti.

7

Domenico Gaetano Donizetti, admitted on a three months' probation as a student of voice and clavicembalo.[1]

Music in Bergamo, however, was not the exclusive province of the churches or Mayr's school. The town, like any self-respecting Italian centre, was addicted to opera. During most of the eighteenth century a temporary theatre was put up each year for the summer Fair. Before long the town was to boast two opera houses. The older, the Teatro Riccardi in the lower town, was rechristened the Teatro Donizetti for the centennial celebration of 1897. It originally opened its doors in 1784 with a performance of Sarti's *Medonte*. Fire destroyed this theatre in 1797, but the opera-minded Bergamascs rebuilt their theatre so promptly that it was in use the following year. The other opera house, the Teatro Sociale (or di Società) was built by a group of dilettantes who wanted a theatre in the upper town run to suit their tastes. It opened in 1807, usually running a second best to the older house, but it lasted until 1892; today the building is used as a *trattoria*. While the Teatro Sociale held its season in Carnival, beginning on the traditional opening date of San Stefano (26 December), the Teatro Riccardi gave its performances starting in August, at the time of the Fiera, or Fair, a gala season in Bergamo because the lakes and highlands of the region have long been a popular summer resort.

Mayr served as a bridge between the two worlds of religious and operatic music. Although his local fame was increased by his labours at S. Maria Maggiore, he was known at that time, throughout Italy and beyond, as a composer of operas. Indeed, in the years between the death of Cimarosa (1801) and Rossini's triumph with *Tancredi* (1813), Mayr was generally regarded as the most important operatic composer in Italy.

For all Mayr's celebrity the name of Bergamo was associated in the popular mind not so much with him, but with a series of remarkable tenors who were born there. The oldest of this group was Giacomo David (1750–1830), famous for the purity of his voice and for his artistry as an inventor of embellishments and variations; even the fastidious Lord Mount-Edgcumbe gave him unstinting praise. David retired from the stage in 1812, and returned to Bergamo to serve for some years as tenor soloist at S. Maria Maggiore, where the young Donizetti had

---

[1] Clavicembalo was then the usual term in Italy for the harpsichord but, confusingly, it was also applied to the early pianos.

many opportunities to hear him. David's son, Giovanni (1790–1864), was also a famous tenor and was celebrated in Naples during the years Rossini was associated with the theatres there, singing in the *prime* of five Rossini operas, but since he was born in Naples, he cannot strictly be counted a Bergamasc. Domenico Viganoni (1754–1823) achieved great celebrity during the 1790's, particularly in the operas of Cimarosa, singing them in Milan, Vienna and London. Like the elder David, Viganoni retired to Bergamo, and his villa at nearby Almenno was the scene of many an evening of impromptu music-making; on many occasions Donizetti was among the guests. Andrea Nozzari (1775–1832) studied with David *père* and made his début in Naples, where he was still active when Donizetti settled there in 1822. The name of Marco Bordogni (1788–1856) is more associated with France than Italy. After a great success at the Théâtre-Italien in 1819, Bordogni was appointed, at Rossini's urging, to the faculty of the Paris Conservatory, a post he still held during Donizetti's days in that city. Domenico Donzelli (1790–1873) pursued a long and illustrious career. Today he is best remembered as the first Pollione in *Norma*, but nearly ten years earlier he had sung the leading role in Donizetti's first important success, *Zoraide di Granata*. Donzelli, a pupil of Viganoni, sang until 1846, when he retired to Bologna, enjoying a close friendship with Rossini. The last of this group of Bergamasc tenors was one of the greatest singers of all time, Giovanni Battista Rubini[1] (1795–1854). The great days of Rubini's career began with his Parisian triumphs of 1825, but his contract with the impresario Barbaja kept him singing in Italy six months of the year until 1831, an arrangement that permitted him to take part in the premières of major works by Bellini and Donizetti. For all his later celebrity, it is fitting to remember that Rubini began his stage career as a chorister at the Teatro Riccardi in Bergamo. After his retirement in 1844, Rubini settled in a lavish villa near his birthplace, and from there he came to visit Donizetti shortly before the composer's death, hoping to bring his old associate some glimmerings of lucidity by singing him a passage from *Lucia*.

This group of tenors—dynasty seems a more appropriate word, for as Nozzari was a pupil of the elder David, so did

---

[1] Rubini was born at Romano, a small town in the province of Bergamo. Today an interesting Museo Rubini may be visited at Romano.

Rubini study with Nozzari—summarizes one striking aspect of the musical traditions of Bergamo. The fame and wealth achieved by this constellation of singing stars explain in part Donizetti's natural gravitation, once his great aptitude for musical composition had manifested itself, towards the opera house as his chief arena of activity. Not only was the musical stage the surest—one is tempted to say the only—road for an Italian composer of Donizetti's generation to make his mark, but the métier was one for which many forces in his environment had a hand in shaping him.

Of all the formative forces that helped to mould Donizetti into a composer, none was more influential than Johann Simon Mayr (1763–1845). As teacher, benefactor, and friend, Mayr, for as long as he lived, gave Donizetti assistance and encouragement; his satisfaction in his pupil's success was never corrupted by any jealousy. Donizetti reciprocated Mayr's friendship and esteem. His many letters to Mayr are consistently respectful and solicitous, testimony to one of Donizetti's most admirable traits, his loyalty. Such was their relationship that Mayr did not call his former pupil by that much-abused title Maestro until after the major success of *Anna Bolena* (26 December 1830), a compliment that takes on its full meaning only when we remember that *Anna* was Donizetti's thirty-fifth opera.

Mayr first crossed the Alps and came to Bergamo as a student in 1788. Born in Mendorf, Bavaria, Mayr had been introduced to music by his father, the village organist. After further study under the Jesuits at Ingolstadt, he came to Italy, like many other German composers during the eighteenth century, to complete his musical education. At the suggestion of a patron, he arrived in Bergamo to study with Carlo Lenzi, then the *maestro di cappella* at S. Maria Maggiore; when Mayr found his proposed teacher knew less about counterpoint than he did, he moved on to Venice, where he made his mark first as a composer of oratorios and later of operas. *Saffo* (1794), Mayr's first opera, achieved a notable success. Thus encouraged, he turned out almost seventy operas in the next thirty years, sometimes as many as five a year. Such fecundity was not uncommon then, and if at times Donizetti's operas tumbled on each other's heels with astonishing rapidity, a persuasive example is not far to seek.

When Mayr accepted the post as *maestro di cappella* at S. Maria Maggiore in 1802, he settled down to spend the rest of his life at Bergamo. Two years later Mayr, a widower, married Lucrezia Venturali, the sister of his first wife. Although Mayr received flattering offers from London, Paris, and St Petersburg, he accepted engagements only for Italian theatres, leaving Bergamo only to rehearse his operas and see them through the prescribed first three performances. His added duties as director of the Lezioni Caritatevoli tied him even closer to his adopted city. In 1813 Mayr suffered severe financial reverses, but his losses in no way dimmed his spirits or made him any less eager to help his students. After this, he composed less frequently for the stage, his final opera *Demetrio* coming out in Turin in 1824, and turned his attention more and more to church music, until blindness and then a paralytic stroke finally halted his career as a composer.

Today the almost total disappearance of Mayr's music represents the judgement of history upon his interest as a composer; yet Mayr enjoyed a decade of popularity and a lifetime of respect. On every side he was lauded for his correctness and erudition, but when Rossini exploded upon the scene with his irresistible verve and *brio*, the fatal lack in Mayr's music stood exposed. That great Rossini partisan, Stendhal, preferred Mayr's serious works; 'in opera buffa, on the other hand, [he] reveals all the clumsy elephantine gaiety of a good, dull-witted burgher'.[1] Rossini customarily referred to Mayr with respect, and well he might, for he owed him a musical debt. The big crescendo, the trademark of many a Rossini overture, had earlier been used by Mayr in *Lodoiska* (1796) and in *Ginevra di Scozia* (1801). Although Mayr is generally regarded as an extinct composer today, many people may have heard one of his melodies without realizing it. The story is told[2] that as a compliment to his old teacher, Donizetti borrowed a melody from one of Mayr's Masses to use as the B major chorus, *Fur le nozze a lei funeste*, in the final scene of *Lucia*. When Mayr learned of this gesture, he is supposed to have said: '*Donizetti mi ha fatto troppo onore*' (Donizetti has done me too great an honour).

[1] Stendhal, *Life of Rossini*, translated Richard N. Coe, p. 20.
[2] Alborghetti, Galli, and Zendrini, *Donizetti-Mayr* (Bergamo, 1875). I made a brief search of a thematic catalogue of Mayr's religious music in the Biblioteca Civica di Bergamo and was unable to corroborate the story.

If history has been unkind to Mayr's music he is still remembered by the double-standard of musicology for his contributions to the form of opera seria. In the first years of the nineteenth century Mayr served as a link between German and Italian music. He managed at times to achieve an almost Mozartian warmth and suppleness in his vocal melodies, which, by contrast, made the serious operas of Piccinni and Cimarosa seem cold and austere. Mayr was a conscientious orchestrator, continually striving for richer sonorities, and writing more liberally for the woodwinds than was then the custom in Italy. Occasionally he wrote florid solos for these instruments, incorporating them in his operatic scores. Mayr's fondness for the orchestra can be seen in his carefully elaborated introductions to arias and in his penchant for experimenting with musical descriptions of storms. Perhaps Mayr's most important achievement lay in his handling of recitative. Instead of relying heavily on the convention of *recitativo secco*, in which little characterization is possible, Mayr worked to expand the expressiveness of accompanied recitative, thereby strengthening the dramatic cohesiveness of his work by his use of what came to be called *canto caratteristico*. Mayr then laboured more to increase the dramatic expression in opera than to titillate an impressionable public. His influence is strong in Donizetti's work, and it might well be urged that it was not until Donizetti reconciled his master's approach with his own efforts to absorb Rossini's idiom that he began to develop a personal style.

In Italy during the first decades of the nineteenth century, Mayr was one of the first to make a thorough study of the works of Haydn, Mozart and Beethoven. His opinion of the last of these composers may be gauged from his composing, in 1827, a cantata entitled *In morte di Beethoven*. Mayr was eager to make the works by these composers known in Italy. In his memorial to the Congregazione di Carità of Bergamo, urging the establishment of a school of music, he wrote that the oratorios of Haydn and the Mozart *Requiem* had not yet been performed publicly in Italy because of the lack of choral groups. In Bergamo, in 1809, Mayr directed the Italian première of Haydn's *Creation*. The performance, in which Donizetti almost certainly took part, was given on the occasion of the founding of another project dear to Mayr's heart, the Pio Istituto Musicale, an organization to assist indigent musicians, their widows and children. Through Mayr, Donizetti had further and more extensive opportunities to become familiar with music of the Viennese masters, as he often accompanied Mayr to the home of Alessandro Bertoli, where from 1814 a group met regularly to play the chamber music of Haydn, Mozart, Beethoven, Reicha and Mayseder. On these occasions Mayr would from time to time play the viola parts. These experiences made such an impression on Donizetti that he was moved to compose fifteen string quartets between 1817 and 1821. These experiences, coming to Donizetti at a most impressionable age, were then scarcely to be duplicated in Italy.

Clearly, it was Donizetti's good fortune to come early into the hands of such a man as Mayr. For, whatever his limitations, Mayr was above all a teacher, a man compelled to share his knowledge. According to Marco Bonesi,[1] one of Donizetti's fellow students at the Lezioni Caritatevoli, Mayr could not take a walk with his pupils without delivering a lecture, nor was he happier than when analysing a score for his scholars. Besides his knowledge of composition Mayr was an experienced man of the theatre who could give much practical advice about the ways of the operatic world as it was then constituted. Further, Mayr had the uncommon humility to recognize his own limitations. When he had taught his star pupil, Donizetti, all he could, Mayr made all the arrangements to send Gaetano to study with the famous Padre Mattei at Bologna, the man who had been Rossini's teacher, to learn counterpoint and fugue. Mayr rounded up patrons to help defray the cost of this further education and even contributed what he could himself. From such a man as Mayr, generous with his learning, his experience, and his money, an eager and talented youngster could not fail to profit. Small wonder that Donizetti loved him as a second father.

Domenico Gaetano Donizetti[2] came to the Palazzo della Misericordia on 24 April 1806 to be tested for his musical

---

[1] Bonesi (1796–1874), wrote *Note biografiche su Donizetti*, an unpublished MS. in the Biblioteca Civica, Bergamo.
[2] Both first names were used in the reports from the school during the first year of Donizetti's attendance, and then Domenico was dropped permanently.

aptitude. 'He has a good ear, his voice is not outstanding, and he should be admitted for a three months' probation,' was the judgement of the examiners. The report is signed by the four men who comprised the original faculty of the school: Mayr, Salari, Capuzzi, and Gonzales. Francesco Salari (1751–1823) was born in Bergamo, studied in Naples with Piccinni, moved to Venice where he was long a singing teacher, finally returning to Bergamo in 1805 to assume the duties as second *maestro di cappella* at S. Maria Maggiore. Antonio Capuzzi (1755–1818) was born in Brescia and had studied the violin with Tartini before settling in Bergamo. Antonio Gonzales (1764–1830) was born at Giomo and had come to Bergamo as organist at S. Maria Maggiore.

Gaetano's name was entered on the rolls of the school on 6 May 1806. The rules of the institution limited the number of free pupils to twelve: eight to study voice and cembalo, four for violin and cello. Donizetti's studies included lessons in singing and declamation with Salari, in piano with Gonzales, the first of the boy's masters to recognize his unusual aptitudes, and in the elements of theory with Mayr. At the end of the probationary period Gaetano was admitted as a regular pupil. The first report from the faculty of the Lezioni Caritatevoli to the Congregazione di Carità, who provided the funds for the school, is dated 13 September 1806 and says of Donizetti:

> In singing class: diligent, attentive, has made progress in reading music, but his voice is defective and throaty. In piano class: diligent in attendance, quiet and attentive. His progress is in accordance with his good disposition and his attention to his studies.

Seven months later, Mayr reported that Gaetano surpassed all the other students in musical progress.

On 10 September 1807, the Congregazione awarded Gaetano a prize of two and a half scudi milanesi. Exactly one year later, however, his continuing in Mayr's school was questioned. The faculty report for 10 September 1808 stated:

> In singing: punctilious in attending lessons, attentive, diligent, has made progress in reading music, but it has not been possible to correct his organic defect. In piano: punctilious, as above, has made progress.

Exactly a week after this report of Donizetti's vocal deficiencies, he was suspended from school.

The Congregazione announced that since his teachers saw no hope of successfully correcting his defective voice, he would be suspended, '*definativamente*'. This action makes it clear that the Congregazione regarded the free school's principal function as the training of soloists and choristers; any boy who had no value to the choir was dropped as not worth the expenditure, no matter what other musical promise he might demonstrate. Then, as if to try to soften the blow to his hopes, it was announced that Gaetano had again won a prize of two and a half scudi.

Prompt steps were taken to reinstate the boy. In short order, Andrea Donizetti wrote to the Congregazione on his son's behalf. His cumbersomely expressed request revolves on the argument that it is a pity Gaetano should lose his cembalo lessons just because of the physical constitution of his throat. Of whatever pressure Mayr put upon the Congregazione no record remains, but the desired effect was achieved, at least temporarily. On 28 October 1808, a few members of the governing board, acting for the whole, ruled that Gaetano and another borderline case be re-admitted 'conditionally, until such time as the Congregazione meet in full session, unless in the meantime some better endowed candidates should present themselves, in which case the decree of 17 September will take effect.'

Fortunately Donizetti's vocal limitations were not sufficient to keep him, aged almost eleven, from making a public appearance in that same year of 1808. For the final concert of the academic year, Mayr had composed an oratorio, *Sisara*. In this work, both Gaetano and his companion of the suspended sentence, Antonio Bosio, were entrusted with a duettino. Assuming that Mayr had all a director's desire to put his pupils' best foot forward on such occasions, one would like to know how he tailored his music for these vocal misfits and how he felt as they performed it. Apparently the results were not entirely hopeless, because for the following year's Accademia, Mayr composed a one-act farce, *Alcide al Bivio*. In this work, which marked Gaetano's début as an operatic singer, he took a contralto role. According to Alborghetti and Galli, in this performance 'Donizetti knew how to contort his voice with such comic effect that he brought smiles to the faces of not only the bystanders, but even to the Teutonic rigidity of Mayr.'[1]

Bonesi's rather ingenuous account of Donizetti's school-days was written nearly sixty years after the event, but, even allowing for the unreliability of memory, a picture of a handsome, high-spirited, likeable boy emerges. Bonesi tells how Gaetano would leave home early to get to school, the only time his father permitted him out without his mother, and he would play under the arches of the Palazzo Vecchio until classes began. He had a knack for imitation, and, when making fun of his fellows, he did it in such a way that he seemed to be laughing with them rather than at them. In class his quickness was the pride of the school. At church he followed attentively any service in which there was music, but, Bonesi rather sententiously adds, he found the music of the untrained street musicians tiresome. Gaetano attended operatic performances whenever he had the opportunity, and when that was lacking, he would gather his schoolmates to improvise comedies and farces with whatever material lay at hand. Nowhere does Bonesi mention Donizetti's problems at school, perhaps through a sense of propriety, perhaps because he had forgotten them.

The threat of suspension remained poised over Gaetano's head. Again the situation looked hopeless when, on 9 March 1809, the Congregazione announced that Donizetti and Bosio were dismissed. At once Mayr wrote, earnestly begging that the boys be permitted to continue. On 6 April the favour was granted until 'further instructions', a condition that left Gaetano's status as precarious as before. Whether it was part of Mayr's original intention, or whether Donizetti, whose obvious talents lay in other directions than singing, crystallized the problem for him, Mayr began to campaign for expanding the scope of the Lezioni Caritatevoli. To start any kind of free musical instruction he had to begin in terms of the need most strongly felt by those who supplied the financial support. Working from the Congregazione's concern for the choir of S. Maria Maggiore, Mayr managed to have the regulations of the school amended to permit boys whose voices were changing to continue their studies of organ and cembalo. This amendment was all to Gaetano's advantage: in mid-puberty his vocal defects were no worse than any other boy's.

[1] *Donizetti-Mayr*, p. 23.

There is evidence, however, that Gaetano had some doubts about the length of time he would be permitted to continue in Mayr's school, for on 7 November 1810, he addressed the Accademia Carrara, petitioning to be admitted among the 'dilettanti' to study design and figure. It is possible that he planned to study art as an alternative to a musical career, or he might have intended to take classes at the Accademia as an adjunct to his musical studies. The date of Donizetti's letter shows that it was written before Mayr had succeeded in getting the Congregazione to amend the regulations; therefore, it seems more likely he was considering art as an alternative to music. His application was granted on 15 November. How often or how long Gaetano attended classes at the Accademia Carrara is unknown. All his life he showed a facility in sketching, but whether this was the result of training or aptitude cannot now be determined.

Further evidence that at some point there was a real question about Donizetti's pursuing a career as a musician turns up in a letter he wrote in 1833 to the impresario Alessandro Lanari. As there had been some misunderstanding about the terms of a contract, Donizetti humorously explained the derivation of the verb *convenirsi* (to come to an agreement), and then continues:

> ... let me inform you that I ... was to have been a lawyer, and my parents started me out on that road; therefore I can give you a lesson in Latin, and in Italian, and in the value of words. . . .[1]

There seems to be no concrete evidence that Gaetano ever received any formal training in law. Since Andrea distrusted music as a sufficiently rewarding career for his son, he may well have tried to steer his youngest boy toward a more stable and remunerative occupation. But it seems highly unlikely that Gaetano himself ever thought very long and hard about either art or the law as alternatives to music, for he continued his studies with Mayr. And Mayr continued to use all the considerable influence he could muster to keep his talented pupil on the road he was clearly destined to follow.

[1] Z. No. 112, p. 327. (References to letters in Zavadini's *Epistolario* will be given in this form. The A series of letters are those written by others to Donizetti. Letters prefixed by B are those written by others to someone else about Donizetti. And those with no prefix are by Donizetti to others.)

By September 1811, Gaetano was obviously reinstated in Mayr's school, after his overture to the Accademia Carrara the preceding year, and his teacher was obviously intent on keeping his prize pupil as may be seen from the libretto of the farce, *Il piccolo compositore di musica*,[1] concocted by Mayr for performance at the exercises marking the end of the term. The interest of this libretto is heightened by the fact the young students portray themselves. The hero of the piece, 'the little composer' of the title, is Donizetti himself. A reading of the text suggests that Mayr had a double purpose in putting this work together. Besides affording a showcase for the talents of the most advanced pupils, the plot is an argument that Donizetti should be allowed to continue his studies at the school. This farce has the additional attraction of permitting a glimpse of the life within the school, because, like any performance designed for a restricted audience of relatives, friends, and patrons, it makes its points through local allusions.

Il piccolo compositore di musica calls for a cast of five. Besides Donizetti, the others were Antonio Dolci, Giuseppe Manghenoni, Giuseppe Pontiroli, and Antonio Tavecchi.[2] The setting for the work is the classroom, fitted out with two pianos, a desk, chairs, and a supply of music paper. Donizetti is the first

[1] Mayr's own printed copy of the libretto is preserved in the Civica Biblioteca of Bergamo. It bears this impressive title: *Il Piccolo Compositore di Musica/Farsa Giocosa per Musica/in due atti/da eseguire/Nell' Accademia Finale/ degli Allievi/delle Lezioni Caritatevoli di Musica/addetti alla Cappella della Basilica/di Santa Maria Maggiore/Sotto la direzione della Congregazione di Carità/di Bergamo/Il giorno 13. Settembre 1811/Bergamo/Dalla Stamperia Crescini.*

[2] These fellow-students occupied a special place in Donizetti's affections. Antonio Dolci (1798–1869) was Gaetano's closest friend. Remaining in Bergamo, Dolci was associated with the music school in various capacities from 1831 to 1866. The closeness of the tie between Dolci and Donizetti may be gathered from the fact that Dolci acted as his friend's agent in disbursing an allowance to Francesco Donizetti. Later, he was the executor of Donizetti's will.

Giuseppe Manghenoni died young, but he was a close friend of Donizetti's until their careers separated them. By 1819 Manghenoni was established as a voice teacher in Venice.

Giuseppe Pontiroli (1797–1854) was an unusually talented vocalist. After winning recognition as a boy soprano soloist at S. Maria Maggiore, he turned into a fine tenor. In 1832, he succeeded Salari as master of voice and declamation in Mayr's school, sharing these duties with another alumnus, Girolamo Fiorini (b. 1807).

Antonio Tavecchi died at twenty-two, shortly before 1819. Mayr had been confident that his career would have rivalled that of the elder David.

character to appear.[1] Even though it is holiday time he has come to the school to work in peace on an aria that he has just been inspired to write. Pleased with himself, he envisions his great success and the favourable reviews in the papers. While he is working on his aria, a pastorale with references to quail and cuckoos, his schoolmates tiptoe in in the best 'zitti, zitti, piano, piano' conspiratorial tradition. Donizetti writes on, unaware of their presence, until they start to add an accompaniment of derisive birdcalls to his aria. When Gaetano scolds them, Tavecchi asks him if he thinks he is the master of the school. Donizetti's reply is anything but modest, but his words have the force of prophecy:

> Vasta ho la mente, rapido l'ingegno,
> Pronta la fantasia, e nel comporre
> Un fulmine son io. . . .

'Huge is my mind, speedy my talent, ready my fancy, and I am like lightning when I compose.' Claiming that it has only taken him seven weeks to compose a waltz, he goes to the piano and plays it. A note in the libretto affirms that the waltz was 'expressly composed' by Donizetti.

As the farce continues, each student has an opportunity to perform. The scores of Sebastiano Nasolini, Stefano Pavesi, and Mayr himself were drawn upon for the operatic selections, but the original texts of the numbers were freely adapted to suit the situations of Il piccolo compositore. The main thread of the plot concerns Donizetti's conceit and the efforts of the others to puncture his self-esteem. At one point in the first act Tavecchi refers ironically to 'our Donizetti, who will eclipse the Cimarosas, the Paisiellos and the Paërs', but his ego is really damaged when three of his fellows begin to perform what purports to be a trio from Donizetti's opera Didone.[2] Before they have sung much, one of the group throws down his music, exclaiming, 'I can't stomach any more of this!' Soon they are all dancing

[1] The lines are in cheerful doggerel. By a strange coincidence, Donizetti's opening words, Qual insolito fuoco, are very close to those of a famous passage in Don Pasquale.
[2] The libretto does not indicate what music was used at this point. Considering the farcical situations, it is entirely possible that they sang whatever came into their heads. The author of the text of the trio, however, is facetiously identified as Rubaversi (literally: line-stealer).

around the supposedly furious Donizetti, taunting him. On this stage picture, the first act ends.

The brief second act begins with Donizetti bemoaning his schoolmates' insolence. When they appear, he refuses at first to speak to them, but soon they persuade him to accompany a duet from Mayr's *Adelasia ed Aleramo*. Donizetti's spirits improve to the extent of singing an aria from Mayr's *Che originali!* His performance is greeted by deafening whistles, a frank estimate of his vocal shortcomings that causes him to run away, desperate. Contrite, the others go to find him, all but Manghenoni, who sings a scene from Pavesi's *Aristodemo*, with a new text beginning: 'Indeed it saddens me that I have mortified my friend Donizetti. . . .' When Donizetti returns, he reads a formal edict that states 'whoever is bold enough to discourage another's talent deserves rigorous punishment.' He encourages the others to join him in studying hard to win the favour of their benefactors. They readily second this sentiment.

Thus it appears that *Il piccolo compositore di musica* was designed to deliver a message to its audience. Besides demonstrating the unusual abilities of his star pupil, Mayr is clearly making the point that Gaetano's vocal limitations are not a crippling impediment to his talent. The edict at the end of the farce is directed to the members of the Congregazione di Carità, urging them not to frustrate Donizetti's musical training. There is another interesting aspect to this little farce: Mayr's treatment of the problem of vanity. That all his life Donizetti was unusually fair in his treatment of rival composers, that he was seldom vain, indicates that he took to heart the lesson of this farce. Furthermore, *Il piccolo compositore* seems to be part of Mayr's continuing campaign to enlarge the scope of his school, to make it something more than a factory for choirboys. The most appealing aspect of this little work is the lively glimpse it affords of Donizetti in his student days.

In 1812, Mayr's hopes that the Liceo would broaden its range were strengthened when he secured the services of Abbate Giovanni Battista Baizzini, a prefect and teacher in the local Ginnasio, to instruct the boys in mathematics, geography, history, Italian and Latin. Mayr had expressed his belief that a singer should be thoroughly familiar with the structure of language and with literature, and for this end he secured the services of Baizzini. This teacher of the *scienze ausiliare* was shortly to cause further tensions for Gaetano at the Liceo.

Every year so far Donizetti's name had appeared on the prize list. His sense of progress made was further strengthened when the faculty unanimously chose him as the outstanding piano student and permitted him to enter special classes in harmony. What must have seemed at the time the greatest boon of all occurred when Donizetti's voice emerged from the process of changing and was judged *una sufficiente voce di basso*. In January 1814, he petitioned the Congregazione to be allowed to fill a secondo buffo role at the Teatro di Società, and his request was granted. In time, his voice developed to the point where he sang bass solos in the services at S. Maria Maggiore.

During the year of 1814 a new note obtrudes in the reports from the school. That of 15 April describes the sixteen-year-old Gaetano in these terms:

> Not too diligent in his responsibility of teaching the younger students . . . nor wholly punctual in attending the classes in outside subjects; it seems that these failings might be the result of his not too regular conduct outside of school. . . .

On 28 May 1814, the Congregazione earnestly admonished all those students whose behaviour was unfitting, 'and especially the pupil Donizetti, whose negligence in all the responsibilities placed upon him has been verified.' The report at the end of the term showed no improvement.

> Gaetano Donizetti, extra student, full of talent both in music and in the auxiliary subjects would make much greater progress if he attended class more often, but his irregular life prevents his profiting from the means for greater improvement. It is believed necessary that the Ill. Congregazione suggest and specify some means of correction. . . .[1]

In the meantime Gaetano was awarded eighteen lire

---

[1] The reports of Donizetti's school years are printed in Giuliano Donati-Pettèni, *L'istituto musicale di Gaetano Donizetti* (Bergamo, 1928), pp. 35 ff.

milanesi, although after his name on the prize list appear the
words 'to be seriously rebuked'. And, indeed, the next month
the Congregazione got around to threatening him with
expulsion, although this threat was never carried out.

The specific causes of Donizetti's unrest seem to be un-
documented, but the general reasons for his rebellion seem
clear. He was sixteen, eager to broaden his limited horizons,
anxious to make his way in the musical world. His parents lived
in severely straitened circumstances. Their oldest son, Giuseppe,
had come home from the army briefly, but instead of staying to
help support his parents, he had gone off again to join Napoleon's forces on Elba. Francesco had no employment, but he
was of an age when he was liable to be called up for military
service, as in fact he was the following year. Undoubtedly
Gaetano bore the brunt of his parents' anxieties and fears; he
was frustrated by their limited hope that he might go as far as
becoming the organist in some nearby parish. Gaetano's loyalty
to his parents was deep-rooted and permanent, but the lack of
understanding he received must have been hard for a boy of his
high spirits to endure.

His truancy at the Lezioni Caritatevoli probably sprang from
boredom. To a boy who learned quickly, whose curiosity was
far ranging, the pedantry of Baizzini and the task of teaching
beginner students were no small burden. It is a double tribute
to Mayr's understanding and to Donizetti's musical gift that the
older man, whatever his feeling about his prize pupil's 'irregular
life', continued to support Gaetano and planned to help him
reach the career that lay before him.

Although there are no existing reports of Gaetano's work at
the school after those of September 1814, he continued on the
rolls for thirteen months longer. In the month of October 1815,
Mayr managed to bring his great scheme to fruition. To send
Gaetano off to Bologna to study with the famous Padre
Mattei, he had to overcome considerable opposition. First of
all, Andrea Donizetti felt additional training was unnecessary
for a boy who could attract people to come from a distance to
hear him play the organ at Seriate, a little village near Bergamo.
Andrea had to be persuaded that his son deserved such an
opportunity, even though it meant postponing the time when
he would begin earning a regular salary. Further, there was the
matter of the bad impression the more strait-laced members

of the Congregazione had received of him during the past year or so; but set against this was the undeniable promise Gaetano had publicly demonstrated and the recommendations of some of his teachers. In August 1815, Donizetti had appeared most successfully in an Accademia at the Teatro Riccardi. The greatest force in the boy's favour was Mayr's belief in him and his willingness to support him enthusiastically.

Mayr's appeal to the Congregazione to enlist their support for his plan to send Gaetano to Bologna conveys much of his feeling for his pupil.

> If in the founding of the free school of music, an institution that has many times enjoyed the approbation of the Superiors, of the first Magistrates, and of the public, it has particularly taken as its aim the cultivation of budding musical talents, which deprived of financial support would have remained buried, and which only through the generosity of this Congregation could be placed in a position to earn by means of their art their sustenance and that of their families. Certainly this consideration has been the basis for the founding of that Institution, and because of the philanthropic sentiments that have always guided the illustrious Members and Rectors of the Pii Luoghi to remember needy families in various ways, and because of the present need, let me hope that the Illustrious Congregation will permit me to put forward my humble prayers on behalf of *Gaetano Donizetti*, a young student who is about to leave the school. Although not overly favoured by nature with an outstanding voice, he is, however, gifted by inclination, talent, and genius for composition, particularly with his readiness of fantasy in conceiving musical ideas which are not unsuitable for the setting of words. He leaves me the most solid hope for his certain success in the study of counterpoint. It would be a loss if this not mediocre talent were not cultivated in the most useful manner, and by the most solid and valuable means of instruction that Italy can boast today, which is that of the distinguished Padre Maestro Stanislao Mattei of Bologna. However, this youngster, lacking the means wherewith to aspire to such an advantage, and furthermore calculating the benefit that would derive to himself and to his parents, who are

deprived of the help of two other sons who are serving in the armies, and who must base their hope of help for their declining years on this son, and considering the honour that might redound to his native city that it should have formed a distinguished composer of music, several charitable souls have had the goodness to offer generous support to maintain this youth for two years. But these funds not being sufficient for everything, I am so bold as to beg the Illustrious Congregation, by an act of true charity directed toward the worthiest end, to deign to concur also in this support. . . . The certificate of good and punctilious behaviour given by his teachers yields the firmest hope that he will profit from these generous gifts with tireless study, the most effective means of showing himself grateful to his benefactors; while I myself will feel an immense obligation toward the Illustrious Congregation for the many repeated favours it has always deigned to shower upon me. And now, full of the sentiment of gratitude and respect, I have the honour of calling myself,

Your most humble, devoted, and obedient servant,

Bergamo, 28 Oct. 1815   s/Gio Simone Mayr[1]

On the same day that Mayr wrote to the Congregazione, Donizetti, just a month before his eighteenth birthday, set out by diligence for Bologna. Besides giving Gaetano money for the journey out of his own pocket, Mayr sent him on his way with two letters. The first recommended him to the publisher, Giovanni Ricordi of Milan; the second, to Marchese Francesco Sampieri of Bologna, asking his assistance in helping the lad find a cheap, comfortable room.

Before following Gaetano to Bologna, we might glance at the manuscripts of half a dozen compositions from his student days in Bergamo. The earliest is a sextet for two sopranos, two tenors, and two basses; on the manscript Donizetti has written in his own hand the date 1812. While these works are of negligible musical interest, but of notable surety of form, one of them, a set of variations on a theme from an opera by Mayr, is the earliest of Donizetti's published works. It was printed by Ricordi in 1815, the year of its composition. That this student

---

[1] Z. No. B. 3, pp. 910–11.

work was so favoured is probably explained by Mayr's employ-ment by the firm of Ricordi as a consultant, a post he held until his failing eyesight forced him to relinquish it.

When Donizetti arrived in Bologna he found lodgings on the third floor of the house now numbered as Via Pepoli 1. Lodging in the same house was Tommaso Marchesi, one of the masters at the Bologna Liceo Musicale. It should be remembered that at this period there were few conservatories in the modern sense of the word in Italy, except those of Naples—for whom the eighteenth century was a golden age. Mayr's little school in Bergamo was just two years younger than the Bologna Liceo, which had been inaugurated only in 1804. Although the decree authorizing the foundation of the Liceo dates back to 20 October 1798, political events had delayed its opening. The Conservatory in Milan was not founded until 1808, upon a decree by the Viceroy, Eugène Beauharnais; the Conservatory of Venice dates from 1811, and although there had been important music schools there earlier, they were administered by various religious organizations. Before the establishment of these conservatories, most of the musical instruction had been carried on, as indeed Mayr's had been, by *maestri di cappella*.

The principal attraction of the Liceo Musicale in Bologna was the classes in counterpoint conducted by Padre Stanislao Mattei (1750–1825). Mattei had been the favoured pupil of the famous Padre Martini (1706–84), the most learned musician of his time, and Mattei's predecessor as *maestro di cappella* at S. Petronio, Bologna. When the monasteries were suppressed in 1798, Mattei, who was a Minorite, returned to the world, but only to live with his aged mother and to teach his pupils.

Rossini, who attended the Liceo at Bologna between 1806 and 1810, has left vivid impressions of Padre Mattei as a teacher. Rossini told Ferdinand Hiller that 'Mattei with a pen in his hand had few equals, but for the rest he was terribly taciturn. Every word of explanation had to be dragged from his mouth by force.' Later, Rossini told Fétis that when he would ask his teacher about a correction, he got a stock answer: 'It is the custom to write it that way.' On the other hand, when the conservative old priest examined Rossini's early scores, he exclaimed that Rossini had dishonoured his school; however, he seems to have relented somewhat when Rossini's growing fame brought great credit to his teacher and to his school.

Judging from the absence of Mattei's name in the over seven hundred of Donizetti's published letters, written after he left Bologna, Gaetano seems to have felt little affection for his uncommunicative teacher, especially when the lack of references to Mattei is compared to the abundant allusions and letters to Mayr. In the notebooks of Gaetano's counterpoint classes preserved in the Museo Donizettiano, there is a weekly succession of exercises in counterpoint and fugue on subjects assigned by Mattei. These studies increased in difficulty, until Donizetti was writing six-part fugues with counter-subjects. These notebooks testify to his diligence, proof that he worked hard to justify Mayr's faith in him. From the marginalia in these notebooks, we learn that Mayr came to Bologna to pay his former student a visit in mid-September 1816 and that Gaetano was anxious to demonstrate what he had learned under Mattei.

There is only an occasional glimpse of Donizetti in these days at the Liceo. Alborghetti and Galli,[1] without explaining their source, tell how Donizetti on the day of his lessons would wait until Mattei had finished with Vespers at S. Petronio and follow him home. After Mattei had gone over his exercises, Gaetano would play tarot with Mattei's aged mother. Others, such as the composer Carlo Coccia, who knew Donizetti during these days, have testified to the good opinion Mattei had of his young Lombard pupil. A rather different view of Donizetti at Bologna is afforded by Corrado Ricci.[2] Mentioning the stories of Donizetti haunting the church and playing cards with mamma Mattei, he says:

That this, and only this, should be the life of Donizetti between the ages of eighteen and twenty, especially in a city like Bologna, where the carefree atmosphere suggested diversions of every sort, is difficult to believe. At Bologna, he certainly studied, but there he would have diverted himself as well with companions, with university students, and with . . .

[1] *Donizetti-Mayr*, pp. 32–3.
[2] Corrado Ricci, 'Donizetti a Bologna: Appunti e documenti', *Numero unico* (Bergamo, 1897), pp. 10–13.

One of Gaetano's companions in those days was Piero Maroncelli, who was combining his course of study at the University with lessons at the Liceo. Maroncelli (1795–1846) was a political liberal; in 1820, as a member of the Carbonari, he was arrested, tried and condemned to death, but his sentence was later commuted to twenty years in the infamous Austrian fortress of Spielberg, where together he and his friend Silvio Pellico were tortured. After his release Maroncelli drifted to Paris and married a mezzo-soprano named Amalie Schneider. Together they came to the United States where Maroncelli maintained a precarious existence as a chorus master for various opera troupes and as a teacher of singing and Italian. He died in New York, blind and mad. In a letter Maroncelli wrote to Donizetti in 1843, he alluded nostalgically to their days together at Bologna.

> . . . You will not have forgotten the beautiful youthful years we spent together at Bologna. You at the Liceo Musicale, and I there and at the University; and, besides, the dear conversations in the house of the degli Antonj.[1]

When Maroncelli first came to Bologna, he already belonged to a secret political society, La colonna armonica. That music loomed large in their 'dear conversations' there is the evidence of a *Laudamus*, composed by Maroncelli, which Donizetti thought enough of to copy out in his own hand.[2] That liberal politics as a topic had much influence on Donizetti would be difficult to support. For one thing, his active career as a composer left him little time, and his commitments involved his staying in good repute with the powers the liberals despised, i.e. the Bourbons and the Hapsburgs. In the extensive published correspondence of Donizetti, there are almost no references to political matters. At first glance, this might seem a case of simple discretion in a period of rampant censorship, a time of spies and counterspies, but Donizetti's silence on such things is so consistent that it speaks more of a lack of interest than of simple carefulness. Unless additional and contrary evidence

---

[1] Z. No. A. 38, pp. 895–6.
[2] MS. in Museo Donizettiano, Bergamo.

should be forthcoming, it appears that Donizetti should be quite simply regarded as apolitical.[1]

Undoubtedly Donizetti's chief concern in Bologna was music, both his studies and his composing. Most important in terms of his future career were Donizetti's first attempts at writing operas. The autograph score of the first of these, *Il Pigmalione*, a one-act comedy, bears this note: 'begun on 15 September and finished 1 October [1816] at two in the morning.' As far as is known, *Pigmalione* was not performed until 13 October 1960, when it was brought out as one of the novelties for the Teatro alla Novità in Bergamo and was well received. At the much-delayed *prima*, Orianna Santunioni Finzi (Galatea) and Doro Antonioli (Pigmalione) comprised the cast, while the orchestra was conducted by Armando Gatti. Still to be performed are two operas from the following year: *Olimpiade* and *L'ira d'Achille*. Of the former, only one scene is known to survive; the holograph score of the latter is in the library of the Paris Conservatory. These three attempts were student work, but to judge from the known quantity of *Il Pigmalione*, they are of considerable competence and verve, confirming the opinion of a fellow student of Donizetti's at the Bologna Liceo, who told Cicconetti:

> . . . the compositions written while [Donizetti] was a student at the Liceo revealed the directness of an expert

[1] I should add, however, that in Italy I repeatedly encountered an oral tradition that Donizetti was 'active' politically. I heard rumours of compromising letters by Donizetti burnt as soon as read and of his serving as a courier, taking advantage of his position to smuggle letters from one town to another. These rumours may have some foundation, but such actions leave no traces. Further, there is the undeniable fact that some of Donizetti's close associates in Paris, Michele Accursi and the Ruffini brothers, were engaged in political intrigue.

I must confess that I couldn't help feeling my informers were motivated to urge the view of Donizetti as a political conspirator because they wished him to seem as great a patriot as Verdi, say, and because they further wished to counteract the once current gossip that Donizetti had not been active enough politically. To set against the rumours I heard is the significant evidence that in all Donizetti's many published letters there is no mention of public events or figures, except where they relate directly to his professional life. If political intrigue was a natural sphere of activity to Donizetti, at least some oblique traces of it might be expected to survive in the mass of his correspondence. That the course of Donizetti's career depended on his keeping in the good graces of a number of courts is a point of considerable importance.

composer and made evident through the easy, florid theatrical style that he had nothing more to learn from Mattei's school.[1]

Donizetti's other compositions of these Bologna years include some vocal works to both religious and secular texts, as well as a number of Sinfonie. These last were not what we think of today as symphonies, but rather what we would call overtures, in either the French or Italian style, depending on the sequence of tempo changes.

One of these latter works, which Donizetti called a Sinfonia concertata for orchestra in C major, was composed, according to a note on the score, on 17 September 1816, and performed at the annual exercises of the Liceo, 9 June 1817. Ten days later Donizetti received a letter from Malvezzi Ranuzzi, the Secretary of the Liceo, complimenting him on his diligence as a student and on his progress, informing him that he had been awarded a prize. Later, this Sinfonia concertata was published by the Milanese house of Carish.

Donizetti returned home to Bergamo for several weeks during the summer of 1817. Two of his compositions, bearing the dates of 16 July and 1 August, were written there. Now almost twenty years old, Donizetti was eager to launch his career and to win fame. He had received a musical education which then could scarcely be surpassed in Italy, and he had consistently proven himself an outstanding student. But the great question was: how and where. As always, Mayr was willing to offer his support. And as always, Andrea Donizetti was anxious that his son begin to contribute to the financial support of his home. No letters survive from this period and so nothing definite is known about what decisions, if any, were reached.

In any event Gaetano was back in Bologna on 7 August, for on that date he composed a Kyrie for chorus and orchestra, which was duly performed on S. Cecilia's Day, 22 November 1817, at the celebration in the church of S. Giacomo in Bologna. The young composer's chief concern in these days was the ever-puzzling question of his future. On 16 November he had written to Mayr to tell him of an arrangement he had heard of from Tommaso Marchesi. A group of aristocratic

[1] Filippo Cicconetti, *Vita di Gaetano Donizetti* (Roma, 1864), p. 25. Cicconetti is here quoting from a letter he had received from a certain Gaspari, dated 17 October 1861.

families in Ancona had lost their music master and were looking for a suitable replacement, one who would teach the modern style of singing and play the piano 'discreetly'; in return for the lessons he would be paid just as 'discreetly'. From a sense of duty to his family he felt he should accept the post as it would make him independent; on the other hand, he was reluctant to consign himself to a limbo from which it would be difficult to accept engagements necessary to the pursuit of his career. As he put it to Mayr:

> . . . Marchesi asked me if I wanted to go there. I answered that without your consent I would not accept the proposal, and he got me this courier. Hereby I let you know what I told him: Note well, signor Maestro, that if I went, I should want to be free for Carnival each year, and until I know whether you have even now some engagement for me, I said, or if I should be writing this Lent for some place, I could not be there until the first days of March.[1]

From this letter it is clear that Donizetti's thoughts of a career already turned towards the operatic stage and that Mayr had promised to help him secure an engagement. Carnival was the chief operatic season, and if Donizetti were free at that time he could supervise the production of his work. Clearly, he regarded the proposed arrangement at Ancona as a stop-gap until he could establish his independence as a composer of operas.

Apparently Mayr answered Gaetano's letter, telling him that he knew of no immediate prospects, for young Gaetano replied in the following mood:

> I understand from your most kind letter that I ought to take advantage of this opportunity and go to Ancona. You should know, however, signor Maestro, that they do not consent to a leave in Carnival, saying that is just the time when they need a maestro because of the continuous concerts that are given and that in them perform most of those people whose Maestro I would be. Furthermore, the salary would be ten scudi a month, giving lessons to five families twice a week, and a gentleman would give me board and lodging in return for teaching his wife and young son. Truly, these arrangements do not seem too

---

[1] Z. No. 4, p. 226.

suitable to me. In any event, I shall accept them only if they leave me free for Carnival. . . .[1]

From this letter it is obvious that Donizetti preferred the uncertainties of an operatic career to the dull routine of music master in Ancona. Apparently his condition of remaining free for Carnival proved an insurmountable obstacle because two weeks or so after this second letter to Mayr, Gaetano had returned to Bergamo to see what he could do about launching his career from there.

Back in Bergamo Donizetti awaited his opportunity impatiently. In these next months he was far from idle. He entered into the amateur musical life of the city. One of his favourite resorts was the weekly gatherings at the villa of Alessandro Bertoli, an excellent amateur violinist. Marco Bonesi played second violin, Mayr viola, and Capuzzi cello. Proof of the interest these informal evenings had for Gaetano is found in his turning up shortly after his return to Bergamo with four movements of a string quartet in E flat major, a composition he had written the day after Christmas 1817— significantly the date was the beginning of the Carnival season. In his memoirs, Bonesi described how Donizetti composed these quartets, for the first one was followed by sixteen more in the space of the next four years.

> . . . I was surprised when he produced quartets written *alla* Haydn, *alla* Beethoven, etc. ; . . . writing them he never approached the piano, not even for an instant. He drew out his composition at his desk in his room, as though he wrote a note to a friend. . . . [He could compose] in the midst of confusion, [but] if he heard anyone playing or singing, he quickly interrupted his work, saying he could not proceed. . . .[2]

While the facility and power of concentration credited to Donizetti by this account are not unparalleled—Schubert, born the same year, was a phenomenon along these lines—they account clearly for Donizetti's future productivity. This

[1] Z. No. 5, p. 226.
[2] Bonesi, unpublished MS.

31

evidence further shows that the emphasis of his musical training stressed practice rather than theory.

Another incident reported by Bonesi points to Donizetti's natural inclination towards composing for the stage. In the countryside beyond Bergamo, at Almenno, lived two men who were well disposed toward Donizetti. One of these was a lawyer named Antonio Quarenghi, who was passionately fond of singing and the possessor of a delightful tenor voice; the other was Domenico Viganoni, one of the famous Bergamasc tenors, who had retired to that place. Their houses were frequently the scene of musical parties, and Donizetti with his agreeable manners and ready humour was a regular attendant. Bonesi recollects that another of the habitués of these evenings was a violinist, A. . . C. . . (Antonio Capuzzi?)

> who was already advanced in years, in bad health and almost toothless. These infirmities notwithstanding, he was always anxious to be with us because he played the violin and was always ready to sing buffo airs. . . .
>
> Donizetti . . . amused himself by improvising an accompaniment. . . . One only needed to hear that composition to recognize the portrait of A. . . C. . . , even though it was presented on the piano keys! Not only did one hear the way he pronounced his words in his raucous voice, but he included his limping and the continuous tic-tac of his cane. One can easily imagine how Viganoni, Mayr, everyone laughed. . . .[1]

Here Donizetti's sense of characterization in musical terms, his grasp of the traditional buffo premise of the pretentious old man whose vanity insists upon exposing his ridiculousness, foreshadows the achievement of *Don Pasquale*.

In the spring of 1818 Gaetano became involved in a venture that speaks of his anxiety to get on somehow with his career. Among the singers at the Teatro di Società that Carnival were two of the leading artists of the period, Giuseppina Ronzi de Begnis (1800–53) and her husband, Giuseppe de Begnis (1793–1849). They sang a season of performances of Paër's *Agnese* and Rossini's *La Cenerentola*.[2] Donizetti struck up a friendship with this couple, probably by arranging music to fit

[1] Bonesi, unpublished MS.

[2] Giuseppe de Begnis, a buffo, had been a member of the original cast of *La Cenerentola* at its first performance in Rome, 25 January 1817.

their voices for their benefit evenings.[1] In those days such events were stipulated in a singer's contract and the programme was designed to show off the star of the evening to maximum advantage. With the hope that their friendship might result in the performance of one of his compositions, Donizetti accompanied these singers to their next engagement at Verona, but apparently he was never called on to act in any capacity but arranger. Disheartened, Donizetti returned to Bergamo.

Here he learned that Antonio Capuzzi, one of the original members of Mayr's faculty, had died on 28 March. To express his duty towards the late Maestro, he wrote a Sinfonia in D. Mayr copied the orchestral parts of this work himself, and it was performed at a concert in Capuzzi's memory. About this same time Donizetti completed his first cantata, *Il ritorno di primavera*, which had been requested by the Liceo in Bologna to be performed at the annual exercises in July of 1818. The authorities of the Liceo had become anxious about the promised cantata and had written to Donizetti to remind him of his obligation. Gaetano wrote to them from Verona on 11 April to assure them the score would be in their hands in good time for its performance, as in fact it was.

Back in Bergamo and still waiting for an opportunity to materialize, Donizetti returned to the writing of string quartets. All the musical parties did nothing to fill his pockets, and Andrea Donizetti, who 'never encouraged' his son, must have complained increasingly at Gaetano's refusal to settle down in a position with a fixed salary. However, some time during 1818 an opportunity to compose an opera fell Donizetti's way. Today it is probably impossible to recover the exact details. The most helpful account available is that in a little pamphlet entitled *Cenni biografici di Donizetti e Mayr raccolti dalle memorie di un vecchio ottuagenario dilettante di musica*,[2] which tells of a Sicilian

---

[1] An evening in which the designated recipient is awarded the proceeds from the box-office.

[2] This pamphlet appeared in 1875 as a by-product of the interest re-aroused in these composers by the removal of their remains to the church of S. Maria Maggiore, Bergamo. The aged octagenarian from whom these memories were gathered seems to have been Bartolomeo Merelli (1794–1879). The author's chronology gets a bit muddled—not surprising since the events related had occurred almost sixty years before—but the statements about these events, although they suffer the same disadvantage, come supposedly from one of the major participants in the arrangements.

impresario, Paolo Zancla, then in Bergamo giving a season with an undistinguished company at the Teatro di Società. Hearing Donizetti well spoken of, Zancla decided to engage him to compose an opera for the opening of the newly redecorated Teatro San Luca in Venice. As the author of the *Cenni biografici* puts it: 'he spoke of the project first with the young Merelli, and the business was settled. Donizetti promised to write the music to the libretto *Enrico di Borgogna*, furnished him by Merelli, who then went to stage the opera.'

The young Merelli was then just turning twenty-two. He had been born in Bergamo, where his father was overseer of the estates belonging to a noble family named Maironi da Ponte. In spite of his father's desire that he study law, Merelli followed his own bent which was to lead him to celebrity and ultimate notoriety as one of the leading impresarios of his time. When Merelli took a course of cembalo lessons as a dilettante-pupil of Mayr, he formed a friendship with Donizetti that was to last until 1821; but when their careers brought them together later their companionship was not renewed. By 1818, Merelli, whose ambitions were literary as well as musical, had set out to gain a place in the operatic world by establishing himself as a librettist. Surely the author of the *Cenni biografici* erred in implying that Merelli persuaded Zancla to put on *Enrico di Borgogna*, when Mayr's recommendation would have carried more weight than that of a scarcely proven librettist.[1]

Again the author of the *Cenni biografici* seems to over-urge Merelli's role in the history of *Enrico di Borgogna* when he says that the librettist went to Venice to stage the new opera. The presence of the composer at the first production of a new work was regarded as so essential that it was customarily insisted upon in the terms of the contract, as was his attendance in person at the first three performances. Merelli certainly went

[1] Merelli's first libretto was for Mayr's *Lanassa*, produced at the Teatro Fenice, Venice, during the Carnival season of 1817–18. For this work, Merelli is listed as a co-librettist with Gaetano Rossi, but who revised whose work is not clear; more likely it was Rossi who, as a librettist of twenty years' experience, tidied up Merelli's maiden effort. Merelli's second libretto was also for Mayr, an *Alfredo il grande*, produced at the Teatro Argentina, Rome, February 1818. His third text was set to music by Nicola Vaccai (1790–1848); the work was entitled *Il lupo d'Ostenda* and was brought out at the Teatro S. Benedetto, Venice, in the spring of 1818.

to Venice,[1] but, more important, Donizetti arrived there early in October, bringing with him his completed score of *Enrico di Borgogna*.

On 13 October, Donizetti wrote to Mayr in Bergamo, uncertain whether Mayr had left yet to go to Rome to produce his opera, *Le Danaidi* at the Teatro Argentina. He sent his teacher these details:

> . . . I inform you that instead of Petrali as prima donna, Catalani *iuniore* has been engaged. She has a very beautiful voice, and I hope for the happiest outcome. I have to rewrite a few things for this soprano. It does not bother to do this to have a singer who is much better than the first one.[2]

Catalani *iuniore* had the first name of Adele (or Adelina) and is not to be confused with the redoubtable Angelica Catalani (1780–1849), of the phenomenal vocal agility and execrable taste. The process of rewriting passages to suit a particular singer's voice was known as *puntature* and was commonplace in those days. Later, Donizetti came to feel that a composer performed this function less capably when it came to his own music than could another competent musician. Unfortunately, the exact nature of Donizetti's *puntature* of Elisa's music so that it suited the voice of Catalani *iuniore* cannot be ascertained now, because the autograph score, like those of other operas he wrote for Zancla, is lost. A manuscript score in a copyist's hand is in the Malherbe Collection in the library of the Paris Conservatory.

Enrico di Borgogna was first performed at the Teatro S. Luca, Venice, on 14 November 1818. Besides Adele Catalani as Elisa, the cast included Fanny Eckerlin, singing the title role of Enrico; Giuseppe Spech, as the usurper Guido; Giuseppe Fosconi, the faithful Pietro, and Andrea Verni in the buffo role

---

[1] Merelli's career is badly in need of accurate reporting. The encyclopaedia *Spettacolo*, a praiseworthy project in many ways, is mistaken when, in the article on Merelli, it states that in 1818 he took a troupe to Vienna and soon became Inspector-General of the Imperial Theatres at 12,000 florins a year. Actually, in 1818 Merelli divided his time between Bergamo and Venice.

At present the best available account of Merelli is to be found in Frank Walker's *The Man Verdi*, pp. 38–95.

[2] Z. No. 7, p. 228.

of Gilberto; the minor roles were in the hands of Adelaide Cassago and Giuseppe Fioravanti.[1]

In the Venetian paper, the *Gazzetta privilegiata* of 14 November 1818 appeared a brief notice that at the 'Teatro Vendramin S. Luca—would be performed *Enrico di Borgogna*, music by sig. maestro Donzelletti [*sic*].' Five days later the same newspaper printed this terse, noncommittal reference to the new opera.

> As to the restoration of the theatre, a superb spectacle. Novel, if not exactly new, the work of the forementioned poet; new as well the composer, who, endowed with good talent, now ventures upon these demanding labours for the first time.[2]

That same season Zancla's company also performed Rossini's *L'Italiana in Algeri*, which made the expenses.

If *Enrico di Borgogna* was not the unalloyed triumph that Donizetti had hoped, the work pleased sufficiently for Zancla to ask for a second opera to be given the following month. In that short time, apparently, the libretto to a one-act farce[3] was

[1] Two of these singers were to be associated with the premières of other operas by Donizetti. The more important of the two was the mezzo-soprano Fanny Eckerlin (1802–42) then at the very beginning of a career that was to take her to La Scala for the spring season of 1820, to Vienna with Rossini and Barbaja in April 1822, and to Paris and the Théâtre-Italien, where she sang Arsace the night Giulia Grisi made her début as Semiramide. The baritone, Giuseppe Fioravanti, was likewise at the beginning of a stage career. Some three years later he sang in the *prima* of Rossini's *Matilde di Shabran*. His services for Donizetti include appearances in more than half a dozen premières over a period of almost twenty years, the most important of his 'creations' being the role of Max in *Betly*. [2] Quoted in Z., p. 15.

[3] There are major puzzles about this work. In the *Cenni biografici* it is referred to as *Il ritratto parlante*, which Zavadini and most biographers of Donizetti associate with *Una follia*, the name by which Donizetti referred to the work composed at this time. Until some concrete evidence (the score, a printed libretto, or a newspaper reference) turns up, everything about this farce must remain conjectural.

Granted there was only a month to write the work from scratch, a limitation that probably sent Merelli in search of a proven libretto. The question of *Una follia* and *Il ritratto parlante* is complicated by the existence of two successful French opéras-comiques: Grétry's *Le tableau parlant* in one act (1796) and Méhul's *Une folie* (1802). Either of these, or both, may have been used as a source by Merelli, and the confusion may well result from which of the works Donizetti and Merelli respectively remembered as the principal source. Since Méhul's work is in two acts and Grétry's in one, this fact may weigh in the favour of the latter work as the principal source of Donizetti's one-act farce.

written by Merelli and set to music by Donizetti, who thereby gave his first professional demonstration of his ability to compose quickly under pressure. The work was staged at the Teatro S. Luca, 15 December 1818, by the same company that had sung *Enrico*, but the distribution of the parts is unknown. The only extant comment about the reception of the work is the word of the author of the *Cenni biografici*, who speaks of it as lucky (*esito fortunato*). *Una follia* (or *Il ritratto parlante*) seems never to have been produced elsewhere, and the neglect of the work, even at the time of its première, may well be explained by its being a one-act curtain-raiser and consequently not heard by the fashionable audience who arrived late at the theatre. The only positive evidence that the opera did not fare ill is that Zancla later commissioned still another opera from Donizetti.

About the beginning of 1819 Donizetti returned to Bergamo, where *Enrico di Borgogna* was staged at the Teatro di Società in the upper city. This production seems to have been less than a howling success as it is scarcely mentioned by Donizetti's biographers. The omission is surprising since the occasion marked the first professional production of a Donizetti opera in his native town. The months that followed must have been a frustrating period for Donizetti. Although he had started his career creditably, he was back where he had been, waiting for a new opportunity to compose for the stage. Certainly it was not easy for Gaetano to return to his friends whose expectations for his success had been more than sanguine, nor to his father, who was still waiting to hear that his youngest son had some permanent employment.

It was impossible for Donizetti to remain idle. On 19 March there was held in Bergamo a benefit concert for the survivors of a spectacular fire, which had cost the lives of two children, while the anguished mother, clutching an infant in her arms, watched helplessly. Ferdinando Arrivabene wrote an ode on the event, and this poem supplied Donizetti with the programme for a sinfonia bearing the descriptive title *L'incendio*, which was duly performed at the concert.

Besides the various minor compositions whose dates attest to their having been written during this period, little is known of Donizetti during this time. But there is one strange little piece of evidence which sheds a tantalizing ray of light on another aspect of Donizetti's life at this time. On the margin of the manuscript of one of his string quartets is written a rather one-sided dialogue. After quoting some verses from the libretto of his still unproduced *Il falegname di Livonia*, Donizetti has written:

> Tell me then, is it yes or no; I have not understood, but I do not believe it—Giuditta Paganini, dear, dearest—and when I have understood, it is sweet to hear it repeated. I would give you my heart, if once given it could remain with you. . . .

Then he continues in French:

> *Giuditte, très aimable, très chère, aimez-vous, oui ou non. Oui? Bien . . . Veux-tu donc faire avec moi une chose?*

And then, suddenly, in English:

> Of the Victory Bonaparte. . . .

He reverts to Italian once more:

> You deny me the surest sign—of the love that binds you to my love. Now I clearly perceive that you have never loved me. . . .

The next words Donizetti wrote are hastily crossed out. The conclusion of this written conversation is in another hand, presumably in that of Giuditta herself:

> Happy and unhappy Gaetano Donizetti . . .
> Sister and brother.[1]

This little dialogue raises a number of questions. First of all, who was Giuditta Paganini? She may have been the daughter or some other relation to Angelo Paganini, who conducted the orchestra at the Teatro Riccardi between 1803 and 1805 and again in 1818 and 1819. To judge from the quotation from *Il falegname* which introduces the conversation, this encounter took place in 1819, a supposition corroborated by the dating of the quartet. Donati-Pettèni reported[2] that Zavadini told him that Giuditta Paganini came from Bologna. Nothing else is known of her.

[1] This conversation is quoted in Donati-Pettèni, *Donizetti* (Milano, 1930), pp. 40–1.
[2] Donati-Pettèni, *L'istituto musicale Gaetano Donizetti*, p. 175.

The most important question is how should this little *entretien* be taken. Although Donati-Pettèni and Fraccaroli used it as a base for sentimental conjecture, it seems difficult to take these words entirely seriously. Donizetti had a well-developed sense of humour, and the whole tenor of this dialogue becomes more plausible if it is considered as a teasing proposition, nothing more. The surprising shifts of language and the bluntness of *Veux-tu donc faire avec moi une chose?* swing into sharper focus if we think of Donizetti more than half in joking, yet perhaps ready to take advantage of any chance favour that might come his way. The chief interest of these jottings is that they afford a glimpse into an area of Donizetti's life about which there is little concrete evidence.

Still another glimpse of Donizetti from the same year of 1819 is found in a memorial written by Mayr as a formal protest against a move by the Congregazione di Carità of Bergamo to cut off the funds of the Lezioni Caritatevoli. Some of the more literal-minded members of the Congregazione had decided that to underwrite a music school was to support non-essentials. Mayr, with the encouragement of several influential members of the group, wrote a defence, basing it upon the argument of accomplishment. After recounting the budding careers of Manghenoni and Bonesi among others, he continues:

> . . . and . . . Donizetti, formerly the bass soloist in the Chapel, at the age of twenty-one has composed three operas for the theatres of Mantua and Venice, while Bergamo from the days of Legrenzi, who lived at the beginning of the past century, has had no operatic composers. . . .[1]

The three operas of Donizetti's that Mayr mentions are *Enrico di Borgogna* and *Una follia*, both produced in Venice, and

[1] Mayr's memorial is quoted in Donati-Pettèni, *L'istituto musicale Gaetano Donizetti*, pp. 54–5.
Giovanni Legrenzi (1626–90) composed at least eighteen operas between *Nino il Giusto* (Ferrara, 1662) and *Ifianassa e Melampo* (Venice, 1685). What is generally regarded as his finest opera, *Totila* (Venice, 1677), was edited by Giovanni Tebaldini in 1891. Legrenzi's career was chiefly centred in Venice, where he was at one time *maestro di cappella* at St Mark's. He wrote oratorios and important instrumental works as well. His most famous pupil was Antonio Lotti (*c.* 1667–1740).

Le nozze in villa, which, although it was composed in 1819, was not produced at Mantua until the Carnival season of 1820–21. Some of the music from the score of *Le nozze in villa* was, however, heard in 1819. That year, for the little farce to be presented at the annual exercise of Mayr's school in September, the director turned the assignment over to Donizetti, who wrote a work entitled *I piccioli virtuosi ambulanti* to a libretto by Merelli. The introduction and an aria with chorus were drawn from *Le nozze in villa*, one of the earliest examples of Donizetti's self-borrowings. That Mayr asked Donizetti to arrange the farce for the school's Accademia seems consistent with his desire to give Donizetti opportunities to display his talent; further, it was an extension of Mayr's argument to persuade the Congregazione di Carità to continue their support of his school.

The author of the *Cenni biografici* gives some particulars of the first performance of *Le nozze in villa*, although he writes of the opera as though it had been performed directly after Zancla's autumn season 1818 at the Teatro S. Luca. He says:

> Further, for that Ducal theatre [Mantua] Zancla wanted a third work; and this, again, with a libretto by Merelli, was the score entitled: *Le nozze in villa*. This opera, in spite of many successful numbers, could not maintain itself because of the caprices and ill will of several singers and especially of the prima donna. Donizetti did not lose courage, being sustained by his already established reputation, and further because he had already been engaged to compose another opera, which was given and applauded the following spring at the Teatro S. Mosè [Venice]. . . .[1]

The prima donna in question was the mezzo-soprano Fanny Eckerlin, perhaps chafing at the contract which still bound her to Zancla. When *Le nozze in villa* was sung in Mantua, she had already sung at La Scala, appearing in a highly successful run of forty-one performances of *La gazza ladra*; in contrast, she may well have found Donizetti's early work dim. The score of *Le nozze in villa* is lost; the *Cenni biografici* suggests that Zancla may have taken it back to Sicily with him, where he died shortly after. A libretto of this opera is in the library of the Naples Conservatory; it bears the title *I provinciali ossia Le*

[1] *Cenni biografici*, p. 14.

nozze in villa; this copy was not printed for the *prima* in Mantua, but for a subsequent production in Genoa for the spring season of 1822,[1] evidence that the opera enjoyed more of a career than had previously been recognized.

The other opera that the author of the *Cenni biografici* refers to as being written for the Teatro S. Mosè was a two-act opera buffa, *Il falegname di Livonia ossia Pietro il Grande, Czar delle Russie*, which was given at the Teatro S. Samuele—not the S. Mosè—on 26 December 1819. Although this opera was composed after *Le nozze in villa*, it was produced first. The libretto was the work of the Marchese Gherardo Bevilacqua Aldovrandini, who may well have based his libretto on Felice Romani's book on the same subject, which was set by Giovanni Pacini, his *Il falegname* having been produced at La Scala, 12 April 1819. The popularity of this subject is proven by Merelli's writing a third version of it which was set by Vaccai and brought out in 1824.

Although Donizetti's new opera was criticized as improvised rather than studiously written and its first reception described as chilly, nevertheless *Il falegname* proved hardier than the *Gazzetta privilegiata*'s lukewarm review would indicate. At its première the opera was sung by the prima donna Amati, the tenor G. B. Verger, the bass Vincenzo Botticelli, and the buffo Luigi Martinelli. Later, *Il falegname* was put on at Bologna during the Carnival season of 1823-24—the first of Donizetti's operas to be produced in the city where he had studied with Mattei—at Verona in September 1825,[2] at Padua in 1826, at Venice in 1827, and at Spoleto in 1829.

Between *Il falegname* and Donizetti's next opera a little more than two years were to elapse. Again, Donizetti returned to Bergamo to await some change in his fortune. Again, he kept himself busy by turning out a surprisingly large quantity of

[1] The cast for this Genoa production included Carolina Contini (Sabina), the well-known tenor Giovanni Battista Verger (Claudio), the buffo Carlo Pizzocchero (Trifoglio), and the bass Andrea Verni (Don Petronio).

[2] I have seen Maestro Tenaglia's copy of the libretto of the Verona production and it contains a different finale to Act 2 to that in the autograph score. Whether Donizetti made this change for the Verona production, or had made it earlier for Bologna, or even whether Donizetti made the change himself, cannot now be determined.

miscellaneous music, including more string quartets for the *casa* Bertoli. For Donizetti this was a period of concern, a time for re-evaluation.

There are few clues to his state of mind at this time, but, such as they are, they reveal his troubled spirits. In his memoir of Donizetti, Bonesi makes an interesting point as he speaks of this period:

> . . . I participated in his first vicissitudes and at the same time shared with him my frank opinion of his music. . . . Appreciating his talent more than anyone, I wanted to see him emerge with glory.. . . . Straightforwardly he told me that he had to attach himself to the Rossinian style, according to the taste of the day. If once he made his own way a little, nothing would prevent him from developing his own style. He had many ideas how to reform the predictable situations, the sequences of introduction, cavatina, duet, trio, finale, always fashioned the same way. 'But,' he added sadly, 'what to do with the blessed theatrical conventions? Impresarios, singers, and the public as well, would hurl me into the farthest pit at least, and—*addio per sempre*.'[1]

Although Bonesi was writing years later than the events he described, his account is true in spirit, for Donizetti was clearly faced with the problem of being forced to meet the public's expectations and preconceptions if he were to gain its favour. Even today, Italian audiences have no great tolerance for novelty, and while in the early nineteenth century they had an almost insatiable appetite for new operas, they had fixed ideas about the general form and style that should obtain in a new work. To win the favour of a public who wanted operas in the Rossinian vein, Donizetti set himself to master the idiom. How well he learned his lessons may be seen from a comparison of the scores of *Il falegname* and its successor, *Zoraide di Granata*. In the latter work, typical Rossinian turns of phrase and figures sound from many pages.

But while Donizetti was concerned with the practical aspects of putting his career in motion, a question arose which threw doubt upon his liberty to follow that calling just then. According to Zavadini,[2] the Austrian governor of Milan issued in

---

[1] Bonesi, unpublished MS.   [2] Z., p. 229n.

December 1820 a call to military duty for the five classes born
between 1795 and 1799, the conscripts to report for active
service between 15 and 24 December. At this time both of
Donizetti's brothers were under arms, but he was not to join
them. Contrary to the often-repeated and erroneous story that
Gaetano was in uniform as early as 1818 and that his early
operas won him a discharge from the army, he was able to win
an exemption from military service.

One of the few surviving letters Donizetti wrote in these years
bears directly on this matter. On 15 December 1820, he wrote
to Mayr, who was in Milan for the staging of his opera *Fedra*:

> ... Pontiroli tells me to let you know that he too has been
> hit by the conscription, but the hectic ones will be exempted
> I believe.[1]

'The hectic ones' (*gli etici*) are Donizetti and his friend Antonio
Dolci. Additional light is shed on this matter by a letter Donizetti wrote to Dolci nearly twenty years later. He speaks of a
'worthy woman' who did 'a favour for you and me in the matter
of the conscription when we needed money.'[2] This generous-
minded woman, Marianna Pezzoli-Grattaroli, was sufficiently
impressed with the talents of these young men to purchase their
exemptions. Donizetti had written and dedicated a number of
piano compositions to her.

Within six months of the time the vexatious problem of his
military service had been settled, Donizetti entered upon the
project that was to serve as the cornerstone for his future
career. The situation can best be surveyed from the letter he
wrote on 17 June 1821 to Giovanni Paterni, the impresario of
the Teatro Argentina in Rome.

> From Sig. Corini I have received the contracts, one of
> which I return to you by him, asking that you will grant
> me my lodging, being sure that this will not bother you in
> the least.
>
> Further, I appreciate your praiseworthy uncertainty
> about which one of us will secure the libretto, and I am
> cheered by that, as I have already spoken to Sig. Merelli.
> Do not fail to inform me about the singers: whether they

[1] Z. No. 7, *bis*, p. 229.
[2] Z. No. 323, p. 499. Ltr. dated 26 July 1839.

are adapted to tragic or to comic works. I believe it will be the former, because at Carnival the remodelling of the Valle will not be completed.

At the appointed time you will have the text in Rome, so that it can be passed by the censors, and I hope it will be excellent since the poet has already worked for Mayr, for Naples, for Milan and for Venice, etc. Corini will be able to confirm this.

I remain, looking forward to the pleasure of meeting you personally, and assuring you that I am,

Your most devoted servant,

Gaetano Donizetti.

P.S. I beg you to answer promptly.

Signing the contract, I have found 500 scudi written in. Since the currency is not explained, I assume Roman is meant, since it is not otherwise indicated. I need to know so that I can settle with the poet. . . .[1]

With this letter, Donizetti returned a copy of the signed contract for the opera that was to be *Zoraide di Granata* to Paterni. There seems to be no concrete evidence just how Donizetti entered into negotiations with the Roman impresario. A persistent tradition asserts that Paterni had originally approached Mayr, who had written several works for the Teatro Argentina in recent years, but that composer, nearing sixty and soon to give up composing for the operatic stage, persuaded Paterni to accept his prize pupil as his substitute. In the absence of any contradictory information, there is no reason not to accept provisionally a tradition which confirms what we know of Mayr's generous nature and of his abiding concern for Donizetti's future.

From Donizetti's letter it is clear that the opera had not yet been begun in the middle of June 1821, but on 9 August, he again wrote to Paterni, telling him that the poet is 'at work on the libretto' and that 'as soon as possible I hope to see some pieces of it'.[2] It is possible, therefore, to date the composition of

[1] Z. No. 8, pp. 229–30.
[2] Z. No. 9, p. 230. Most of this letter is given over to recommending a second tenor, Vincenzo Fraccalini, to Paterni's consideration. If the impresario had engaged Fraccalini, Donizetti might have been spared the crisis that threatened *Zoraide*.

Zoraide di Granata as having been started after 9 August 1821 and completed by 1 October of that year. On the latter date, Mayr wrote a letter to the Roman librettist Jacopo Ferretti (1784–1852), introducing Donizetti. It is typical of Mayr's goodness and modesty that while he praises his pupil warmly, he mentions only that he has studied in Bologna with Padre Mattei.

In the first days of October, Gaetano left Bergamo, taking with him his score of *Zoraide*, Mayr's letter of introduction to Ferretti, and a passport. In those days of a divided Italy, a passport was required to travel between the Austrian province of Lombardy and the Papal States. On Gaetano's passport he was described as twenty-three years and eleven months old; hair, chestnut; eyes, blue; colouring, fair; height, tall; physique, slender; purpose of travel, to produce an opera at the Teatro Argentina.

Thus, Donizetti set out from the city of Bergamo, 'taking flight like an owl', on the journey that was to bring him not only fame and wealth but also humiliation and tragedy.

CHAPTER 2

Launching a Career

Before we return to Donizetti and the unexpectedly successful production of *Zoraide di Granata*, it might prove helpful to review some of the conditions which prevailed in the operatic arena at that time.

First of all, it is essential to understand the role of the composer in connexion with the people he was forced to deal with. Certainly, as far as material rewards go, or the matter of being able to dictate his wishes about a performance, or to retain any appreciable control over the music he composed, Donizetti was in a far less favourable position than Verdi in his latter years, or Puccini. Certainly the conditions under which Donizetti worked had a profound effect upon his operas.

In the 1820's a composer was rarely engaged as long as six months before the new opera was to have its first performance. The composer's contract with the impresario characteristically specified both the librettist and the subject—not necessarily a new one. The composer was expected to pay the librettist out of his own fee. The librettist was most frequently a local poet, one perhaps who, like Checcherini or Cammarano, was connected with the theatre in the capacity of stage manager, or one who, like Ferretti, was a literary jack-of-all-trades. If the composer lived in another town, he would have to compose his score with little chance of personal consultation with his librettist. In fact, the composer could exercise only limited control over the libretto; he might sometimes manage to refuse a subject outright and he might manage to have some lines altered to suit his purposes, but the ultimate authority over the plot and wording of an operatic text lay in the hands of the censors.

The role of the censors, especially in the celebrated cases of Verdi's *Rigoletto* and *Un ballo in maschera*, is well known, but the extent of their influence in Italy during the first six decades of the nineteenth century can scarcely be exaggerated. In the north, the Austrian censors supervised the stages of Milan and Venice; the exigent Papal authorities had to be appeased in Rome; in Naples and Palermo, the sensibilities of the Bourbons were assiduously protected. In the Kingdom of the Two Sicilies, although the law decreed that a libretto be submitted for approval a full year in advance of its first performance, the uncertainties and last-minute arrangements of operatic management frequently caused the submission of the libretto to be delayed until the opera was ready to go into rehearsal. It is clear, for example, that Donizetti characteristically composed his works to texts before they had been censored, for the autographs of such operas as *Imelda de' Lambertazzi*, *Francesca da Foix*, and *L'assedio di Calais* show that words were altered after the music had been written.

Among other things, the censors were adamant in refusing to permit such subjects as regicide, treason, suicide and adultery to be enacted upon the stage. To present a priest,[1] part of a religious service, or a crucifix would be sacrilege. Such potentially offensive or subversive words as *Dio*, *angelo*, *tiranno*, or *libertà* were stricken out, and the censors would replace them with others which, though antiseptic, did not invariably make good sense. The Roman censors were perhaps the most touchy. At one time they would not permit any mention of France on the stage, while their religious scruples are most exquisitely revealed on the occasion of the first production of *La favorita* there, when the title was changed, the king's liaison called an engagement, the setting shifted to Armenia, and that most static of all Fathers Superior, Baldassare, transformed into a whirling dervish! In contrast to the censorship in Italy, that in France was considerably more lenient, and Paris held for Italian composers the attractions not only of greater réclame and fatter

[1] This explains why operatic marriages are customarily performed by notaries.

fees than they could earn at home, but much greater freedom in choice of subject.

The most crippling aspect of censorship in Italy has not perhaps been sufficiently emphasized. In Naples, for example, the librettists who worked there regularly, such as Tottola, Gilardoni and Cammarano, had little desire to gain reputations as trouble-makers. Their adaptations of plots avoided potentially censorable situations, even when their changes and omissions did not make dramatic sense. This intimidation of librettists is undoubtedly the most insidious aspect of the whole ugly situation, as well as the most far-reaching in view of its ultimate effect upon the composer seeking his inspiration in such a compromised text.

A matter of major concern to a composer was the company of singers assembled by the impresario for the season in which the new work would be produced. Unlike the great repertory opera houses of England and the United States today which may have as many as a hundred singers on the roster for a long season, the usual company of those days consisted of a soprano and usually a mezzo-soprano, who would be expected to sing both female and male-hero roles, a first tenor, sometimes a second tenor, a first bass for serious roles, and a basso buffo to appear in comic works as well as in those of the semi-serio genre. Any small parts were customarily filled by the more prepossessing members of the chorus which often totalled no more than sixteen to twenty. In the larger opera houses and for the gala seasons in the smaller theatres, a lavish impresario might provide understudies for the leading parts. With such a limited choice of singers at any given time, a composer had to be familiar with their vocal strengths and weaknesses, and their dramatic aptitudes and limitations. The complaint that a particular company is ill-suited (*non adatta*) for this work or that runs like a refrain through the letters of Italian composers of this period.

The composer had to take advantage of the singers' talents because he had to rely on winning, if possible, a decisive success for his new opera during its first three performances. It was usually stipulated in his contract that a composer had to be physically present, seated at the cembalo, for these crucial performances. In this way the impresario could assure himself that the composer would be on hand for the rehearsals and to take responsibility for the originality of his score. The impresario usually did not pay the balance of the fee for the opera until after the first performance. Further, a composer would frequently find himself harassed by a penny-pinching manager who hoped to economize in matters of scenery, costumes and properties.

A hazard of a different sort sometimes beset the composer—his rivals. While Donizetti himself almost invariably regarded his fellow composers benignly as fellow sufferers pursuing an uncertain career, he was not always so well treated in return. Not only a rival but a rival's enthusiastic partisans could create difficulties for anyone who threatened to dim the favourite composer's lustre. As in the case of Countess Samayloff for Pacini, and Giuditta Turina for Bellini, a woman of influence might use any means at hand to smooth her lover's path by roughening the road for his rivals. A hostile demonstration from a faction in an audience; a scathing review purchased from an accommodating critic; the sowing of disaffection among the singers and musicians, all these methods and others were common practice in the gentle art of arranging a fiasco. A composer's birthplace might help or impede his career, for in those days of a divided Italy, the triumphs of a *forestiere* were galling to less successful native sons. Such examples of pettiness are not, of course, unique to Italy nor to this period, but at a time when there were many operas composed each year and a large number of men of widely varying talents writing them, the occasions for such harassment are more frequent than in a period less prolific of operas.

For a composer to achieve his prompt and decisive success, he had therefore not only to cope with impresarios and their sometimes niggardly preparations for staging the work, but with the incontestable power of the public. In this period, opera houses occupied a place of unusual significance in the social scheme. Primarily they were centres for a form of entertainment that provided, as could not other institutions, a community of interest and a sense of national identity that permeated the whole peninsula. The performance, though, was often a backdrop to the other diverting activities in the social centre that was an opera house, a salon away from home where gossip reigned supreme, where liaisons were formed, fostered and finished, where political enthusiasms could find indirect means of expression. To many the opera itself was merely an accompaniment to these engrossing occupations. Some others, who self-consciously played the roles of connoisseur and musical detective, heeded the performance, keenly observant of the vagaries of the singing, on the alert for any music that seemed to echo that of another opera or another composer, and were immovable in their judgements. The audience sat in a theatre that was not darkened, held supper parties in the antechambers to their boxes, and might break into noisy laughter and conversation at any provocation unless they were severely shushed by their neighbours. They tolerated the practice of interspersing long sequences of ballet between the acts of an opera instead of insisting the opera and the dance be arranged in logical sequence, and consequently they had two confusing plots to muddle them. For all the other interests that conflicted for their attention, these audiences were still capable of finding themselves overwhelmingly amused or moved by a performance and receiving it with impulsive enthusiasm; their boredom or displeasure could, on occasion, find equally direct expression. They were quick to respond to fine singing, to an effective bit of dramatic characterization, to music that was immediately assimilable. It was in the hands of such an audience—unpredictable, demanding, jealous of its traditional prerogatives —that the fate of a new opera was decided.

Even though a composer were to win a success, or even that utmost pitch of enthusiasm that the Italians call *fanatismo*, his difficulties were by no means over. The greater a success the more eager other towns were to hear the new sensation. But since a composer was not protected by copyright laws at this time, many an unscrupulous impresario who wished to avoid paying the rental of the music from its owner would try to persuade a copyist to make an extra copy of the parts, or he would hire a hack to orchestrate the work from a printed piano score. Although there were laws designed to protect an author's rights in many parts of Italy, they were often flouted. Complaints against the musical pirates recur again and again in the correspondence of Bellini, Donizetti, and Verdi, and when they could they took legal action against the offenders, but the dishonest practice was slow to die. Donizetti was himself the victim of such piracy which worked a double disadvantage to the composer, for not only did he lose royalties by the inept production of a work with wildly incorrect parts, but such a presentation damaged both the reputation of the mutilated opera and of the composer who wrote it. When *Anna Bolena* was first staged in Rome (Teatro Apollo, January 1833), it failed utterly because it was given in a woefully corrupt version patched together by the conductor, Carlo Valentini.[1]

It is easy to call this period one of debased taste and look upon it as a sort of inartistic disaster area; yet this is to dismiss it too glibly. It was a transitional era in which the petrified conceptions of eighteenth-century opera seria were slowly giving way to the more elastic forms of romantic opera. It was a time of great ferment and a time in which conservative forces exerted strong pressures to resist change. If one takes a partisan view of this struggle, opera, certainly then the most representative form of artistic expression in Italy, seems trivial and artificial; but if one observes the struggle objectively, the operas of the period, from the escapist comedies of Rossini through the strange anomaly of works with wildly melodramatic plots set to rigidly formalized music, serve as a clear reflection of the forces in opposition during this transitional epoch.

When Donizetti arrived in Rome he delivered Mayr's letter of introduction to Ferretti's house.[2] The librettist lived in a fourth-floor apartment in an old palazzo, via dei Lucchesi, No. 24. His wife, the former Emilia Terziani, was a member of a distinguished musical family; as yet there were no children—the eldest was not born until September 1822. At thirty-eight, Ferretti was easy-going, genial and extravert. Not a wealthy man, he had made numerous friends with his facile literary talents, and his hospitable nature had caused his home to become a meeting-place where anyone interested in poetry, in the theatre, or in music, could find a warm welcome. Mayr could not have made a wiser choice of a man to befriend Gaetano on his first visit to Rome. Not only was Ferretti familiar with the cross-currents of the Roman opera stages, but

---

[1] See Alberto Cametti, *Il Teatro di Tordinona poi il Apollo* (Tivoli, 1938).
[2] The principal sources for the details of Donizetti's first stay in Rome are three invaluable books by Alberto Cametti: his biography of Jacopo Ferretti (1898), his *Donizetti a Roma* (1907), and his two-volume history of the Apollo theatre (1938). Cametti has a praiseworthy respect for fact.

he had a wide acquaintance among persons whose support and friendship would prove invaluable to Donizetti. In any event, Ferretti seems to have taken an instant liking to the personable young man and to have served him well.

Although Ferretti had never written an opera libretto[1] for Mayr, he had come to know him well during his three months' stay in Rome in 1808, and the friendship had been maintained at Mayr's later visits. Ferretti had, however, supplied many composers with books: the younger Guglielmi, whom he regarded as the most difficult composer he ever worked with; Nicola Zingarelli, who never asked for a single change in a libretto; Giovanni Pacini; and most noteworthy, Rossini, whom he had supplied with the texts for *Cenerentola* and *Matilde di Shabran*, this last work having had its première in Rome the previous February. To someone like Donizetti, whose experiences as a composer had been confined to Bergamo, to Mantua, and to the smaller theatres of Venice, it must have seemed that he had been brought to the banks of the mainstream of the operatic swim. For if Rome had no single theatre that boasted the zealously cultivated prestige of Milan's La Scala or Naples' San Carlo, it had three important opera houses: the Argentina, the Valle, and the Apollo, this last proud of a tradition that extended back to 1675,[2] while at the Argentina on 20 February 1816, had occurred the most important première of the first quarter of the nineteenth century: Rossini's *Il barbiere di Siviglia*.

For the Carnival season of 1821–22 only two of the three theatres were open. The Valle was closed for a whole year as it was being completely redecorated by Valadier. The company that usually performed opera buffa at the Valle had moved to the Apollo until its regular quarters would be ready; the Argentina confined its activities to opera seria. Both companies were under the management of Giovanni Paterni (1779–1837), a wealthy Roman industrialist, who indulged his fondness for speculation and the opera by skilfully managing opera troupes in Rome until he retired from this activity some time after 1832.

---

[1] He had, however, written an oratorio text for Mayr, *Il voto di Jefte*, which was given at the Valle in March 1814.
[2] The Apollo was originally called the Teatro Tordinona, but the name was changed to the Apollo in 1795, with the hope thereby of ridding the theatre of its associations with a notorious prison.

Both theatres opened their season on the traditional date of San Stefano, 26 December. The Apollo began with a new opera by Carafa, in which Luigi Lablache made his Roman début, entitled *La capricciosa e il soldato*: the libretto was by Ferretti, but it had been so badly manhandled by censorship that he refused to own his work. The Argentina opened its season with another new opera, *Cesare in Egitto* by Pacini, sung by Maria Ester Mombelli, and the tenors Domenico Donzelli and Americo Sbigoli. Both operas were well received, and performed for about a month.

While singing the second-act quintet of Pacini's opera the tenor Sbigoli had the misfortune one night of bursting a blood vessel in his throat when he attempted, in his repetition of a phrase that Donzelli sang with magnificent effect, to imitate the leading tenor's robust tones. Within a few days the unfortunate Sbigoli was dead, leaving a pregnant wife and four young sons.[1] This calamity produced a crisis for Donizetti, as he had written the important role of the General Abenamet in *Zoraide di Granata* for a second tenor. Sbigoli's fatal accident would seem to have occurred about the middle of January 1822, because Donizetti was confronted with the problem of revising the part of Abenamet for a contralto named Mazzanti,[2] there being no time to secure another tenor. In fact, there was so little time before the first performance that three numbers had to be eliminated from the score. Undoubtedly Sbigoli's death and the unlooked-for labour that befell Donizetti and the uncertainty of entrusting an important role to an unknown singer caused him to look forward to the first performance with some trepidation. His whole future hinged upon the outcome of his first encounter with an important centre.

The hastily recast *Zoraide di Granata* was given at the Argentina on 28 January 1822, sung by Maria Ester Mombelli (Zoraide), Mazzanti (Abenamet), Donzelli (Almuzir), Alberto Torri (Ali), Gaetano Rambaldi (Almanzor) and Gaetana Corini (Ines). The performance was interspersed by two ballets, *Le amazzoni di Boemia* and *L'avaro*.[3] Both of them failed, while

[1] Pacini tells the story in his *Le mie memorie artistiche* (Florence, 1875), pp. 28–9. Pacini also states that he formed a firm friendship with Donizetti, dating from these days in Rome.
[2] It is not clear if Mazzanti took over Sbigoli's role in *Cesare in Egitto* as well.
[3] The choreographer for these ballets was Antonio Landini.

Donizetti's opera won a major success. The success was not tepid or merely polite, the opera aroused enthusiasm and fervour, the sort of reception that Gaetano had dreamed of but not dared to expect.

Luck was with him. The failure of the ballets only served to enhance the merits of his opera. There was no competition from the Apollo, for two days earlier the new work there, *La festa in villaggio* by Vincenzo Puccita, who was known as Angelica Catalani's tame composer, had been received in stony silence. Another situation favoured Donizetti. For most of 1821 Pacini had remained in Rome, enjoying the favours of Princess Pauline Borghese (1780–1825), one of Napoleon's sisters, and the Roman public felt a desire to demonstrate to the princess (whose character was epitomized in Canova's famous statue of her as Venus) that there was more than one composer capable of creating a stageworthy opera. Further, the general knowledge of the hardship worked on the new composer by the untimely death of Sbigoli may well have roused the audience's sympathy. And Donizetti was fortunate to have Donzelli,[1] then at the height of his powers, in his cast, for the popular tenor seems to have exerted himself to contribute to the favourable reception of this opera by a fellow Bergamasc.

These circumstances, however, could do little more than predispose an audience to concentrate on the solid merits of Donizetti's score. They heard an opera that revealed the composer's gift for fluent melody, his knowledge of orchestration, and his sure handling of concerted pieces. Few of his contempories, save of course Rossini, launched a career for which he had training comparable to that Donizetti had received.

The occasion had all the unique aura of a first success. For this Roman audience there could be no invidious comparisons with Donizetti's past achievements; and there was all the thrill of discovering a new composer of indisputable talent.

Abbé Celli has left an account of the response to the première of *Zoraide* in his criticism which appeared in the Roman weekly, *Notizie del giorno*.[2] He describes the applause as 'unanimous,

---

[1] In 1808 Donzelli had made his début on the stage, singing in Mayr's *Elisa* at the Riccardi in Bergamo. Giuseppe Donizetti had also sung in these performances.

[2] No. 5, 31 January 1822.

sincere, and universal', adding that 'every piece was received with particular pleasure; enthusiasm greeted the introduction, the duet, and the quartet of the first act, as well as the romanza, the big tenor aria, and the finale of the second act.' Celli believed the reception would have been even warmer if the audience could have heard the three pieces which unfortunately had to be omitted.[1] He continues:

> That excellent singer and most competent actor Donzelli drew as he pleased upon the emotions of those who heard him; la Mombelli, always up to her best, was ravishing with the sweetness of her singing and with her expressive pathos. All thoughts, however, revolved round the young composer tacitly urging him not to desist from his chosen path and not to deviate from the beautiful style that does him honour.

The seal was set on Donizetti's success after the third performance, on 30 January, when he and Donzelli were serenaded by a military band and marched in a torchlight procession to a banquet in a restaurant. Earlier that day Donizetti had written to Mayr about the fate of *Zoraide*, 'I limit myself to saying it was very happy (*felicissimo*).'

The good fortune that attended *Zoraide*'s first production made Donizetti's name known from Naples to Milan; it opened the way for new engagements. This would seem enough to make Donizetti's first visit to Rome an event of great importance to his future, but another occurrence was to prove of almost equal significance. At some point during this four months' stay in Rome he was introduced to the household of Luigi Vasselli (1770 or 1771–1832), the man who was to become his father-in-law.

Vasselli was a distinguished lawyer, coming from a family associated with the law. His probity and acumen had been recognized by Pius VII, who had commissioned him to codify the laws of civil procedure.[2] Some time before 1795 he had

---

[1] Apparently Celli had heard these pieces played on the piano, probably by Donizetti himself at Ferretti's home, for Celli was a frequent guest at the house. Part of Celli's review is quoted in Cametti, *Donizetti a Roma*, p. 20.

[2] Luigi Vasselli was the author of *Formulario di tutti gli procedura analogamente al Codice pubblicando con Notu proprio del 22 Novembre 1817* (Rome, 1818).

married Rosa Costanti, two years older than he. They lived on the *piano nobile* of the via delle Muratte, No. 78, with their four children and a daughter-in-law. Their oldest son, Antonio or Toto,[1] then twenty-seven, was at the time a surgeon assigned to the papal troops, but he was eventually to follow the family profession of the law. Francesco, named for his paternal grandfather, was just twenty-two and barely launched on a career as a lawyer to the Papal Curia. He died, tragically young, in 1826, leaving a twenty-five-year-old widow, Serafina. The youngest son, Gaetano, was still a schoolboy of sixteen. The only daughter was Virginia,[2] thirteen, who had shortly before left the convent school of the Monastero delle Vergini. The Vassellis' household was completed by two servants: one, an old woman in her eighties; the other, a youth from Riofreddo, the country place from which the Vassellis originally came.

The Vassellis formed a closely knit family, bound together by strong bonds of affection, and dominated by the austere but kind-hearted Luigi. Virginia, the youngest child and the only daughter, was idolized by her brothers. As in most families in their position, there was music in the home, and Virginia was on the way to becoming an accomplished pianist and singer. While Donizetti's first friendship in this family group was with Toto, a young man with a robust sense of humour and a profound loyalty to his family and friends, he can scarcely have been unaware of the promise of the dark beauty and gentle disposition of young Virginia.

Besides the Vassellis, Donizetti formed a friendship with another important family in Rome. The Carnevalis were of a deeply musical bent; although, like others of their class, they had never considered a professional career appropriate, they had developed technical aptitudes and musicianship that would have been the envy of many who earned their living by singing and playing. That Roman society possessed its share of amateurs who were musicians of the first class is attested by the formation of such groups as the Accademia filarmonica, which gave performances of difficult works which on occasion surpassed those in the theatres. Anna Carnevali, the wife of

[1] According to Cametti, this name was pronounced with the accent on the first syllable.
[2] She was born 27 November 1808 and christened Anna Maria Virginia. Her baptismal certificate is to be found in the records of S. Marcello.

Dr Paolo Carnevali, and her daughters, especially Clementina who sang with the Accademia di S. Cecilia for many years, were in the centre of this circle of highly talented amateurs. Donizetti offered proof of his friendship and esteem for this family by composing music for them.

Donizetti remained in Rome as long as *Zoraide* held the stage. He had entered into an environment new to him; he was treated with admiration and affection by distinguished people. It speaks well for Donizetti's pleasant and unassuming manner, for his poise and wit, that he took his new surroundings in his stride, forming attachments that were to last him the rest of his life. That he missed Rome is proven by his wry comment in a letter to Ferretti: 'Naples does not please me, Rome very much, and therefore I live at Naples for Rome.'[1]

The exact date of Donizetti's departure from Rome is not known, but he seems to have left in the latter half of February for Naples. He arrived with a contract in his pocket to write an opera, coming to Naples just at the end of one of the most celebrated periods in the history of opera there. Before the middle of March, Rossini and Isabella Colbran abandoned the city that had seen their triumphs, never to return. Rossini had been brought there in 1815 by the celebrated impresario Domenico Barbaja to produce *Elisabetta, regina d'Inghilterra*, a great success in which la Colbran, an established favourite in Naples, attained the pinnacle of her career. Rossini's tenth and last opera for the San Carlo, *Zelmira*, had been brought out on 16 February 1822, just about the time Donizetti was preparing to leave Rome. As soon as the run of *Zelmira*, which had obtained little more than a *succès d'estime*, was over, both Rossini and Colbran were to proceed to Vienna to rejoin Barbaja, who in December 1821 had given up the management of the Neapolitan theatres for that of the Kärthnerthortheater. On their way to Vienna, Rossini and Colbran stopped off near Bologna to get married, thereby legalizing a relationship that had endured since Isabella had deserted Barbaja's bed for Rossini's.

One of Rossini's last functions in Naples was to conduct a Lenten performance of Mayr's oratorio, *Atalia*. Donizetti, who

[1] Z. No. 12, p. 233, dated 26 March 1822.

was present at some of these rehearsals as the composer's surrogate, gave Mayr a revealing picture of Rossini's last days in Naples:

Naples, 4 March 1822

Most esteemed signor Maestro:

I don't know to what to attribute the fact that since my departure I have been deprived of letters from you. Have I perhaps involuntarily displeased you in some way? If so, I beg a thousand pardons, but I beseech you not to deprive me of news of you.

I have been brought to Naples before the end of this month by my contract, which enables me to assist the performance of your oratorio as much as possible, but I see that it will all be in vain. They expect to put it on now three years after it was written—in a moment as unfavourable as it could be. Suffice to know that Donzelli takes the role of *David*, Cicimarra that of *Natan*, and Fabré[1] that of *Atalia*, although she has not sung for two years. As if that were not enough, she has a very husky contralto voice, and signor Rossini has to adapt all her part for her. This last [Rossini] complains jesuitically to the singers that they have not performed well, and then at the orchestral rehearsals he stood there gossiping with the prima donnas instead of conducting. . . . I believe this should suffice, but as though this were not enough, I tell you that la Dardanelli does not sing the first-act aria, that they have cut some recitatives, some choruses, the little finale of the second act after Atalia's aria, etc. etc.

. . . and then not to perform this music—that is the gratitude of la Colbran, after having been such a favourite. . . . As for me, I stay out of sight, and so this morning they asked for me. They say, however, that Barbaja will perform it in Vienna, too, and there it will be done complete. . . .[2]

From this letter we get a clear picture of Donizetti, angry, jealous of his teacher's reputation, as he watches the easy, cynical behaviour of the most famous composer of the day. If Donizetti had any inkling of the developments shaping for

[1] Fabré was the daughter of Beaumarchais's cook.
[2] Z. No. 11, pp. 231–2.

Rossini, he certainly regarded them as no excuse for the slipshod treatment of Mayr's oratorio.

Soon Donizetti settled down to a busy routine in Naples, dividing his time between the preparation of operas and composing his own. One of his first responsibilities was to assist in the rehearsals of Carafa's *La capricciosa e il soldato*,[1] which had received its first performance while Donizetti was in Rome. As Ferretti's libretto had been badly mauled by the Roman censors, Donizetti wrote to Ferretti to ask for the original text, before monsignor Piatti had got to work upon it. In this same letter, Gaetano alludes to his own plans:

> . . . I write as hastily as possible (*precipevolissimevolmente*) in order to speed my opera's going on stage, which will be after the Novena of S. Gennaro,[2] towards the middle of May.
>
> . . . and if you see Vasselli, tell him that I have received his letter and that everything is going well. . . .

To this letter Donizetti appends these postscripts:

> . . . Tell me, is it true that they are saying in Rome that I wrote the new overture for Mayr's oratorio? I beg you to give the lie to this gossip, because, among other things, the overture wasn't even played, the work being sufficiently long. . . .
>
> Mercadante is writing *Alfredo d'Inghilterra*.[3]

Donizetti concludes this letter[4] by observing he has written more postscript than letter.

His first composition to be performed at Naples was not the opera he mentions to Ferretti, but a cantata for two sopranos, written to celebrate the birth on 6 April 1822 of the Prince of Salerno's daughter, Maria Carolina Augusta, who was later to become Donizetti's pupil. The opera, *La zingara*, had its first

---

[1] This opera has the same subject as Vicente Martin y Soler's *La scuola de' maritati*, to a libretto by Lorenzo da Ponte, which had been produced at the Haymarket, London, 27 January 1795.

[2] Traditionally the Neapolitan theatres were closed for the Novena of S. Gennaro (St Januarius), the patron saint of the city.

[3] Mercadante's opera was never given, perhaps never finished, as he was soon composing *Adele e Emerico* for La Scala. It may well be that the libretto for the opera on Alfred was the same one by Tottola that Donizetti set to music the following year.   [4] Z. No. 12, p. 233.

performance at the Nuovo on 12 May 1822. The title role was sung by Giacinta Canonici; among others in the cast were Caterina Monticelli (Ines), Giuseppe Fioravanti (Don Sebastiano), Carlo Moncada (Don Rinuccio), Marco Venier (Fernando) and Carlo Casaccia (Papaccione). The libretto was written by one of the hardest working poetasters for the Neapolitan theatres, Andrea Leone Tottola. Tottola was an impoverished Abbé, an errand-boy for Barbaja and Colbran. Tottola's limitations have been neatly caught in a famous epigram:

> Fu di libretto autor, chiamossi Tottola,
> Un' aquila non era, anzi fu nottola.

'There was a writer of a libretto named Tottola; no eagle was he, but a bat.'

The favourable reception of La zingara was chronicled by the Giornale del Regno delle Due Sicilie.[1] 'This new work by our young composer was crowned with a success that sustained the reputation he acquired in the first test of his music at Rome. The public called him out many times, according him animated applause. The singers all competed in revealing the merits of the opera.'

The following day Donizetti wrote his own account of the première to Anna Carnevali in Rome.

> I hope that already you have kindly pardoned my silence, and thus I hasten to give you news of my opera, since I know my true friends will enjoy it, and especially you who have the kindness to call me 'son'.

> So the lucky Donizetti appeared on stage Sunday with La zingara, and the public was certainly not stingy of compliments. I could almost say they lavished them, all the nicer since here in Naples they applaud very little. Those who contributed most to the happy outcome were Moncada and Fioravanti. I assure you they sang their pieces divinely, even though the former was not much impressed with his aria (later he saw that he had been mistaken), and the latter sustained a most exhausting scene.

> Although la Canonici was almost overlooked in the preceding opera, she aroused unusual applause in this, not through any merit of mine, but rather that of the poet who

[1] No. 113, 13 May 1822.

created for her a very effective character . . . the audience did not neglect some pieces which had slipped by the first evening. I was called out again and earned applause which perhaps the cast deserved more than I. This evening, for the first time, the King will come.[1]

The favour *La zingara* found with the Neapolitans can be measured from its preliminary run of twenty-eight consecutive performances; it was put on again in July and played for twenty more. *La zingara* was given in Germany in 1823 and was performed from time to time as late as 1859, when it was sung in Havana.

Donizetti's next opera followed fast on the heels of this success. On 29 June at the Fondo, a one-act farce, *La lettera anonima*, was performed by Giuseppina Fabré (the Countess), De Bernardis (Lauretta), Rubini, who was yet to be recognized as an extraordinary singer (Filinto), De Franchi (Don Mercario), Pace (Giliberto), and Calvarola (Flageolet). The libretto was the work of Giulio Genoino, the only time he so served Donizetti, or anyone else that I have been able to discover. The farce was mentioned rather obliquely in the official newspaper on 1 July; the only thing the critic found to praise about the work was the absence of a cabaletta after the quartet—a classic example of negative reviewing. That the composer was not happy with his work and its reception is shown by a letter to Mayr of 22 July.

> . . . On the 29th of last month I gave my farce, which even though half-ruined by a beginning singer, did not have the most unhappy outcome.
>
> Strange that these prima donnas declare war on my productions without knowing me at all. The aforementioned came *herself* and begged me to let her sing . . . and then the baggage did not sing: the direction has suspended her pay for now; and if she will not sing, she will be brought to the police station! As for me, I am lucky that her waywardness is public knowledge! I send you the article from the paper, not to let you know the praise, but rather to show you how much I seek not to stray from a sound style. At least if I do not have the ability to restore

[1] Z. No. 13, pp. 233–4. The King was Ferdinando I (1751–1825), the Bourbon ruler of the Two Sicilies.

music to its former glory, at least I don't have the reputation of being one of the corrupters (*depravatori*). I leave
Friday night and will be at Milan about the twentieth. I
hope to see you there. . . .[1]

By 3 August, Donizetti was already in Milan,[2] for on that
date he and the librettist, Felice Romani, signed a contract to
write the third opera for the autumn season at La Scala.
Romani's libretto was to be ready by 20 September so that it
could be passed by the censors.

Coming to Milan was a momentous step for Donizetti. In
less than a year he had made his mark on the stages of Rome
and Naples, and now he was come to confront the most exigent
audience in Italy, one notoriously unimpressed by reputations
made elsewhere. Donizetti came with misgivings, with pre-
monitions of disaster, and with the feeling that he was perhaps
pressing his luck too far. At this time Donizetti had no illusion
about his limitations as a composer. Even if he would have
preferred to postpone his début at La Scala, the force of circumstances was against him. Mayr had recommended him to
the management. Mayr was eager to see his pupil bring the
Milanese public to his feet. Furthermore, Donizetti was in no
position to pass by such an opportunity.

As early as 17 April of that year, Donizetti's name had been
mentioned by Franchetti, the government official who was
responsible for overseeing La Scala. He had written a report to
the Austrian governor of Milan, recommending that new
operas by young, coming composers might add a fillip to the
autumn season. He mentions Mercadante first and then Donizetti, describing him as 'a young man who has already distinguished himself in Rome during the last Carnival season and
who is now composing in Naples.' To clarify his description of
Donizetti, he had added the phrase '*sul fare di Mercadante*' (on
the general order of Mercadante), but then he thought better
of it and crossed it out. Franchetti goes on to say that Donizetti
'could be engaged for two hundred zecchini or two thousand

---

[1] Z. No. 14, pp. 234–5. The article Donizetti mentions is obviously not that
in the *Giornale del Regno delle Due Sicilie*.
[2] The chief source of Donizetti's stay in Milan in 1822 is Verzino, *Le opere di
Gaetano Donizetti* (Bergamo, 1897), pp. 20–48.

francs at the most.'[1] On the basis of this report, Donizetti was made an offer and accepted it.

Donizetti was to find that collaborating with Romani could be an unsettling business. Felice Romani (1788–1865), was even then known as the most literate librettist in Italy, although his great fame was to come later as a result of his association with Bellini. Romani had the annoying habit of accepting more commissions than he could reasonably fulfil and of agreeing to deadlines that he had no intention of meeting. Such was the case this autumn of 1822, for Romani had also engaged himself to provide the libretto for the opera to be produced directly before Donizetti's. This work was Mercadante's *Adele e Emerico*, and its juxtaposition to Gaetano's was scarcely to his advantage because Mercadante's *Elisa e Claudio* had been the hit of the spring season of 1821 at La Scala[2] and had been put on again that spring for an additional twenty-seven performances. Thus Donizetti found himself in direct competition with a composer who seemed to be at the crest of his popularity.

The 20 September, the day appointed for the submission of Romani's libretto, came and went without a sign of the poem. The following day Mercadante's *Adele e Emerico* had its successful première, launching a series of fifty performances, which makes it one of but a handful of operas to have been given that many times in a single season at La Scala. It was not until 3 October that Romani turned over to Franchetti just the first act of his text for *Chiara e Serafina, ossia I Pirati*. Franchetti passed it on at once to Torresani, the Chief of Police, for censoring, and it was returned the same day with one slight change. On 3 October, then, it is definite that the first act of the libretto was written—had the second act been finished it stands to reason it would have been submitted, too—yet by 15 October, *Chiara e Serafina* was ready to go into rehearsal! It may be assumed that the first half of October 1822 was a busy time for Donizetti.

Knowing the importance of his first opera at La Scala, Donizetti worked himself into a state of anxiety and frustration.

---

[1] Quoted in Verzino, *Le opere di Gaetano Donizetti*, p. 24. The original document is in the State Archives of Milan.

[2] *Elisa e Claudio* was Mercadante's first opera to be produced at La Scala, and it is the best of his early stage works. Much of its intitial success was due to a fine cast, headed by Teresa Belloc-Giorgi, Donzelli, and Lablache.

Every day he saw more clearly the unfavourable position he occupied. He had had to sit idle while Romani completed the text so that he had a perilously short time to compose his score. His feelings are clearly revealed in a letter to Mayr.

> ... I must inform you that the [first performance] unfortunately will be the 26th, as only yesterday was the first run-through held. I hope, however, that I will have the pleasure of seeing you, if not at the first performance, at least at the third. I suggest you bring a *Requiem*, for I shall be slaughtered, and thus my funeral will be taken care of —women with such grumbling dispositions, buffos who scorn the music, singers of small parts who complain. Only la Fabbrica is left; she is the very best—therefore, be cheerful. I tell you no more so as not to wear you out and so I can finish scoring a bitch of a sextet. ...
>
> Mercadante joins his greetings to mine.[1]

Another clue to Donizetti's state of mind is found in a sentence scrawled on the final page of the autograph score of *Chiara e Serafina*, 'Così finirà l'opera, o bene o male'.

As Donizetti told Mayr his opera was performed on the 26th, although it had seemed that it might be delayed as Fabbrica caught a cold and had to miss several rehearsals. Still not completely recovered, she sang the first performance on the scheduled date. Besides Isabella Fabbrica (Chiara), who had graduated from the Milan Conservatory a few months before and proved herself a personable singing-actress in her début in Mercadante's *Adele*, the cast included Rosa Morandi (Serafina), Maria Gioia (Lisetta),[2] Savino Monelli (Don Ramiro), Antonio Tamburini (Picaro), Nicola de Grecis (Don Meschino), Carlo Poggioli (Don Fernando), and Carlo Pizzochero (Don Alvaro). Between the first and second acts of Donizetti's opera, Gioia's ballet, *Gabriella di Vergy*,[3] was danced, while the

---

[1] Z. No. 15, p. 235.

[2] Like Fabbrica, Gioia was singing her first season. She was the daughter of the noted choreographer, Gaetano Gioia; later she married the baritone Tamburini.

[3] Like many ballets of the period, *Gabriella di Vergy* employed a plot which had been successful as an opera, in this case Carafa's *Gabriella di Vergy* (1816). The plot was to be used again; Mercadante in 1828 and Donizetti in 1826 each wrote operas entitled *Gabriella di Vergy* (although the latter work was not performed until 1869 and then in a *rifacimento* by someone else).

evening's entertainment was concluded with a second ballet, *Il merciaiuolo in angustie.*

Chiara e Serafina was reviewed in the *Gazzetta di Milano*,[1] by Francesco Pezzi, who began with a long diatribe against the *longueurs* and reiterations found in operas based on French plays. There was some aptness to this stricture as Romani's libretto was derived from de Pixérécourt's *La cisterne.* Finally Pezzi gets around to discussing the opera of the evening:

> . . . Proof of the foregoing is the new score by Donizetti, which, although it lacks originality and resembles much music that several modern composers give us every day, is out of the same mould, all of them having the same distribution of pieces, and always reproducing the same melodies so that hardly has a singer uttered a measure, but the hearer knows how it will continue. The new score, I say, might have been tolerated perhaps, if, along with its prolongations and repetitions, the composer and the poet had not displayed themselves too openly, for which it is no little thing that the public maintained a certain composure of indulgence that it has not shown on other similar occasions.
>
> . . . To sum things up, I will say that after sparse applause for the diligence of la Morandi and la Fabbrica, and after some sign of discontent for the weakness of the music, the audience with faces of bronze watched the curtain descend.

This is severe, probably too severe, since the opera managed to total twelve performances before it was put aside.[2] As far as I can discover no theatre has put on *Chiara e Serafina* since. Donizetti was deeply hurt by the chilly reception of the Milanese audience. If he had counted on some leniency in the face of the adverse conditions that surrounded the composition of the work, conditions he could little control, or if he relied on some tolerance from his fellow Lombards, he was sadly disappointed. Even more disappointing was the decision of the

[1] Appendix of 27 October 1822.

[2] Herbert Weinstock (*Donizetti*, p. 35) has pointed out that there was an important treason trial in Milan at this time. As La Scala was under close surveillance, many people avoided the theatre. The chief reason for the failure of *Chiara e Serafina*, however, lies in the inadequacy of Donizetti's music.

La Scala management not to offer him a contract for a new opera after they had seen the reaction to *Chiara e Serafina*. Nearly ten years were to elapse before Donizetti won an unconditional success in Milan.

The exact date of Donizetti's departure from Milan is unknown. Almost certainly, he did not go to Bergamo, having little stomach to face his townsmen after his discouraging experience at La Scala. As a matter of fact, a surprising number of years were to pass before Donizetti's music aroused enthusiasm in Bergamo. Part of this disaffection arose from their dislike of his busying himself on the 'foreign' stages of Rome and Naples, part from the fact that Bergamo was in effect a summer resort for the Milanese, and the mezzo-fiasco of *Chiara e Serafina* produced inevitable repercussions there.

By 19 December Donizetti was back in Rome. On that day he composed and dated a soprano-bass duet he wrote for Clementina Carnevali and Nicola Cartoni. Cartoni was one of the distinguished amateur singers in Roman society, a friend of the Carnevalis and Vassellis, and a pupil of Teta Ferretti's uncle, Pietro Terziani. The text of the duet is highly dramatic, a dying woman protests her innocence to a disbelieving man;[1] the music is routine. Besides this duet, Donizetti also composed three other songs while he was in Rome. He seems to have spent his time in the company of his friends who tried to help him regain his equanimity after his set-back in Milan. The Ferrettis had a three-month-old daughter, Cristina, for him to dandle. Anna Carnevali gave him a commission to buy her gloves and shoes when he got back to Naples. The most important business of this stay in Rome was the signing of a contract with Paterni, whereby he agreed to make a *rifacimento* of *Zoraide di Granata*, Ferretti was to make the necessary changes in the libretto, and to write an opera buffa for the Valle. Paterni agreed to pay him 500 scudi for both works.

Donizetti was back in Naples by the end of March 1823, faced with a heavy programme. First, he had to write a cantata, scheduled for performance at the San Carlo in May, then an opera seria for the same theatre, and still later an opera buffa for the Nuovo, all this work in addition to that he had contracted

---

[1] This very interesting MS. is still in the collection of Arturo Toscanini.

to do for Paterni in Rome. The cantata, *Aristea*, was a setting of a stereotyped pastoral libretto by one of the lesser Neapolitan 'regulars', Giovanni Schmidt. Donizetti wrote to Mayr that the libretto was typically bad and the audience excessively noisy. To Ferretti, he described the plot succinctly as 'shepherds (bitchery, in a word)'. At this time, Donizetti was writing to Ferretti about the proposed changes in Merelli's libretto to *Zoraide*.

Before he was able to get very far with that project, he was deeply involved with his opera seria, *Alfredo il grande*. This opera, to a libretto of Tottola's that indulged historical licence to unheard-of limits, was produced at San Carlo, 2 July 1823, with Elisabetta Ferron[1] (Amalia), Teresa Cecconi (Enrichetta), Andrea Nozzari (Alfredo), Vincenzo Botticelli (Edoardo), Michele Benedetti (Atkins), Gaetano Chizzola (Rivers) and Antonio Orlandini (Guglielmo). While Donizetti was composing this opera, he had written to Mayr: 'I will go on stage with *Alfredo* within thirty-five or forty days at the most. I speak sincerely (it will be as it will), but I don't know how to do more.'[2] Donizetti's modesty was strikingly confirmed; *Alfredo* seems to have had a run of just two performances. The critic of the *Giornale del Regno della Due Sicilie* dismissed it by writing: 'one could not recognize in this work the composer of *La zingara*.'

During the late summer Donizetti's plans were thrown into confusion by the death of Pius VII on 20 August. During the conclave the theatres of Rome were closed, and since the selection of Pius's successor involved bitter controversy, there was considerable uncertainty how long it would be until the theatres reopened. On 16 September, Donizetti writes to Paterni in a state of consternation:

> . . . I want to know whether our contract for the coming Carnival will be in effect as soon as the Pope is elected, true? Because I only undertake the journey [to Rome], counting on your friendship. Here the custom in the

[1] Ferron was a Londoner by birth, active in the major Italian theatres during the 1820's. Her husband, Joseph Glossop, briefly held the leases to San Carlo and La Scala. If Ferron's name is forgotten by opera enthusiasts today, that of her grandson is not. He was Augustus Harris, the *doyen* of Covent Garden from 1884 to 1896.
[2] Z. No. 18, p. 238.

theatres is only to suspend, not to abolish, contracts, and I believe the same thing will hold in Rome.[1]

Leo XII was elected on 28 September 1823, and once again the Roman projects were activated. But before Donizetti left Naples, he had put on his newest opera, a two-act[2] farce, *Il fortunato inganno*. The libretto, a satire on the manners of theatrical people, is better than average Tottola. The opera was sung by Teresina Melas (Aurelia), Francesca Checcherini (Fulgenzia), Carlo Casaccia (Lattanzio Latrughelli), Giuseppe Fioravanti (Il Colonello), Marco Venier (Edoardo), Carlo Moncada (Bequadro), Raffaele Casaccia (Vulcano), but the pungent irony of the opera was endured by the Neapolitan audience for only three evenings. No critic reviewed it; Donizetti doesn't mention it in the few of his letters to survive from this period; the opera seems to have had no subsequent productions.

Donizetti came to Rome about the middle of October to prepare for the revised version of *Zoraide*, but this work had been much in his thoughts even before he left Naples. On 1 April he had written to Ferretti asking him not to make too many changes in the second act. He continues, 'What concerns me is that the rondo for the *musico*[3] be affecting and awesome: *amen.* Also the cavatina in the first act needs doing over, you know.'[4] Ferretti completed his revisions by 25 July, for on that date they were passed by the ecclesiastical censor.

Donizetti's next substantial reference to the matter of *Zoraide* is in a high-spirited letter to Vasselli, written on 7 October. Although Cametti[5] claims that Paterni had sent the contract to Donizetti on 29 September, the day following the election of Leo XII, Donizetti, in this letter, is still awaiting the notification that will ensure his being granted a leave of absence from his duties in Naples.

> ... I am very sure that Paterni will write soon. The rest of my letter is all for Ferretti, and do you know why? Because

[1] Z. No. 19, p. 238.
[2] Zavadini errs in speaking of this work as a one-act. The libretto of the original production is in the Naples Conservatory Library, showing the farce to be divided into two very long acts.
[3] *Musico* is the traditional term for a contralto singing an heroic male role. Donizetti's operas, from *Enrico di Borgogna* to *Pia de' Tolomei* contain a number of such parts.   [4] Z. No. 16, p. 236.   [5] *Donizetti a Roma*, p. 33.

I firmly believe that he who drinks from the fountain of Hippocrene swears eternal hatred for money, thus placing Ferretti in that number, I, desperate, direct this letter to you which is intended for the ruined man.[1]

Donizetti then describes his difficulties in getting hold of Ferretti's text, which had been sent to a man named Agnesi, whom Donizetti never found at home. But now he has the manuscript at last.

... What has got into friend Ferretti? five pieces? and pieces of this sort? . . . This awful Ferretti (*Ferrettaccio*) . . . comes bounding along with a *choral cavatina, choral aria, choral duet, choral introduction*, and besides we have choruses. . . . Doesn't it mean, however, that *Zoraide*, instead of being a fine thing, will be a great bitchery, because everything is done over again. Up to the cavatina and aria of Pisaroni I was in agreement, but then a duet, a final rondo with all those people on stage who have to sing! Ah by God, the business got too big. . . . The finale, yes sir, I wanted it changed, . . . but this time I see the impresario has taken advantage of me.

... Listen, Ferretti *mio*, tell the Impresario that I will do all this and more too if he wants it, but I hope then he will be grateful. I wanted to write a new finale, but that was only done out of friendship. Then he makes me compose a chorus and an aria for Patriossi and a duet for Donzelli and Pisaroni, all of which should not be done without some recognition. Yet I understand everything is for the good of the opera, and if everything goes as swimmingly as I hope, I will not have wasted my labour—I hope for reciprocal friendliness from him.

Tell him to write to me at the earliest when he wants me to come, because besides the difficulty of my leaving, the quicker it takes place, the more I can find time to do. You see, my big old Vasselli, that, by God, I must work like a stevedore, and I get 500 scudi, while Mercadante gets 700 for a single opera. However, if all goes well, I will be happier than anyone. I hope it does. . . .[2]

[1] Donizetti is here referring to the practice that then obtained: the receiver of the letter paid for the handling.
[2] Z. No. 20, pp. 239–40.

If Donizetti had started on the new music for *Zoraide* before he left Naples, he had not completed it until some time after he arrived in Rome. On 10 November, he sent round by hand the final rondo, an aria with bravura variations, along with an accompanying letter to Rosamunda Pisaroni.[1] The startlingly obsequious tone adopted by Donizetti might seem to reveal much about the relative standing of young composers and operatic stars at that time.

> . . . I will call myself thoroughly content if I might be honoured by your approval, and I beg you frankly to take advantage of my friendship and tell me your opinion of every piece of your music. I assure you that only scarcity of talent has hindered my desire to do better. . . .[2]

But it should be remembered that Donizetti is merely imitating the tone of elaborate protestation then customary in what might be called the 'dedicatory' style.

Zoraide di Granata in its revised form was presented at the Argentina on 5 January 1824. It was to have been given on the customary opening date of San Stefano, but the inauguration of the season had been postponed because the Pope had been severely ill.[3] In spite of the excellent cast that included Luigia Boccabadati (Zoraide), Pisaroni (Abenamet), Donzelli (in his old role of Almuzir), Domenico Patriossi or Patriozzi (Ali), and Giocamo Galassi (Almanzor), and in spite of Donizetti's new pieces, the opera failed to arouse the anticipated enthusiasm. What had seemed original and striking had come in two years' time to seem *déjà vu*. The commendable craftsmanship of the score could not conceal the lack of inspiration. Only one number of the score, the new duet for Pisaroni and Donzelli,

---

[1] Pisaroni (1793–1872), was the foremost contralto of the decade. She began her career in Bergamo as a high soprano. She made her début in 1811 in the title role of Mayr's *Ginevra di Scozia*. Several years later a very severe case of smallpox took away her voice and left her terribly disfigured. When she regained her voice, it had settled into a deep contralto. Her first great success as a contralto was her singing of Malcolm in the original cast of *La donna del lago* by Rossini. Her imposing voice and extraordinary technique enabled her in large measure to overcome the handicap of a singularly unprepossessing stage appearance. By 1829 her career had started to decline.
[2] Z. No. 21, pp. 240–1.
[3] Indeed, Leo XII seems to have been elected with the expectation that he had not long to live, but he survived until 1829.

produced a fervid response. In fact, the critic of the *Notizie del giorno* went so far as to claim that this duet alone would suffice to assure Donizetti 'the most glittering crown among composers of opera seria.'[1]

A more jaundiced account of the revision of *Zoraide* comes from Stendhal.

> Donizetti, over whom the Romans went mad two years ago, and whom they followed home the night of the first [it was the third] performance of *Zoraide di Granata* with shouts of admiration, has bored us fatally the 7th of this month with this same *Zoraide*, strengthened by new pieces. La Pisaroni, who plays the lover's role, is admirable in it; the tenor Donzelli very fine. His voice, however, does not please me at all; it is veiled and, in the upper notes, resembles a yell. . . . Donizetti is a tall, handsome young man, but cold and without a shred of talent; it seems to me that they applauded him two years ago to give affront to the Princess Pauline, who protected young Pacini.[2]

Zoraide managed to hold the stage of the Argentina until 7 February, on which date it received its last performance in Rome. This revised version was later sung in Italian in Munich and Lisbon (both in 1825) and at the San Carlo in 1829. Whatever chagrin Donizetti felt at the weak showing made by the reworked *Zoraide* was banished by the substantial success of his opera buffa for the Valle. For most of his life it was Donizetti's nature to regard the mixed fortunes of his career as a composer with objective eyes; after an opera had been launched he could let it go its way as he lost himself in the labour of composing and rehearsing his next stagework.

L'ajo nell'imbarazzo, set to a libretto by Ferretti, was first performed on 4 February 1824 at the Valle by Maria Ester Mombelli (Gilda), Agnese Loyselet (Leonarda), Savino Monelli (Enrico), Nicola Tacci (Don Gregorio), Tamburini (Marchese Don Giulio), Giovanni Puglieschi (Pippetto) and Luigi de Dominicis (Simone). This was the first of Donizetti's operas to give strong evidence of his flair for operatic comedy. Although the music is predominantly cast in the Rossinian mould, much of it is apt and has authentic sparkle. The reviews of the first

[1] No. 3, 15 January 1824.
[2] Stendhal, *Correspondance inédite* (Paris, 1855), p. 257.

performance were enthusiastic, praising the score for its spontaneity, inventiveness, clarity and the originality of ideas. The opera held the stage for the remainder of the season, being applauded with increasing fervour at every performance.

L'ajo was the earliest of Donizetti's operas to win wide approval. Within the year it was performed in Palermo, and the following year there Donizetti conducted it himself. For the Neapolitan première (Nuovo, June 1826), Donizetti revised the score, omitting some music, rearranging numbers, and adding new pieces. The recitatives were put into prose, and the buffo role of Don Gregorio translated into Neapolitan dialect. The cast for this *rifacimento*, which had been rechristened *Don Gregorio*, included Giacinta Canonici (Gilda), Francesca Checcherini (Leonarda), Antonio de Bezzi (Enrico), Carlo Casaccia (Don Gregorio), Felice Pellegrini (Marchese) and Giovanni Pace (Simone). Two months or so later, on 21 August, *L'ajo* was staged at La Scala under its original title, the second of Donizetti's operas to appear on that stage. While the Milanese critics acknowledged that the opera had earned warm applause, they levelled the charge that the music was derivative, finding echoes of Rossini, Mercadante, and Pacini in the score. Of the cast, the soprano Girolama Dardanelli (Gilda), Monelli (repeating his old role as Enrico) and an excellent buffo Andrea Bertolucci (Don Gregorio), were singled out for particular praise. At its first appearance at La Scala, *L'ajo* ran twenty performances, and the official rating of the production was *buonissimo*. The opera was given in Vienna[1] on 2 April 1827, with Lablache making a great impression as Don Gregorio.[2] However, when *L'ajo* was put on in Bergamo during the Carnival season 1829–30, having been prepared by Mayr, the production unfortunately was an utter fiasco. On 28 July 1846 Lablache introduced his famous role of Don Gregorio to London,[3] but the opera failed to please. Chorley dismissed it as 'not among Donizetti's happy comic operas'.[4] Besides these

[1] Loewenberg errs when he claims *L'ajo* was the first of Donizetti's operas given in Vienna; *Emilia di Liverpool* was performed there in the summer of 1824.

[2] Four days earlier, Lablache had been one of the thirty-six torchbearers at Beethoven's funeral.

[3] Others in the London cast were Jeanne Castellan (Gilda), Mario (Enrico), Federico Lablache (Pippetto), and Luciano Fornasari (Marchese).

[4] Chorley, *Thirty Years' Musical Recollections*, p. 174.

performances in England, *L'ajo* was sung in Germany, France, Spain, Portugal, and Brazil, but never, apparently, in North America.

After the successful launching of *L'ajo nell'imbarazzo* at the Valle in February, Donizetti was required by contract to be present in the theatre for the first three performances. He seems to have gone back to Naples as soon as this obligation was met. Some time before the end of February, he signed a contract there with the impresario Francesco Tortoli for a new opera and for the *rifacimento* of *L'ajo* (*Don Gregorio*) to be given at the Nuovo. For these labours Donizetti was to receive 300 ducats. The new opera was *Emilia di Liverpool*,[1] first performed at the Nuovo on 28 July 1824. The principal parts were sung by Teresina Melas (Emilia), Francesca Checcherini (Candida), Carlo Casaccia (Don Romualdo), Giuseppe Fioravanti (Claudio), and Domenico Zilioli (Federico). The opera was given only eight times before it was allowed to lapse. The critical reception was lukewarm.

> . . . Composers, not finding a shade of passion in the midst of the sea of impassioned words in these wretched dramas, are forced to utilize strong or surprising situations found in the poet's work and to capitalize on the contrast of characters and coincidence, permitting them some effects of light and shade, to obtain some variety in the composition. That is the condition, for example, of Donizetti who recently wrote the pretty music of *Emilia di Liverpool*.[2]

That Donizetti was dissatisfied with the first version of *Emilia* but felt the work could be salvaged is apparent from his subsequent attentions to the score.

On 18 August 1824 he writes to Mercadante, who was then in Vienna assisting in the production of a season of Italian opera. One of the works scheduled for performance was *Emilia*.

---

[1] An earlier opera based on the same source, Scatizzi's *Emilia di Liverpool*, bore the orthographically original title of *Emila di Liverpaut*. The composer of this work was Vittorio Trento and it had been produced at the Teatro Fiorentino in 1817. The librettist is anonymous and judging by the similarity of the names of the characters, Donizetti probably set substantially the same libretto. Two of the singers in his cast had sung the same roles in Trento's version: Francesca Checcherini (Candida) and Carlo Casaccia (Don Romualdo). Rubini was the Federico in 1817.

[2] *Giornale del Regno delle Due Sicilie*, 9 October 1824.

This letter contains some insights into Donizetti's attitude towards his work and responsibility as a composer.

> . . . My *Emilia* will be given in Vienna: in the second act there are some new[1] pieces, because the old ones were of lesser effect than these. I recommend them to you, but not only these, I recommend the whole opera to your care; you know my manner of composing and you know well some alteration of tempo is needed. Do what you will then, for I entrust it entirely to you. The role of Lablache, which Fioravanti sang [Claudio], I know will have to be adjusted a bit for him. I have made *puntature*[2] for some things, but in most cases the composer is the worst one to do these things because he lives with his original ideas. Between you two you can adjust everything. . . .[3]

In 1828 Donizetti made an even more extensive revision of the opera. Giuseppe Checcherini (1777–1840) re-arranged the libretto.[4] Checcherini was a stage director for the Neapolitan theatres; his wife, Francesca, had sung at San Carlo since 1812 and had been a member of the original cast of Donizetti's *Emilia*. The revision of *Emilia* was given at the Nuovo during the Lenten season of 1828. The title role was sung by Annetta Fischer.[5] While Fioravanti retained his old role of Claudio, the buffo role (that character's name having been changed from Don Romualdo to Conte Asdrubale in the revision) was in the hands of Gennaro Luzio, then at the beginning of his illustrious

[1] It is possible that by 'new' Donizetti means 'new' to the score rather than newly composed. One of the pieces by Donizetti that saw yeoman service in a large number of scores is the original rondo to *Il falegname*. In the Naples Conservatory library there is a copy of this aria that clearly shows that it was once used in *Emilia*; yet for the Nuovo in 1824 the score ended with a finaletto, for the 1828 *rifacimento*, the final number was a rondo borrowed from *Alahor di Granata*. Perhaps Donizetti sent the aria from *Il falegname* to Mercadante in Vienna along with this letter.
[2] This is what amounts to a technical term, meaning the changing of notes in a part to accommodate the range of a particular singer. Lablache was a bass whose effective range stopped at the E above middle C; Fioravanti, on the other hand, was a baritone.
[3] Z. No. 23, p. 242.
[4] For a detailed discussion of this revision see Jeremy Commons, 'Emilia di Liverpool', *Music and Letters*, 40 (1959), pp. 207–28, and also see p. 418.
[5] She was the adopted daughter of the bass Ludwig Fischer who was a close friend of Mozart's. Later Fischer married the tenor, Marco Venier, and returned to Vienna, where she conducted a famous vocal academy.

career. Not only was Checcherini's wife still in the cast, but his daughter Marianna as well. But for all the care lavished on it, the new version of *Emilia* seems to have fared no better than the earlier. It has been revived at least twice since: once at the Nuovo-Nazionale in Naples in 1871, and again at Liverpool in 1957, when Joan Sutherland sang Emilia. On the latter occasion, *Emilia* was broadcast by the B.B.C.

The year 1825 began quietly for Donizetti. As it was a Holy Year, the Roman theatres were closed, and there was no chance for a contract there which would allow him an extended stay in that city near his friends. On 3 January, Ferdinando, King of the Two Sicilies died, and the Neapolitan theatres were shut for a period of mourning. When his eldest son, Francesco I (1777–1830), was crowned, Donizetti's part in the celebrations was to provide the music for a cantata, *I voti dei sudditi* (*The prayers of the subjects*), to one of Schmidt's pseudo-Arcadian texts. This cantata was performed on 6 March, the leading shepherds' roles being sung by Adelaide Tosi and Nozzari. Just about the time of this performance, Donizetti was visited by a Don Francesco Morabito from Palermo, who engaged him with a season's contract to act as *maestro di cappella* to the director of music for the Teatro Carolino there, and to compose a new opera for that theatre. His engagement was to run from 15 March 1825 to 15 March 1826; for his services he was to be paid the splendid sum of forty-five ducats a month, with a month's vacation. On these terms Donizetti set out for a highly unpleasant year in Palermo.[1]

The Teatro Carolino, the principal theatre in the Sicilian capital, had fallen on bad days. The theatre was small and poorly equipped; it was one of a handful in the Italian world that attempted to put on opera the year round. The financing of operatic projects is a risky business, and in Palermo the hazards were unusually great in those days. In 1824 the lessee of the Carolino had been dismissed for fraud. For the following season there had been much infighting for the vacant post, which was finally won by Morabito with the backing of Duke

[1] The principal source for Donizetti's Palermitan adventure is Ottavio Tiby, *Una stagione lirica di 125 anni fa: Gaetano Donizetti a Palermo* (Rome, 1951).

Branciforti. Once Morabito was assured of his lease, he came to Naples to assemble a company. Besides Donizetti he engaged the English soprano Ferron, even though she was in the last stages of pregnancy, and the tenor Berardo Calvari Winter, who in 1848 was himself to sample opera-house keeping when he spent two years as director of the San Carlo. Antonio Tamburini and his wife, a mezzo-soprano, were also members of the company. In contrast to Donizetti's forty-five ducats a month, Ferron was to receive 517½, and Winter 350. Besides their pay, the singers, the director, everybody in fact down to the prompter and *macchinista*, were permitted a benefit evening.

On 6 April Donizetti arrived in Palermo aboard the *S. Ferdinando*. His fellow passengers included the tenor Winter and his retinue, as well as the mezzo-soprano Caterina Lipparini. The season had been announced to begin on 21 April, but as the company was slow in assembling, the event was postponed until 4 May. The first opera was Pacini's *Il barone di Dolsheim*, new to the theatre. The most prominent feature of the performance was the catastrophic playing of the orchestra. So acute were the complaints that the following day Donizetti, his assistant, Andrea Monteleone,[1] and the first violinist were called on the carpet by the Superintendent of Public Spectacles, the Duke di Serradifalco. The upshot of this meeting was the dismissal of three members of the orchestra, and a promise to adjust the hood of the prompter's box to permit clearer vision between stage and pit. This beginning was an ill omen of events to come.

The second opera of the season was Rossini's *L'Italiana in Algeri*, which went somewhat better because Tamburini and his wife had made their tardy appearance. The baritone soon established himself as the one member of the company to win real popularity with the Palermitan audience. Ferron had not yet arrived; she was in Portici, recovering from the birth of a son. The understandable reason for the delay in her coming in

---

[1] Tiby seems to exaggerate when he says that relations between Donizetti and Monteleone were not good because the latter was a close friend of Bellini. Since Bellini's first opera to be publicly performed was still a year away, it would seem a rather premature partisanship. If Donizetti and Monteleone had their difficulties, there were to be provocations aplenty within the walls of the Carolino. And if they had their difficulties, Donizetti bore no grudges as his amicable letter to Monteleone (Z. No. 32, pp. 251-2, dated 14 May 1827) will show.

no way mitigated the displeasure of the audience at the Carolino at being denied the services of the prima donna. To fill in the time until she was fit enough to undertake the journey to Palermo, *Il barbiere* was put on, and only the excellence of Tamburini's Figaro kept the audiences attending the theatre. In June, Donizetti managed at last to find out where Ferron was recuperating and sent her urgent word to come by the next boat. The prima donna made her tardy appearance in Palermo on 28 June, but she was still ailing. By now Donizetti was feeling the pressures of an insistent but unco-operative management, the hostility of the audience, and the discontent of his very uneven company of singers. Donizetti's position was doubly uncomfortable since he was responsible for the musical aspects of the season and he had had as yet no opportunity to display his true talent as a composer.

To launch Ferron under the most favourable circumstances, it was decided to introduce her in Rossini's *Aureliano in Palmira*, which had not yet been given at the Carolino. The plan was to give the opening on 6 July, a gala evening as it was Queen Maria Isabella's birthday. As luck would have it, *Aureliano* could not be readied in time, probably because Ferron's health did not permit her to attend all the rehearsals. As a last-minute substitute, Cimarosa's *Il matrimonio segreto*, and a pastiche-farce entitled *Il trionfo della musica*, the latter score being an anthology of popular operatic airs by a variety of composers, were given. Ferron made her début in this last work, which turned out to be neither farcical nor triumphant, as her capabilities lay in the line of tragedy rather than comedy and as her voice was not in its best estate. The tone of the evening may be imagined from a critical review which told the audience to reserve its judgement until la Ferron should appear in a work better suited to her talents. Eventually she sang in *Aureliano in Palmira*, but that work succeeded as little in persuading the Sicilians that it was one of Rossini's major works as it had elsewhere, and consequently played to sparse houses.

Early in July Donizetti found an opportunity to make his début as a composer, even though it was with an ephemeral cantata, extemporized to speed the departure of the Lieutenant-General of the island, the Marchese Ugo delle Favere, whom the King had summoned to Naples. This work was briefly alluded to in the newspaper, *La Cerere* (15 July 1825), as being 'dashed off in a few hours' by 'Mo. Dorizzetti [*sic*]'. For the King's birthday, 14 August, Donizetti whipped up another cantata, but the papers were silent about this effort.

These cantatas made no impression on the sad fortunes of the season, which dragged on painfully. As the public displayed its discontent more openly, bad feeling developed between the Superintendent and Morabito. Matters reached such a low ebb at one point that the impresario was arrested and put in jail for a day. These difficulties had serious effects on the morale of the company. One day at rehearsal the sorely tried Donizetti emphatically rebuked the second bass, Antonio de Rosa, who decided that his honour as an artist had been compromised and made an insulting scene. When de Rosa refused to apologize, he too went off to jail for a day, and emerged at the end of it impenitent.

As the storm clouds gathered, Donizetti produced a work of his own, *L'ajo nell'imbarazzo*, on 5 September, with Caterina Lipparini (Gilda), Carlotta Tomaselli (Leonarda), Winter (Enrico), Tamburini (Marchese Don Giulio), the role he had created the year before at the Valle, Nicola Tacci (Don Gregorio), and Salvatore Patti, the father of Adelina (Pippetto). For this last role, Donizetti must have made extensive *puntature* as Patti was a tenor singing a part written for a bass; his presence in this part may well reflect Donizetti's desire not to have de Rosa in the cast. *La Cerere*, 8 September, described the performance in these terms:

> ... The opera season has not really begun until now, when a spectacle capable of producing real pleasure is offered. *L'ajo* ... has received the applause that a work by a '*professore*' full of taste, philosophy, and sentiment, performed by able executants, ought to arouse in an intelligent audience. We are convinced that particularly for opere semiserie we have a company that would be difficult to surpass.

Donizetti wrote to Mayr saying that only *L'ajo* and his master's *Originali*[1] succeeded in drawing people to the theatre.

[1] It is difficult to tell what Donizetti means by this reference to Mayr's *Che originali!* That farce was not performed at the Carolino that season. Perhaps, as Tiby suggests, some of the score was included in the pastiche, *Il trionfo della musica*; perhaps it was given at another theatre in Palermo.

During the run of *L'ajo*, a crisis was fast developing about the ballet season, which was due to start early in October. Morabito does not seem to have concerned himself much about it, thinking he had only to send to the Ballet School in Naples to be supplied cheaply with a full company of dancers. Apparently it was not until the ballet should have begun rehearsals that Morabito discovered that the student dancers in Naples were permanently on call at the San Carlo and not free to pirouette at the Carolino. While Morabito temporized about the ballet company, Serradifalco became increasingly impatient in his demands for a prospectus. When he could hedge no longer, Morabito submitted a roster of five dancers that he had succeeded in rounding up. Later he found enough to put on four ballets, but the first was not produced until 8 November. Donizetti was bitter about these dancers as he wrote to Mayr: 'There are some dancers who for two months get 2500 ducats to trill with their feet, and we poor devils are in a state of degradation—we get no consideration . . . and the trills of those people do not bring in a single ducat more.'[1]

Serradifalco's irritation with Morabito arose not only from the mismanagement of the ballet season, but also because Morabito had given a quarter fewer operatic performances than he had contracted to put on. His basic problem was financial. He was so badly in arrears that he owed Donizetti two and a half months salary. He owed the singers so much that in December they threatened not to sing another note until they had been paid, but some money must have been forthcoming because the unhappy season continued. Serradifalco tried to counter Morabito's fecklessness by appointing a commission of three trustees. Morabito and his backer, Duke Branciforti, protested against this move, saying they wanted to terminate the present season at once, although they claimed they would give the next year's season they had agreed to, as Morabito's lease had four more years to run. The lessee's appeal was denied, and thus the season was condemned to run its course.

At the end of October Rossini's *L'inganno felice* was staged, but the affairs of the Carolino were now of so little public interest that no review of it appeared. Late in November Donizetti prepared the first performances of Spontini's *La*

[1] Z. No. 25, p. 244, dated 21 December 1825.

vestale in Sicily; Ferron sang Giulia. This work did not fare
well, for two week's later Mercadante's *Elisa e Claudio* took its
place. For this last opera Donizetti provided a final aria to take
the place of Mercadante's, but this aria may well have been
from one of Donizetti's other operas, not a rondo expressly composed for this occasion.

Some time about the middle of December Donizetti put into
rehearsal the new opera he was under contract to write for the
Carolino. Donizetti's letter to Mayr, which has already been
alluded to, affords a glimpse of the difficulties that beset him at
this time. The letter begins portentously with a German
quotation: *Die Vergebung ist die beste Rache*, which he assures
Mayr he understands and puts into practice. The thought of
Mayr is a comfort to him.

> ... I know that the good Mayr loves me; I have seen it on
> thousands of occasions. To receive one of your letters from
> time to time always relieves me of agitation, and it was
> high time you sent me one.
> ... I have heard you wrote to my friends the Vassellis in
> Rome. They were delighted because they esteem you. . . .
> I am completely convinced that we will leave here with a
> broken head, that is to say with several months' salary owing.
> For me it is certain, but patience, this worries me less. My
> real displeasure is to see myself forgotten by everyone and
> to come to the close of an engagement without hopes of
> beginning another. . . .
> You wanted to know about the progress of the music
> school here?[1] It is pitiable; there are horrors, ragged
> youngsters, the worst voices, without teachers who know
> anything about singing; all in all, a synagogue, *sinagoga
> perfetta*. For the instruments, there are some pupils that
> show promise, but they have dogs for instructors in my
> opinion. I don't even speak of the recitals. In my own
> way, I don't go around flattering people behind their
> backs, but here it is not at all worth the trouble. They look
> on people of the theatre as infamous and consequently pay

[1] Since Mayr's Lezioni Caritatevoli was one of the earliest conservatories in
Italy, he was naturally interested in similar schools elsewhere. In 1825 the
Palermo Conservatory was directed by Isidoro Gatti, and Donizetti's
description seems not to have been exaggerated.

us no attention, while we care nothing for them. The trade of the poor writer of operas I have understood from the beginning to be most unhappy . . . but I assure you, dear Maestro, that I suffer very much from the sort of beasts we have need of for the execution of our labours.

If the devil came from . . . eh, who knows!

I put on Spontini's *La vestale* in nineteen days, or more accurately, in nineteen mornings, for in the evening there were performances. I defy anyone to do more . . . When I think of all this, I sweat. Indeed dear Maestro, only you and I in all the summer have drawn audiences with the *Originali* and with *L'ajo nell'imbarazzo*, and the trills of the dancers did not bring in a single ducat more. I was to have given my opera by now, but because of Ferron's illness, I will go on towards the first of the year. I have no little fear. . . . They don't want to hear Ferron, the wife of Tamburini (the daughter of Gioia) is a dog, the tenor Winter, etc. etc. And in the midst of this I have had to joke with music that requires some intelligence . . . may the prayers of Mayr and mine too be granted, but this time it is difficult. . . .[1]

The opera of Donizetti's that was postponed by Ferron's indisposition was *Alahor di Granata*; it was produced on 7 January 1826, with the English prima donna singing Zobeida, with Gioia-Tamburini (Muley-Hassem), Winter (Alamor), Tamburini (Alahor), and Salvatore Patti (Ismaele). The newspaper review was favourable without being in any way enthusiastic. Its main thesis was that public apathy ought to be checked by this new opera which deserves applause, for Donizetti 'has the prudence to hold a middle road between the beauty of the old school and the energy of the new.' *Alahor* was produced at the San Carlo the following summer, sung by Henriette Méric-Lalande, Brigida Lorenzani, Winter, Lablache and Gaetano Chizzola. The score for this opera is lost; only one florid contralto aria was published, while the rondo seems to have been grafted on to the revised version of *Emilia* (1828). In Palermo *Alahor* held the stage until 25 January, when it was replaced by *Tancredi*. It seems unlikely there were any more performances that year, as Ferron left Palermo on the 26th.

[1] Z. No. 25, pp. 243-4.

Alahor was played again at the Carolino, when it opened the 1830–31 season, and that was the end of its career.[1]

A traditional, but mysterious, item in the long list of Donizetti's operas is the farce, *Il castello degli invalidi*, which is supposed to have been given at the Carolino in February or during the spring of 1826. No trace or mention of this opera has been found in Palermo, but all the biographers dutifully repeat the name, as the composer included its name in a list of his works he sent his brother-in-law on 24 October 1841.[2] Tiby, however, affirms his belief that there is no such opera because he could find no reference to it. In the absence of any concrete evidence for its existence, particularly since no score, autograph or otherwise, nor a libretto is known, any comment about *Il castello degli invalidi* can only be conjecture.[3]

The season in Palermo finally closed on 18 February 1826. The following day the theatres were closed for a period of jubilee decreed by the Pope. Donizetti, however, had left Palermo on the 14th. The eleven months he had spent there were a time of harassment and frustration. The bay of Naples must have looked welcome indeed when he saw it again.

Just about the time Donizetti left Palermo, an event occurred in Bergamo which afforded him some consolation for the shabby treatment he had experienced in Sicily. Mayr wrote to him that on 23 February the Unione filarmonica of Bergamo had decided to honour Donizetti by ordering his portrait painted by Moriggia and by giving a concert of his music. Donizetti described his feelings about this event in a letter to Mayr:

> ... I have heard of the things from another world done for me at the Accademia. ... How the world lives by illusions. There they celebrate and honour one who has no other merit than to have been away from home for a few years, while this person lives under another sky with the same qualities and perhaps worse ones than those he possessed at home. It is enough that Mayr loves me and I

[1] If the missing autograph of *Alahor* survives at all and is to be found anywhere, Palermo is the most likely place to start looking for it.
[2] Z. No. 378, p. 558.
[3] The possibility of a connexion between the mysterious *Il castello degli invalidi* and the *pasticcio Il trionfo della musica* ought to be checked out.

A drawing of Donizetti by an unknown artist dated Rome 1827 and dedicated to Mayr

Donizetti's birthplace in Borgo Canale, Bergamo

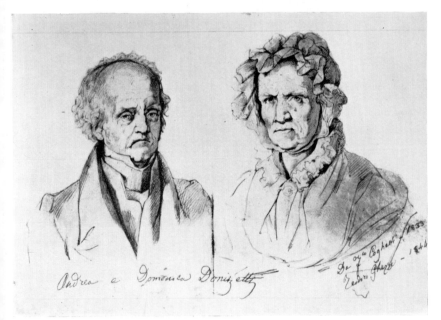

Andrea and Domenica, Donizetti's parents. A copy by Teodoro Ghezzi of a drawing by Francesco Coghetti

The building where
Mayr opened his
music school

Giovanni Simone
Mayr. Portrait by
Gaetano Barabini,
1827

Giacomo David

Giuseppe Viganoni

Giulio Marco Bordogni

Andrea Nozzari

Four Bergamasc tenors associated with Donizetti

will never be puffed up by all the rest and a thousand times more.[1]

Elsewhere in this letter, Donizetti refers to the tenor Ignazio Pasini, whom Mayr had armed with a letter of introduction to Gaetano. Pasini had been engaged by the Carolino in Palermo. Donizetti tells Mayr that he had supplied him with letters to Pietro Generali, his successor as director of the theatre, and to the singers Fischer and Tamburini who would be the best persons for him to know in Palermo. He wishes Pasini 'an entirely different fate as far as his salary than was mine and that of my companions, but I am very much afraid. . . .'

Donizetti also reports to Mayr on his impression of Bellini's first opera to be publicly performed. His first, *Adelson e Salvini*, had been given in 1825 at the Conservatory.

> . . . This evening at the San Carlo will be given *Bianca e Gernando* (Fernando no, because it is naughty)[2] by our Bellini, his first work. Beautiful, beautiful, beautiful, especially since it is the first time he writes. It is unfortunately beautiful as I give my opera in two weeks time. . . .[3]

The opera of his own that Donizetti refers to is *Don Gregorio*, the *rifacimento* of *L'ajo*. The opera was well received and became a favourite with Neapolitan audiences. At this time Donizetti had hopes that this opera might soon be produced in Bergamo, and so he sent word by way of Mayr to Paolo Agazzi, the impresario there.

> . . . Tell Agazzi that *L'ajo* needs a very good woman and principal buffo, a *tenore contraltino* who is adequate but not one of the better ones, and a serviceable basso cantante. If there is a good second woman for the part of the old servant, there is a duet with the leading woman that pleases very much here.[4]

Alahor di Granata was to have been given in Naples on 21 June, but the performance was delayed because Winter was anxious

---

[1] Z. No. 26, pp. 245–6, dated 30 May 1826.
[2] Not Fernando because the censors forbade it. The late king was Ferdinando, also a Ferdinando was the heir apparent.
[3] Z. No. 26, p. 245.
[4] Z. No. 28, p. 248, dated 21 July 1826.

to make his début in the role of Alamor, which he had created
in January. Because Winter counted on making a favourable
impression in the tenor aria in the second act, it was agreed to
postpone the rehearsals until he could participate in them.
This arrangement did not allow Donizetti to be idle, however,
for he was busily preparing a new one-act serious opera for
the San Carlo. *Elvida* had its first performance on 6 July,
with Méric-Lalande (Elvida), Brigida Lorenzani (Zeidar),
Almerinda Manzocchi (Zulma), Rubini (Alfonso), Lablache
(Amur) and Chizzola (Ramiro). Schmidt's libretto was another
exercise on the warfare in the last days of the Moorish kingdom
of Granada. Donizetti wrote about *Elvida*: 'Little money, a
great deal of work; if I have much honour for it, I will be well
paid.' At the first performance, a gala for the Queen's birthday,
the royal family was in the theatre and, contrary to their
usual custom, applauded the opera. In spite of this auspicious
beginning, the work did not draw well, justifying Donizetti's
view of it, written to Mayr before the first performance:

> . . . It is no great thing to tell the truth, and if I catch them
> with Rubini's cavatina and the quartet, that will suffice
> for me.[1]

Alahor was finally produced at the San Carlo 10 July. Donizetti
gave his impression of it in a letter to his father:

> . . . On the 19th I gave *Alahor*, the opera for Palermo, and
> it made no great impression; all that pleased were the
> overture, the cavatina for the heroine, the tenor aria, and
> the final rondo, but for Naples that is not enough—here
> they want everything excellent, meanwhile it is enough
> there were no whistles and some applause. . . .[2]

So far this year had been the busiest one of Donizetti's career.
In January he had produced *Alahor* in Palermo; since his return
to Naples he had composed the additions for *Don Gregorio* and
rehearsed it; for the San Carlo he had rehearsed *Alahor* and he
had composed and produced *Elvida*. Except for the opera buffa,
these works lacked the staying power to survive once their
novelty had worn off. Donizetti worked on them conscientiously,

---

[1] Z. No. 27, p. 247, dated 15 June 1826.
[2] Z. No. 28, p. 248, dated 21 July 1826.

but he had no illusions about the limits of his conscientiousness. Forced by economic necessity to write more than he should, and enabled by his own technical proficiency to produce and keep producing operas under adverse conditions, he was aware that he still had much to learn. And so he addressed himself to a project of a different kind.

In his letter of 15 June to Mayr, which describes all his other activities, he ends with these words:

> . . . Dearest Maestro, for my diversion I am writing the *Gabriella* of Carafa. I know his music is beautiful, but what I do now I do to please myself.

Carafa's *Gabriella di Vergy* (San Carlo, 1816) was one of the most successful operas by this old crony of Rossini. The libretto by Tottola is based on a gruesome play by du Belloy. Donizetti composed an opera to this libretto, although he had no contract for it, or, apparently, any plans for producing it.[1] He wrote it, as he says, as 'a diversion', or as an exercise. The gory plot, dealing with a heroine who dies when her husband hands her a casket containing the freshly-excised heart of Raoul, afforded Donizetti the opportunity to treat situations stronger and more violent than those in the librettos offered him by impresarios. In those days there was a marked preference for plots which ended happily; the tidal wave of romantic melodrama was not to break for another decade on Italian stages. Thus, with *Gabriella*,[2] Donizetti seems to have been addressing himself deliberately and privately to the problem of enlarging his range as a composer of operas.

After all his intense activity of the early part of the summer Donizetti fell ill. On 11 August he wrote to Mario Aspa in Messina that he had been stricken by 'a most tiresome fever that only today seems to have left me'. On the last day of August Donizetti left Naples for Rome, where he signed a contract with Aniceto Pistoni for an opera buffa to be given at the

[1] Donizetti's *Gabriella di Vergy* was produced, after his death, in 1869 at the San Carlo. The version used was a fairly free one, involving among other changes the giving of the *musico* role of Raoul to a baritone.

[2] The interesting autograph of this score is in the Museo Donizettiano. In 1828 Mercadante brought out in Lisbon his version of this subject, but it did not reach Italy until 1832. At best, the vogue of Mercadante's *Gabriella di Vergy* was modest.

Valle in the coming Carnival season. Donizetti seems to have remained in Rome until after the production of *Olivo e Pasquale* at the Valle on 7 January 1827. The libretto for this work was by Ferretti, who took his plot from a popular play by Sografi. Ferretti's text must have been ready and waiting for Donizetti when he arrived in Rome, for he writes to Mayr on 30 September that the opera is far advanced. 'Here I am working and am already at the middle of the second act, not the scoring however. Now I leave it there for the qualms that can follow or rather that do go following me. Anyway, the ensemble is done.'[1]

With most of his opera out of the way, Donizetti was able to settle down in the congenial atmosphere of his Roman friends. Because of his collaboration with Ferretti he was seeing much of him and his family, which had grown now to include three daughters. His friendship with the Carnevalis was as close as ever. Shortly before he left Naples, he had written to Signora 'Nanna' a letter to greet her on her name-day. Clementina Carnevali had married three years before Natale Mongardi, a high-ranking officer in the Papal Guard. From Donizetti's affectionate greetings and his warm, easy tone, it is clear that he still enjoyed his brevet status in this family circle. But of all his attachments in Rome, none grew closer than that with the Vassellis.

It must have been during this time that he was drawn toward the seventeen-year-old Virginia. Toto's young sister was just out of a convent when he had first met her, and now she had developed into a beautiful dark-eyed girl. Certainly, not the least of her attractions for him was her musical ability. During this stay in Rome, Gaetano wrote and dedicated two compositions to Virginia. The first is a scherzo for violin and piano, employing twenty-seven themes from his operas. On the last page of the autograph, he lists the operas whose melodies he employed. The most recent of the operas mentioned is *Alahor*, but one name on the list catches the eye, *La bella prigioniera*.[2] With this scherzo then, Donizetti was symbolically dedicating

[1] Z. No. 31, p. 251.
[2] Only two numbers of this work survive, perhaps all that was ever composed. Oddly enough, the music was written to piano accompaniment. Therefore it was not designed for the stage. It may have been intended for the amateur musicians in Rome.

to Virginia all the operas he had written up to this time. His second composition for her is a duet for two sopranos. This autograph bears the date 30 November 1826, three days after Virginia's eighteenth birthday and one day after his own twenty-ninth.

At some time during these days Gaetano asked Luigi Vasselli for his daughter's hand. By the following May, in any event, the terms of her dowry were well under discussion. To put himself on a better financial footing and to insure his ability to support his own household, Gaetano signed a contract with Barbaja to write four operas a year for three years in return for 200 ducats a month; in addition to this he was to receive an additional 50 scudi a month acting as musical director for the Teatro Nuovo in Naples. By consigning himself to these intensive labours, Donizetti was at least assuring himself a regular income, if not a lavish one.

Domenico Barbaja (1778–1841) was one of the most remarkable impresarios who ever lived. A completely self-made man, he combined the conflicting talents of extraordinary shrewdness and little knowledge, but in his thirty-year reign, during which at various times he controlled the fortunes of the San Carlo, the Kärthnerthor in Vienna, and La Scala, he fostered and exploited the greatest operatic talents of his time. Barbaja had a contract with Pacini similar to the one he entered into with Donizetti. In his memoirs Pacini makes two interesting observations about the impresario he knew so well. With Barbaja his word was as good as a contract. 'Where are there honest, solvent impresarios today?' and later, 'Barbaja used to call those he liked *assassino, mariolo, ladro*, and I used to use the same words right back at him.'[1]

But before Donizetti could return to Naples and take up his duties for Barbaja, he had to supervise the birth of *Olivo e Pasquale*. The opera opened the season at the Valle on 7 January 1827, the opening having been delayed from San Stefano. Donizetti's opera was sung by Emilia Bonini (Isabella), Anna Scudellari-Cosselli (Camillo), Agnese Loyselet (Matilde), Giovanni Battista Verger (Le Bross), Domenico Cosselli (Olivo), Giuseppe Frezzolini (Pasquale), Luigi Garofolo (Columella) and Stanislao Prò (Diego). None of Donizetti's printed letters refer to the outcome of this performance, but the

---

[1] Pacini, *Le mie memorie artistiche*, p. 16n. and p. 43.

account in the *Notizie del Giorno* makes it clear the opera was not an unqualified triumph. The music is praised for the excellence and aptness of the orchestration; several numbers, particularly the quartet for men's voices, were lauded, but the performance was found wanting, especially the performance of la Bonini, who seems to have been out of her element in a comic role. This criticism aroused the prima donna to the extent of writing a letter in her defence to the paper, asserting that she had been well applauded and charging that the management is unhappy over the bad success of the opera and the certain and true proof of it is the small sale of tickets each night.[1] The opera, however, managed to hold the stage of the Valle for a month. Shortly after Donizetti's return to Naples, he put on *Olivo e Pasquale* at the Nuovo with more favourable results than in Rome. The excellent cast included Annetta Fischer (Isabella), Vincenzo Galli (Olivo), and Gennaro Luzio (Pasquale). The opera survived on many Italian stages until about 1870, while it was also sung in Spain, Portugal, Germany, and Austria. London heard it on 31 March 1832, sung by de Méric[2] (Isabella), Vincenzo Galli (Pasquale), Rosa Mariani (Camillo) and Alberico Curioni (Le Bross). According to Chorley, the opera 'fell dead on the hour of [its] appearance.'[3]

After the third performance of *Olivo e Pasquale* Donizetti left Rome to assume his position in Naples. After producing *Olivo e Pasquale* at the Nuovo, he brought out on 13 May the first of his operas written under the terms of his contract with Barbaja. This was *Otto mesi in due ore*, which was sometimes called *Gli esiliati in Siberia*. The cast included Caterina Lipparini (Elisabetta), Vincenzo Galli, Giuseppe Fioravanti, Gennaro Luzio, Giuseppe Loira and Raffaele Scalese. The opera enjoyed a run of fifty performances. Usually well received wherever it was produced, *Otto mesi* was judged at La Scala, however, as no better than a mediocrity and at Genoa it failed to survive a cataclysmic first performance. According to Verzino,[4] *Otto mesi* deserves attention, for in 1831 a Modenese audience employed the third-act march from Donizetti's score in a

[1] Quoted in Cametti, *Donizetti a Roma*, p. 56.
[2] This excellent soprano is not to be confused with the more widely known Henriette Méric-Lalande.
[3] Chorley, *Thirty Years' Musical Recollections*, p. 33.
[4] Verzino, *Le opere di Gaetano Donizetti*, p. 75.

turbulent patriotic demonstration, the earliest example of Donizetti's music being used in that way. After Donizetti's death, *Otto mesi* underwent a metamorphosis when a conductor named Ugo Fontana added quite a bit of his own music to the score and brought it out in Paris (1853) as *Elisabeth ou La fille du proscrit*.

On 25 May 1827 Donizetti wrote a letter to his father which gives some idea how the plans for his marriage were progressing.

> Dear Papa,
> I hope to find you less displeased now that you know the name of the young lady that perhaps I will marry, because certainly I could not have found a better person in regard to character; I will not say beauty because that lasts a short time. Now I want you to know that they give 2000 colonati payable in three years, that is for three years yet one enjoys only the six per cent; afterwards I am master of the sum and able to place it where I please; earlier no, because her father made a contract for six years with the bankers and only three have passed. There is another thousand for her household goods and silver; therefore it seems to me that a man who has not one soldo can afford to marry her. And last, what more would other girls have? And then, who knows, but what I might come and settle near you? The young lady does what I want, so —?
> At the Nuovo I have given my opera, *Otto mesi in due ore*. I have written the good news to Mayr, but there has been no reply. It goes very well indeed. Love to mamma, my brothers, my friends, my teachers, and wishing you a thousand years of good health, I call myself your,
>
> Gaetano.[1]

From this letter it would seem probable that the arrangements between Gaetano and Luigi Vasselli were initiated during the months from September 1826 to January 1827 when Donizetti was in Rome. If he later returned from Naples to discuss the dowry, there are no documents at present that

[1] Z. No. 33, pp. 252-3.

confirm it. From Gaetano's letter of 25 May to his father, it is apparent that he had written earlier giving some inkling of his plans, for Andrea seems to have written back protesting at his son's plan to marry a stranger. Donizetti's father was afraid that if his son, who had not seen his parents in six years, established a home of his own, he would be less likely and less able to give financial support to them. Gaetano's mention of 'other girls' suggests that Andrea may have urged the choice of some Bergamasc girl as daughter-in-law, hoping thereby to strengthen Gaetano's ties at home and to establish a handy relationship with some well-to-do family there. To ease his father's anxieties Gaetano spelled out the terms of the marriage settlement, and to the same end he threw out the suggestion that he might settle in Bergamo again. For all the genuine love Donizetti always retained for his birthplace, there is no confirmation that he ever seriously, or for very long, considered such a move. Indeed, the evidence all points the other way. After Virginia married Gaetano, she never met her husband's parents nor came to Bergamo. From this, it would seem that Gaetano was not particularly anxious for his wife to meet his family or to see at first hand the humble circumstances in which he had been born and in which they still lived. The only time a proposal was made for such a meeting, an invitation was issued to Andrea, and to none of the others, to come to Naples.

At this point it might be helpful to digress briefly from Donizetti's busy career and glance at his family. His parents had moved from the Borgo Canale in 1806 to quarters in the Piazza Nova (today the Piazza Mascheroni), and later moved again to Contrada S. Grata, No. 150. From this address Andrea continued to carry out his duties as porter of the municipal pawnshop. Domenica Donizetti's health, it seems, no longer permitted her to engage in the needlework with which she used to supplement the family income. The elderly couple—in 1827 they were both about sixty-two—were looked after by the granddaughter Beppina, the daughter of Maria Antonia Donizetti Tironi, who died in 1823.

Gaetano's eldest brother, Giuseppe, had permanently left his parents' home in 1808. He had been trained as a musician, studying with his uncle Corini and receiving some private lessons from Mayr, for at eighteen Giuseppe had been beyond the admissible age for acceptance in the Lezioni Caritatevoli when they were instituted in 1806. The climax of Giuseppe's musical career in Bergamo was his singing of a bass role in Mayr's *Elisa* at the Riccardi during the Fiera season, 1808. Soon after, the twenty-year-old Giuseppe was conscripted into the 7th Regiment of the Army of the Kingdom of Italy. In 1809 he was fighting the Austrians, while in 1810 he accompanied his regiment to Spain where he remained until 1813, taking part in the siege of Saragossa. In 1814, at the dissolution of the Italian army, Giuseppe returned to Bergamo for two months, but then he made his way to Elba to join the service of Napoleon, taking up the duties of a military flautist. On 12 February 1815 he married Angela Tondi, a native of Portoferraio.

At the time of The Hundred Days, Giuseppe accompanied Napoleon's armies to France, now serving as an infantryman, but on 1 May 1815 he left this service and returned to Italy. In October of the same year he resumed his career as a military musician by assuming the duties of bandmaster in a Sardinian regiment. In Alessandria, Piedmont, the couple's only child, a son, Andrea, named after his paternal grandfather, was born on 29 April 1818. Giuseppe continued as bandmaster with various Sardinian regiments until 1827. Then it came about that the Sultan of Turkey, Mahmud II (1785–1839), as part of the reforms that earned him the name of 'infidel' from the zealots of Islam, wished to introduce Westernized military music to the Ottoman armies. For advice on this matter, the Sultan turned to Marchese Grappallo, the Sardinian minister at Constantinople, who in turn inquired for a likely bandmaster with one of his sovereign's regiments, and so in 1828 Giuseppe moved to Constantinople.

In one of his letters to his father, that of 21 July 1826, Gaetano alludes to Giuseppe's desire to find another service, but the proposal from Turkey was apparently not made until the following year. When he received one of his father's anxiety-ridden letters, this time about the Sultan's offer, Gaetano reacted sharply:

> I have heard and with great astonishment of my brother Giuseppe's resolution. I tell you sincerely, because I am unprejudiced, that one can love and adore God even in the deserts, and for a good Christian there is no need for

churches to be the determining factor; one loves God in
one's heart and the presence or absence of sanctuaries
makes no difference. His decision seems to me altogether
bad at the times in which we find ourselves. I will never
applaud such a decision, and it must be that the 8000
francs have blinded him, but you should make him consider that if he finds things don't go well there, he will find
it more difficult to find employment in Italy. I would have
written to him about this, but he tells me that during this
month he will be at home; thus it is useless since letters
take 15 days from here to Chambery. If however he comes
home decided to do this, let him see this letter of mine,
and tell him moreover that I highly disapprove of such a
resolution, not for the journey, not because he would lose
a regiment that he loves so much, but for the dangerous
times[1] in which we find ourselves. Tell him that in this
world it is necessary to be discreet in one's desires, and one
lives happily. I don't want to become a millionaire, for the
little I earn satisfies me, and I live without debts and am
very happy. Perhaps he desires too much and will find
himself sorry. I wish him all possible good things, but when
I see him at Genoa, I will not fail to talk clearly to him,
although then it will be entirely useless.

On the other hand, there are many whom I have known
who have undertaken both journeys and services worse
than his, and they have come back with goods and
money. In sum, I cannot advise him about this, since I do
not want either to be blessed or cursed. I tend to my own
affairs, to my soul, further he is older than I; therefore he
must think, consider, and decide. . . .[2]

But when Gaetano got to Genoa in February 1828, he found
that his brother had already started out for Turkey. On the
day of his arrival in Genoa, the 28th, Gaetano wrote to his
father to learn what Giuseppe has decided to do and how he is.
Constantinople was to be Giuseppe Donizetti's home for the
rest of his life.

By 1827 only Giuseppe and Francesco survived of Gaetano's
brothers and sisters. The details of Francesco's life up to this

[1] The naval Battle of Navarino had just taken place on 20 October 1827.
[2] Z. No. 37, pp. 255–6, dated 5 December 1827.

time have only been sparsely recorded. According to Verzino,[1] Francesco served in an Austrian regiment, a situation which suggests that he could scarcely have been inducted until 1814, when he would have been about twenty-one or two. Francesco was also a musician of sorts, probably playing the trumpet in a regimental band; but he also included among his few talents an aptitude for the cymbals. By 1821 Francesco was back in Bergamo a civilian once more, as we learn from a petition to the Delegazione di Bergamo, in which it is stated that 'fifteen young amateurs of music desire to form a civic band under the direction of Francesco Donizetti.'[2] Besides this activity he seems to have had no regular occupation until after his father's death in December 1835, when it was arranged by Gaetano and Dolci that the unenterprising Francesco should succeed to the portership of the pawnshop.

The family situation explains Andrea's rather selfish fears when, in the spring of 1827, he heard that Gaetano planned to marry Virginia Vasselli. It was to Gaetano that his father looked first, and he had already formed the habit of applying to him for funds. Gaetano's letter of 21 July 1826 is only one of many that deals with this problem.

> . . . You need money? Alas! Honours I could give you, but money. . . . Here at the Teatro Nuovo I have sold a score [the revision of *L'ajo*], I received for the rehearsals and everything 40 ducats; at the San Carlo with *Elvida* 200 ducats; but with the other opera I don't know if they will even say thank you to me. Suffice it that in every case I will try to help you as best I can. . . .[3]

Meanwhile Gaetano remained at his post in Naples, turning out operas to satisfy the terms of his contract. At the Fondo, on 19 August 1827, appeared *Il borgomastro di Saardam*, to a libretto by Gilardoni; the best-known operatic treatment of this subject, however, is Lortzing's *Zar und Zimmermann*. For Donizetti's première the role of Marietta was entrusted to one of the leading sopranos of the day, one who was to introduce many of

[1] Edoardo Clemente Verzino, *Contributo ad una biografia di Gaetano Donizetti* (Bergamo, 1896), p. 15.
[2] Quoted ibid.
[3] Z. No. 28, p. 248.

his operas—Carolina Ungher (1803-77).[1] The others in the cast included Almerinda Manzocchi (Carlotta), Celestino Salvatori (Czar Pietro), Winter (Flimann), Raffaele Casaccia (Timoteo), Carlo Casaccia (Borgomastro), Giovanni Pace (Leforte), and Gaetano Chizzola (Ali Mahmed). The opera was well received in Naples and ran for more than thirty-five performances, but at La Scala, where it was heard with Ungher heading a very inferior cast, the opera was an utter fiasco. Bellini, who was in Milan at the time, wrote to his friend Florimo[2] on 2 January 1828, that he had heard from someone who attended the general rehearsal of *Borgomastro* at La Scala that 'in the first act there is nothing, in the second a duet that just might please, but as a whole the work will have a fiasco.'[3] Bellini's not impartial expectations were completely realized. Elsewhere *Borgomastro* fared better, holding the stage until about 1840.[4]

In his letter to his father of 30 October 1827 Donizetti refers to his next project.

   . . . I am engaged in writing a farce for my benefit evening. I will give it in November, and all this to draw a crowd.

[1] This is the way her name was characteristically spelt in Italy. Ungher was born in Hungary, came to Vienna, where she studied singing with Aloysa Lange, Mozart's sister-in-law. She made her début as a mezzo-soprano singing Dorabella in *Così fan tutte* (1821). In 1824 she sang the contralto solo in the first performance of Beethoven's Ninth Symphony, and it is she, according to tradition, who turned the deaf composer round so that he might acknowledge the applause. She was brought by Barbaja to Italy, where she sustained a brilliant career until she retired from the stage at her marriage in 1840; she spent the remainder of her life in retirement at Florence. Besides her services for Donizetti's operas, she sang the first performance of Bellini's *La straniera* (later Bellini described her every note as a *stilettata*) and of Pacini's *Niobe*. When Rossini heard her during her only season at the Théâtre-Italien (1833-34), he is supposed to have made this *mot*: '*Elle a ardeur du sud, énergie du nord, poitrine de bronze, voix d'argent, talent d'or.*' (She has southern ardour, northern energy, a chest of bronze, a voice of silver, and a talent of gold.)
[2] Francesco Florimo (1800-80) was a fellow student of Bellini's at the Conservatory, his dearest friend, his most ardent partisan, consequently he was not given to boosting Donizetti. Florimo became director of the library at the Conservatory of S. Pietro a Majella, where he exerted much influence, wrote biographies and histories of music in Naples, but, alas, he was not an impeccable scholar.
[3] Bellini, *Epistolario*, ed. Luisa Cambi (Milan, 1943), Ltr. IX, p. 31.
[4] Acccording to Loewenberg, it was sung in Budapest in Hungarian (1839).

Excuse me if I send you little money, but if I can later, I will send you something more. You should write more often, for Mayr does not even answer. Make my Quarenghi[1] write to me. I hope soon to give you a fine piece of news. Enough, we shall see. Goodbye, my greetings to Francesco.[2]

This farce was *Le convenienze ed inconvenienze teatrali*, produced at the Nuovo, 21 November 1827, with Gennaro Luzio in the baritone-harridan role of Agata. For this work Donizetti turned librettist and fashioned his own text from two plays by Sografi. Donizetti's libretto is full of high spirits and verbal felicities, testifying to his genuine flair for this activity and to his great good humour in these months before his marriage. His letter to his father shows his concern for raising money at this benefit, and it is quite possible that not the least of his reasons for turning librettist is to avoid splitting his fee. Whatever Donizetti's motives, the quality of this libretto, and of those he was later to write for *Il campanello di notte* and *Betly*, make one wish he had availed himself more frequently of his own talents for ready verse.

Le convenienze enjoyed a fine success. It was still playing in Naples in 1831, at the Fondo. Berlioz heard it then and reports:

At the Fondo the opera buffa is played with such fire, spirit and brio as to raise it above almost every theatre of its class. While I was at Naples they were performing a most amusing farce of Donizetti's, *Le convenienze teatrali*.[3]

Donizetti later expanded this work into two acts and made substantial changes in the plot. The revisions bear no date, but it is possible that they were made for the Milanese première at the Canobbiana, 20 April 1831. Here the work was well received and ran for twenty-two performances, but at La Scala,

[1] Antonio Quarenghi, a Bergamasc lawyer who owned a villa at Almenno, was one of Donizetti's dearest links with Bergamo. Almost all of his letters to Mayr of this period contain jovial greetings to Quarenghi, whom he once refers to as *ubbriaco* (drunken) Quarenghi. Unfortunately, none of Donizetti's letters to him, if indeed he wrote any, seems to have survived.
[2] Z. No. 36, p. 255.
[3] Berlioz, *Memoirs* (ed. E. Newman), p. 170.

in the autumn of 1842, it had a single disastrous performance. It played successfully in other towns, such as Palermo. In 1831 an unnamed Milanese journalist found 'the melodies fresh, vivacious, everything attractive and pleasing; the orchestration is worthy of proven maestros. . . .'[1] Near the end of his career, Donizetti thought of making a further revision of this opera, but the deterioration of his health prevented him from carrying out this project.

A month and a half after the première of *Le convenienze*, Donizetti won one of the greatest successes of this period of his career with *L'esule di Roma*. The opera was given at the San Carlo, 1 January 1828, with Adelaide Tosi (Argelia), Edvige Ricci (Leontina), Rubini (Settimio), Lablache (Murena), Giovanni Campagnoli (Publio), Gaetano Chizzola (Lucio), and Capranica (Fulvio). The libretto was by Gilardoni, but the censors had insisted on a last-minute change of title, the opera being given as *Il proscritto*. It was enthusiastically received, particularly the trio at the end of the first act. Of this trio, Rossini is supposed to have said that it would suffice to make a composer's reputation. That Donizetti regarded this trio as an independent step toward freeing himself from the patterns of Rossini is demonstrated by his letter of 2 February to Mayr. After thanking his teacher for his congratulations on the success of *L'esule*, he goes on:

> . . . Next year I will finish the first act with a quartet and the second with a death, according to my fashion. I want to break the yoke of the finales . . . but for now to finish with a trio, never again, since everyone tells me that if I were to die, if I were to return to the body of Signora Domenica and be born again, I could not do such a thing again—but I am encouraged and feel myself capable of doing better things.[2]

At Milan, 12 July 1828, *L'esule* was given at La Scala with Henriette Méric-Lalande (Argelia), Winter (Settimio), Lablache (Murena), and Domenico Spiaggi (Publio). Although the work was much applauded and received ten performances, the opera had been severely mauled by Monsignor Rolla, the

[1] Quoted in Verzino, *Le opere di Gaetano Donizetti*, p. 71.
[2] Z. No. 38, p. 257.

censor. Pezzi, the critic of the *Gazzetta di Milano* (15 July 1828) judged it with characteristic grimness.

> With *L'ajo nell'imbarazzo*, with *Il borgomastro di Saardam*, Donizetti made known to us his great fondness for imitations. Constant to his love also in his *L'esule di Roma*, he shows himself only fleetingly unfaithful. In a trio, a duet, and in the *largo* of an aria, one recognizes an inspired pupil of Mayr; in the rest there is more reminiscence than inspiration. If rumour does not lie, *L'esule di Roma* made a furore on the stage at Naples. This reception justifies choosing it for our theatre. Donizetti's opera was applauded also by us.
>
> If this applause was not a furore, it will be perhaps the fault of the air, less volcanic along the Olona than along the Sebeto.[1]

L'esule was given in England, Germany and Austria, but its most meaningful triumph for Donizetti occurred at Bergamo in the summer of 1840. Here the opera was conducted by Donizetti's fellow-student, Marco Bonesi, and sung by Eugenia Tadolini, Domenico Donzelli and Ignazio Marini. These last two singers were Bergamascs. For the occasion Donizetti had composed a new cabaletta for Tadolini and a new aria for Donzelli. He attended the performance and was greeted with a delirious ovation. This evening marked at long last, the unstinting recognition of Donizetti's talent—although he had begun his career more than twenty years before—by his fellow citizens of Bergamo.

In Naples on 16 January 1828, Donizetti signed a contract with Barbaja for two operas, for which he was to receive 500 ducats. In Milan, on 16 January 1828, Bellini, still flushed over his triumph with *Il pirata* at La Scala the previous October and still gloating over the fiasco of *Il borgomastro* at La Scala, wrote again to Florimo: 'I believe Donizetti has been forced to take two bottles of Le Roy[2] to make his anger pass.' Donizetti, for his part, was on the crest of the wave. Exhilarated by the success of *L'esule* and looking forward to his departure for Rome and the sight of Virginia, he needed no physic. He arrived in

---

[1] Quoted in Verzino, *Le opere di Gaetano Donizetti*, p. 80.
[2] This was a formidable purgative of the period.

DONIZETTI

Rome on 2 February, as we learn from his letter to Mayr of that date. 'I arrived today and today I found your letter. That Romani, who promises everything, keeps his word about nothing (*che tutto promette, nulla mantiene*)! I have written to him; he does not answer. He chose the subject and it does not please me too much. Enough. I am going to Genoa in a few days and I will overturn Heaven, Earth and Sea. . . .'[1] There is no record where Donizetti stayed during these few days in Rome, but certainly he saw Virginia whenever the opportunity offered. It may well have been at this time that it was agreed they would be married upon his return from Genoa.

Donizetti arrived in Genoa, dead tired, on 28 February. He wrote to his father:

> This morning I arrived happily, but with broken bones and so tired that I cannot express it. Tonight I will have my revenge.
>
> Tell me what Giuseppe has resolved to do and how he is.
>
> Do not forget to send me my baptismal certificate.
>
> Here they do not have too good an opinion of me because of the fiasco at Milan of [*Il borgomastro*] the work that pleased so much at Naples. Perhaps it is better. The book however is truly a great pastiche and tell Mo. Mayr that Romani has served me in his fashion.
>
> I expect however something agreeable, and I hope it will be. In April I put on my opera and afterwards leave at once for Naples, where things go particularly well for me, and if I can find three soldi a day, I would prefer it to travelling and to writing for the theatre.
>
> Tell me your news and command me in whatever I can do. . . .[2]

At Genoa, for the opening of the new opera house, the Carlo Felice, the authorities had seen fit to plan a season with works by the leading Italian composers of the day: Rossini, Bellini,

[1] Z. No. 38, p. 257.
[2] Z. No. 39, pp. 258-9. Donizetti's mention of leaving 'at once for Naples' may well be a deliberate falsehood, hoping to keep his prospective marriage a secret from Bergamo.

Donizetti, and Morlacchi.[1] If this list seems strange, it is because 'leading' can be a most subjective adjective. Of the four, Bellini was the only Southern Italian, although at the moment the lion of Milan; the other three had all been pupils of Padre Mattei. Rossini did not leave Paris to come to Genoa, but the others were present to stage their operas. Two *prime* were scheduled: Donizetti's *Alina, regina di Golconda* and Morlacchi's Genoese compliment, *Colombo*. Much of the drama of this season was behind the scenes, for this marked the first season in which Donizetti and Bellini were in direct serious competition.

The season opened on 7 April with a gala. First there was a 'melodious and well sung' hymn for the occasion, a compliment to the royal house of Savoy, who were present in force. This hymn was composed by Donizetti and performed by Letizia Cortesi, G. B. Verger, Tamburini, and the chorus; it was the first score officially performed in the house. The evening continued with a performance of Bellini's *Bianca e Fernando*, sung by Tosi, Giovanni David, and Tamburini. Between the two acts of Bellini's opera, a new ballet by Giovanni Galzerani, entitled *Gli adoratori del fuoco*, replete with spectacular pyrotechnic effects, was danced by la Paul, Elisa Vaque Moulin, Aubert Noblet, and Stefano Gastillon. The greatest triumph of the evening went to the ballerina, Vaque Moulin.[2]

Bellini arrived in Genoa, almost three weeks after Donizetti, on 19 March. His frequent letters to Florimo are full of his anxieties about his 'enemies'. For instance, he is sure that Pacini has tried to cause trouble in Milan and that Pacini's father, a basso buffo, had succeeded in causing him trouble in Vienna. He is concerned about the new numbers he has written for *Bianca e Fernando*, especially a new cavatina and cabaletta for Tosi. On 5 April he writes to Florimo that the soprano was unhappy with her new music, and that only with difficulty could he persuade her to sing it as he wanted it. Then he reports that he has found the reason for her behaviour.

---

[1] The most famous associations of Francesco Morlacchi (1784–1841) are that he was a co-Kapellmeister at Dresden with Weber and later Wagner's precedessor. Morlacchi's best-known opera is *Tebaldo ed Isolina* (1822).
[2] Giovanni Battista Vallebona, *Il teatro Carlo Felice: Cronisteria di un secolo 1828–1928* (Genoa, 1928).

. . . David, however, tells me that the changes had come from [Donizetti] and I had suspected that because Tosi herself told me that when she showed the part to D— he had said that the stretta was worthless. That, I believe, he said from his own judgement and without malice and because he was concerned for her. But then he gave her back the parts with such changes of tempo and everything contrary to my notions, that it makes me certain that it is *completely impossible* to have friends in the profession. And his turn coming after my opera does not make me believe that he inclines toward my success.[1]

At the slightest sign of criticism a man of Bellini's neurasthenic suspiciousness was quick to see a plot. For his part, Donizetti had found *Bianca e Fernando* at its Neapolitan première, *bella, bella, bella*. . . . After the Genoese première of *Bianca*, Bellini wrote a glowing and detailed account of his success. The opera ran for twenty-one evenings with, according to the official record, increasing success. Bellini's letter of 12 April to Florimo confirms the growth of enthusiasm, and he adds that because of the theatre's excellent acoustics, Donizetti had said that 'Tosi seems to have doubled her usual voice.'

The second opera of the season was *Il barbiere*, which, according to Bellini, 'made a fiasco such as you wouldn't believe.' Since the season was being given by two overlapping companies, one for the serious operas and one for the comedies, Donizetti was naturally concerned by the weakness of the latter group, since *Alina* was an opera buffa. With reason Bellini describes 'poor' Donizetti as 'very agitated'. The prima donna, Cortesi, the tenor Verger, whom Bellini sums up as '*mediocrissimo*', and the buffo Frezzolini left the audience cold; only Tamburini aroused any enthusiasm. In fact, Cortesi was so bad that the management sent off at once to try to find a replacement for her. The third opera of the season was Rossini's *Otello*, with Tosi and David, but the tenor role of Rodrigo was sung by the mezzo-soprano Brigida Lorenzani, for whom Bellini wrote a new cavatina. *Otello* played to full houses for fourteen evenings.

Very pleased with himself, Bellini had already left Genoa when *Alina* had its first performance on 12 May 1828. This

---

[1] Bellini, *Epistolario*, Ltr. XXV, p. 75.

opera was sung by Adelaide Comelli-Rubini[1] (Alina), De Vincenti, an eighteen-year-old pupil of Pasta (Fiorina), Verger (Seide), Tamburini (Volmar), and Giuseppe Frezzolini (Belfiore). By a felicitous gesture, the score of *Alina* was dedicated to Donizetti's true friend, Antonio Dolci of Bergamo. The *Gazzetta di Genova* (13 May 1828) praised the new opera. 'All the pieces of the score, and especially the ensembles with chorus, proved the excellent skill of the young Lombard composer. Through it all shines a certain exuberance that is always rousing and pleasingly sustained.' In spite of the tone of this review, the later performances of *Alina* were not particularly happy due to the vocal deficiencies of Comelli and Verger, both of whom suffered from chronic indispositions. On the 15th of May, Gaetano wrote an account of the first performance to Mayr.

> I was obliged to put on my opera with a week's preparation because the Director had told His Majesty that it would be put on on Monday, and they were performing an opera every evening. Enough! When Heaven wants to give protection one can go on even without rehearsals, and my *Alina* won a most happy reception. His Majesty had the complacency to applaud Alina's cavatina, the tenor aria, the duet for the bass and the soprano, and the final variations. I could have been more pleased. The tenor was sick, the woman was . . . enough with all this, at the end of the performance, the singers were called out twice and twice the composer—I swear to you that by the disorder at the general rehearsal, held the same morning and lasting until three, I believed I was going to be slaughtered. Yesterday *Otello* was given because of the illness of my tenor Verger. . . .[2]

While this letter explains the unpropitious circumstances that almost shipwrecked the première of *Alina*, the charm and balance of the delightful score kept it on the stage through most

[1]Born Adelaide Chaumel and trained at the Paris Conservatory, she was brought by Barbaja to Naples about 1818. She Italianized her name and enjoyed an extensive career, although she was never regarded as a singer of the first class. She ultimately retired to further the career of her husband, the tenor G. B. Rubini, whom she had married in 1819.

[2] Z. No. 40, p. 259.

of the nineteenth century. Strangely enough *Alina* seems never to have been produced in either England or America.

Sometime between 12 and 19 May, Donizetti wrote a new cabaletta to insert in Rossini's *L'assedio di Corinto*.[1] Donizetti's addition, *Pietosa all'amor mio*, was first sung at Genoa by Tosi and Tamburini and much applauded. This cabaletta was included in numerous later performances in Italy.

On 19 May, Donizetti set out for Rome; he was to have left two days earlier, but the courier had been delayed. This fact is found in his letter to Mayr of 15 May, which also contains some of Donizetti's reflections on his career.

> . . . The disappointment of not being able to see you is greater for me, dear Maestro, because I had set great store by it, but what can I do? On 16 August I must go on stage, and the subject is not even decided yet. I don't live for profit, but honour, and I assure you that if I could write a *Medea*,[2] I would be content to die afterwards. I am making you a little *Souvenir* of my music, including *L'esule* and various other parts of operas that have pleased in Naples. Among these is *Ugolino*[3] of Dante. I have received some indulgence for it, and I want yours. . . .[4]

It seems curious that in this letter, written just a few days before he left Genoa to go to Rome for his marriage, Donizetti makes no mention of it to the man he called his 'second father'; the truth of the matter is that he had made up his mind that the best way to break the news to his 'first' father was to announce a *fait accompli*. The opera for 16 August is just an excuse. Donizetti did not want to face his father in

---

[1] This is the Italian translation of *Le siège de Corinth* (Paris, 1826), in turn, a *rifacimento* of *Maometto II* (Naples, 1820). *L'assedio* was first introduced into Italy at Parma, 26 January 1828.

[2] *Medea in Corinto* is Mayr's most solid opera.

[3] This curious composition was written in Naples during January 1828 and dedicated to Lablache. The vocal setting shows an occasional dramatic impetus, but the piano accompaniment is woefully inadequate. Rossini once wrote: 'I heard that Donizetti had the melancholy idea of setting a canto of Dante to music. It seems to me that this is much too proud. I believe that in such an undertaking not even the Eternal Father would succeed, admitting that he had been a *maestro di musica*.' Quoted, G. Radiciotti, *Rossini*, vol. II, pp. 321–2.

[4] Z. No. 40, p. 260.

Bergamo just then, nor did he want to postpone his arrival in Rome.

Gaetano Donizetti married Virginia Vasselli on Sunday, 1 June 1828, in the Roman church of S. Maria in Via. The witnesses were Antonio Vasselli and Giovanni Battista Zampi.[1] In a few days the newly married couple left for Naples with their household goods, including a piano, and moved into an apartment on the Vico Nardones, No. 14. The only extant letter from Gaetano to his father that deals with his marriage is that of 19 July, and in it he tries to make peace with the offended old man.

> Dearest Papa,
> I do not thank you for the letter you have written me before this. I understand that you might be offended not to have been present at the wedding, but also I planned to spare you the expense and to have you soon receive with a single letter news from both your children, but my consideration was not understood. Then you say that you know more about politeness than I do (and this may be so), but I have shared news of this blessed marriage with you for a long time now; therefore I think I have not failed in any great measure.
> If for now I cannot send you a portrait of my wife, I will send you her handwriting,[2] that is she wants to write to you, so be patient for now. Whether you see her or not is up to you, since either here or at Rome you would be welcome, and I will try to pay your way back. Therefore make an effort. At the first of October her papa and brother will look for you, you will see Rome, and come here and leave together; after all, we are not *in finibus terrae*. Take courage. To come to Rome will require a few *bajocchi*. When you are there, I assure you, you will not need a farthing more. Apply for a leave of three months, and everything is arranged. Now we will see if you are a

---

[1] The marriage certificate, as Cametti reports, is difficult to find, as the bridegroom's name is spelled Bonizetti.

[2] Donizetti uses the word '*carattere*' which is a double play on the word character.

man of your word. In the first days of next month I go on stage with the opera *Gianni di Calais*. Now I will write to Mayr.

I beg you to keep this invitation to yourself and not extend it to Francesco, for then the thing changes aspect. I know that Giuseppe has left. Let me hear that Mamma is well and you too, and greet all my friends for me.

Gaetano.

Interpolated at this point is a note added in Virginia's hand.

Signor Andrea,

I take the liberty of writing these few lines to unite my prayers to those of good Gaetano, in regard to the wish of your coming and spending some little time with us. I flatter myself that you would not deny us that favour, while [a refusal] would be too great a disappointment for us.

I beg you to convey my greeting to your most estimable Consort.

Persuaded of your goodness, as also of that of your Lady Consort, I beg you to accept me among the number of your children; certain of being able to obtain so fair a favour, I go now to sign myself with all my esteem, your affectionate daughter and servant,

Virginia Vasselli Donizetti.

Gaetano continues the letter.

Tell the excellent Maestro Mayr that I have received his much appreciated letter by the hand of his pupil engaged by Barbaja. As far as I can, I will help him as I would a brother, as soon as I know in which opera he makes his début.

I have just paid a little tribute to the climate with a little fever for two or three days; now I am well. . . .[1]

On 10 July, Virginia's father had written a courtly letter to Andrea Donizetti, in which he acknowledged receiving an earlier letter from him. If any of Andrea's hurt feelings appeared in his letter, there is no hint of it in the formal phrases of Luigi Vasselli's reply.[2]

[1] Z. No. 41, pp. 260–1.
[2] See Z. No. B. 5, p. 913.

For Donizetti, the rest of the year 1828 was given over not merely to settling down to domesticity, but to engaging in intensive bouts of composition. *Gianni di Calais* was brought out at the Fondo on 2 August, sung by Comelli-Rubini (Metilde), Maria Carraro (Adelina), Rubini (Gianni), Tamburini (Rustano), Michele Benedetti (the King), Tati (Ruggiero), Giovanni Pace (Guido), Gaetano Chizzola (Corrado), Ricci (Arrigo), and Capranica (an Official). The opera won a striking success; particularly admired was the barcarolle sung by Tamburini in Act 1. Its luck held when it was put on at the Carcano in Milan exactly a week after the triumphant *prima* of *Anna Bolena*. In this production the leading roles were sung by Elisa Orlandi, Rubini, and Frezzolini (Rustano). But Rubini's fondness for the role could not make the opera viable in Paris when it appeared at the Théâtre-Italien, once in 1833 and once the following year.

Gianni di Calais was followed in the autumn of 1828 by a one-act farce, *Il giovedì grasso ossia Il nuovo Pourceaugnac*. The first cast included Comelli-Rubini (Nina), Maria Carraro (Camilla), Rosalinda Grossi (Stefania), Rubini (Ernesto), Lablache (Raimondo), Arrigotti (Teodoro), Giovanni Campagnoli (Colonnello) and Giovanni Pace (Cola). Although this unpretentious work was well received, due to the fine cast, it soon slipped out of sight. This opera seems to have had no other productions until recently when it was performed and broadcast in Switzerland. During the last two months of 1828, Donizetti was deeply engaged with the composition of still another opera, *Il paria*. At the end of the year he wrote to his father, who had not managed to make the trip to Naples to meet his new daughter-in-law.

Also this year is over, thanks be to God, without disaster. This letter of mine will not arrive in time to wish you the best of all new years; it will arrive after Epiphany, but have patience. I learned from your letter of your troubles, and especially the illness of mamma, and of the death of the good Maestro's mother-in-law.[1] These things I have been feeling very much. I hope Mayr and all his family will be granted peace, and I hope just as much that mamma

[1] Signora Venturali was twice Mayr's mother-in-law. After the death of his first wife, Angela, in 1799, he married her sister, Lucrezia, in 1804.

will be cured. Age itself brings frequent illnesses, and therefore one must be resigned to it.

In regard to my sending you something. I would not know how to find another method than this, which is that Sig. Agazzi would give you six, seven, or eight scudi, and I would pay them here to Nozzari, since to make a bill of exchange for such a small sum is impractical, nor would anyone be found who makes one nearer than Milan. In any event, if you should find a quick way to let you have something every so often, that would please me, too . . . and I will do as much as I can!

It displeases me that little Andrea does not show talent for music,[1] after all the praises I have heard from Giuseppe. Remember that he should change his occupation at once, so that he will not remain among the mediocrities as I do, because that way one can never hope for good fortune. As he is young he can undertake some other line of work. I will go on with my new opera at the Teatro S. Carlo the 12th, title: *Il paria*. . . .

My wife greets you, and now I cannot write since there are things to do around the house. . . .

Love us and live happy. Farewell. Your

Gaetano[2]

The little Andrea that Gaetano mentions in this letter is the ten-year-old son of Giuseppe, who had been left behind by his parents to continue his education in Bergamo. In an earlier letter to his father, on 21 October, Gaetano had spoken of his nephew and of Giuseppe's concern that his son receive good training. Andrea was to go on to study law at the Royal College of Genoa, receiving his degree in 1841.

Il paria was given on 12 January 1829 at the San Carlo. Gilardoni's uncommonly expressive libretto was drawn from a tragedy by Casimir Delavigne. The opera was sung by Adelaide Tosi (Neala), Edvige Ricci (Zaide), Rubini (Idamore), Lablache (Zarete), Giovanni Campagnoli (Akebare) and Chizzola (Empsaele). Donizetti reports on the performance in his letter of 19 January to his father. After expressing his

---

[1] Donizetti's nephew entered Mayr's school in Bergamo in 1828 as a student of voice and cembalo. He left the school in 1829.
[2] Z. No. 43, p. 263, dated 30 December 1828.

pleasure that his father has got money from Agazzi and telling him to apply again if in need, he continues:

> ... I am very well. I have given the opera and was called out. However, I tell you that I have erred in several places, and I will make it good by adjusting it. I know myself!
>
> Every time you have news of Giuseppe, I beg you to write to me about it. I believe we are going to increase in family . . . we shall see! . . .[1]

The year of 1829, however, did not augur well for Donizetti. Although *Il paria* enjoyed some measure of success because Donizetti was a genuinely popular figure in Naples, its vogue did not last; and this opera, which shows more striving toward an original mode of expressiveness than any other opera he wrote before *Anna Bolena*, sccms not to have been produced elsewhere. Instead, Donizetti used it as a mine for music to go into several of his later scores.

During the spring Donizetti was seriously ill. His letter to his father of 7 May tells the story.

> Dearest Papa,
>
> I write to you after the storm. I have been very sick with convulsions, bilious attacks and, even worse, internal haemorrhoids, and therefore, bleedings, baths, purges, a régimen, and afterwards—I fell sick again. Now, however, the cure is making me well, and I am on my way to recovery. I was to have written for the S. Carlo for 30 May, but my illness has made me postpone it to 6 July, the Queen's gala. I will write *Elisabetta al castello di Kenilworth* with la Boccabadati, la Tosi, David, and Winter. I am at the second act, and there are three acts of three piecos each. . . .

Then after another discussion of money for his father, he goes on:

> ... I am concerned about mamma's health, and I beg you to write to me about it frequently. Giuseppe has written to me and described an immense number of diversions that he finds there and that appeal to him, so much the better. . . .[2]

[1] Z. No. 44, p. 264.   [2] Z. No. 45, pp. 264–5.

Two weeks later he writes again to report that Virginia has sent her mother-in-law a lock of her hair and a ring with her name and Gaetano's on it. Gaetano sent his father a tie-pin. He also reports that they are sending a portrait of Virginia painted by a friend of theirs. This painting is the work of Teodoro Ghezzi and hangs today in the Museo Donizettiano in Bergamo. The portrait, Gaetano explains, is so that father 'can have an idea at least of my taste in the female species.' He concludes the letter with a facetious reference to Virginia's pregnancy. *'La bestia di consorte vi saluta.'* On the following day he writes to his father again—the prospects of becoming a father himself seem to have driven him closer to Andrea—and mentions his hopes of seeing them in August. The most nostalgic note of all occurs in the postscript. 'Ah, if I could have a panorama of Bergamo—as it used to be—I would pay for it, you know.'

Gaetano and Virginia remained in Naples for the production of *Elisabetta al castello di Kenilworth*, which came out at the San Carlo on the Queen's birthday. Tottola's wretched libretto comes from Scott by way of Scribe's libretto, *Leicester ou le château de Kenilworth*, for Auber (1823). Donizetti's newest opera was sung by Tosi (Elisabetta), Luigia Boccabadati (Amelia), Eden (Fanny), David (Alberto, Conte di Leicester [*sic*]), Winter (Warney), and Paolo Ambrosini (Lambourne). Of the fate of this work, Donizetti wrote to Mayr on the 24th that the dress rehearsal was a great success, but on the first night it was *'quasi disapprovata'*. Then Tosi fell ill, and the next performance was postponed until the 12th, and on that night everything went well. But he sums up his own judgement of the opera: '[Between ourselves] I wouldn't give one piece of *Il paria* for the whole of *Il castello di Kenilworth*.'[1]

Almost at once after the date of this letter, Gaetano took Virginia to Rome so that she might bear his child in her family home. Gaetano had been granted a short leave of absence by Barbaja. According to the birth certificate,[2] the baby was born on 29 July 'at the second hour of the night' and was christened Filippo Francesco Achille Cristino. Virginia's brother, Toto, was the proxy for the godfathers; the godmother was the Countess Virginia Rusponi. In a pitifully short time the child

---

[1] Z. No. 49, p. 268.
[2] Quoted in Cametti, *Donizetti a Roma*, p. 68.

died, on 11 August 1829, after only thirteen days of life. On the same day Gaetano wrote Barbaja an anxious letter, pleading for a longer leave of absence because his wife needed at least forty days to recover. His grief and agitation show clearly in his phrases:

> ... About the blow you delivered to me about my leave of absence, dear Barbaja, it is too cruel. You have granted me a month and a half. Only two weeks ago I arrived here. My wife you know needs at least 40 days, and much more now that tonight my son has died. And you want me to leave? Have pity, my Barbaja, pity. If truly you should need me, I would want to serve you, but now for the 19th you have Guglielmi, and on 4 October there is Pacini, and Gilardoni is working and cannot do anything for me. Why do you make me travel to Naples. *I have barely delivered* and you want me to become pregnant? You are too unfeeling then. I hope to stage an opera of mine, so that I will not have everything snatched from me. If however you really need me then I am here; but if you can let me have a little rest, I will work with more talent on my return.[1]

The clearest description of the melancholy events of these days is to be found in Gaetano's letter to his father of 20 August.

> Your congratulations are most welcome to me although they come too late. I say late since the baby, after the twelfth day, went to heaven. The uncertainty of the pregnancy and the visit made to her by the best doctors in Naples who denied the danger to the uterus caused her to follow the remedies prescribed by these beasts, with the result that the baby (*creatura*) was born at seven months. But he had a very large vein on the top of his head that ran from one ear to the other across the top of his skull. The facts are that after seven days of life he went into convulsions, he twisted up his eyes, he did not eat any more, and after a little life, barely prolonged by feeding him spoonfuls of milk, he remained two days with his mouth closed and died. It is better so, than to have a boy devastated by illness, for they say that if he recovered, at

[1] Z. No. 50, p. 269.

the least he would have remained crippled. Let's not say anything further about it. . . .[1]

While Donizetti was in Rome, he retouched the score of *Alina* and, so Cametti says, prepared it for its production at the Valle. The opera was given on 10 October with Annetta Fischer making her Roman début in the title role; others in the cast were Agnese Loyselet, the tenor Pietro Gentili, Crespi, and the buffo Spada. The work won a solid, if not a brilliant, success. On 20 December, also in Rome, a cantata entitled *Il genio dell'armonia* was put on to celebrate the accession of Pius VIII. Donizetti was responsible for part of this score, the rest of it being the work of the Roman composers Costaguti and Capranica. There is no record whether Donizetti was still in Rome or whether, as he had informed his father on 20 August, he had carried out his intention of leaving for Naples about the middle of September.

From Naples on 10 January 1830, Gaetano reported to his father all his reading, including the poetry of 'Bayron' for his opera about Noah, which would be called *Il diluvio universale*. For this opera, he had supplied Giraldoni with a scenario for the libretto, and already completed the first act. He promised to send news of his one-act farce which would be given for his benefit night, 7 February, while *Il diluvio* would have its first performance exactly three weeks later. Donizetti, however, did not indicate that he felt anything unusual about having two new operas come out in such a short time.

The farce for his benefit evening was *I pazzi per progetto*, with Boccabadati (Norina), Carraro (Cristina),[2] Lablache (D'Arlemont), Luzio (Venanzio), and Ambrosini (Frank). The opera was much applauded, but as Donizetti wrote to his father, 'indeed in this case I would rather have had less applause and more money, but because the Russian Minister gave a ball the same evening the theatre was half-full.' *I pazzi per progetto* was favoured with a number of revivals in Naples and Palermo.

[1] Z. No. 51, p. 269.
[2] Florimo reverses the singers for Norina and Cristina, but it is too much to believe that Boccabadati would not sing the role which is allotted the final rondo.

Elsewhere in the letter briefly quoted above, of 13 February, he reacts to the news of the fiasco of *Alina* at Bergamo.

> Bravo, bravo, bravo! I am displeased that the good, the excellent Mayr laboured over it; for the rest, I laugh at it. There, they whistle at me; here, I am applauded . . . *I pazzi per progetto* succeeded most brilliantly . . . here everything I do goes well. And you others in Lombardy never give my works credit, never, never; the papers have discredited me too much. . . . I gave *Alina*, all the papers cried fiasco, and yet one should speak the truth against everyone; meanwhile my pieces are heard everywhere in society, all the singers put them in other operas, even now in *Corradino*, and in the same cities and in the same theatre; nevertheless they say fiasco—very well—I laugh at it.[1]

The rehearsals of *Il diluvio universale* began on 13 February and the first performance was given on the 28th. Luigia Boccabadati (Sela) almost wrecked the première by coming in twenty bars too soon in the first finale. The others in the cast were Carraro (Ada), Winter (Cadmo), Lablache (Noé), Lorenzo Salvi (Cam), Ambrosini (Iefte), Arrigotti (Sem), and Chizzola (Artoo). According to Ghezzi, who jotted down his reminiscences of Donizetti in 1860,[2] not only did Boccabadati's contretemps, which both Festa the conductor and Lablache vainly tried to avert, evoke whistling, but also the final scene of the flood. On 4 May, Donizetti describes the reception of this work to his father.

> . . . The oratorio, the first evening, received many favourable and many unfavourable reactions, but it seems now the favourable party has won, not by my being called out on stage, but by the work continuing all through Lent. I am rash to say that I worked very hard on this score, and I found myself quite satisfied with it. If you think you will find *cabalette* in it, then do not expect to hear them, but if you want to learn how I have understood to distinguish the profane genre of music from the sacred, then be tolerant, listen, and whistle if it does not please you. . . .[3]

[1] Z. No. 53, p. 272.
[2] Teodoro Ghezzi, 'Ricordi su Donizetti', *Omnibus* (7 March 1860). On the whole, Ghezzi's memories are disappointingly unreliable.
[3] Z. No. 55, p. 274.

On 29 May, he wrote to his father that he was already at work on his next opera, *Imelda de' Lambertazzi*, and that he was to write a cantata to celebrate the return of the King and Queen from their travels. His work was hampered by his poor health, for, as he wrote to his father on 24 June, 'Here it is very hot and working as I do I suffer very much between pains in my head and haemorrhoids in my. . . .' *Imelda* was finally produced in the latter part of August,[1] with Antonietta Galzerani (whom Donizetti had likened to a 'straw fire growing more feeble from night to night') in the title role. The male members of the cast were more impressive: Winter (Lamberto); the twenty-three-year-old tenor, Giovanni Basadonna, then at the outset of his notable career (Orlando); Tamburini (Bonifaccio); Michele Benedetti (Ugo); and Ambrosini (Ubaldo). It is not surprising that *Imelda* promptly disappeared from view, as the censor had made Tottola's feebly violent libretto almost incomprehensible.

On 1 August 1830 Donizetti had signed an agreement to compose a new opera for the Teatro Carcano in Milan, where a gala Carnival season was planned with an unusually strong company. In the early part of September, Gaetano and Virginia left Naples for Rome. Here, several weeks later, Donizetti left his wife to stay with her family and proceeded north alone. On 5 October he wrote his father a brief note from Bologna, a city he had not visited since his departure from Padre Mattei and the Liceo Musicale.

> I will be in Bergamo on Sunday, and I beg you not to meet me in Milan so that we do not miss each other on the road. Tomorrow I will leave here and find my lodgings in Milan, leave my things there, and then with speed I will speedily come (*col veloce verrò velocemente*).
>
> Do not upset yourself if I should be delayed, because who knows how many times I shall have to negotiate with the poet, but I hope not. I am alone, so you will not be able to see my wife, who is staying in Rome. If she did not, our earnings would suffer. . . .[2]

[1] The date of *Imelda* is in question. Zavadini on p. 38 says 28 August, but on p. 172 he says 23 August. Cametti says 5 September. The printed libretto for this production merely says 'summer'.
[2] Z. No. 61, p. 280.

For the first time in nine years Donizetti saw his beloved Bergamo on 10 October. He stayed only a few days, but this must have been a time of deeply felt renewals, not only seeing his parents again, but Mayr and Dolci and other old friends. From Bergamo he returned to Milan.

Although Romani's libretto was supposed to be ready in September, it was not in Donizetti's hands complete until 10 November. To compose his opera he went to Como to stay in the villa belonging to the great soprano, Giuditta Pasta. Within a month he had completed his score and returned to Milan, ready to commence the rehearsals of *Anna Bolena* on 10 December.

With the triumphant reception of *Anna Bolena* Donizetti's career entered a new phase. Never again would he seem a talented mediocrity capable of flashes of something better, just one of Barbaja's stable of abjectly prolific composers. With one stroke he became a figure to reckon with in that musical empire, the world of Italian opera.

CHAPTER 3

Establishing a Reputation

While Donizetti was rehearsing *Anna Bolena*, Virginia remained in Rome, anxiously awaiting news of the opera's reception. On 21 December she wrote to her father-in-law in these revealing terms.

> . . . I am very glad to hear from my Gaetano that you are both in good health, and I pray that Heaven may conserve it always. As soon as my Gaetano's opera comes out, I beg you please to give me precise news of the outcome, because to tell the truth I do not trust him; therefore I turn to you, and I am sure you will relieve my anxiety, since you can imagine in what agitation I am living, all the more so because I am familiar with the sensitivity of his character; therefore I recommend myself to you, because during the time when his opera is put on, you go to keep him company. . . .[1]

When word of the opera's success came to Virginia, however, it came from her husband himself. (The existence of Donizetti's letter describing the first night of *Anna Bolena* was long unsuspected; Zavadini learned of it only after his massive *Epistolario* was completed, but he found space to reprint it in his preface, where he affirms his convictions of its authenticity.)

> My respected and most beloved Wife:
> I am pleased to announce that the new opera of your

[1] Z. No. B. 7, p. 914.

beloved and famous husband has had a reception which could not possibly have been improved upon.

Success, triumph, delirium; it seemed that the public had gone mad. Everyone said that they could not remember ever being present at such a triumph.

I was so happy that I started to weep, just think! And my heart came close to you and I thought of your joy had you been present, but you know that I do not want to expose you to such strong emotions, because it would be to no purpose. There are emotions that seem like dying, when one is still uncertain of the audience's reactions.

Even though I had faith in a favourable reception, because everyone spoke well of the opera, artists and orchestra, and even the impresarios, in the first quarter hour, I was suspended between paradise and hell. . . .

Now I am in paradise, and I cannot express my happiness. I lack only a kiss from my Virginia, which I will come to collect at the first chance. I beg you then—*deh t'en priego*, as Romani would say—to prepare me the reception a great maestro merits who comes home full of ardour wanting first thing to embrace his own wife.[1]

Anna Bolena, the cause of Donizetti's elation, had its memorable first performance at the Teatro Carcano, Milan, 26 December 1830. The impressive cast included Giuditta Pasta (Anna), Elisa Orlandi (Giovanna Seymour), Enrichetta Laroche (Smeton), G. B. Rubini (Percy), Filippo Galli (Enrico VIII), Lorenzo Biondi (Rochefort), and Antonio Crippa (Hervey). While the review of the performance in the *Gazzetta di Milano* does not match Donizetti's enthusiasm, the notice contains little of that publication's wonted acerbity in judging his operas.

The cabaletta of an aria sung by Rubini, one of those phrases of great sentiment, that perhaps would expire unobserved on another's lip, but not that of Pasta, and the animated ideas in the finale: here is the essence of what truly pleased in the music of the first act. The other applause that was heard was not due only to the singers.

But in the second act the aspect changed and the talent of the Maestro demonstrated itself with unusual strength.

[1] Z., pp. xvii–xviii.

A duet, a trio, and three arias are of beautiful and grandiose structure. As for the performers one has to have heard Pasta and Rubini in their two arias of differing type and structure to form an idea to what point the power of declaimed song and the enchantment of perfect sounds may attain. In the trio Pasta, Rubini, and Galli showed themselves not only at their best but truly masters in the perfection of their ensemble . . . in this piece, particularly, with its most complicated and beautiful harmonies, Donizetti has shown himself a worthy and favourite pupil of Mayr. It is just to place the youthful Orlandi in a prominent place near these three, for, with a great model before her, she shows that she has profited from it. . . .[1]

If the critic of the *Gazzetta* approached the performance of *Anna Bolena* impartially, that of *L'eco*, another Milanese periodical of the time, certainly did not. On 3 January, *L'eco* reported that the audience 'remained somewhat cold, except for the applause given the singers'. On 4 February, *L'eco* turned its attention to *Anna Bolena* again. 'This opera was corrected in some places by Maestro Donizetti. In the first performances (after an interruption) we will hear changes in it which we hope will bring greater glory to the composer.' This last comment is a dig at Donizetti, who was reputed to compose without ever making an erasure or a revision; but even a casual examination of his autograph scores and sketches will show that he frequently reworked his music. On 25 February, *L'eco* returned to the attack: Donizetti's opera 'has been heard coldly for a month or more, and in a theatre I will not call empty, but which was certainly not entirely full.' By its typical coolness, if not its downright hostility, toward Donizetti, and by its enthusiasm for Bellini, *L'eco* demonstrates clearly to which camp it belonged.

A great deal of romantic rubbish has been written about the relationship between Donizetti and Vincenzo Bellini during this Carnival season of 1830–31. The principal source for it is the fervid imagination of Emilia Branca Romani whose unctuous memoir of her librettist-husband has been quoted by many writers who deal with these events. She reports, even to the extent of supplying the dialogue, a conversation that was

---

[1] Quoted in Verzino, *Le opere di Gaetano Donizetti*, p. 95; from *La gazzetta di Milano*, 27 December 1830.

supposed to take place between Romani and Bellini shortly after the première of *Anna Bolena*. Bellini is pictured as being in such despair over Donizetti's success that he begged Romani to abandon their plan for collaborating on an *Ernani*, as Bellini felt their chances for a success depended on coming forward with an opera entirely different in type and mood. And that is how, as Emilia Romani's pretty invention goes, Romani came to provide Bellini with the libretto for *La sonnambula*. Bellini's letters prove the circumstances to have been quite different.

On 3 January 1831, Bellini wrote to his friend Giovanni Battista Perucchini:

> ... I am not writing *Ernani* any longer because the subject would suffer some modification from the censor, and therefore Romani, in order not to compromise himself, has abandoned it. And now he is writing *La sonnambula ossia I due fidanzati svizzeri*, and I have just started the introduction yesterday.[1]

This letter effectively refutes Emilia Romani's tale. Romani voluntarily gave up the idea of *Ernani* because he did not want to get into trouble with the authorities, and his decision had nothing to do with *Anna Bolena*.

Since this passage from Bellini's letter also establishes the date on which he commenced composing *La sonnambula*—2 January 1831, when Bellini was in Milan—it also disposes of another myth. Many writers have mentioned the remarkable coincidence that while Donizetti was Pasta's guest at her villa on Como, busily composing *Anna Bolena*, Bellini was at a nearby villa on the lake, the guest of his mistress, Giuditta Cantù Turina, busily composing *La sonnambula*. This story is simply not true, for Donizetti had substantially completed his opera when he returned to Milan to begin rehearsals on 10 December, when Bellini had not yet started his opera.

There is still one more false impression about Bellini and the première of *Anna Bolena* that needs dispelling. Some biographers of Donizetti, such as Fraccaroli,[2] have described Bellini as sitting in a box at the Carcano the night of 26 December 1830. This detail is ancillary to Emilia Romani's story, because it seems logical to base Bellini's anxiety over the success of *Anna*

---

[1] Bellini, *Epistolario*, Ltr. CI, p. 265.
[2] Arnaldo Fraccaroli, *Donizetti* (Milan, 1945), p. 118.

Bolena on his having been present at the première. Bellini was not at the Carcano that night, but at La Scala, where the Milanese première of his opera, *I Capuletti ed i Montecchi*, put him in a foul humour, as we learn from his letter to Perucchini.

> . . . I did not write to you after the first evening because my poor opera could not have been more badly performed, so that even though it produced some effect and the public wanted me on the stage, I was so furious that I did not wish to go out. . . .[1]

If at the start of that Carnival season in Milan, Donizetti's *Anna Bolena* produced a stronger impression than Bellini's *I Capuletti ed i Montecchi*, the score was evened when *La sonnambula* won a resounding triumph at the Carcano, on 6 March 1831, with Pasta (Amina), Rubini (Elvino), and Luciano Mariani (Rodolfo). It would be difficult to find a parallel of two operas of such outstanding merit as *Anna Bolena* and *La sonnambula* having their premières the same season in the same theatre. From this time on the names of Donizetti and Bellini were linked as the first outstanding composers to emerge in Italy following the retirement of Rossini. At this time Bellini was twenty-nine, four years younger than Donizetti, but his position had been established in 1827 with *Il pirata*, while it was not until *Anna Bolena* that Donizetti was admitted as being on a somewhat equal footing with Bellini.

Anna Bolena was the first of Donizetti's operas to be presented in London and Paris. Henry Chorley describes its reception in London in these terms:

> For a while, however, the new composers were received timidly. *Anna Bolena*, brought hither under the protection of Madame Pasta's royal robes, was permitted rather than admitted, though in this historical English opera might be discerned something of Donizetti's own; and though three of the characters—those of the Queen (Pasta), Percy (Rubini), and Henry the Eighth (Lablache), were played and sung to perfection. Donizetti, however, was not an utter stranger here. A duet of his, introduced into a pasticcio opera by Bochsa, called *I Messicani*, had, a season or two earlier, excited attention. But he was credited with

[1] Bellini, *Epistolario*, Ltr. CI, p. 264.

small individuality by those who then ruled public opinion. So it is curious to recollect how Bellini's second opera, introduced here (also by Madame Pasta), *La Somnambula* [*sic*], was treated on its introduction with contempt; the want of science on the part of its composer dwelt on, and that which is true in expression, and which has kept the opera alive, utterly overlooked. It may have been that possibly truth in expression was not then much cared for by those who frequented our Italian opera. The time of Donizetti and Bellini, though at hand, was still to come.[1]

It was not long before the musical and dramatic performances of Pasta, Rubini, and Lablache in *Anna Bolena* were appreciated for the consummate achievements they were. As long as these singers continued their careers, and even when Giulia Grisi and Mario replaced Pasta and Rubini, Donizetti's opera was a cornerstone of the repertory.

Before Donizetti left Milan, where the success of his opera had won him influential friends, he composed on 24 January a cantata for the marriage of the Austrian Archduke Ferdinand to Anna, the daughter of Victor Emmanuel I. The actual wedding ceremony took place in Turin, 27 February 1831, but Donizetti was not present on that occasion. If Donizetti could have exercised prescience as he composed his cantata, he would have taken particular pains over it, for in 1842 he was to become the Hofkapellmeister to Ferdinand, who had become Emperor in 1835. Also in 1842, Donizetti was to dedicate his opera *Linda di Chamounix* to the Empress Anna. Composing a cantata for this royal wedding may have increased Donizetti's impatience to see his own wife, for he left Milan on 31 January.

He arrived in Rome at an exciting time. A revolution had broken out, and the followers of Mazzini, encouraged by the French, had driven the newly elected Pope, Gregory XVI, from the Papal States. Donizetti describes what he sees in a letter he wrote his father on 15 February.

> I am writing to you so that you will not think I am lying dead among those who have been shot. I am a man whom few things disturb, or rather only one: that is, if my opera

[1] Chorley, *Thirty Years' Musical Recollections*, pp. 17–18.

goes badly. For the rest, I do not care. I live because they let me live. Also I want to live, for when one can no longer live, etc.

The fact is that I am well, that I could leave Saturday for Naples, but there are assassins around. The government here provisionally recalled the troops that garrisoned the roads of the Pontine marshes, and hardly had that happened than the carriage of the same courier who came with me from Bologna to Rome was riddled with shot coming by Terracina. I am waiting until the soldiers go back to their posts and then I am going.

Here Carnival has been suspended for three days; and at sunset everyone is indoors. . . .

Tonight at the house there was a big dinner for the end of Carnival, since one cannot amuse oneself at the theatre.[1]

This is one of the very few letters in which Donizetti mentions the political events of his time. His reticence on this subject seems to spring from something other than mere discretion at committing his feelings to paper. Anyone who was deeply involved in political activity would, it seems reasonable, be unable to refrain from an occasional hint or allusion to matters which concerned him deeply, but one looks in vain for evidence of this sort in Donizetti's published letters. Rather, he only describes events as they bear directly upon his person and his career. In fact, Donizetti's personality as it is revealed in his letters seems completely without the humourlessness and instinctive deviousness that incline a man towards conspiracy.

If politics had little appeal for Donizetti, a politician tried to convert Donizetti into a symbol. Giuseppe Mazzini, in his *Scritti letterari*,[2] hailed *Anna Bolena* as 'approaching epic poetry in music'. He goes on to mention some of the arias and a duet, praising them for their melodic inspiration and the work for its felicitous orchestration. Mazzini's purpose seems to be to make Donizetti's art a rallying point for feelings of national identity. Donizetti's operas seem to have served this non-musical function only incidentally, unlike those of Verdi, who deliberately chose libretti that contained crowd-rousing lines and situations.

When conditions in Rome permitted, Gaetano and Virginia

[1] Z. No. 64, pp. 281–2.
[2] Mazzini, *Scritti letterari*, vol. II, p. 313.

proceeded to Naples without incident. When next Donizetti wrote to his father, on 19 April, he begins:

> I have told you a hundred times that when I do not write, it is a sign that I have nothing to tell you, and not because I have been sick. For if I had been, if I could not write, Virginia would write; therefore, do not trouble yourself about this. We are both well, and I hope you are the same. . . .[1]

The rest of the letter contains not a word about the political troubles, nothing about their journey, nothing about his musical activities. The facts of this year in Donizetti's career must be gathered from the evidence of the works themselves.

Some time during 1831,[2] Donizetti wrote an opera for Rubini, using an old libretto by Romani, entitled *Gianni di Parigi*. As Rubini was no longer singing in Italy, but dividing the year between Paris and London, Donizetti hoped that the tenor, on the strength of their long association, would appear in it on one of his benefit evenings. Rubini was familiar with Romani's libretto from having sung in an earlier opera written to that text, Francesco Morlacchi's *Gianni di Parigi*, when it was given at the San Carlo in 1820. The plot was not original with Romani; he had derived it from a most successful opéra-comique by Boieldieu.

Rubini never availed himself of Donizetti's generous gesture. The choice of subject was not particularly appropriate, for Rubini would scarcely be tempted to sing Donizetti's opera in Paris while Boieldieu's *Jean de Paris* was still being performed there with some frequency. Further, Rubini's unsuccessful adventure with Donizetti's *Gianni di Calais* at the Théâtre-Italien would not make him anxious to appear in another *Gianni* opera by Donizetti.

In any event, Donizetti composed the opera and sent it to Rubini, and as time passed, and there was no sign that the work would be given, he felt hurt. Donizetti's disappointment shows in a letter he wrote to Mayr.

> . . . All the tenors from my home town have shown me the thousandth fraction of friendship that those from elsewhere

---

[1] Z. No. 65, p. 282.
[2] As the autograph score of *Gianni di Parigi* bears no date, it is difficult to establish the time precisely.

have. Rubini, in particular, to whom I gave *Gianni di Parigi* written expressly for him, so that he might give it in Paris or in London for his *serata*, retaining for myself only the rights of the reduced scores . . . Rubini said he had it . . . I have not even had an acknowledgement. . . .[1]

Gianni di Parigi remained unperformed until 1839. At that time Donizetti was living in Paris and presumably retrieved his score from Rubini. The opera was then given at La Scala 10 September 1839 with Antonietta Raineri-Marini (Principessa), Lorenzo Salvi (Gianni), Ignazio Marini (Pedrigo), and Agostino Rovere (Siniscalco). In Milan the opera obtained only a mediocre success. Besides a production at the San Carlo in 1846, *Gianni di Parigi* did not enjoy an extensive career.

Likewise, neither of Donizetti's other new operas written this year made any substantial impression. The first, *Francesca di Foix*, was produced at the San Carlo on 30 May 1831, a gala night as it was the name-day of the new King, Ferdinando II. The singers taking part in the performance were Luigia Bocca-badati (Francesca), Marietta Gioia-Tamburini (the Page), Giovanni Campagnoli (the Count), Tamburini (the King), and Lorenzo Bonfigli (the Duke). This opera was never produced elsewhere. The second of Donizetti's one-act works was *La romanziera e l'uomo nero*. Boccabadati sang Antonina in the *prima* at the Fondo, while Tamburini, Luzio, and Ambrosini were also in the cast. *La romanziera* was later given at the Carolino in Palermo, but its career was brief.

One of the visitors to Naples in 1831 was Mendelssohn. At the house of the hospitable Cottrau, who directed the important Neapolitan music publishing house of B. Girard, he met Donizetti; on another occasion Cottrau and Donizetti took Mendelssohn to call on the celebrated singer Josephine Fodor-Mainvielle. Mendelssohn has left his impressions of Donizetti as he was in 1831. He took a severe view of what seemed to him Donizetti's too great confidence in his facility, his willingness to rely on one or two carefully prepared pieces to carry a whole opera, and his composing too much, which must finally compromise his reputation. The occasion for Mendelssohn's observations was the première of *Francesca di Foix*, an opera that

[1] Z. No. 95, p. 310.

in Cottrau's own opinion, written to his sister directly after the first performance, was 'very feeble'.[1]

When Mendelssohn made these comments, he had little knowledge of Donizetti's music; for example, he had not yet heard *Anna Bolena*. Donizetti's career was undergoing a transition when Mendelssohn saw him. Donizetti realized that his engagement with Barbaja to compose a set number of operas a year for the Neapolitan theatres had become a trap from which he now longed to extricate himself. His two farces of 1831 were the final works extracted from him under the old, intolerable terms. Mendelssohn did not always retain the low opinion of Donizetti he formed in the late spring of 1831. Chorley tells a delightful anecdote of an evening party in London. A group of pedants were excoriating *La fille du régiment* and appealed to Mendelssohn, hoping that he would cap their denunciations with a well-turned phrase, but imagine their embarrassment when Mendelssohn said: ' "I am afraid I like it. I think it very pretty—it is so merry." Then, bursting into one of those fits of hearty gaiety which lit up his beautiful countenance in a manner never to be forgotten, "Do you know," said he, "I should like to have written it myself!" '[2]

Donizetti remained in Naples the rest of 1831. Several of his letters to his new friend in Milan, Count Gaetano Melzi (1786–1851), a well-known bibliophile, survive. In them Donizetti gives a good deal of space to his efforts to fill the Count's commissions for books and harpstrings and the like, and to accounts of activities in the Neapolitan theatres, but certain details shed light on Donizetti's concerns. On 30 July he mentions the threat of the epidemic of Asiatic cholera, which had already appeared in Rome. This outbreak was mild compared with the devastation of the epidemic six years later. Donizetti speaks of the performances continuing in Naples

> . . . while still the cholera lets us amuse ourselves, considering that we have fumigated letters brought by two couriers from Rome, etc. The miserable traveller must stay at Terracina for 20 days before being admitted into the Kingdom, when whoever stays in that place at this time of

[1] Guillaume Louis Cottrau, *Lettres d'un mélomane* (Naples, 1885), p. 13.
[2] Chorley, *Thirty Years' Musical Recollections*, p. 108.

year dies there because of the unhealthy air, without the cholera finding him. . . .[1]

Again to Melzi, he alludes, on 8 September, to his difficulties with Barbaja over the coming production of his *Fausta*.

. . . Tomorrow I hope to break my engagement with Barbaja; since I am not free to choose whom I want in my new opera, so be it then, for I want it very much. . . . Already we are both free by verbal agreement, and tomorrow I conclude the matter. . . .[2]

Although Donizetti went ahead and composed *Fausta*, which was brought out the following January, he had broken the tie that bound him to compose several operas a year for Naples. After *Fausta*, Donizetti can no longer be thought of as primarily a composer for the Neapolitan theatres; although he continued to write for them, he wrote even more for other opera houses. From now on his chief tie to Naples was his position as director in charge of the musical preparation of productions, except when he obtained leave to mount one of his new operas elsewhere; later he was prominently connected with the Naples Conservatory. His active connexion with Naples lasted until 1838 when an intolerable situation drove him away from that city.

During the last months of 1831 Donizetti was occupied with the composition of *Fausta*, but his labour on that opera was complicated by the death of Domenico Gilardoni, his librettist, before the text was completed. The final portion of the poem was written by Donizetti himself. The suggestion has been put forward that Donizetti left Naples in the month of December and made a hurried trip to Milan to attend the *prima* of *Norma*, which occurred on 26 December 1831 at La Scala. The basis for this suggestion is the existence of two letters, purportedly by Donizetti, giving enthusiastic descriptions of the first night of *Norma*. These two letters are very probably not authentic. First of all, it is highly unlikely that Donizetti would dash up to Milan (a journey that was no small undertaking in those days) while *Fausta* was in rehearsal being readied for its première on 12 January 1832. Secondly, the autographs of these letters have never been produced; one was printed in a book about Bellini

[1] Z. No. 67, p. 284.   [2] Z. No. 68, p. 285.

by Florimo, the other supposedly coming from a Genoese publication of 1854. Next, the style of these letters lacks the characteristics of Donizetti's other letters. In one of them he is supposed to have written that 'Verdi also agrees', but it seems unlikely that Donizetti would consult the opinions of a then unknown youth of eighteen! There seem abundant grounds for believing that Donizetti stayed in Naples, preparing *Fausta* for its successful première.

This opera was sung by Giuseppina Ronzi de Begnis (Fausta), Edvige Ricci (Licinia), Eden (Beroe), Giovanni Basadonna (Crispo), Tamburini (Costantino), Giovanni Campagnoli (Massiminiano), and Revalden (Albino). *Fausta* achieved a few vigorous years of life, but by the end of its first decade it had largely vanished from the stage. For the production at La Scala on 26 December 1832, Donizetti provided a new overture to the opera, and the tenor Pedrazzi interpolated into the performance an aria by Pugni. When *Fausta* was sung at the Fenice in Venice the following year, by Pasta and Donzelli, Donizetti added a new opening scene and a duet for the soprano and tenor in the second act. *Fausta* was put on in London in 1841 with Grisi, Mario and Tamburini, but these three could not succeed in making the English take to the opera. The opera deserves a better fate than the total neglect it has received for over a century; the final aria is one of Donizetti's finest pages.

Ten days before the *prima* of *Fausta*, Donizetti's father-in-law, Luigi Vasselli, died of apoplexy. There being no extant letters by Donizetti of this period, it is not clear if Virginia preceded her husband to Rome, or if she travelled with him when he left Naples for the north on 27 January. As was his usual custom, he left his wife with her family, for he was engaged at Milan to write a new opera scheduled for production in March.

This work was *Ugo, conte di Parigi*, written to a libretto by Romani, which had been sent to Naples[1] before Donizetti's departure. The censors maltreated this libretto so drastically that Romani refused to allow his name to appear upon it. The resulting changes show up in the autograph score, evidence which suggests that Donizetti had already started work upon the opera in Naples. In its botched, anonymous form, the opera was given at the Scala on 13 March 1832 with a fine cast: Pasta (Bianca), Giulia Grisi (Adelia), Clorinda Corradi-Pantanelli

[1] So claims Verzino, *Le opere di Gaetano Donizetti*, p. 103.

(Louis V), Felicità Baillou-Hillaret (Emma), Donzelli (Ugo), Vincenzo Negrini (Folco of Anjou). The opera was adjudged a mediocrity and was only performed four times and never again anywhere. The *Gazzetta di Milano* records that 'generally speaking Donizetti's music pleased very much at the first performance and had an almost equal success at the second', but the reviewer goes on to say that the work had been hastily produced, the singers did not seem familiar with their parts, and several of them were visibly fatigued. No wonder, for it had been an exhausting season, opening with *Norma*, which, after its initial cool reception, played for thirty-four performances to scenes of frantic enthusiasm. Whatever its merits or shortcomings, Donizetti's opera stood little chance, coming at the end of such a season.

For the ground he lost in Milan with his compromised *Ugo, conte di Parigi*, Donizetti soon had a chance to redeem himself in the eyes of the Milanese. For the spring season at the Teatro Canobbiana, the impresario, Alessandro Lanari, was in need of a new opera; he appealed to Donizetti and Romani to supply the work. It is not known just when this appeal was made, but in a short time the composer and librettist came up with *L'elisir d'amore*, one of the happiest successes of Donizetti's career. There is a certain type of writer who enjoys compressing the time in which operas are composed; such a writer would urge that *L'elisir* was planned and finished in two weeks. Until concrete evidence decides that matter it should be recognized that the time could have been as long as a month.

For the libretto Romani turned to the text that Scribe had written for Auber's *Le philtre*, which had been put on at the Opéra, 20 June 1831, a little over ten months before Romani and Donizetti set to work on their version. Romani followed the Scribe poem very closely for the most part, the most notable additions being the soprano-tenor duet in the first act and famous tenor romance, *Una furtiva lagrima*, in the second. The point has not been sufficiently made that Romani had at hand someone who was an authority on *Le philtre*. Henri-Bernard Dabadie[1] had sung the role of Jolicœur in the

---

[1] Dabadie (1797–1853) is a singer whose name is practically forgotten today, but he deserves to be remembered as the first Guillaume Tell; for Rossini he also sang Moïse and Raimbaut (*Le comte Ory*) in the first performances of those works.

première of *Le philtre*, and he was soon to be the first to sing the Italian counterpart, Belcore. Romani with his materials ready at hand and with his experience of the theatre, did not need much time to write his libretto.

On 24 April Donizetti mentions the opera in a letter to his father.

> . . . I am here, and at any rate in the coming week I will hold the first rehearsals, even though I have not finished (I am lacking only a little). Romani was obliged to finish quickly, and now he is adjusting certain things about the staging for me. Yesterday evening was the first performance [of the season] and the only tenor is moderate; the woman has a pretty voice but you know what they say. The buffo is a dog. . . .[1]

On 4 May he wrote to Papa again; most of his letter deals with the question of his nephew Andrea's education. Giuseppe had written that he wanted his son to enter college at Genoa, but Gaetano thought it would be better if the boy continued his education at Bergamo. Andrea, now fourteen, was to go to Genoa. Then Gaetano reverted to the subject of *L'elisir*.

> I am well. . . . Tell Dolci that I will go on stage either Saturday or Tuesday. And don't you come, I beg you, you know. I don't like to have you at the first performances.
> I will come to Bergamo instead. *Addio*.[2]

L'elisir d'amore had its *prima* at the Teatro Canobbiana on 12 May 1832. Besides Dabadie as Belcore, the cast included Sabine Heinefetter[3] as Adina, the tenor Giambattista Genero as Nemorino, and Giuseppe Frezzolini, whose daughter Erminia became a celebrated prima donna, was the first Dr Dulcamara. The opera enjoyed a run of thirty-three performances. The enthusiastic review of the performance in the *Gazzetta privilegiata di Milano* (14 May 1832) sums up the new opera by saying: 'To lavish greater praise on the Maestro would be

---

[1] Z. No. 72, pp. 288–9.
[2] Z. No. 73, p. 289.
[3] Sabine (1809–72) was one of the three Heinefetter sisters, all of whom sang opera. Sabine, the eldest, sang at the Italiens and at La Scala, dying insane. Maria (1816–57), who sang in Vienna as Mme Stöckl-Heinefetter, also died insane. Kathinka (1820–58) sang in Paris and Brussels after 1840, but she was spared the fate of her sisters.

unfair to the opera; his work does not need exaggerated compliments.' Two days later Donizetti wrote to Mayr: 'The *Gazzetta* reviews *L'elisir d'amore* and says too many good things; too many, believe me . . . too many!' Donizetti's reaction may be read both as an example of his humility and of his pleasure at receiving fair treatment at the hands of the Milanese critics who had dealt with him harshly for the better part of ten years. *L'elisir*, the fortieth score completed by Donizetti, is the earliest of those which are performed with any frequency today.

That Donizetti did not go to Bergamo after the first performances of *L'elisir*, we learn from his letter to Mayr on 16 May.

> . . . I leave this evening; signor Andrea will be displeased, but what can one do? Greet him for me and tell him that I have written to Genoa about the boy and that he will have the answer himself. . . .[1]

By the 21 May, Donizetti was in Rome, for on that day he signed a contract with the impresario Alessandro Lanari for an opera to be produced at the Pergola in Florence. For this Donizetti was to set a new libretto by Romani, but because the librettist was so slow in writing the book and turning it over to the composer, the first performance had to be postponed until the very end of the Lenten season of 1833. On 14 June, Donizetti signed another contract, this one with Giovanni Paterni, whereby he agreed to compose an opera to Ferretti's libretto, *Il furioso all'isola di S. Domingo*, the work to be performed on 26 December 1832. For his opera Donizetti was to receive 570 scudi which would be paid to him in three instalments: the first at his arrival *alla piazza*, the second when he turned over the first act of his score to the impresario, and the balance after the third performance.

After signing this contract Donizetti returned to Naples, taking Virginia with him. Here, his first occupation was to prepare for the Neapolitan première of *Anna Bolena*, which occurred at the San Carlo on 6 July. The opera was sung with Ronzi de Begnis (Anna), Adelaide Toldi (Seymour), Diomilla Santolini (Smeton), the Russian tenor Nicolai Ivanoff (for many years Rubini's understudy at the Italiens, as Percy) and Lablache. Donizetti wrote to Count Melzi on 12 July that the

[1] Z. No. 74, p. 290.

opera had 'a happy success, and (as is rare on gala evenings) the court applauded four times and called out the cast and the poor maestro.'

By 2 August, Donizetti had received the first act of Ferretti's libretto for *Il furioso*, for on that day he writes:

> Bravo, bravo Ferretti! The first act pleases me very much, and therefore the second will be beautiful! There are a few very little things that I will tell you in person (perhaps they will be nonsense), and so we are off at a gallop with the poem! . . .
>
> Now, day after tomorrow, *Otello Malibran* . . . I cannot yet make a comparison. . . . I wait! Now Ronzi will do *Fausta* and soon, so la Malibran should be dumbfounded![1]

A week later he wrote to Ferretti again. He had started setting parts of the libretto, and there were changes he wanted Ferretti to make. To take some of the sting out of his suggestions he cast his letter in the form of a bantering dialogue.

> Here I am . . . it annoys you perhaps? have you something to do? ! — No? — Now? Yes? ! — Hear me then; and where I make nonsense, set me straight and you will be thanked. Put quotes[2] . . . (alas) — Hear me! Don't tremble!
>
> Duetto Bar[tolomeo] Marc[ella]—Marcella '*Va da tutti abbandonata*' (leap) '*Voi dovete ritrovarlo*' etc. (you can print them if you like). That tempest in the stretta annoys me, because, the thundering interferes with the *hearing*. If I have to set the words without thunder, then yes, but I will set perhaps only two triplets! (Don't sweat dear friend.) The cavatina of Eleonora beginning: '*Ah! lasciatemi, tiranni*' up to '*poi gli squarciavo il cor*'. Then I skip this: '*Fuggi L'amai*', etc. I leave however the chorus '*Chi può frenar*' and I attack the cabaletta that you will change the metre of '*ma il ciel non ode i miei lamenti, ma il fato gode dei miei tormenti, degli astri provo la crudeltà. Qual cor sensibile a tante pene, pietose lagrime negar potrà.*' (You understand the reason.) Yes, yes, I understand, go on. Don't sigh, Ferretti, for pity's sake (in an heroic tone).

[1] Z. No. 78, p. 292.

Here Donizetti is alluding to the common practice in those days of setting quotes round those lines of a printed libretto that were not set to music.

Duetto Card[enio] and Kaid[amà] after Kaid. says *'Chi la man gli consegnò'*, I go . . . *'La conosci?'* etc. etc. that business then of Kaid. falling down and staying there, does not please me, and I would like it changed, so that I can keep a larghetto right up to the stretta, and I use that *'era il sorriso'* etc. and not the last; I leave it be however from *'Deciditi'* up to *'Il tuo cor qui fermerà'* and, changing colour, he replies: *'Era il sorriso'*; at which point you see the buffo cannot be on the ground, it must be rather that he holds him by the hand.

Cavatina for the brother. Chorus *'Ecco alfin'*, yes. — *'Se verace,'* up to *'le sue lagrime'*. No! The Cavatina, yes; I omit however *'Nel lasciar'* etc. up to *'Ah! dammi ciel pietoso.'* Now I breathe. The finale, very good, only I should like 4 verses instead of 2, where it says: Fernando. *'Voglio al mio petto stringerlo'* etc. and when Eleonora says *'(Se) a piedi suoi (morrò)'* and thus 4 for everyone; and resuming then Bart [olomeo] *'Fra sprechi'* etc. I take up the allegro. If not, the finale all stays in one tempo. On the other hand if Cardenio hearing the 4 verses of Bart[olomeo] that will soften his heart, if he would want to say to him *'non piangere, lasciate a me le lagrime,'* he could say it then. The stretta is made, and if it does not please . . . it will be a sign . . . that it will cause bad humour! (*Ca* . . . says Ferretti, what a castration.) One sees that Donizetti comes from the place where they make eunuchs. Farewell, excuse your

Donizetti

(Prepare and send.)
La Malibran is la Malibran, but la Ronzi is la Ronzi; *Fausta* this coming week with Lablache.[1]

This is one of the most interesting of Donizetti's surviving letters because it shows his detailed concern with the construction of a libretto, although here he is suggesting omissions rather than textual changes. The cuts that Donizetti desired made are in keeping with his belief that brevity and clarity are traits essential to an effective opera. Donizetti's sense of dramatic values was sharpened by his practical experience as musical director in the theatres of Naples. That this letter and the others Donizetti wrote to Ferretti about the libretto of *Il furioso* form

---

[1] Z. No. 79, pp. 293-4.

an isolated instance of such an analysis does not mean that
Donizetti was not deeply concerned in the details of the construction of the texts he set; rather his practice was to work
with his librettist at hand and carry on his discussions verbally.
The following note from Cammarano illustrates this point.

> I shall wait for you in the Two Sicilies café until two
> o'clock. . . . The finale strikes me as not too bad. We will
> read it together: four eyes are better than two, or rather
> eight are—counting my glasses and your two eyes which
> are equal to four.[1]

Cammarano's remark about Donizetti's eyes being equal to
four is persuasive testimony of the regard this competent
librettist had for the composer's acumen.

On 18 August Donizetti wrote to Ferretti again about the
text of *Il furioso*. 'In the second act, let your eternal rule be
brevity—for pity's sake—brevity.' Early in September he sends
another letter. After worrying about various minutiae in the
duet for Cardenio and Kaidamà, he brings forth this precept:
'The good consists in writing little and beautifully, and not in
singing too much and being boring.' By the time Donizetti left
for Rome on 10 November, he had completed the music for the
first act of *Il furioso* and begun the second.

But before he left Naples he had composed and brought out
another opera. Donizetti had hoped to have a libretto by
Romani for this opera, but the poet wanted too much money.

> . . . *Romani mi ha fottuto*, and now he denies he will be
> satisfied with 500 francs, which is what (I swear to you
> before God) he asked me for: *ahead with old texts, for I must
> go on in October*. . . .[2]

By 18 September Donizetti had decided to use a text by the
Palermitan librettist, Pietro Salatino, entitled *Sancia di Castiglia*,
and had already begun to compose the music.

> . . . I am roaring and writing my Newborn, which consists
> of seven numbers in all. *Sancia di Castiglia*—poisoned
> children—death of the mamma. . . .[3]

---

[1] Spike Hughes, *Great Opera Houses*, p. 204. The original of this note, relating
to the time of *Roberto Devereux*, is in the Lucchesi-Palli Library in Naples.
[2] Z. No. 80, p. 295. Ltr. of 18 August 1832 to Ferretti.
[3] Z. No. 84, p. 298, to Ferretti.

This opera of attempted filicide and successful suicide appeared at the San Carlo on 4 November with Ronzi de Begnis (Sancia), Diomilla Santolini (Garzia), Edvige Ricci (Elvira), Giovanni Basadonna (Rodrigo) and Lablache (Ircano). Donizetti made the *beau geste* of dedicating this opera to Mayr. The opera was well received; two days after the *prima* Donizetti described to Ferretti how the singers and composer were called out and cheered. Unfortunately, the initial enthusiasm did not last, and *Sancia* soon disappeared from the stage.

The chief excitement of the San Carlo season had occurred earlier, in August and September, when the celebrated Malibran sang her first season in Naples. Malibran appeared in three of Rossini's operas, *Otello*, *Cenerentola*, and *La gazza ladra*, with great success, especially in the last opera. During the same period Ronzi de Begnis was appearing in *Anna Bolena* and *Fausta*, and she was shortly to create *Sancia*. Donizetti's interest in this rivalry of the two prima donnas was, not surprisingly, weighted on the side of the one appearing in his works; further, his friendship with Ronzi dated back to Bergamo days.[1] Donizetti made a joke of the rivalry of Malibran and Ronzi in a letter to Ferretti.

> . . . La Ronzi is rehearsing *Fausta*, and that should even the balance, that is put her higher than Madame, who with *Otello* and *Cenerentola* has made one high and one low. Thus, Ronzi is making two highs, and the balance weighs in her favour (because actually she has a bigger ass—that adds weight—besides more flesh elsewhere).[2]

[1] Giuseppina Ronzi de Begnis (1800–53) made her début in 1817 and married the successful buffo, Giuseppe de Begnis. At first she was a successful prima donna buffa, whom Stendhal characterized as 'brilliant and attractive'; she sang at King's Theatre in London during the 1820's. Later she separated from her husband and returned to Italy to launch what amounted to a second career as a singer of dramatic and tragic parts. An interesting description of her as she appeared in 1832 has been left by Cottrau (*Lettres d'un mélomane*, p. 16).

'I don't know if I have spoken to you of Mme de Begnis. I am scarcely one of her partisans, and I form thereby an exception not only to our coterie [of which Donizetti was a member], but of almost all the public, for her voice displeases me completely and her expression always seems to me a little outrageous. I should say too nuanced—do you understand me?— on every word and almost every note. But I must admit she has an admirable method of singing, much taste, and above all she is a superb figure of a woman.'　　　　　[2] Z. No. 80, p. 295.

Besides the excitement of the rivalry of the prima donnas, Donizetti also kept his Milanese friends, Count Melzi and his wife, supplied with the news of the latest scandal. Pacini, who had enjoyed the experienced favours of Pauline Bonaparte at the time of Donizetti's *Zoraide*, had caught the eye of a Russian Countess, Giulia Samayloff. She had deserted her headquarters in Milan, where she had equipped her palazzo with a private theatre, where one of the most frequent performers on her private stage had been the tenor Giovanni David. All this she had abandoned to follow to Naples both Pacini and David, who had an engagement there. The alignment of this trio was an object of fascinated scrutiny to all Naples. That Pacini had won at least a temporary victory may be inferred from the noisy demonstration engineered by the Countess at the *prima* of Bellini's *Norma* (La Scala, December 1831).

Gaetano and Virginia left Naples on 10 November and spent the night of the 11th at Terracina, arriving in Rome the following day. They stayed at the Vasselli's apartment on the via delle Muratte, where a commemorative plaque has been affixed to that building, announcing that Donizetti composed *Il furioso* and *Tasso* there, although in actual fact he brought more than half of the score of *Il furioso* already completed in his luggage. On the 13th, Ferretti, sick in bed with asthma, sent Gaetano a note, informing him that he was assembling his libretto to submit to the censor. Donizetti, laid up with a pain in his side, answered in doggerel that he still waited for the words of the final rondo. On 1 December, the libretto was approved for performance; on the 6th, as Donizetti wrote to Ricordi, the rehearsals had not yet started. He continues:

> . . . with what I have done I tell you candidly I am not displeased . . . if it doesn't please Rome (since here there is neither the best company nor the best orchestra) that will not depress me at all, for I will do as I did with *Olivo e Pasquale* which they whistled at here, and I took it to Naples, etc. etc. etc. . . .[1]

The rehearsals of *Il furioso* may not have started until the middle of December, since the first performance of the opera

[1] Z. No. 88, p. 303.

was not given until after the new year. At about the same time Donizetti received a letter from his father containing an anonymous clipping, one of several such that had appeared in Bergamo, containing digs at Donizetti. On reading this latest example, Donizetti's pride was so stung that he answered his father in a strong letter which reveals a good deal about Donizetti's view of himself at this time.

I do not know that I hurt one of my fellow townsmen if I write little or if I write much, or if I am paid much or little, so that all the way to Rome . . . come . . . anonymous letters, giving me advice that is more insolent than anything else. How does he know if I am paid a little or a lot? What does it matter to him if I write a dozen scores a year? For this should I be called the *lackey* of the Maestros, the man who writes *incorrectly*, the man full of *reminiscences*, the man without *judgement* and *philosophy*?

Will this person then recognize true judgement? I fear not. If he recognized it, he would see that I certainly do not deserve this imputation. I don't know anyone who does not employ reminiscences; and if he would have the goodness to reveal himself, I would take him for a little stroll through the scores of *that one* whom he does not name, and I would make him put his hand on whichever one he chooses, not to show him reminiscences, but whole pieces taken from I know where. He advises me to write for better theatres, while I travel only from the S. Carlo of Naples to La Scala of Milan, and next year to the Fenice of Venice. Perhaps he believes the Seriate[1] a better theatre and that I should engage myself to write there? The Valle in Rome is certainly not one of the secondary houses because Rossini has written all his most beautiful operas there. What does he want of me then? That I should use better texts? Let him give them to me. Let him find me a poet for the theatre less a rascal than Romani at keeping his word and I will offer 100 scudi to the one who makes me a good text. The writer makes a fine speech on that note. I do not live gratis in the house of a beautiful woman who can make me a present of the poet, and do favours for

[1] The Seriate was a third-rate, provincial *teatraccio* in the country near Bergamo.

others to satisfy her protégé, as is happening now. I have protested to Florence for the book I should have had in October, for up to this very day I have not had one line of it.

For the rest, then, it is not that I scorn anybody's advice, but when it is someone like this man, whom with good reason I call more insolent than anything else, I dislike the writer and advise him on one point: he who is concerned for my reputation does not come anonymously to give his opinions, but one who says, 'I am the one, etc., I am your friend, etc.'; then I will thank him as thoroughly as now I despise and scorn that partisan. . . .[1]

Writing this letter when he was angry, Donizetti was driven by his emotion to make several exaggerations, but his general tone of indignation is justified. The composer that the anonymous writer did not name is, of course, Bellini, whose liaison with Giuditta Turina had undoubtedly helped his career in Milan. It was no comfort to Donizetti that in Bergamo Bellini had scored a great success that past summer with *Norma*, sung by Pasta and Donzelli, and Bellini's scrupulous attention to the gentle art of paying court to influential people in no way diminished his success. Donizetti's irritation with Romani's easy promises and tardy accomplishments dated back to the time of *Chiara e Serafina* but it had become more intense recently. Although their collaborations had brought them both honour and would continue for more than a year, theirs was never to be a truly warm friendship. Donizetti had learned from painful experience to distrust Romani's assurances, while the Torinese librettist, who had more than a suspicion of pomposity in his nature, never found the uninhibited Donizetti completely congenial. Of the three, Bellini, Romani, and Donizetti, the last was the most forthright and the least conceited.

At the Valle, 2 January 1833, Donizetti's self-respect, jarred by the anonymous attacks from Bergamo, found justification in the valid success awarded *Il furioso all'isola di S. Domingo*. There was long applause for the singers: Elisa Orlandi (Eleonora), Marianna Franceschini (Marcella), Giorgio Ronconi (Cardenio), Lorenzo Salvi (Fernando), Ferdinando Lauretti (Kaidamà), and Filippo Valentini (Bartolomeo), especially for

[1] Z. No. 89, pp. 303–4.

135

Ronconi, not yet twenty-three, who, with his imposingly sung and affectingly acted Cardenio, proved himself to be the most promising baritone to appear in Italy since the emergence of Tamburini.[1] On the following day Donizetti wrote to Ricordi:

> . . . Yesterday the opera went on . . . Ronconi in *furioso* bears himself very well, and Orlandi too, and the buffo too, and the tenor too, and the second woman also. And more than everything the public bears itself well and shouts and calls us out.[2]

The newspaper reviews of the first production were uniformly enthusiastic. In October of the same year, Donizetti personally adapted and staged *Il furioso* at La Scala where, with Eugenia Tadolini, Winter, and Orazio Cartagenova (Cardenio), it had a popular success, running for thirty-six performances. Although some of the Milanese papers reported the work's success frankly, others, such as *L'eco* and *Il barbiere di Siviglia*, continued to carp and find fault with Donizetti. *Il furioso* contains some of the composer's most original dramatic characterizations, and as long as Ronconi and baritones of his ilk kept the work in their repertoire, the opera held the stage.

The same night that *Il furioso* earned its triumph, *Anna Bolena*, in a pirated version, made a solemn fiasco at the Apollo. Several days later Donizetti had his revenge for this infringement of his rights and this debasement of his score when he conducted the first performance of a concert version of *Anna Bolena*, put on by the Filarmonici romani. This performance met with such an enthusiastic response that it was repeated on three subsequent evenings. Then, buoyed up by his Roman successes, Donizetti took leave of his wife and set out for Florence on 10 January. On the 13th he announces his arrival to his father.

> Here I am at Florence, *without the libretto*, and I am supposed to go on the second Sunday in Lent. As usual

---

[1] Giorgio Ronconi (1810–90) was the son of a famous singing teacher; he made his début at Pavia in *La straniera* (1831). Early recognized as an outstanding singer, he pursued a career that took him to France, England, the United States, and Spain; in this last country he was also an impresario and singing teacher, dying in Madrid. His distinguished career lasted into the 1870's, but although his voice declined early, he was one of the most striking singing actors of his time. In his *Thirty Years' Musical Recollections*, Chorley has left a vivid picture of him. [2] Z. No. 90, p. 305.

Romani has failed me, but Donizetti has not failed to protest, at the specified time, and here I am, being paid without working.

As I understand that the fault is not the poor impresario's, I offered to make an adjustment rather than to file suit. It would be this: put on *Fausta*, which is very well adapted to the company, write several new pieces, and I can get more money.

The impresario, however, is not here but at Venice, and his agent agrees fully with me, and we wait his [Lanari's] yes or his no.

At Naples it is freezing, at Rome it is freezing, here one freezes. There never was such a season as this! . . .

I am waiting for another anonymous letter from the partisan on *Furioso* so I can correct those places his musical knowledge will point out. . . .[1]

While Donizetti waited in freezing Florence for Romani to provide the text and for word to come from Lanari, he passed his idle hours with a contralto named Giuseppina Merola. This affair is alluded to in a letter that Lanari wrote Romani on 1 August 1833. The impresario was looking forward to the opera he hoped Romani and Donizetti would write for the following year, and mentioned the singers available for it. 'If you should need a *musichetto*, I could give you La Merola, who has an excellent figure, is handsome and competent, and with her Donizetti gave me horns;[2] using her, you would do Donizetti a service.'[3] La Merola is a shadowy figure. She had sung the role of Smeton in *Anna Bolena* in 1831 when that opera was first given in Venice. She was then a member of Lanari's company, and still was when the impresario brought his company into the Apollo in Rome for the Carnival season of 1833–34; there she sang Smeton again and Cavino in *I Normanni a Parigi*. At the end of the same year she was still with the company, as we learn from a letter of Bellini's to Florimo, in which he mentioned Merola as a possibility for the role of Queen Enrichetta

[1] Z. No. 92, pp. 306–7.
[2] Lanari does not mean this literally, as he was married to someone else, but rather he seems to be stretching the term to apply to the province of an impresario's traditional prerogatives.
[3] Iarro (Giulio Piccini), *Memorie d'un impresario fiorentino* (Florence, 1892), p. 133.

in the proposed Neapolitan performances of *I Puritani* with
Malibran. Donizetti's published letters refer to her but once.
When he wrote to Lanari on 22 August 1833, on the occasion
of that impresario's having taken his company to Foligno, a city
lately damaged by earthquake, this is all he said:

> . . . Give my greetings to the couple Duprez, to Cosselli, to
> Porto, to Merola, and to everyone you have taken with
> you to the city of the earthquake, which I pray heaven
> holds off during the course of your performances. Tonight
> I begin the rehearsals of *Tasso*. . . .[1]

There is no reason to believe that this encounter between
Donizetti and Giuseppina Merola was anything more than a
passing affair. It is worth mentioning only because it is the one
example of such a relationship with a singer that is known to
have left behind even this much concrete evidence. In the long
view there is some justification for regarding this instance as
representative.

Donizetti's period of enforced idleness in Florence came to an
abrupt halt when he learned that Lanari had set his heart on
producing a new opera by Donizetti in his Lenten season.
Finally, Romani, who had been bitterly involved with Bellini
over the libretto to *Beatrice di Tenda*,[2] was able to concentrate
on the text for *Parisina*, which Donizetti apparently did not
receive until about the middle of February. The opera was
composed with great speed, rehearsed, and brought forward
on 17 March 1833, at the Pergola with Ungher (Parisina),
Marietta Sacchi (Ismelda), Gilbert Duprez (Ugo), Domenico
Cosselli (Azzo), and Carlo Ottolini Porto (Ernesto). The opera
was accorded a warm greeting by the audience, especially the
great scene in the second act between Parisina and her husband,
Azzo, which according to the critic of the *Commercio* 'could not
help but move the hardest heart'. *Parisina*, as long as Lanari
retained the rights to the score, formed one of his frequent
offerings. By 1850 the opera had been heard as far afield as
Rio de Janeiro and New York, and it was given in Siena as
recently as 1964.

As soon as *Parisina* was safely launched, Donizetti returned to

[1] Z. No. 115, p. 333.
[2] The arguments became so severe that there was a cessation of friendly
relations between Bellini and Romani until late in 1834.

Rome. Soon he and Ferretti were deeply engaged in writing a new opera for the Valle, which they hoped would duplicate the success of *Il furioso*. For a long time Donizetti had entertained the notion of writing an opera about Torquato Tasso, as the famous poet had many associations with Bergamo. Part of Donizetti's original intention had been to write the opera for Rubini, but since that tenor had departed for Paris and London, and since he had displayed no interest in *Gianni di Parigi*, he turned his mind to Ronconi, who had won a personal triumph as Cardenio in *Il furioso*. Donizetti seems to have played a prominent part in shaping the new work, and through most of April and May he and the poet were occupied with it. Oddly enough Donizetti did not sign the contract for *Tasso* until 6 June; and although Paterni offered him 600 scudi for the work, Donizetti held out for, and apparently got, 650. The libretto was approved by the censors on 10 July, and the following day he wrote to Lanari that his score was finished. Cicconetti[1] tells a story of Donizetti one evening at the Vassellis suddenly excusing himself from his assembled friends and re-appearing half an hour later with the finale of the first act of *Tasso* finished. This feat of rapid composition assumes a different perspective when we learn that this finale employs the same music as the final quartet from *Il paria*. Although Donizetti had finished composing and assembling his score before the middle of July, *Tasso* did not go into rehearsal until 22 August.

The summer of 1833 was in some ways a most frustrating time for Donizetti. He was bothered by a flurry of pirated editions of his operas. His letters to Ricordi of this time are full of elaborate precautions that his music be delivered safely. In spite of their care, a copy of *Il furioso* fell into the wrong hands; further, a fraudulent *L'elisir* was staged in Naples. His greatest difficulties, however, were with Lanari. There was much evasive bandying of words on the impresario's part before Donizetti could pin him down to a mutually agreeable time for production of the new opera he had contracted to compose for him. Donizetti believed he deserved some consideration from Lanari because he had behaved fairly over the matter of *Parisina*, for he would have been justified in bringing suit. To strain their relationship further, Lanari, who owned the rights to *Parisina* had put such an exorbitant price on the score that

[1] Cicconetti, *Vita di Gaetano Donizetti* (Rome, 1864), p. 80.

Robert and Severini, the co-directors of the Italiens, refused to consider it. Since Donizetti was anxious to go to Paris and eager to have his music performed there, he felt that Lanari had done him a great disservice. By the end of August they seem to have settled their differences, but not before Donizetti had written to the impresario on 6 August, mincing no words:

> . . . You speak to me of *friendship* and *esteem*, etc., but that is an old song now. If you had friendship for me, I had it for you; if you feel esteem for me, I esteem you, but what you have not yet given me, and what I have given you, is the proof of disinterest. . . .
>
> Then if you have lost 11,000 lire in Florence, that is something to take up with [Romani] and not with Donizetti, who finished the opera for you in a very few days, who staged it, who even corrected the proof of the libretti.
>
> At Venice you have lost more and you have not reproached anyone. I have no regrets. I have done my duty and more than my duty. I advise you then that the season *to be agreed upon* should please us both. In Carnival I don't know if I can serve you. I advise you again, and for the last time, that if you want me in the coming Carnival or in the coming Lent, advise me of it by the next courier; if not, I propose to you the cancellation of the engagement, with the same terms for the receipt of money we had for *Parisina*.
>
> The courts do not frighten me, and I will always be in every way
>
> your,
Gaetano Donizetti.[1]

During the latter stages of the resolution of his disagreement with Lanari, which was finally settled by Lanari accepting the new opera for the spring season, Donizetti was engaged in rehearsing *Tasso*. On 9 September 1833, that opera had a successful *prima* at the Valle, being performed by Adelina Spech (Eleonora d'Este), Angelina Carocci (Eleonora, Duchess Scandiano), Ronconi (Tasso), Antonio Poggi (Roberto Geraldini), Antonio Rinaldi (Alfonso d'Este), and Ferdinando Lauretti (Don Gherardo). Although the opera was substantially applauded, especially the first finale and Tasso's scene in

[1] Z. No. 112, pp. 328-9.

Act 3, the response to the opera did not quite achieve the intensity of the acclaim meted *Il furioso*. Ronconi won a personal success as Tasso and sang the role for many years, but when he retired, the opera virtually disappeared from the stage.

On 13 September 1833, Donizetti wrote a brief note to the tenor Gilbert Duprez, reporting that *Torquato Tasso* had been 'most happily' received, and continues with a ribald reference to Alexandrine Duprez, the tenor's wife who also sang for Lanari: 'be careful my friend not to make my prima donna pregnant so that instead of a maiden on the stage we would have a deflowered girl'.[1]

From this missive it is clear that Donizetti was looking forward to writing for Lanari the following spring.[2] Not long after this letter was written Donizetti left Rome alone for Milan, where he made the necessary *puntature*, added some new music, and rehearsed *Il furioso* at La Scala. As early as 19 June he had been approached by Teodoro Gottardi, who was the agent of Duke Carlo Visconti and oversaw the affairs of La Scala, which the Duke was then managing. The middle man in these negotiations was Ricordi, who had bought the score of *Il furioso* from Paterni. On the 30 September Donizetti signed an agreement in Milan to do the desired work on *Il furioso* for what amounted to 720 Austrian lire.

During the next few days there was a revolution in the managerial offices of La Scala.[3] Gottardi, who had succeeded in thoroughly botching the plans for the coming season and in antagonizing many people, was sacked by Visconti, who assumed the management of the theatre himself. One of the first tasks facing him was to straighten out the tangle so that the Carnival season could open on 26 December. Visconti called Donizetti to his office and offered him a contract to

[1] When I examined this letter it was unpublished, but it has since appeared in *Studi Donizettiani*, *I* (Bergamo, 1962), p. 17.
[2] It is just possible that Duprez failed to heed Donizetti's injunction, for Mme Duprez did not sing in the *prima* of *Rosmunda d'Inghilterra* the following spring of 1834.
[3] The principal source for these events, and the history of the first performance of *Lucrezia Borgia* is Verzino, *Le opere di Gaetano Donizetti*. Verzino made a thorough search of the Archivio Visconti, and he was the first to contradict the erroneous story, propagated by Cicconetti, Royer, Alborghetti and Galli, that Donizetti took over Mercadante's contract because the latter was stricken with ophthalmia.

write a new opera for the opening night, his libretto to be *Lucrezia Borgia*, written by Romani. Before Donizetti left the Duke he had agreed to write that opera as well as another one for the following Carnival. Only when he had signed the agreement did he learn of the existing confusion. While Gottardi had still been in charge, he had completed an engagement with Mercadante to compose the opening opera for the Carnival season. Mercadante had his heart set on writing an opera about Sappho, but Henriette Méric-Lalande, the prima donna of the season, strenuously objected to this proposal, because she had never played such a role and felt it would be ill-suited to her. Therefore, Romani had begun a second libretto based on Hugo's *Lucrèce Borgia* which had scored a definitive success in Paris on 2 February 1833. Although Romani was later to seek to obscure the time at which he started this libretto, it is clear that some, if not all of it, existed by the time Donizetti entered the picture.

Henriette Méric-Lalande (1798–1867) was to play an important part in the creation of *Lucrezia Borgia*. She had been singing in Italy for about ten years, but she had been born in France and had studied in Paris with Garcia and Talma. In her best days she possessed phenomenal vocal agility, as is proven by the score of Donizetti's *Elvida*, which was tailored to her prowess in 1826. Time had not been kind to her, and however voluble her vocal mechanism, the quality of her voice had deteriorated, for when she appeared in London in 1830, Chorley had succinctly characterized her appearance as 'too late'. By 1833 Lalande had arrived at that nerve-racking point in her career when she felt she could take no chances with the unfamiliar and that she must appear at what, in her view, was the best advantage. Lalande had become an arch-conservative about her career, more than reluctant, afraid, to try anything new.

The affairs of the coming season were at an impasse. Mercadante wanted to write an opera on a subject unacceptable to the prima donna. The librettist had two subjects under construction. Two composers had been contracted to write an opera for the same night in the same theatre. It was at this point that Visconti cut the Gordian knot. Since Donizetti would write *Lucrezia Borgia*, a role that Lalande found agreeable, the Duke wrote to Mercadante asking if he would agree to postpone his engagement until the following autumn. Mercadante was then deeply involved in his newly assumed duties as *maestro di cappella* at Novara and could not well get away; thus Visconti's proposition came as a relief, and he agreed to it for the same terms, 4500 lire, he was to have had.[1]

Learning that Donizetti had been engaged, Romani wrote to Visconti for an explanation; he was poised between Lesbos and Renaissance Ferrara and wanted some direction which way to proceed. As soon as it was clear that *Lucrezia Borgia* was what the Duke wanted, Donizetti sent, on 11 October, a complete list of the characters in *Lucrezia Borgia*—there were an even dozen of them, an unusually large number in those days—with the names of the singers who would fill each role; thus, from the start Donizetti planned this score with individual voices and requirements in mind.

Everything seemed to be proceeding smoothly until 28 October, when Romani wrote a letter to Visconti claiming that he was being unfairly treated, for having written a *Saffo* and now 'engaged in writing' *Lucrezia Borgia*, he was only being paid for one text, and therefore the management of La Scala was getting one free. Romani's desire to get as much money as he could for his work had caused Donizetti difficulties before. For all Romani's claims of still being 'engaged in writing' the libretto, it seems probable that Romani had all but finished it and was merely engaging in a mild form of blackmail before he turned it over to Donizetti. Not until 26 November did Romani consign the complete libretto so that it could be approved by the censor, but as the rehearsals for *Lucrezia Borgia* began on 3 December, Donizetti must have had the poem, or substantial parts of it, in his hands for some time.

Acutely sensitive to his position, Romani knew that the subject of *Lucrezia Borgia* was not likely to win the censors' approval easily. In his covering letter of 26 November to Visconti, he had written, almost sulkily, 'I could not treat this subject better, nor go more carefully as far as the censors were concerned,' adding a hope for Visconti's protection. Although the original suggestion for using the subject came from Romani, as he worked with it he grew progressively colder towards it. And with reason, for the censors, provoked by a Milanese

[1] Mercadante's opera, *La gioventù di Enrico V*, was produced as the last opera of the autumn season of 1834 and won a mediocre success, five performances.

family that claimed descent in some degree from Lucrezia, threatened to forbid the performance. Employing all his tact and influence, Visconti finally managed to obtain approval for the work.

Almost immediately new trouble developed when Lalande turned intransigent. She objected strenuously to the stage direction that bade her appear at her first entrance wearing a mask. This dramatically effective business was repugnant to her sense of a prima donna's position, because there was a possibility she might not be recognized at once and welcomed by the applause her status, in her view, warranted. This problem was settled by a compromise: Lalande first entered carrying her mask in her hand. Her second objection was more drastic. By her lights, a proper opera should end with an elaborate vocal show-piece for the prima donna. In vain did Donizetti try to argue that dramatically such an aria would be disastrous, that the spectacle of a grief-stricken mother, indulging herself in a lather of coloratura as she stands over the body of her son, dead through her machinations, would be repellent. Lalande stubbornly insisted on her prerogatives. With time running short and well aware of the damage a disaffected prima donna might wreak, Donizetti yielded against his will and prevailed upon the equally reluctant Romani to provide eight lines of verse for the cabaletta, *Era desso il figlio mio*.

Lucrezia Borgia opened the Carnival season on schedule. Besides the strong-willed Lalande, the cast included Marietta Brambilla (Maffio Orsini), Francesco Pedrazzi (Gennaro), Luciano Mariani (Alfonso), Napoleone Marconi (Liverotto), Giuseppe Visanetti (Apostolo Gazella), Ismaele Guaita (Ascanio Petrucci), Giuseppe Vaschetti (Oloferne Vitellozzo), Domenico Spiaggi (Gubetta), Ranieri Pochini (Rustighello), Francesco Petrazzoli (Astolfo). The opera was applauded, but it by no means produced the effect that made it throughout the nineteenth century one of Donizetti's most popular works. Certainly the failing powers of Lalande were small help on the occasion. The second performance, however, was felt to be markedly superior to the first, and the opera was given thirty-three times in its first 'edition'. In its early years, the opera had a chequered career due to the cavilling of local censors and, consequently, appeared under a great many different titles: *Alfonso, Duca di Ferrara*, at Trieste; *Eustorgia da Romano* at

Florence and Bologna; *Giovanna I di Napoli*, at Ferrara; *Elisa da Fosco*, at Rome; and *Nizza de Granade*, at Lyons. When the opera was first sung in Paris, due to the objections and threatened legal action of Hugo, the score was sung to a newly improvised libretto set in Turkey, and entitled *La rinnegata*. The opera was given a second 'edition' at La Scala (11 January 1840), with Erminia Frezzolini as Lucrezia and Napoleone Moriani as Gennaro, but that production was nearly banned entirely by the censors. Only when Merelli—Donizetti's first librettist, who had recently become manager of La Scala—succeeded in making the point that *Lucrezia Borgia* had been sung and enthusiastically applauded in Vienna the previous May were the pretensions of the censors in the provincial capital of Milan overcome. For this second production at La Scala, Donizetti provided a new finale, scrapping Lalande's incredible cabaletta, and substituting a most affecting death scene for the tenor. In this revised form, *Lucrezia Borgia* won a major triumph.

During the troubled days that preceded the first performance of *Lucrezia Borgia*, Donizetti received what was at once a compliment and a reminder that he had been gone a long time from Naples. On 29 November, Donizetti's thirty-sixth birthday, the genial Leopold, Prince of Salerno, the uncle of the King of the Two Sicilies, appointed him his *maestro di cappella*, and word of his appointment reached Donizetti about a week later. This sign of Bourbon favour appeared to be a happy augury for the future of Donizetti's career in Naples; that it was a deceptive sign was not apparent for several years to come.

On 29 December 1833, Donizetti left Milan and went to Genoa to visit his nephew Andrea, who was enrolled at the Royal College there. If Donizetti wrote reports of his visits to his father, such letters seem not to have survived. The only document that sheds even a little light on this visit is a letter from the fifteen-year-old Andrea to his grandparents, written not long before Christmas, 1833.

Dearest Grandfather and Grandmother,
    I don't know what to think or what might be the matter since I haven't had your news for a long time, and since I

have written to you more than once, as I told you in my last letter. I don't know if this has happened because of your illness or forgetfulness, or whether I have fallen into your bad graces. Excuse me if I speak with such arrogance, but the need of your news makes me do it, seeing that I have been deprived of it for a long time. Nevertheless I hope that it is not because of your carelessness nor because I have fallen into your bad graces, since the fault is not mine.

For now these few lines suffice, but as soon as I receive your news, I will answer. For now, wishing you all a good feast at Christmas and a good New Year, I declare myself
Your most obedient grandson,
Andrea Donizetti.
In my name greet Grandmother, Beppina,[1] the relatives, friends, and my companions. Your news, your news.[2]

This letter still speaks aloud with the homesickness of a young boy away from his family and in a strange school at Christmastime. It would seem, then, that his Uncle Gaetano's visit was to cheer him up. The letter, however, exhibits a trait in young Andrea's character that was to grow stronger with the years: his facility at bluntly imputing blame to another, while being equally convinced of his own innocence. Granted the circumstances in which he found himself in December 1833, his complaints, though tactless, had had some justification. Fourteen years later this trait was more evident and not so easy to justify.

Donizetti was back in Genoa after having staged *Fausta* in Turin, on 19 January, for on that date he wrote a very interesting letter to Visconti. For the rehearsals of *Lucrezia Borgia*, Donizetti had re-arranged the seating of the La Scala orchestra. Apparently there had been some complaints at this change, for Donizetti explains that he seated the first chairs of the string quartet close to the leader merely to bring the arrangement of the La Scala orchestra into conformity with the practice that had been successfully adopted by other theatres. In this letter

[1] Beppina was the name of the daughter of Maria Antonia Donizetti Tironi, who was young Andrea's first cousin and took care of her grandparents.
[2] An unpublished letter in the library of the Conservatory of Naples, No. 63794. There is a transcript in Zavadini's hand in the Museo Donizettiano, Bergamo.

Donizetti also informs Visconti that he is leaving Genoa that very day.

He travelled to Florence, where he was under contract to Lanari, to compose a new opera, *Rosmunda d'Inghilterra*. His libretto was by Romani, but instead of having to wait until the last minute for a new one, he was setting an old text that had already been put to music by Carlo Coccia (Venice, 1829). Donizetti had the libretto in his hand at least by 11 December 1833, for on that date he sent a list[1] of the characters (including one with the remarkable name of Worcesto) and a description of the scenes and their settings, to Virginia in Rome, with instructions for her to hand it over to Lanari. Therefore Donizetti received the book from Romani during the time *Lucrezia Borgia* was in rehearsal. The active collaboration of Donizetti and Romani ended with the turbulent preparation of *Lucrezia*; although they were still to discuss projects in an occasional letter, nothing ever came of them. Except for two librettos which had been set before, those of *Rosmunda d'Inghilterra* and *Adelia* (Rome, 1841), Donizetti was never again to set a text by Romani. After 1834 Romani practically stopped writing opera texts, for in that year he assumed the editorship of the official *Gazzetta* of Turin, a post he held until 1849.

Rosmunda d'Inghilterra is ultimately derived from the story of 'Fair Rosamund', the ill-fated mistress of Henry II. Donizetti's opera was performed 27 February 1834, at the Teatro Pergola in Florence.[2] The role of Rosmunda was sung by Fanny Tacchinardi-Persiani, whose greatest claim to fame dates from the following year when she sang in the première of *Lucia*. Persiani (1812–67) was the daughter and pupil of Nicola Tacchinardi, one of the greatest vocal technicians of his time. In 1830 she had married the composer, Giuseppe Persiani, seven years her senior, and had made her stage début two years later, at the age of twenty. Writing to Lanari about her in the previous October, Donizetti had described her as 'more than a little cold (*freddina, freddina*), but precise and absolutely on pitch'.[3] Associated with her in the première of *Rosmunda* were

[1] This unpublished memorandum-letter now appears in *Studi Donizettiani I*, p.17.
[2] The establishment of the exact date of the *prima* of *Rosmunda* was finally made possible by the appearance of *Studi Donizettiani I*, which contains a letter Donizetti wrote to Rossini on 22 February 1834 from Florence. (See *loc. cit.*, pp. 21–2.)   [3] Z. No. 122, p. 338.

Anna Del Serre (Eleonora), the obliging Giuseppina Merola (Arturo), Gilbert Duprez (Enrico), and Carlo Ottolini Porto (Clifford). The opera seems to have made little impression, for it held the stage but a short time, and was never performed outside Italy. Three years later, at the urging of Cottrau's publishing firm who had bought the rights to the score, Donizetti made a *rifacimento* of the work, which was brought out at Naples under the title of *Eleonora di Gujenna* (*Eleanor of Aquitaine*). The most notable thing about the score of *Rosmunda* is the heroine's scena which Persiani introduced into *Lucia*, at least by May 1837, to replace *Regnava nel silenzio*; Anna Thillon also sang it in the 1839 French production of *Lucia*; Jenny Lind used it for the same purpose in London. Except for this scena,[1] *Rosmunda* has long disappeared.

From Florence Gaetano returned to Rome, collected Virginia, and continued on to Naples. Seventeen months had passed since he had left that city. On 12 April he signed a contract with the management of the San Carlo for a new opera to be produced in August; this opera, however, did not see the stage until October and then only after drastic changes. The contract was not the only important news of his career in April 1834, for his letter to Mayr of the 24th is brimming with news.

> Fifty thousand greetings!
> First of all, how are you? Well, I hope. Your wife? Your daughter? Yes!
> Yes! All well and God be praised!
> First a trouble (for you).

Then Donizetti tells Mayr that the maestro of the Royal Chapel in Naples wants a Mass composed by him, and continues:

> Here we are!
> His Majesty absolutely bestows on me the honour, the favour, of being a Maestro in the Royal College of Music, and as soon as I put before him that I had already contracted various engagements, he replied, 'It is only right that I should give you leaves of absence'—is it come to this?

[1] Joan Sutherland recorded it as an annex to her complete recording of *Lucia* for Decca Records, a service to history that deserves a vote of thanks from all who care about Donizetti.

His Highness, the Prince of Salerno, the King's uncle, has made me his *Maestro di camera* to teach his daughter singing, and shortly I will enter upon these two posts.

The news isn't finished yet!

Rossini had written the most flattering letter to come and compose in Paris and I have accepted. If at Milan my opera is the first in the Carnival season, I will fly at once to Paris. Don't say a word about this: that is, don't mention the time of my going to Paris because the management at Milan might schedule me for the second work in Carnival; and as my time there is not fixed yet, I try to smuggle myself in without an agreement about it, the prima donna having already asked that my opera be the first.

Dear Maestro, I must have written in big letters—since I've already filled up the page to where I started.

I tell you the latest!

My brother hopes to come from Constantinople after the marriage of one of the Sultan's daughters. Have the goodness to tell Signor Andrea and add that he [Giuseppe] and she [Virginia] and I are all well.

I write here in August!

Many greetings to Dolci, Pontiroli.

To all who remember.[1]

Donizetti's elation comes from this constellation of fortunate occurrences, all of them materially rewarding, all of them holding promise for the future of his career. Thus Donizetti announces that he has been appointed a professor of counterpoint and composition at the Naples Conservatory. By 18 July he had assumed his duties, for on that day he writes to his father that he has just discovered he must serve the first six months without pay. The news of Donizetti's appointment to this post aroused a different reaction in another quarter. On 24 July, Bellini writes to Florimo from France:

> . . . Then Donizetti has been elected Maestro? I don't find it bad, however Mercadante was very much more worthy of it; and I hope they will not give him Zingarelli's post, but give it to one who will have a name worthy of such a position.

[1] Z. No. 134, pp. 347–8.

But how will Donizetti now go here and there composing? Isn't he obliged to remain rooted in Naples? I believe
that with such a post he will have to give up touring
around, otherwise how can the boys follow a course of
study? Tell me clearly how matters stand on this: if
Donizetti will not be able to take himself to Milan after
the last opera he writes in December, I will be able to
use pressure on that Duke Visconti, who has never been
my friend. While Milan itself as much as Naples asks for
my new operas and shouts against the Duke, he coldly
asks me if I want to write and his offers do not go beyond
what they were; but if Donizetti will not be able to go
there any more, and he is the only Maestro the jealous
ones and the former partisans of Pacini have wanted to
support, then the dear Duke must turn to me and vomit
thousands of lire. . . .[1]

The difference in tone between these two letters, Donizetti's
announcing his appointment and Bellini's reacting to it,
crystallizes the fundamental difference in point of view of the
two men. While Donizetti is anxious to gain recognition, it is
never at the cost of anyone else's reputation. Bellini, on the
other hand, lives in a state of perpetual neurotic anxiety, a
living exemplum of the principle he had stated back in 1828,
that 'It is *completely impossible* to have friends in the profession'.

As Donizetti wrote to Mayr, he had already received a letter
from Rossini in Paris, offering him a chance to compose for the
Italiens. For several years this had been Donizetti's greatest
ambition. To be able to arrive in Paris on time, he had used the
offices of Ronzi de Begnis, who had been engaged at La Scala
for the coming Carnival, to persuade Visconti to let his opera
open the season.

Donizetti's operas continued their popularity in Naples
during that summer of 1834. Ronzi de Begnis re-appeared in
Anna Bolena. In July, when *Parisina* was given its Neapolitan
première with Ungher, and Cosselli—the same singers who had
sung the first performance in Florence the year before—Donizetti was not in the theatre, but so great was the applause that
the performance was halted until he was found and pushed out
on stage to receive the acclamations of the audience. At this

[1] Bellini, *Epistolario*, Ltr. CLXXVIII, p. 419.

same period, he had just completed his most recent score, *Maria Stuarda*, to a libretto by Giuseppe Bardari that was closely based on Schiller's play.

The rehearsals of *Maria Stuarda* began about 1 August, and in the opera Ronzi di Begnis had been cast as Elisabetta and Anna Del Serre as Maria. At one of the rehearsals occurred what proved to be one of the famous scandals of the day. When Del Serre turned on Ronzi in the second act, she had these pointed lines to deliver:

> MARIA: *Figlia impura di Bolena,*
> *Parli tu di disonore?*
> *Meretrice—indegna, oscena,*
> *In te cada il mio rossore.*
> *Profonato è soglio ingelese,*
> *Vil bastarda, dal tuo pie!*

(Translated: Impure daughter of Boleyn, do *you* speak of dishonour? Obscene and unworthy prostitute, I blush for you. Vile bastard, the English throne is sullied by your feet.)

Anna Del Serre delivered these lines with such conviction that Ronzi took them personally. She charged her rival, seized her by the hair and started pommelling her with her fists, bit her, and hit her in the face and breast. Not surprisingly Del Serre lost her footing under this onslaught and fell, but, deciding not to faint, she struggled up and returned the attack. Ronzi so outweighed her adversary that Del Serre fainted in earnest and had to be carried home.[1] Donizetti reported a sequel to this skirmish in his letter to Ferretti of 7 October.

> . . . You know of the conflict between the women, but I do not know if you know that Ronzi spoke against me, believing me out of earshot. She said: 'Donizetti protects that whore[2] of a Del Serre': and I unexpectedly answered: 'I do not protect either of you, but those two were whores, and you two are whores; be convinced, either be ashamed or be quiet'—I said no more, the rehearsal continued, she sang, the matter went no further. . . .[3]

[1] The details come from *Teatri, arti e letteratura* (Bologna), 23 October 1834.
[2] Donizetti merely writes 'p . . . .', meaning *puttana*.
[3] Z. No. 150, p. 362.

More serious trouble, however, awaited Donizetti. Some time not long before 1 October, Queen Maria Cristina attended the dress rehearsal of *Maria Stuarda*. She watched the enactment of the Queen of Scots' fate with such horrified empathy that she came close to fainting during the third act. The next day Donizetti was officially informed that the performance of his opera was forbidden. Trying to salvage his labour and collect his fee, he sought a way out of the impasse. First of all he suggested revising the libretto, proposing the subject of Lady Jane Grey, but as that story also involved a royal beheading, permission to use it was denied. By 2 October the story of *Buondelmonte* was approved. Donizetti produced some new music, including a string of new recitatives, and by 7 October the *rifacimento* was put in rehearsal and first performed on 18 October. The cast included Ronzi (Elisabetta), Del Serre (Irene), Francesco Pedrazzi (Buondelmonte), Carlo Ottolini Porto (Tebaldi), Crespi (Mosca), and Achille Balestracci (Lamberto). The original form of the opera was reconstructed and presented at La Scala in December 1835 with Malibran as Maria, but the story of that ill-fated production will be told in its chronological sequence.

Shortly after he had finished composing *Maria Stuarda* Donizetti started writing his opera for Paris, *Marino Faliero*, to a libretto by Emanuele Bidera, who had based his text primarily upon a play by Casimir Delavigne, and, in part, on Byron. Originally Donizetti had hoped to have a libretto by Romani, but he soon yielded this notion. He had almost completed the score of *Faliero* by 8 October, but he still had to compose another opera, this one for the Carnival season at La Scala. For this assignment, too, he had first thought of using a text by Romani. His letters to Ricordi and Visconti of that summer and early autumn are full of queries about Romani and complaints about his failure to produce the libretto. On 27 September he suggested as a subject a play by the Roman dramatist Marsuzi, entitled *Giovanna I di Napoli*. On 11 October he wrote to Ricordi:

> . . . I believe that one will not suffer more in hell—
> Imagine my fear of not being the first in Carnival—I am
> looking for a letter from the Duke as the Jews await the
> Messiah. . . . I have already ordered a text here, but if the

Duke doesn't answer me how I should proceed and what I should write, I waste time uselessly. . . .[1]

On 14 October Donizetti writes to Visconti that he will not give Romani longer than the 20th. He has already heard that the Duke is opposed to the subject of *Giovanna*; therefore, he suggests the possibility of Bidera, who had already written the libretto to *Marino Faliero* for him, and who could write a book for Milan.

About 20 October Gaetano sent Virginia overland to Rome to stay with her family while he took ship for Genoa to meet Giuseppe. Together they went to Bergamo where they spent several days about 21 November. It would seem to be on the occasion of this visit that Donizetti strengthened his bonds with Dolci and increased his friendly standing with the Basoni family. Although he had known them earlier there is no record of his mentioning the Basonis by name in his published letters dating from before this visit, nor is there a known letter to Dolci, although he mentions him by name, for their friendship went back to the days of the Lezione Caritatevoli. In 1828, Donizetti had dedicated the score of *Alina* to Dolci.

After this brief but important visit, Donizetti returned to Milan where he gave his attention to readying the score of *Gemma di Vergy*.[2] The opera was sung on 26 December with Ronzi de Begnis (Gemma), Felicità Baillou-Hillaret (Ida), Domenico Reina (Tamas), Orazio Cartagenova (Conte di Vergy), Ignazio Marini (Guido), and Domenico Spiaggi (Rolando). This opera, for which Donizetti received 6500 Austrian lire, had a good, but not an outstanding, success at its première, its first 'edition' achieving a run of twenty-six performances. Today it is a little difficult to understand the great vogue which this opera enjoyed for nearly forty years, but by the last quarter of the nineteenth century it was rarely given and soon not at all. By a strange coincidence, when the opera was introduced to Naples in 1837, the roles of Gemma and Tamas were sung by Caterina Barili and Salvatore Patti, whose

---

[1] Z. No. 151, p. 363.
[2] This work is not to be confused with the minor *Gabriella di Vergy*, which Donizetti wrote in 1826, but was never produced during his lifetime. The libretto to *Gemma di Vergy* is based on Dumas's *Charles VII chez les grands vassaux*.

greatest claim to attention is that they became the parents of
Adelina Patti.

On 31 December 1834 Donizetti left Milan for Genoa where
he took a ship for Marseilles and then proceeded by diligence
to Paris. The date of his arrival in Paris has not been recorded,
but it is more than probable he arrived in time to witness the
première of Bellini's *I Puritani* which took place at the Italiens
on 25 January 1835, being sung by Giulia Grisi (Elvira),
Rubini (Arturo), Tamburini (Riccardo), and Lablache
(Giorgio). During this Paris season the rivalry between Bellini
and Donizetti was to have its last and climactic chapter.

Bellini had been in France for most of 1834, hoping to arrange
his entrée to the French theatres under the most auspicious
circumstances. Bellini had begun composing his opera during
the summer to a libretto by Count Carlo Pepoli, as he had not
yet made peace with Romani. His bitterness over their disagreement at the time of *Beatrice di Tenda* is apparent in a letter
he wrote on 4 August. '[Romani] is born to compromise all the
poor maestros.'[1] However, by December of that year he had
received a conciliatory note from Romani, which he answers
enthusiastically calling him his dearest friend, swearing he had
never stopped being fond of him in his heart, and, rather
typically, insisting in italics that from now on Romani should
write librettos for no one but Bellini, only Bellini. By 21
September Bellini could report that his opera was almost completed. Shortly after this he began to make a series of visits to
Rossini, which he describes to Florimo, 4 October:

> . . . Rossini pays me compliments. You should know that
> I have begged Rossini (to pay him court and also be-
> cause I believe he can give me golden advice) to be kind
> enough to give me his counsel. . . . That has pleased
> me, and if I have the protection of Rossini, I am off at a
> gallop. Up to now he has only spoken badly, very badly,
> of me, saying that the one with the most genius in Italy
> is Pacini, and for the working-out of pieces the best is
> Donizetti.[2]

[1] Bellini, *Epistolario*, Ltr. CLXXIX, p. 422.
[2] Ibid., Ltr. CLXXXVII, p. 443.

How typical that is of Bellini, to believe that Rossini was speaking badly of him, when he didn't mention him at all, but happened to compliment other composers! Rossini helped Bellini revise his score of *I Puritani*. By 30 November, Bellini had become increasingly anxious about Donizetti, for he writes to Florimo:

> . . . Who has written the book of *Marino Faliero* for Donizetti? You tell me that he has written some beautiful music, but it had better not be like that of *Buondelmonte* that you have lauded as something glorious at the first performance, but which ended by being whistled. . . .[1]

On the day after the *prima* of *I Puritani*, Bellini gloated to Florimo 'O my good Florimo, how happy I am!!' and gives him a detailed account of the performance; on the same day he wrote to his uncle, Vincenzo Ferlito, to say: 'I am at the apex of happiness.' It cannot be denied that the first production of *I Puritani* was a great immediate success. Florimo, in his *Bellini—Memorie e Lettere*, has printed what purports to be a letter from Donizetti to Romani describing the first evening of *I Puritani*:

> I have arrived late, but better late than never. The success of Bellini has been very great, in spite of a mediocre libretto; the opera continues to hold its own, although we are now at the fifth performance, and it will be thus until the end of the season. I tell you about it, because I know you have made peace. Today, for my part, I begin the rehearsals, and I hope to give the first performance at the end of the month. I do not at all deserve the success of *I Puritani*, but I hope that I shall not fail to please at all.[2]

It is difficult not to believe that this letter is cut from the same piece of cloth as that purported to describe Donizetti's view of the *prima* of *Norma*. For one thing, Donizetti did not feel very cordial towards Romani at this point, and it is difficult to believe that he wrote in such a way about *I Puritani*; for another, the mealy-mouthed sentiments in the final sentence are unlike the tone of Donizetti's authentic letters, but, on the other hand, they sound very much like Florimo's own style, and he was a

[1] Ibid., Ltr. CCII, p. 482.
[2] Zavadini reprints this letter as No. 157, p. 367.

man not beyond inventing dialogue years after it was supposed to have been spoken. Like the *Norma* letter, the autograph for this has not been produced; and until it is—if it can be—there seem better grounds for doubting the authenticity of this letter than for accepting it as genuine.

The few extant letters by Donizetti from this first stay in Paris give little clue to the events at the Italiens; Bellini's copious letters give more details, but they are observed by a malevolent eye. On 6 February, three days after Bellini received the Legion of Honour, he writes: 'Yesterday Donizetti began his rehearsals.' On the 27th he informs Florimo:

> . . . I know also that Donizetti and his friends (my enemies) intrigue here and there, both to see he has a resounding reception and then to see he gets the cross [of the Legion of Honour]. We will see if they succeed. Meanwhile the news of the rehearsals of his *Marino* is not encouraging. They say that the first act is weak, in the second there is a good aria for Rubini; I know only the dramatic part, but the music is thin. I believe that it will sustain itself with the great dramatic situations the subject presents, but it will depend on how Lablache's part goes, and on whether the melodies are new and effective. I know that Rossini has made him revise the introduction, the finale and many other pieces. Thursday, 5 March, they say, it will go on stage. Whether it goes well or very well, it will be a matter of indifference to me. . . .[1]

On 13 March, again to Florimo:

> . . . Yesterday evening Donizetti's new opera went on; *Marino Faliero* has made a semi-fiasco. Perhaps the papers will not be hostile to it, but the public remained discontented, and the proof of it will be the prompt reappearance of *I Puritani*. . . .[2]

Bellini was one of these people who developed his attitudes through copious repetition, and through his own intense concern for himself, he moved appreciably from the facts. Such a hardening of the narrative can be readily perceived in

[1] Bellini, *Epistolario*, Ltr. CCXIV, p. 529.
[2] Ibid., Ltr. CCXXVII, p. 533.

Bellini's effusive account of his career in Paris, written to his uncle on 1 April 1835. Only a substantial quotation can give the real flavour of this remarkable letter.

> ... Rossini, who truly exercises a great deal of influence here in Paris, especially with the papers, decided to engage Donizetti also, because thus putting him in opposition to me, he would suffocate me, exterminate me, sustained by Rossini's colossal influence, etc. etc. In fact at the announcement that Donizetti had also been engaged, I had a fever for three days, seeing the veritable trap that had been prepared for me. In fact one of my acquaintances told me not to hope for a good reception in Paris, and that, if there were a success, it would be Donizetti's, because Rossini was supporting him. Then I, once this first impression had passed, took courage and began to think how to vanquish such diabolical intrigues that would have compromised me in the face of all Europe, and I would have been, had I remained their victim. Discussing this with myself, I resolved before everything to study my new score more than usual and then to pay court to Rossini and to let him know how much I esteemed his immense talent etc., etc., also to draw near to his lady friend[1] and see them both often, to put myself almost in an intimate relationship with them, so that they themselves would resolve to protect me rather than to persecute me. For all this I needed no urging, for I have always adored Rossini. I succeeded happily. Meanwhile I worked with all my power in the country, well lodged in the house of my English friend, Mr Lewis.
>
> Having won Rossini's friendship, I said to myself: Let Donizetti come now! It was the third time I found myself with him in the same theatre. In, I believe, 1831, at the Carcano in Milan, he wrote *Anna Bolena*; I replied with *Sonnambula*. The following year he wrote *Ugo* for La Scala (which had a fiasco); I gave them *Norma*. Finally I found myself here with him, and having tamed Rossini's hatred, I feared nothing further, and with more courage I finished my work that bore me so much honour, as Rossini predicted three months before I went on stage.

[1] Olympe Pélissier, who became the second Mme Rossini in 1846.

The good things that these people have said about
Donizetti have influenced the papers much. The madness
of faction showed itself at the first performance of *Marino
Faliero*, on 12 March. However, at the general rehearsal
(as at mine) the management invited many people; but
with a difference: for mine they were invited by note, and
for Donizetti's the management offered tickets to whoever
wanted them. Therefore, at the general rehearsal there
was immense applause, so much so that, finding myself
with Rossini in a box, we both laughed at this furore; for
at all the other rehearsals the opera had been condemned
as one that would live a little while, a very little while,
because it is the worst of all the operas Donizetti has composed, which up to now number 48. At the first performance, the hall, or the pit, was filled with the claque,
but as the Teatro Italiano is full, very full, of subscribers,
the claque was not able to impress anyone, and the effect
of *Marino Faliero* was mediocre. At the second performance
it was judged worse, at the third everyone deemed it a real
funeral, so much so that the management, having wanted
to support it and give it at Lablache's benefit, has lost
3200 francs.[1]

At this point, let us interrupt Bellini's mean-spirited account of
his rival to read what Donizetti wrote to his friend Dolci on
16 March about the same events.

I wanted to send you just the article from the *Messager*,
but I am thinking of sending you a couple of words about
the second and third performances, which were brilliant.
Rubini sang as I have never heard him, and for this
reason I have had to repeat his cavatina and aria both
evenings. The reception of Bellini with *I Puritani* has made
me tremble not a little, but as our works are of opposite
character, thus we have both obtained a fine success without displeasing the public. Don't take it in your head to
answer me as I leave the end of the week for Naples. . . .[2]

What a contrast! Donizetti knew that he won an honest, if
not overpowering success, but Bellini would not allow one

[1] Bellini, *Epistolario*, Ltr. CCXXX, pp. 536–8.
[2] Z. No. 160, pp. 368–9.

shred of merit to his rival. He continues his account to his uncle:

> ... *Marino* had 5 performances and *I Puritani* 14, plus the benefit of Tamburini and the last two of the season, in all 17 performances between 24 January and 31 March, an unheard-of thing in Paris, where the public, fickle by nature, will not endure in the six months of the season to see an opera more than about six times from the stage. ... Therefore the field is left to me. The just public has decided, and already had, since the first performance of *Marino Faliero* as had the government and all the impresarios, for the first did not distinguish the composer with any honour, nor have the second made him any offers, and he left the 25th, I believe, for Naples, convinced of his fiasco.
>
> What an opera he has written! It is an incredible thing —he who in *Anna Bolena* showed talent. This work for Paris is deprived of novelty, most ordinary, and most ordinarily orchestrated—without concerted pieces—in a word worthy of a young student. And Rossini, who protected him, has said that had Donizetti sought the most trivial music he could find, he could not have done worse. ... [1]

Marino Faliero was sung by the same singers who had appeared in *I Puritani*; Grisi, Rubini, Tamburini, and Lablache sang the roles of Elena, Fernando, Ismaele and Faliero the Doge; the others in the cast were Santini (Steno) and Ivanoff (a Gondolier). The opera was given in London on 14 May 1835 with the same company. Chorley's account of that production explains in part why *Marino Faliero* made less impression than *I Puritani*.

> In spite of the grandeur of Lablache as the Doge of Venice, in spite of the beauty of the duet of the two basses in the first act of *Marino*, in spite of the second act containing a beautiful moonlight scene with a barcarolle, sung to perfection by Ivanoff, and one of Rubini's most incomparable and superb vocal displays, *Marino Faliero* languished, in part from the want of interest in the female character—a fatal fault to an opera's popularity.[2]

[1] Bellini, *Epistolario*, Ltr. CCXXX, p. 539.
[2] Chorley, *Thirty Years' Musical Recollections*, p. 65.

Marino Faliero continued to enjoy revivals and to hold the esteem of competent critics for a good many years. It proved itself to be far more than the failure that Bellini crowed over.

There was more to Donizetti's first visit to Paris, however, than his production of *Marino Faliero*, although that was his primary concern. Of importance to his future were the people he met. Some of them he had known before he came to Paris. For the leading singers of the Italiens he had composed on many earlier occasions; Rossini he had known from February 1822, when the young Donizetti first came to Naples. Robert and Severini, the co-directors of the Théâtre-Italien, he had encountered in Florence in 1833, if not on one of their earlier scouting expeditions into Italy to recruit talent for their theatre. Some people he met for the first time. For instance, there was Michele Accursi, whose name he had mentioned in a letter to Ricordi of 15 April 1834, directing the music publisher to send a contract to 'Monsieur Michel Accursi (*Accursi*, I repeat the last name because I wrote it badly the first time), *poste restante*, Paris'. Since the contract in question was that for *Marino Faliero*, this fact suggests that Accursi was an *homme d'affaires* connected in some capacity with the Italiens. Actually, Accursi posed as a political exile—Paris was full of fugitive Italians in those days—but he was really a counterspy who sent detailed reports to the Vatican of the activities of his fellow countrymen in Paris.

Of Paris Donizetti writes to Dolci: 'It is very beautiful, but I prefer quiet! I am most handsomely received, invitations rain and dinners shower, the soirées deluge, and therefore I prefer quiet.' Certainly in the round of all this social activity he met people who were to form part of his world when he settled in Paris. There was Count Rudolf Appony, the Austrian Ambassador, and his wife; the de Coussys, Auguste, a banker, and his socially influential wife, Zélie; there was the Bergamasc tenor, Marco Bordogni, who had become a singing master at the Paris Conservatory; there were the music publishers Troupenas, Pacini, and Latte; there was the wife and sister of his friend Cottrau; there were the French composers Adam, Auber, and on through the alphabet.

While Donizetti was in Paris he attended the other theatres. At the Opéra, he saw *La Juive* which had its première on 25 February 1835. In several letters he mentions this production and his harrowing impressions of the realism of the acting and lavish staging, while the music left him cold. On this last point Bellini agreed with him, dismissing it in a letter to Florimo, as '*una vera porcheria*'. He must also have heard Adam's *Le chalet* at the Opéra-Comique, a relatively new work then, having been first performed the previous September; Donizetti was to remember *Le chalet* when he wrote his own libretto for *Betly* the following year. That Donizetti was dazzled by Paris there seems little doubt; that he found it at first rather more sophisticated than the lazy, gossiping Naples, which had been his headquarters for many years, is probable, though his innate tact and humour won him many friends; that Donizetti left Paris with his heart set on returning and conquering the city is certain.

On 25 March he departed from Paris. He was in Leghorn on 10 April, on his way to collect Virginia and return to Naples, where his leave of absence had expired the last day of February. He was returning to Naples to compose still another new opera, *Lucia di Lammermoor*.

CHAPTER 4

Triumph and Bereavement

On his return from Paris, Donizetti spent several days in the Vasselli household, seeing Ferretti and other friends in Rome, before he and Virginia returned to Naples about the third week in April. Their first days were busy ones. Gaetano found the Neapolitan theatres, when he again took up his duties as musical director, were in confusion. Barbaja had given up his post as impresario, and he had been succeeded by a Società d'Industria e Belle Arti. This direction by a committee of aristocratic dilettantes was to result in an unhappy year for the professional musicians. While Gaetano was occupied with these difficulties, Virginia was preparing to move her household to new quarters. Since their marriage the Donizettis had lived on the third floor, Via Nardonnes, No. 6; on 3 May 1835 they transferred their possessions to Vico Corsea, No. 65, where they were to live on the fourth floor over the Black Eagle inn for two years.

Donizetti's difficulties with the new management began almost immediately upon his arrival in Naples. Learning that the company was in need of a workhorse prima donna, Donizetti volunteered to help to provide one. To this purpose he wrote to Ricordi on 23 April a letter which contains some interesting details of the working conditions at the San Carlo in those days.

> Instead of answering your letter of yesterday which would take too much time now, I beg you to have the goodness to undertake as carefully as possible this commission at this very moment, almost without finishing

reading. If Signora Boccabadati should be in Milan, you will hurry to her and make these proposals.

The said Signora Boccabadati would engage herself for three months to begin on the day of her arrival in Naples, which should be at the earliest moment, taking a carriage on receipt of the enclosed contract and accepting the conditions in it. It would be in the power of the Commission to secure her again after the three months of the present engagement. She would be engaged as prima donna *assoluta* for the Royal Theatres, S. Carlo and Fondo, obligating herself to sing in all the opere serie, semiserie, buffe, farse, cantatas, as in the printed contract. Her monthly salary would not go beyond the sum of 600 ducats without a benefit evening, and only 500 if she should give her benefit in the first three months. The management would notify her of the renewal of her contract not later than fifty days after the beginning of her engagement. It is always understood that the renewal would be by the same conditions and salary. She would sing no more than five times a week and no less than three. The benefit evening would be accorded in the case of her accepting the re-engagement after the first three months and will be held in the Teatro S. Carlo, but the subscriptions would not be suspended.

If the said soprano is disposed to leave at once, all goes well. If the least delay occurs, see Signora Blassis and deal with her for 400 ducats a month for the first three months. . . .[1]

From the hasty, business-like tone of this letter, Donizetti was trying to bring some order into the affairs of the opera house by decisive action. Chaos, however, continued to reign. On 3 May he writes to Ricordi again, saying that the Società, after asking him if he knew anyone in Milan he could write to for assistance in engaging a prima donna, had now written to Ricordi themselves to exclude Boccabadati because they have heard conflicting rumours about her vocal condition. 'A cage of madmen,' Donizetti calls the members of the Società. For the eighteen days of the Novena of S. Gennaro, when all the Neapolitan theatres were closed, they could not agree upon a new opera to

[1] Z. No. 163, pp. 370–1.

put on and brought back Donizetti's *Gemma*, which had not
pleased before the closing and pleased even less after the
re-opening. 'Poor singers . . .' he adds ambiguously. He reports
that there are many people who want the Società to name
Barbaja as the administrator for the group, but this move would
only anger Lanari, who was then serving in that capacity.

> Ronzi renounced thirty performances because the
> audience would not tolerate her for a full hundred.
> She has very little tact, and only shouts: *money, money,
> and the whistling means little to me*, this aggravates the public.
> She is wrong, and the public is wrong to whistle at her, for
> in Italy now we know no one better than she since the
> departure of Madama Pasta and Malibran. . . .[1]

Under such upsetting conditions Donizetti carried on his work
in the theatre.

Of the various offers that reached Donizetti during this year,
one came from the impresario in Turin, Giuseppe Consul. He
proposed that Donizetti should write an opera on an old
libretto of Romani's entitled *Gl'Illinesi*; the natives of this title
come not from Illinois but from India. Romani's text had
already been set by Francesco Basili (La Scala, 1819) and by
Feliciano Strepponi[2] (Trieste, 1829), but Consul hoped that
Romani could be prevailed upon to revise it extensively. On
1 July, Consul wrote that he had discussed the matter with
Romani, who instructed him to inform the composer that the
first act of the libretto would be ready in August. Consul also
told Donizetti that the leading parts would be sung by Giuditta
Grisi, the elder sister of the more famous Giulia, by Donzelli,
who would sing the romantic lead, and by the bass Schober.

Donizetti's reply to Consul's letter affords insight into his
awareness of how much the success of a new opera depended
upon the singers' suitability to their roles.

> I believe that Romani, that Consul, that Lampieri him-
> self[3] have lost their minds; what, Donzelli in love? But you
> know Donzelli must be 50 years old! and with 50 years on
> his rump to play the lover, or, *per Bacco*, at my time of life,
> no! I know that Donzelli in 1822 was already playing a

[1] Z. No. 164, p. 372.   [2] The father of Giuseppina, Verdi's second wife.
[3] Alessandro Lampieri was Consul's right-hand man in conducting the
affairs of the Teatro Regio, Turin.

tyrant's role; I know that at Milan in *Norma* he seemed already too mature as he did in *Ugo*, and I know further that when Strepponi wrote his *Gl'Illinesi*, with the same Grisi, Ungher was the young Frenchman. . . . I have the old libretto; it does not please me greatly for today's time, unless Romani, who could do everything for it, revises more than just three parts. I believe la Grisi would much prefer to play a *musico* since she has been accustomed to it for a long time. . . .[1]

For goodness' sake, dear Consul, brevity; and punctuality in sending me the book finished early in September. . . .[2]

On 21 July Donizetti was no happier about the proposed *Gl'Illinesi*, for he writes to Consul again,[3] saying he wants a completely new text, not a cobbled one. He is worried about the plot's lack of romantic interest: 'I want love, without which operatic subjects are cold, violent love.' This last statement is interesting because it reveals Donizetti at this time already oriented toward the vehemence of romantic melodrama.

By 14 September the project had not advanced one jot. On that date Consul reported to Donizetti that 'the more than blessed' Romani had yet to write the first line. 'I can no longer believe in his always vain and false promises, and I foresee that as already happened to me last year, I will be thoroughly disgusted....'[4] On receiving this letter from Consul, Donizetti wrote back on the 24th, asking to be released from the engagement. Although this letter of Donizetti's does not appear in Zavadini, the unpublished reply by Consul, dated 12 October, is in the Naples Conservatory library. His attitude is sympathetic:

> . . . Such inconvenience displeases me particularly because it has deprived me of the pleasure of having with me this Carnival a friend whom I esteem and love very much, but on the other hand, I cannot condemn your reflections

[1] Giuditta Grisi's most famous *musico* role was Romeo in Bellini's *I Capuletti ed i Montecchi*, which she sang at the première in Venice and in the first performances at La Scala.   [2] Z. No. 168, pp. 375–6.

[3] This letter (Z. No. 171, p. 135) was apparently carried to Turin by the fourteen-year-old ballerina, Fanny Cerrito, who had made a great hit in her début at the San Carlo the previous year.

[4] Unpublished letter in the library of the Naples Conservatory (No. 63818), and a transcription at the Museo Donizettiano, Bergamo.

which are only too just. I assure you that both Lampieri
and I together have done everything possible to have the
book sent to you at the stated time; but what do you want
us to do, when from that blessed Romani one can no
longer obtain anything. . . .[1]

Thus, the project of *Gl'Illinesi* came to nothing, and Donizetti
was never to write a new opera for Turin. The details of this
negotiation show the friendly relationship between Donizetti
and an impresario and his whole-hearted concern for such an
undertaking. The incident sheds further light on the difficulty
of extracting a libretto from Romani.

On 9 November 1834, not long before he left for Milan to
rehearse *Gemma di Vergy*, Donizetti had signed a contract with
the management of the Royal Theatres of Naples to write three
operas for the company, the first to be ready for production in
July 1835. This contract,[2] which was signed by Prince Ottojano
and Antonio Santorelli, provided, among other things, that the
choice of the plots and of the poets would be made by the Commission with the concurrence of Maestro Donizetti, that the
Commission would place the libretto, already approved by
the censors, in Donizetti's hands at least four months before the
opera was to be produced, that for each opera Donizetti would
receive 2500 ducats, payable in one sum after the first performance, and that the Commission would receive all rights
whatsoever to the scores.

The first news of the subject for the opera to be given in July
1835 is found in a letter Donizetti wrote to Count Luigi
Spadaro del Bosch of Messina, on 18 May:

I am most grateful for the memory you retain of me. I
advise you that the impresario from Messina will go at 7
today to Barbaja where he will hear a prima donna and a
tenor with whom I am unacquainted. I hope they will be
excellent both for you and for the excellent Messinesi who
deserve a reward after the misfortune of last year. I would
advise him, had not the matter been placed in the hands

[1] Unpublished letter in the library of the Naples Conservatory (No. 63819),
and a transcription at the Museo Donizettiano, Bergamo.
[2] Donizetti's copy of the contract is in the Museo Donizettiano, Bergamo.

of Barbaja, who is angry with me because I am writing for the Società, not reflecting that with the same zeal I have served him, I will serve anyone—*Fiat!*

The delay of my poem for the S. Carlo, which will be *The Bride of Lammermoor* of Walter Scott, makes it difficult for me to accept in August your very kind proposals—*malheur à moi*—but it is the poet's *fautte* [*sic*]. . . .

I fear that the *Parisina* performed in Messina was pirated, and also *L'elisir d'amore*. . . .[1]

On this date little more than the subject could have been decided, for it was not until the 25th that Donizetti submitted to the Società a plan for the text and a list of the performers. It was his usual practise to submit such a statement as soon as he had reached an agreement with his librettist; for example, listing the proposed cast for *Lucrezia Borgia* Donizetti sent the statement to Visconti the very day after his first conference with Romani about that text. By 29 May, Donizetti had still heard nothing from the Società, and so he wrote them a tart statement, reminding them of the terms of his contract, by which the approved libretto should have been in his hands the preceding March.

After having developed for you as clearly as possible with my letter of 25 May the reasons that have induced me to write *Lucia di Lammermoor*, I do not understand how you can want to attribute to my long indecision on the choice of the subject the delay of the staging of the opera, in the course of the month of July; permit me to tell you with my customary frankness that you should find among the terms of the contract there is that one that says you should have given me the book, approved by all authorities, on the first days of this past March. While only a few days ago you placed at my disposition, as a result of my repeated urgings, the poet Signor Cammarano, with whom I came to an agreement directly on the subject, above stated. You should remember that when I myself placed in your hands a few days ago the plan on which was indicated the performers, not only did you approve the choice, but personally sent it to the censor, whence it came back approved for the scenic part, a formality which you could have well

[1] Z. No. 165, p. 373.

dispensed with, considering that urgency has often got us out of some difficulty. The delay then does not come at all from my part; rather I would be within my rights to protest did I not trust in your loyalty.

Time flies, and I assure you that I can no longer remain in such perplexity, since I have other obligations. Therefore, either be pleased to authorize the poet Signor Cammarano to busy himself without delay on the plan of *Lucia di Lammermoor* already presented to and approved by the censor, and in that case I would regard myself as obligated to finish the work by the end of August, without insisting on the four-month period, allowed by the contract; otherwise allow me to regulate myself, reverting to my rights strictly according to the terms of the contract and cancelling every easement offered by me in my earlier letter of the 25th of this month and in this letter.[1]

This letter reflects both Donizetti's direct tactics in business and the state of disorganization within the Società. Donizetti was still willing to seek some reasonable compromise so that his opera might be written and performed. This is the same pragmatic policy he followed with Lanari over the much-delayed libretto of *Parisina*.

Donizetti was uncommonly fortunate in the Commission's recommendation of Salvatore Cammarano, for they were to enjoy a mutually stimulating collaboration over the next several years; although they were never quite to succeed in duplicating their first triumph with *Lucia*, the operas they worked on together are among the most interesting Donizetti wrote. Cammarano came by his feeling for the theatre honestly; it was in his blood. His grandfather Vincenzo[2] had come from Sicily to Naples in 1764, where he became a famous Pulcinella. He had four sons, all of whom were on the stage at one time or another. The eldest, Filippo,[3] succeeded his father as leader of

[1] Z. No. 166, pp. 373-4.
[2] There is an interesting account of the Cammarano family to be found in an article by Vittorio Viviani, 'Libretti e librettisti,' published in *Cento Anni di Vita di San Carlo: 1848–1948* (Naples, 1948). An English reduction of the material about the Cammaranos is found in Spike Hughes, *Great Opera Houses*, pp. 201–3.
[3] The *Enciclopedia Italiana* says Salvatore was Filippo's son, while Viviani (and Hughes after him) says he was the son of Giuseppe, Filippo's next younger brother.

the troupe at the Teatro San Carlino, but at the age of ten he had written a play, *Il comico inglese*, and later translated Goldoni into the Neapolitan dialect. Salvatore (1801–52) was one of Filippo's nine children. As a boy he attended a so-called Accademia Poetica, run by a lawyer named Cascini; at eighteen he wrote a play, *Baldovino* which was successfully produced at the Teatro Fiorentino. As Salvatore early showed an interest in becoming a librettist, his father introduced him to Barbaja, but as the impresario had a whole stable of librettists already, he would not engage him. Salvatore tried to show him a sample of his work, a text entitled *Belisario*, but Barbaja refused to read it. At some time in his youth, Salvatore also attended a school in scenic design at the San Carlo, the classes being under the direction of the famous Niccolini. It was not until the death of Domenico Gilardoni, which occurred while he was writing the book of *Fausta* for Donizetti, that Barbaja was willing to engage Cammarano, but then not as a librettist but as a stage manager. He continued in this capacity until the Società gave him his first opportunity, a collaboration with Bidera on a subject for Giuseppe Persiani's *Ines de Castro*. It was on the basis of this creditable performance that the Società finally recommended him to Donizetti.

The desire on Donizetti's part to treat, as he wrote to Consul, subjects that dealt with 'love, without which operas are cold, violent love', found an answering spark in Cammarano. His style was terse, energetic, rather formalized, but he had a true man of the theatre's sense of what was dramatically effective. The librettos he wrote for Donizetti are full of striking scenes, although it must be frankly admitted their motivation is not always lucid. Perhaps the best example of Cammarano's strengths and weaknesses is to be found in the last libretto he wrote, and dying, left not quite finished, *Il trovatore*. Certainly, Cammarano's association with Donizetti was fortunate for him, giving him the chance to work with a craftsman of vast experience and one able to analyse and describe his reactions to a text precisely.

All through the month of June, Donizetti and Cammarano were intensely involved with the writing of *Lucia*. From this month Zavadini was unable to find any correspondence, nor do any letters from this time appear in *Studi Donizettiani I*, a lack which may well reveal the intensity with which Donizetti was

working. One indication of how this month passed comes from
a letter of the 14th by Cottrau to his relatives in Paris. He
reports that he and his wife Jenny customarily passed their
evenings with Donizetti and Virginia at the Cottrau's Villa
Majo at Infrascata 'where we are in *villeggiatura*, where we talk,
we make music, we take tea. . . .'[1] In spite of the leisurely sound
of this, Donizetti must have worked with extraordinary concentration, because the final page of the score is dated 6 July
1835. Between the last days of May and 6 July the whole
opera, libretto as well as music, was written. On 8 July Donizetti wrote to Spadaro in Messina that he expected *Lucia* would
be produced about 20 August; on 16 July to Gaetano Cobianchi
in Paris, he announces that 'my *Lucia* is already finished'.

When 20 August rolled round *Lucia* was not yet in rehearsal.
The mismanagement of the Società had produced such a state
of crisis by the end of July that the King personally intervened,
dismissed the former directors and appointed in their places
Prince Torella, Capacelatro, and Santorelli. On 5 September,
Donizetti wrote to Ricordi that the Società was in imminent
danger of failing, that la Persiani had not been paid and refused
to rehearse and that he had no idea when he would be paid
himself. This difficulty seems to have been overcome so that
Donizetti could announce to Ferretti on 16 September that the
first performance would take place on the 28th; actually it
occurred two days earlier, on the 26th.

The first performance of *Lucia di Lammermoor* was one of the
greatest triumphs ever to take place at the San Carlo. Throughout much of the evening most of the audience was dissolved in
tears; there was frantic applause for Persiani (Lucia), and
Duprez (Edgardo), and, particularly, for Donizetti. The others
in the cast that memorable evening were Teresa Zappucci
(Alisa), Domenico Cosselli (Enrico), Carlo Ottolini Porto
(Raimondo), Balestrieri (Arturo), and Rossi (Normanno).

On 29 September Donizetti sends the good news to Ricordi,
but with uncommon restraint.

> . . . *Lucia di Lammermoor* has gone on stage, and kindly
> permit me to shame myself and tell you the truth. It has
> pleased, and pleased very much, if I may believe the
> applause and the compliments received. Many times I

[1] Cottrau, *Lettres d'un mélomane*, p. 33.

was called out and also the singers, even more times. His Majesty's brother Leopold, who was present and applauded, paid me the most flattering compliments. The second evening I saw a most unusual thing for Naples: that is, in the finale, after great cheers for the adagio, Duprez in his curse was applauded to the heights before the stretta. Every piece was listened to with religious silence and hailed by spontaneous cheers. I have dedicated it to His Excellency the Minister Marchese Del Carretto (of the Police)....[1]
... If you tell my friend Cerri to send two lines to my Mayr at Bergamo with the news, I will be most obliged.

Already you will know that I have broken off with Turin, therefore if I had a place in Milan to come for making adjustments, if needed, or to stage *Maria Stuarda*, I could do it ... *La Tacchinardi*, *Duprez*, *Cosselli* and *Porto* carry themselves very well, and especially the two first-named are wonderful....[2]

In the years since 1835, *Lucia* has been the most frequently successful of Donizetti's operas. It was to be a symbol of romantic sensibility for more than one generation.

About a week after the première of *Lucia*, the shocking news of Bellini's death reached Naples.[3] At first it was received with incredulity that the thirty-three-year-old Bellini could have been struck down in the fullness of his promise. When the news was confirmed that Bellini was indeed dead at Puteaux, not far from Paris, from an acute infection of the large intestine, complicated by an abscessed liver, a tremendous outburst of grief exploded, particularly in his native Sicily; and Naples, the city where he had received his musical training and won his

[1] Marshal Marchese Francesco Saverio Del Carretto is thus described by Harold Acton, *The Last Bourbons of Naples*, p. 56: '[He] was detested by the liberals as a renegade, and ... has therefore gone down in history as a monster. But nobody holding his office at such a time could expect to be popular, and all parties had to admit that he performed his odious duties efficiently.'
[2] Z. No. 177, p. 385.
[3] In his history of the Teatro Carolino, Tiby reports that the news did not reach Palermo until 13 October; therefore it cannot have arrived in Naples many days before that.

first success, mourned him with almost equal fervour. Since Bellini died on 23 September, just three days before the *prima* of *Lucia*, and since word of the tragedy took time to arrive in Naples, mere chronology gives lie to the often-repeated tale that Donizetti was supposed to have said he composed his opera as a memorial to Bellini, inspired by his spirit.

That Donizetti was moved by Bellini's death is undeniable. He knew nothing of the tone of Bellini's letters, and it is clear that Bellini's behaviour to Donizetti's face gave no indication of the expressions he confided at his writing desk. The not always reliable Florimo[1] tells a story that while Bellini was still a student at the Conservatorio di S. Pietro a Majella, he heard a performance of Donizetti's *La zingara* and was so impressed by the septet that he copied it and studied it. Since Donizetti had known Bellini from his student days through those of his successes, he felt a genuine admiration for the accomplishments of the younger man. The only time he seems to have judged Bellini harshly was when he was provoked by the anonymous report from Bergamo. It was consistent with Donizetti's pragmatic view of his profession that he was little prone to envy another his success; that, after all, was what they all worked for, and Donizetti had had too much first-hand experience of the vagaries of singers, impresarios and audiences, not to be pleased when one of his colleagues managed to overcome these hazards. With the increased confidence that his own success with *Lucia* gave him, and from the depths of his own sensitive nature that gave him keen insight into the emotions of others, he could not help but be profoundly stirred by the death of Bellini.

Donizetti's first expression of his feelings about Bellini is shown in a letter he wrote to Ricordi on 17 October.

> From my bed with a most severe headache!
> I myself offered to conduct at the Conservatory Winter's Mass for the memorial service for the unfortunate Bellini. Now they urge me to write a mass expressly and I have consented. Now a third thing, they tell me that this will take place 2 December. That is too late and I will not be in Naples to conduct.[2]

[1] Francesco Florimo, *La Scuola musicale di Napoli* (Naples, 1880), vol. III, p. 247.
[2] Z. No. 178, p. 386.

On 20 October, Donizetti, again writing to Ricordi, reverts to the same subject.

> ... I am very happy to be able to give in Milan the last token of my friendship to the shade of poor Bellini, with whom I found myself writing four times, and every time our relationship grew more and more close. . . . Everything I prepared was cancelled by fate, which caused me to engage myself for Milan. . . . I only stand waiting the verses of the most famous Maffei, who will have a double subject to weep: that is, the death of a friend and the union of his verses to my music. I have much to do but a token of friendship to my Bellini goes before everything. . . .[1]

In all, Donizetti composed three 'tokens of friendship' for Bellini. The first was a Requiem Mass, a work for soprano, contralto, tenor, baritone and bass soloists, chorus, and orchestra. It consists of an *Introito, Requiem, Te decet hymnus; Kyrie, Dopo l'Epistola; Requiem e graduale, Antifona; Dies Irae; Tuba mirum;* and *Judex ergo.* The *Requiem* is a strangely ambivalent work, partly quite operatic in feeling and partly illumined by a real religious spirit; for example, the soprano and contralto solo parts are simple and restricted in range, suggesting they were intended to be performed by boys' voices, while the music for the male soloists is more extensive in range and emotional content. While in no way a pretentious work, its total effect is oddly beguiling, as though Donizetti were sincerely trying to depict his own view of Bellini's spirit, rather than to explore the awful mysteries of the religious text. The other two memorial pieces for Bellini were apparently not completed until the following year. The first of these is a *Lamento in morte di Bellini,* for voice and piano, setting a threnody by the Milanese poet Count Andrea Maffei. The other is a Sinfonia for orchestra, which is little more than a pot-pourri of Bellini's melodies, although they are handled with no little skill. Of the three pieces occasioned by the death of Bellini, there is no question that the most abiding interest resides in the *Requiem.*

After *Lucia,* Donizetti's next stint of operatic composition was a work for the Fenice in Venice. Donizetti had long been in

[1] Z. No. 180, p. 388.

negotiations with this theatre, but three times the plans had fallen through. As he wrote on 6 June to the Milanese journalist Luigi Previdali he had:

> ... the desire to see again the city where, either well or ill, I began my musical career. Unfortunately the offers made me by the management were so meagre that every time I put them out of mind. ...

He enlists Previdali's help, explaining about his agreement with Consul, which had not yet been dissolved, and asking him to explore the ground in Venice.

> ... I would have to know however what the company is ... and this is a very delicate note, in regard to the payment; to let you see how much I want to do this, I will content myself with 8000 francs as was offered me last year and the sole right of reduction for pianoforte of the said opera. Tell him that here without travelling I have 12,500 francs, thus I hope he will appreciate the sacrifice I make. As to the treaty, however, use immense secrecy for here they would turn to stone knowing it. The poet should be Sig. Cammarano, the poet of the royal theatres of Naples, to save time thereby. And I only ask to go on stage after the middle of Carnival. ...[1]

Previdali did his work well, for on 25 July Donizetti signed a contract with Natale Fabbrici, then the impresario of the Fenice. Although Fabbrici tried to engage him for 7000 francs, Donizetti held out for 8000 and got it. Further, he agreed to be in Venice by 1 January with the completed score. This commitment reveals Donizetti's assumption that the Turin contract for *Gl'Illinesi* would fall through. Fabbrici accepted Cammarano as the librettist and *Belisario* as the subject.

With *Belisario* Cammarano, as a much younger man, had hoped to win an engagement with Barbaja; now the poem was closely scrutinized by Donizetti, who modified it to suit his purposes as the annotations in his hand on Cammarano's text testify. In any event during October the composer and librettist were hard at work on this opera. On 24 October Donizetti writes to Fabbrici that he is progressing with *Belisario* and that he has no need for verses by a poet named Beltrami, whom

[1] Z. No. 167, p. 375.

Fabbrici had obviously recommended to him. He goes on to give the impresario some particulars about the opera.

> ... I suggest to you a really good second bass for the part of Giustiniano. Remember that since this character is the Emperor, it should not be derided by the public. Sig. Ambrogi would be offended by such a part, and therefore I respect him and would not offer him anything so small.
>
> For goodness' sake tell me who the tenor is, and though it is either Pasini or Poggi, at least let me know.
>
> ... Here there is talk of many cases of Cholera in Venice, is it true? ...[1]

As soon as Donizetti had *Belisario* well under way, he could turn his attention to Milan, where he had offered to supervise the production of *Maria Stuarda*, the first production of the original form of that opera, whose performance had been banned in Naples, causing it to appear thoroughly disguised as *Buondelmonte*. As early as 3 May he had been thinking seriously of this proposed production of *Maria Stuarda* at La Scala with Malibran in the title role. On that date he wrote to Ricordi that if Malibran were definitely to sing his opera, he would write a Sinfonia for the Milanese production. The plan proceeded according to schedule, for on 7 August Malibran wrote to Visconti from London saying that she was studying her part and had been to Westminster Abbey to copy the costumes of Mary Stuart and Elizabeth. A month later Malibran was back in Milan for the autumn season, singing with fine success Rossini's *Otello*, *L'elisir d'amore*, *Il barbiere di Siviglia*, and a single performance of Vaccai's *Giulietta e Romeo*, on 17 November.

Five days earlier the libretto of *Maria Stuarda* had been approved by the censors without any modifications, and the opera was ready to go into rehearsals. Although Donizetti was not to arrive in Milan until 3 December,[2] the initial preparations

---

[1] Z. No. 181, p. 389.

[2] Verzino, *Le opere di Gaetano Donizetti*, pp. 159–60, assumes that Donizetti was already in Milan at least by 28 November and quotes a letter from Calisto Bassi, librettist and handyman around La Scala, which speaks of the troubled rehearsals of *Maria Stuarda* and of a '*Maestro Orgasmo*' whom Verzino takes to refer to Donizetti. Bassi's letter bears the date 28 November, but either it is misdated, or else '*Maestro Orgasmo*' refers to someone else, for on 30 November Donizetti had only got as far as Genoa on his way to Milan.

for the opera commenced during the latter days of November, in the composer's absence. This whole production of *Maria Stuarda* was doomed to be cursed by bad luck.

In Naples, Donizetti had applied on 30 October for a two-month leave from his duties there, his absence to run from the beginning of December to the end of January, a period that would allow him both to stage *Maria Stuarda* in Milan in December and to proceed to Venice in January for *Belisario*. That Donizetti had other problems on his mind appears from a letter he wrote to Dolci on 29 October, just the day before he applied for his leave.

> Dearest friend,
> In all secrecy.
> My brother Francesco torments me continuously with two things; the first is the more painful, that papa is dying, that he stays up all night; that he absolutely needs money is the other thing, and on this he presses me terribly.
> If it is true that papa is in need; give him everything that mamma might ask, but if this is not true, write to me at once that I may calm myself.
> I just had a letter from Giuseppe of 25 days ago, and he says he sent 200 francs. If they have not received it, tell mamma to write as usual to *sig. Paolo De Gris, registrar of the R. Senate of Genoa*, who I believe is the usual one to send the money to them.
> I am composing for Venice and have no head for such sad news. Write me the truth.
> Greet Mayr, and forgive your
> > > > Donizetti.[1]

He took Virginia, who was nearly five months pregnant, to Rome and took a ship at Leghorn, arriving in Genoa near the end of November. On the 30th, his father's name-day, he writes to Signor Andrea, wishing him a hundred more such days.

> I had wanted to answer you from Milan, but as I stay here three days, thus I say I know you should have received the 200 francs. If not, I will arrange for you to have them. ... Do not come to Milan for now, as I do not know if I will stay there or if I will come at once to Bergamo. From there

[1] Z. No. 183, p. 390.

I will write to you. I leave Wednesday, today is Monday, Thursday I shall get there. Goodbye. Greetings to everyone.[1]

From this letter it is clear that Donizetti arrived in Milan on Thursday, 3 December 1835.

He got there to find the company at La Scala at cross-purposes. Besides Malibran as Maria, the role of Elisabetta had originally been assigned to Sofia dell'Oca-Schoberlechner, but she was dissatisfied with her part, feeling that it was not extensive enough in comparison to Malibran's to be worthy of a prima donna. She withdrew from the cast in a foul humour and succeeded in stirring up further dissension among the company. Donizetti found this situation confronting him when he got to the theatre, but before he was able to pacify the angry singers, he heard that his father had died on 9 December. He wrote at once to Dolci:

> I have received a letter from Marieni. It tells me a thing I cannot believe. If I could only have been there; in my true distress I turn to you so that you, so that Mayr, so that all, might make my filial duties for me. Spend a hundred, two hundred scudi, but let the funeral show the gratitude of one son, since [Giuseppe] cannot help because of distance and [Francesco] will not be able to help because of lack of funds.
>
> I will write to you. . . .
> Think of mamma in everything that she might need.[2]

This was a time of grief for Donizetti. Although on occasion he had been almost exasperated with his father, although he felt that his father had never understood or sympathized with or encouraged him in his career, he was nevertheless deeply aware of his obligations to his parents, and there is no question that Donizetti was keenly sensitive to the thought of death. He could not bring himself to go to Bergamo, and he could not leave La Scala where everything was in turmoil over *Maria Stuarda*.

It was not until 16 December that he signed a formal agreement with Visconti for his labours over that score, writing a new cabaletta and overture, supervising the rehearsals, for

---

[1] Z. No. 186, p. 392.   [2] Z. No. 187, p. 392.

which duties he was to receive 250 bavare. It is clear from a list of singers and their roles appended to the contract that the role of Elisabetta had not yet been filled after the defection of la Schoberlechner. That such a vital part was still open suggests that Donizetti's distress over his father's death prevented him from giving his full attention to the rehearsals.

Before the first performance, Malibran fell ill. She was unable to sing when the season opened on 26 December with a performance of *I Puritani*, the first in Milan, given with Schoberlechner and the tenor Antonio Poggi. On the 28th, Donizetti wrote to Dolci that he had no idea which day the first performance of *Maria Stuarda* would be, and his doubts about the opera were such that he recommended his friend to wait until he heard about the opera's reception before he came down from Bergamo to see it.

The first performance was given on 30 December; although Malibran was, according to Donizetti's description, 'voiceless', she insisted on singing anyway so as not to lose her fee of 3000 francs.[1] The others in the cast were Giacinta Puzzi-Toso, whom

[1] Since Malibran was the most famous singer of her day and much romantic nonsense has been written about her, it is interesting to recall a frank description of her by one who knew her well and had frequent opportunities of observing her at home.

Guillaume Cottrau's brother in Paris had written to him at the request of Countess Merlin for anecdotes of Malibran, shortly after the diva's death. Cottrau supplied the requested information, but he also appended his private observations, telling his brother Félix to keep them to himself: 'Is it good that I should tear aside the veil and show poor Malibran in all the nakedness of her egotism, of the poverty of her feelings where a crude education never allowed one ray of poetry to penetrate? This last assertion will doubtless seem exaggerated to you, but know that she never opened any other books but librettos, newspapers and the novels of Paul de Kock; that all ideas of the future, of devotion, of sacrifice to a sincere conviction were foreign to her; that she called trickery all other manner of thought; and that finally, to portray her in a word, I have seen her interrupt de Bériot, when he was reading a letter from Brussels with news of his son, to chat about business of the theatre! Yes, alas, this was the true heartless woman Balzac wrote of. Enough of this sad subject, for it is very sad, I assure you, for me who has realized the truth about this famous woman only little by little (and in the last days of a liaison that had grown very cold) at the time of her last departure [from Naples, March 1835].

'You see by the nature of these details that they are only for you, for I never open myself this way to anyone, not even to Jenny [his wife], who still preserves a lively enthusiasm for la Malibran....'

(*Lettres d'un mélomane*, p. 56.)

Donizetti also described as 'voiceless' (Elisabetta), Teresa Moja (Anna Kennedy), Domenico Reina (Leicester), Ignazio Marini (Talbot), and Pietro Novelli (Cecil). The audience was thoroughly displeased with Malibran for appearing in such poor vocal condition and made their displeasure manifest. Although the second and third performances went better, the damage had been done,[1] and the opera was removed from the bill after seven performances; however the first act (in which Maria Stuarda does not appear) was performed on four later evenings in conjunction with two acts of Rossini's *Otello*, in which Malibran enjoyed a triumph. It seems altogether probable that Malibran, for one reason or another, became prejudiced against Donizetti's opera and disliked appearing in it. She was a singer whose remarkable success stemmed from her strong will-power and her astonishing control of her recalcitrant voice. When she was out of sorts and out of voice, the results were not impressive. The English manager, Alfred Bunn, said of Malibran that to check her powers was to annihilate them! She performed a real disservice to *Maria Stuarda*, one of the best of Donizetti's unfamiliar operas, for it has gone down in history as an opera that not even Malibran could save.

This disappointment with *Maria Stuarda* did nothing to raise Donizetti's spirits. His frame of mind is shown in a series of letters he wrote to Dolci during these days.

On 28 December:

> ... For my coming home it is too soon. I don't have the courage. It will be instead on my return from Venice. Only to think of it makes me feel bad. I am not yet resigned and only distance distracts me. ...[2]

On 3 January:

> I have not seen you yet, and perhaps it is better, for (not the second nor the third) but the first evening you would have suffered and not a little from the ups and downs of *Stuarda* ... I don't go near the theatre any more. My brother writes that now mamma seems troubled by a blow on the arm—Everything is in order for me!
>
> I leave with Ricordi a hundred bavare for you. I don't know what I owe you, what you have spent for — Write

---

[1] The censors intervened, objecting to the scene where Maria and Elisabetta exchange insults, among other things.   [2] Z. No. 189, p. 393.

to me at Venice my debt and forgive me if I bother you. May the new year be better for my family. . . .

. . . through you . . . I hope to ease poor mamma so that she may live if not happily, at least tranquilly. . . .[1]

On 4 January:

Forgive if I send double letters, but yours reached me after I had posted mine. And in yours, the explanation of my debt is not too clear to me. . . .

Give me mamma's news often and yours. If there should be Cholera there, go to bed early at night and get up late in the morning, drink a lot of very hot tea, give up fruit and all vegetables, eat little, stay always hungry. Thus people lived at Genoa. Dissolve coralline in the evening and drink it in the morning.

Make my brother write to me often. Goodbye, greet everyone, everyone, everyone. I recommend to you the commendation to Antonio Bassi of my brother [for the succession of his father's position].

Tonight I leave by diligence.

P.S. How is Quarenghi? Write to me everything about everybody.[2]

Donizetti's inability to face Bergamo at this time, his not being able to bring himself to write the word 'funeral' when he asked Dolci how much he owed him for the expenses, both speak of a highly sensitive temperament. Just as Donizetti sought to avoid painful experiences, so he tried to dismiss them by losing himself in his work, by keeping himself so occupied that he had no time for distressing thoughts. In his earlier years his copiousness of composition resulted from his drive to establish and support himself; now, and even more so in the next few years, his continuing flood of music becomes something in the way of a compulsion. Donizetti escaped from Milan to lose himself in the preparations for *Belisario*.

Donizetti arrived in Venice on Wednesday, 6 January 1836, but a week was to pass before the rehearsals of *Belisario* began. On the 10th he wrote to Dolci to inquire about his mother and to report that there was no sign of cholera in Venice. On the 13th,

[1] Z. No. 190, p. 394.   [2] Z. No. 191, p. 395.

the day the rehearsals for his opera were to start, he writes again to Dolci, having heard that Francesco is planning to sell some of the things he and Giuseppe had sent their father.

> . . . Giuseppe sent 200 francs in November. Mamma, before I left, said she needed nothing. Now Francesco writes that he must sell those little gifts that Giuseppe and I sent to poor papa from time to time. What is going on? Does mamma need anything or doesn't she? It is impossible that they have used up the 200 francs besides the rest. But if this is so, go to mamma and ask her if it is true she is in need, and then make me the customary pleasure of a gracious loan; be careful however that Francesco is not offended. Tell him that I sent my answer to you instead of to him. Recommend him to Bassi in my name, I beg you, so that he will favour him, and so that mamma will not have the distress of seeing herself chased out. Answer me, calm me, and tell me if you have got the 100 bavare I left for you with Ricordi.
>
> Greet everyone. Mayr especially. How is the Cholera going?[1]

The recommendation to Bassi refers to Gaetano's hope that Francesco would be appointed to succeed his father at the Monte di Pietà. Lodgings were granted along with the post, and Gaetano was anxious that his mother should not have the additional trial of moving so soon after her bereavement. Since Francesco had filled his father's place during the old man's illness, Gaetano believed that his brother should be preferred for the simple duties, which amounted to little more than writing from dictation, and therefore were not too taxing to one of Francesco's limited intelligence. This matter was not settled at once, much to Donizetti's annoyance, for he believed that in this simple affair his appeal should carry some weight with his fellow Bergamascs. Eventually, Francesco's appointment was confirmed.

The season at the Fenice did not proceed auspiciously. In a production of Rossini's *L'assedio di Corinto*, the singer Antonietta Vial did not please, although she was popular outside the theatre because of her good looks. Her lack of success bothered Donizetti as she was to sing an important role in *Belisario*. With

[1] Z. No. 194, pp. 396–7.

the first performance of that opera, on 4 February, however, the fortunes of the season greatly improved, for *Belisario* won a clamorous success, attaining a run of twenty-eight performances. The strong cast included Carolina Ungher (Antonina), Vial (Irene), Badessi (Eudora), Celestino Salvatori (Belisario), Ignazio Pasini (Alamiro), De Giorgi (Giustiniano), Dell'Oro (Eutropio), and Giovanni Rizzi (Eusebio and Ottarino). The rousing choruses and other spectacular elements of the music insured the opera's early popularity. It opened the autumn season of 1836 at La Scala, where it was enthusiastically received, as performed by Eugenia Tadolini, Marietta Brambilla, Francesco Pedrazzi, and Salvatori repeating his Venetian success in the title role. *Belisario* was performed all over the world and found particular favour in Germany, where it held the stage throughout the nineteenth century.

Donizetti's own view of his work is expressed with his usual disarming frankness to Antonio Pacini, a Paris music publisher:

> ... *Belisario* is less thoroughly worked out [than *Lucia*], but I know that in the theatre it had an effect, that it did not deceive a population without some merit. — In any event I myself place it as a work below *Lucia*. ...[1]

The Venetians liked it so much that after the third performance, on 6 February, they escorted Donizetti home with a band and torchbearers.

On Monday, 8 February, Donizetti left Venice and started his journey back to Naples. He was anxious to get on his way, not only because his leave of absence had expired the last day of January, but to rejoin his pregnant wife. His journey started inauspiciously, as he informed Salvatori from Milan on 11 February.

> I don't write to you yet to thank you, for I should have to use more ink than St Thomas Aquinas, but only to tell you that past, present, and future generations should flee from the *Diligenza Franchetti* as (they say) the devil flees the cross. ... To leave Monday evening at 8 and to arrive in Milan Tuesday morning at 4. There is not a grain of truth in the excuse that the roads are very bad; it is the swinish greed either of the drivers or the agents who have

[1] Z. No. 205, p. 407, dated 19 April 1836.

the nerve to hitch 4 horses when there is a load of 600,000 weight.

. . . I leave from here Monday morning and go to Genoa. If you remember me when Eustacchio makes his famous meatballs, sigh in my direction and open your mouth to put in four. . . .

A thousand kisses to you, to Ungher, to Pasini, to Vial (and I will give them to her).

From Naples you will hear the rest. . . .[1]

On 15 February Donizetti sailed from Genoa; the voyage was stormy and the sea so rough that Donizetti despaired of reaching Leghorn safely. Badly shaken up, he disembarked and hurried on to Rome, but here was greeted by the news Virginia had been delivered prematurely of a still-born daughter. A few days later he was struck another grievous blow. On 5 March he wrote to Dolci:

> Then all is over? If I did not have such a strong constitution that I amaze myself by it, I too would forever join the others. Only three months on tour, and in three months I have lost father, mother,[2] and baby daughter, besides my wife is still sick because of a premature birth at seven and a half months.
>
> I have had my strength sustained a little by the outcome of *Belisario*, by having received the Legion of Honour, but only yesterday having learned of the loss of mamma too, I am in such a state of excessive dejection from which time alone can retrieve me, if I have that much will to live. I saw Francesco's letter, sent to me from Naples (since I am here in quarantine, and I leave the day after tomorrow).
>
> From that I learned that you thought of everything, and I for the second time am ready to pay you, and I beg you to send me the bill as soon as possible.
>
> It will be my responsibility to write to Giuseppe.
>
> As Francesco wants to know if everything that is left is for him alone, I will tell him this: that only the gold box I would love to have back. Of any jewellery there is, I, for my part, give it to him, and not only those things but

[1] Z. No. 196, p. 398.
[2] Domenica Nava Donizetti died 10 February 1836, aged seventy-one, of a stroke.

whatever would be owing to me in dividing what we have at home there.

I hear that you want my portrait, and he too makes a point of having it. Myself, I am for you, but if Francesco should make great difficulties, I will send you another. He will have a copy made of it and could let you have it, but —who knows!

As far as Giuseppe giving up his share, I am going to write to him now, and I hope he will think as I do. Further; if the granddaughter should want some of the women's clothing, he could give it to her, if he wanted, for the company she was to those poor things. See to it he doesn't get the idea of selling the portrait of my wife, for goodness' sake.

Let me know if he gets the job in the *Monte*, if Bassi remembered me.

My friend, it is very unlikely that I should see those places again, where I have lost everything; but you, I hope, will come to Naples, and I tell you now and forever, remember that you have house, bed, fire and table. I find no way to thank you, and I beg you to give my greetings to our good Mayr.

I hope to have a good trip. Greet Sig. Rosina [Basoni], her pretty daughter, Pontiroli, and tell my brother that I did not answer his letter until now for they held his letter a secret from me. Greet him and may he stay well, and you too.

Addio. . . .[1]

The letter poignantly reveals Donizetti's state of mind. Even in this state of shock and grief, he thought of Francesco's welfare and that of his niece, but the idea of going back to Bergamo was unendurable to him then. On the evening of 6 March he and Virginia started their sad journey back to Naples.

There he found things in a not very encouraging state. Both the San Carlo and the Fondo were closed, the Società having given them up. Only the Nuovo remained open, but it was not drawing well. Not until 4 June,[2] when Barbaja resumed control of the Royal Theatres on a four-year lease, did operatic

[1] Z. No. 197, p. 399.
[2] On this date Barbaja signed the lease; Donizetti was apprised of Barbaja's plans by at least 31 May (the day before the *prima* of *Il campanello*), for on that date he wrote to Lanari: *Barbaja è finalmente impresario.*

activity in Naples resume its normal patterns. With nothing to occupy him in the opera houses, Donizetti could only resume his classes in counterpoint and composition at the Conservatory. He also reverted to a form of activity that had not engaged him for the past eleven years—he wrote a string quartet, his eighteenth, and the opening allegro in E minor he was later to use in the overture to *Linda di Chaumonix*. Some of the emotional intensity generated by his recent sorrows finds its way into this restless, sombre music.

Helping to brighten these dark days was his pleasure at being made a Chevalier of the Legion of Honour. Louis-Philippe had decreed the honour on 2 February and the official notification of it had been dispatched from Paris on the 13th. Along with his formal acceptance, Donizetti had to send a copy of his birth certificate. He wrote to Dolci for it, admonishing him that his name was spelled with a single 'z' and not the 'zz' that most people in Bergamo used. His most revealing comments about the Legion of Honour, however, appear in a letter he wrote to the Paris banker, Auguste de Coussy on 24 March:

> After a thousand and one quarantines I came to Naples and from here I girded myself to write to the famous Rossini to thank him for the act of friendship in sending me himself the letters from M. Thiers. Now I hear from many people that Rossini is in Rome. Imagine my discomfort in thinking that my letter of thanks to the Minister will remain in the post office until the great Maestro returns to Paris. . . .
>
> . . . would you tell M. Severini that if he should have an order to open Rossini's letters coming from Italy, would he have the further kindness to forward the letter to President M. Thiers at the earliest opportunity so that I should not pass for ungrateful or uneducated. . . .
>
> Would you believe it? When I first heard of my nomination, my first thought after you was that of saying: How Zélie will have rejoiced! I can still see her happiness just at the idea of being able to succeed in this difficult assignment. Imagine how it is waiting for the thing to be done—and imagine how touched I am by such friendship.
>
> I tell you that if there is any expense you have only to speak. . . .

I have needed this and the most fortunate success of my *Belisario* in Venice, for I have lost in three months, father, mother, and daughter. I do not wish to distress you.

If the news is false that Rossini is in Italy, greet him for me. . . .[1]

Soon after writing this letter to de Coussy, Donizetti was harassed by more disquieting news from Bergamo. Francesco wrote to him that their brother-in-law, Tironi, was advancing a claim for part of the inheritance. This news exasperated Gaetano as Tironi had already received a marriage settlement when he married Maria Antonia. If he wanted to make a claim now, Donizetti wrote to Dolci, he should be willing to pay a share of the funeral expenses, which Gaetano and Giuseppe had borne alone. Gaetano asked his friend to remind Francesco to be careful to make an affidavit that everything in the house, except the clothing for the granddaughter, was bequeathed to him orally by their mother. He told Dolci to insist that Francesco keep this affidavit as well as the receipt for Maria Antonia's dowry. After worrying about Francesco's getting the job in the pawnshop, he reverted to the phrases that run through the letters of this time like a litany:

> For the rest let it be as heaven wills. I have had more vicissitudes in three months than anyone else. I lost father, mother, daughter, my wife is still sick, a most praiseworthy friend of my brother-in-law died, I survived by a miracle a storm between Genoa and Leghorn, here the theatres are closed hence the money is stopping. *Pazienza!* . . .[2]

Donizetti's spirits did not begin to improve until the chance to compose a new opera appeared. In May he entered into negotiations with Lanari, who had secured the lease of the Fenice for the coming Carnival. It is possible to follow the details of these parleyings because Lanari's side of the correspondence is in the library of the Conservatory of Naples.

The earliest of the extant letters is Lanari's of 5 May from Florence, in which he alluded to an earlier letter of Donizetti's dated 28 April, apparently lost. In this letter Lanari informed Donizetti of the proposed company, consisting of Persiani, the

[1] Z. No. 200, pp. 401–2.   [2] Z. No. 203, p. 405.

contralto Rosina Mazzarelli (whom Lanari believed could cope with a good part), the tenor Poggi, and either Marini or Coletti as basses. It was still not perfectly certain if there would be funds for the season, but Lanari would leave for Venice the following day to confer with Count Berti, the President of the Spectacles at the Fenice, to get the matter settled. In the meantime he would offer Donizetti 8000 francs for the score and promise to publish it after a year, further he would pay 100 scudi to Cammarano for a libretto.

Donizetti's reply, written 12 May, begins: 'It would cost you much less trouble to say *I don't want you* than to make me such a ridiculous proposal.' Lanari, however, had already written to him again, on the 9th from Venice, repeating his offer and adding that he was doing his best to make a better offer than Fabbrici had made for *Belisario*. Then Lanari reverts to la Mazzarelli, whom he hoped would be capable of taking a principal part in Donizetti's opera along with Persiani. On the 17th, Lanari, now back in Florence, replied to Donizetti's letter of the 12th, saying he could not understand how Donizetti could call 8000 francs ridiculous, but as proof of his good faith he would send Donizetti two copies of the contract with the amount left blank to allow him to name his own price and to put forward his own conditions. He also asked Donizetti to write a letter recommending Mazzarelli to Count Berti.

The very day that Lanari's letter was sent from Florence, Donizetti in Naples was writing to Count Berti to give his opinion of Mazzarelli, not because he was psychic, but because on 10 May the Count had written to him asking Donizetti to pass judgement on her. Donizetti's terms were guarded.

> . . . It would be difficult for anyone to give a just opinion of the talent of Signora Mazzarelli for the theatre. She has not yet made a début. Who can foresee what will be the outcome of her first appearance? She is endowed with a beautiful contralto voice; the first and only time I heard her she sang with sufficient expression. . . .
>
> As for me I have not been able to reach an agreement with Sig. Lanari. . . .[1]

On the 19th, Lanari wrote to report that the first production in Florence of *Marino Faliero* was a great hit. '*Furore! Fanatismo!*'

[1] Z. No. 209, p. 409, dated 17 May 1836.

By the 21st, Donizetti had received the blank contracts, but before he returned them he wanted to assure himself of the operas that would be performed before and after his. He wanted to avoid the situation that happened with *Lucia*, which had been given directly after Giuseppe Persiani's *Danao* when 'that good Fanny' did not sing well; everyone said that it was because she preferred to sing in her husband's compositions. Since he had received 8000 francs from Fabbrici for *Belisario* and 2000 more from Ricordi for the rights of 'reduction', he was now asking Lanari for 10,000 francs to be paid in gold napoleons and for that sum he would cede him all rights whatsoever to the score. On 31 May Donizetti signed the contract on those terms.

On the 4 June, Lanari had received the contract, and felt that Donizetti was receiving 'a pretty wage for a Maestro. . . .' He reports that the enthusiasm over *Marino Faliero* keeps growing in Florence, and that Mazzarelli will shortly make her début as Adalgisa in *Norma*. The true reason for all this interest in Mazzarelli emerged only gradually. When Donizetti and Cammarano agreed on the plot of *Pia de' Tolomei*, which appealed to them as a suitable vehicle for Persiani, they decided there was no place in the plot for another female character, which meant no role for Mazzarelli. When Lanari heard of this, he was resigned to it; but Count Berti, when he got wind of it, absolutely refused to approve *Pia* unless it contained a role for his protégée. Donizetti yielded to this pressure and wrote to Lanari on 28 June to insert into the contract the clause that Berti insisted upon: that the opera be written for two prima donnas.

> . . . [Mazzarelli] will do the role of Pia's brother. She will have a Cavatina, not much in the Finale as she has to escape, and a big *scena* with chorus in the second act. An understudy's part and nothing more. If this is enough for you, if this is convenient, you write at once that I accept, and tell him further that Dante speaks of Pia and Sestini at greater length in a novella. I am working on the introduction for Poggi. . . .[1]

On 2 July, Lanari reported he had written to Count Berti of Donizetti's agreement to use Mazzarelli in a *musico* role, and

[1] Z. No. 214, p. 413, dated 28 June 1836.

again he added his belief that she had the makings of a major artist. When Lanari took his company to Leghorn she would sing in *Il nuovo Figaro* by Ricci, in *Tasso* with Ronconi, and then in *L'elisir*. In his next letter, he reminds Donizetti that she is a mezzo-soprano with good low tones, a fact that suggests her roles, especially in *L'elisir*, would have to be extensively transposed.

The last extant letter in this series is by Lanari from Leghorn on 19 August. He had not written earlier, he explains, because he had been very busy. He said that Berti had been pressing him hard to have the plot of *Pia*. 'Hurry, because you know as well as I the prolixity of that President.' He wants to know the ordinance of the work: notes of the costumes, the supernumeraries, and whether there is a band, reminding Donizetti that the Fenice chorus consists of eleven men and twelve women. In this letter there is nothing about Mazzarelli, suggesting that her appearances at Leghorn were not up to expectation. Nor did she make a hit in Venice; in fact, the following year when Lanari gave *Pia*, he eliminated part of the music of Mazzarelli's role and assigned it to a second tenor.

While Donizetti had been engaged in his dealings with Lanari and Count Berti, he was writing an opera for the Teatro Nuovo. Adam[1] tells an apocryphal tale, which many writers on Donizetti have mindlessly perpetuated, of the manager of a little theatre who had fallen in dire straits and appealed to Donizetti to save him by writing him an opera and of how in a week's time Donizetti presented him with the complete score of *Il campanello*. The actual story of the origin of the opera seems to be rather different. For one thing, the date of 7 June 1836 usually given for the first performance of *Il campanello* is wrong; both Loewenberg and the current Ricordi score give the right date. That this is correct is corroborated by a letter written by Cottrau on the 4th.

I send you two duos from a charming comic opera by Donizetti, *Il campanello*, which has just been given here with an unheard of success the first of this month. The subject is taken from a very droll vaudeville, *La sonnette de*

[1] A. Adam, *Derniers souvenirs d'un musicien* (Paris, 1859), p. 307.

nuit, that Benedict sent me and which I proposed to our composer.

The music in it is delicious in my opinion. . . . I have just bought the rights of *Il campanello* and I send you a letter from Donizetti with the address left blank for the relinquishing of printing rights for France.

Barbaja just took over again the theatres, the San Carlo and the Fondo, for four years with the help of stock-holders. . . .

At this moment Donizetti is composing *Pia de' Tolomei*; it will be performed at the Teatro Fenice of Venice towards the end of January. I have bought in advance the rights to this work, and I should like to negotiate it in advance. . . . I could also dispose of these ariettes and six little chamber duos that Donizetti composed at the Villa Majo and which are of the same type as the *Soirées musicales* of Rossini. . . .[1]

This letter provides much useful information about *Il campanello*. It explains the provenance of the libretto, which Donizetti wrote himself. It reminds us that the Nuovo did not count as a minor theatre, and on 1 June was the only one then open in Naples, as Barbaja, just having resumed the director-ship of the Royal Theatres, would not have been able to commence performances immediately. The letter also makes it clear that by 4 June at least two of the duets from *Il campanello* were already printed, which suggests that the score had not been written as hastily as the apocryphal anecdote would suggest.

Il campanello was performed by Amalia Schütz (Serafina), Giorgio Ronconi (Enrico) and Carlo Casaccia (Don Annibale). The personnel of this cast further gives the lie to the old story, for Ronconi was one of the leading baritones of the day and would scarcely be appearing in a minor theatre. *Il campanello* held the stage for a long time in Naples, but it does not seem to have been very widely performed until comparatively recently, when it has become a staple of the workshop repertory.

Nor was *Il campanello* the only opera written by Donizetti in the summer of 1836. On 24 August he brought out another one-act opera, *Betly*, for which he also wrote his own libretto, this time adapting Scribe's libretto for Adam's *Le chalet*. *Betly* was

[1] Cottrau, *Lettres d'un mélomane*, p. 44. The songs by Donizetti written at the Villa Majo are known as *Nuits d'été à Pausilippe*.

sung at the Nuovo by Adelaide Toldi (Betly), Lorenzo Salvi (Daniele) and Giuseppe Fioravanti (Max). The contrast between the rowdy, satirical farce of *Il campanello* and the pastoral naïveté of *Betly* delighted the audience. Cottrau gives us some idea of the flavour of the early performances when he writes to his relatives in Paris on 11 October.

> Launer has had the idea of buying the pieces of *Betly* and intends to have the opera performed at the Italiens. As I am the proprietor of the score, and since a success in Paris would make it the fashion, you can imagine how this project pleases me. *Betly* has only three roles, soprano (Toldi), tenor (Salvi), bass (Fioravanti). Grisi could undertake the first, the second would suit Ivanoff marvellously, for it depicts a simple type and it is well placed for the voice, and without roulades, of a sort that Rubini would probably refuse. The third role was sacrificed here by Fioravanti, who has no voice left and had to change the cavatina after the second performance, but he is a very good actor. The role is the best of the three and the opera would be a fiasco at Paris if it was not played by Lablache. . . . You could tell him that besides the cavatina that Donizetti had to change and the duo with the tenor, there is another with the soprano in the best situation in the work. . . . Use then your most persuasive arguments to urge him and also so that he will put in a good word for the choice of the opera.
>
> I want to tell you another essential thing, *Betly* is only the pendant to *Il campanello*, a charming farce that is a burst of laughter from beginning to end. I would like the two pieces together. As to the later, it is marvellously well adapted for Lablache and Tamburini. . . .[1]

Betly was subsequently produced in Paris, but not at the Italiens. In 1853 it was sung at the Opéra to a new libretto by Hippolyte Lucas, carpentered to fit Donizetti's music, but it played only five performances in spite of the presence of the charming Angiolina Bosio as the heroine. Earlier *Betly* had undergone another change when Donizetti expanded the work into two acts for the Teatro Carolino in Palermo. This version was first sung on 29 October 1837 by Irene Secci-Corsi,

[1] Cottrau, *Lettres d'un mélomane*, pp. 47–8.

Ambrogio Danini, and Eugenio Mazzotti. In its new form the opera became a great favourite, and Betly's cavatina one of the popular airs of the day. After suffering an eclipse at the end of the century, *Betly*, like *Il campanello*, shows signs of taking a new lease on life, having been successfully revived in a number of small Italian theatres in the last decade or so.

To Ferretti in July, after twitting his friend that he had become his rival as a librettist, Donizetti gave an inkling of his next project. 'I am writing, with an appropriate ballet, *L'assedio di Calais*. Eustachio di Saint-Pierre will be sung by your Barroilhet. With la Manzocchi as a *musico*.' At first he had believed the opera would be produced in September, but fear of an outbreak of cholera delayed its production. In September he told Dolci that people were not going to the theatre, but apparently he meant the San Carlo, for in the same letter he told him 'half of Naples is running to see *Betly*'. The rehearsals got under way in October, for on the 19th Donizetti wrote to Spadaro:

> . . . I am rehearsing for the 19th of the coming month . . .
> *L'assedio di Calais*. The rabid rages begin, and with them
> the ravings, the palpitations, and the fears. . . .[1]

Exactly on 19 November, the evening being a gala for the Queen Mother, *L'assedio di Calais* was given at the San Carlo with Almerinda Manzocchi (Aurelio), Caterina Barili (Eleonora), Pierre Barroilhet (Eustacchio), Federico Lablache, the son of the great Luigi, (Edoardo III), Tucci (Edmondo), Pietro Gianni (The Unknown), Ferdinando Cimino (Giovanni d'Aire), Freni (Giacomo de Wisants), Revalden (Pietro de Wisants) and Giuseppe Benedetti (Armando). Three days later Donizetti describes the evening to Ricordi:

> *L'assedio di Calais* has gone well. I was called out six
> times (the evening after the gala). The third act is the least
> effective (you see my sincerity). Who knows but I might
> retouch it. . . . It is my most thoroughly worked out opera.
> Barroilhet, Manzocchi, Barili, Gianni, all applauded. But
> the cholera keeps everyone in the country. I leave early
> next month.
>
> If you print it all, wait until I see it again in Milan, and

[1] Z. No. 223, p. 420.

on the first page of the score perhaps I will put: *dedicated to H.M. the Queen etc.*

The King sent a chamberlain to congratulate me, and tomorrow I go to thank him. But the cholera distresses everybody and the theatre will be deserted just the same. . . .[1]

Writing to Dolci the same day he repeated much of this, but added his observations that the ballet slowed down the action and he was considering cutting it. For an opera of unusual interest and merit, *L'assedio di Calais* had a very disappointing career. After these few performances to a half-deserted house in Naples, it was never again given in Italy. The following year, Donizetti toyed with the idea of adapting it for the Opéra in Paris, but nothing came of that project. More than a century has passed since *L'assedio di Calais* was performed.[2]

When Donizetti sailed from Naples on 6 December, Virginia stayed behind as she was in the early months of her third pregnancy and to the normal hazards of travelling that winter was added the discomfort of lengthy quarantines due to the fear of cholera. The following day Gaetano sent her a letter from the roadstead of Leghorn, the ship not being permitted to dock for fear of the epidemic, to inform her that he had got that far safely. When the letter arrived, it had been heavily fumigated.

The next day Donizetti reached Genoa, where he had to undergo a period of sixteen days' isolation in the Lazaretto. Rather grimly he resigned himself to this dreary prospect, especially since it meant he would still be there at Christmas. He was not cheered to learn that on the night of 12 December, the Fenice in Venice, the opera house where *Pia de' Tolomei* was scheduled to be performed, had been destroyed by fire. Next, he received a letter from Venice informing him that everyone connected with the proposed season had been asked, because of the disaster, to give up a quarter of their salary. He wrote back

[1] Z. No. 225, p. 421.

[2] Umberto Manferrari, *Dizionario delle opere melodrammatiche* (vol. 1, pp. 321–35), gives a not very accurate listing of performances of Donizetti's operas. He mentions a *rifacimento* of *L'assedio di Calais*, given at the Imperial Theatre, St Petersburg, in 1851. Loewenberg does not mention this opera.

that he would give up a thousand francs but no more, since he had all the expense of travelling and of his long quarantine to pay. He waited, half-expecting the management to break his contract. On 28 December he explained to Mayr from Milan why he could not get to Bergamo:

> The fire at the Fenice, the quarantine at Genoa, and the indecision in which the directors at Venice leave me, make it impossible for me to come to Bergamo. I leave tomorrow. . . .[1]

Donizetti arrived in Venice shortly before the end of the year. The performances that were to be given at the Fenice had been moved to the Teatro Apollo, Venice. Not only was the season late in starting, but the rehearsals were delayed when the baritone Salvatori fell ill and had to give up his contract; they could not begin until his replacement, Giorgio Ronconi, arrived on the scene. Sometime before the rehearsals of *Pia* started, Donizetti went back to Milan, but he had returned to Venice by 24 January. At long last the first performance of *Pia de' Tolomei* was given on 18 February 1837. Persiani sang Pia, while Rosina Mazzarelli, Antonio Poggi, and Ronconi filled the roles of Rodrigo, Ghino, and Nello, respectively. On 20 February, Donizetti sent a brief report to Dolci.

> It seems strange that you and our good Mayr are expecting me now in Bergamo, when a month ago from Milan no one answered me. Know that it is impossible for me now as then to make the excursion, since my leave of absence expired on the 6th of the month. I am leaving the day after tomorrow by way of Ferrara to make the best time. *Pia* pleased, all except the finale of the first act. . . . Remember me to our Mayr and to all his household, to Signora Rosina, to my brother and friends and I will see you next year since I return to Venice for the re-opening.[2]

In the last phrases of the letter Donizetti alluded to the fact that on that same day he had signed a contract to compose an opera for the following year when the Fenice would be rebuilt and re-opened.

Donizetti had not been back in Naples long and had hardly resumed his various duties, when he received a letter from

[1] Z. No. 231, p. 425.   [2] Z. No. 233, pp. 426–7.

Lanari, written from Venice on 25 February, with news of *Pia* and reminding him of a promise.

> ... The noisy stretta of the finale of *Pia* does not produce any effect. ...
>
> As a whole, the opera continues to please, especially the duet in the first act and all of Ronconi's *scena*. I beg of you to think of me for a new finale since you have planned it and have promised me, being assured of my gratitude. With this new piece *Pia* will be an opera equal to or perhaps better than *Belisario*. La Samayloff and Poggi are furious with you for leaving without going to see them, since Poggi has been the support of your opera. ...[1]

On 22 May, Donizetti sent Lanari the new finale, which was introduced into *Pia* when the opera was put on in Sinigaglia in July.[2] *Pia de' Tolomei* was given at the San Carlo in October 1838 and for this production Donizetti made some alterations, including a revised closing scene. On this occasion the opera was sung by Ronzi, Buccini, Basadonna, and Barroilhet.

At about the same time Donizetti wrote the first finale, he also composed a *pièce d'occasion* which could not have taken much of his attention; this was a Sinfonia for a cantata to be sung at La Scala in memory of Malibran, the proceeds of the performance going to a monument to the singer who had died the previous September in England as the result of being thrown and dragged by a horse. The other composers who contributed music to the cantata, *In morte di Maria F. Malibran*, were Pacini, Mercadante, Vaccai, and Coppola; the singers taking part in the performance included Sofia Schoberlechner and Francesco Pedrazzi; unfortunately, the evening must have been far from a success, for the official records of La Scala starkly describe it as having: *esito cattivo*.

Some time at the beginning of May, Donizetti wrote to his brother-in-law that he was cursing as he tried to find a subject for his new opera. At that moment Donizetti held contracts for two operas: one for the San Carlo for the summer or autumn, the other for Venice the following Carnival. He also tells Toto

---

[1] Unpublished letter in the library of the Naples Conservatory. A transcript is in the Museo Donizettiano, Bergamo.

[2] Cammarano's text for the new finale to Act 1 of *Pia* is printed in *Studi Donizettiani I*, pp. 146–51.

Vasselli that on 5 May, he and Virginia were moving from their quarters on the Via Corsea to an apartment he had bought the previous November, situated on the fourth floor of Strada Nardonnes, No. 14, just a few minutes' walk from the San Carlo.

On 5 May another event occurred which was to have a more drastic effect on Donizetti's future. On that day Nicola Zingarelli, the director of the Royal Conservatory in Naples, died. Donizetti was named pro-director and, according to Florimo, given verbal assurances that it was just a matter of time until appointment as director would be verified. At his death Zingarelli was eighty-six and had held his post since 1816. Neapolitan by birth, a schoolmate of Cimarosa, he was a conservative old man, without sympathy for the innovations of Rossini, and a passionate perpetuator of the old traditions of the school of Naples. Bellini had been a pupil of Zingarelli's, and of his pupils then living in Naples Florimo and Mercadante were easily the most prominent. To them Donizetti was scarcely a happy choice as Zingarelli's successor, for he had been educated elsewhere, and in those days of a divided Italy, Donizetti was regarded in Naples as a 'foreigner'. That all was not to go smoothly with Donizetti's future at the Naples Conservatory is no cause for surprise.

Donizetti wrote a Mass for Zingarelli which was performed in June. At this time he was also engaged in making a *rifacimento* of *Rosmunda d'Inghilterra*, rebaptized *Eleonora di Gujenna*, which was sung at the San Carlo that year without winning any more favour than its earlier version. He was also involved in a correspondence with Lanari about the opera for Venice. There were questions first of all whether Lanari would get the lease for the season, whether the restoration of the Fenice would be complete and the interior dry enough to perform in, whether this singer or that would come. Lanari, as always, hoped to please Donizetti by sending him reports of successful performances of his operas. From Bologna on 22 May he writes:

... You will be happy that this evening is the last performance of *Lucia* which has made what must be called a furore. In this opera Moriani made himself immortal. Strepponi, following the example of Palazzesi, has changed her aria and replaced it with that of *Fausta*, which pleases.

The adagio of the finale [the sextet] is repeated every evening. . . .[1]

The first hint of tragedy appears in a letter Donizetti wrote Mayr on 21 June, telling him about the Requiem Mass for Zingarelli.

> . . . Dear Maestro, I am not indolent by nature, and 57 works for the stage prove it.
>
> In three days I wrote a mass for the dead for poor Zingarelli. But if it will be performed, perhaps it will not give a wicked effect. I remembered one of your imitations. . . . What after so many years? Yes, sir, after so many years. The beautiful remains ineradicably engraved like the word of God. I could tell you many sad things, but to what good?
>
> Stay well. . . .[2]

The 'many sad things' that he might mention, but did not refer to, was his grief over the unhappy termination of Virginia's third pregnancy. She had been delivered of a son on the 13 June at four in the afternoon, but the child lived a very short time. According to the child's death certificate, the pitiful little body was brought the following day at six to the registry of the S. Ferdinando district by two of Donizetti's closest friends: Aniello Benevento, a lawyer thirty years old, and Tommaso Persico, a business man aged thirty-one. That Virginia had puerperal fever seems clear from a letter Gaetano sent to Cottrau a few days later:

> . . . Donna Virginia has been very ill, but now she is better. Diarrhoea, milk drying up almost completely! She coughs —We hope for the best. I stop because Barbaja is here bothering me. God knows what he wants. . . .[3]

To add an unindelible atmosphere of horror to this trying time for Donizetti, Naples was in the grip of a violent epidemic of cholera. It had broken out in April, and by the end of June there were more than five hundred new cases each day and more than three hundred fatalities. One of the Queen Mother's

---

[1] Unpublished letter in the library of the Naples Conservatory. Transcript in the Museo Donizettiano, Bergamo.
[2] Z. No. 240, p. 431.   [3] Z. No. 243, p. 433.

ladies-in-waiting was seized by the disease and carried off in less than two hours, just before King Ferdinando left Naples to take the royal family to the safety of Manfredonia. There were even cases among the students at the Conservatory. Donizetti wrote these details to his friend Spadaro at Messina, and adds:

> ... we are alive. I cannot go to the country because of the forty days of Donna Virginia; therefore I stay and wait to see if it attacks me—
> Meanwhile I am well. . . .[1]

The forty days he refers to is the traditional period for which a woman was immobilized following childbirth.

A week later, Donizetti, hearing of the cholera in Messina, sent to Spadaro the regimen which he and Virginia had been following to protect themselves from the disease.

> A true preservative against the cholera! Don't be attacked by it! By that you will understand that it is necessary to set your heart at peace as I do, for already I have been exposed to it four times. My regimen and that of my household, where everyone stays perfectly well, is this: Banish every sort of vegetable except cooked onions. Then soup with noodles, and rice: boiled, fried, and moist. And roast meat: either veal, or beef, or chicken; no lamb. Never salad; instead of fruit, sweets, but made at home and iced. Less fat than you normally use; I make much use of very fresh butter. Eggs, but only the freshest. Potato *vol au vent*, pasties of rice with chicken giblets. In the morning, coffee, then later lunch also with coffee, and in the evening (even tonight the 8th of July), boiling tea and a biscuit. If one is seized with diarrhoea, one must cure oneself at once and not wait until the third day; for pains in the belly decoction of camomile is excellent. It is most difficult to die if the cure in the beginning is not upset. It is necessary to understand that it is easier to have a relapse in the time of convalescence than to catch it in the first place. My very existence and my health I believe I owe to the last wine you sent, and on this point I recommend you drink it. . . . I was not even attacked by the grippe. It will be perhaps a mockery, but I recommend you eat

[1] Z. No. 242, p. 432.

lightly if you can, and in the evening drink only tea or a crouton in wine. . . .

Farewell. If you are afraid, come here, for every day it lessens and will end soon. At Palermo it is deadly. The soldiers go, the money goes . . . there is a disaster. And as usual they believe things are poisoned as they do everywhere. Farewell.[1]

Although the cholera began to lessen in Naples, it raged in other parts of Italy. Gaetano and Virginia followed their regimen faithfully, but if his wife's condition had improved for a time following the birth of their child, the improvement was illusory. Virginia caught a very severe case of measles. In an effort to ease her discomfort, she was given a bath, which produced a violent reaction. The details of her last moments were sent by Donizetti's friend, the painter Teodoro Ghezzi, to Toto.

. . . I am distressed to have to touch a wound that will cause you pain, but not speaking of it would be very much worse, therefore . . . for now I tell you that that angel of a woman died truly like an angel, that her last words were of her distress at having to leave a dear mother and brother, and her Gaetano whom she loved so much on earth, and more than anything she asked of her mother, in a moment of calm, for her blessing before leaving her forever, without being able to embrace her, without being able to see her brother, without at the last having around her her dearest ones! In the final ten minutes of agony, only so long did her last suffering endure, she lost consciousness, she did not speak again. . . .

Write often to Donizetti. . . .[2]

Virginia Vasselli Donizetti died at four o'clock in the morning on 30 July 1837, at the age of twenty-eight. A memorial service rather than a funeral was held at S. Maria delle Grazie on the via Toledo, for Virginia had been buried the day she died. Since the grief-stricken Donizetti could not face going back to the Strada Nardonnes, Persico took him home with him. For several days he stayed in bed, unable to get up. It was Persico who sent the first news of the tragedy to Toto.

[1] Z. No. 244, p. 434.   [2] Z. No. 250(b), p. 439.

On 5 August Donizetti began to try to pick up the pieces of his life. He wrote to Toto:

> Oh! My Toto, my Toto, let my grief find an echo in yours, because I need someone who understands me. I will be unhappy eternally. Don't drive me away, think that we are alone on earth. Oh, Toto, Toto, write to me, for good-ness' sake, for love of your,
>
> Gaetano[1]

He also wrote to Spadaro:

> I am a widower—what more to say! Excuse me if my grief does not let me give you long descriptions—*I am a widower*, and you will understand how much pain it exacts to feel it and to write such a word! . . .
>
> Tomorrow the wine is finished and the cholera. And it is an original thing, that as the last time, one passed, and the other finished! . . .
>
> Don't speak to me, in answering, of my being a widower. . . .[2]

On the same day he tried to transact some needed business. He had Cottrau write a letter to Lanari for him. At the end of this letter, Donizetti added a few words in his own hand. After speaking of his operas, he wrote: 'I am a widower. Nothing more. Pray for her. *Addio!*'[3]

From Rome on 10 August, Toto sent a letter to Donizetti, but it was written before he had received the first news from his brother-in-law.

> Our misfortune does not offer room for comfort. Perhaps time will lessen the grief, but for now it is impossible. I ought to preserve myself for mamma, Gaetano, and Irene, who would enter a convent, if I should die. If I were alone, I would go travelling through the hospitals to catch the cholera.
>
> You do not write to me, and I do not know how you are, and finally I do not know how and in what circum-

[1] Z. No. 246, p. 436.
[2] Z. No. 247, p. 436.
[3] From an unpublished letter in the library of the Liceo Musicale, Bologna. Reproduced with kind permission. Since published in *Studi Donizettiani I*, pp. 41–2.

stances the death of that Angel occurred. Oh Gaetano, how much we have both lost!

My poor old mother is with me in my suffering.

Write to me, and tell me that I am

your Toto.[1]

To this letter Gaetano replies on the 12th.

Do not torture me by believing that I have not written to you. I have done it when I hardly could, and you are the first to whom I addressed letters. The how and when I have lost the one I loved so much, excuse me, my Toto, but I am not yet able to tell you. I still believe I am dreaming, still the fatal door is closed, and still I do not trust myself to stay alone.

The pain that I feel for you all is equal to my own. But, believe it, Toto, that I did not spare anything: three-day services, prayers, three doctors, *the mid-wife*—

And what good is saying anything?—I will be eternally unhappy! I do not dare tell you to come in October, because of the pain I cause you, but perhaps an outburst will help us both. They are not dying of cholera here, for I would already be underground. Never invoke death as now you do. Patience!

This morning I gave away the new cradle, that was to have served—Everything, everything I have lost.

Without father, without mother, without wife, without children—for whom do I work then? Oh! My Toto, come, I beg you on my knees, come in October.

Perhaps you will be of comfort to me—and I to you. For the disease, it will be finished because today there were seven cases. The house was for her, the carriage for her— She never even tried it. God—God—Toto *mio*, write and forgive me if I bother you more than usual. I will be unhappy, you alone are left me, until she will have interceded with God for my death and our eternal union. Farewell, greet mamma. . . .[2]

On the 15 August Toto answered Gaetano's most recent letter.

In reading your letter I started to weep like a child, and I felt better. The continual grief that I feel is so deaf, so

[1] Z. No. A. 9, p. 869. [2] Z. No. 248, pp. 436–7.

deep, so persistent, that if I had such an outburst of tears on the 6th or 7th of this month, I would suffer less. It is impossible that I should find peace.

My Virginia, you went to heaven to join the other Virginia, and the angel of our Father. Your loving soul caused you suffering in this world, and while you wrote to me you were happy, you were taken away.

You, my Gaetano, must feel more than I the loss we have endured. How much that poor creature adored you! She guarded you like a treasure and feared that all the women wanted to steal you away. I know, my friend, that you loved her, and that you spared nothing for her, I know it. But what is the use? We are both unhappy. I must preserve myself so as not to send my mother to poverty, and my brother, my niece, otherwise I would go to find the Cholera as one searches for peace. I am inexpressibly weary of life.

I promise you nothing for October, but be certain that I need you as you need me. Write to me when you can. You have attached your life to something glorious, and you have the Italian spirit, you know how to feel this vital illusion. But I am lost in the herd. I vegetate in my tedious life like a plant in a bog. . . .

. . . Remember that evening of July 1826 in the Piazza Colonna when I promised you Virginia.[1]

The other Virginia that Toto mentions in this letter was his fiancée who had died not long before.

The intensity of feeling generated by this correspondence sometimes brought Donizetti a feeling of numbness, as is shown by his letter of 17 August.

. . . I risk wounding you justly, because it seems to me that we feel no remorse, and God knows whether I speak the truth and whether I have failed to keep my promises. Forgive if I open the wound. . . .

He urges Toto to come to Naples in October because:

. . . perhaps then it will be decided if I must die here for the Conservatory, or whether I can flee for some little time from these places, from this furniture, from these stairs.

[1] Z. No. A. 10, p. 870.

My Toto, come, come, come. You need it, I can't do without it!

Write to me always. . . .[1]

That Toto appreciated Gaetano's feelings is clear from his answer of 22 August.

Ah, if I could, as if I will ever stop writing to you, oh my Gaetano, as you say to me in your last letter. But how can I come if I should have to leave this poor old woman alone in such danger, and what would I do in the solitude of an eternal quarantine? . . .

As the cholera had now broken out in Rome, where the epidemic was to nearly equal the intensity it had reached in Naples, Toto was reluctant to leave his widowed mother. Toto asked if they had cut off a lock of Virginia's hair because he would like to have one to cherish.

I keep looking at the portrait by Teodoro that I keep before me. Oh, face of an ingenuousness rare in your sex, I see your beautiful soul full of fire, incapable of moderation, and most ardent in love. But what good is it, oh my Gaetano, this customary outburst of mine. I can only write of Virginia and I distress you. . . .

Mamma has not yet the strength of spirit to write to you. She has insisted I tell you it. My Gaetano, preserve yourself for her. The cholera, which takes its victims strangely, could have liberated me from my annoying life; you could give a piece of bread to this poor old woman so that she does not go begging through the streets, her hand outstretched. The disease winds about, and it has wound its way into the monasteries and into the prisons. Two of my friends died, although they were well off and led orderly lives. Thursday 252 dead. . . .[2]

As soon as Donizetti heard of the cholera he rushed a description of his regimen to Toto, urging him to follow it closely. His distress of mind is clear because he skipped back and forth between injunctions about diet and avoiding crowded churches to outcries that he had been spared to live. He assured Toto that he understood why he could not abandon his mother

[1] Z. No. 250(a), p. 438.   [2] Z. No. A. 11, pp. 870-1.

now, but since his most recent letters had not been fumigated (*profumate*), he hoped that soon it would be possible to travel without having to stay in quarantine.

> . . . If the closing of the courts causes you financial loss, write to me what you need, so that you can draw on me as though it were your own money. I tell you this once and forever. . . .[1]

On 26 August Donizetti wrote scolding Toto for writing to Persico but not to him, and assuring him that he did not want to spare any bad news so that he could share it with them. Toto on the same day gloomily described the epidemic in Rome.

> . . . I share your desire, that is to see your letters as you love to see mine. We are both unhappy. Only time can ease the violent state in which we are. I am certain I will have a stroke, but when will it come? I do not care a rap for the Cholera. . . . Yesterday opposite the windows of my office the sister of that Tota, Mamma's niece, died of a fulminant Cholera, and when I saw the coffin that took away the poor girl, without priests, without ceremony, I envied her fate. Yesterday the Sanitary Bulletin read 186 dead, but there are twice that many at least. . . .[2]

Three days later he sent another description of the ravages of the disease in Rome.

> . . . The mortality rate is greater than that at Naples, considering here the population of 150,000 souls, but from that figure you must subtract 17,542 families that left before they closed the road, as happened beginning at Albano, Tivoli and Monteraso, where they admit no one coming from Rome.
>
> The disease increases. The Sanitary Bulletin of the 26th reads 184 dead, of the 27th, 186, of the 28th, 194, but they are short many that go unreported.
>
> The Quirinal and the Vatican were not spared and there have been deaths, but they were servants. The Holy Father is very well, thanks to the Omnipotent, and Sunday he will go to St Peter's for the Beatification of two Servants of God. This sacred solemn function will attract

[1] Z. No. 251, p. 440.   [2] Z. No. A. 12, p. 872.

many people. The Prisons, the Ghetto are breeding places of death. Every quarter has a hospital. The sick refuse to go there because none is seen leaving it. No hearses having been made, the dead are carried in pushcarts with the coffin exposed. The gravediggers, without any distinguishing mark are found in all the inns, where they sleep and drink, leaving the stretcher with the sick person or the corpse outside the door as though it were a bale of merchandise. . . .[1]

At Naples Donizetti seemed imprisoned in his grief. He was still so deeply stunned by the most recent, the most severe, blow of the many he had sustained in a few short months, that he could not accept it. On 31 August he admitted his weakness to Toto:

If you have wanted her hair, if it has pleased you, if you have the courage to see it, wear it, then you are more philosophical than I; it is a sign that you are stronger than I. Then, what does this mean? It means that I can not yet accustom myself to believing my misfortune, that I can not yet send you a letter without tears hindering me as I write it.

That will come with time, because I see every day so many who accustom themselves to live having lost beings in the same relation as she to us—But the door is closed, I cannot open it, I still run away from that door—My temperament was not such to lose itself in words of endearment; it had come to need that object, it had found an existence in her! Ah, let us stop![2]

On the same day Toto was writing him another report of the cholera. Between 28 July and 29 August there had been 4002 cases reported in Rome, and the official count of deaths stood at 2140. The Vasselli family was still spared the disease. Donizetti was horrified with the cholera reports, but he assured Toto, writing on 4 September, that the epidemic had been twice as severe in Naples. He adds:

. . . Always give me news of you, of your house, of everything. This morning I went to His Majesty so he could tell

[1] Z. No. A. 13, p. 873. [2] Z. No. 254, p. 442.

me yes or no, nothing more! He answered that he would oblige me very soon.

In a few days I begin the rehearsals. This will be for me the opera of my emotions, but I don't want to begin the labours, when at every page....[1]

With all the other strains on his nerves, the uncertainty about the directorship of the Conservatory was an added exacerbation, and Ferdinando's notorious reluctance to commit himself on any matter was no help to Donizetti at this time. Nor could he help but dread the start of the rehearsals of *Roberto Devereux*, the music that he composed during his days of anxiety and bereavement.

On the 7 September Toto wrote a further description of the cholera to his brother-in-law. In his letters there had appeared a note of that strange sort of rivalry which leads people to argue that the disaster which touches them personally is worse than that which strikes another. Certainly, in his morbid frame of mind, Vasselli found a deep interest in the disaster. In his last letter he had described the hospitals on the Corso, set up in the churches of S. Giacomo and Gesù Maria, and told of the crowd of corpses there and the resulting stench. In this letter he lists some of the distinguished people who have succumbed and describes the protective measures that have been taken. On the same day Donizetti wrote to him: 'Don't tell me anymore about the cholera, you tell me enough when you say you are all all right.'

On the 12th he writes again.

... The beginning of my rehearsals is postponed; meanwhile, head either good or poor, I must think of the opera for Venice for January. The poet has yet to think of a subject and I have to deliver it in December. I will have to write a dozen songs, as usual, to earn twenty ducats each, that in other times I made while the rice cooked, and, the pen falls from my hand. I don't know how to do anything but I have to do everything, because everything is promised! Oh! my life, how sad you have made me, abandoning me alone on this earth. I seek to laugh, to distract myself; I would do anything to find a little rest from my internal pain—only half an hour without thinking

[1] Z. No. 256, p. 444.

of my condition—it is useless—I see the precipice from which I have fallen, without having the strength to raise myself. The soul cheers us in sadness, but the spirit is discouraged, and for me who has to write and to please, it is more painful to seek pleasant images than to kill oneself in the heat of happiness! Don't fear your coming because we will not be alone, since I will avoid every occasion in which we could fall into sadness through solitude. My friends are still sleeping in the house, and they will not leave us then. . . .[1]

In the days since Donizetti had left Persico's home, where he had been taken after Virginia's death, and returned to the Strada Nardonnes, his friends, Teodoro Ghezzi and Aniello Benevento, had been staying with him. The loyalty of these friends, even of the sensitive Aniello, was to remain constant while he lived and true to his memory as long as they lived.

On the 13th Donizetti wrote to Toto again. His stream of letters to his brother-in-law proves his need to unburden himself, to confess to someone who cared for him the thoughts that tormented him.

. . . My opera will go on stage in October and you will be here. I find your comparison to Petrarch accurate as to the situation, but my sadness proves on the other hand how distant we are, how distant in feeling. There are moments when I could give myself in hand to a hundred women if they could distract me for half an hour, and I would pay what I could. I try, I laugh, I hope, but I fall back further. No one would believe it, because I never reveal to anyone my internal sadness, but you, only you know me, and to you alone is given to imagine it. . . .[2]

This passage contains some of the most revealing self-analysis that Donizetti ever wrote, for it shows his understanding of the drive that led him to seek women. It was not from wantonness, not from depravity, but only an irresistible desire to escape from himself and from the intolerable grief and loneliness that never gave him more than half an hour's peace.

On 16 September he wrote to Toto again, still urging him to come, even though there was still a two-week quarantine in

[1] Z. No. 258, p. 445.   [2] Z. No. 259, p. 446.

force. He reports that he has yet got no concrete decision from Ferdinando about the directorship. He reverts to his eager desire to have Toto come to Naples, saying that certain times he would rather have him by his side than his brother Giuseppe. He continues:

> . . . Of the opera I cannot tell you because they have not yet begun the rehearsals. I have no will to do anything. I have songs to write at twenty ducats apiece that last year I wrote while the rice cooked. Now, paid, urged—I cannot. I have no head for it—I am depressed—I seek every way of distracting myself. I laugh, I joke, and the more I let myself go, the more I fall back. Teodoro and Aniello are still here, but there are moments when I would beg them on my knees to leave me alone that I might weep. I know I need him who sympathizes with me, and I find no one for that purpose.
>
> I am glad the cholera is diminishing. . . .[1]

On 19 September he wrote at length about Toto's coming. Then he announced that he would be leaving Naples at the end of the November to go to Venice. He still had heard nothing definite about the appointment at the Conservatory, perhaps the following week the King would give him an answer. Two days later he wrote to Toto again. He told him that the quarantine has been reduced to ten days. Then his grief breaks out again:

> . . . I read of the death of the Princess Massimi and of the pallor of Franci, but believe it, my Toto, nothing moves me; and I do not even grieve about it as something as awful as what happened to me. At your coming perhaps I will have opened her door, but now until my return, it will remain as it is. Did I tell you? I seem to be waiting for her —It seems to me that she must come back—that she is in Rome—I still weep for her as on the first day. Oh Toto! . . .
>
> I have written a song sadder than I am—I cannot, yet I must write an opera for 15 December, and I do not know the subject, or just barely.[2]

In his next two letters, of the 23rd and 26th, Donizetti wrote almost exclusively about the theatre. Toto had promised to

[1] Z. No. 261, p. 447.   [2] Z. No. 263, p. 449. The sad song is *È morta*.

send him Bulwer-Lytton's *Rienzi*, which he thought might make a good opera, and Donizetti said he would willingly read it. It is an interesting juxtaposition that Donizetti considered making an opera from the novel that five years later served Wagner with the plot for his first operatic success. Besides the English novel Donizetti was interested in a French play, Lockroy's *Un duel sous le Cardinal de Richelieu*, as a possibility for the opera for Venice. Bellini had once considered using this plot, but he died before he could make anything of it; Donizetti, however, was not to write an opera on that subject this year, although in 1843 he returned to it, basing *Maria di Rohan* on Lockroy's play. But apart from these future prospects Donizetti was again actively engaged in the opera house, superintending a production of *Betly* at the Fondo. Only once in the letter of the 26th did his composure crumble, when he cried out: 'Oh, if I could speedily join my . . .' but he cannot bring himself to write the name of Virginia, and it appears in no letter he wrote after her death. 'What use is it to make wishes?—Here nothing, nor yesterday either, nor the day before!'

On the 30th he wrote that *Rienzi* arrived with the post the previous day and he had already almost finished the second volume. The plans for the opera in Venice were in trouble again, because Cammarano saw too many difficulties in the Lockroy drama. Such uncertainties gave him 'the pangs of purgatory'. He was upset, too, by the appearance of three French frigates in the bay and by the cannon being set along Posillipo in case the ships were planning a military attack. 'Peace, peace, for pity's sake,' he wrote, 'after all that cholera!' The French ships soon sailed away and in Donizetti's next letter no more is heard of them. He still had no word from the King, but at last the order had come to turn over the score of *Roberto Devereux* to the copyists, a sign that the rehearsals would soon begin. On 7 October: 'At last I begin the rehearsals of the opera Monday and I will lose my head, as usual.' Besides this time-consuming chore, he reports that he has yet to see 'a comma' of the libretto for Venice, and in nine weeks he must deliver the finished score.

> . . . I try to force myself, but I am depressed at certain times. Now work is so heavy to me, that no more—I am

always saying: For whom am I working?—Why?—I am alone on earth—Can I live? And such ideas make me drop my arms, dear Toto!

It little matters any more, if I have or if I don't have what I ask. I am apathetic—So many beautiful things decided for October and here is the month begun, and I am nailed down to work, and for whom?—for no one. . . .[1]

Roberto Devereux, which was derived by Cammarano from Ancelot's tragedy, *Elisabeth d'Angleterre*, was first performed at the San Carlo on 29 October 1837. The opera was sung by Ronzi di Begnis (Elisabetta), Almerinda Granchi (Sara, Duchess of Nottingham), Basadonna (Roberto Devereux), Paul Barroilhet (Lord Nottingham), Timoleone Barrattini (Lord Cecil), Rossi (Sir Gualtiero Raleigh) and Giuseppe Benedetti (A Companion to Lord Nottingham). Two days later Donizetti wrote to Ricordi:

> . . . I gave my opera the day before yesterday at the S. Carlo; it is not for me to tell you now how it went. I am more modest than a whore; therefore I should blush. But it went very, very well. They also called out the poet. . . .[2]

The same day he wrote to the Ferrarese composer, Angelo Lodi, that the opera's reception 'could not have been more flattering'. *Roberto Devereux* won a solid success, not only for the singers, especially Ronzi, but for the music, a welcome reminder to Donizetti that when all else failed him he could lose himself in his career.

At the same time Donizetti composed a Requiem Mass for Abbate Fazzini, which was performed on 7 November 1837. This work had unusual significance for Donizetti, coming on the heels of all the deaths that the past two years had brought him, for he planned its performance with special care, as he wrote to Mayr on 20 December from Venice:

> . . . I risked doing in Naples a Mass for the dead (for my soul was inclined for such a thing). There it was performed, and on such an occasion I did it according to my fancy. I had the altar moved almost into the middle of the church, and the half of the rotunda behind the main altar I had covered with a black hanging, over which one could see

[1] Z. No. 268, pp. 452–3.   [2] Z. No. 270, p. 454.

only an immense golden cross from the arch to the floor. In such a manner the orchestra remained behind, and the public heard and did not see them. The church all in black, the only light, that of candles, made the mood of the service very sad; and thus was removed the public's distraction of seeing who plays and who sings, because for me in things pertaining to death I love very much this religious sadness.

The idea pleased generally. . . .[1]

Although this performance of the Mass for Fazzini satisfied Donizetti's need of expressing his grief in a ritualistic way, there were continuing annoyances which kept him ill at ease. The matter of the directorship continued to hang fire. The performances of *Roberto Devereux* were interrupted by Barroilhet's indisposition that required him to stay in bed for two weeks.

One great satisfaction to him in the last part of October had been a visit from Toto, who had finally been able to make the journey once the danger of cholera had completely subsided. There is a significant change in tone between the letters that Donizetti wrote to Toto before his visit and in those afterwards. The morbid tension begins to disappear, although from time to time he was still to sound a desperate cry of grief and despair, but in place of his morbid dejection a tone of rowdy, sometimes almost hysterical, jocularity gradually appears. Not that either forgot Virginia, but together they found some terms on which it was possible to express their feelings, a level of communication that by its apparent lack of constraint reveals ineradicable pain in the heart.

One uncomfortable piece of business was amicably settled between them before Toto returned to Rome. On 31 October Toto gave his brother-in-law a receipt for the objects that formed Virginia's dowry. This receipt was to become a matter of contention between Vasselli and Donizetti's heirs after his death.

After Toto's return to Rome Gaetano writes to him on 7 November:

. . . My opera for Venice proceeds so slowly that I have done nothing more, the labour, my raging at my irresolution, all this deprives me of all my will.

[1] Z. No. 282, p. 463.

. . . Sunday at the table a little anger between Teodoro and Aniello broke out. We started whistling and it finished thus. It is good that at my return everyone will be in his old home. . . .

Teodoro has given me a copy of the note and your other paper that I have not read yet, and it stays sealed. He says that they are all receipted.

My Toto if there ever is anything beside this that it would please you to have, speak, because everything is at your disposal. I am most grateful to you for all that you do, but remember my things are yours, and that your desire will be law to,

your
Gaetano.[1]

On 3 December Donizetti left Naples on his way to Venice. He stopped for a few days in Rome and then proceeded north by way of Florence and Ferrara. He arrived in Venice some time before the 20th, waiting to begin the preparations for *Maria di Rudenz*.

This opera was composed under the most difficult circumstances and with the greatest reluctance by Donizetti. His letters to Toto contained references to the long delay in finally settling upon a subject. The letters of Lanari to Donizetti, in the latter part of 1837, are also full of this problem. On 13 October he wrote to Donizetti from Bologna to say that he had glanced hastily at the sketch of *Maria di Rudenz*. He wondered whether the part of Matilde was intended for Tadolini or for a lesser singer; because if the role was for Tadolini, it would have to be augmented, as she had been engaged as a prima donna *assoluta* and her part would have to be equal to Ungher's. The book strikes him as too gruesome.

Count Berti shared this last opinion. He reported to Lanari that he did not find the book admissible to the stage of the Fenice because there were too many atrocities in it, too much confusion and obscurity of treatment. Such dramas were, in his opinion, 'the shame of the Italian theatre.' He sent for Donizetti to examine a libretto by Pietro Beltrami, entitled *Ghismonda di Mendrizio*, which he thought would be more appropriate.

On 31 October Lanari wrote to Donizetti again, hoping that

[1] Z. No. 273, pp. 455–6.

Cammarano had made the libretto less grim by cutting out one of the victims, 'because without that President Berti would never approve it.' On 21 November, Donizetti was at work composing the opera, but, as he told Toto, it did not please him at all. His peace of mind was further disturbed just then by the efforts around the San Carlo to marry him off. He resisted such manœuvres, although later he was to toy with the idea of remarriage. On 25 November he informed Toto that he had completed half the opera.

When *Maria di Rudenz* was finally given at the Fenice on 30 January 1838, with Ungher (Maria), Napoleone Moriani (Enrico), and Ronconi (Corrado), it ran just two performances, and *Parisina* was hastily put on in its place and given sixteen times. Although the opera was later given in Milan, Genoa, and Naples, nowhere did the gruesome melodramatic plot win favour, and although certain parts of the music, such as the baritone aria in the first act and the sextet, were applauded, the score did not have enough vitality to maintain itself. While it is risky to write a final epitaph for any opera, it is difficult to believe that *Maria di Rudenz* will ever see the stage again.

On 3 February 1838, Donizetti left Venice and returned to Naples, reaching there before the end of the month. Donizetti avoided going to Bergamo while he was in Venice. On 16 November he had written to Toto:

> . . . I should go to Bergamo—A new place of grief—No one any more!—I am like an orphan—I should go to my house —How can I? Why not? What would my brother say? And if I don't go, what will Mayr say? Who knows if we shall ever see each other again! Oh, no one knows me, because I do not speak, and I suffocate. . . .[1]

When he had written to Mayr from Venice the following month he told him that he had heard he was a grandfather and happier than he who would not even be a father now. He wished the old man happiness, and said that if it were not for the power that music possessed for him, he would be dead. 'I still weep as on the first day.' But not a word did he utter about going to Bergamo.

One of the first things that Donizetti did upon his return to Naples was to seek an audience with the King and present

[1] Z. No. 276, p. 458.

another memorial about the directorship of the Conservatory. He wrote to Toto on 7 March a brief but graphic account of the interview.

> . . . Yesterday I was with His Majesty. He said to me, smiling: Goodbye, *cavaliere*—I, seeing him joking, followed along, and said that if he did not ever believe me worthy of that post (gently, however, you know), I would have accepted Paris, and therefore I begged him to give an answer soon—He laughed, took the paper, shook my hand affectionately, and said:
> *Va bene: addio, cavaliere.*
> I laughed, he laughed, and I will see then what this laughter will produce. . . .[1]

Ferdinando was fond of the expression *va bene* because it gave an impression of cordiality without committing him to saying a definite yes or no. The King's reluctance to give his final approval to Donizetti's appointment suggests manœuvring behind the scenes. While the King did not want to offend his subjects by selecting Donizetti, neither did he wish to deny Donizetti the post outright, hoping that time would solve the problem.

Donizetti's mention of the offer from Paris shows that his interest in going back there had in no way diminished, but had, in fact, increased. Even before Virginia's death the matter had been in the forefront of his plans. As early as 21 May 1837 he had written to Duprez, who had returned to France and made a sensational début at the Opéra in *Guillaume Tell* (17 April 1837), first of all to congratulate the tenor on his success and to suggest the production of several of his operas. He had heard that the Italiens was considering putting on *Lucia*, but if that plan should fall through, he could arrange it for the Opéra.

> . . . I could make as many *ballabilli* as they want, I could change or lengthen what you wanted . . . I want to frighten M. Duponchel about this as little as possible. I believe that the opera I would rather give at the Opéra would be *L'assedio di Calais*, because it is the most studied, the most conforming to the French taste, and as such, everyone believes that it was written for Paris. . . .

[1] Z. No. 286, p. 466.

I do not tell you that to obtain an engagement from M. Duponchel, who does not esteem me, I know. I have received offers a thousand times, and two thousand times he has refused me, but I tell you this only for my self-respect that would enjoy it. I never talk of financial interests, thus you see my wish is noble. I leave you free to choose, although I incline toward *L'assedio*; in any case, if *Lucia* is not given at the Italiens, I urge you to say a word to him from time to time, since you know my intentions. . . .

Greet Levasseur, Nourrit and Abreck [Habeneck] who, although he does not know me, will not disdain a greeting. . . .

P.S. Do you know M. and Mme De Coussy? Give my greetings to those amiable people. . . .[1]

From this letter it is clear that Donizetti was hoping to use the offices of his friend the tenor Duprez to gain favourable consideration of Charles Duponchel, then the director of the Opéra. Duprez, however, was not Donizetti's only ally working for him in Paris. Michele Accursi and the de Coussys were each working in their separate ways. But the decisive person in Donizetti's coming to Paris turned out to be himself and this influence was brought to bear by the great success of *Lucia* when it was first produced at the Italiens, 12 December 1837, with Persiani, Rubini, Tamburini and Bortolo Morelli. This decisive conquest made Donizetti the composer of the hour, and the doors of Paris swung wide for him.

Donizetti heard favourable reports from Accursi of the rehearsals of *Parisina* which was being put on at the Italiens to capitalize on the vogue of *Lucia*. *Parisina* was given on 24 February 1838 with Grisi, Rubini, and Tamburini, but it was given only seven times before it was dropped from the repertory. This opera's failure to win high favour in no way compromised Donizetti's popularity, as *Lucia* continued to fill the theatre. By May 1838 negotiations with the Opéra were under way, and Scribe had promised to send Donizetti a libretto; concurrently, parleyings with the Italiens were in progress. Donizetti did not consider a move to Paris until the autumn, and therefore he signed a contract with the San Carlo for an opera in September.

---

[1] Unpublished letter in the Museo Donizettiano. Since published in *Studi Donizettiani I*, pp. 39–41.

In May, Accursi was in Naples and doubtless there was much conversation about Donizetti's going to Paris.

Donizetti's conditions for an agreement with the Opéra are set out in a letter he wrote to Duponchel on 25 May.

> I hasten to answer the letter that you honoured me by addressing to me, and I begin by thanking you for all the flattering things it says of me.
>
> A success at the Théâtre de l'Académie Royale de Musique is a glory that all composers seek, and it is with joy that I receive and accept the proposition that you have wanted to make me, to open the stage of this theatre, famous for so many great names, to two of my works.
>
> But however natural the desire that I have to enter upon this fine career, I cannot close my eyes to the gravity of such an enterprise. My début in France must correspond to what I have done up to the present in Italy, and I can only worthily commence at the Opéra of Paris with a work of the importance of those one is accustomed to see in this theatre; therefore I ask you for a libretto in five acts and to have placed at my disposal all your singers, reserving to myself the choice of M. de Candia [Mario], as you appear to want him in this first work, if the success of his début realizes the hope that his fine talent and voice have already made conceivable. When the great masters, after whom I must appear, have had in their hands for their success all the resources that your Theatre offers, you will find it just, Monsieur, that I wish for my protection the same assistance, otherwise the struggle would be too unequal, and it would be foolhardiness in me to expose myself there.
>
> In the contract signed by you and that you have had the kindness to send me two copies so that I may sign it, the time when my two works should be performed must be stated precisely, and above all the first (for which I ask three months of rehearsals of three hours a day) for I must arrange my travelling to France with my engagement and my position. At the same time the libretto would have to be sent to me, for I want to busy myself with this work as soon as I receive the poem for it. . . .[1]

[1] Z. No. 293, pp. 471–2.

A few more details of Donizetti's Paris arrangements appear
in a letter he wrote to Dolci the following day. He reported that
he was flattered by the offer from the Opéra, but that everything was still in the air. He had received a text from Scribe,
but as it did not please him, he was going to send it back. On 1
June he wrote to Toto that he had received long letters from
'Accursi, that long-winded person. I am very fond of the poor
little fellow; he is truly a good person. He wants to see me and
that is all. But I want honour, and it is about that that we
debate.'

One of the long-winded Accursi's letters from this period is
extant, or at least part of it, but it must have been a very long
letter indeed. On 11 June he wrote from Paris that he had
received Donizetti's letter for Duponchel, but that he could not
deliver it, as the director was in the country for a few days. He
had heard that, beginning in 1840, as Robert the manager of
the Italiens planned to retire, the lease would be taken up by
Berlioz and his friend Viscount de Ruolz. He was interested that
Donizetti come to Paris to personally stage the opera that he
was currently writing for Naples for the French tenor Adolphe
Nourrit, who had left the scene of his triumphs at the Opéra
when he was seized by uneasiness at the engagement of Duprez
at that theatre.

> . . . the opera that you are writing for Nourrit . . . would
> make a fine effect if it were given at the Italiens soon; the
> opera, if you like, could be *L'elisir* or *Roberto Devereux* or
> *Belisario*, indeed that which would make the most secure
> effect. Of these operas one should be for Tamburini,
> another for Lablache, or at least one for Lablache and the
> other for both; one for Grisi, the other for Persiani. . . . I
> reflect that poor Rubini would have to be on the tracks
> continuously for lack of another tenor. I have prompted
> the management to exchange Ivanoff for Moriani; I have
> told them to inquire whether he wants to come to Paris. . . .
> It seems that Auber, who had a contract with the Opéra,
> had barely heard that you were coming to write for the
> same theatre, but he has hurried to go on stage before you;
> thus he will go in October, and you in February or March.
> This week I also hope to terminate this business. Now we
> are off at a gallop; if you wanted to, you could give

Adelaide[1] at the Italiens, and the new opera at the French theatre, but having this last it would be better to replace the other with that you are now writing for Nourrit. . . . *What is the title of your new opera for Nourrit?* Could it be adapted for Lablache, not for voice naturally, but for the dramatic part? Could it be for the principal quartet? Now that I have worked and spoken of you, it is fair that I ask you a favour for me. . . .[2]

Accursi wanted Donizetti to write him a letter of recommendation to de Ruolz. Viscount Henri Catherine Camille de Ruolz (1808–87) was a wealthy dilettante of music who had been in Naples in the late autumn of 1835, when he had an opera entitled *Lara* produced at the San Carlo. Donizetti had befriended de Ruolz on that occasion, which has been racily described by Dumas *père* in his travel book, *Corricolo*. Now Accursi hoped that Donizetti could persuade de Ruolz that he would need 'a bright and honest Italian' to act as his agent. He also suggested that Donizetti write to Rossini to urge him for the post. He went on and on in copious detail how Donizetti could best help him; for instance, he asked Donizetti not to date his letter to de Ruolz, allowing him to submit it at the best moment. In his prolix sentences, Accursi reveals himself as an irrepressible opportunist. However insistent his sense of a *quid pro quo*, Accursi helped Donizetti in this instance at least.

An echo of Accursi's letter appears in Donizetti's to Toto, of 27 June.

. . . Michele wants recommendations to certain French impresarios who will have the Teatro Italiano after 1840, and I have helped him. . . .[3]

Donizetti's 'opera for Nourrit' was *Poliuto*, a setting of Corneille's *Polyeucte*. Donizetti had chosen the subject especially for the French tenor, who worked with Cammarano on the libretto. Nourrit had earlier performed similar offices for Meyerbeer's *Les Huguenots*, in which he had sung Raoul in the first

[1] *Adelaide* was a comic opera, to an Italian libretto, that Donizetti never finished; some parts of his score would turn up ultimately as parts of *La favorite*.
[2] Unpublished letter in the Naples Conservatory Library.
[3] Z. No. 300, p. 478.

cast, and for Halévy's *La Juive*, in which he had been the first Eleazar.

On 11 July Donizetti informed Toto that the opera was almost finished, but he foresaw difficulties as the censorship was frowning on the representation of a saint's life on the operatic stage. On 15 July, he mentions the opera to Toto again. He is incensed over an article that had appeared in *Patria*, accusing him of making his new opera out of equal parts of *Anna Bolena* and *Tasso*. 'I am not a man to do such things!' he insists, repeating his assertion for emphasis. '*Poliuto* is entirely, entirely, or at least almost entirely, new, except for the adagio of the first finale. The rest is entirely new, and at Naples they have heard too many of my things not to know.' The adagio is the sextet from *Maria di Rudenz* which Donizetti grafted on to the score of *Poliuto*.

This letter to Toto of 15 July also contained news of his affair in Paris and of the still unresolved question of the directorship of the Conservatory.

> ... As to Michele, he embroils me in the controversies of Paris, so that after four months of correspondence I still do not know what will become of me, whether I will have an engagement or not.
>
> I will go there in October, and I will do more in two days than he in two years.
>
> This morning I went to see the Minister of the Interior to hand in my resignation, and he believed it was a political move, as I had asked to have the Directorship, but I answered coldly: 'Excellency, no! I interpreted His Majesty's long silence to mean a refusal, and now I only ask the acceptance of my resignation.' It appeared it was the wish of His Majesty to form a Commission of which I would be the head, and that I would have a raise in salary —But I answered: 'If it was for money, I earn two thousand ducats in three months. It was for *honour*. I was not worthy of it, now I ask to be dismissed.' At my dry answer, he turned a little surly, but he is good and I hope to obtain my resignation. ... [1]

As far as Donizetti was concerned the blow that fell on 12 August, when *Poliuto* was formally prohibited performance, was

[1] Z. No. 305, pp. 481–2.

not the overwhelming disappointment it might otherwise have been. He had already determined to go to Paris in October; he had already accepted the situation at the Conservatory at Naples as impossible and had submitted his resignation. He was prepared to leave the city that had accepted with enthusiasm and steadfast loyalty almost everything he wrote for its audience; the city where, as well, he had experienced shattering grief. Although perhaps it is too much to say that he left Naples completely on his own terms, at least he left to meet a new future which he had desired and worked toward for years. He took his departure early in October from the city which is forever associated with the première of *Lucia*.

A postscript to the tragedy of Donizetti's life in Naples was made by the death of the tenor Adolphe Nourrit. It has been suggested that his suicide was a result of his disappointment over the prohibition of *Poliuto*, a further check to his career after the great blow of fearing himself supplanted in Paris by Duprez.

Since the facts of Nourrit's suicide are little known and often misconstrued, some light on this matter might well be welcome. Guillaume Cottrau, who because of their mutual French origin was a close friend of Nourrit's, wrote a vivid account of the event the day after it occurred.

First of all, Nourrit's suicide did not occur until 8 March 1839, nearly eight months after the ban on *Poliuto*. His death was, rather, the result of an increasingly morbid sensitivity. Here is how Cottrau describes the events of that fateful morning.

> Yesterday morning at the hour at which I write to you, five-thirty, he arose suddenly after a horribly agitated night. His wife, who after watching him, had just become drowsy, said to him: 'Aren't you taking a light, Adolphe?' He answered: 'I don't need one', and he left the room. Accustomed to his insomnia, Mme Nourrit went back to sleep, but she was soon awakened with a start by a strange distant sound. After a struggle of several minutes between drowsiness and dark foreboding, she hastily dressed and looked around the apartment. (The one that Lablache occupied the last time in the Palazzo Barbaja, and in

which Rossini composed several operas.) She crossed the salon, three other rooms; a pale light coming through an open door gripped her attention, she rushed to the landing. It occurred to her that her husband had gone down to see Barbaja, who is a very early riser and who lives on the next lower floor, the third. Her glance, after surveying the closed windows, went down to the courtyard. In the doubtful light of the dawn, a mixture of material, green, white, and red drew her attention. She ran down the staircase; soon she could no longer doubt her misfortune. . . .[1]

[1] Cottrau, *Lettres d'un mélomane*, pp. 65–6.

CHAPTER 5

Widening Horizons and Gathering Shadows

Donizetti arrived in the French capital on 21 October 1838 and took lodgings in Rue Louvois No. 5, the same house that Adolphe Adam, the French composer, then occupied. The Paris that Donizetti came to was the self-acknowledged musical capital of the world. Its theatres set the fashions of the time, and even today their shadow still touches parts of the repertory and practice of any great international opera house.

Chief among these theatres was the Académie Royale de Musique, usually known simply as the Opéra, where massive works, frequently in five acts, featuring elaborate ballet sequences and huge, lavish sets, were performed before the *haute-monde*. In the past decade, the Opéra had been the scene of stirring premières, those of *Guillaume Tell*, *Robert le Diable*, *Les Huguenots*, and *La Juive*, a series of works that established a whole new *genre* of spectacular grand opera. About a month before Donizetti's return to Paris, the Opéra had produced a flamboyant failure. After twenty-nine rehearsals, Hector Berlioz's *Benvenuto Cellini* ran only seven performances, an experience that profoundly embittered Berlioz against the state-run opera houses of Paris. Berlioz knew, as did every other opera composer of his generation, that a success at the Opéra marked the pinnacle of a career.

Next in importance was the company known as the Italiens. This group had entered upon its greatest decade in 1830, with the accession of Robert and Severini as co-directors, Rossini acting as their adviser and ally. It was they who brought Giulia Grisi, Tamburini, and Lablache to Paris, and re-introduced Rubini there, forming thereby a legendary constellation of operatic talent. On 15 December 1837, just three days after the triumph of the first Parisian performance of *Lucia*, the Salle Favart, where the Italiens had been giving their performances, was destroyed by a disastrous fire that consumed all the sets and costumes, cost Severini his life, and left Robert physically hurt and financially crippled. The company moved to the Salle Ventadour, where it continued to give performances as best it could. In spite of the economic problems, heightened for poor Robert by the fact that the terms of his lease for the Ventadour prevented him selling one-third of the seats for every performance, these being reserved by the owners, the musical quality remained what it had been before. The Théâtre-Italien enjoyed considerable social prestige, although it never possessed the aura of a national institution that surrounded the Opéra.

Third in the Parisian hierarchy of lyric stages in those days stood the Opéra-Comique. The traditions of this company stretched all the way back to the Fairs of Saint-Germain and Saint-Laurent in 1697, yet for all its longevity and the loyalty of its own bourgeois public, the troupe never had the réclame of the Opéra or the Italiens. The Opéra-Comique, after occupying the Salle Ventadour for some years, had moved in 1832 to the Salle des Nouveautés, a site on the Place de la Bourse, where the company remained until April 1840. Perhaps the easiest way to recapture the flavour of the Opéra-Comique in those days is to look at the list of works, almost all of them completely forgotten today, which were performed there most frequently in 1838: Ambrose Thomas's *La double échelle* (eighty-one times), Auber's *Le domino noir* (sixty times), Adam's *Le postillon de Longjumeau* (fifty-one times), Clapisson's *La figurante* (forty-four times), Adam's *Le chalet* (forty-three times), Thomas's *Le perruquier de la régence* (thirty-seven times), Adam's *La marquise* (thirty-three times), *Marguerite*, by the son of the famous Boieldieu (thirty-two times), Adam's *Le brasseur du Preston* (thirty-one times), and Plantade's *Le mari de circonstance* (thirty-one times).

Between the time of his arrival in Paris and the end of 1840, a period of not quite twenty-seven months, Donizetti was to write two new operas for the Opéra, one for the Opéra-Comique; he was to introduce three of his old works to Paris at the Italiens, and to bring out the very well received French 'edition' of *Lucia di Lammermoor* at the short-lived Théâtre de la Renaissance. His success, added to his ease in dominating every lyric stage of importance in Paris, brought him mixed popularity. In society he was lionized; his handsome appearance, his attractiveness to women, his ready wit and easy manners, even the faint aura of scandalous behaviour that surrounded him, all contributed to his being readily picked up by the powerful hostesses of the day. Among the large Italian population in Paris, the musicians, the exiles, and the opportunists, he was treated as a symbol of national success in what was then the only readily exportable product of that politically divided peninsula. Not surprisingly many of the French composers regarded his coming not as an invasion, but an infestation. However politely they treated him in public they were, as a group, eager to intrigue against him behind his back and to use what journalistic power they could command to blunt the edge of his triumphs.

There were two composers in particular who hoped to bring about musical revolutions; to them Donizetti became a symbol of all that was debased and wrong in the musical taste of the day. To Berlioz, who dreamed of reviving the great traditions of French music and enriching them with his own brand of romanticism, Donizetti was the most repulsive, because the most ubiquitous, symptom of the Italianization of French musical taste. To Richard Wagner, who came to Paris in September 1839, aged twenty-six, hoping to arrange a production of *Rienzi* at the Opéra, the spectacle of Donizetti's fortune was an object of envy and contempt, especially when Wagner's desperate financial straits forced him to earn his bread by making transcriptions for the publisher Schlesinger of such hits of the hour as Donizetti's *Les martyrs* and *La favorite*. Granted a traditional bias in favour of the unappreciated man of genius, the partisans of both Berlioz and Wagner have tended to dismiss Donizetti out of hand, their attitudes in part crystallized by the polemical essays of these composers. Such people reject Donizetti, rolling up his best with his worst and tossing it into the ashcan, without taking the trouble to examine him for what he was in terms of his own tradition. If there is such a thing as an historical prejudice against Donizetti, and almost any history of music written by a non-Italian would give this impression, it dates from these years of his Parisian successes.

Donizetti's view of himself when he first arrived in Paris appears in a letter he wrote to Dolci on 13 November 1838.

> . . . I have been in Paris more than twenty days. To tell you what I am doing is quickly said. I am staging at the Italiens *Roberto Devereux* and *L'elisir d'amore*. To tell you what I will do afterwards, here it is: I will give the opera that at Naples was forbidden, in the French language at the great French theatre, the Académie Royale. After that I cannot tell you what I will do. . . . If I am set free, however, after *Poliuto* is given at the Opéra, I will return to Italy to breathe a little, since among all the friendliness, the dinners, the portraits, the busts in wax, etc. all that, even though it flatters my pride, nevertheless annoys a poor artist such as I am. Here I clearly see there is a way to gain on every side, but I, accustomed to little, to want little, I cannot adapt myself even to earning money. I am not Rossini, and I do not have his fortune, but when a man has what he needs to live and to amuse himself enough, I think that he should retire and be happy. I live well, I will put away after this French opera three thousand other scudi; what more do you want me to seek? . . . I do not want to play the fool like my brother, the Bey, who after having earned more than I perhaps, stays there in ancient Byzantium to scratch his belly between the plague and the stake. I offered to make a home together, and I do not know, but I believe his wife dissuaded him fearing perhaps that I would live off them. I am alone—it is painful to say this word—you will understand how much grief is enclosed in it, but, inasmuch as God wanted it this way, my brother could stand to improve his condition. Then we would have asked Francesco to come with us—ah! vain illusions. He loves Constantinople, to which he owes everything; I love Italy because to that country, after my debt to Mayr, I owe my existence and my reputation.

I have given His Majesty the King of Naples my resignation from the conservatory, and that to make my life more tranquil if that is still possible. His Majesty did not answer, and I have meanwhile asked for three months' leave. This absence expires in December and I have already written for another three; either he accepts my resignation or grants me the leave. Then in March I will come back to Italy for some time, then I go back to Paris for three months, and then *I leave France forever*. I don't want the Theatre to leave me, I want to leave it. . . .[1]

Donizetti's coming to Paris, as this letter proves, was to seek a way to end his career on his terms. He had already asked for whom he was working now that Virginia was dead and his hopes of children with her, and had faced the answer that there was no one, certainly not his brothers. Yet he could not extricate himself from his career; his *amour-propre* drove him on, just as it drew him to Paris with the hope that he could retire with the accolade of a success at the Opéra upon his career. His career became an addiction, however, for behind each success lurked the possibility of another. During the next five years the alternatives to activity became less and less conceivable to him, as his personality began to undergo the changes that were the first warnings of his collapse. In this letter to Dolci, written just after his arrival in Paris, the alternatives were still possible, but this tone of frank self-evaluation was never to sound so clearly and so objectively again, as he became increasingly involved in the pathetic pursuit of surviving that he might continue his career, going on that he might somehow evade and deny the dreadful changes that obtruded upon him from within.

Donizetti's first musical activity in Paris was to assist the production of *Roberto Devereux* at the Italiens; for it he composed a new overture, featuring the tune of *God Save the Queen*, a new tenor romanza, and a new duet. The work was sung for the first time in Paris on 27 December 1838 with Grisi (Elisabetta), the English mezzo-soprano Emma Albertazzi (Sara), Rubini (Roberto), and Tamburini (Nottingham). Donizetti sent a report of the first performance to Dolci on 10 January 1839, containing a sentiment that any Italian composer might feel when his operas were given abroad.

[1] Z. No. 316, pp. 491–2.

> . . . Last month I gave my *Roberto* with good success, the sub-
> sequent performances go still better since here the Italian
> language is not too well understood by all the habitués
> of the theatre, and as I seek to emphasize the text, it
> happens that they often do not understand the dramatic
> situation. . . .[1]

A little less than a month later, he performed the same offices at
the Italiens for *L'elisir d'amore*, adding to that opera a rondo for
Persiani and a duet for the soprano and Tamburini. This opera
was produced on 17 January 1839 winning a great success with
Persiani, Ivanoff (Nemorino), Tamburini, and notably the
splendid Dulcamara of Lablache.

Meanwhile, Donizetti had begun to think seriously about the
revised version of *Poliuto*, to a new libretto by Scribe, which
would serve to introduce him to the stage of the Opéra. In
January 1839 he estimated that when all the necessary work
was done, the opera would be ready to go into rehearsal in
October of that year. At the Opéra each composer who signed a
contract to compose for that theatre was granted a turn, but if
his work was not ready when his turn came round, or for some
reason he chose to cede his place, he would then be assigned a
later date. Donizetti had originally been assigned a turn for the
spring of 1839, to follow Auber's five-act *Le lac des fées*, but
realizing that he could not complete his revisions by that time,
he wrote to Halévy on 14 January 1839, ceding his place to him.
Halévy's *Le drapier* had been scheduled to follow Donizetti's
opera. This system of 'turns' was cumbersome, affording opportunities for all sorts of delaying actions and petty annoyances.
Donizetti came to resent it thoroughly in time.

On 8 April Donizetti sent Mayr a description of his labours
on *Poliuto*.

> . . . My health is excellent in the midst of my work, and
> here is an account of what I am doing.
> I will give at the Grand Opéra my *Poliuto* which was
> banned in Naples as being too sacred. It will be enlarged
> into four acts instead of three as it was, and translated and
> adjusted for the French stage by Scribe. This means that I
> have had to rewrite all the recitatives anew, to make a new
> finale for the first act, to add arias, trios, and appropriate

[1] Z. No. 317, p. 493.

dances such as they use here, in order that the public will not complain that the texture is Italian, and in this they would not be wrong. The music and the French stage poetry have a *cachet* all their own, to which every composer must conform, whether it is in the recitatives or in the lyrical sections; for example, no *crescendi* etc. etc., no customary cadenzas, joy, joy, joy; then in between one verse of the cabaletta and the other, you should always have some lines that heighten the emotion, without using the customary repetitions of the lines which our poets employ. This *Poliuto*, now transformed into *Les martyrs*, will be given within the year.

I am obligated, under a penalty of 30 thousand francs, to deliver the score by 1 September. By 1 January 1840 I am obligated to hand in the finished score of my second grand opera, which however is in four acts and which I have already under way, under the same penalty. In the middle of these occupations I am finding and will find the time to finish my three mates [*conjugi*], the other being the opera I will give to the Italiens here, for their opening upon the return of the company from London. I hope that suffices.

Perhaps you will ask where I find the time? I find it, I also go walking in the middle of the day, and while walking I work more. I love art and I love it with passion. . . .[1]

The second opera for the Opéra, which Donizetti had 'already under way', was *Le duc d'Albe*, also to a text by Scribe. Although he had started on this score early in April 1839, he was to put it by unfinished before the year was out, and it was to remain incomplete at the time of his death. This score had a most chequered career; and it was not to see the stage until thirty-four years after the composer's death, when it was produced in an Italian translation and finished by other hands.

During his first six months in Paris Donizetti's first rush of enthusiasm abated somewhat, and his spirits took a darker turn. He sounds this sombre note quite plainly in a letter to Mayr, dated 15 May 1839.

Oh how glad I was to see your handwriting, just as I am always pleased to hear you are in good spirits! Then you do not feel your age. And I who am sad feel it strongly

[1] Z. No. 319, pp. 494-5.

already. I am grey and tired of working. . . . The world believes me what I am not, I do not care for the world, but rather for myself. I have a hundred thousand francs in capital, should they not suffice to live on moderately? Now I am writing two operas here. . . .

He also tells Mayr that he still does not know whether his resignation has been accepted in Naples. He had hoped to go back there, returning to Paris in October to start the rehearsals of *Les martyrs*, but he was afraid that he might not be allowed to leave Naples if he went there. That his dark mood is caused by working too hard is revealed by another passage from the same letter.

. . . Here I am always at my desk. I have finished *Les martyrs* and already begun *Le duc d'Albe*. Oh, my Maestro, I will give the theatre a bitter farewell as soon as possible. I say bitter, although it has made me rich, but I'll say it from the heart, wanting to get away from so many *souffrances*. . . .[1]

Except for his successes at the Italiens, there is no doubt that he was uneasy about the crucial test at the Opéra. Certainly, he found little comfort in such duties as directing a concert, on 17 March, at the Salle Herz, to launch a new periodical, *Il bravo*, where he shared the platform with the principal stars of the Italiens. This was one of the onerous activities that engage a composer who feels he must not neglect such an opportunity to stand well with the press and public. Donizetti's depression continued all that spring and in mid-summer it was deep as ever.

In July he heard from Dolci that among the effects of their benefactress, Marianna Pezzoli-Grattaroli, were found some of his youthful compositions that he had dedicated to her in 1819 and 1820. She had died of the cholera in 1837; both Donizetti and Dolci retained fond memories of this woman because she had advanced the money to purchase their exemptions from military conscription almost twenty years before. Donizetti was curious to see these juvenilia, but he did not want to have to pay an exorbitant price for them. After explaining his position on this matter, Donizetti speaks of his feelings about Bergamo.

. . . Oh how much I would like to see you all again, but I fear that it is not to be. I cannot, I lack the courage to go

[1] Z. No. 320, pp. 495–6.

where I had father, mother, and not see anyone again. I had a wife who took the place of them all. I have lost her! I am alone on earth. The climate of Paris does not agree with me. I am growing thin. I will leave right after my first opera is given and come back for the second. . . .[1]

He was encouraged by the success of the French version of *Lucia di Lammermoor* at the Théâtre de la Renaissance, 6 August 1839, sung by the English soprano, Anna Thillon, Ricciardi (Edgard), Hurteaux (Henri), Zelger (Raimond), Gibert (Sir Arthur), and J. Kelm (Gilbert). This last character is Normanno in the Italian version, but in the French version, made by Alphonse Royer and Gustave Vaëz, he is combined with the role of Alisa, which is omitted. There are other substantial differences in the French version, changes that required Donizetti to re-arrange his score and compose new recitatives. The opera is also simplified to meet the modest talents of the company at the Renaissance, which Donizetti cheerfully described as 'beginners and dogs'. In spite of this unpromising cast, only Thillon being a first-rate singer, the work made a great impression. He informed Persico of the event:

. . . Suffice it to know that I was in bed with a headache, but after the opera I was obliged to get up as the singers, chorus, and orchestra came with torches to repeat the choruses of *Lucia* under my windows, and from above (like royalty) I thanked them amid the cheering. Yesterday evening, second performance, theatre crowded. . . .

The opera in this form will make the tour of France and from time to time I will have some francs from the provinces too. . . .

Mme Nourrit succumbed of grief from her loss, day before yesterday, leaving many orphaned children. . . .[2]

This French version was put on at the Opéra in 1846, and over a number of years attained a total of over two hundred performances, although the complete score was not performed during part of its career at the Opéra, as *Lucia* became a curtain-raiser for mixed bills. It is this French version that Flaubert alludes to in the famous scene of Emma Bovary attending a performance of this opera at Rouen. All the while the French

[1] Z. No. 326, pp. 500–1, dated 9 August 1839. [2] Ibid.

Lucie maintained her popularity her Italian *alter ego* continued to hold the stage at the Italiens.

On 9 October Donizetti wrote to Persico again. He had heard many rumours that the directorship of the Naples Conservatory was to be offered to Rossini, and he felt relieved that at last this matter was to be settled. Actually, the post did not go to Rossini, but to Saverio Mercadante, who accepted it in 1840.

> ... The post of director then is for Rossini, as many, many people write here; for me, no. All for the best, and I will prove it to you. In the coming week I begin rehearsals at the Grand Opéra with *Les martyrs*. Further, having written, scored and delivered, a little opera to the Opéra-Comique, which will be given in a month or at the most forty days, and it will be for the début of la Bourgeois. You will see by the announcement that I send you with Leopoldo [Persico's brother], that I have promised two to the Renaissance. One, the *Fiancée du Tyrol*, will be *Furioso* amplified; *L'ange de Nisida* will be new; and thus I will pass my winter in three theatres, besides the grand opera that I have to deliver now to the Opéra by the first of the coming year. You will understand that when there is so much to do, there is no time to play the rooster either with the old women or the young ones: in any event I bore myself and I amuse myself. See to it that after the leave of absence expires, that the affair passes in silence, because it would be shameful to ask for a post refused by Mercadante and not wanted by Rossini. Act as though I never had anything to do with the Conservatory, and if His Majesty should question you, say that, not seeing an acknowledgement of my memorial, I have believed myself unworthy of such a post and assumed that because of his kindness he had not dared answer me and give me a refusal; that, furthermore, in such a state of uncertainty I accepted these engagements, and that I will accept as many as will be offered, since the moment is come and gone. ...

He gives Persico some instructions about his apartment in Naples.

> ... If the furniture is ruined, sell it, for God knows what will become of me. Now that I have my heart at peace

over the Conservatory, I will lead a vagabond life, and I will keep well. I will come to Naples to sell the furniture, perhaps, and farewell. None of this is certain for now, but it will end thus. . . . I am going to take an apartment now, you know! . . .[1]

From this letter it is clear that his opera for the Opéra-Comique, *La fille du régiment*, had already been completed by early October. Of the works for the Renaissance, one of them, *L'ange de Nisida*, was to be finished, but Antenor Joly, the impresario of the company, went bankrupt before the work could be performed. Donizetti was later to salvage most of this score when he converted it into *La favorite*; the other, *La fiancée du Tyrol*, was to involve the adaptation of much of the score of *Il furioso* to a new text, but apparently Donizetti never embarked on this project because of the failure of the theatre.

Uppermost in Donizetti's mind these days were the rehearsals of *Les martyrs* scheduled to begin before the middle of October. These rehearsals did not run smoothly, however. Halévy's *Le drapier*, which was to have been produced before *Les martyrs*, had been delayed, and did not obtain its first performance until 6 January 1840.[2]

The director of music at the Opéra, Habeneck, told Donizetti that he wanted to alternate the rehearsals of *Les martyrs* with those of *Le drapier*. Donizetti refused to agree to this arrangement, for he felt he must insist upon being treated with all the consideration the Opéra accorded its regular composers. He wrote to Persico on 6 December 1839:

... I coldly took my score, I carried it home, and I did not bring it back until I received a written statement from Scribe and Halévy, assuring me that *Le drapier* would be given in this month, and they would leave January to me so that I too can give my opera. I wrote the new aria for Duprez, who was enthusiastic about it. God protect us. . . .

This contretemps helps explain, in part at least, the delay of the production of *Les martyrs*. In these days Donizetti's sensitivity went beyond his treatment in Paris, however, to the gossip

[1] Z. No. 328, pp. 502-3.
[2] *Le drapier* was one of the last works Mario sang at the Opéra before he joined the company of the Italiens.

about him going the rounds in Naples. He was concerned about the mezzo-soprano Almerinda Granchi, the original Sara in *Roberto Devereux*. She had written to him that she was without an engagement for the current season, and Donizetti told Persico that he would help her if he could. She had reported on the tales about Donizetti current in Naples.

> . . . La Granchi has written to me that here I have an old woman who makes me lavish gifts. You can say that the money I make comes in, and this should be enough to justify me. For the rest, I have no need of anyone, and I have had no cravat-pin from anybody. As to my house, we will talk about it, because I do not have the courage to sell it, since Paris is not my city. I stay here to earn money, if that is possible; then we will see what I can or must do. Greet Campagnoli and tell him that I have never received His Excellency's reply, thank him, but do not ask for any more leaves of absence, do not talk any more about the Conservatory, as it does not exist. We count upon what I earn, and leave the position to someone worthier or with more renown than I. . . .[1]

Of the new operas Donizetti wrote for Paris, the first to be given was *La fille du régiment*, although it was composed after Donizetti had finished transforming *Poliuto* into *Les martyrs* and after he had begun *Le duc d'Albe*. *La fille* was first given at the Opéra-Comique on 11 February 1840, with Euphrosyne Bourgeois, or Borghèse (Marie), Marie Julie Boulanger[2] (Marquise de Berkenfeld), Blanchard (Duchesse de Crakentorp), Mécène Marié de l'Isle, father and teacher of Galli-Marié (Tonio), Henri (Sergeant Sulpice), Riquier (Hortensius), Léon (Notary), and Plainati (Caporal). The first night, as Duprez recorded in his *Souvenirs d'un chanteur*, was almost a failure. There seems little doubt that the opera was greeted by organized hostility because this work by Donizetti had penetrated the stage of the most French of Parisian opera houses at the very time he had another opera in rehearsal at the Opéra. The clearest evidence of the move to discredit Donizetti at the start of his career in Paris is found in a witty, basically inaccurate

---

[1] Z. No. 330, pp. 505–6.
[2] Mme Boulanger *née* Hallinger (1786–1850) sang at the Opéra-Comique from 1812 to 1845. She was the grandmother of Lilli and Nadia Boulanger.

review by Berlioz, which appeared in the *Journal des débats* (16 February 1840).

These are the salient passages in Berlioz's review:

... The music of this work has already been heard in Italy, at least in great part; it is that of a little opera imitated or translated from *Le chalet* of M. Adam, and a success to which M. Donizetti does not probably attach the slightest importance. It is one of those things that one writes by the two dozen a year, when one has his head furnished and his hand light. The composer of *Lucia* and *Anna Bolena* was wrong to allow such a feeble production to be performed at the *Théâtre de la Bourse* at the moment when the attention of the dilettante public is concentrated on that work being prepared at great expense at the Opéra. Without any doubt, he could not gain any advantage for the success of *Les martyrs* from this effort; we are bold to answer that it could only be more or less unfavourable to him. When one is on the point of producing a work written *per la fama* [for fame], as M. Donizetti's compatriots would say, one must guard carefully against exposing a *pasticcio* concocted *per la fame* [for hunger]. ...

The score of *La fille du régiment* is not at all one that either composer or the public takes seriously. There is some harmony, some melody, some rhythmic effects, some instrumental and vocal combinations; it is music, if one will, but not new music. The orchestra wastes itself in useless noise; the most heterogeneous reminiscences are mingled in the same scene; one discovers the style of M. Adam next to that of M. Meyerbeer. The best parts, to my mind, are the pieces that M. Donizetti added to his Italian score to make it viable at the Opéra-Comique. The little waltz that serves as an entr'acte, and the trio *dialogué*, which was mentioned before the performance, are of this number; they lack neither vivacity nor freshness. The finale of the first act is not well defined; one looks in vain for a striking idea. A phrase by Marie in Act 2 is well launched; its design is elegant. I will say nothing of the overture. M. Donizetti does not bother himself much, very probably, with the criticisms of this score, but again, he is wrong, because of *Les martyrs*. The public does not like to be treated so cavalierly. . . .

What, two major scores for the Opéra, *Les martyrs* and *Le duc d'Albe*, two others at the Renaissance, *Lucie de Lammermoor* and *L'ange de Nisida*, two at the Opéra-Comique, *La fille du régiment* and another whose title is unknown, and still another for the Théâtre-Italien, will have been written or transcribed in one year by the same composer! M. Donizetti seems to treat us like a conquered country; it is a veritable invasion. One can no longer speak of the opera houses of Paris, but only of the opera houses of M. Donizetti. . . .[1]

On the same day that this insidious review appeared, Donizetti wrote a letter of protest which was published in the *Moniteur universel*, 18 February.

. . . The author of the article was not afraid to claim that my score has already been heard in Italy, at least in great part, and that it is a little opera, imitated or translated from *Le chalet* of M. Adam.

If M. Berlioz, who correctly places conscience among the first duties of the artist, had taken the trouble to open my score of *Betly*, of which the poem is in fact a translation of *Le chalet*, a score which has been engraved and published in Paris by M. Launer, he could have assured himself that the two operas which he cites have no music in common between them. May I be allowed to affirm, in my turn, that the music which makes up *La fille du régiment* was all written expressly for the Opéra-Comique, and that not one piece of it has figured in any score whatever.

I must conclude, M. le Rédacteur, by pointing out this crucial error on which rests, after all, the entire article by M. Berlioz, and I have the confidence that your lofty impartiality will not refuse the appearance of this correction.[2]

The false assertions and loaded arguments of Berlioz failed to achieve their purpose. *La fille du régiment* was performed at the

[1] Hector Berlioz, *Les musiciens et la musique* (Paris, 1903), pp. 149–52.
[2] Z. No. 332, p. 507.

Opéra-Comique forty-four times in 1840, eleven in 1841, and then, successfully revived in 1848, it held the stage for the rest of the century, finally achieving a total of 1044 performances at that theatre alone. Donizetti went to Italy to prepare the first Italian performance. The French text by Bayard and Saint-Georges was translated and adapted by Callisto Bassi, Donizetti supplying recitatives to take the place of the spoken dialogue. In its Italian form, as *La figlia del reggimento*, it was performed at La Scala, 3 October 1840 (just a little less than a month after the foundering of Verdi's *Un giorno di regno*). Sung by the nineteen-year-old Luigia Abbadia (Maria), Lorenzo Salvi (Tonio), and Raffaele Scalese (Sulpizio), it was cordially, if not enthusiastically received. About a month after the Milanese *prima* of *La figlia*, a pirated edition was brought out at the Teatro Nuovo, Naples, the music being sung to a text by A. Passaro. *La fille du régiment* has never been as popular in Italy as in France. In England the opera enjoyed a great vogue when the role of Marie was sung by Jenny Lind, Henriette Sontag, and Patti; in the United States it was very frequently given during the Civil War, and it is still revived from time to time.

On 7 April 1840 Donizetti wrote to Persico:

> ... You believe that *Les martyrs* has been given and regiven, eh? Not yet, and yesterday for the fourth time the dress rehearsal was announced and then called off because of sickness.
>
> Every singer, everyone except me, has fallen sick, and today we still have one invalid. Imagine if I am not bursting, or could not feel more like dying. You know very well the agitation a dress rehearsal produces. Four times in that condition, until an hour before time to begin, and then everything is postponed.
>
> Imagine how I am now. I suffer horribly from my nerves. Oh, if you only knew what one suffers when one puts on an opera here! You have no idea; enough to tell you that they annoyed Rossini. Enough of that. The intrigues, the hostilities, the journalism, the direction—*auff!* But, by God, I will bring it out, you know. . . .
>
> In a few days I will write to you of the outcome. Now I

predict it. First act—good enough; 2nd—cold; 3rd—very good; 4th—will bear up. If you could see the changes, the abridgements and lengthenings! This morning I am still working on it.

... Don't be astonished if you see me arrive in Naples at one moment or another. Until October I will be free, perhaps I will come, marry Carolina, and come back here. Is that all right? Yes! It is done then—that is—it will be done—that is—These delays make me horribly sad. . . .[1]

Carolina Giusti, whom Donizetti mentions in this letter, is the daughter of a wealthy merchant who hoped to marry her off to the successful composer. For his part, Donizetti never considered the possibility seriously, only toying with the idea when he was depressed. There had been much in the many delays of the first performance of *Les martyrs* to depress him.

Three days after he wrote this letter to Persico, *Les martyrs* was at long last produced on the stage of the Opéra, 10 April 1840. The work was sung by Julie Dorus-Gras (Pauline), Duprez (Polyeucte), Eugène Etienne August Massol (Sévère), Prosper Dérivis (Félix), Wartel (Néarche), and Serda (Callisthènes). The score was dedicated by Donizetti to Queen Marie Amélie.

A most interesting, and by no means unfavourable, review of *Les martyrs* was written by Théophile Gautier, appearing in *La presse*, 15 April 1840. Gautier takes a dim view of Scribe's libretto.

... Scribe ... has made of Félix a feeble and irresolute character, a pagan fanatic, a religious Brutus, as one can see in the sufficiently cavalier preface that precedes the libretto. We have already expressed our opinion of the versification of M. Scribe, which is without rhythm, without rhyme, without caesura, without number, in a word, the most anti-musical versification one can imagine. This explains why the furnishing of libretti is exclusively confided to him. . . .

Most of the music pleased Gautier, but especially the overture with its prayer for the chorus. To him the high point of the performance was the finale of the third act.

... The finale of Act 3 is a piece of construction very ably designed by M. Donizetti. Here, all the elements of the

[1] Z. No. 334, pp. 508–9.

drama were present; the struggle of the two worlds was established. On one side, the Pagans, having at their head the high priest Callisthènes, sacrificing to Jupiter; on the other, the Christians, with Néarche and Polyeucte, exalting the glory of Almighty God. On the first level we have Pauline and Sévère; on the second, Félix. M. Donizetti has understood in a superior way all the beauties that this situation should contain, and he has known how to render the emotions of the crowds and the feelings of the principal characters with incontestable talent. The hymn to Jupiter, executed by the priests and the people is *fatale*, as is all that belongs to religious paganisms. The profession of faith by Polyeucte roused the audience and decided the success of the work. . . .

Gautier talks at great length about the spectacular scenery and costumes. He was especially taken with the second act, representing the great square at Melitene, but since the act was entirely occupied with décor, costumes and scenery, 'the musician could not do much there'.

. . . A triumphal arch, of elegant and noble architecture, occupies much of the stage; the rest of the curtain at the back is filled with structures of all sorts: temples, colossi, colonnades, obelisks and porticoes. An immense crowd covers the square, and the painted people harmonize very happily with the live ones; this difficult transition from painting to reality is managed with much art; for brightness of light, ardour of tone, powerful effect of relief, it is difficult to go further. The antique is well understood, and all the architectural details are of . . . perfect exactitude. . . .[1]

This description helps convey some idea of the lavish staging at the Opéra in those days.

If Gautier was largely pleased with *Les martyrs*, Berlioz, on the other hand was not, contemptuously dismissing it as a 'Credo in four acts'. Donizetti, for his part, was relieved by the initial reception of his work and sent back favourable reviews of it to his friends in Italy. The work won little more than a *succès*

[1] Théophile Gautier, *L'art dramatique en France, depuis vingt-cinq ans* (Paris, n.d.), pp. 46–9.

d'estime, but circumstances were against its making a place for itself in the Paris repertory. After the fifth performance the series of presentations was interrupted by the illness of Duprez; at his recovery they were resumed only to halt in June, when Duprez was engaged to sing in the provinces during the summer. *Les martyrs* encountered a further setback when, sometime before August 1840, the director Duponchel ceded the Opéra to Léon Pillet. Although the new director opened the autumn season with *Les martyrs*, the work was allowed to lapse after its twentieth performance because the role of Pauline was suited to neither the voice nor the temperament of Mme Rosine Stolz, Pillet's mistress and a woman determined to dominate the stage of the Opéra single-handed. In the provinces, however, *Les martyrs* found greater success than in the capital city.

In Italy *Les martyrs*, which was sung in an Italian translation of the four-act version as *Paolina e Poliuto*, was soon replaced by the original three-act version, *Poliuto*. The original form of the work was first performed at the San Carlo on 30 November 1848, seven months after Donizetti's death, by Eugenia Tadolini (Paolina), Carlo Baucardé (Poliuto), Filippo Colini (Severo), Marco Arati (Callistene), and Ceci (Nearco). In this form the opera was frequently revived, particularly when Tamberlik and Tamagno won great successes in the role, and it is still revived occasionally in Italy. Now it is characteristically sung in a composite version which adds parts of the French version to the original 1838 score.[1]

At the end of May 1840 all the harassments that Donizetti had endured for the past year boiled over when he learned from Persico that the newspaper clippings reporting the good reception of *Les martyrs* had not been reprinted in the Neapolitan papers, due to the machinations of Florimo and Gennaro Giarrattelli. Having resigned from the Naples Conservatory, he was hurt by the treatment he had received in the city where he had worked long and hard. He told Persico that when he saw

[1] Perhaps the only occasion when a city could compare the French and Italian versions the same season occurred in Buenos Aires in 1854, when a French company gave *Les martyrs* at the Victoria, while an Italian troupe performed *Poliuto* at the Argentino.

239

his name praised so much in the Paris papers and in those of most of Italy, but reviled in the Neapolitan journals, 'then I laugh, I eat, I drink, I do what my heart and what friendship prompts me to'. He also reports that the Théâtre de la Renaissance has gone bankrupt and that he is left with the finished score of *L'ange de Nisida* on his hands.

A few days later Donizetti received an offer to compose an opera for Rome, the proposition coming from the impresario Vincenzo Jaccovacci, who had just assumed the direction of the Apollo, a post he was to hold honourably for more than thirty years. This opera for Rome was to be *Adelia*, but before Donizetti composed it he came to Italy and returned to Paris to put on *La favorite*.

He left Paris about the middle of June and came to Milan by way of Switzerland. There he busied himself with the preparations for *La figlia del reggimento* at La Scala, but soon he was drawn towards Bergamo, learning that his old opera *L'esule di Roma* was scheduled for performance at the Teatro Riccardi. On 1 August he wrote to Dolci:

> You believed I was in Paris, while I was travelling over the awful but splendid mountains of Switzerland, and now you may think I am at Naples, but I am writing to you from Milan. I very much want to come to Bergamo to see our Mayr, my brother, you, and my friends, but now I do not know, as here I am engaged in a suit against Ricordi,[1] and I cannot leave the city for very long. Thus I should like to combine the useful with the pleasant and come to Bergamo on the day of the first orchestral rehearsal of *L'esule*, and explain the staging and cut or adjust anything that needs it. To do this I entrust myself to you; you are (I hope) still the director for the operas, but if you are not because you made too much money or are too fat, then consider such a thought. Write to me at least two days in advance, and thus I will do one act one time and the other the following day. What I tell you you know is just between you and me. Marini, they tell me, cannot sing above C. . . .
> I want to stay in Borgo so as not to bother either you

---

[1] This suit against Ricordi was the composer's legal protest against the unsanctioned production of *Gianni di Parigi* at La Scala in 1839. Ricordi and Donizetti were soon on their old amicable terms.

or my brother nor myself with comings and goings in the warm hours. I want it well understood that none of you go to any trouble. Do not contradict me, so I shall not have to swear.

After ten days I will go to Naples, I will write the opera for Rome, and after Carnival Paris. . . .[1]

Donizetti went to Bergamo and stayed for the first performance of *L'esule di Roma* which opened the Fiera season, sung by Eugenia Tadolini, Donzelli, and Ignazio Marini. For Donzelli, Donizetti wrote a new aria. The performance was a brilliant success; but, more important, a great personal triumph for Donizetti. After this unstinting reception by the people of his own city Donizetti never again felt his reluctance about Bergamo that had been marked in his attitude and letters for almost twenty years. On 15 August, after his return to Milan, he wrote Dolci a glowing letter, full of his gratitude and appreciation.

On the same day he replied to a letter he had received from Léon Pillet, the new director of the Opéra. Pillet had written that he wanted an opera for the end of the year, but he apparently rejected the notion of doing *Le duc d'Albe*, or he planned to postpone it until some future date. He suggested that *L'ange de Nisida* be amplified to fit the requirements of the Opéra. Pillet's letter to Donizetti has apparently not survived, and even if it had, there is no assurance that it contained the real reason for rejecting *Le duc d'Albe*; the usual assumption has been that the exigent Mme Stolz did not find the role of Hélène to her taste. On the strength of this commitment for Paris, Donizetti negotiated a delay for his Roman opera from the opening of the Carnival season until February 1841. With these matters attended to Donizetti hastened back to Paris, arriving there on 2 September, having eliminated his trip to Naples.

During September 1840 Donizetti made the necessary adjustments to convert *L'ange de Nisida* into *La favorite*.

The history of no opera by Donizetti has been more consistently misrepresented than that of *La favorite*. When the

[1] Z. No. 340, pp. 516–17.

impresario of the Renaissance, Antenor Joly, gave up producing operas,[1] the score of *L'ange de Nisida* remained the composer's property. That *L'ange di Nisida* is the principal source of *La favorite*, many writers have reported; some of them have also noted that *L'ange di Nisida* incorporates parts of the earlier (1834) incomplete score of *Adelaide*. It is generally known, as well, that the famous tenor aria, *Spirto gentil*, in the last act of *La favorite* was taken from the unfinished score of *Le duc d'Albe*. So far accurate enough, but then we turn to the often-repeated story that Donizetti composed the fourth act in a single night, a story perpetrated apparently by the composer Adolphe Adam,[2] and dutifully repeated by writers on Donizetti ever since. Quite simply, this legend is not substantiated by the facts. The true story is not better known because for a long time the autograph score of *La favorite* was thought to be lost, but now the autograph is the property of Count Luigi Treccani degli Alfieri. However, a microfilm of the autograph, made to facilitate the sale of the manuscript, is in the New York Public Library and may be consulted on written permission from Count Treccani.[3]

It has been assumed that since *L'ange de Nisida* was an opera in three acts and *La favorite* is in four, the principal adjustment to the score was the addition of a new last act tacked on to the existing ones. A moment's thought about the realities of dramatic structure should reveal the implausibility of such an

[1] The last days of the Renaissance were not bolstered against financial disaster by the production of a monstrously inept four-act opera by Hippolyte Monpou, entitled *La chaste Suzanne*, which was first put on 27 December 1839 with Anna Thillon in the title role. The autograph contract for *L'ange de Nisida* is in the Bibliothèque de l'Opéra, Paris, and is dated 5 January 1840. It binds Donizetti and the librettists Royer and Vaëz to deliver the score by 1 February 1840.

Joly's company performed in the rebuilt Salle Favart, opening on 8 November 1838 with plays. He went on to giving opera, but as he was losing money he disbanded the opera company during January 1840. In February he produced a ballet, *Le zingaro* with Carlotta Grisi, but in spite of her success, Joly continued to lose money and he ceased his activities altogether on 16 May 1841.

[2] Cicconetti, the earliest of Donizetti's biographers, cites Adam as the source for this tale (Cicconetti, p. 129), but here the time is reduced to three hours. The traditional retelling of specious anecdotes customarily tries to 'dramatize' them by making short times even shorter.

[3] I am indebted to Mr Walter Toscanini, among many other things, for helping me to consult this microfilm.

Virginia Vasselli Donizetti painted by Teodoro Ghezzi in 1829

Elizabeth (Elisabetta) Ferron, the English prima donna

Carolina Ungher as Antonina in *Belisario*, 1836

Gennaio 1817
Real Teatro di S. Carlo

Il Sogno di Partenope
Cantata

Apollo
Sig Rubini

Two stars of the première of *Anna Bolena*
above Giovanni Battista Rubini, the greatest of the Bergamasc tenors; he sang in the premières of eight of Donizetti's operas
below Giuditto Pasta, the greatest singing-actress of her generation

Fanny Eckerlin

Rosamunda Pisaroni

Maria Ester Mombelli

Domenico Donzelli

Four singers associated with Donizetti's early operas

Henriette (Enrichetta) Méric-Lalande   Anna Thillon

Fanny Tacchinardi-Persiani   Giuseppina Ronzi di Begnis

Four prominent sopranos associated with Donizetti's operas

Jacopo Ferretti, who supplied Donizetti with four texts, besides revising the book of *Zoraide*

Felice Romani, the most famous theatre-poet of his day; he supplied Donizetti with seven librettos

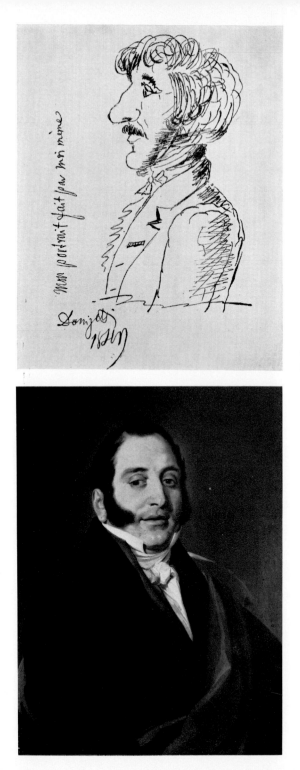

Caricature of Donizetti,
drawn by himself in 1841

Antonio Dolci, a lifelong
friend of Donizetti

Donizetti's piano which he acquired in 1822 and used until his departure from Naples in 1838

arrangement. If *L'ange de Nisida* had come to a logical dénouement, as one would expect of a libretto written by two such
knowledgeable men of the theatre as Royer and Vaëz, is it
likely that a new, second dénouement could be appended to the
already existing one? To put this problem another way, consider the dramatic situation at the end of Act 3 of *La favorite*.
Fernand has learned that his bride is the King's discarded
mistress; he accuses the King of robbing him of his honour; he
breaks his sword and casts it at the King's feet; and, thoroughly
disillusioned with the world, he allows Balthazar to lead him
back to the monastery. Certainly there is no dramatic resolution
here, and yet if one is to accept the story that the last act of
La favorite was composed later and appended to the existing
score of *L'ange*, one is forced to the conclusion that this situation, or something very much like it, was the end of *L'ange de
Nisida*.

A clue to this problem may be found in the account written
by one of Donizetti's librettists, Auguste Royer, in his *Histoire
de l'Opéra*. Royer writes:

> The work [*L'ange de Nisida*] had three acts; the first was
> enlarged to make two. The other acts remained as they
> were. A minor character disappeared; a duo subtracted
> from the score went into *Maria Padilla*, performed in Milan
> in 1841. In the duo of the fourth act, Mme Stolz had
> the romance, *Fernand, écoute ma prière*, added during
> rehearsals; the tenor's romance, *Ange si pur*, was borrowed
> from the manuscript of *Le duc d'Albe* (an unperformed
> opera). The entire fourth act was written in twenty-four
> hours by Donizetti, who had in mind only the melody of
> the famous duet.[1]

The contradiction in Royer's description is obvious. If the
first act of *L'ange* was enlarged into two, then the second and
third acts of that score would become the third and fourth acts
of the new work. Yet Royer repeats the old tale about the last
act being written in twenty-four hours. However, if the first
act of *L'ange* has been enlarged into two acts, then there is
already a fourth act. If one of Royer's statements is right, the
other must be wrong; he cannot have it both ways. But if the
fourth act is *already* composed, the process of making a few

[1] Auguste Royer, *Histoire de l'Opéra*, pp. 152–3.

textual changes, and of adding a tenor aria, likewise *already* composed, of adding some musical splices, would not seem excessive for a twenty-four-hour period, particularly for a composer who customarily worked under pressure.

But let us return to the plausibility of the idea of dividing the opening act of *L'ange* into two acts. Obviously, if a dramatic work is to be expanded, the rising action lends itself most readily to such treatment. Only a short time before Donizetti had followed precisely this pattern in enlarging the three-act *Poliuto* into the four-act *Les martyrs*. Furthermore, in both cases of *Les martyrs* and *La favorite* Donizetti was adapting a work composed for a theatre of more modest possibilities to that arena of the spectacular, the Paris Opéra. One of the special requirements for the Opéra was the inclusion of a ballet divertissement, and in both these scores the dances were spliced into the second act.

To examine the autograph of *La favorite* is to confirm these suppositions. All through the fourth act one finds the names of Sylvie and Léon, the heroine and hero of *L'ange de Nisida*, crossed out and the names of Léonor and Fernand written in above. These changes of name recur throughout the final act, except for the tenor aria, *Ange si pur*. Instead of Balthazar's name, we find Le supérieur.[1] In some of the stage directions the names have not been changed at all: for example, one reads, '*Léone sortant avec agitation de la chapelle*'. In the final duo, the names of Léone and Sylvie are again crossed out and those of Fernand and Léonor written in. Certainly Donizetti had more than 'only the melody of the famous duet' in mind as Royer claims when he made the necessary adaptation for the last act of *La favorite*; he had, in fact, the whole act already on paper and scored.[2] One passage in the final act where there is no changing of names is Léonor's prayer, *Fernand, imite la clémence* (the passage that Royer erroneously alludes to as, *Fernand, écoute ma prière*); clearly this music was composed after *L'ange de Nisida* had definitely become *La favorite*. But after this prayer, the names of the former characters recur up to the end of the

---

[1] This character, also sometimes referred to in the score as Le Moine, accounts for the changing of Balthazar, originally a purely secular character in the Leonora di Guzman story, into a priest.

[2] That it was already scored may be deduced from those passages which Donizetti discarded; the instrumentation for them is complete.

act. The most telling evidence of all occurs on the final page where, in his own hand, Donizetti has supplied the date *27 Xbre* [December] *1839*! This date demonstrates conclusively that almost all of this act had been composed more than *eleven* months before the première of *La favorite*.[1]

The autograph score of *La favorite*, especially when it is considered in relation to the materials in the Paris Conservatory, affords a fascinating glimpse of Donizetti the craftsman at work. The remarkable thing about *La favorite* is that in performance it produces a powerful, homogenous impression, scarcely suggesting the disparate origins of the score.

On 1 October 1840 Donizetti wrote to Toto that his work on the score of *La favorite* was completed.

> . . . I am being killed by the rehearsals. At this moment I finish my four-act opera, and it is a thing to make one die to be rehearsing every day. I have the compensation that all the singers are all well acquainted with their parts, except the secondary ones (as usual), but no one is absent, *et voilà tout. . . .*[2]

La favorite had its première at the Opéra on 2 December 1840, conducted by Habeneck, with Stolz (Léonor), Elian (Inès), Duprez (Fernand), Barroilhet, making his début at the Opéra (Alphonse), Nicholas Prosper Levasseur (Balthazar), and Wartel (Don Gaspar). Gautier reviewed *La favorite* for *La presse*, 7 December 1840, writing that the work aroused neither great enthusiasm nor opposition; although there were some happily conceived melodies, there were negligences which even though they might be forgiveable in Italy, were not appropriate to the 'serious habits' of the Parisian stage. He continues:

> . . . The performance is very elegant and very satisfactory. Barroilhet, the débutant, placed himself at once among singers of the first rank. His method is large and recalled the good days of the great Italian school. His voice is perhaps a little veiled; however it has much bite and easily cuts through the musical texture. He possesses a rare

---

[1] There is a further interesting note at the end of the autograph score of *La favorite*, signed by Gustave Vaëz, attesting that 'the changes of the words were written in this manuscript by me'.   [2] Z. No. 349, p. 524.

quality in bass voices, that of *smorzatura*, the art of the singer sweetly extending the sound which he carries to the highest degree.

Duprez was excellent in the scene of the confession and where he breaks his sword before the King.

Madame Stolz acted and sang the difficult role of Léonor with great dramatic feeling. In the fourth act, which recalls a little the tale of the Comte de Comminges, she projected in a superior way the devoted and melancholy mood of the character.

Levasseur often seemed to us to have trouble with his memory, but he impressed on the role of Balthazar an entirely appropriate character of unction and austerity. . . .

This splendour is worth much in winning success . . . at the opera prodigality is the best economy. . . .[1]

The reaction of the general public seems to have been somewhat more favourable than Gautier's review indicates because the work drew well and made money steadily during its first two months at the Opéra. On 8 December, Donizetti sent the Milanese publisher Francesco Lucca a bundle of favourable reviews, urging him to get them reprinted because 'every good Italian who loves his country and music should read them gladly.' The fate of *La favorite* was decisively settled on 12 February 1841, when Carlotta Grisi[2] made her début at the Opéra in the ballet divertissement of Donizetti's opera. Her success, which roused Gautier to raptures and much of the Parisian public to enthusiasm, brought new interest to the performances of *La favorite*, which was heightened when the dancer became the latest rage with her performance in the première of *Giselle*; after that she drew crowds to any work she appeared in. While Grisi's popularity did not exactly make the fortune of *La favorite*, it endowed the performances with added interest, enabling Donizetti's opera to become a great favourite, but the work held the stage long after Carlotta Grisi had left it, ultimately totalling more than six hundred performances at the Opéra.

La favorite made its way more slowly in Italy, due to the subject which, with its presentation of monks and monasteries

[1] Gautier, *L'art dramatique en France depuis vingt-cinq ans*, p. 83.
[2] Carlotta Grisi was a first cousin of the sisters Giuditta and Giulia Grisi.

and adultery, contained much to agitate the censors. As a result *La favorite* first appeared in far-fetched disguises under such titles as *Léonora di Guzman*, *Elda* and *Daila*, but it was not until the 'sixties that the opera established its great popularity, winning at La Scala alone six 'editions' in that decade. As long as Italy produces star mezzo-sopranos of the calibre of Ebe Stignani, Giulietta Simionato, and Fiorenza Cossotto, *La favorite* will continue to be heard in that country.

Donizetti had already composed the score of *Adelia* before he left Paris on 14 December 1840, starting to work on this opera as soon as he had completed the arranging, rather than the composition, of *La favorite*, an activity which had engaged him throughout September. His libretto for *Adelia ossia la figlia dell'arciere* was an old one by Romani, already set by Carlo Coccia and by several other composers, none of whom had had much success with it. As the conclusion of Romani's plot was regarded as unsatisfactory for Rome, the audiences of that city still preferring happy endings, Girolamo Maria Marini supplied the libretto for a new last act. Donizetti was not pleased with the composite botch, and against his better judgement he went ahead and set it to music. In November he had sent the first two acts to Jacovacci; the third he brought with him.

If Donizetti had been superstitious he would have had qualms about *Adelia*. Shortly before he planned to leave Paris he heard a rumour that the Pope had died, an event that would mean the closing of the Roman theatres until a new Pontiff could be elected. Only when he learned the rumour was false did he set out for Rome. His journey was a terrible one. Taking a ship at Marseilles he was immediately swept up in a violent tempest that left the vessel after five days of buffeting in the harbour of Toulon! There Donizetti spent Christmas; when the storm subsided the ship got to Leghorn in a day and a half. Shortly after he reached Rome, the Tiber overflowed its banks in a menacing flood that threatened to shut down the Apollo which was situated close to the river. Such were the omens that preceded the first performance of *Adelia*.

An omen of a different sort reached Donizetti by courier not many days after he came to Rome. He received a letter from his Paris banker, Auguste de Coussy, a strange missive that shows an almost unseemly eagerness to get his hands upon Donizetti's money.

> My dear friend,
> I have received your letter of the 19th by which you send me four bills of exchange on Persico. I do not know how to prove to you my gratitude at this new mark of your affection. I am cruelly harassed at present, and it is in your friendship that I trust; you have proven to me that it will not be wanting. You have made no error; it is precisely to me that the bill of exchange must be sent, only you would have to write to Persico that you draw on him four bills of exchange for 4000 each for three months, on Rothschild of London; this is the customary commercial practice and that will obligate him. You will urge him strongly not to fail to accept it, because then Rothschild could demand a reimbursement plus expenses.
> Now that you are close to Naples, do not fail to consider your interests and to liquidate your assets as far as you can. You will do me a service in sending me at once what you would receive, and it will not run any danger in my hands. My wife tells me that you should withdraw from Michele what he will have received. She will order it of Accursi in your name.
> Goodbye, my friend, accept again my thanks and the assurance of my friendship and gratitude.
>
> de Coussy

Directly following this letter on the same paper is an effusion from Zélie, Mme de Coussy.

> How grateful I am for all that you do for us, my dear sir! I do not know how to thank you, but God will bless you! Believe that my wishes and prayers for your happiness will be granted. You will be happy! Glory, fortune, health, you have gained them for ever. Your opera will be received with delight; triumphs will follow you everywhere; the tale of your success will sweeten my regrets. I am very depressed and very unhappy! Since your departure not a day, not a night without shedding tears. I am obliged to conceal my flowers from my husband, he is so unhappy! I should console him, it is my duty. I submit to it without

complaint, but, alas, still calling for an end to this suffering from all my desires. It is too strong, my courage deserts me.

Monsieur is unhappy. Charles naughty, you . . . absent; what is left for me? Sleep has deserted me! I take long, long drives to tire myself out; then I have a fever, and dejection brings me a few moments rest. My only distraction is to go to hear your last composition, and to enjoy the success which, alas, has brought you no benefit. So far I have gone twice to *La favorite* without being able to stay for the last act. I am so weak and in such pain that I must avoid emotions that are too strong, and this romance and this duo reminding me of a happier time tear my heart to tatters.

Accursi dined here last Thursday. His presence made me feel badly. I thought of our arrival in Italy, then he too was present. This trip to Rome ought not to have taken place! Today you get to Rome! This evening you will go to a great dinner at your brother-in-law's, Accursi told us. Have a good time! As for me, I weep and I suffer! Tomorrow, Christmas day, you will see all your friends, your artists and the Director; you will be honoured, received, you will be absentminded. You wished to be in Rome for this holiday, you told Mme Walsh. As for me, I will think of the proofs of affection that you have given to a lady by going two hundred and fifty leagues to spend this day with her. I will pass all this day in church, praying God for you, for Monsieur, and asking for myself to forget all my misfortunes. My heart tells me that my prayer will be promptly granted. I suffer too much.

Farewell, my dear sir, will you accept my wishes for happiness for the year 1841, and believe in my very sincere gratitude.

Zélie de Coussy.[1]

Zélie's letter shows that she wished to gain sympathy, that she resented Donizetti's absence in Italy, and that she was quick to advise her husband in his business. Zélie's protestations were in the nature of an omen, too, but some years would pass before she showed her hand more plainly.

Her predictions of how Donizetti spent his time in Rome

---

[1] Z. No. A. 29, pp. 887–9.

were in part correct. He arrived there shortly before the end of the year and stayed with the Vassellis. He amused himself by playing billiards with Toto and his circle of friends at the Casino de' Carbobagni. He attended the theatre.

The season at the Apollo had opened the day after Christmas with *Marino Faliero*, sung by the Bergamasc soprano Benedetta Colleoni-Corti, in place of Giuseppina Strepponi who had contracted a case of rosolia. *Faliero* did not please, and Colleoni-Corti was demoted to singing at the Valle, where she did better with *L'ajo nell'imbarazzo*. The next opera at the Apollo was the Paris version of Rossini's *Mosè*, which was well received, being sung by the three artists who were scheduled to sing in *Adelia*: Giuseppina Strepponi, Lorenzo Salvi and Ignazio Marini. Although *Mosè* drew well, the public was impatiently waiting for the première of Donizetti's opera.

Adelia was finally presented on 11 February 1841, with Giuseppina Strepponi (Adelia), Clementina Baroni (Odetta), Lorenzo Salvi (Oliviero), Ignazio Marini (Arnaldo), Filippo Valentini (Carlo di Borgogna), Pietro Gasperini (Comino), and Luigi Fosso (a Shield-Bearer); the excellent conductor Emilio Angelini directed the orchestra. In spite of all the enthusiasm built up in the audience in anticipation of the première, in spite of all the merit of the cast assembled to perform the new work, the opening night of *Adelia* was a colossal débacle. The difficulty was caused by the great demand for tickets, which was met by the unscrupulous and disastrous expedient of selling many more tickets than there were seats in the Teatro Apollo. When the huge throng descended upon the theatre, many, who felt they had every right to be inside the theatre, could not get in; those who managed to gain admittance were deeply resentful of the audible tumult, few could hear the performance, and the singers themselves were unnerved by the shouts and challenges both inside and outside the theatre. When Strepponi made her first appearance near the middle of the first act, the uproar was at such a height that she hesitated to begin her cavatina, seeing there was small likelihood that anyone could hear it. A little later Angelini halted the orchestra until some semblance of order was restored. There were fisti-cuffs among the box-holders, one hot-headed young fellow resenting the aspersions he heard cast upon the directors of the theatre, one of whom was his uncle, a noble duke. Before the evening was over, Jacovacci was arrested and hauled off to jail, along with the cash box.

Surprisingly enough with all this confusion, some attention was paid at least to the latter parts of the performance. A trio for the principals and a soprano-tenor duet were enthusiastically applauded, and Donizetti was even called to the stage four times. The second performance went more smoothly and the audience was more gracious with its approval. Jacovacci was released from prison, having paid a fine of 100 scudi, and the aristocratic pugilists were reconciled at the home of the French Ambassador. When all the confusion had completely died down, *Adelia* was seen to be a tame opera, saddled to an unfortunate libretto. One of Donizetti's Roman acquaintances reported that the composer, with his characteristic frankness, accepted the blame for the non-success of *Adelia*, admitting he had accepted a libretto not to his liking, without situations, without passions, without effects, and with verses incapable of exciting inspiration.

Donizetti did not stay in Rome for the end of the Carnival season of 1841, which terminated on 23 February with *Mosè*; he left on the 19th and moved directly to Paris. His visit to Rome, for all the pleasure of being with his brother-in-law's family and his other old friends, had been a trying time for Donizetti. Under the most favourable circumstances he found rehearsing an opera and enduring the first performance an agonizing ordeal, and what he suffered from the tempestuous opening night of *Adelia* can well be imagined. With these days is associated a rumour that is false in fact, if not in spirit. It has been alleged, and countless times repeated, that the bass Marini sang flat during the performances of *Adelia* to spite Donizetti, because he was angry at the composer's over-zealous attentions to his wife. Another more immediate explanation exists for Marini's vocal shortcomings; he was notoriously short-ranged, as Donizetti wrote to Dolci at the time of *L'esule di Roma* in Bergamo in 1840, and the tessitura of the role of Arnaldo is better suited to a baritone than to a bass. That it was Marini's wife who engaged Donizetti's attention is by no means certain, nor would it seem to have been, as some have claimed, Strepponi; but it does seem part of a pattern that Donizetti, when he was agitated and upset, sought to escape from his unhappiness in a woman's company. There are two revealing sentences in Donizetti's letter to Dolci of 30 January 1841, written from Rome. 'Find me a wife, for being alone bothers me. You could make yourself still richer by becoming a marriage broker, which in Paris is a recognized occupation.' That Donizetti again reverted to the notion of marriage suggests he felt the need of a stabilizing influence; that he never got beyond writing about it casually suggests he felt himself incapable of assuming a serious commitment, or it might mean that he had some inkling of the true nature of his physical condition, for the odds are that he had by this time contracted the disease that was to kill him.

The day before Donizetti left Rome, he wrote to Dolci (18 February 1841).

> On leaving Rome I send a greeting to you and to my native town. *Adelia* continues well . . . I return to Paris for an opera buffa, then to Milan in Carnival, then to Vienna in the spring. I received from the great Sultan, in return for an Imperial March I composed, the Order of Thourat like my brother. Napoleon belongs to two centuries, I to two religions. Don't speak of this ridiculous comparison, understand. They will be embarrassed if they take it as serious. Thus I will do as that Turk who became a Christian and having come to the last moments of his life, on one hand prayed with the priest, then he turned and cursed in Turkish; for this the priest asked him why if he prayed with him, had he turned his head and muttered in Turkish; he answered that he had been born a Turk but died a Christian, and that not knowing in the beyond whom he would find to judge him, Christ or Mohammed, he wanted to take care of both contingencies, and therefore he prayed in both languages.
>
> Joking apart, this honour has given me great pleasure, and I believe that you too will be pleased. . . .[1]

The day after Donizetti left Rome he reached Civitavecchia, accompanied by some of his friends, but not by Toto, who was ill. At Civitavecchia, on the 20th, he was fêted at a performance of *L'esule di Roma*. Here he took a ship to Marseilles and was

[1] Z. No. 356, p. 530.

back in Paris on 2 March, taking up lodgings at the Hôtel Manchester, Rue Grammont No. 1.

Back in Paris Donizetti was approached by Scribe, who suggested a subject that did not please Donizetti; he went to see Pillet to have it changed. On the strength of the success of *La favorite* Pillet was anxious to have another score from Donizetti, and the suggestion of a new libretto indicates that the production of *Le duc d'Albe* was still in abeyance, that the conditions making for its postponement still obtained.

About the opera buffa Donizetti mentioned in his letter to Dolci, written just before he left Rome, there is some mystery. This work may have been the second opera he was supposed to write for the Opéra-Comique, but he was never to finish another work for that theatre, although in 1842 he composed seven numbers for a score entitled *Ne m'oubliez pas*, which was intended for that house. In the spring of 1841, in fact, Donizetti was not occupied with composing an operatic score. He wrote a collection of songs, *Matinées musicales* which he dedicated to Queen Victoria, and in May he improvised a cantata to be performed on the occasion of Mayr's seventy-eighth birthday in Bergamo.

On 14 June a big concert or Accademia was given in Bergamo to celebrate the grand old man's birthday. On 18 May, Donizetti received a letter from Bergamo announcing the plans, and in a very short time he had composed the cantata to hastily adapted verses. Far more than the musical value of his contribution is the promptness and warm-heartedness of Donizetti's response to the man he revered above all others. He wrote Dolci a letter accompanying the cantata:

> I am sure, dear brothers (*confratelli*) that you will laugh in looking at what I have made, but consider—that today the 18th I received your letter, that this very day if there is time I will put it in the post, but I am afraid not (there is only a quarter of an hour before it leaves), that for such a fine occasion I would have wanted to speak or sing or play to heaven and earth, that the time presses, that afterwards it would be too late, that the doing of it, either for better or worse (the latter certainly) made me seize the time—that I did it then! Thus you see—He is named Giovanni, San Giovanni is the patron of music, which

everyone knows to be made on the notes of the scale *ut, re, mi*, etc., after that, I found a poem on Genius, then I changed the words of the first verse, and made it seem that his genius guided mine in the time of my youth (period of the Middle Ages), he encouraged it, sustained it, as he did (and here forgive if I dare to call genius my good intentions). Thus I take flight, and traverse the reaches of the sky to its flaming edge, until from too much boldness I try to approach the sun, and the wings of wax melt and I fall into the sea of oblivion. For this time alone I can follow the precept; *do not mingle the sacred and the secular.* As one many times in a single meal mixes lean and fat foods, could I not be with you and shout *Viva Mayr*: 'Our Father who art on earth' in two languages? . . .[1]

Donizetti gave instructions to Dolci just how the cantata was to be performed, especially at the final cadence, when everyone, including the orchestral players, were to shout 'Viva Mayr', saying he wanted to hear the uproar all the way to Paris: 'of both my shouting and my wish, his heart will be the best interpreter.' When the concert was given, Donizetti's cantata was the final composition on the programme, which included performances by Mayr's pupils and admirers and some of the old master's compositions. One of the most interesting numbers on the programme was a set of variations on *Tu che a Dio spiegasti l'ali* from Donizetti's *Lucia*, performed by the cellist, Alfredo Piatti, one of the most celebrated alumni of Mayr's school.

Sometime during this summer of 1841, apparently feeling a little at a loose end because his negotiations with the Parisian theatres were still in the air and the final arrangements for his new opera for La Scala not yet settled, Donizetti turned his hand to something a little more substantial than concert songs and improvised cantatas for Mayr. In a very short time he wrote a one-act farce called *Rita ou le mari battu*. The story is told that he met the librettist Gustave Vaëz out walking one day and asked him to suggest a subject. Out of this chance encounter, and without any settled contract for its production, Donizetti composed his charming farce. The opera remained unperformed until after his death, when it was brought out at

[1] Z. No. 363, p. 537.

the Opéra-Comique, 7 May 1860, with Caroline Lefebvre (Rita), Warot (Beppe), and Barrielle (Gasparo). Because of its genuinely funny plot and blithe score, this little work has enjoyed a flurry of performances in the last twenty years, totalling more than it received in the first eighty-odd years of its existence.

After Donizetti's elation over Mayr's cantata, his spirits slumped once more. Victor Hugo had raised trouble about Donizetti's operatic treatment of *Lucrèce Borgia*. In May, the opera had been performed with great success for three evenings in Metz, when Hugo applied to the courts to have the representations stopped, claiming that Donizetti's work was a misuse and infringement of his own property. Donizetti's librettist sued and won his case, but the whole affair seemed a symptom of the many annoyances that plagued him.

At the end of July Donizetti wrote to Toto, telling him that every week *La France musicale* was printing 'horrors' about him.

> ... however I do as everyone does, I let them talk, I laugh, and I pass on. There are many others who speak well of me. Philosophy, dear Toto. ...

His deep-lying sensitivity, morbidity even, is shown in the same letter when Donizetti refers to his feelings on the fourth anniversary of Virginia's death, two days before.

> ... On the 29th I wept as if it had been the first day of my misfortune. I could not do anything less. In the midst of my joys if one thought of her presents itself, the tears follow. To whom can I tell this? Who would believe it? In me? In me, whom everyone believes busy, gay. ...[1]

As long as he was able Donizetti's one method to conquer his low spirits was to lose himself in work. Soon he was deeply involved in his next opera, *Maria Padilla*, which was to open the Carnival season of 1841–42 at La Scala. For this opera Donizetti found himself collaborating with one of the oldest and most prolific, if not the most talented, librettists in Italy, Gaetano Rossi (1775–1855). A native of Verona, Rossi had

[1] Z. No. 369, pp. 549–50.

written a text for Mayr, *Che originali!*, as early as 1798, the first
of eighteen librettos he was to write for him. Among the more
than a hundred opera books he had produced the best known
were two he supplied to Rossini, *Tancredi* and *Semiramide*. For
Maria Padilla, his first text for Donizetti, Rossi had turned to a
French play of the same name (1838) by François Ancelot. He
had sent the first portion of his libretto to Donizetti probably in
July, for by 10 August the composer could report that he was
already 'sufficiently advanced' with his score.

A week later Donizetti had left Paris and gone to Baden.
From here he wrote to Rossi, sending his letter via Merelli,
who was then the director of La Scala, asking for the rest of the
drama and making suggestions for the treatment of various
episodes. One passage from this letter shows Donizetti's skill at
conceiving a dramatic situation.

> . . . For the big duet in Act 3, I leave everything to you;
> it seems best to me, however, that Maria should begin the
> story of her life since she has been the King's mistress and
> that her father should listen to her distractedly. Afterwards
> by his few broken words unrelated to what she said, Maria
> perceives his madness; but it is necessary that the first
> time, that is in the middle of Maria's narrative, he should
> give an answer that she can believe relevant to what she
> has been saying, so that she continues. Then finally he (if
> it is wanted), instead of answering his daughter, can begin
> in tearful phrases an adagio, where he reproves her
> behaviour without seeing her, without looking at her, etc.,
> and stopping all of a sudden in the middle of the last
> phrase, he perceives at his feet his daughter (or a woman)
> and goes into a rage etc., but it should finish with both of
> them still weeping. . . .[1]

It is not clear how long Donizetti remained in Baden. From
the letters of Accursi and de Coussy of April 1845,[2] it is possible
that this is the occasion when they were all together in Baden
and Donizetti watched his banker lose 10,000 francs by following a gambling system. In any event, Donizetti was in Milan by
the end of September.

There he wrote to Toto on the 29th that he was still working
on *Maria Padilla*. Originally, he had hoped to have Erminia

[1] Z. No. 372, pp. 552–3.   [2] See pp. 294–8.

Frezzolini[1] create the title role, but she was pregnant and expecting her first child in December or January. The role of Maria was finally assigned to Sofia Löwe (1816–66), who had been singing the previous summer in England without arousing great enthusiasm. On 10 December the rehearsals began, all the company being present but Donzelli, who was due in a day or two. The book had been approved by the censors, but with an alteration that did not at all please Donizetti. In the original libretto Maria had committed suicide, but the authorities objected to such terminations and insisted that she 'die of joy'![2] *Maria Padilla* opened the Carnival season 26 December 1841 at La Scala, being sung by Löwe, Luigia Abbadia (Inès), Donzelli (Don Ruiz di Padilla), Giorgio Ronconi (Don Pedro), and Gaetano Rossi (Don Ramiro). The opera was enthusiastically applauded, but there was a widespread feeling that the work was hampered by Rossi's libretto, a judgement that it is difficult not to share. At the first performance Donizetti was called out twice, and six pieces were applauded. The second performance went even better, as Donizetti was to send Toto a detailed account on 28 December, soon after the performance was over.

> Maestro on stage.
> Cavatina *Inès*—Maestro out once.
> Cavatina *Maria*—Maestro out once.
> Appearance of *D. Pedro*—Applause: maestro out once.
> Duet for *D. Pedro* and *Maria*—Much applause. Artists out, maestro no.

Act 2

> Chorus—Applause.
> Cavatina *Ruiz*—Donzelli out.

---

[1] Erminia Frezzolini (1818–84) was the daughter of the buffo Giuseppe Frezzolini, the original Dr Dulcamara. She had made her début in 1838 in *Beatrice di Tenda*; and was such a sensation that she opened the Carnival season at La Scala, 26 December 1839; less than a month later she won a major triumph there in the version of *Lucrezia Borgia* with the new ending. Shortly after this she married the tenor Antonio Poggi. Her name is best remembered today as a member of the first casts of two of Verdi's operas: *I Lombardi alla prima crociata* and *Giovanna d'Arco*.

[2] Those who object to the vague and unconvincing methods of demise encountered in operas of this period should remember the censors and their restrictions.

Duet for *Maria* and *Inès*—Maestro out twice.
Duet for *Ruiz* and *D. Pedro*—Much applause.
Stretta finale—Little applause.

Act 3

Trio for the two women and second tenor—Applauded.
Duet for *Ruiz* and *Maria*—Maestro out after the adagio,
   and afterwards everyone.
Chorus—Nothing.
Romance for Ronconi or *D. Pedro*—Maestro out once.
Finale—Maestro out after the adagio. Afterwards everyone
   out. The Maestro twice alone and twice with the artists.[1]

Maria Padilla did not hold the stage long. It was produced in
Naples with Tadolini, Basadonna and Filippo Coletti in 1842,
and again at Milan, this time at the Canobbiana in 1849, but
in neither place did it make a lasting impression. The libretto
was translated into French by Hippolyte Lucas and was played
occasionally in the provinces of France, but apparently, never
in Paris, except for the duet for the two women which became
a warhorse for Fanny Persiani and Jeanne Castellan, these
ladies interpolating it into other scores. The footlights have not
come up on a performance of *Maria Padilla* for over a century.

During the time that Donizetti was concerned with *Maria
Padilla* he composed a *Miserere* for the Vatican choir, at the
request of Toto; as a reward for this composition, he received
the Order of San Silvestro, a Papal honour limited to three
hundred recipients. Donizetti's letters reveal that he had
developed an almost childish delight in orders and recognitions
of this kind; in this matter he never lost the wonder and pleasure
of one who knows that he was born poor and without social
backing.

During this stay in Milan, at the time of *Maria Padilla* and in
the months following, Donizetti went out often in Milanese
society. He was the musical lion of the day; although he was
soon to be seriously challenged in this role by the twenty-nine-
year-old Giuseppe Verdi, whose *Nabucco* in March 1842 was to
provide one of the greatest triumphs La Scala had ever seen.

[1] Z. No. 390, p. 571.

Donizetti became a frequenter of various salons, especially that of Giuseppina Appiani in the Borgo Monforte.[1] This charming and forthright woman seems to have had no romantic attachment for Donizetti, but rather a sincere friendship and concern, and took him to live in her house where she had already lodged another waif, Sandrini, who was apparently a friend of the family. It was in the home of this hospitable woman that Donizetti lived during the months before his departure for Vienna while engaged in composing *Linda di Chamounix*.

On 16 February 1842 Donizetti announced to Toto that 'the opera is almost finished'; thus, *Linda di Chamounix*, the opera with which he hoped to impress the demanding Viennese public, was written in large part in the month and a half following the production of *Maria Padilla*. On Christmas 1841, just prior to the first performance of that opera, he had sent Toto a description of the plot of *Linda*, that libretto being also the work of Gaetano Rossi.

> . . . Do not go searching in history for the subject for Vienna. They are youngsters who leave Savoy for Paris where they earn their bread. There is one who is good and one who is bad. Many times the girl is on the point of allowing herself to be seduced, but every time she heard a song from her home and thinks of her father, of her mother, she resists. Then she does not resist any more—the seducer wants to marry another girl. Then she becomes mad (*auff*); then she returns to her home with a poor boy who makes her walk by means of playing the song; if not, she stops. Both of them almost die of hunger; the seducer arrives—he has not married. The girl regains her senses when she learns of it. . . .
>
> Do not speak ill of it to me, because I have seen the play in Paris. It is short and serves my purpose. . . .[2]

This letter is interesting because it hints at the original form of the plot which was later diluted for Viennese sensibilities. According to this summary Carlo succeeds in seducing Linda,

[1] Frank Walker, *The Man Verdi*, pp. 96–116, exposes much of the romantic nonsense that has been written about Peppina Appiani, Donizetti, and Verdi, putting it to the test of reason and common sense.

[2] Z. No. 389, p. 570. The play on which *Linda di Chamounix* is based is *La grâce de Dieu* by d'Ennery and Lemoine.

while, in the final form of the story, she has innocently allowed herself to be compromised by Carlo, and although she accepts his hospitality she will not even allow him the compensation of a kiss until she is lawfully married to him.

Before Donizetti left for Vienna he was invited to take part in an historic series of performances. Rossini invited him to conduct the *Stabat Mater* at its inaugural performances in Italy, on 18, 19, and 20 March 1842. This work, though parts of it were ten years old, had not been completed by Rossini until late the preceding year; it had had its first performance in Paris at the Salle Ventadour on 7 January 1842 with Grisi, Albertazzi, Mario and Tamburini as the solo quartet. Rossini was not present at this wildly successful performance in Paris; he was in Bologna where he had assumed the care of the Liceo Musicale two years previously. Obviously, an important new work by Rossini was eagerly anticipated in Italy, and equally obviously Bologna was the site for its introduction to the composer's native country. At this stage of his retirement Rossini's neurasthenia had reached such an acute form that the notion of personally directing the performance was out of the question; indeed, Rossini was not even present for the first two evenings, and on the final night was only with difficulty persuaded to overhear the performance from an adjoining room. Since he could not bring himself to conduct his *Stabat Mater*, Rossini turned to Donizetti for a variety of reasons. For one thing Donizetti was the nearest approach to Rossini's successor then active on the Italian scene;[1] for another, Donizetti was currently the most distinguished graduate of the Bologna Liceo Musicale, with the exception of Rossini himself; and last, Rossini hoped to persuade Donizetti to assume the directorship of the Liceo. Donizetti was flattered by Rossini's invitation to conduct the *Stabat Mater* and hastened to accept it.

Donizetti sent word of the invitation to Toto, on 4 March.

> . . . I leave this coming Tuesday [10 March]. For where? For Bologna. Ah, you are making fun of me—But—I don't believe it. If I arrange with my singers, who are travelling with me . . . I am going to Bologna, for the *Stabat* which is

---

[1] The arrangements were obviously completed before the *prima* of *Nabucco* (9 March 1842); therefore Verdi could scarcely have been considered for this assignment.

being given on the 18th and later; then, by diligence via Ferrara, Padua, etc. I go to Vicenza on the 22nd and there I meet my companions for the Viennese trip. Do you know why I am doing this? Because Rossini, as soon as he heard I was going there, wrote to me that he wanted by all means to entrust me with the direction of the *Stabat* and put at my disposition *his life and all his possessions*. You see that such an invitation is not repeated. To be sure I do not want to conduct, because I would tremble before him, but I want to show my gratitude to him.

My opera for Vienna is finished, orchestrated, retouched, etc.; it leaves today for Vienna. . . .[1]

Donizetti left Milan on the day following the *prima* of *Nabucco* at La Scala, and an often-told anecdote relates that he kept talking all the way to Bologna of the beauties of Verdi's score and of the brilliant future before that young man. Donizetti conducted the rehearsals for the opening performance of the *Stabat Mater*, which turned out to be a brilliant success. The solo quartet was Clara Novello, the English soprano; a dilettante contralto from Bologna named Degli Antonj; the Russian tenor Ivanoff, who had left the Italiens to continue his career in Italy; and for the bass solos, Count Pomeo Belgioioso, a Milanese who was one of Rossini's dearest friends. Of all the singers connected with these performances, the one whose name was ultimately to be the most widely known appeared, modestly enough, in the ranks of the chorus—the nineteen-year-old Marietta Alboni, the famous contralto, then studying singing with Rossini.

Donizetti's own reactions to the triumph of Rossini's *Stabat Mater* appear in several letters he wrote to his friends. On the day of the final performance, 20 March, he wrote to Persico:

. . . Today we have come to the third and final performance. The enthusiasm is impossible to describe. At the end of the general rehearsal, which Rossini attended, he was, in full daylight, amid the shouts of more than five hundred people, accompanied home. The same thing the first evening, under his windows; nevertheless he was not in the auditorium; and yesterday the same thing. . . . We are *écrasés* by applause and shouting and poems etc. . . .

[1] Z. No. 399, p. 579.

. . . Rossini besieges me and lures me to accept the direction of this Liceo and the chapel [S. Petronio]. If it does
not suit me, I can leave when I want. Leave twice a year.
What do you say to it? I will write to you from Vienna. . . .[1]

On 30 March he sent Persico a few more details of the per-
mances:

. . . Let me tell you that the din made at Bologna over
Rossini and me was indescribable. Bands, cheers, poetry.
Finally Rossini, whom I obliged to attend the third
performance, was fêted as he deserved and came to the dais
where I conducted and embraced me and kissed me and
shouts deafened us both. At my departure he presented me
with four studs as a souvenir and he wept openly with his
arms around my neck saying over and over: *Don't abandon
me, dear friend.* Everyone was astonished by his demonstrating so much emotion. . . .[2]

When Donizetti got to Vienna he repeated his performances of
the *Stabat Mater* that spring of 1842; first a private hearing for
the Imperial Court, and later an enthusiastically received
performance in the Redoutensaal.

As Donizetti had planned he met the company of singers who
were journeying to Vienna for the Italian season at the Kärthnerthortheater in Vicenza, and travelled with them to the
Hapsburg capital, arriving there on 27 March 1842. The
principal Viennese opera house was then under the management of Merelli, who had close and influential friends in Vienna.
In fact, Merelli's sympathies were such that after 1850, when he
released the reins of La Scala, he continued his activities in
Vienna for some time, even contributing, in 1854, as part of
celebrations of the marriage of Emperor Franz Josef and
Elisabeth, a cantata entitled *Un viaggio a Vienna*, to which he
had written both words and music! In 1842, however, Merelli
kept his principal headquarters in Milan and operated the
Kärthnerthortheater through a partner, Carlo Balocchino
(1770–1851), who had been associated with Barbaja during his
Vienna season of 1822. In Vienna the Kärthnerthortheater

[1] Z. No. 401, p. 581.   [2] Z. No. 402, p. 582.

gave performances all the year round in German, except for the months of April, May, and June, when many of the most prominent Italian singers were free of engagements after the principal Carnival season in Italy to journey to the Austrian capital.

At first Donizetti was much taken with Vienna; '*bella, bella, bella*', he had written to Persico. He had come armed with a very warm letter of recommendation from Rossini to Metternich, and this missive, promptly presented, opened many doors for him. Donizetti, on 4 April, described Vienna in slightly less enthusiastic terms to Toto:

> ... In Vienna things do not go badly, but if I told you that it is more expensive than Paris, perhaps you would not believe me, but so it is.

In this letter he mentions that he is still considering the offer from Bologna.

> ... You cannot believe the pleasure that your letter which I found here urging that I accept the two posts at Bologna has given me. I think as you do, I am altogether tired of this gypsy life. If (as says Donzelli, who is living in Bologna) *they will give me everything, and more yet if I had asked for it*, the thing is not unpleasant. Mercadante asked 50 scudi a month; and I 60; he would have been satisfied with most modest quarters near S. Petronio; I want 80 collonati a year and to choose my quarters where I please. He wanted three months' leave a year, and obligated himself in his free time to make up lessons; not I. I asked up to six months, if it was needed, of vacation, at the same pay. The copying of the music paid by them, because the copies stay at the church. To give lessons for two hours instead of three; to write only one composition a year for S. Petronio; to be able to bring all the pupils from the school to S. Petronio and have them sing free any music that I write. You see, by God, that the only thing lacking is the saying: *Look at me and you pay me*. We shall see if Donzelli speaks the truth. Then my life is finished, then all the prophecy that I made about myself comes true; then I will be nothing but the school.

Michele does not stop writing to me: *come, come, you*

must, you are most necessary, but I hang back, because not even Paris attracts me, nor ever could attract me. I continue to wait for the answer from Bologna, because the *yes* or the *no* or the modifications of my proposal cannot be long coming. . . .[1]

Donizetti's feeling towards the proposal from Bologna cooled the longer he was away and the more he saw of the cordiality of the Austrian capital.

As soon as Donizetti had arrived in Vienna the rehearsals for the Italian season began. He sent many reports of the shade of success or failure enjoyed by each production. Donizetti's position with the company involved not only producing his new opera, but serving to help with the necessary musical modifications that each production involved. It is clear from his report about this season of 1842 that Merelli did not always engage a company well adapted to the works that were scheduled; Merelli's remissness on this score over the next three years was to become a matter of increasing vexation to Donizetti.

Donizetti was anxious about the success of *Linda di Chamounix*, and accordingly he kept the opera in rehearsal longer than was his custom: through most of April and the first half of May. The first orchestral rehearsal took place on 10 May. On the 15th, he wrote to Dolci about the approaching production:

> . . . Up to now it is going not badly. If I were to tell you what the singers thought, they are pleased; but the Theatre, dear friend, is a beautiful woman and one tempts you with applause, and the other with caresses, and when you are as certain of the success of the opera as you are of that one's love, she turns her back on you and the theatre converts the certainty into a fiasco; thus, for one or other, you remain with your face in your hands. . . .[2]

The first performance took place on 19 May 1842 with Eugenia Tadolini (Linda), Marietta Brambilla (Pierotto), Napoleone Moriani (Carlo), Felice Varesi (Antonio), Prosper Dérivis (Prefetto), and Agostino Rovere (Marchese). The opera, dedicated to the Empress Anna, was an immediate success.

[1] Z. No. 404, p. 585. [1] Z. No. 415, p. 601.

Donizetti described the happy evening to Toto two days later.

> . . . The composer called out seventeen times alone and with the singers. The theatre packed. Second performance: an enormous crown of flowers thrown to the composer. Monday, third performance (and then Moriani did not feel very well). Moriani's benefit. The composer conducted in person. The papers speak with much enthusiasm. . . .[1]

Shortly afterwards he sent word about it to Ricordi.

> . . . Moriani's benefit made 2200 florins. I believe that is the best praise that can be given to my poor music. Last evening the whole Imperial family were there; and they did not leave until they had seen me come out twice, joining their applause to that of the public. . . . Last evening after the second act another immense crown of flowers was given by the public to the worthy Tadolini. All the singers compete in zeal, all know how to win applause, but la Tadolini stands revealed in a surprising manner. She is a singer, an actress, everything, and imagine that she is applauded just at her appearance in Act 3. I believe that if you saw *Linda* with Tadolini you would truly see a new type of madwoman, for she has been obedient to my directions. She weeps, laughs, remains stupefied as required, and I say myself that this scene is superior (performed thus) to all the mad scenes I have written. . . .[2]

The next important production of *Linda* was at the Italiens on 17 November 1842, the production being prepared by Donizetti. The role of Linda was a great success for Persiani, and for her Donizetti composed and wrote the words to what is now the most famous excerpt from the opera, *O luce di quest' anima*, which was not part of the original Viennese score. The rest of the cast for the Paris *prima* included Brambilla, Mario, Tamburini, and Lablache. Gautier found the opera more worked out than most of Donizetti's scores and called it irreproachable. La Scala did not hear *Linda* until 2 March 1844, when it again earned a great success as sung by Tadolini, Alboni, Italo Gardoni (Carlo), Filippo Colini (Antonio),

[1] Z. No. 417, p. 604.   [2] Z. No. 418, p. 605.

Camillo Fedrighini (Prefect), and Rovere. The opera was performed regularly all through the nineteenth century, and still enjoys occasional revivals today.

The rest of Donizetti's first season in Vienna was taken up with official duties and overseeing the opera season. On 4 May he had presented the private performance of Rossini's *Stabat Mater* for the Imperial Court, and on 30 May he staged the still-remembered first public performance at the Redoutensaal. For the first performance Donizetti was rewarded with a diamond cravat-pin, and he retaliated by composing an *Ave Maria* for five voices and string accompaniment which he dedicated to the Empress. It seems obvious from Donizetti's attention to official duties and from his diligence in the matter of compliments to the court that he hoped some kind of appointment would crown his efforts. Until he was assured on this point, he was more than usually uncertain about his future plans.

On 15 May he had written of his uncertainty to Dolci.

> . . . At the end of this month I will no longer be in Vienna; already for the 30th I have given up my lodgings. Where I will go then, I myself do not know if it will be to Naples, to Paris or Milan. Everything can be decided from one moment to another by the letters that arrive. I would most like to go to Milan; but it is four years and more since I went to Naples, and I want at last to settle my affairs, then go away quietly if that is possible. In any case with my letter in which I will inform you of the outcome [of *Linda*], you will learn my fate for the future and whatever it is, one or the other, I believe that it will not stop our travelling together. Today I did not eat because I was tired from the rehearsals. . . .[1]

His indecisiveness continued for more than a month; he was alternately buoyed up by the continuing success of *Linda* and depressed by the heat (only a month before it had been snowing and freezing) and by an attack of tonsilitis. His letters of this time are full of complaints of the changeable climate of Vienna. He was also concerned about a pupil, Matteo Salvi (1816–87),

[1] Z. No. 415, p. 602.

266

who had come from Bergamo to study with Sechter and, hoping to become a writer of operas, had attached himself to Donizetti. Salvi, who was in 1881–82 to prepare the incomplete score of *Il duca d'Alba* for performance, followed Donizetti like a worshipful puppy. As Donizetti reported to Dolci, Salvi—

> studies, but he needs scolding. He is rather cool of temperament, and I do not know whether it is fear or respect or whether he does not dare enough, and thus I seek to encourage him as much as I can. He is possessed to follow only me. . . .[1]

Later, reverting to Salvi's want of fire, Donizetti told Dolci that the young man did not even seem like a Bergamasc![2]

As an antidote to Donizetti's frustrations over the opera season, a largely undistinguished one except for the triumphant *Linda*, and over his efforts to cheer Salvi, he had the satisfaction, on 28 May 1842, of being made an Honorary Member of the Gesellschaft der Musikfreunde, one of the most distinguished of the Viennese musical organizations. An even greater honour was in store for him, as he hints to Dolci on 16 June:

> You must know (and this is a secret for now and I urge you strongly to keep it one) that I was called to Court to know if I would accept the post that Krommer[3] formerly, Mozart and Kozeluch,[4] etc. held, that is Kapellmeister to His Majesty the Emperor, receiving orders only from him through the Grand Chamberlain. There would be the obligation of directing concerts in the royal apartments only two or three times a year, paying me separately for every cantata that might be commissioned, every year

[1] Z. No. 411, p. 597.
[2] Salvi was later to write four operas, none of which earned much success. One, *La prima donna*, a one-act farce, was brought out at the Kärthnerthortheater the following year with Tadolini and promptly disappeared into the dustbin. His *Lara* and *I burgravi* both had very brief careers at La Scala; his *Caterina Howard* came, and promptly went, in Vienna (1847).
[3] Fritz Krommer (1759–1831) a violinist and composer, had held the post of Hofkapellmeister from 1818 until his death. Schubert as a young man thought Krommer's symphonies laughable.
[4] Leopold Kozeluch (1754?–1818) succeeded Mozart, whom he treated shamefully, as Hofkapellmeister in 1792. Beethoven, with considerable justice, habitually referred to Kozeluch as '*miserabilis*'.

having five or six months' leave, and there is attached to the post an honorarium of three thousand a year. I said if His Majesty wanted it, I would serve for nothing, but, if His Majesty wanted to raise his benevolence to the summit, I would accept such conditions for four thousand florins, making him understand that in two months with a single opera I had received the same amount.

My remark was not found unjust. I was told to put it in writing, and I did so and gave it to him so that it could be presented; perhaps today His Majesty will see it. And that is why I urge you to keep it secret for now. . . . Before my departure I shall know, I hope, yes or no. . . . [1]

On 3 July 1842 the appointment was formally made with a salary of 12,000 Austrian lire a year, and accepted. Donizetti found great satisfaction in this honour, which seemed to insure him a place in history.

On 1 July Donizetti left Vienna for Milan, after having taken leave of the Imperial family. At Milan he once again stayed in the Appianis' house. After a few weeks in Milan he made a short trip to Bergamo on the 8th, seeing Dolci and Mayr and the Basonis. That summer was unusually hot and Donizetti was troubled with severe headaches. When he returned from his brief stay in Bergamo he wrote to Dolci assuring him that he had not been in a bad humour, but only suffering from a headache. On 30 July he left Milan for Genoa where he took a ship for Naples.

When the ship put into Civitavecchia Donizetti sent a brief note to Toto. A portion of this letter is symptomatic of the nervous agitation that made the final years of his career restless and erratic.

. . . Your blame for my accepting the most honourable post is unjust. Six months free are a fine thing; a thousand lire a month at Vienna and away are not to be despised. Do you know that at Bologna they only wanted to grant three months' leave at a time? Do you know that I would have to be without fail in Bologna on S. Petronio's Day? That it would not be enough to compose new music, I would be wanted there in person? . . . Do you know, on the other hand, that my post was Mozart's? That His Majesty

[1] Z. No. 428, p. 616.

asks only two concerts a year and that if I am commissioned to write music, I am paid for it?

Reflect more and encourage me, because it breaks my heart in two to leave Naples, and this is not because of Naples, but myself. You speak to me of other women? Oh, laugh, then, and believe that I still weep as on the first day. Oh, if I could find some distraction! Believe it, I seek to stupefy myself. Enough. . . .[1]

Toto's anger at Donizetti's acceptance of the post of Hof-kapellmeister to the Hapsburg Emperor and his concomitant refusal of Bologna has probably a double explanation. With the rising tide of national feeling in Italy during the 'forties, the fact of Donizetti's acceptance of an official court post to the Emperor of Austria did not sit well at all, and it is possible that Toto shared to some extent this point of view. His chief reasons for wishing that Gaetano had accepted the offer from Bologna were his concern over the vagabond life that his career forced upon his brother-in-law and his deep-seated conviction that Donizetti needed a more settled, a more orderly environment.

Gaetano reached Naples on the 4 or 5 August. Not only had he come to see about his business and his apartment there, but also to visit his old friends Persico, Ghezzi and Benevento. While he was there *Maria Padilla* had its first Neapolitan performance at the San Carlo, the occasion was a warm personal tribute to Donizetti although the opera enjoyed no longer life there than anywhere else. He came to negotiate a contract with Edouard Guillaume, then the director of the Royal theatres in Naples. In return for 2400 ducats he agreed to write an opera for October 1843, but months elapsed before the subject was finally agreed upon, and even then the première of the opera was delayed until January 1844.

The excitements of his visit to Naples and the memories awakened in him by being back there for the first time in more than four years affected his health. Twice in a little over three weeks he went to bed with a fever. On the second occasion a gratifying incident occurred which he duly reported to Dolci, on 29 August.

. . . It has given me great pleasure to see Naples and to find all my friends still the same, and to see a large crowd that

[1] Z. No. 437, pp. 623-4.

assembled almost spontaneously at the theatre to see me again! Kept in bed by a fever, I had to get up and go and show myself, being almost obliged to do so by the police. . . .[1]

He could not, however, bring himself to sell his possessions there, postponing his decision until the following year when he planned to return to Naples. He left Naples on 6 September but because of stormy weather it took him more than a week to reach Genoa.

On 15 September he wrote to Dolci to inform him of his plans.

> . . . After three months in Paris I will go to Vienna to fill my position. It is right! I am very sad, although smothered with honours, applause, fêted everywhere. It makes no difference! Nothing fills a void. The weather is very fine, the sea is calm. I suffered much for two nights—horrible storms. Yesterday we were forced to stand in at Leghorn for twenty-four hours because of the foul weather. It is the equinox. What difference does it make? If God wants me, *here I am*. I found many in Naples to whom I have done good, they will intercede for me; if I have done harm to anyone it was without wanting to. . . .[2]

Arriving at Paris before the end of September and unsure what engagements he would accept, he made tentative plans to work with Hippolyte Lucas on French translations of *Maria Padilla* and *Linda*; the latter opera he had agreed to stage at the Italiens. There had been negotiations with the Opéra, but since Pillet had not yet shown any interest in staging *Le duc d'Albe*, he had made no definite commitment.

On 27 September 1842 he signed a contract for a new opera for the Italiens, the first new opera he was to write for that company since *Marino Faliero* almost eight years before. This was to be *Don Pasquale*. At that time he had already started on another work for Vienna, to be given there in the spring of 1843. He had secured for this work a libretto, entitled *La regina di Cipro*, from Giacomo Sacchero, based on a recent French success by Halévy to a text by Saint-Georges. Composers turned to French operas as the sources of plots with such frequency during the first half of the nineteenth century because in those days few French scores were performed outside their native land, until the international vogue of the works of Meyerbeer and Gounod in Italian translation, beginning about 1850.

Donizetti's work on his *La regina di Cipro* came to an abrupt halt when he had written about two-thirds of the score. He learned that the German composer Franz Lachner had also composed a work to the same subject, and, even worse, Lachner's score was scheduled for production in Vienna in a newly revised form the same season that he had hoped to produce his opera. Donizetti, annoyed by this turn of events, put by his music and turned his attention to the opera for the Italiens.

As his librettist for his new work he secured the services of Giovanni Ruffini, paying him 500 francs to provide the text. For their plot they turned to an old opera, Stefano Pavesi's *Ser Marc'Antonio*, which had had its *prima* at La Scala in 1810. Pavesi's opera enjoyed a score of years of great popularity both in France and Italy before it began to lose its grip on the stage. Ruffini and Donizetti adapted the plot, simplifying and eliminating many of the characters.

For many years there was considerable mystery about the authorship of the libretto of *Don Pasquale*, that text being signed M.A. (for Maestro Anonimo?). Some had assumed that those initials belonged to Michele Accursi, whose prolix letters and obsessive repetitiveness make him an unlikely choice indeed as a librettist; while others have suggested that Donizetti had turned librettist again, as he had done on earlier occasions. The question was solved by Alfonso Lazzari, who discovered in Ruffini's correspondence clear references to his experiences as Donizetti's librettist. Ruffini's letters even explain why he choose not to put his name to his work: he said that he found working so closely with Donizetti 'paralysing' and that he was forced to work in such haste that he did not recognize the libretto as his own.

On 12 November Donizetti wrote to Toto to announce that the Paris première of *Linda* was imminent.

> . . . Afterwards I start rehearsing a new opera buffa that cost me more than ten days of labour, written for la Grisi, Mario, Lablache and Tamburini. Title: *Don Pasquale*. It is

the old *Marcantonio* (don't tell). Before giving it I have got 6000 francs here, 6000 at Milan for Italy and Germany. The theatre, without retaining the rights, gave me 3000 for it, and London 4000. I pay the poet, the copying, and 15,000 still remain for me. . . . As soon as Lablache is recovered, the rehearsals begin, because the parts are copied. I was in the middle of the opera for Vienna, when, the other day, the management wrote to me that the subject is forbidden. Imagine whether I am depressed! What to do now? What subject, old or new? . . .[1]

Don Pasquale was first given 3 January 1843, at the Italiens, with Giulia Grisi (Norina), Mario (Ernesto), Tamburini (Malatesta), and Lablache (Don Pasquale). The first evening was an unadulterated triumph for all concerned. Gautier's review gives a clear picture of that historic evening. Here is his description of Lablache:

. . . The uncle, played by Lablache in the most fluttering manner, wearing a house coat of white dimity, nankeen trousers, and a black silk bonnet, is like all uncles everywhere, very displeased with his rascal of a nephew. Following ancient and solemn precedent he seeks to disinherit him. It is entirely just. Why should he be anybody's uncle? Don Pasquale, in spite of his 68 years and his gout, finds himself still enough of a gay blade, still green enough to make heirs less collateral than M. Ernest. He consults Dr Malatesta on this delicate point. . . . The doctor returns with a young woman wearing a dress of the most virginal *carmélite* and with a black lace veil that hardly lets one suspect her pretty face.

To receive this angel of youth and beauty, Don Pasquale makes a most extravagant toilette: a superb perruque the colour of mahogany dressed with ridiculous curls; a green frock coat with engraved gold buttons, which he could never fasten because of the enormous rotundity of his figure. All this gives him the look of a monstrous beetle that wants to open his wings to fly and cannot succeed. With the most gallant air, he advances with popping eyes, his mouth heart-shaped, to take the girl's hand. She emits a cry as though she had been bitten by a viper.[2]

[1] Z. No. 452, p. 636.   [2] Gautier, *L'art dramatique*.

Gautier is enthusiastic about the score as well, calling the quartet 'a piece fashioned by a master's hand'. He also singles out the chorus of the servants and Ernesto's serenade, the former as original in construction, the latter as full of colour and charm.

The day after the first performance Donizetti wrote to Toto that every piece of *Don Pasquale* had been applauded, while he was called out after the second and third acts. He thought the cast, both for their singing and acting, was unsurpassable. The following day he wrote to Ricordi that the success was not entirely due to his music, because Lablache was the pivot of the plot and conducted himself most skilfully. Later he wrote to Ricordi about the dedication of the opera, which Donizetti placed at the feet of Zélie de Coussy.

There is little to report about the subsequent performances of *Don Pasquale*. This work, ranking as the greatest Italian operatic comedy between Rossini's *Il barbiere* and Verdi's *Falstaff*, still holds the stage and is frequently performed all over the world, but nowhere more often than in Germany. It is difficult to foresee a time when this delicious comedy will cease to amuse and delight audiences.

On the last day of 1842 Donizetti was nominated a corresponding member of the French Academy. On the occasion of his acceptance of this honour Donizetti delivered himself of his views on music. The minutes of his speech survive, and although his remarks are anything but a profound contribution to musical theory, they are frequently pungent and reveal much of his sincere and pragmatic approach to his craft.

On that occasion, among other things he said:

> Music is only a declamation accentuated by sounds, and therefore every composer must instinctively apprehend and give rise to vocal melody based on the accent of the declamation of the words. Whoever does not succeed in this, or does not do it felicitously, will only compose music devoid of feeling.
>
> A German student says: 'Ah! Here there is too much rhythm! Ah! Here there is too much melody!' I would tell them, as Rossini did, imitate the good where you find it,

since to avoid one or the other will cause music to lose that which gives pleasure.

I will not say melody before everything since, if we have a defect in certain periods of Italian music, it is because it has sinned too much on this side, and from that I believe came a neglect of orchestration. But I will never say, however, as some do, that what is rhythmical is not sublime.

Many preach: imitate Beethoven; and may God will it so. Imitate him then, but imitate something beyond the instrumental effects and the rhythm. Have musical science before everything; afterwards take all the liberties that are taken in the symphonies and the last writings; but write me a *Septet*, a *Mount of Olives*, a *Fidelio*, etc., and everything will be pardoned you.

The intellect is a rough stone that when it is worked becomes polished, but not in every part. For example, the painter practises his art and is nothing when it comes to music. Michelangelos appear rarely. One can have musical science and no taste; one can have practical taste and lack science; one can have everything—and be a genius.

With assiduity musical science can be learned by anyone; it is acquired with opportunity and labour. Taste and genius must be innate in a composer. Here is the effect of it: Rossini is a genius and as such he has opened the imagination of his contemporaries. After him—I am speaking of Italy—every other composer lived or lives with the science and with the taste and with the practice born from the style created by this genius.

Rossini appeared and accomplished that which was granted only to a genius to achieve. Although young and almost ignorant of Art, he divined the effects of Mozart in *Don Giovanni*, of Beethoven in the symphonies. . . . The public, shaken from a species of musical apathy, encouraged the new composer, and he much emboldened by his successes, endeavoured, and succeeded. . . . Not by study, but by frequent opportunity to write, he improved and made himself severely correct in his art. By means of so much genius, so much practice, and, in spite of himself, such musical science, sprang *Guillaume Tell*.

German composers should sing a little more; Italians, a little less. The French do not have this contempt, for they

send their students to Italy, making them perfect themselves in the taste for vocal melody. . . .[1]

Certainly Donizetti's view of Rossini as the genius who learned
and refined his art by constant practice points out the example
that he himself followed. Donizetti never regarded himself as
Rossini's equal; he was one of the generation who followed him
and profited by his new style. When Donizetti began to evolve
his own characteristic tone, freeing himself from the Rossinian
formulas, he continued to practice the precept of seeking
frequent opportunities to compose so that he might broaden his
expressive vocabulary and refine his style. That Donizetti's
progress was not rapid nor unfaltering nor extraordinarily
extensive is due in no small measure to the conditions under
which he was forced to work, and in part, undeniably, to the
restless compulsion of his personality. But those who scoff at
Donizetti merely because he wrote too much would do well to
consider the precept he stated to the members of the Academy,
and to consider the loss to music since the opportunities for
constant practise and performance of new works are almost
infinitely fewer in the strangling economy of musical organizations today.

On 7 January 1843, four days after the première of *Don
Pasquale*, Donizetti left Paris to start the long journey to Vienna
proceeding by Strassburg, Munich and Linz. Exhausted by the
strain of launching *Don Pasquale* and by his anxiety over the new
opera he had begun to write for Vienna that spring, he stopped
a few days in Strassburg to gather his strength to proceed on his
journey. When he stopped in Munich he made a setting of
Victor Hugo's poem, *La fiancée du timballier*.

Donizetti arrived in Vienna on 16 January to find the city in
the grips of severe winter weather. Almost immediately after
his arrival he took to his bed with a fever. By the end of the
month he seemed recovered and immersed himself in a variety
of projects. On 30 January he informed Toto of them.

. . . For Vienna I am writing a *Duello sotto Richelieu* (a
French drama), for Naples, *Ruy Blas*, set in a different
location; for Paris, at the Opéra-Comique, a Flemish

[1] Donati-Pettèni, *L'istituto musicale Gaetano Donizetti*, pp. 193 ff.

subject. For the Opéra if they call me instead of Meyer-beer, I will compose a Portuguese subject in five acts. And all this for the current year. And first, I will restage *Les martyrs* which has made a furore in the provinces. And the following spring I will give the other, that is, *Le duc d'Albe*, in four acts. And all this without fakery and with a new—illness caught at Paris, that has not gone yet and for which I am waiting your prescription—Farewell.[1]

These multiple activities require some explanation. The opera for Vienna was finally called *Maria di Rohan*, set to Cam-marano's libretto based on Lockroy's play, *Un duel sous le Cardinal de Richelieu*, a subject Donizetti had considered as early as 1837. For the opera at Naples, Donizetti soon renounced the subject of *Ruy Blas* for nothing more is heard of this idea from him; he turned instead to the score of *La regina di Cipro* that he had put by the preceding year; this work was rechristened *Caterina Cornaro*. The project for a Flemish subject or any other to be mounted at the Opéra-Comique was allowed to lapse. The Portuguese subject for the Opéra, however, did materialize; this was to be *Dom Sébastien*, the last complete score Donizetti ever wrote. Nothing came of the revival of *Les martyrs*, perhaps because la Stolz could not begin to sing the tessitura of Pauline as the part was written, and an important new production or revival without her services was scarcely to be considered during the management of the compliant Pillet.

Besides his extensive programme of composition, Donizetti also had to concern himself with the musical management of the Kärthnerthortheater. The Italian season was to open with the first Viennese production of Verdi's *Nabucco*. On 6 February Donizetti wrote to Ricordi to send the chorus parts for that opera post-haste so the rehearsals could begin. Donizetti had a sincere belief in Verdi's talent and promise, doing his best in Vienna this year with *Nabucco*, and the next with *Ernani*, to see these operas were worthily performed. For his services on his behalf, Donizetti won Verdi's gratitude.

On 14 February Donizetti sent Dolci a report of his activities, beginning with an apology for his long silence.

---

[1] Z. No. 470, pp. 652–3. Although Donizetti gives no further details of this new illness (*malanno*), it is not unreasonable, in view of Donizetti's medical history, to suspect that he refers to a new venereal infection.

... You want news? Here it is! The winter is very fine, the balls follow one another with great rapidity. In the month of March concerts of classical sacred music will be given, and they will perform amongst the music of Haydn, Mozart, and Beethoven, my poor offertory, and that gives me great pleasure, since there will only be sacred, classical music and the performers will be very numerous. My tragic opera in three acts (*Maria di Rohan*) is finished. I have begun that in five acts for Paris (not *Le duc d'Albe* which is already written in four and which will be given later, but another). I am waiting for the poem from Naples. I wrote there to ask if they wanted to break the engagement, but I am afraid not, and thus I must go to Naples in July, then run to Paris for August. In the midst of all these labours I am feeling well, travelling does not kill me. From time to time I have my usual fever that makes me a visit, but it does not last more than twenty-four hours; its force leaves me beaten down for some time, then, back to work, and with more eagerness. ...

A few days more and I will send Francesco as much as I can. For you now. Why not come here for Salvi's operetta and my opera? You know that in a short time you would hear *Linda*, *Pasquale*, and the farce? If, for example, you came in May! Come, oh pot-belly, then the weather will be fine. On the first of May you will see the opening of the Prater, good theatre, a fine time to see the environs. After you leave, or at the end of June, we could go together as far as Padua. Come on then. ...[1]

Although Dolci did not visit Donizetti in Vienna, this invitation shows the deep regard the composer had for his friend and his longing for companionship. While Donizetti had made a wide circle of social acquaintances and had many comrades of long standing among the singers and musicians of the company, he was without the presence of any of his dearest friends. He tried to sound cheerful about the state of his health, but he could no longer disguise the fact that his bouts of fever were now 'usual'.

The opera season progressed with its usual ups and downs. Pauline Viardot, then at the beginning of her distinguished

[1] Z. No. 474, pp. 657–8.

career, sang *Barbiere*, and inserted the rondo from *Cenerentola* in the Lesson Scene; but this singer made a fiasco of a revival of *Alina, regina di Golconda*. Tadolini won a success in *Nabucco* and repeated her distinguished *Linda* of the previous year, but when she sang the cavatina Donizetti had written for Persiani in Paris, she was forced to transpose it down. During May and early June, Donizetti finished *Caterina Cornaro* and sent the score to Naples; and meanwhile *Maria di Rohan* went into rehearsal.

That opera had its première on 5 June 1843 at the Kärthnerthortheater with Tadolini as Maria, Carlo Guasco as Chalais, and Giorgio Ronconi in one of his most celebrated creations as Chevreuse. Donizetti conducted the performance himself. The following day Donizetti informed Toto, to whom he dedicated the opera, of the outcome.

> With the utmost sorrow I must announce to you that last evening, 5 June, I have given my *Maria di Rohan* with la Tadolini, Ronconi and Guasco. All their talent was not enough to save me from a sea of—applause. Called out after every act. In sum, a complete fiasco, splendid! Everything went well, everything, everything. Write it to Naples; write it to your wife and daughter, to all your household and friends.
>
> All the Imperial family came in from the country expressly, and remained to the end of the opera, to— whistle. And you will see this evening how it will go. What a sinfonia, *sor* Toto!
>
> *Bergamus et non plus ultra!* . . .[1]

Thus, teasingly, Donizetti announced the great success of this opera, which, as he wrote to his brother Giuseppe a little later, 'is going divinely'. *Maria di Rohan* is another of Donizetti's works which enjoyed great popularity, especially in Italy, for many years. It is still revived there occasionally today. Musically, it is one of Donizetti's most cohesive scores, but it demands great acting to make its true effect.

As Donizetti had written to Toto in January, he had tried to break his contract with Naples, but when the authorities insisted, he finished *Caterina Cornaro* and sent the score there.

[1] Z. No. 486, p. 667.

Because of his concern for the five-act work for the Opéra, on which he pinned great hopes, he decided to forego attending the première of his opera in Naples. He was concerned about the casting for it, and he was afraid of the treatment his work would receive at the hands of the censors and of those musicians in Naples who might mistreat his score if he were not there to defend it. In spite of his concerns, he decided to leave *Caterina* to her fate.

On 14 June he wrote to Persico that he by no means wanted the notorious Anna Bishop, then ensconced in Naples, to take the title role. In Vienna, Bishop had made 'the stones laugh' and besides she had 'not much voice'. The alternative prima donna was Fanny Goldberg, but Donizetti would not accept her without some concrete information about her capabilities and her range of voice. A few days later he wrote to Ghezzi about the proposed production of *Caterina* in Naples.

... It grieves me even more than it does you that I cannot come in person to be present at the rehearsals and staging of *Caterina*, but how can I do it? How to go to Naples in a month, rehearse, and run to Paris according to my very old contract with the Académie Royale? I would have to fly. At least it will be like this: when I am feeling better, I will leave in my carriage, I will sleep when I want to, I will stop when I feel badly, nor will I count the hours as I would, had I made the trip to Naples. I have written to Signor Flauto, and I have given up 500 ducats besides; I believe that when a Maestro sends a certificate of ill-health, he cedes money and renounces the staging of his new score. I believe that such claims must be recognized, if the Maestro is considered a man of honour.

I have urged that the woman be a soprano, that Fraschini be the tenor, and the baritone Coletti; or this good bass they are said to have (Beneventano, I believe). If they were not eager to give my opera, and they kept it for la Tadolini, then I too could come (if I do not die) and stage it; but this way, and now, it is impossible for me.

If la Goldberg (whom I am not familiar with), enters into the public's good graces; if as you say she has some spirit, and if the part suits her with small changes, then they can go ahead and give it. Urge whoever knows the disposition of the censors that the text be changed as little as possible. . . .

I . . . pray for the text, since I am ready to take back my opera if I have to see it sacrificed like *Padilla*, where in one place it had formerly said *quale orror* and they substituted there *oh gioia estrema* to the same music: I have laboured conscientiously, and I would not want for the caprice of a few people, or for bad intent, to see an interesting subject made ridiculous. That is a matter for the management, and I hope that they will take an active concern.

I have already sent both the first act and the libretto; the second and third are already in Persico's hands. I beg you then, if it must be given soon, that the most scrupulous attention be paid to the ritardandi, crescendi, accelerandi, etc., so that thus the colours, the light and shade are not hidden. . . .[1]

Vincenzo Flauto, the general manager of the Royal theatres of Naples, for all his eagerness to put on *Caterina Cornaro*, did not get the work on the stage until the following January. There seems no doubt that in Donizetti's absence the work was granted no special consideration. The composer was not able to come for the première in January 1844, because his six months' leave of absence from the Imperial Court had expired at the first of the year, and he had to return to Vienna. When *Caterina Cornaro* was finally performed, the cast included Fanny Goldberg (Caterina Cornaro), Salvetti (Matilde), Gaetano Fraschini (Gerardo), Filippo Coletti (Lusignano), Marco Arati (Andrea Cornaro), Rossi (Strozzi), and Ceci (a Knight).

Before Donizetti left Vienna in July 1843, he took care of one matter which lay close to his heart. One of the consequences of his nomadic life was his inability to supervise the few possessions which were dear to him. On 7 June he wrote to Persico:

. . . Give the pianoforte to Toto and tell him that I would not give it to anyone for all the gold in the world because it was—hers; then because I owe my reputation to it. The bell attachments (*i campanelli levati*) are in a cupboard in the library. Send him all my printed scores. Greet him and all his family. . . .[2]

[1] Z. No. 490, pp. 671–2.   [2] Z. No. 487, p. 667.

The significance this instrument held for Donizetti becomes even more explicit in his letter to Toto of a few days later, when he informed him what he had done.

> ... Do not sell the pianoforte for any price, for contained in it is my whole artistic life. From 1822 I have had the sound of it in my ears; there murmured the *Annas*, the *Marias*, the *Faustas*, the *Lucias*, the *Robertos*, the *Belisarii*, the *Marinos*, the *Martyrs*, the *Olivos*, *Ajo*, *Furioso*, *Paria*, *Castello di Kenilwort*, *Ugo*, *Pazzi*, *Pia*, *Rudenz*—Oh! let it live as long as I live —With that piano I lived my time of hope, my married life, my solitary time. It heard my joys, my tears, my deluded hopes, my honours—it shared with me my sweating and my labour—my talent lived there, in that piano lives every period of my career, of yours, or of your careers. Your father, your brother, all have seen it, been familiar with it, all have tormented it. It was everyone's companion and may it be one forever to your daughter as a dowry of a thousand thoughts, sad and gay. . . .[1]

Thus, Gaetano hoped that Toto's infant daughter, Virginia, would possess the piano, preserving it for all its associations with the deepest emotions of his life. Today the piano is to be seen in the Museo Donizettiano in Bergamo. To read the excerpt from the letter to Toto quoted above, which is engraved on a brass plaque upon the piano, to graze the discoloured ivory of the keyboard with one's own fingertips, is to feel a sudden closeness to Donizetti the man.

On 11 July 1843 Donizetti left Vienna, riding in his newly acquired carriage, accompanied by Matteo Salvi and his servant Antony. By 15 July he had reached Munich, and here he made a point of visiting Johann Caspar Aiblinger (1779–1867). Aiblinger was one of Mayr's oldest friends, sometime Kapellmeister of the Italian opera in Munich, and best known as a composer of church music. In 1833, while he was engaged in collecting ancient music, Aiblinger had visited Bergamo, and on that occasion he had renewed his friendship with Mayr; in the summer of 1838 Mayr had returned the visit and had been fêted in Munich and given an emblazoned wreath. From

[1] Z. No. 494, p. 676.

Munich Donizetti sent an account of his meeting with Aiblinger to his beloved teacher.

> I will begin by telling you that Aiblinger is well, and his
> sister, too, who spoke very often and affectionately of you.
> He was our guide for a good two hours. . . . Now we are
> leaving, *we* because Salvi is with me. We are well. . . .
> Salvi will remain in Paris a month and some days, and
> leaving, he will bring with him the chief parts of his opera
> already written. I will help him as much as I can, but you
> who are over us, master and lord, will be able to give him
> further advice after you have heard the work. . . . I am
> now writing the opera in five acts for Paris, D. Sebastiano
> of Portugal. You are well acquainted with the unfortunate
> expedition of this king against Algeria, the loss of all his
> army, and the mystery still surrounding his death. The
> subject deals with this. We have Camoens, the Inquisition
> that secretly schemes to enslave Portugal to Spain, a little of
> everything in fact. They are spending a large amount for the
> staging. The newly engaged painters are already at work. . . .
> As usual, when I get to Paris, I will work from 7 in the
> morning until 4 in the afternoon, and the thing will progress.
> At Aiblinger's I saw a painting of the place where you
> were born [Mendorf], and the thing gave me the greatest
> pleasure. My birth was more secret however, since I was
> born underground in the Borgo Canale. One went down
> by a cellar stair where no ray of light ever penetrated. And
> like an owl I took my flight, bearing with me both sad and
> happy omens, unencouraged by my poor father who
> always kept saying: it is impossible that you should com-
> pose, that you should go to Naples, that you should go to
> Vienna. The only shield against such humiliations is moral
> strength. I say it and I boast of it. I have had many
> unhappy experiences. It was only a secret tear that came
> out of a greater will to work. How can one not shed such a
> tear over a work lost, over new difficulties in finding better
> opportunities. . . . Yet I always found them, now I do not
> seek them any more! I am happy, beloved, esteemed—
> what more? I have in heaven one who prays for me, for
> you, for everyone. . . .[1]

[1] Z. No. 496, pp. 678–9.

This letter to Mayr, with its nostalgic memories of his grim youth before he entered Mayr's school, placed in conjunction with his reverie over the piano he had sent Toto two weeks earlier, shows the sadness of spirit that engulfed Donizetti at this time as he tried to evade his feelings of the transitoriness and purposelessness of his life. His taking the trouble to seek out old Aiblinger is a symptom of his desire to understand his past in view of the uncertainty of his future.

His trip to Paris was a miserable one in fact. His carriage was badly made and constantly broke down; he finally abandoned it in Munich and took the railroad part of the way to Paris. He arrived there about 20 July to find Paris in the grip of an unseasonably cold spell.

Dom Sébastien went into rehearsal about the middle of August. On the 23rd he wrote to Ricordi that many things were being changed which would influence the outcome of the opera. On 2 September he told Mayr that he was amusing himself because the rehearsals of the opera were 'almost finished'. He was also preparing *Belisario* and *Maria di Rohan* for the stage of the Italiens; for the latter he was composing some new music by transforming the part of Gondi into a *musico* role for Marietta Brambilla. But *Dom Sébastien* was not nearly as ready for production as he had hoped.

On 15 September he wrote to his librettist, Scribe:

> Since your departure yesterday I torment myself over one word. *Mourir pour ce qu'on aime*. I have tried a thousand times *Sauver celui qu'on aime*; and I am not at all content that the same music works as well for one word as for the other.
>
> I would much rather do it over—but the time! And the artists are also long accustomed to sing the text and the music, would they want to start again with something else? Oh! I beg you, leave the word *mourir*, it seems to me that this phrase is more African. At least, see if I am wrong.
>
> In the Duo also, this re-entry of the Inquisitor destroys for me the effect that I had conceived. You, with your dexterity, with your immense talent, you will find a way. . . . Come to a rehearsal, hear what I have done, and perhaps, on the scene itself, you will find a happy way to do this, or better you could leave things as they are.

Think that I have still the ballet music to write; think of the new arrangements that must be made; they must go to be copied; they must be learned, in the studio, on the stage, etc.

I do not draw back before this work, but be good enough to hear for yourself what has been done, and to assist us for several days, for I value your advice very much.

Once more, heed my prayer, have the goodness to bring your changes yourself so that before having them carried out, I can submit to your judgement the music that I have attempted. As to the fourth act, I have finished the music of it, and you could try it when you wish. . . .[1]

From this letter it is apparent that Donizetti was being besieged by last-minute changes sent along by Scribe, who had not bothered to familiarize himself with either Donizetti's music or his approach to the dramatic situations.

On 18 September Donizetti informed Toto that he had so far orchestrated four acts of *Dom Sébastien*, as well as writing a duettino to insert in the last act of *Maria di Rohan*. On 10 October he told Toto, writing in doggerel Latin, that the first performance of *Dom Sébastien* would take place about 20 November. On the 18th he wrote to his Viennese friend, Leon Herz, that the first rehearsal of the fourth act had taken place the previous evening, 'besides the first and second acts for the second time, perhaps the opera will not be bad.' That all had not gone well with these rehearsals becomes clear when it is remembered that six weeks before Donizetti had reported to Mayr that they were 'almost finished'.

Belisario was given its first Parisian performance at the Italiens on 24 October 1843, with Grisi (Antonina), Leone Corelli (Alamiro), and Luciano Fornasari (Belisario); the last won a personal success, but the score failed to please the French public, and it was dropped after the sixth performance and never revived by that company. During the time that Donizetti was concerned with this production, *Dom Sébastien* struggled closer to its first performance. On 30 October, Donizetti wrote to Herz:

. . . My grand opera approaches its end. Today the rehearsals are halted for a change in Act 4 (the Inquisition).

[1] Z. No. 505, pp. 687-8.

When that is made, all will be ready. Before 15 November
D. Sébastien (saving some misfortune) will be given. . . .
    Today I begin my rehearsals of *Rohan*. . . .[1]

On 9 November he sent Herz a more detailed report.

> . . . You want news of *D. Sébastien?* Very well, here it is
> before the performance. Let all this remain between us and
> be easy for in 5 days you will have the opinion of the world,
> and you will say then: my friend has enough experience
> to know the public. Here is the résumé according to me:
> First act—it will please. Second, with the dances, a duo
> and the final romance above all, will also have a success.
> Third, a romance (perhaps), the men's duo and the
> funeral march with the trappings, will be applauded. But
> the rest has been spoiled by the continual changes, thus,
> *no.* Fourth act, much action, the ensemble will not dis-
> please, without exciting enthusiasm. There is in the 4th
> act a scenic effect that comes off very well. In the fifth, a
> little cavatina (not much), the grand duo will seize
> attention—a barcarolle afterwards, which I had to cut in
> half or else the situation will be lost.[2] A very short trio,
> unaccompanied almost, will go neither hot nor cold. After
> that the dénouement, in which the music can do nothing.
> From all this you can understand that my opera finishes
> with a rat's tail, as they say, or like wax in the sun. Today
> they are going to change the setting of the funeral march
> completely (and here it is Thursday and Monday the
> whole thing is to be performed). They have cut an adagio
> in the finale of the third act and moved it to the 4th, and
> this poor finale is now only a garrulity (*bavardage*). Here is
> the finale of the third act lost because M. Scribe (stub-
> bornly) says that the scene will gain from it. There will
> always be enough pieces of music, but I complain about
> my finale. On Tuesday I am going to give *Maria di Rohan*
> also. . . .[3]

---

[1] Z. No. 513, p. 695.
[2] At rehearsal Rosine Stolz flatly refused to stay on stage for two verses of
the barcarolle. Furious, Donizetti finally compromised by cutting the
second verse, and Stolz stayed on stage.
[3] Z. No. 516, pp. 698–9.

At long last *Dom Sébastien* had its first performance at the Opéra on Monday, 13 November 1843. The opera, which Donizetti dedicated to the Queen of Portugal, was sung by Rosine Stolz (Zaïde), Duprez (Dom Sébastien), Barroilhet (Camoens), Massol (Abayaldos), Levasseur (Dom Juan de Silva), Octave (Dom Antonio), Hippolyte Brémond (Ben-Selim), and F. Prévot (Dom Enrique). The opera was applauded, but it failed to arouse the enthusiasm that Donizetti had counted on. It was performed thirty-two times at the Opéra before it lapsed from the repertory. The work was not the utter fiasco that it has traditionally been described. In Italy, in a translation of the text by Giovanni Ruffini, the opera has been performed with regularity, if not exactly with frequency, and it has enjoyed the respect of a discerning public.

CHAPTER 6

Disintegration

It was during the rehearsals of *Dom Sébastien* in November 1843 that Donizetti's appearance and manner began to make people suspect there was something seriously wrong with him. Everyone knew that rehearsal time strained nerves and provoked explosions of 'temperament'; everyone knew that Donizetti had been driving himself too hard for years and that he drove himself hardest at rehearsal times; but no one who had worked with him before had ever seen him in such a state. Sometimes he would forget what he was saying in mid-sentence and stare at those he was talking to in such a queer, fixed manner that he made them uncomfortable. Other times he would fly into violent rages that left him incoherent, shaking all over. Always he was convinced that he was the victim of a conspiracy to sabotage his opera.

If rehearsal times are difficult at best, many things combined to make the preparation of *Dom Sébastien* unusually explosive. There was Donizetti's anxiety that his latest work would be greeted by critics and public alike as his masterpiece, a triumph to surpass the success of *Don Pasquale* the previous January and to silence forever the insinuations of the critics. Donizetti resented the way he had been treated by the French press; they in turn resented him as a ubiquitous foreigner who pre-empted all the opera stages of Paris. And now he was doing it again, for while *Dom Sébastien* was being rehearsed at the Opéra, his *Maria di Rohan* was being readied at the Théâtre-Italien for its

Paris première. The French composers who were under contract to the Opéra resented Donizetti's success, envied him his facility, derided him as an Italian opportunist, and intrigued against him at every opportunity. On the stage Donizetti faced another exasperating situation. He was confronted by the pretensions of Rosine Stolz—the mistress of the Opéra's director, Pillet—and Madame Stolz was one of the most paranoid prima donnas who ever wrecked the morale of a theatre. The tenor Gilbert Duprez, who was also in the cast of *Dom Sébastien*, described this time as one when Donizetti was spared 'no chicanery, no opposition'.[1]

When the success of *Dom Sébastien* fell far short of Donizetti's expectations, he felt the failure more deeply than he cared to admit. For all his talk about the receipts (130,000 francs by the nineteenth performance), he could not disguise his bitter disappointment. In the past he could forget a fiasco by losing himself in his next work, but now he found he could not induce the intensity of concentration he had so long relied on. A sort of automatism set in. He followed his deeply-grooved habits, but his former vivacity returned only fitfully. In his letters of 1844 he mentions new contracts, great plans, but he seemed incapable of summoning the energy to carry them through. His headaches grew worse and more frequent; he was restless, often feverish. In addition there were the inadmissible changes he felt in himself, the symptoms of the disease that was soon to shatter and humiliate him.

The last of his operas to have its *prima* during his lifetime, *Caterina Cornaro*, fell flat. Unable to go to Naples for its first performance, Donizetti had sent off the score with misgivings, but when he heard its failure had been complete and, worse yet, that ill-disposed people were saying that he did not even write the music himself and had palmed off on them someone else's weak opera just to revenge himself on the Neapolitans, his pride was stung. He rejected such talk proudly. He admitted the blame for the failure was his, but he had not thought his opera so 'infamous' as to deserve an irretrievable fiasco. While he soon managed to forget the disappointment of *Caterina Cornaro*, his bitterness about *Dom Sébastien* remained and rankled.

The story of the last years of Donizetti's career has been told in the preceding chapter, but certain events of that time point

[1] Gilbert Duprez, *Souvenirs d'un chanteur* (Paris, 1880), p. 95.

towards his collapse. Throughout the early months of 1844 he complained frequently and bitterly of the long Viennese winter, a sign of the increasing exacerbation of his nerves. In the latter part of June, when his brother Giuseppe came on from Constantinople, Gaetano took to his bed with what was called 'intestinal inflammation', suffering again from convulsions as he had in April 1829. Although his doctors prescribed rest, he set off on a tour of Italy that took him to Bergamo, to Lovere, back to Bergamo, to Milan, to Genoa, to Naples, to Rome, back to Naples, to Genoa again, Milan again, Bergamo for the third time, and finally back for another winter in Vienna. Not an itinerary to rest a dangerously overworked man! One day, while he was in Italy, he was accompanying a famous singer at the piano when his memory unaccountably went blank; the lady choose to interpret his lapse as a purposeful effort to make her look a fool. Had not Donizetti's friends intervened there would have been a scandal. Undoubtedly other incidents took place as well that seemed ominous in retrospect.

Back in Vienna, Donizetti continued to experience alarming alterations in his health. Sometimes when he tried to write or compose, a sort of cloud seemed to obscure his intellect, but this disturbance would seem to pass again as mysteriously as it had come. His apparent recuperative powers at this time deluded his associates about the seriousness of his condition. His gait altered; sometimes his legs would not support his weight. His face became deeply lined; sometimes his facial muscles suddenly grew rigid, producing an alarming change in his expression. He seemed to have lost much of his former self-control; there were sudden outbursts of irritability, unaccountable lapses of memory, deep fits of depression, periods of profound apathy. The Viennese doctors he consulted prescribed baths and applications of boiling mustard on his neck.

Perhaps his growing sense of dislocation is best symbolized when he conducted his revised *Dom Sébastien* at Vienna, 6 February 1845. The opera was sung in a German translation made by Donizetti's friend Leon Herz. As he knew only a few words of the language, Donizetti felt uneasy and out of touch with the production. 'How I sweated,' he wrote of it, 'scampering through the notes of the recitatives, not knowing what the singers said.'[1]

[1] Z. No. 613, p. 792.

That same year the Italian season at the Kärthnerthor-theater, which ran from April to June, was far from successful. The company assembled by Merelli was not as strong as in past years and included some singers with little experience and less aptitude for the roles they were to sing. 'What are you going to do with singers who have no voices, beginners who don't know music and who have never stepped on a stage, who jump ten and twelve measures, and who are satisfied they have sung like gods or goddesses?'[1]

Of his onerous duties at the theatre his letters are full, but there is scant mention of his health. On 20 May he writes to Persico that he is *nervosissimo*, that the cold is killing him. On 7 June he informs Dolci that the Viennese climate has given him '*la febbre nervosa*'. A few days later he writes to Peppina Appiani in the same vein:

> I have spent a horrible winter. Under the influence of this climate my nerves have become so sensitive that to stay a year would kill me. I will leave for Paris about 10 July.[2]

A revealing glimpse of Donizetti during that last year in Vienna comes from Felice Varesi. Shortly before his death in 1898 the baritone told Raffaello Barbiera of his shock at encountering Donizetti in the Prater late one night. The composer was following a girl down a dark path.[3] At the time such behaviour was not apt to be interpreted as still another symptom of the disease that was soon to declare itself openly.

One final piece of evidence corroborates the spirit of Varesi's anecdote. Annibale Gabrieli, Toto's grandson, writes of a tale told by the violoncellist Domenico Labocetta (1823–96) to Persico. Before Labocetta lost his voice and turned to the cello, he had been an operatic tenor and a member of Merelli's company in Vienna that spring of 1845. He said that Donizetti's lodgings in Vienna were open to frequent visits by complacent ladies who came accompanied by elderly chaperons. Gabrieli commented on this story: 'To deny out of hand this sort of eroticism in Donizetti's final years does not seem possible to me. But it was one sign among many of the dissolution that

[1] Z. No. 636, p. 811.
[2] Z. No. 640, p. 815.
[3] Raffaello Barbiera, *Vite ardenti nel teatro* (Milan, 1931), p. 165.

had already begun; it was not a cause or among the causes of his condition.'[1]

Donizetti arrived in Paris at the beginning of August. On the 9th, his name day, there were signs of serious mental disturbance. Doctors were summoned. Two days later he wrote to Toto (this is Donizetti's last letter to his beloved brother-in-law) and tried to let him know what had happened.

> . . . This morning I was examined by 3 prominent doctors *Andral, Ricord, and . . . and . . .* They concluded between them after putting a thousand questions to me that I should go away . . . that I should travel . . . have a change of climate. . . . I chose at once either Rome or Naples, because I would be in my own house. Rome (they said) is too far from the sea. Better, Naples: there you can take sea baths; but you have to stay at *Castellamare.* Imagine whether I accepted! I leave everything! I am going. I must not write for two years, for the past two years I haven't because I didn't want to. Now that I am eager to, the doctors don't want me to. . . . Twelve leeches on the anus. Decoctions four times a day (Boiled Arnica). My head (to tell the truth) was very heavy and only said *no* aloud. Now I move it and it is the effect of the climate because I could move it already before the medicine.
>
> A foot bath of hot water every other day, is scheduled . . . I am *nervous*, and you know it, and you have always known me . . . and you can always tell me anything when I get to Naples. Don't answer me now! 5 Operas!!! *Only* one thing holds me back from ending it all [*Una sola mi torebbe a tutto*]; one must wait for it when one is a *Christian.* You are going to tell me? *How is that? You haven't the strength* to write an Opera? . . . You? . . . . ! I? *Yes!* I have it!— *The head?* It's free! *The imagination?* It's free! *Will you write it?* It wouldn't hurt me! But an imperceptible secret of the doctors tells me, *that I have nothing,* but *I might come down again with the same sickness from the blood going to the head, and then it might congeal.* Have I appetite? I digest! The prescribed foods are light. The beverages likewise. I avoid

wines—I drink Bordeaux and *Vichy water*. I go out; I walk;
but only in the morning *Andral* pressed my *chest*; he
thumped on all the ribs (right side), and said to me: you
must *take these remedies*, so that next winter will not work
on your nerves, as the past one does now. Therefore: we
order you to travel a little; and when you get accustomed
to all the rigours of winter, you may write as much as you
want—You must avoid the strong emotions of *popular
drama. Your* nature is too sensitive. *Your head is too* tired! . . .
I choose Naples because . . . I hope to see you . . . we will
be close! . . . I have my house!—I write to you, and I beg
you to copy this to Aniello. Tell him that if in 4 or 5 days
things don't keep improving I will leave! Marseilles etc.
but don't let all this reach anyone's ears, as I must avoid
pain, and emotion. I will write to you from Naples etc.
etc. Now I will dress and go out. . . .[1]

The disjointed tone of this letter alarmed Toto even more
than the news it contained. His concern would have been
greater if he recognized the names of the doctors, especially that
of Phillipe Ricord (1800–89), whose chief contribution to
medicine, demonstrating the error of Hunter's theory that
gonorrhoea and syphilis were the same disease, has won him a
niche in medical history. Ricord's presence at this the first of
many consultations held over Donizetti shows that the true
nature of his disease was no longer in doubt.

Toto waited anxiously for some further word, news that
Donizetti had arrived safely at Naples, a further medical report,
anything; but no information reached him directly. Malicious
gossip sprang up like weeds: people whispered stories about Donizetti's irregular behaviour, about his being surrounded in Paris
by people whose only thought was to use him, about his family
and friends, not one of whom went to be near him. Daily this
talk grew louder and more open, adding to Toto's distress. He
wrote to Aniello Benevento, to the other friends in Naples,
Teodoro Ghezzi and Tommaso Persico, and to Antonio Dolci
in Bergamo, but no one knew very clearly what had happened
to Gaetano in Paris. Their frequent, anxious letters remained
unanswered; the few Donizetti wrote were scarcely encouraging.
The doctors had been called in because Donizetti had fallen

[1] Z. No. 646, pp. 820–1.

on the pavement in front of his house, the Hôtel Manchester, Rue Grammont No. 1, and had been carried inside still unconscious. When he came round, his speech was incoherent, his articulation indistinct. About this time he was the victim of *idées-fixes*. Verzino[1] relates a story that Royer had told him which illustrates this observation. One day Donizetti went with some friends to the country for a picnic. As he had been asked to provide the pastries, he had the carriage stop in front of a bakery and soon re-appeared with a large box; but when he kept repeating this performance, buying many more pastries than the party could possibly eat, he was asked for an explanation. As the realization of what he had been doing dawned on him, he turned pale and said, 'Ah, I don't remember; I don't remember anything.'

After the bad time early in August, Donizetti's condition underwent a temporary improvement. On the 21st he wrote to Dolci that the doctors had been to see him, and he repeated their instructions. The tone of the letter is less disturbed than of that to Toto.

> That dog of an *Andral* (very handsome face) kept looking at me because he had never met me before. Then he grabbed my wrist . . . and I had no fever. He thumped me very hard on my right ribs, and I said: you are not hurting me at all; and he laughed.

He even makes a little joke, comparing the climate of Paris with that of Vienna: 'Here in Paris the air is much lighter, and the rain heavier.' And then he continues:

> My head is cured, and that's enough for me.
> My nerves are irritated so that every time someone writes? . . . Patience!
> The tomb! It is finished![2]

While by these last words Donizetti possibly may have intended to refer to the mausoleum for his beloved Virginia that had been completed in Naples not long before, they could not have but struck the tender-hearted Dolci as a fateful premonition.

Donizetti's seeming recovery marked only a brief pause in the inexorable advance of the paresis. On 30 August, Drs Andral

---

[1] Edoardo Clemente Verzino, *Contributo ad una biografia di G. D.* (Bergamo, 1896), p. 129.   [2] Z. No. 648, pp. 822–3.

and Rostand held another consultation on his case. Louis Léon
Rostand's speciality was cases involving softening of the brain.
The treatment they prescribed was much like that earlier
reported by Gaetano to Toto, except for the addition of dry
cuppings on the neck and dorsal region. They concluded he was
suffering from a disease involving the nerve centres; therefore
he should abstain from all mental fatigue, immediately giving
up all work. Later, they felt, travel and sea baths might be
beneficial.[1]

For the time being Donizetti was being kept in Paris under
doctor's orders. This situation gave a strong argument to
Michele Accursi and the de Coussys, Donizetti's agent and
banker, for keeping close to hand the goose that laid their
golden eggs. Not long before Donizetti returned to Paris he had
received an incredibly long-winded letter from Accursi, dated
Paris, 10 April 1845. After much not very coherent advice to
Donizetti, in the course of it berating him for his 'mulish
obstinacy' Accursi turns to the matter which is really troubling
him.

> . . . Now listen, [my sister Elisa and I] find ourselves in
> deep water in these last days, to the point that I was forced
> to ask Mme de C— for a loan of 500 francs to be able to
> proceed. She proposed to advance me the money from
> what had been received for you, and that I should inform
> you of it. I could do nothing less but accept it because I
> was forced by circumstances, because I am in debt to you
> already for larger sums, but I told myself that if you were
> in my shoes and I in yours, I would not have hesitated one
> moment in the face of such embarrassments. Don't think,
> dear Gaetano, that I have forgotten my earlier debt. No
> indeed, but what do you want? You know it was based on
> the hope, the certainty, of restitution, on putting into use a
> gambling system that cost us 7000 francs. . . .

He continues at length about the system, telling Donizetti that
it is infallible, that it has been proved for three consecutive
seasons at Baden, and that if he only had 7000 francs he could
repay it along with the interest that sum would have earned.
There are several highly significant passages in this letter.

[2] Alborghetti-Galli, *Donizetti-Mayr*, Appendix. The text of more than a
dozen medical reports on Donizetti's condition are reprinted here.

> ... I have spoken about it to Mme de C. ... She made me despair; she told me that it was useless to send a letter to you about it. She said that if she had the money she would give it to me, but that from you there was no hope, that if she had the money it would draw us all out of an abyss, etc. etc. These words were the consequence of her angry state of mind towards you. ...

and later on in the same letter:

> ... and so we are come to the moment when I had to appeal, as I told you, for assistance to Mme de C. ...; then I sought advice, not being able to find this capital, before turning to the last resort of asking you for it. I revealed my position to Mme de C., she advised me not to do it as it would be useless. On the other hand, Mons. de C. encouraged me. ...[1]

On 24 April Accursi returned to the same subject swearing it would be for the last time. This letter sheds further light on the habits and attitudes of these people.

> ... From your letter it seems to me you thought my gambling system was the same as the system of de C., whom you have seen lose under your own eyes, but it is not the same, rather it is strikingly different. ...
>
> ... I have asked for this capital of 7500 francs which is necessary to carry out the operation, one which for three years has occupied all our efforts. On it depends our future, our fortune. ... To refuse me this loan, when only this loan can save me, is truly a barbarous thing.
>
> ... M. de C. having bought in your name an investment of 2450 francs at 5% with money that he owed you, he has asked me to turn over the receipt he gave you, because you told Mme that you left it with me. I don't have it. I have only bills that are in that box: old useless papers. ...

Accursi went on then to discuss the rumour that Mario had been killed in a duel in London and reported on Barroilhet's successful début there in *La favorite*. He had found an Italian play, *Una lezione stravagante*, which he thinks would make Donizetti an excellent subject for an opera buffa. At the end of this lengthy letter, he came back to the topic uppermost in his mind.

[1] Unpublished letter in the library of the Naples Conservatory.

... All of us embrace you with true hearts and we hope to call you our *Saviour*, *Addio*, *addio*. Just today de C. has told me that he wrote to you. He knows that three years' experience with the system at Baden were fortunate. He tells me that if you wish, he could give me the money at once. Gaetano, I recommend myself to you. I await your answer.[1]

The letter that Auguste de Coussy wrote to Donizetti on 24 April is also in the Library of the Naples Conservatory, along with two from Accursi just quoted. De Coussy's letter reveals that Donizetti had not instructed him very clearly what to do for Accursi. The banker wrote:

... My dear friend, I have made an error *on paper*, understanding that you really wanted me to lend 7500 to Accursi. It was of the loan at Baden which has become necessarily a gift that you meant to speak. I understood your letter better when I read it again. This error has gone no further than on my paper, so that you don't need to swear at me too much: *che bestia, che*. ...

Besides, the letter you wrote to Accursi left no doubt and limited the gift to 500 francs. Your kindness! I believe that you have done well and that Accursi's system is another deception like that of Lacoste—

It is quite bizarre that just as I wrote the foregoing, someone rang. It is Accursi who comes to beg me to write to you that his system of gambling is not at all that of Lacoste, that his is much better, etc. etc. I admit that Accursi's system is another than that which made me lose 10 thousand francs, but you do not have a big enough fortune to undertake such ways of speculation. It is too dangerous, and the most acute people leave their money be.

Nothing yet is certain about the life or death of Mario. What is certain that it was caused by the scene of the slaps administered by Grisi to Mlle Castellan during *Lucia*, which were returned by the last. ...

Next de Coussy took up the matter of the receipt for Donizetti's loan, which Accursi could not find. Since de Coussy repaid the

[1] Unpublished letter in the library of the Naples Conservatory. Note on letter 'found in Vienna—1849'.

money, he wanted a receipt; in the absence of the original, he suggested that Donizetti send him the following statement, which seems couched in very general terms:

> I declare that the second entry in my name of 2540 francs at 5% interest is the amount of reimbursement which M. de Coussy made me for all the sums that I have lent him.

After signing his letter de Coussy adds a postscript to the effect that not only has he given Accursi no money, but he has allowed him to read nothing.

A longer postscript is added to the letter by Zélie de Coussy herself.

> Do you still recognize my handwriting? After such a long silence, you should be surprised to see it again. If you only could imagine that, although mute, I have never stopped for a single instant occupying myself with you and with your interests. The poor woman, whom you scorn without pity, whom you treat like an old fool who has bored you for too long, should be silent so that you are spared the weariness of reading this letter, but she continues none the less to watch over your affairs. Accursi has begged me to write to you to support his request. I have refused him cold, now he begs me to tell you of the certainty of his system, which I don't believe at all. You have done well to give him the 500 francs. . . . This poor unfortunate is, I believe, sore pressed at this time. He has done you services; your fortune permits you to recognize them; you have acted nobly in making him a present of the 500 francs, besides the former 250 francs, but that is enough.
>
> You should not go further. Now be perfectly calm. Your letter was misinterpreted at first, but a second reading was clearer. Nothing has been done, nor will anything be done.
>
> Vatel[1] will have great need of you, having lost Mario; the occasion is marvellous for you; profit by it. Make him engage the tenor who will suit you, making the condition that his début take place in your opera. The Escudiers will buy this work at whatever you should ask, engaging themselves to pay you the day the contract is signed. You know

[1] Vatel was then the manager of the Italiens.

it, for you have already received their letter. It is a fine occasion to see your friends again. For you know how last year when I begged you to come, you said: above all, Madame, do not cause me to make a useless journey for if I came what would I do at Paris since I am giving no opera there? Now this is a situation that will decide you to come, and whatever the motive, it will bring your friends the happiness of seeing you. Believe me, they will be very happy at your return. You are sick; the climate kills you; why do you continue to stay there? Believe me, give your resignation, come and settle in Paris. You will be surrounded by attention, by affection. Your glory, your talent, will increase in France. Your purse and your income will grow. All the press will be devoted to you. I am always busy at cultivating the journalists. I know many new ones who are very influential. They will be useful to you. You spend your evenings reading the newspapers! Oh! That is very dull, and it would be better to pass them in my boudoir. . . .[1]

These are the people whom Donizetti relied on in Paris: the agent, who wanted to secure the old age of himself and his sister by using a gambling system at Baden; the banker, who lost 10,000 francs gambling himself, who borrows money from Donizetti, who lends Donizetti's money without asking permission; the banker's wife, who is supposed to be angry with him, yet is anxious to get him to Paris, where she promises him her influence and the hospitality of her boudoir. On 29 April Donizetti wrote to de Coussy to tell him not to let Accursi have any more money, promising to write to Accursi himself to say that it would be the last money he would have from him. These three all had their motives for wanting Donizetti in Paris, perhaps to re-invest his money there. It makes no difference to what extent they connived or exerted pressure to keep their composer on a short leash—the obstacles the Donizetti family encountered when they tried to get Gaetano away from Paris make some connivance seem probable—the course of Donizetti's illness very nearly let them have their way.

Sometime during this August Donizetti, with a little twist of irony, performed a gesture which proves he was still capable at

[1] Unpublished letter in the library of the Naples Conservatory.

times of his old generous feelings. Always willing to support his fellow composers, even those who had behaved harshly towards him, Donizetti gave Berlioz a letter of introduction to Leon Herz.

> *Je crois te faire un véritable cadeau en te presentant M. Berlioz qui veut bien visiter Vienne et y faire entendre quelques unes de ses brillantes compositions.*[1]

This '*véritable cadeau*' of a Berlioz was not above accepting this letter, with its request that Herz be 'an adviser, a guide, a friend', from the man whose motives he had repeatedly traduced in the pages of the *Journal des débats*.

Hopes that Donizetti might be on the road to recovery were soon blasted. On 9 September he wrote to his old friend Guillaume Cottrau, a music publisher in Naples, a letter that could only have caused consternation.

> What do you say? that I am going to die? Here is what I tell you—that I fell out of bed at night . . . that I was found in the morning on the floor in my nightshirt, . . . that for 12 hours I did not come to my senses. . . . How thin I have become, you would not believe!
>
> I am forbidden excitement. I had four operas to write, but I had to give up everything. I told him I wanted to die in Italy! I wanted our mineral waters for my lung.[2]

The nightmare-like experience of falling out of bed has been dismissed by some as an hallucination, but Donizetti kept referring to it in subsequent letters, and the truth of the matter is confirmed by the doctor's consultation of 28 January 1846. Donizetti was deceived, perhaps intentionally, in believing there was anything wrong with his lungs. After his death they were found to be perfectly normal.

On the 18th he wrote again to Cottrau. Just two sentences: one to say that he was feeling better, although still in bed and being treated with leeches and mustard plasters; the other, that he was revising *Gemma di Vergy* for a production at the Théâtre-Italien with Grisi and Mario. Obviously, both these letters to Cottrau were intended to answer the flood of mail anxiously inquiring about his health. There is no doubt that Donizetti found all this correspondence annoying.

[1] Z. No. 649, p. 823.   [2] Z. No. 650, p. 824. Complete.

Aniello Benevento, to whom Toto was supposed to send a copy of the letter of 11 August, had always been touchy about any signs he interpreted as meaning Donizetti preferred his other Neapolitan friends over him. Like the others he had been eagerly waiting for some word that Gaetano would soon arrive in Naples. On 23 September he wrote an anxious letter urging Donizetti to come ahead. He was dismayed to hear that Gaetano stayed in Paris and, worse yet, talked of returning to Vienna. There is no doubt of Aniello's sincere affection as he continues:

> But don't you understand the pain we all feel in knowing you are unwell and far away from us. Besides we would prepare for you all the attention our affection is capable of. If however our affection does not move you, let the desire to save yourself stir you. But why don't you want to come to Naples where you could begin a new era of life and happiness?[1]

The discouraging answer to this plea came not to Aniello, but to Teodoro Ghezzi. The letter is dated 2 October.

> As proof of the friendship and affection I feel for you, I am writing to you three hours after a surgical operation on my brain, a vescicant, after 25 leeches behind my ears, then another 20. . . . Since last night my poor brains have made me suffer. . . . I suffer! The surgeon this morning peeled, pulled, and cut! . . . They held me with my head high. What pain! . . . I am seized with melancholia, which my tremendously sensitive nerves feel and I want to weep. I pretend to be happy with tears in my heart. I have completely changed. . . . My nerves are so wrought up that I fell out of bed one night, and it seemed to me as though the bed were turning over on top of me. I don't know if I'm still alive, since I fell with my head down without trying to break my fall with my hands, like someone who had been strangled. . . . Perhaps with a night-light I won't fall again? No, oh silence![2]

This letter with all its evidence of his physical and mental suffering, only served to increase the agitation in Naples.

He wrote there again five days later, this time to Tommaso Persico, and throughout most of it he seems determined to

[1] Z. No. A. 53, p. 905.   [2] Z. No. 652, pp. 824–5.

reassure his friends. He mentions the many letters he has received, even one from Madama Marotta, the porteress of his old apartment on the Via Nardones. Although he says he will come to Naples sometime, he is anxious to reassure Tommaso that the climate of Paris is not harmful to him. Then he makes the interesting admission that he was aware of his illness the year before in Naples. Being again in the city where his wife died had brought on a crisis marked by 'the difficulties encountered, the resemblance . . . the silence!' Again he reverts to the advantages of the Parisian climate, making one wonder who had been dinning this idea into his poor muddled head. The letter ends with a cry of despair:

> Do you know that the flow of blood to my head did not make me die because God does not wish it? I fell out of bed at night and beat my head on the floor to escape. . . . Therefore, can you guess? I want to stay with the lamp lit and then at the hour when I fell (2 in the morning or 3) I feel my heart thumping and I wake up . . . I see the light . . . all is still . . . I become calm again, and then besides I make the servant sleep in my room. Tell the doctors that night is the saddest thing for someone with blood rushing to his head and with sensitive nerves, besides the strictness in diet, in drink, in hours set for waking and sleeping.
>
> Light, light! Either that of God, or that of oil and wax! 12 hours of convulsions—24 leeches, bathing, medicine for vomiting. Hot poultices on my thighs. . . . Nothing. Nothing.[1]

Donizetti's very disturbing letters, clearly revealing the anguish of his mind struggling against the implacable inroads of disease, increased the consternation of his friends in Italy. The contents of these letters were circumspectly shared by the anxious little groups in Naples, Rome, and Bergamo. Their eagerness for accurate news led them not only to write to Rue Grammont No. 1, but to anyone in Paris who might be trusted to send an accurate account of Donizetti's condition.

Antonio Dolci, in Bergamo, was particularly distressed.

[1] Z. No. 653, pp. 825–6.

Besides his grave concern for Gaetano, he was a daily visitor at the house of their old teacher. Gaetano's beloved Maestro, Mayr, at eighty-two, was slowly dying after a stroke. Keenly aware of the old tie that bound Mayr and Donizetti, Dolci could not share his double grief with either. When Mayr finally died, on 2 December 1845, Donizetti's mind was shrouded in darkness.[1]

One of those to whom Dolci wrote was Marco Bordogni, one of the famous Bergamasc tenors, who for some years had been a successful *professeur du chant* at the Paris Conservatory. On 9 October he sent this reply:

> . . . His health is a little changed, but the doctors hope rest and a change of climate might restore it. I believe his friends should engage to take him away from Paris, and to break up his relationship with a woman who is in great part the cause of his illness![2]

Bordogni's letter made it seem imperative to get Donizetti away from the influences of Paris, but Dolci was bound to Bergamo by his own family responsibilities as well as by the dying Mayr. The only available member of Gaetano's immediate family was his good-for-little brother Francesco, whose chief concern about Gaetano's illness was whether his allowance would continue to be paid regularly. On 22 October Toto wrote to the other brother Giuseppe in Constantinople, urging him to go to Paris at once, but in the meantime Dolci continued to elicit information from friends in Paris.

On the 28th he heard from Lorenzo Monterasi, a Bergamasc musician residing in Paris.

> You cannot imagine my pleasure at receiving your dear letter of the 20th which I got the evening of the 25th. The day before yesterday I went to Donizetti's, but he had gone out early and I did not see him all that day. Yesterday I went back and found him in a bad humour, because he was giving a lesson and his servant had gone out without his knowledge, obliging him to go and open the door himself. He said he had received your letter and I told him

---

[1] Dolci succeeded Mayr, becoming acting director of Mayr's school and *maestro di cappella* until May 1847, when Alessandro Nini formally assumed these functions. Dolci's duties prevented him leaving Bergamo to come to Gaetano in Paris. [2] Z. No. B. 22, p. 927.

of your anxiety, caused by his long silence; to which he answered that a few days before he had written you a somewhat sad letter (in his words) *with friends I must say what I feel in my heart; but now I almost regret having done it.* I could not keep him very long, because (as I said above) he was busy. Afterwards I went to find signor Accursi, his personal agent and secretary, who told me that all the time the Maestro receives letters from Rome and Naples which urge him to come and spend the winter peacefully. To these requests it seems he does not wish to comply, rather he seems to have decided to leave for Vienna. Although they cannot make him leave for Italy, they will do everything possible to keep him in Paris, and it seems certain that he will not leave.

To report on his physical and moral condition, I will tell you: I was in London when I heard that Donizetti had lost his mind. Although I did not believe it, none the less it made a great impression upon me. I got to Paris the 21st of September, and the following day I went to see him and great was my pleasure to find that he was eating in such a way as to leave me no doubt that he was perfectly well both as to his *head* and his *stomach*. Since then I see him almost every day, and I have never recognized in him any symptoms of mental derangement. Someone told me that when he was talking at length he had hesitated sometimes over his words, but very *rarely*. They have put leeches, plaster and vescicants on the nape of his neck, for that reason some have taken him to be stupefied, but he merely could not turn his neck freely. It seems that the vescicants have done him good. A week ago, they lifted up the vescicant, and it seems that some little disturbance [*una piccola cosa*] occurred.

I report on the former relationship he had in Paris with Madama. . . . I am convinced that it would be helpful to him, rather than harmful; because this woman has the Maestro's health more to heart than has any other woman. Her only wish is to procure him every possible means of assistance and distraction, but not in the manner that many badly informed persons are disposed to believe. I repeat that it is better that he had an old acquaintance, while it might also be, as the badly informed believe, injurious; I

say that with an *old partner* one does not abandon oneself
to it with the same ardour as one would *with a new one*.[1]

While this last suggestion may well have startled Dolci, he
found the news of Donizetti's condition, as reported by Monterasi, encouraging. The Madama . . . of this may be that
solicitous widow from Nice, Sophie von Löwenstein, whose
concern for Donizetti was shortly to bring her some painful
experiences—or the Madama might even more probably be
Zélie de Coussy. Whatever consolation Dolci may have been
able to find in the letter from Monterasi, who can not have been
a very perceptive observer, it was not bolstered by receiving the
letter Monterasi told him Donizetti had written him.

> It was one of our townsmen who showed me Prelli's
> letter which speaks of me, of my nervous illness—Why
> afflict my friends?—I have told you thousands of times
> that when I am sick then another will write for me; if I die,
> the papers will announce it; but, until then silence
> (although I wrote to you), if I am silent, it is a sign that
> things are going better! I thank you for your concern.
> Didn't I answer you a little while ago perhaps? I have no
> *fever*, no more vescicants, no more *leeches*. I do not fall out
> of bed at night any more. The twelve and a half hours of
> unconsciousness out of the bed and on the floor did not
> recur. I will leave for Vienna, and very soon! God send
> me there well. They have not bled me . . . greet everyone
> . . . Mayr will see and know that his musical sons . . . die a
> few at a time—Rossi—Tavecchi—Manghenoni—Next!
> . . . God knows. . . !
> A thousand greetings to Madama Basoni.
> Three operas for the Académie Royale, I have let them go.
> Farewell friends. I will not even go to Vienna; I am
> weak; I cannot turn my head much. But . . . I live! I live
> for the others! . . .[2]

While these forebodings increased Dolci's apprehensions,
Toto had already, on 22 October, written to Giuseppe in Constantinople urging him to go to save Gaetano. This letter was
received on 5 November, and the same day Giuseppe answered
that he could not go himself, too much time would be lost

[1] Z. No. B. 23, pp. 927-9.   [2] Z. No. 656, p. 828. Complete.

applying for leave of absence from his post as director of the Sultan's military bands, but he would send his son Andrea in his place to act as official representative of the family. Accordingly, Andrea sailed from Constantinople on the 13th, armed with instructions to take Gaetano back to Italy, preferably to Naples.

The twenty-seven-year-old Andrea, who not long before had completed his studies for the law, arrived in Milan on his way to Paris to find two letters waiting for him. One was from Toto, who spoke of his regrets at having lost his influence over Gaetano and urged Andrea to get his uncle away from France and Austria as soon as possible and bring him safely back to Italy. The other was from Francesco, who reported that Dolci had heard that his Uncle Gaetano was soon leaving for Vienna; therefore he advised Andrea to write to Paris to learn if his uncle was still there before he went. Apparently Andrea followed Francesco's advice because he did not reach Paris until Christmas Day. Andrea had little enthusiasm for this family mission and postponed his arrival as long as he dared. Even for those days, forty-two days seems an excessive time to travel from Constantinople to Paris.

Andrea was upset by what he found when he got to Paris. His description of Gaetano's condition put Dolci 'in the greatest turmoil'. The effort of holding up his head, even for a short time, was too much for Gaetano. Every movement of his muscles caused him pain. His thin body slumped inertly; his lifeless eyes caused his face to appear expressionless, even stupefied. His ideas were few and confused; his memory would suddenly go blank. He was prey to profound apathy. His disposition had radically altered: he had moods when he was gloomy, taciturn, angry, and suspicious. He had delusions of persecution, sometimes shouting that he had been poisoned. Worst of all, he was periodically gripped by compulsive eroticism.[1]

In answering this distressing news, Dolci shows himself an incurable optimist. He writes that he had been talking to Giovanni Pedroni, one of the editors of the Casa Ricordi, who had lately returned from Paris where he had seen Gaetano. Pedroni had reported that Gaetano's health was good and that he was in pain only when he tried to write. Then, clutching at

[1] T. Oliario, 'La Malattia ed i Medici di Gaetano Donizetti'. *Minerva Medica*, vol. XXIX, Pt. 2 (1938), p. 12.

straws, Dolci wonders whether the arnica prescribed for Gaetano
could have affected his mind. He had been talking to a doctor
about this, and he knew of a woman who grew weak in the
head after taking arnica. The inconsistencies in the reports of
Gaetano's condition arise from the fact that it was not constant,
more often bad than good, and clearly worsening. In any event
Dolci's optimism did not sit well with Andrea, who was finding
his uncle increasingly difficult to deal with. The month of
January 1846 marked a crisis in Gaetano's condition; clearly
things could not continue much longer as they were. Andrea's
anxiety caused him to write quite unsympathetically to Toto
on the 21st.

Although this letter is lost, Toto's reply of 2 February gives
a clear indication of its contents.

I have never suspected either you or Michele, but the
stories that circulated referred to the de Coussy household,
and it is said the 20,000 ducats that Gaetano drew out of
the Neapolitan banks have been entrusted to Sig. de
Coussy, who paid the interest, but who had not guaranteed
the principal. It is said that Madama had ensnared
Gaetano with inconceivable wiles, and so many other
things have been said that you have given the lie to with
your convincing assurances. I was sorry that you challenged me, if I didn't believe your assertions, to come to
Paris. I, dear Andrea, would have flown faster than you
to be close to the man who is dear to my heart and to my
family, but Heaven has denied me the means of carrying
out this desire. Don't ever speak to me again with the
language you used in your last letter, since it was I who
urged your father to take personal care of Gaetano, and
consequently I shall always be your defender and pane-
gyrist for the fine proof of affection you have given your
uncle. Don't write any more, I beg you, on the subject of
diffidence, but let us speak of Gaetano.

If the doctors prefer the trip to Italy, and if one of these
doctors must accompany him, it seems that the wishes of
Gaetano need not be consulted; but the doctor accompanying him must have everything prepared, and then put
your uncle in the carriage and start out. The season will
soon be favourable, and you must hasten your departure

as much as possible. Your talent and your learning should make you philosophical enough not to be put out by the bad treatment an invalid, in spite of himself, might give you. If you should bring Gaetano to Rome, I will show you by my example how I can endure whatever rudeness he might show me. I feel myself cut to the heart to read this letter of yours. Oh! my poor Gaetano that you should be reduced to such a dreadful state of health! I am moved to tears. I urge you not to abandon him. . . . Ronconi writes from Naples with not very good news of Gaetano's health. In Rome and Bergamo terrible things are going the rounds. . . .[1]

To this letter Toto appends an equally revealing message to Michele Accursi.

After so many years of silence you have taken up your pen to upbraid me and to call me a slanderer . . . who has little friendship for Gaetano and is no help to him. I do not need to justify myself; what I wrote pertained to Mad. de Coussy and to her family, because people coming from Paris have told me about it and I had no reason not to believe it, because no one had torn away the veil from this relationship. By your assertions I see my error. Then I heard from Gaetano that you have a sister-in-law, a woman of rare qualities, and believed that she might be involved in taking care of the invalid; because of your silence to me it followed that you were disgusted with him and wouldn't go near him. Now from your bitter words I learn that I was deceived. . . . I beg you to bring your help to him to an end by arranging Gaetano's departure for Italy. . . . Sustain Andrea patiently, and if I did not have thirteen persons to support, I would come to your side and give you a lesson in patience. . . .[2]

But while these misunderstandings were being straightened out in Rome, things were taking place in Paris which soon put an entirely different complexion on the case. Finding his uncle by now impossible to deal with and resenting the inability of

[1] Franco Schlitzer, *L'Ultima pagina della vita di Gaetano Donizetti, Quaderni dell' Accademia chigiana*, No. 28 (Siena, 1953), pp. 8–9.
[2] Ibid., p. 9.

the other relatives and friends, who were so quick to advise and criticize, to come to Paris and help him, Andrea turned to the doctors. On 28 January 1846 (ironically, the date was the twenty-fourth anniversary of Donizetti's first successful opera, *Zoraide di Granata*), Calmeil, Mitvié, and Ricord wrote a comprehensive report. Juste Louis Cameil was an authority on mental disorders. Jean Mitvié was a nephew of the famous Esquirrol, and in 1824 they had established together a private asylum at Ivry; later Mitvié was to serve as Donizetti's personal physician.

The report on Donizetti's condition begins with a history of his symptoms. This report is the source for one of the most frequently repeated anecdotes about Donizetti: how each time he composed music it seemed to him that only one hemisphere of his brain was engaged and that a sort of partition seemed to separate the two halves. The rest of the report is worth quoting in detail because it was the basis for an important decision.

> In 1843 M. Donizetti complained one evening of feeling an extraordinary sensation in his head, and when he tried to give an idea of it he said that it was as though lightning had just flashed across his brain. Afterwards, in Italy, one day a sort of swelling of his face and dullness of expression were noticed. Still later he showed himself distracted on one occasion when it was to his advantage to keep up his usual high standards, and an accomplished singer complained of his accompaniment.
>
> Finally, since the middle of 1845, signs of a morbid condition in his brain became more common, and each day less equivocal. M. Donizetti was no longer able to compose as in the past; his ideas seemed less numerous than before; he easily gave way to frequent drowsiness; his walk seemed laboured; his body bent until he appeared stooped; his whole physical appearance became unfavourable; a host of nuances which could be perceived in his behaviour betrayed a relative lowering of his faculties of judgement and imagination.
>
> In August 1845 the weakness of his legs became so pronounced that he was subject to falling; at times his memory left him completely; an increasingly marked change occurred in the habits, the tastes, and the mode of

living of M. Donizetti. The learned doctors called in to examine him announced the existence of a disease of the major nerve centres, and prescribed treatment which was religiously followed under the direction of Dr Ricord.

The autumn of 1845 marked some periods of relief which permitted M. Donizetti's friends to hope to see him cured; however, there followed new symptoms of undeniable gravity. Several times at night when M. Donizetti left a horizontal position to move his arms, a sort of disturbance within his brain caused him to become painfully frightened. It seemed to him as though the floor pitched beneath him, that something crossed his brain from back to front, and that the house would come crashing down. In the morning after such a shock M. Donizetti was found stretched on the floor, and it was not until after he had been properly treated that he completely regained consciousness.

Finally today M. Donizetti's illness tends to reveal itself in its true light. The heaviness of his movements is obvious; the invalid barely gets out of the way of obstacles and dangers in the street; his pronunciation is at times thick; his posture, the poses of his head and body reveal that his muscles lack energy.

Not only do his memory and other intellectual faculties reveal a failure of breadth and understanding, but he confuses false and unreasonable ideas with rational ones. He believes that he is being robbed, that some one is stealing from him sums of money which are not at his disposal at all.

Also his character has become either irritable or taciturn; the excitement of his genitals no longer allows M. Donizetti to resist the satisfaction of his desires, and more and more he compromises his health by yielding to his partly unhealthy needs.

The undersigned are brought to think after all that has been revealed, that M. Donizetti is afflicted with a chronic disease of the great nerve centres, that this disease is located principally at several points in the pia mater and in the superficial substance of the brain, that it has at times been complicated by congestion of the capillaries, and complicated by a serous exudation into the cell structure of the meninges, which tends in time to soften the consistency of the nerve pulp.

They are of the opinion that now an exacerbation is taking place in several affected parts, and that the aggravation of his symptoms should be attributed to the action of this cause.

They are of the opinion that M. Donizetti is no longer capable of estimating sanely the consequences of his decisions and actions, and that if he were left free to follow his impulses, he can only hasten the progress of his illness.

They cannot advise a prompt departure from Paris as had been considered at first; they fear that the journey would be the occasion of irrational acts. . . .

In conclusion, they believe that for the present M. Donizetti should be placed in an establishment designed for the treatment of mental derangement, and that it will always be possible to reconsider a journey later, if it is deemed necessary.[1]

On 31 January, three days after the preceding report, a formal certificate was drawn up committing Donizetti to a mental institution. The following day a tawdry drama was enacted. In the morning a carriage drew up in front of the Hôtel Manchester; the bundled figure of Donizetti, supported by his Austrian servant Anton and by Andrea, was escorted out of the building and helped into the waiting vehicle. As the carriage started off, another, with Dr Ricord for its passenger, followed. Since their destination was a closely guarded secret the word had been given out that Donizetti was leaving for a rest cure at Nice. Donizetti himself believed he was setting out for Vienna, where his duties as Hofkapellmeister required his presence on 12 February. He felt compelled, at whatever the cost to his health, to meet the terms of his Viennese engagement, convinced he could not afford to lose his stipend of 12,000 Austrian lire. Since Donizetti believed that precisely this amount had been stolen from him (the delusion the doctors referred to in their report of 28 January), his determination to get to Vienna reflects, in some measure, the determination of his relatives, friends and doctors to prevent such a disastrous undertaking. In fact, some time earlier Donizetti had signed a

[1] Alborghetti-Galli, *Donizetti-Mayr*, Appendix: '*Consultation pour le 28 janvier 1846.*'

request for a leave of absence, pleading the state of his health, but he could not have remembered signing it when he drove out of Paris the morning of 1 February.

After the carriage had travelled about three hours it came to an abrupt halt. Donizetti was told that there had been an accident to the vehicle which would take several hours to repair. Fortunately, however, they had stopped near to a comfortable inn where the travellers might wait until their journey could be resumed. Donizetti was helped inside, where he was greeted by Dr Moreau, the director, who tried to pass himself off as an innkeeper. The unsuspecting Donizetti was shown to a suite of three rooms, opening on a garden.

Shortly after his arrival at the supposed inn at Ivry, Donizetti became aware that Andrea and his servant, who had slept in the same room with him every night for the past two months, were no longer with him. When he tried to leave he was told he could not. Convinced that he must get to Vienna, and keenly aware of the honours and responsibility of his official post, Donizetti became increasingly agitated. When the story of the damaged carriage no longer satisfied his overwrought patient, Moreau told him the flimsy tale that Anton had robbed his master and therefore the trip to Vienna must be postponed until the police had investigated the crime thoroughly. To lend some slight air of versimilitude to the story, Anton had been given some money, urged to keep what he knew to himself, and shipped back to Austria to find a new position.

But the fabricators of this tale underestimated Donizetti's ability to see through it. By the 5th Donizetti understood that he was being held against his will and that he was not being told the real reason why. He began to write a series of notes, turning to his friends to help him escape, crying out in anguish against the obviously trumped-up excuse of the robbery.

These notes were never delivered. Although they were exhibited in Bergamo in 1897, their tragic message was not published until Guido Zavadini brought out his invaluable *Epistolario* in 1948. A few excerpts should suffice to reveal the agony and despair so movingly expressed in these hastily scrawled notes.

If Donizetti's dates are to be trusted, and even in better times he was uncertain of the day on which he wrote, the first of these notes was written on the 5th, and although it has no address it was certainly intended for Countess Appony, the wife of the Austrian Ambassador in Paris.

Excellency!

Have pity! Pity! They have arrested me; why? My servant, it seems that he might be a thief. Hold the carriage; but, to arrest me too? In my carriage? To steal! . . . They defame me! . . . it's a mistake!

Meanwhile; I await your help:—

Donizetti

I must before the middle of this month, be in Vienna— Have pity, pity; I am innocent! the carriage is mine. I must be in Vienna by the 12th—Oh! You alone, Countess, know that I must write a mass for the Imperial Chapel of the Court at Vienna—Speak about this to H. E. your Excellent husband. This will be my last letter. I steal . . . my own property? Oh! Error! I will go back if *you* want it. Steal from myself. . . .[1]

Then on the following day he wrote in French, probably to Mme de Coussy:

Go Madame, *chez la S. E.*, and beg her . . . then beg through her and you will give me the answer . . . Excuse. *Ivry:*—

I am in the service of *Austria*—beyond France: They arrested me in my carriage, my things are stolen and I am alone! . . .

Madame la Comtesse. She will speak to you of me, and will not repulse my earnest prayer.

I beg this of you: my health is weak, but I have not lost my mind.

I weep. Have they found the crime? or not?—Give my entreaty.

And then on the back of the same sheet:

Pietá, Pietá, m'han arrestato — Ivry . . . venite, venite, per amor di Dio — (Gaetano) — Che ho fatto? — Oh mio Dio.[2]

The next day he wrote again to Zélie de Coussy the longest of these heart-breaking letters, with all their indications that Donizetti was far from oblivious to his surroundings, again intending that his letter should be passed on to Countess Appony.

[1] Z. No. 661, pp. 831–2.   [2] Z. No. 663, p. 833.

Madame come to *Ivry* . . . in an hour. . . ! Me, I have been arrested too—My servant has stolen another time?—My nephew's grief gives me courage! The young man is innocent—Set him free. . . . Oh! God! what sorrow. . . .

They arrested my nephew, and it was my *Servant*! they have arrested him . . . I haven't seen him again; Come! . . . may the blood of God descend on you: cursed be he who *lies*—Come; but if you cannot . . . prevent the death of my poor friend! He has 4 thousand plus 8—*I am innocent*. Everything has been returned! . . .

The letter is signed: *Le pauvre Donizetti*[1]

For all the efforts to keep Donizetti's seclusion in the asylum at Ivry a secret, the word soon leaked out and tongues wagged harder than ever. On 3 February Andrea had written to Toto in Rome and a joint letter to Dolci and Francesco in Bergamo, justifying the move. Sophie von Löwenstein, getting wind of the rumour that Donizetti was headed for Nice, drove to the frontier in her carriage day after day in the hope of meeting him and bearing him off in triumph to her villa.

At first Toto was prostrated by the news, but on 2 March he pulled himself together to warn Andrea of the possibly harmful effect isolation might have upon Gaetano.

> . . . What does he do in this *casa di salute*, how does he pass the time? I am very much afraid of the isolation. Remember that for a man who can have lucid intervals this isolation is a terrible spur to melancholia, even if he were sane. How much more prejudicial it will be for Gaetano, who has such a disease. This thought makes me tremble.

After expressing his concern for Gaetano's financial arrangements, he hoped that Andrea and Michele together would see that the patient had everything he needed to be comfortable. He concludes:

> I will keep your secret, but you know that gossip accuses me and Gaetano's relatives of having dumped him in a public hospital. My God, what scoundrels![2]

[1] Z. No. 666, pp. 834-5.   [2] Schlitzer, *L'ultima pagina*, p. 11.

313

On 27 March Toto wrote again to Andrea. In this letter his annoyance with Andrea's manner of writing to him shows itself even more plainly than in his earlier letters. He had received another communication from Andrea on the 16th.

> Your letter . . . although sad, gave me some comfort for all that pertains to your description of *La Maison du Santé* where Gaetano is living and for that which concerns the unhappy state of his health; but for all that which relates to the justification of your conduct, permit me to tell you that for me the thing is harmful or inconclusive. You must not justify yourself, because the good do not accuse you, and the gossips are not put down by such means, but by scorn. If you were in Rome, you would hear how I am accused of egoism and cruelty, because I haven't gone to Paris and because I didn't put a stop to his relationship. I have received from Naples in addition various letters written by lady acquaintances or friends of Gaetano who are bold enough to accuse me of being an accomplice to the death, or the loss of Gaetano, and they conclude that I would still be in time to save him if I left immediately for Paris. You can imagine my dismay at not being able to move from Rome. In such a state of excitement I have proposed to Aniello and to Don Teodoro that one or the other of them should go in my place to Paris, with a letter from me, where they could give the lie to the slander of those who have written from Paris to Naples, that Gaetano has been thrown into a Public Hospital like a beggar and when he is violent the paid attendants restrain him. . . .[1]

For all his reluctance and touchiness Andrea deserves some sympathy for his was a very difficult task. Many of Gaetano's friends and supporters were never to forgive him for being a party to the confinement of Donizetti at Ivry, but it should be remembered that Andrea continued his efforts to have his uncle moved to Italy even in that dark spring of 1846. And what is more Andrea had to bear the brunt of the gossip even more than Toto and Dolci and Francesco, and, besides, he had to keep reassuring them in their anxieties and complaints. Small wonder that sometimes his patience wore thin! His feelings can well be imagined on receiving a letter consisting of one sprawling

[1] Schlitzer, *L'ultima pagina*, pp. 11–12.

sentence, a grammatical morass, from Francesco, in which he complains that he is being kept in the dark about Gaetano's condition, but his real reason for writing is his concern for his allowance. Dolci apologised for Francesco's letter, writing on 4 April, by saying that Francesco had written without his knowledge.

> . . . I kept Gaetano's true state even from Francesco, but he, hearing contradictory gossip on every side, wanted to know the truth from me, and it was then I was, I should say almost, obliged to read him yours of the 17th and your last of the 28th, begging him to keep the secret and not to reveal the true condition of Gaetano. . . .[1]

In this same letter, Dolci says that he expects Ghezzi will have already arrived in Paris. Ghezzi, in fact, left Naples on 31 March bearing a letter of introduction from Guillaume Cottrau to his family in Paris.

> This note will be delivered to you by Teodoro Ghezzi, a distinguished painter and intimate friend of Donizetti, who is going to Ivry to learn for us whether the poor Maestro is in a condition to undertake the journey. Ghezzi is an excellent fellow, whom you will probably remember. Try to see Donizetti with him and give him many affectionate greetings from us. Poor Donizetti![2]

Ghezzi duly arrived in Paris, and Andrea took him out to Ivry at the earliest opportunity. Ghezzi found Donizetti slumped in a chair. Smiling briefly, he relapsed into a state of apathy. Ghezzi tried to engage his old friend in conversation, mentioning all sorts of things in his anxiety to elicit some response, but when Donizetti failed to give any sign at the name of his adored Virginia, Ghezzi left heart-broken and convinced that Donizetti was so beyond the help of friends that transferring him anywhere would be useless.

On the other hand a startlingly different impression of an interview at Ivry on a day when Ghezzi was present was written by Sophie von Löwenstein in a long, diffuse letter to Rosa Basoni, dated 10 October 1848.[3] In January 1846 Sophie

---

[1] Ibid., pp. 13–14.
[2] Guillaume Cottrau, *Lettres d'un mélomane*, p. 89.
[3] Z. No. B. 33, pp. 942–8.

expected Donizetti to come to her at Nice, but when he failed to arrive, she sent a spy to Paris who sent her the shocking news that Donizetti was confined at Ivry.

She left her invalid son at Nice and came to Paris at once. At first Andrea refused to let her see his uncle, but she threw herself at his feet and wept, thereby winning his consent, but only on the condition that she would swear never to ask to see Donizetti again. Willing to promise anything, Sophie accepted Andrea's condition. In her eagerness to make Andrea out a villain, she says that the day before her interview with Andrea he had received a letter from Dr Moreau, the director of the asylum at Ivry, urging Sophie be given permission to see Donizetti because it might be of some benefit to him.

In any event, on the appointed day Sophie, accompanied by Andrea and Ghezzi, went to Ivry and was met by Moreau, who led them to Donizetti's rooms. Moreau went ahead of them, saying, 'There is a lady here who is very anxious to see you.' On his feet, about to go into the garden, Donizetti was turned round by his new servant, Antonio Pourcelot, so that he could see who had come. Then Donizetti opened his arms and cried, '*Ah, Contessa mia!*' He found her hands were cold, and he wanted a fire lighted. Then he asked Sophie about her son, although he had not seen him for years, speaking, Sophie claims, 'with all his old lucidity'. Next, she reports, he begged her to take him to Italy with her, complaining they kept him locked up and treated him like an imbecile.

Just then, from close by, they heard one of the women patients shriek. Terrified, Donizetti asked, 'What is it? Where did that scream come from? From *here* in this house?' Sophie tried to assure him the sound came from the street, but she suspected then that Donizetti knew he was in an asylum, 'and that thought was sufficient to make him mad'.

When she started to leave, Donizetti urged her to come again. Then, says Sophie, he turned to Ghezzi and took his hands, saying over his shoulder, 'You from Nice, he from Naples, come *here for me.*' At that moment she claims Andrea reminded her in a furious whisper that she had sworn an oath never to ask to come to Ivry again. He was angry, as she saw it, because he was afraid that seeing her had benefited his unfortunate uncle's health.

Obviously Sophie exaggerated, but how much is difficult to

assess. She misses no opportunity to snipe at Andrea, whom she swears was insanely jealous of his uncle. Her story rings truest when she speaks of Andrea's opposition to her visit, because in view of his efforts at secrecy and in face of all the gossip, he could scarcely be anxious to let everyone who wanted to, go to Ivry. Certainly, if Teodoro Ghezzi had found Donizetti as Sophie describes him, he would not have been as discouraged as he undoubtedly was. On 16 April Andrea wrote to Dolci describing 'the tragic scene' of Ghezzi's encounter with Gaetano. Even if this letter is lost, some idea of its contents may be gained from Dolci's reply. 'I would not have believed it possible that Gaetano would not be moved by the name of his Virginia, and that the visit of Teodoro, his intimate friend, should have provoked a crisis.'[1] Significantly, after Ghezzi's visit the talk of bringing Donizetti to Naples begins to diminish and that urging Bergamo starts to increase.

That Donizetti's condition varied from day to day may be assumed from the consultation held on 7 April by Drs Javille and Félix Voisin. They found him unable to sustain the simplest conversation, and they observed his efforts to walk and even took him to a billiard table to test his co-ordination. His movements, they found, were tentative and they detected symptoms of progessive paralysis. They were convinced he needed the supervision and care of skilled attendants, all of which were to be found 'd'une manière parfaite' at Ivry. They would be opposed to any effort to move Donizetti.[2]

Four days later there was another consultation, this one by Drs Voisin and Fovis. A copy of their report was sent to Dolci by Andrea, and although it is not printed in Alborghetti and Galli, its discouraging contents can be surmised from Dolci's letter to Andrea of 20 April. 'I find the physical condition of my Gaetano, after having read the consultation of 11 April, is such that there is no hope of his being able to undertake a Journey.'[3] That there were two consultations within a few days suggests that between the 7th and the 11th of April there was an alarming change in Gaetano's health, perhaps the crisis provoked by Ghezzi's visit.

Dolci, however, was not discouraged by this bad news to give

[1] Schlitzer, *L'ultima pagina*, p. 16.
[2] Alborghetti-Galli, *Donizetti-Mayr*, Appendix: '*Consultation pour le 7 avril 1846.*'   [3] Schlitzer, *L'ultima pagina*, p. 16.

up his hope of bringing Gaetano home to Bergamo. He consulted Baroness Rosa Rota-Basoni and her daughter Giovannina, who had established a sympathetic relationship with
Donizetti over the past ten years. Deeply concerned for the
hapless Donizetti, the Basonis declared themselves ready to
provide him with whatever care and comfort he might require
and ready to welcome him no matter what his physical condition might be. Andrea favoured the move to Bergamo, and as
Gaetano's condition seemed to have remained relatively constant during the latter part of April and May, he arranged for
still another consultation. On 12 June 1846 Drs Cabarrus,
Fouquier, and Roche—the first two held the Légion d'Honneur
and the last was President of the Académie Royale de Médecine
—examined Donizetti and concurred that a journey would not
be harmful and that he should start for Italy without delay.[1]

Armed with this report Andrea went to the Austrian Embassy in Paris with a request that he be granted a passport for
his uncle, who as a Lombard was an Austrian citizen, and also
in the service of the Imperial Court. Count Appony consulted
Moreau and the staff at Ivry before answering Andrea's
request. They responded with the opinion that under no
circumstances should Donizetti be allowed to travel. These
opposing opinions were then sent to Count von Spaur, Governor
of Milan. In view of the interest that both the Imperial family
and Metternich had expressed in Donizetti, Spaur was asked to
ascertain whether Francesco was in a position to assume care
of his brother and whether Bergamo could provide adequate
medical care for Donizetti. Appony informs Spaur that only if
his answers are favourable would he be willing to assume
responsibility of issuing a passport to Donizetti and his nephew.
After urging a prompt reply Appony says that it would seem
advisable to appoint a trustee for Donizetti.

The day after he received it, Spaur sent the letter with its two
contradictory enclosures to Cavaliere Giambattista Bozzi, the
Delegato Provinciale at Bergamo. The next day Bozzi, with
Dolci, went to La Dorotina, the Basoni's summer villa at
Lovere. Their arrangements to care for Donizetti met with his
enthusiastic approval. In his reply to Spaur, Bozzi reported

[1] Alborghetti-Galli, *Donizetti-Mayr*, Appendix: '*Consultation pour le 12 juin 1846.*'
[2] Verzino, *Contributo*, pp. 135 ff.

that although Francesco was unable to care for his brother, the widow Basoni would provide him with every possible sort of assistance. The medical care in Bergamo, he went on, leaves little or nothing to be desired. As to a trustee, the matter could easily be attended to. Spaur in due course forwarded Bozzi's report to Count Appony in Paris. Dolci, believing now that it would be only a brief time until Gaetano was back in Bergamo, was full of happy plans, but his optimism was not to last long.

At this point Gabriel Delessert (1786–1853), the Préfet of the Paris police since 1836, begins to cast a shadow over the negotiations of the Donizetti family. Today it is difficult to disentangle the motives of Delessert. One of his friends described him as a thoroughly honest man who had no shred of imagination. A variety of hypotheses may account for Delessert's antagonism toward Donizetti. A wealthy member of the *haute monde*, whose wife was for years the *amie* of Prosper Merimée, Delessert may well have been prejudiced against artists as a class and against those who were the subject of scandalous gossip in particular. There is evidence that Delessert took a narrow view of public morals; it may be that this man, who put into effect and enforced rigid statutes governing behaviour and dress in public places, was unfavourably disposed towards Donizetti because of complaints made to the police during those crucial months before he was confined at Ivry. It is also possible that he took a dim view of Donizetti's close companions Accursi and Ruffini, both of whom were political exiles. Whatever his motives, Delessert proved himself a powerful and stubborn opponent to Donizetti's returning to Italy. He flatly refused to give Andrea permission to remove his uncle from Ivry. On 3 July he sent official word to Moreau that Donizetti was not to leave the premises until further orders.

Andrea protested. There were heated discussions which soon spread to Bergamo. On 11 July Dolci wrote: 'And when will all this infamous trickery end?' Two days earlier Delessert had ordered three doctors attached to the Préfeture, Bonneau, Béhier, and Trélat, to go to Ivry. Examining Donizetti, they found further mental deterioration. They expressed concern over the chronic stoppages of his bowels and bladder. They were distressed by his frequent mental congestions. They claimed that since he was impervious to all external impressions, the proposed journey to Bergamo would not only be useless but downright dangerous. They conclude, a little smugly, 'While according full justice to the noble feelings that prompt the nephew of Sig. Donizetti, we are of the opinion that the journey should be formally prohibited.'[1] Receiving this report Delessert, on 16 July, sent a formal order to Andrea restraining him from any further action.

But Andrea did not give up yet. Finally he managed, after 'repeated and pressing urgings' to arrange yet another consultation, this one held on 20 August. The assembled doctors were Calmeil, Ricord, Mitvié, and Moreau. Here is their report:

> They were struck by the state of weakness to which the paralysis had reduced all his muscles.
>
> M. Donizetti can still stand and walk on a level surface, supported by the arm of his servant, but his steps are very uncertain, his walk is a stagger, his body is decidedly bent to the right and in front, in such a way that falling is a constant danger, and his progress would be impossible if his servant did not take pains to maintain his master's balance.
>
> For several days his head has been bent far down on his chest, where it seems set due to the rigidity of the flexor muscles.
>
> Any effort to raise his head produces a painful sensation; on his neck there is no redness, nor warmth, nor any appearance of tumescence.
>
> His faeces are expelled only at very long intervals; his urine flows drop by drop without the invalid's being aware of it.
>
> His pulse has little strength. M. Donizetti seems to have no awareness at all of his condition, such is the progress of the cruel disease upon his fine faculties.
>
> The undersigned do not know positively if the type of contraction now noticeable near the cervical region is due to increased irritation of the great nerve centres or to a rheumatic condition . . . for all practical purposes a precise diagnosis is not necessary because the condition is not influenced by treatment.
>
> The undersigned are definitely of the opinion, basing it

[1] Alborghetti-Galli, *Donizetti-Mayr*, Appendix: '*Rapport pour le 10 juillet 1846.*'

upon the striking number of morbid symptoms, that the changes which have developed in M. Donizetti's brain are slowly approaching their greatest degree of intensity. They share the opinion that at the point he has reached, there also exists in the cerebral cavities a certain amount of fluid, and thus its accumulation contributes to the diminishment of his moral and intellectual strength.

They believe that one should have to wait only a short time for a termination as regrettable as it is inevitable.

As they have been obliged to pronounce judgement on the possibility or impossibility of M. Donizetti making a journey, they answer with the assurance of perfect conviction:

that at present no experienced man endowed with the least prudence would dare to assume the responsibility for moving an invalid in M. Donizetti's condition;

that even the movements of the smoothest, best balanced carriage would expose his head and neck to a dangerous seesawing;

that the relaxation of the bladder could be suddenly followed by a constriction which would require the use of a catheter, a painful and often delicate operation;

that the *erosions* which make paths through the convolutions of the brain would, under the pressure of fatigue, be liable to a sudden flux of blood, and could bring on at once *violent convulsions.* . . .

Some considerations of another degree, although very secondary, should be added to those which oppose his being moved: M. Donizetti's fame makes it imperative to dissemble as much as possible to avoid the impressions that his present state would give rise to in those who see him; out of respect for him his last moments must be kept from the eyes of strangers.

Finally, devotion itself is obliged at a certain point to submit to the yoke of opinion. M. Donizetti's career has drawn to him the good opinion and the protection of the great; even the appearance of wrong must be avoided when one has only praiseworthy sentiments and good intentions as have the family of M. Gaetano.

The undersigned do not advise any particular treatment; it is only a matter of hygiene to prolong the number of days left to M. Donizetti; and if any medical concerns present themselves, they should be treated by the experienced doctors in whose hands Donizetti has been entrusted.[1]

When Andrea read this decision he felt as though he had come up against an insuperable obstacle. Meanwhile in Bergamo, Dolci and Francesco, although they had been disappointed by the news of the consultation of 12 July, did not despair. They continued to write to Andrea of the arrangements being made in Bergamo to receive Gaetano. Directly after the consultation of the 20th (the report was not written up until ten days later), Andrea wrote to Dolci the discouraging results of this last medical opinion, adding that he had had a letter from his father in Constantinople reporting his mother's poor health and ordering him to return as soon as possible.

On 1 September Dolci replied to Andrea.

I was much surprised to read in your last these terrible words; the unhappy Gaetano is lost . . . and forever!!! What a blow this was for me you cannot imagine. I trust in heaven that there might still be some hope . . . and I still hope that one day or other he may be moved to Bergamo. . . . I had a letter from your father which surprised me very much . . . he absolutely wants you to return to Constantinople, because you have not been able to drag poor Gaetano from Paris. . . . What is the use of insisting? Everything has been tried, everything has been attempted, but everything in vain. He is right, but to abandon the poor invalid in an establishment in the clutches of who knows what people, that is also a very hard thing. By the same courier I am also writing to your father and I advise him again to make the final sacrifice of coming to Paris. . . . Here in this locality everyone asks me with great interest how is the health of the good Maestro, but I cannot give them the news. Francesco, too, was surprised to read your father's letter. He writes that perhaps you will pass through Bergamo. Finally, somehow write me something.[2]

This letter reveals Dolci's good heart and invincible optimism. In spite of Dolci's urging Giuseppe was not able to get to Paris.

[1] Alborghetti-Galli, *Donizetti-Mayr*, Appendix: '*Consultation pour le 30 août 1846.*'   [2] Schlitzer, *L'ultima pagina*, pp. 26–7.

He applied for a passport, but his request was denied. Verzino, in his *Contributo*, explains this surprising refusal as an example of unforgetting and unforgiving bureaucracy, reaching back thirty years to the time when Andrea Donizetti, Giuseppe's father, wrote a letter to the Austrian Governor of Milan requesting the release of his eldest son from the army for reasons of economic hardship. Verzino claims that since Giuseppe had served in the Sardinian army and was an emigrant, the Austrian government was not, even after all this time, willing to accord him any favours.

Andrea left Paris on 7 September. On that day he went out to take leave of his uncle, who very shakily wrote these few words: *Gaetano Donizetti fà saluto—Andrea parte oggi—7 settembre 1846*.[1] Andrea arrived in Bergamo about the middle of the month. He brought a box of Gaetano's jewels and orders which he gave to the Basonis for safe-keeping; he also brought two sealed boxes, the larger containing the autograph score of the uncompleted *Le duc d'Albe*; the smaller, the finished score of the one-act farce *Rita*. These were turned over to Dolci, who, on 17 September, signed a formal receipt for them, stating that he had received orders from Andrea and Francesco not to consign them to anyone, unless it be to Gaetano himself or to those who had entrusted him with them. On the 20th Andrea, who had been the guest of his uncle Francesco in the old house on the via Arena, left for Milan to continue his journey home. Before he left, Andrea had asked Francesco to give him power-of-attorney, but Francesco refused, explaining that maybe in a moment of sanity Gaetano might reproach him with it and cut off his allowance. Andrea and his father both betray an increasing anxiety over Gaetano's property, which, as his illness moved toward the inevitable, was each day closer to being theirs.

Of Andrea's departure from Bergamo, Giovannina Basoni wrote in her *Memoirs*,[2] that he left orders that no one was to dare try to move Gaetano from Ivry. An even less encouraging reminder he left behind were the detailed instructions for the funeral and embalming of his uncle. Giovannina was outraged with Andrea for abandoning his uncle. She refused to believe him when he said his uncle was *in extremis*, had to be fed by a machine and could no longer speak nor recognize anyone. She

[1] Z. No. 672, p. 839, in facsimile.   [2] MS. in the Museo Donizettiano.

323

claims to have heard that none of these things was true. Thus she shared the point of view that prevailed in Bergamo, of resolutely clinging to every shred of hope, of refusing to believe the worst. A year later she was to have a chance to see for herself just how things stood.

While Andrea was in Constantinople the situation at Ivry fell into dull routine, marked only by the almost imperceptible stages of the invalid's decline. For days on end Gaetano was left with only the companionship of his faithful servant, Antonio Pourcelet. He receded further and further into a state of apathy. As his ability to move about lessened, he passed his days seated in an armchair, his hands knotted into fists, a hand-kerchief placed around the ends of his fingers so that his nails would not pierce his palms, his head sunk upon his chest, either dozing or staring dully into space. At Bergamo, Dolci and the Basonis worked to keep up each other's spirits, praying the time would soon come when they could demonstrate what loving care and attention would do for the Maestro they idolized. Toto in Rome and Ghezzi and the others in Naples were disappointed that if and when Gaetano returned to Italy he would probably go to Bergamo, yet they continued to wait anxiously for any scrap of news about the invalid.

In Paris, too, Donizetti was not forgotten. Occasional visitors made the long trip to Ivry and back. On 9 November Alphonse Royer and Gustave Vaëz, the librettists of *La favorite*, came to see him. As Royer describes the episode nearly twenty years after it occurred in his *Histoire de l'Opéra*, Donizetti stared at them fixedly, but gave no sign of recognition, nor did he speak. When a bowl of soup was brought to him, they fed it to him because his paralysed hands could no longer hold a spoon. Royer says he lapped up the soup *'comme aurait fait un animal'*. A slightly more encouraging account refers to the following day, which Accursi describes as 'one of his good days'. Writing to Dolci, Michele says he took his sister and her son to call on Donizetti. He smiled at them, and when he learned the boy was attending the Conservatory, he tried to embrace him. They asked if he wanted to go back to Paris with them (an incredibly heartless question under the circumstances!), and poor Donizetti tried to struggle to his feet.

Gilbert Duprez has also left a vivid picture of his visit to Ivry, which he did not write down until the late seventies. Finding Donizetti completely withdrawn, the tenor tried to evoke in him some sign of life by speaking of the events they had shared in Italy a decade or more before. When words brought no response Duprez began to sing the final aria from *Lucia*. The first Edgardo was amazed when Donizetti suddenly offered to accompany him and started to grope towards the piano. The effort had been too much; his knotted hands fell on the keys, his head slumped down, his features drained of any sign of intelligence. The following year a still more famous tenor than Duprez was to sing a part of *Lucia* to him, eliciting no response whatsoever. Francesco Florimo, the Neapolitan archivist and biographer of Bellini, went to see Donizetti about this time and came away in tears.

By the end of the year there was widespread feeling among those concerned for Donizetti that there was, in view of his helpless condition, no useful purpose to be served by keeping him in confinement any longer. Accursi was of this opinion. Dolci wrote to Giuseppe that he shared the view, and that both Accursi and de Coussy were writing to him to the same effect.

The most significant of the visitors to Ivry during the final days of 1846 was none of these, however, but Baron Eduard von Lannoy,[1] an official of the Hapsburg court and a true friend of Donizetti, who came from Vienna expressly to see what could be done about the unfortunate inmate of Ivry. This influential friend was distressed by all the loose talk and criticism which put Donizetti and his family in such unfavourable and un-dignified light. At Paris he made a thorough investigation of the situation and visited Ivry several times. On 22 January he sent Giuseppe a letter, or ultimatum rather, that is a masterpiece of directness.

> . . . it is with full knowledge of the law that I write to you, not to reprove you nor from any desire to offend you, but to fulfil my obligations towards my friend and to present the thing to you in its true light.
>
> A year ago confinement was necessary, now it is no

[1] He was concerned with the stage, too, having written a melodrama, *Emmy Teels* in Vienna about 1830.

longer. Gaetano can no longer walk without being supported by his two custodians and cannot even rise from a sitting position without their help; and, as a result, he can no longer abuse his liberty. He is sinking little by little, the paralysis makes slow but continuous progress. No longer is there any hope of saving him, but what can be done is to make the last months of his existence less lugubrious, less melancholy.

He is still aware of the presence of his friends, his face grows animated, he struggles to talk, he smiles and weeps. Dr Moreau says the visits he receives are beneficial to him rather than harmful; now to go to Ivry to spend an hour with the poor invalid takes five hours, carriages are expensive. The unhappy Gaetano spends too much time alone with only his custodians.

If he were moved to Paris, he could be cared for by the same doctors, have the same custodians and the same care; furthermore physically he would do as well there as at Ivry and his morale would be a thousand times better because his friends could see him any day at any hour. They would cheer the last days of his life, and the famous maestro would not die in an institution, but in his own apartment.

His maintenance now costs 500 francs a month; in Paris it would cost 1000, perhaps 1500. Gaetano has about 20,000 francs income yearly. Now is it better that he should save 14,000 francs a year and succumb drearily in gloomy desolation or that he should save little or nothing and live a few months as happy as it is possible for him to be?

I beg you, sir, to think deeply about these alternatives, and to give me your answer. His friends are disinterested; they neither want to profit by Gaetano's misfortune nor live at his expense. The bills will be perfectly in order and supported by all the vouchers.

If neither brotherly feeling nor all the other considerations bring you to agree to Gaetano's leaving Ivry and being situated and cared for in his own house in Paris, I beg you to write to Count von Lesser. The other relatives will be forced to have recourse to the law. The French Civil Code expressly says: a person who is of age, who is in a state of imbecility, of dementia, or of violence *must* be interdicted, even when there are moments when he is lucid.

It would be necessary in this case to direct the courts not to fail to pronounce the interdiction, to name a *trustee*, and to obtain for him what you, sir, would have refused.

You have too noble a heart, sir, to permit matters to come to this extremity. Then give your consent to the just demand of the friends of the unfortunate Gaetano, and, fulfilling thus your duty as brother and good relative, you would spare yourself the remorse that doubtless would torment you later, and which a few thousand francs would certainly not spare you.

Excuse my frankness, but I have believed it my duty to tell you all I feel in my heart and to neglect nothing to brighten by however much they may be the last days of the life of my ill and unhappy friend.[1]

Giuseppe responded to this purposeful letter by once again dispatching Andrea, who took with him a miniature of his father, to see what could be done to procure Gaetano's release from Ivry. Andrea did not leave Constantinople until 4 March, when he sailed at six in the evening on the Austrian Lloyd steamer, *Die Kaiserin*.[2] He disembarked at Trieste on 13 March. Two days later he happened to read in the *Vendemmiatore* (a journal published in Parma) an article by a man named Checchetelli, which was a violent attack on the Donizetti family for their neglect of Gaetano, imputing self-interest as their motive in keeping their famous relative immured at Ivry. This article[3] infuriated Andrea and he was determined to answer it.

He arrived in Milan on 21 March and the following day went to see Count von Spaur, the Governor of Milan, to arrange for the publication of his answer. On the 26th Andrea went to Bergamo and there he prepared his article, taking the precaution of having it examined by a lawyer. On 3 April he was back in Milan, making the necessary arrangements for the

[1] Z. pp. 152–3.
[2] Andrea's activities for 1847 can be followed closely, because his MS. journal or daybook for this year is in the Museo Donizettiano.
[3] It was reprinted in the *Vendemmiatore* from another periodical, *Pallade*.

publication of his defence, which appeared in the *Gazzetta privilegiato di Milano*, on Monday, 12 April.

Andrea's defence was to give a reprise of all his activities in Paris, of all the consultations, to publish the addresses of all the doctors involved, inviting any interested persons to write to them for confirmation of his story. Once his article was safely in print it became one of Andrea's chief concerns to see that it was reprinted and circulated as widely as possible.

He left Milan for Turin on 14 April where he went to see Romani, who, as editor of the *Gazzetta privilegiata di Torino*, promised to write something in Andrea's favour. On the 16th he left for Chambéry, where he visited old friends. The evening of the 19th he set out for Lyons, where he again broke his journey for a day and a half, leaving there the 21st and arriving in Paris at 11.30 p.m. on the 23rd. The following day he went to Ivry and wrote this account of it in his journal:

> April 24. I went to Ivry at high noon and I saw Gaetano. Oh God! in what condition!! He keeps his eyes closed constantly! He recognized me, and his servant assured me that he had not seen him so observant of anyone for many months as he was of me. He kissed me at my request, often he looked at me. I saw Moreau, what things he told me! He gave me the address of Mad. Löwenstein.[1] I did not find her because she has moved elsewhere. I went to the Hôtel du Havre where it was believed she was staying, but in vain. I will write her a letter to *poste-restante*.

On the 25th he went back to Ivry; but gives no details. The next day he called at the Austrian Embassy where he was shown a letter from Delessert which stated that Donizetti was not only unable to leave for Italy, but he could not even be brought back to Paris. On 2 May Andrea moved to the Hôtel d'Italie and here he saw that a French translation of part of his answer to Checchetelli had appeared in *France musicale*. He also received a letter from Zélie de Coussy. On the 3rd Andrea went back to Ivry where he saw Donizetti walking supported by the servant Pourcelot. Andrea was sure that Pourcelot 'only wanted that Gaetano should recognize me and show me some friendliness!'

[1] Since Checchetelli said he had learned from Paris of Andrea's supposed neglect and self-interest, it seems likely that Andrea believed Sophie van Löwenstein was Checchetelli's informant.

On 5 May he asked for an audience with Delessert, and sent the article to Sophie von Löwenstein. The next day he went to see Madame de Coussy in the evening. 'Always the same', he noted in his daybook. That same evening he sent his first report to the anxious Dolci.

> . . . I got to Paris on the 23rd ult. at 11 o'clock at night. The following day I went to Ivry to embrace my uncle. Great God! in what a deplorable state I found him!!! . . . Seated in a big chair, his eyes closed and a pleasant expression upon his face which could momentarily delude someone seeing him for the first time that he would answer them, but the situation is quite other! His life, in short, is worse than death! . . .
>
> Although I had been away from the invalid for seven months, nevertheless he recognized me and smiled. I embraced him many times, he responded with several kisses, but only because I asked him to! . . . He pressed my hand often, he looked at me with attention, and I will even say, with interest. One of his servants assured me that for a long time he had not seen Gaetano so preoccupied with a visitor as that day. I spoke to him of his dearest friends, of his late wife; in vain! I presented him with the portrait of my father which he certainly recognized since he held it for a long time looking at it with interest; then dropping it, he almost fell from his chair trying to pick it up, and when I gave it back to him, face down on purpose, he took it eagerly and turned it over. At last, embracing him, as I left to return to Paris, I said to him: *arrivederci a domani, caro Gaetano*, and he answered, stammering, *a domani*.
>
> Since that day I have seen him many times, but always in the same condition. That is the unhappy truth, dear Dolci! . . .[1]

Andrea goes on to assure Dolci that he will do everything in his power to arrange Gaetano's return to Italy, but he believes he will encounter even more difficulties than he did the previous year. He reports that Delessert had sent his staff physician, Béhier, out to Ivry to see if Donizetti could be moved to the de Coussy's house, but Moreau had been opposed to it, even

[1] Z. No. B. 28, pp. 933–4.

suggesting that such a step might hasten the Maestro's death. Although Andrea does not say so explicitly, he cannot have been in favour of the proposed transfer to the home of the excitable Zélie because he told Dolci that both he and his father believed a *chez soi* the most desirable arrangement for Gaetano. This letter was a cruel blow to Dolci who answered it, saying: 'I still want to hope . . . I don't want to delude myself. . . .'[1]

On Friday the 7th Andrea went again to Ivry. He found Gaetano 'always the same'. The next day he had his audience with Delessert.

> . . . I spoke at length of the plans of my family, of our intentions. I let fall several words of my suspicions. The Préfet accompanied me to M. Schayet, of the 1st division of police, who gave me all the papers regarding Gaetano, but I must write again to the Préfet to have copies of them.
>
> In the evening I went to hear Mlle Rachel at the Théâtre Français.

On the 10th Andrea went back to Ivry, and took a straw hat to his uncle. While he was there Madame de Coussy came with her brother. Andrea comments:

> . . . She tried to make me believe that from time to time she cried. She asked me about my plans; I answered that I did not even know myself. She is dying of fury. . . .
>
> 13 May. Bought an inkpot for my office at Constantinople, 18 francs. I don't understand the answer to my letter that I wrote the Préfet. He does not want to let me see the report of Dr. Béhier, which is too much in opposition to that of Mitvié. . . . In any event, this delay disturbs me, since I can do nothing without that report. . . .
>
> 14 May. Went to Ivry. . . . In the evening I went to the Grand Opéra to see *Lucia di Lammermoor*.[2] Gaetano's music makes me feel bad when I think of what he was and what he is now. . . .
>
> 17 May. Went to Ivry. Then to the Préfecture and talked with Schayet and I asked them if they wanted to give me

[1] Schlitzer, *L'ultima pagina*, p. 31.
[2] *Lucia* was first performed at the Opéra 20 February 1846, by Maria Dolores Nau, Duprez and Barroilhet, becoming the six hundredth work to enter the repertory of that theatre.

Béhier's report. He made me understand not, but they have already ordered another doctor to go to Ivry. . . .

20 May. Went to Ivry with Rubini's nephew, Scandrini, and another Roman who knows Checchetelli. When I presented these gentlemen to Gaetano, he shed a tear. Later, asking him why he did not speak, I saw him several times put his hand to head, wanting to speak and raising it as though he felt a weight that pressed on him. He was asked if it was true that he wrote *Furioso* at Rome in Toto's house, he answered yes; if he wrote *Anna Bolena* for Rubini, yes; for the Teatro Carcano in Milan, he answered no, but that it had been written for the Tordinona.[1] He gave, in total, many signs of intelligence which amazed Moreau.

21 May. Went again to Préf. of Police, could not speak to anyone. . . .

22 May. Went to Ivry. Gaetano always in the same state! I saw Moreau, who asked me if there was nothing new. I hope to get myself out of there with everything.

25 May. I am writing to the Préfet, asking another audience, to finish it, if it is possible. Went to see Gaetano, and then Mitvié. I gave him the news about the report that Béhier must make again, and he told me that it will be favourable. . . . He went to Ivry the 10th of this month. Will I be able then to move Gaetano? I hope so at least. I received a letter from Dolci, which contained one from Francesco, who is always the same.

26 May. I received a letter from the Préfet, who granted me an audience for tomorrow. I hope that finally I will know something!

27 May. . . . At noon I went to the Préfet, who told me that he had signed the permission to let Gaetano leave the asylum at Ivry. Finally I have obtained something and I begin to hope of taking Gaetano to Italy. I went to M. Schayet and then to M. Lezeret, the commissioner in charge of the sanitoriums, and I begged him to please write a letter to communicate to me officially the letter of the Préfet. I went to see M. Mitvié and informed him of

----

[1] *Anna Bolena* was, however, first performed at the Carcano.

what had happened, and I begged him to send me a copy of the official disposition, which I am to receive tomorrow. Béhier has met the conditions that I have already proposed. He, however, had reputedly sent a favourable report to Mme de C.

28 May. . . . I received a letter from the Préfet that announced he had given orders that Gaetano could leave the asylum. I went to look over half of Paris to find a house for Gaetano. . . .

29 May. . . . Looked for houses where I could lodge Gaetano. I found nothing that would suit him, although I have learned of several from Michele Accursi, who knows Paris better than I. . . .

30 May. I sent to my father, Ghezzi, Vasselli, Dolci, and de Gris, copies of the current *France musicale* that announces the permissions I obtained to bring Gaetano to Paris. . . .

31 May. I saw Gaetano, as before. . . .

For the next week Andrea is mostly concerned with sending copies of various articles to people, and looking for lodgings. Only once, on Saturday, 5 June, did he go to see Gaetano. On the 7th he finally found a likely looking place on the avenue Chateaubriand for Gaetano.

8 June. Went with M. de Coussy to see the house to have his advice. Later went with Mme de C. She wanted to make difficulties as I would have to take an apartment for a year at least and thus I would commit myself to other, more considerable expenses. [Here something is heavily crossed out.]

9 June. Wrote to my father. Went to Ivry; then I saw a gardener to take care of the garden. I would have to give him 100 francs!

10 June. Gave 20 fr. down to hold the house at disposition for the 13th of this month. Went to Ivry in a carriage. . . .

12 June. Went to Ivry. At 5 had a curious scene with the concierge of the house I rented for Gaetano. He gave me back my down payment and did not want to rent it to me. I was even received rudely. I returned in the evening with

Michele and Garofolini. The same thing. I went to the Commissioner of Police of the quarter and complained. I took the same apartment for Monday. These are certainly the manipulations of Mme.

13 June. I went to see other houses for Gaetano. I received a letter from the gardener who confirmed me in my supposition of yesterday regarding the actions of Mme de C. Tomorrow I must see this man who promises to explain things to me, and I don't know how I can. The object of all this, we will see.

14 June. I went to the Commissioner of Police and then to M. Goudenone. They asked me all sorts of questions, and I discovered that it was an unknown man who whispered in the ear of the concierge not to rent me the apartment because I and my companions were bad types (*cattivi originali*). I believe this can explain everything. Could Mme have played this dirty trick? . . .

16 June. I saw other apartments. I went over others with Mme de C. and I fixed again on this one on the avenue Chateaubriand No. 6, because it is the most convenient.

17 June. Rented the house for Gaetano for 250 francs a month. . . .

20 June. Went to Ivry. Moreau not there. Gave orders that all would be ready for Tuesday, the day I will bring Gaetano to Paris. . . .

22 June. Went to buy a tent to put in the garden for Gaetano. They came to put it up.

23 June. Went to get Gaetano at Ivry to take him to Paris. I cannot describe my feelings this memorable day! Left Paris at 6 in the morning, with Gaetano by 9.30. I arrived in Paris with my uncle at 11.30. . . . Mitvié came and found Gaetano very well, in fact he did not suffer at all during this trip. . . .

Now that Gaetano was free after having spent sixteen months and twenty-three days at Ivry, he could go out for a drive in a carriage every other day, weather and his condition permitting. These rides, which Andrea hoped would ready the patient to undergo the long trip to Bergamo, were gradually extended until their leisurely course lasted three or four hours, taking him as far as Saint-Cloud. Giovanni Ricordi was in Paris in July and went to see his afflicted friend, an association that had lasted thirty-two years since the time when Ricordi had published Gaetano's *Variations* on a theme by Mayr. Ricordi went driving on 15 July with Donizetti, Andrea, and the loyal Antonio, and reported that the invalid rode along with his eyes open, looking around him and seemingly content, a contrast to his apathy indoors.

In a letter to Peppina Appiani dated 22 August, answering her request for news of Donizetti, Verdi, who had come to Paris for the production of *Jérusalem*[1] at the Opéra, wrote in his usual straightforward manner:

> . . . I have not seen him yet because I have been advised not to, and if the occasion to see him without anyone knowing presents itself, I shall certainly do it. His physical appearance is good, except that he always keeps his head on his chest and his eyes closed. He eats and sleeps well and scarcely utters a word, or if he does it is very indistinct. If someone is presented to him, he opens his eyes a moment; if they say to him: *give me your hand*, he stretches it out, etc. It seems that this would be a sign his intelligence is not entirely gone; nevertheless a doctor who is his devoted friend told me that these indications are rather those of habit and that it would be better if he were animated, even *violently insane*. Then one might hope, but this is to want nothing less than a miracle. For the rest, his condition is now as it was six months, a year ago: no improvement, nor worsening! There, that is the present condition of Donizetti. *E' desolante, è troppo desolante.* . . .[2]

On 3 August Andrea summoned a photographer to the apartment on the avenue Chateaubriand. A daguerrotype was taken of Gaetano and Andrea, which shows the composer slumped in his chair, his eyes shut, his chin resting on his chest, his fists knotted. Andrea is seated beside him, his hands resting solicitously on his uncle's right arm. Andrea sent a copy of it to Rosa Basoni to prepare her for the tragic alteration she would see in her long-awaited guest. For a time it looked as though

---

[1] A revision of *I Lombardi alla prima crociata*.
[2] Giuseppe Verdi (ed. Alessandro Luzio), *Copialettere*, p. 463.

the daguerrotype were all she would ever see, because the problem of getting the necessary permission to start Gaetano on his final homeward journey developed into a situation that could only be resolved by international diplomacy.

For all Andrea's inexplicable dilatoriness at times, there is no doubt he worked hard and constantly during his second Paris stay to achieve his long-desired end. To present the appearance of a solid family front and to bolster his position, Andrea summoned the not very prepossessing Francesco to Paris, where he duly arrived 12 August. The preceding week Dr Giovanni Antonio Lorenzo Fossati (1789–1874) came expressly from Milan to examine Donizetti and made a formal declaration that he could, with the necessary precautions, withstand the trip to Bergamo.[1] Andrea submitted Fossati's declaration to Delessert, but the Préfet refused to grant any change in Donizetti's status.

While all these things had been going on Zélie de Coussy had not been idle. Here is the account of her activities which appears in Andrea's journal.

24 June. [The day after Gaetano's removal from Ivry to the avenue Chateaubriand]. . . . In the evening I took a nosegay of flowers to Mme de C. in Gaetano's name, because it was her name-day. I took care, however, that the bouquet contained neither thoughts nor other *sentimental* flowers. . . .

26 June. Mme and Mlle de C. came. . . .

27 June. In the evening Mme and Mlle de C. . . .

29 June. Mme de C. came, but she did not see Gaetano because he was already in bed. . . .

7 July. In the evening Mme de C. came, but I did not see her, as usual. . . .

11 July. Mme de C. sent Gaetano a letter and a jar of sweets. I sent back the jar of sweets, pretending not to be at home. Antonio said he could not receive it, I having forbidden him to accept anything whatever in my absence. . . .

12 July. I received a letter from M. de Coussy. . . .

[1] Alborghetti-Galli, *Donizetti-Mayr*, Appendix: '*Dichiarizione del De Fossati di Milano (4 août 1847).*'

335

13 July. Michele came, who gave me a report of the displeasure manifested by Mme de C. at the sending back of the sweets. I can do nothing about it, since I was not at home! Then let them think what they want. . . . I wrote to M. de C. . . .

15 July. I went to M. de Coussy and drew 2000 francs. . . .

27 July. In the evening Mme de C. came but I did not see her and she made a scene with the servants because they did not let her see Gaetano. There were two strangers with her. I have to know who enters my house, but Mme believes the servants are hers to command. . . .

29 July. Mme de C. presented herself again. . . . My servants repeated the same things they said the other night. They told her to come as others did when I was at home, at eight in the morning. . . . But she flew into a rage with one of them and said she would not come again. May God will it so. . . .

2 August. The de Coussy family came and remained in the foyer. They did not want to enter. . . .

3 August. I saw the Marchesa Cavalcanti and Sig. de Luca, who told me of the scene Mme de C. made at my door. She slammed the door and said that I didn't want to receive her. But when Florimo heard that I ordered that no stranger could be admitted in my absence and that only the strangers who were with Mme de C. were not allowed in, he told them that I was right. . . .

7 August. In the evening at the house of the De C.'s. . . .

This is the last entry about Zélie. Andrea's journal pretty well peters out after 13 September. It is a strange, frustrating record, full of hints, bias, and gaps. It gives a full record of Andrea's running round to see doctors and his efforts to get Gaetano back to Italy, and it reads as though it were intended primarily as a source for a defensive article he planned to write when he finally succeeded in getting Gaetano back to Italy. Only two things are certain as far as Zélie went. There was no love lost between her and Andrea, but since her husband was Gaetano's banker he could not break with the family completely; he was determined to keep her away from Gaetano as much as possible. For his part, Andrea could be petty and childish, and for all his considerable labours on his uncle's behalf, he, as his father's only heir, could scarcely be counted a disinterested party.

As the summer was getting on and the favourable season for the journey with it, the Donizettis redoubled their efforts. In the face of Delessert's repeated refusals, Giuseppe stepped into the arena. On 16 August he made a formal application to Count von Stürmer, the Austrian plenipotentiary to the Sultan's court, laying before him the facts of the case, detailing the careful plans for the journey to Bergamo, and asking him to submit a formal request to Count Appony that Donizetti be permitted to leave while the weather was still favourable. In this *Istanza*, Giuseppe specifies the Préfeture of Police which 'persists in taking the greatest interest in the tragic position of Gaetano Donizetti and persists in making difficulties, just as they did the previous year.'[1] Consolidating the attack from Paris, Andrea arranged what he hoped would be a decisive consultation of six doctors to render judgement on the advisability of the journey. The six doctors convened in Donizetti's apartment at 2 p.m. on 17 August. They debated at length before they would even agree to a consultation and then their opinion was divided: Drs Fossati, Chomel, Rostand and Mitvié agreed to the departure, provided suitable precautions were taken; Drs Andral and Calmeil affirmed their belief the journey would be harmful and that Donizetti should remain in Paris.[2]

There is a further medical report, dated 23 August, and signed by Calmeil, one of the dissenting physicians, but whether this is a detailed statement of his position on the 17th or the record of still a further examination is not clear. Calmeil states his belief that there was a lesion on the medulla oblongata, that with such a lesion even a slight shock could produce fatal results. 'Each day paralytics who are much more robust than Donizetti pass from life to death in the twinkling of an eye. . . .

---

[1] Alborghetti-Galli, *Donizetti-Mayr*, Appendix: '*Istanza, Constantinopoli, il 16 agosto 1847*.'
[2] Ibid.: '*Consultation pour le 17 août 1847*.'

How regrettable it would be to his family if this should happen to Donizetti in a public street.'[1]

Andrea's hope that the majority opinion of the 17th would make an impression on Delessert was soon shattered. As soon as the Préfeture learned of the result, Dr Béhier, the staff physician, called at the avenue Chateaubriand No. 6 to announce, and in a manner that infuriated Andrea, that he was categorically opposed to the move. Next Andrea turned to Count Appony, asking his assistance in securing the authorization. The Austrian ambassador's reply was disheartening: he could not accede to Andrea's request since the opinion of the doctors had not been unanimous. Andrea's next blow was a letter from the police commissioner of the *arrondissement* which bluntly told him that since his uncle's condition had not improved in the slightest, M. le Préfet had decided that he should not leave the country. Andrea was so incensed by this continuous opposition, the true motives of which never showed themselves, that he may well have been moved to make some injudicious remarks in the hearing of the police. In any event, his anger was further aroused on the evening of the 26th, when gendarmes were installed in the *conciergerie* of avenue Chateaubriand No. 6. Dr Mitvié's daily medical report for the 26th noted that his patient's condition was unchanged and that his outings might continue. And so, on the following day when Andrea started to take his uncle out for his usual airing, the police refused to permit them to enter the vehicle. Andrea went at once to the Préfeture and demanded an explanation. Delessert explained that the action of the police had only been a precautionary measure to prevent an illegal departure for Italy.

Writing of these harassments to Leon Herz in Vienna, with the intention that Herz would get the story into the Viennese papers, Andrea expresses his reaction to this last move by Delessert. '*Pour le coup c'est pas trop fort, et je commence à soupçonner les véritables amis de mon oncle trop—dévoués—à qui le mérite de l'invention d'un mensonge si effronté? Ma fois* [sic] . . . *à la personne qu'un lui emprunte un cœur, et qu'elle n'a qu'un méchant esprit. Quel dommage qu'on n'ait encore brevetée!!* . . .'[2] The *personne* Andrea

[1] Alborghetti-Galli. *Donizetti-Mayr*, Appendix: '*Consultation pour le 23 août 1847.*'
[2] Z. No. B. 30, pp. 935–8.

alludes to so spitefully here is probably Zélie de Coussy, who had tried to get Donizetti moved from Ivry to her house about the first of May.

Still seething from his latest interview with Delessert, Andrea went to see three notable lawyers, Marié, Crémieux, and Berryer, who advised him to take the matter to court if any more attempts were made by the police to prevent Donizetti from riding in his carriage. Also on the lawyers' advice, Andrea wrote to Delessert to say that he would never again admit Béhier to his uncle's presence, unless it were for a final consultation, which he would permit provided Dr Mitvié was present. If that meeting was held its report has not been kept.

Andrea's tactic of publishing accounts of the Préfeture's action all over Europe coupled with pressure from Vienna engineered by Baron von Lannoy finally stopped Delessert. The spectacle of the Paris police detaining such a famous man as Donizetti, an Austrian subject and attached to the Imperial Court, and giving no adequate reason for their action, left Delessert no route but retreat unless he chose to provoke an international incident.

The inner workings of this opposition will probably never be known. Zélie de Coussy and Countess Appony were on good terms, as may be deduced from Donizetti's letters written in those first frantic days at Ivry, when he urged Zélie to use her influence on the wife of the Austrian ambassador.[1] A close alliance between them might account for Appony's refusal to help Andrea because the consultation of 17 August was not unanimous. Certainly Andrea's letter to Herz reveals his conviction that there was a woman behind it. Toto in Rome had heard all sorts of stories about Zélie and her harmful influence. The heart of the mystery is the question of what advantage she, or anyone else, would gain personally or materially from keeping Donizetti in Paris when he was reduced to a practically vegetable state. Such analyses of their motives ladies like Zélie do not frequently commit to paper.

At long last the journey to Bergamo began its pitiable course on 19 September. The party consisted of Gaetano, Francesco, Andrea, the servant Antonio Pourcelot, and Dr Rendu,

[1] In one of the frantic letters written in his first days at Ivry, Donizetti describes Countess Appony in these terms: '*Elle est italienne, élève de Mayr.*'

especially engaged to make the journey. They left for Amiens from the Gare du Nord and arrived at their destination at 4.30 p.m. According to Rendu's daily report Donizetti seemed in no way tired by his first day's journey. In the hotel he was helped to walk up and down his room before dinner, and then he ate heartily. He slept well that night. They got to Brussels on the 21st, where Donizetti spent a restless night and awoke feverish. Rendu diagnosed his condition as a congestion of the bladder and performed the necessary catheterization. As a result of this complication the party stayed in Brussels five days. Their journey then continued without incident down the Rhine to Basel and then by carriage over the St. Gotthard pass. On 5 October they reached Como where Dolci came to join them. Here the doctor suggested they shorten their trip by omitting Milan and heading straight for Bergamo, which they reached the evening of 6 October.

The arrival of the carriages at the Palazzo Basoni has been compared to the arrival of a funeral procession. As announcements of Donizetti's progress back to Bergamo had already appeared in the papers, a large crowd had gathered to welcome him. Count Lochis, the mayor of the city, who all along had encouraged the return of this distinguished native son, was there in his official capacity, along with other dignitaries. Marco Bonesi was there to welcome home his fellow pupil of Mayr's school. The Basonis, mother and daughter, anxiously awaiting their long-expected guest, determined by their loving care to try to accomplish what all the doctors could not do. But when the carriage door door opened and the pitiful, emaciated figure was almost carried into the house, the tragic sense of loss caused many to weep. When the Basonis saw the incontrovertible evidence of Donizetti's condition, all their eager hopes, that somehow the medical reports had exaggerated the case, collapsed.

Donizetti was taken to a large bright room on the *piano nobile* of the Palazzo Basoni (now the Palazzo Scotti). It opens on the back of the house; a tall door opens onto a little balcony that overlooks the garden and the patio beneath. In the distance stretches the plain of Lombardy to the south. The walls of the room are a creamy yellow, in the ceiling a large oval painted to represent blue sky and scudding clouds. The furnishings, in Donizetti's day, included a single bed with a high headboard and footboard of polished mahogany, the piano Donizetti had bought for Giovannina in Vienna, and an especially contrived arm-chair with a padded board to support his head and a tray that fitted across the arms.[1] As soon as he arrived he was fed and put to bed.

The following day Rendu made the last of his daily reports.[2] Donizetti had spent a good night. There were no signs the journey had had any ill effect upon him; his condition seemed exactly as it had been before his departure from Paris.

Legal sanction was required to permit Donizetti to stay with the Basonis, and to gain it Rosa and Giovannina appeared in court on 10 October, and made a solemn declaration that they had both ample means and an ardent desire to care for Donizetti as long as he should need their assistance. The following day Rendu officially turned over his patient to two Bergamasc doctors, Giovanni Cassis and Luigi Calvetti, all three signing a statement that they had gone over together the reports of earlier consultations and thoroughly examined the patient. Cassis and Calvetti declared they would watch attentively for any signs of deterioration or of congestion: in view of his hopeless condition, they would limit their treatment to maintaining the patient's hygiene.[3] This limited objective was eminently realistic, but outside Bergamo there was considerable unfavourable speculation and gossip about the care Donizetti would receive at the hands of small-town doctors. A reflection of this talk turns up in a letter the ever-solicitous Lannoy wrote to Dolci on 18 October. He had heard that the doctors of Bergamo intended to subject Donizetti to drastic treatment in hopes of accomplishing what their Parisian confrères had failed to. Lannoy urges Dolci to prevent any such treatment as it can only hasten Donizetti's death. He is anxious for Dolci to recognize the unusual virtues of Donizetti's servant Pourcelot as an excellent person, genuinely attached to his master. Then he addresses Dolci as Donizetti's newly-appointed trustee and tells him the names of

[1] The bed, the piano, and the arm-chair form today three of the most moving exhibits at the Museo Donizettiano, Bergamo.
[2] Alborghetti-Galli, *Donizetti-Mayr*, Appendix: '*Declaration au matin 7 Octobre 1847.*'
[3] Ibid.: *Consulto per il 11 Ottobre 1847.*'

those he should write to in Vienna so that he can make the necessary business arrangements with them.

For over a year the question of appointing a trustee for Donizetti had been in the air. Two very different reasons apparently delayed its solution. For one thing, the family and friends were reluctant to force the issue as long as there was any likelihood of Donizetti being, even momentarily, sane. For the other, there was undercover pressure to avoid or at least to delay Dolci's confirmation as trustee as long as it seemed possible to keep Donizetti in Paris. Ever since Andrea had turned over to Dolci the sealed packages of manuscript music, he had, in effect if not in title, served as trustee. More than that, his function as disbursing agent for the funds that Gaetano and Giuseppe supplied for their brother Francesco had given him a trusteeship of ten years' standing. Through August and September 1847, Dolci's declarations and applications shuttled back and forth, put off with one excuse after another, until the matter was finally settled on the eve of Gaetano's arrival in Bergamo.

While the legal arrangements consequent to Donizetti's condition went through the courts, he was settled into a routine that continued some months with little variation. In the latter part of October Andrea set out for Constantinople to await the inevitable from there. Meanwhile Antonio dressed and shaved his master each morning and helped him to his arm-chair. He was fed, often by Giovannina, and then visitors would drop by. Dolci came every day, often several times a day. The Basonis spent long hours with him, Giovannina played his music on the piano he had picked out for her in Vienna four years before. What changes those years had brought, as now she played for that shrunken, withdrawn figure, anxiously glancing at him to see if this or that melody had brought some glimmer of recognition to those vacant features. Rubini came from his villa at nearby Romano one day and sang the first-act duet from *Lucia* with Giovannina, but in vain. Dr Cassis looked in twice a day. Other friends came frequently and talked to him of the old days, talking Bergamasc, with the ever-present hope that some word or reference might dissipate, even for a moment, the mists that shrouded his intelligence. Donizetti would look at each visitor attentively, as though he were struggling to place him, but his attention would not last long, his eyes would close and his head sink back on his chest. Rarely he would mutter some monosyllable, but no amount of straining helped a listener know for sure what it was he had tried to say.

For some months there was little appreciable outward change as the disease followed its insidious but inexorable course. In February 1848 there was considerable alarm when he ran high fevers and sweated profusely. He was assailed by fits of coughing that interfered with his eating. The doctors modified his diet and increased the number of purges; gradually the symptoms abated. Dr Cassis was convinced that a gastro-rheumatic attack from which Donizetti suffered was not a consequence of his principal disease. By the end of February Donizetti had recovered sufficiently to resume his former routine, but this attack had left him alarmingly thin.[1] Throughout March there was little perceptible change.

The insidious progress of Donizetti's disease, the creeping damage of the lesions in his brain and spinal column, could not be postponed or turned back. The first of April he awoke, seeming much as he had for the previous month. As Antonio and the Basonis followed their usual routine of caring for the patient, there seemed no indication that anything unusual would happen. Until five o'clock. . . . But here is Giovannina Basoni's graphic account of Donizetti's last days:

> The first of April at 5 in the afternoon, while he was eating his supper, which he used to do with a good appetite Signor Donizetti was seized by an apoplectic attack that drew up his eyes and mouth and paralysed his arms and left leg! All through the night the poor invalid remained in this condition in spite of the application of a dozen mustard plasters to his feet and legs. It was impossible for him to eat anything as his teeth were locked. It was not until about seven in the morning that he could be made to swallow several spoonsful of broth, and the features of the famous Maestro became relaxed again and his eyes intelligent.
>
> At 10 a vescicant was applied to the nape of his neck. At noon there was fever and Signor Gaetano's head became very hot. At 2 in the afternoon 16 leeches were placed behind his ears. The fever continued until the following

[1] Schlitzer, *L'ultima pagina*, pp. 35–6.

morning, when he was able to take several spoonsful of broth with ease. We began to hope that the famous composer would be out of danger . . . but, alas! this satisfaction was cruelly shattered. About noon the fever started up again more violently than on the previous day. At 1, 18 leeches were applied to his temples. And when the blood ceased to flow, the unfortunate invalid was seized by a convulsion that twisted his limbs horribly. He could no longer breathe through his nose as his nostrils were shut tight. Everyone thought he had come to the end! The archpriest who lived near us was sommoned at once, and he administered Extreme Unction. The convulsions lasted about three quarters of an hour, and later on the fever rose unbelievably high. The poor invalid sweated so copiously that the moisture wet through everything he had on him, even the top mattress of his bed. At 10 in the evening the sweating stopped and Signor Donizetti's linen and bed were changed. In spite of the weakness of his condition he endured all this moving very well.

By the morning of the 4th the poor invalid was indescribably emaciated. In spite of the rigour of his illness he had, in three days, taken a cup of broth. On the 3rd and 4th Masses were said for him at all the chapels of the Madonna and one was sung at the high altar of the Crucifix in the Cathedral.

The evening of the 4th the famous composer was in great danger, so much so that the priest did not leave him all night. During the evening of the 5th, the fever was very severe.

Until this time, having the original with us, we had never thought of having his portrait painted. But on the fifth day of this illness, having lost every hope of being able to preserve the dear invalid, we hastened to call in a painter, and the surprising thing was (which could be called a gift from Providence as though the famous Maestro had wanted to leave us a faithful reproduction of his handsome face) that his features, which in the preceding days had been contorted by his illness, immediately became relaxed again and his eyes expressive, so that one would have thought he took an interest in what was going on about him, and so that Signor Rillosi could reproduce on canvas

344

all the inspiration of genius that was expressed in the features of this great man.

During the evening of the 5th the fever became stronger. On the morning of the 6th they began to feed him by indirect means nourishment fortified with egg yolk. The 7th and 8th Signor Donizetti kept getting worse and worse.

He was in agony.

On the 8th at 5 in the afternoon, the famous invalid took his last breath, the priest being present, and surrounded by my mother and me, by his intimate friend Dolci and by his affectionate servant. . . .[1]

The following day Dolci wrote to Andrea:

Gaetano non è più.
. . . In these final days I have never left him. You can imagine the Basonis' grief and desolation. . . .[2]

The concern of Donizetti's family and friends was overshadowed by the stirring events of those days. In 1848 revolution ran like a wave across the map of Europe. By March there were disorders even in the streets of Bergamo, while Donizetti sat, head sunk on his chest in the Palazzo Basoni, oblivious even to those who nursed him. While the composer lay beyond the reach of his friends, his music was adapted to the political winds of the hour. In those excitable days audiences seized on anything that caught their patriotic fancy. The military choruses from *Belisario* had aroused the Bolognesi to such a pitch of nationalistic fervour that they had poured out of the theatre chanting them. All shades of opinion could adapt an operatic sentiment to their cause. In December 1848 a phrase from *Gemma di Vergy* caused the Palermitani to stand up, 'waving handkerchiefs and shouting: "Long live the Pope, the King, and the Italian league!" '[3]

In the main, however, Donizetti's music lent itself less easily to the ardours of the *risorgimento* than did Verdi's. The good-hearted naïveté of Nemorino, the bruised melancholia of Lucia, the climacteric fantasies of Don Pasquale, what had these to do with the partisan heroics of nationalism? There is a sort of

[1] Z. pp. 159–61.　　[2] Schlitzer, *L'ultima pagina*, p. 40.
[3] Harold Acton, *The Last Bourbons of Naples*, p. 189.

justice in Donizetti's dying, that he, who in so many ways is vividly representative of the age of Louis-Philippe and Metternich, should remain unaware of the uprising that drove them from power, and succumb in the year that saw the end of this era.

In spite of the uneasy excitement of those April days, when the Genoese and Piedmontese led by Carlo Alberto advanced across Lombardy, Bergamo gave Donizetti an elaborate funeral. The ceremonies began at ten in the morning of 11 April, gathering a crowd of civic dignitaries, of clergy, of the Guarda Nazionale, of four hundred torchbearers. But a few hours later the final scene of the tragedy was played in the tool-shed of the Valtesse Cemetery. The autopsy on Donizetti's corpse was performed there so as not to offend the sensibilities of the grief-stricken Basonis. Eight doctors, including Cassis and Calvetti, assembled there at 2.30 in the afternoon. The actual work of dissection was performed by Drs Giovanni Locatelli and Federico Maironi.

Undressed, the body appeared extremely emaciated. The abdomen was greenish in colour up to the ribs, a sign that putrefaction had already set in. In those days autopsies were relatively uncommon procedures and the findings of this one, performed more than sixty hours after death, reflect the medical knowledge of the period. On opening the skull, they found fluid in the brain. The writer of the report then earnestly records that they noted highly developed bumps *'in corrispondenza della località della musica, della idealità e della meravigliosità'*, evidence of the then widespread vogue of phrenology. The skull was only the thickness of a fingernail. The brain weighed 1391 grams. A deep lesion was found on the pia mater, which adhered so tightly to the substance of the brain that it tore as the doctors tried to separate them. The lateral ventricles were swollen and found to contain three ounces of fluid. The fourth ventricle was in similar condition. The cerebrum was dotted with a few pale spots. The cerebellum was normal. Examining the spinal column, another lesion was found, this one on the dura mater, extending from the fifth dorsal to the second lumbar vertebra. They found more fluid in the spine and signs of lesions on the marrow. Cutting along the pia mater, they discovered the medulla appeared pulpy, so that although it retained signs of its usual state in the area of the neck, the lower the doctors followed it the less it presented its original appearance. The ribs were found to be unusually fragile and brittle. The lungs were normal; the heart appeared slightly dilated. The organs in the abdomen were all declared perfectly normal.[1]

After two and a half hours' work, the doctors finished, and signed the report. All but the upper half of the skull of Donizetti's body was interred in the vault belonging to the Pezzoli family.

The top of the skull was carried off by Dr Gerolamo Carchen, an Austrian military doctor, who had been one of the bystanders during the autopsy. He took it to Astino where he directed an asylum for the insane. After Carchen's death the grisly memento passed to his heir. In 1874 when plans were made to transfer the bodies of Donizetti and Mayr to a fitting resting place in S. Maria Maggiore, there was great consternation when part of the skull was found to be missing. A frantic search was organized, the piece of skull finally retrieved from Carchen's heir and found to fit perfectly with the rest. In 1875 Donizetti's body was moved with great pomp and entombed in S. Maria Maggiore, but still without the top of the skull. It was kept in an elaborate jar in the Museo Donizettiano until 1951, when Donizetti's monument and coffin were moved from one part of S. Maria Maggiore to another. At that time Guido Zavadini placed the top of the skull with the rest of Donizetti's remains.

In spite of the difficulties that abound in basing a judgement on events of over a century ago, on yellowed medical reports, and on an autopsy that lumps together observation and fancy, it seems beyond any reasonable doubt that Donizetti was a victim of cerebrospinal meningovascular syphilis. The original infection must have preceded Donizetti's collapse by a good many years, exactly how many can probably never be determined. His convulsions and other symptoms from which he suffered in April 1829 may well be connected with the progress of the disease that ultimately killed him.

It would be unwarranted to assume that because Donizetti was a syphilitic that he was any more of a libertine than a man of his time, of his disposition, of his profession, of his opportunities, might be expected to be. The few, recurrent obscenities that occur in his later letters to his best friends, and, above all,

[1] Alborghetti-Galli, *Donizetti-Mayr*, Appendix: '*Autopsia.*'

the obsessive sexuality of the '40's are plainly consequences of his disease and of the changes it wrought in him, both morally and physically. This consideration is central to a just appreciation of Donizetti's tragic life.

The greatest tragedy of all is that had Donizetti lived today he could have been cured.

Postscript

The consequences of a man's life continue even after his death.

There was, for example, the question of Donizetti's estate. His funeral cost 761 Austrian lire. Since 1844, Teodoro Ghezzi in Naples, had been accumulating a bill to Donizetti's account. When the heirs settled it in 1849 it had run up to 1188 ducats, most of it for Virginia's mausoleum and for the bi-weekly Masses that were said for her, but there were other items too: bracelets and pins of coral and tortoise shell that Ghezzi sent to Vienna when Gaetano ordered them.

Then there was the matter of the dowry. Toto wrote to Andrea about returning the principal, and the question became bitter before it was finally settled. No matter what feelings he may have acquired regarding other Donizettis as a result, Toto remained true to his affection for Gaetano. Later he became a Roman agent for Ricordi—and it is to Toto that the score of *Rigoletto* is dedicated. He was Verdi's friend, too, seeing him especially in that time when *Un ballo in maschera* had its première at the Teatro Apollo in 1859. Toto lived until 1870.

Francesco Donizetti, on the other hand, died not long after Gaetano, breathing his last in December 1848. He, with Giuseppe, had shared Gaetano's inheritance, but great was the fury of the eldest brother and his son Andrea when they discovered that Francesco had left a will of his own, bequeathing everything he owned to the woman who had taken care of him before he died, Elisabetta Santi Pesenti. Giuseppe until he died in 1856, and Andrea, too, did their best to invalidate her claim. An interesting letter from Dolci to this woman, who by then was calling herself Elisabetta Santi Donizetti, sheds light on the whole situation. He wrote on 2 April 1861:

349

Most honoured Signora,

Moretti has sent me your greetings, and I send you mine with these few lines. [Andrea] Donizetti has become mad; this I read in the paper, *La Lombardia*, of Saturday last. I was very surprised to learn of that misfortune, but God is just. . . .[1]

Dolci's last remark speaks volumes about his judgement of Andrea and his actions. Andrea's life was spent trying to gain possession of Donizetti's estate, but in 1858 he found time to marry Giuseppina Gabuzzi, who bore him two sons, Giuseppe and Gaetano. On 11 June 1861 Andrea was admitted to the insane asylum at Aversa, near Naples, as suffering from: 'Mania—Delusive hopes.' He died there on 11 February 1864 of 'cerebrospinal softening'—a symptom of meningovascular syphilis, the same disease that brought Gaetano low.[2] Andrea's two sons spent their lives clouded by the bogey of the Donizetti estate. In their last years they supported themselves as best they could by the sale of the manuscript music and letters that remained to them. The younger Gaetano perished in an air raid during the Second World War; his brother Giuseppe died about 1949.

Ultimately, it is the other inheritance that matters, the bounty Gaetano Donizetti bequeathed to the whole world. As long as Donizetti's operas are performed, the tragedy that closed over his life and that of his heirs, is important only so far as it sheds light upon his works and upon the conditions that shaped them.

[1] Unpublished letter in the Museo Donizettiano, Bergamo.
[2] These details were communicated to me by Dr Annibale Puca, Director of the Ospedale Psichiatrico at Aversa.

Part Two

CHAPTER 7

Form in Donizetti's Operas

Operatic forms in Italy during the active years of Donizetti's career were relatively stable, and represented considerable variety as the products of two centuries' modifications and refinements. While it is beyond the purpose of this discussion to trace the antecedents of these received forms, it is important to keep in mind two areas which left an impression on these forms: the type of genus of the libretto and the demands of the singers.

The category to which an opera belonged (farsa, opera buffa, opera semiseria and opera seria)[1] conditioned to some extent the formal ingredients of a score. Certain classes of arias and ensembles, such as the aria parlante and the finale in the form of a moral, occur customarily in comic scores, while the gran scena and the heroic duet, for example, are found in serious or tragic works. Opera semiseria contains a mingling of tragic and buffo elements; the comic music of the Marchese in *Linda di Chamounix* is woven in with the romantic and serious music of the rest of the score.

The structure of a libretto may condition the structure of an

---

[1] Although these are the most frequently encountered terms, some of Donizetti's scores bear other classifications. For instance, *Otto mesi* is described as an opera romantica; *Il diluvio universale*, because of its biblical subject, is an azione tragica-sacra; *Gianni di Parigi*, *L'elisir d'amore*, *La fille du régiment*, and *Rita* (although only the last two contain spoken dialogue) are each called an opera comica; *Betly*, on the other hand, bears the title opera giocosa. None of these special terms, however, signifies the presence of elements absent in the more usual categories.

opera in another sense. The necessary dramatic functions of exposition, rising action, climax, and dénouement must be clothed in appropriate musical forms. This consideration accounts for the usual pattern of introductory chorus and opening scena, more often than not for male voices, so frequently encountered in operas of this period. The climax of the plot usually precipitates an ensemble, as the entrance of Edgardo in Act 2 of *Lucia* immediately precedes the sextet. Sometimes the dénouement takes place in a final ensemble, but, more characteristic of the operas of this time, the plot is unravelled in a passage of recitative which was followed by a double aria for the prima donna.

The prerogatives of the prima donna frequently conditioned the placings of her music. When the prima donna came into her own during the early years of the nineteenth century she made her presence felt. The example of Isabella Colbran's influence on Rossini's Neapolitan operas gave her successors a standard to emulate. Often the entrance of the prima donna was delayed until the second scene, an arrangement that whetted anticipation for her appearance and also insured the presence of the tardy boxholders. The leading lady's appearance often took the form of an aria di sortita followed by a brilliant cabaletta. The custom of concluding the opera with a cavatina and rondo for the prima donna soon came to seem a stereotyped effect that blunted the natural working-out of the plot. Donizetti came to detest the custom, as may be seen from his complaints about Méric-Lalande's insistence upon a final bravura aria in *Lucrezia Borgia*. In his later operas, especially those written for theatres outside Italy, Donizetti reverted only rarely to the practice of the final show-piece for the soprano. The pretensions of the prima donna to her solo finale received their *coup de grâce* in 1844, when Verdi refused to appease Sofia Löwe by replacing the final trio in *Ernani* with a rondo.

Although the choice of musical forms and their disposition was conditioned by the nature of the libretto and, usually less so, by the whim of the singer, Donizetti used a fairly restricted number of forms, sometimes modifying them considerably. Briefly to survey Donizetti's representative practice with preludes, overtures, arias, duets, and ensembles will show something of his notion of operatic form.

For Donizetti the term *preludio* means a relatively brief passage, usually in a single tempo, ending on a dominant chord rather than a full cadence, and leading directly into the opening scene which is in a closely related key. The shortest of Donizetti's preludes is that to *Elvida*, only 5 bars long, while the longer ones, such as those to *Lucia*, *L'elisir*, and *Lucrezia Borgia*, run to 33, 40, and 42 bars respectively. Exceptions to the general rule of a single tempo are found in the preludes to *L'elisir* and *Lucrezia Borgia*. In the former, the allegro, 9 bars of chordal sequence, precede a series of variations marked larghetto; in the latter, 33 bars of maestoso are followed by 8 of allegro, a passage modulating to the D major vivace of the opening chorus. Usually the key relationship between the prelude and the opening scene is close. For instance, in *Il giovedì grasso* both the 14 bars prelude, and the opening scene are in C major; while in *Lucia* the prelude is in B flat minor and the introductory chorus is in the parallel key of B flat major.

Donizetti used at least three different types of preludio. The shorter ones, such as those of *Elvida*, *La romanziera e l'uomo nero*, and *L'assedio di Calais*, which are 5, 6, and 7 bars respectively, are little more than fanfares designed to quiet the audience before the rise of the curtain. The brief opening allegro of the *L'elisir* prelude seems designed for a similar function, although here it is to gain the audience's attention to the larghetto body of the prelude. This passage exemplifies a second type of preludio. A set of variations,[1] it shows Donizetti using an autonomous musical form rather than writing music which bears some direct, functional relationship to the plot. The third type of preludio favoured by Donizetti might be called the atmospheric; the preludes to *Lucrezia Borgia* and *Lucia* are examples of this type. The former is built primarily on a sinuous five-note motto, variously harmonized and orchestrated, which establishes the sombre mood of the tragedy; the latter is introduced by a timpani roll and mournful chords, first for the horns and later for trombones, leading up to three climactic dissonances, and ending with a funereal trombone ostinato and the woodwinds sustaining dominant harmonies. Both preludes prefigure and prepare for the tragic action to follow.

Donizetti's chief contemporaries, Rossini and Bellini, preferred

---

[1] These variations, largely in D major, are indebted to Mayr for their colouring and treatment; they bear little resemblance to the rest of the score in texture and mood. Considering the great haste with which this score was composed, it is not inconceivable that for this section of the prelude Donizetti availed himself of a passage he had already composed.

the longer overture to the shorter prelude. One of the great practitioners of the operatic overture, Rossini wrote them even for one-act comic operas, such as *La scala di seta* and *Il signor Bruschino*. Of Bellini's readily available works,[1] only *La straniera*, *Beatrice di Tenda* and *La sonnambula* have preludes; the rest have overtures. Bellini's preludes are all over 40 bars in length. That of *La sonnambula* is in the same key and time as the opening chorus; unlike Bellini's other preludes, that of *Beatrice di Tenda* employs a tune that is later sung by the soprano in the first finale. Characteristically, Donizetti's preludes do not use material which recurs in the opera; however, his overtures, such as that of *Don Pasquale*, sometimes use material found elsewhere in the score. Rossini's overtures, more often than not, have no thematic connexions with the rest of the opera.

Verdi wrote more preludes than overtures. Only three of his essays in the latter form possess conspicuous merit, i.e. the overtures to *Luisa Miller*, *Les vêpres Siciliennes*, and *La forza del destino*. In his preludes, such as that to *Aida*, Verdi's practice differed from that of his major predecessors. Here he states, develops, and combines two themes that recur later in the opera; further, Verdi sets off his preludes from the opening scene by ending them with a full cadence. While the brief introduction to *Il trovatore*, with its drumrolls and fanfares, seems to resemble Donizetti's notion of the very brief prelude, Verdi continues the musical patterns after the rise of the curtain, thereby linking the prelude directly to the opening scene. By the time Verdi came to compose *Otello* and *Falstaff*, he caused the curtain to rise almost immediately and presented the opening episodes of the drama as a sort of musico-dramatic prelude.

Donizetti's use of the preludio is more formal and more restricted than Verdi's. In his longer preludes Donizetti's music possesses interest and musical appropriateness. The preludes to *Lucia* and *Rigoletto* reveal kinship in scope and intention, but Donizetti does not quite equal Verdi's intensity in suggesting a tragic and implacable fatalism.

Donizetti used the term *sinfonia* without reference to its seventeenth-century connotations, usually for extended overtures which are separated from the opening scene by a perfect

---

[1] Excluded from consideration here are Bellini's student work, *Adelson e Salvini* (1824) and the unsuccessful *Zaira* (1829), a score the composer pillaged when he composed *I Capuletti*.

cadence and are separately 'numbered'. By sinfonia, however, Donizetti did not intend to describe a set formal organization; in fact, he did not always limit the term to compositions designed to precede an opera, nor to compositions for orchestra. He wrote several pieces for piano to which he gave the name sinfonia.[1]

Here, for convenience, the term sinfonia will be limited to identify an orchestral work that is designed to precede an opera and is complete in itself, but not following any set pattern. In his earlier years, except in the case of his one-act farces, Donizetti did not distinguish the scope of the work by writing a preludio for shorter works and placing a sinfonia before only full-scale serious operas. For example, *Il borgomastro di Saardam*, an opera buffa, has a full overture, while *L'assedio di Calais*, one of the most moving of Donizetti's serious operas, has only the briefest of preludes. The cause for such apparent discrepancies seems, in part, to have been economic. When *Fausta* was first given at La Scala (26 December 1832) and when *Roberto Devereux* had its première at the Italiens, Donizetti replaced the brief preludes of each opera with new and extended sinfonie, for which he received additional money from his publisher. In his later years, when he was writing primarily for the theatres of Paris and Vienna, Donizetti provided the operas he composed for those stages with overtures. The lone exception is the very lengthy *Dom Sébastien*, which has a prelude of 52 bars connecting directly with the introductory chorus.

An examination of the thirty sinfonie Donizetti wrote[2] makes

[1] A representative example is in the library of the Liceo Musicale, Bologna, dated '19 9bre 1816'. It further bears the information that it was written in an hour and a quarter by order of Mattei. It begins in C minor, largo, after the 24th bar shifting to C major, presto. It seems, however, conceived more in orchestral than in pianistic terms, for there is much writing of tremolandi. Zavadini, in his list of Donizetti's works, erroneously cites this composition (his No. 231) for orchestra.

[2] The state of some of Donizetti's overtures deserves comment. The autograph of the overture to *Alfredo il Grande* is very incomplete. Salvi arranged the overture to *Il duca d'Alba*, since Donizetti never got around even to making sketches for it, from themes that appear later in the opera. When Donizetti made a *rifacimento* of *Rosmunda d'Inghilterra* for Naples, he supplied this new version, which bore the title *Eleonora di Gujenna*, with a new overture. The autograph copy of the overture to *Parisina* in the Museo Donizettiano bears on it, crossed-out but quite legible, the name *Bianca d'Aquitania*; this change suggests that at one time Donizetti thought of this music in connexion with the earlier score of *Ugo, conte di Parigi*, the heroine of that opera being Bianca d'Aquitania. Indeed, he used the same overture for both operas.

it clear that he generally followed a consistent pattern of tempo markings: a fairly short passage in slow time, followed by a longer passage in rapid tempo, and concluding with a coda marked *più mosso*. In the cases of the overtures to *Anna Bolena* and *Don Pasquale*, he prefixed a very brief allegro section to the episode in slower tempo. Donizetti calls the music preceding the rise of the curtain in *Il furioso* a sinfonia, but the passage is only 35 bars long and in a single tempo, larghetto. Although Donizetti calls this work a sinfonia, it more nearly resembles a preludio as it establishes the atmosphere for the drama with a musical description of a storm.

In these overtures Donizetti characteristically uses close key relationships. The earliest of Donizetti's surviving overtures, that to *Enrico di Borgogna*, consists of a slow-fast arrangement, both tempos in D major. In the overtures to *La favorita* and *Linda* he uses parallel major and minor keys. The overture to *Don Pasquale* begins and ends in D major, but the 42-bar andante section is in F major. On occasion, as with the overture to *La fille du régiment*, Donizetti introduces his second theme (later recurring as Marie's *Chacun le sait*) in the key of the dominant (F major), later bringing it back in the tonic key (B flat major).[1] On occasion Donizetti avails himself of more distant key relationships, as when in the overture to *La favorita* he finds himself moving from C minor to D major. In most of his overtures, it is Donizetti's practice to write in extended units of a single tonality, subordinating the passages in foreign keys for contrast and colour.

In his overtures Donizetti followed the general practices of his contemporaries. Although he came to avoid the Rossinian trademark, the stylized crescendo (which, it has been claimed, Rossini adopted from Mayr's *Ginevra di Scozia*), Donizetti builds his overtures climactically so that the greatest point of tension —achieved by dynamics, pitch, tempo, and texture—usually comes shortly before the final cadence. Donizetti wrote overtures that are thematically separate from the scores they precede—for example, those to *La favorite*, *Linda* and *Maria di Rohan*; and he composed overtures with the thematic material

---

[1] Although this practice is reminiscent of sonata form, this overture builds episodically and contains no development section. Rossini used the same key relationships for the second theme in some of his overtures, for example in that to *Semiramide*.

that is heard in the opera—for example, those to *Poliuto*, *La fille du régiment*, and *Don Pasquale*. He seems to have felt no clear-cut preference between the two types.

The predominant texture of Donizetti's overtures is melodic and homophonic. His themes are of contrasting character, and the contrast is reinforced by different instrumentation. Occasionally he overlaps the imitation of a melodic figure, achieving a contrapuntal texture, as in the slow introduction of the overture to *La favorite*. His melodies are usually sharp in profile and markedly rhythmical. As in the overture to *Linda*, he displays a fondness for figures that lend themselves to sequential treatment. From these observations it may be seen how thoroughly Donizetti worked within the same tradition as his contemporaries, for much the same things might be said of Rossini's and Bellini's overtures. In his overtures, Donizetti came to favour a mellower orchestral palette than Rossini's and a more sonorously voiced one than Bellini's.

Deserving special mention are three of Donizetti's overtures which involve departures from his usual approach. For *Poliuto*, he inserts into the overture a brief choral hymn that recurs during the opera. For the Paris première of *Roberto Devereux*, Donizetti composed not so much an overture as a *pièce d'occasion* that employs the tune of *God Save the Queen*.[1] For the overture to *Linda di Chamounix*, Donizetti was so anxious to make a good impression with his first opera expressly composed for a Viennese audience that he adapted the first movement of his 18th string quartet to serve as his overture. This is an example of sonata form; the second theme is in the relative major but completely supported by dominant harmony, while the abbreviated recapitulation modulates into the parallel major, ending with a blatant vivace. In spite of this final blemish, the overture to *Linda* stands besides those to *Don Pasquale* and *Maria di Rohan* as Donizetti's finest accomplishments in this area of composition.

With his arias Donizetti employed a rather wide range of terminology. On occasion he refers to them by the words

[1] With this melody Donizetti seems to have intended a canny stroke, for he knew very well that the stars of the Italiens divided their year between Paris and London.

cavatina and *romanza*; other times, depending on the dramatic situation, he might call one a ballata (Pierotto in Act 1 of *Linda*), another a preghiera (Léonor in Act 4 of *La favorite*), and still another a serenata (Ernesto in Act 3 of *Don Pasquale*). To judge by Donizetti's practice, these terms have no clear-cut connotations of form or genre.

In *Il barbiere*, Rossini calls such divergent arias as Figaro's *Largo al factotum* and Rosina's *Una voce poco fa* cavatinas. Donizetti is as liberal with the term when he applies it both to Dulcamara's garrulous salesmanship in *L'elisir* and to Duke Alfonso's cry for vengeance in *Lucrezia Borgia*. Nor is the term any indication of length. Arturo's 8-phrase passage in the wedding chorus of *Lucia* is described as a cavatina, as is Linda's *O luce di quest'anima*, which runs to more than a hundred measures. Nor does the term cavatina give any consistent indication of tempo. While many of them are marked largo, larghetto, and maestoso, indications such as moderato and allegretto are far from rare; and some, like Don Pasquale's *Un fuoco insolito*, are even marked vivace. Nor does the term necessarily apply to an aria in a single tempo. Some have two movements, following the example of Rossini's *Ecco ridente* and *Una voce poco fa*; Donizetti's usual practice, like Rossini's, is to connect the sections directly without any intervening recitative. In *Udite, udite, o rustici*, Donizetti uses no less than three tempo markings: maestoso, andante, and allegro vivace. Nor is the term any indication of an aria with a cabaletta; for some of them, such as Lucia's *Regnava nel silenzio*, he has written a pendant aria; for others, such as Nemorino's *Quanto è bella*, he has not.

If the term cavatina had any clear implication for Donizetti as regard to form, it would seem that more often than not he planned the aria in two stanzas, but even within this general framework there are a number of modifications. A cavatina with a very regular form is Linda's *O luce di quest'anima*, which has two stanzas, each in ternary form and connected by a 4-phrase transition, and concluding with a coda. Less regular, but of a pattern Donizetti often used, is Ashton's *Cruda, funesta smania*. This cavatina consists of two balanced stanzas connected by a 4-bar transition; each stanza contains 9 phrases[1] and is in binary form. The second stanza of this cavatina is not

[1] The ninth phrase is a cadenza-like repetition of the text but not the melody of the eighth, making a general pattern of 6 plus 2 plus 1.

identical with the first, either melodically or harmonically; the first two phrases are the same, but at the third there occurs a sudden irruption into the key of E flat.[1] Sometimes Donizetti inserts a modulation, often from a minor key to its relative major, before the seventh phrase of a cavatina stanza—a procedure he follows in the second stanza of *Una furtiva lagrima*[2] and in both stanzas of Marie's *Il faut partir*. Lucia's *Regnava nel silenzio* contains even greater freedom of melody and harmony, yet this cavatina follows the pattern of two 9-phrase stanzas. Although Donizetti echoes the contours of the opening phrase at important points in the structure, there is little repetition between the stanzas. The first verse begins in D minor and ends in F major; the second moves from F major to D, the last-named key commencing at the seventh phrase.

The difficulty of associating the term cavatina with any consistent pattern of mood, melodic style, tempo, or harmonic sequence should now seem apparent. Donizetti's most consistent application of the term was to use it, but again, not invariably, for the first aria a given character sings.[3] For example, in *L'elisir*, Nemorino's *Quanto è bella*, Adina's *Dalla crudele Isotta*, Belcore's *Come Paride*, and Dulcamara's *Udite, udite* are all called cavatinas, although each demonstrates notable differences in design.

That Donizetti's use of the term romanza seems more consistent than his use of cavatina may result only from the fact that he employed the term romanza less frequently. The most common form of romanza is in slow tempo, in two varying stanzas, and without a subsequent cabaletta; the text is usually concerned with romantic love.[4] The romanzas in two stanzas usually contain some melodic, and occasionally harmonic, changes in the second verse; however as in Smeton's *Deh! non voler costringere* and Lucrezia's *Com' è bello*—the second stanza is just a more highly ornamented version of the first. Sometimes the two stanzas are separated by a brief transition; sometimes not.

[1] This is one of the striking examples of Donizetti's fondness for the diminished sixth, an interval Donizetti shows a predilection for in *Lucia*.
[2] Donizetti terms this aria as a romanza, but it adheres to the pattern here described.
[3] A typical exception is found in *Anna Bolena*. The page Smeton's first aria is called a romanza, but in Act 1, Sc. iii, he sings a cavatina.
[4] Not all romanzas have amorous texts; Donizetti calls Orsini's narrative of friendship to the death, in the prologue to *Lucrezia Borgia*, a romanza.

There is also a second, less common form of romanza in ternary form. Two examples of this type are Fernand's *Ange si pur* (*Spirto gentil*) and the tenor aria in Act 2 of *Linda di Chamounix*. The sections of these romanzas are shorter than the stanzas of the first type; the middle section uses melodic patterns contrasting with those of the first section and modulates briefly to a different key. Both types of romanza end with codas, repeating the last lines of the text to different melodic patterns and accompanying figures.

Although Donizetti does not use the term *aria* to describe a set form, he uses it most frequently with an aria in slow time followed by a cabaletta. When Donizetti employs the term *aria finale* he is primarily describing the location of the number in his score. A usual counterpart of an aria finale in his earlier works is a rondo, in effect a special kind of cabaletta. A typical rondo is that concluding the 1828 version of *Emilia di Liverpool*; it consists of a 6-phrase melody and a set of two variations with all the changes written out by the composer, while between each solo passage are two phrases for the chorus.[1] Donizetti's cabalettas, other than those in the rondo pattern, are most frequently in binary form with the second section having a more elaborate vocal melody than the first; after a transition the cabaletta is repeated and ends with a coda. Lucia's *Quando rapito in estasi* illustrates this pattern. In these cabalettas Donizetti did not write out the added embellishments for the repetition, but the convention of these works assumed that the singer would provide them.

In his duets, as with his arias, Donizetti employs a wide variety of patterns. These patterns are, of course, modified by the dramatic situation and by the principle of contrasting in design with the numbers that precede and follow them. The harmonic patterns of the duets are understandably affected by the ranges of the voices taking part in them. With soprano-tenor duets, for instance, there is apt to be less modulation in repetition of sections than with other combinations of voices. The simplest arrangement occurs in the duet *Veranno a te* at the

[1] An interesting expansion of this pattern occurs at the end of *Elvida*, which is a rondo *a due* with staggeringly difficult variations expressly composed for the agile larynxes of Méric-Lalande and Rubini.

end of Act I of *Lucia*: here the soprano introduces the binary melody, the tenor repeats it in the same key, and then they sing it in unison, still in the same key. When Donizetti harmonizes the soprano and tenor voice, his usual practice is to give the melody to the tenor. A duet that contains a change of key due to the voice ranges is the contralto-tenor duet, *Onde a lei ti mostri grato* from *Lucrezia Borgia*. The contralto begins the duet in the key of A flat major, but the tenor replies in E flat minor. In the andante of the soprano-buffo duet in Act 2 of *Linda*, the Marchese introduces a melody in G major, but at Linda's entrance there is a modulation to B major. An even more typical example occurs in the duet at the beginning of Act 2 of *Lucia* where the soprano sings a G major melody which the baritone repeats in the dominant key.

To consider Donizetti's duets in the light of their arrangement by movements reveals that he frequently employed from one to three tempo markings. The duets with a single movement are of two general types: binary and ternary. The duet for Linda and Pierotto (Act 2, *Linda*) is in binary form; the first section is a contralto solo, and the second, more elaborate section, combines the voices.[1] A different one-movement, binary pattern is found in *La favorite*. In the duet, *Dans ce palais*, Alphonse introduces a 4-phrase melody that Léonor repeats; the second section of the binary form consists of a passage for the voices together. The *Notturno* in the last act of *Don Pasquale* is an example of a one-movement duet in ternary form. Here the voices sing together from the start, except in the middle section where they are heard in overlapping sequences; the repeat of the first section contains some elaboration of the melody, and the duet ends with a codetta. It is characteristic of these duets in a single tempo that Donizetti allows a single tonality to dominate.

Examples of duets in two movments are the buffo duet for Don Pasquale and Dr Malatesta and the love duet from Act I of *Linda*.[2] The general arrangement of the buffo duet is very simple; there is an allegro moderato 4/4 and a moderato mosso

[1] Although this duet is marked larghetto, the general outline is identical with that favoured by Donizetti in such solo cabalettas as *Quando rapito in estasi*.

[2] *Linda di Chamounix* is a particularly interesting score to examine for Donizetti's various duet forms, as the opera contains eight duets.

6/8, both in the key of F major. The melody in each section is introduced by Don Pasquale and then repeated *in toto* by Malatesta; the voices are not combined until near the end of the second section and then in unison. The two movements are separated by a transition, the dialogue at this point providing the motivation for the second section. The wholesale repetitions and unison passages for the baritone and buffo are an indication that Donizetti thought of these voices as having essentially the same range.[1] The two-movement form of the Act 1 love duet from *Linda* is slightly more complicated than that of the buffo duet from *Don Pasquale*. Here the two sections are marked andantino (2/4, B flat) and allegro moderato (4/4, G). The tenor sings the complete melody (in binary form) of the slow section and the soprano repeats it; the second part commences with a passage *d'assieme* ending on the dominant and leading into Carlo's passage, *A consolarmi afrettisi*, which is repeated first by Linda alone and then by both voices in thirds and sixths. Sometimes in a two-movement duet Donizetti inserts a reprise of the slower movement into the quicker tempo as he does in the love duet in Act 1 of *La fille du régiment*.

There is a strong resemblance in general lay-out between Donizetti's duets in three tempos and his solo scenas. He uses a wide variety of tempo sequences, as may be seen from such examples as the Linda-Marchese duet (larghetto, andante, and vivace), from the Lucia-Edgardo duet (larghetto, allegro, moderato), and from the Lucia-Enrico duet (moderato, larghetto, vivace).

In Donizetti's operas a fast-slow-moderate sequence is most common. While the sequence of tonalities in these duets is affected, of course, by the relative ranges of the participating voices, generally the first and last sections will be in the same key, while the middle will be in a contrasting key. Occasionally a section will be introduced by one voice in a minor key and the second voice will respond in the parallel major, as in the *Sulla tomba* passage of the Lucia-Edgardo duet. The key relationships

---

[1] The distinction between the bass and baritone range was still emerging during the second quarter of the nineteenth century, although some roles were clearly written for 'high' basses and some for 'deep'. Donizetti roles that today are sung by baritones, except those written for singers like Ronconi and Varesi who had powerful top notes, generally have a noticeably lower tessitura than that found in Verdi's baritone parts.

most generally favoured by Donizetti are the usual ones for his period: moving between parallel and relative major and minor keys, moving from the key of the tonic to the dominant, and moving in keys in a third-relationship, either major or minor. Occasionally, however, he will provide a surprise, as when he suddenly moves from B flat major to C flat major in the Lucia-Edgardo duet.

The melodic units of these duets are most commonly in binary form, but the division of phrases between voices, solo and together, singing in harmony or in unison, varies considerably. When he harmonizes two voices, Donizetti stays well within the general practice of his period of keeping the parts mainly at the distance of the third or sixth, except in cadences and cadenzas where he often sets the parts in contrary motion.

Although Donizetti's ensembles vary considerably in complexity, they stand, with relatively few exceptions, as evidence of the solidity of his craftsmanship. Indeed, the sextet from *Lucia* was once, and may well still be, the most widely known of all operatic ensembles. As a writer of concertante, Donizetti's success rests chiefly on the clarity of his formal design, his skill at voice leading, and the sonority resulting from the placing of the voice parts. Only rarely do Donizetti's ensembles seem all top and bass line with little between as Bellini's sometimes sound.

The basic formal arrangements of his ensembles follow patterns already familiar from the discussion of his arias and duets, except that their proportions seem greater, due to the space required for the exposition of three or more parts, as in the splendid Act I quintet in *Anna Bolena*. Donizetti wrote ensembles both in single movements (as in the *Don Pasquale* terzetto and in the unaccompanied quintet in the last act of *Linda*) and in two or more movements. The most usual pattern is slow-fast-stretta.

One aspect of Donizetti's placing of voices is illustrated by his trios. If we allow that there is a common 'trio-situation' in which one character is torn between an opposing pair, it will follow that this conflict will be reflected in the voice parts. For instance, the trio in *Lucrezia Borgia* begins with an agitated phrase for the baritone, answered by the soprano, but the character of the trio changes with the entrance of the tenor's sustained melody, for now the soprano part sometimes echoes the tenor line and sometimes the agitated patterns of the baritone part. The same general sort of interplay is found in the trio in the last act of *Maria di Rohan*. A somewhat different trio-situation occurs in Act 2 of *Don Pasquale*: here the soprano sings a lyric line, an aside, while the baritone and buffo converse in patter figures.

The voice-leading in Donizetti's ensembles is uncommonly effective. The simplest sort is doubling, as when Raimondo reinforces Enrico's descending phrase in the second episode of the *Lucia* sextet. Frequently a figure will be imitated in each part in turn. Sometimes, as in the quartet from *Il paria*,[1] the overlapping parts each in turn announce a descending sequence. Again the voices may enter in fugato style, as at the beginning of the vivace in the finale to Act 2 of *La favorite*.

It must be confessed that one part of Donizetti's ensemble writing seems weak to listeners today. In the cabaletta of a trio, such as that in *Anna Bolena*, or in the strettas of his finales, Donizetti often relies too much on unison lines, on rhythmic patterns repeated *ad nauseam*, and on over-extended codas that harp on predictable harmonic sequences. The stretta at the end of Act 2 of *Lucia* and that to the third act of *La favorite* are cases in point. Fortunately these, and passages like them, are usually shortened in today's performances. These patterns are not, of course, Donizetti's exclusive property; they may be found over and over in the operas of Rossini, Bellini and in Verdi's early works. Undoubtedly they result from a desire to produce the effect of an overwhelming vocal mass, and considering the much smaller forces[2] that participated in performances during this time, the need for and the efficacy of this blatant effect can, perhaps, be extenuated.

Before leaving Donizetti's ensembles, a brief glance at the form of the famous sextet from *Lucia* might illustrate the strengths of Donizetti's ensemble writing. This sextet is conceived in binary form; the first section is introduced by the tenor and baritone and immediately repeated, but this time the soprano and bass sing the opening melody, while the tenor and

[1] Beginning at Zarete's words: *Sei padre qual son io*.
[2] Choruses of a dozen to eighteen, and orchestras of fewer than thirty players, were not uncommon.

the baritone interject counterphrases. The second section begins with a broad descending phrase for the baritone, and it is not until this point that all six voices and chorus are added to the texture. From here on the sextet contains six real parts. The second section is repeated exactly, and the sextet closes with a brief coda. So salient are the outer melodies that only an attentive listener hears the full richness of texture.

The forms used most frequently by Donizetti were the general currency of the Italian operatic stage of his day. A detailed examination of his practice reveals again and again the great variety and apparent spontaneity of effect that he could achieve within them. The attention to detail shown by the changes of melody and harmony in the second stanzas of his arias is just one piece of evidence to prove that Donizetti is often a more conscious craftsman than his detractors are willing to credit him with being.

CHAPTER 8

Some Aspects of Donizetti's Style

To his contemporaries, Donizetti's facility was notorious. The rapidity with which he could produce music impressed the dilettantes of his day, and in time Donizetti grew vain of his reputation for speed, and himself shaded the truth to add to the legend, although many of his non-Italian contemporaries derided him for this touted facility.

In order to see Donizetti for what he was, rather than to dismiss him for what he was not, it is necessary to face up to the question of his facility. We must remember that in the eyes of his first teacher, Mayr, it was precisely the readiness of young Gaetano's musical inventiveness that singled him out from his fellow students as having unusual promise. When he played the part of 'Donizetti' in the little farce, *Il piccolo compositore di musica*, at the annual exercises of Mayr's school in 1811, he was given these lines to sing:

> *Pronta la fantasia, e nel comporre*
> *Un fulmine son io. . . .*

> Ready my fancy, and in composition
> I am like lightning. . . .

These lines, even allowing for their humorous exaggeration, were public acknowledgement of the fourteen-year-old boy's ability to compose like lightning. In Mayr's experience to compose meant the ability to conceive balanced melodies adapted to a received form, complete with an appropriate harmonic structure. The training Donizetti received was largely designed to strengthen his ready gift. And in Italy, during the years when he was growing up, there were but two spheres where a composer might hope to find steady employment, either in a church or in an opera house, both places that demanded music at short notice. The pragmatic base of Donizetti's musical training, the emphasis placed upon facility as a positive virtue, can scarcely be over-stressed.

Of course it is impossible to reconstruct the process by which a composer's creative imagination works; indeed even if we had Donizetti's description of the process as he was aware of it, his account would not be very helpful as the very nature of the experience resists communication. The evidence of the autograph of *Una furtiva lagrima*[1] indicates that Donizetti first jotted down the melody and shorthand indications of the harmony and instrumentation of the melody, filling in all the details later. This autograph (and in the wealth of Donizetti's manuscripts many similar examples may be found) suggests that Donizetti's mind conceived the aria with all its salient features, even the bassoon introduction, simultaneously. Such a performance is not incredible in the light of Donizetti's training, strengthened by years of practice, of his deep-grained reliance on traditional form, which was aided by his setting librettos already tailored to those forms. His working conditions were favourable to a man gifted with his facility.

Gianandrea Gavazzeni[2] has pointed out that Donizetti's scores are apt to seem a sequence of loosely related numbers, rather than musico-dramatic entities that build towards a powerful conclusion, as the best of Bellini's scores or those of Verdi do. While Gavazzeni's observation undoubtedly points to one of the consequences of Donizetti's facility, the qualification needs making that there is an almost direct ratio between the dramatic power of the libretto he had in hand and the musical cohesiveness of his score. The less Donizetti was moved by a text the more apt he was to compose routine music for it. At the same time, it is difficult to point to an occasion when he failed

---

[1] Reproduced in Zavadini, p. 368; the difference in the ink clearly suggests that the melody and bass line was written at one time and the rest of the parts filled in later.

[2] Gianandrea Gavazzeni, *Trent'anni di musica* (Milan, 1958), p. 10.

to be roused by a powerful situation. The spontaneity of feeling implied by this ratio is, at heart, but another phase of his facility.

Further, Donizetti's publicly stated conviction about the nature of music provides his justification for his facility. On the occasion of his acceptance of a membership as a correspondent of the French Academy, he said:

> Music is only declamation accented by sounds, and therefore every composer must conceive and evoke a melody from the accent of the declamation of the text. Anyone who is unsuccessful or unlucky in this will compose only music devoid of sentiment. . . .
>
> The German student says: 'Ah, here there is too much rhythm! Ah! here there is too much melody! . . . ' Imitate the good wherever it is to be found, because to undervalue the one or the other will lose you the end, that is, to give pleasure. . . .
>
> I will not say melody always, for if there is a defect in certain periods of Italian music, it is that it erred too much on this side, and from that I believe stems a negligent attitude towards instrumentation. But I will not ever say, however, as various people do: that that which is regularly rhythmical, is not sublime.[1]

Donizetti's remarks here afford guide-lines to his habits of composition. He frequently altered the repetition of a melodic phrase to fit the sense and accent of the text. His rhythms are characteristically forthright and clearly stressed. His orchestral scores show his detailed concern for instrumental colour and variety. Most important, Donizetti acknowledged that mere facility was not enough. At another point in his remarks to the French Academy, he says: 'Beyond creativity (*fantasia*), a composer must have training, taste, practical knowledge (*scienza, gusto, pratica*).'[2]

These qualities might operate in at least two ways. First, they would serve to censor and reject ideas that seemed inadequate; secondly, they would serve to improve the quality of his *fantasia* by affording him a deeper sense of the possibilities in a musical idea. The autographs and sketches left by Donizetti reveal that he had recourse to second thoughts and that on

[1] Giuliano Donati-Pettèni published the notes for Donizetti's speech in *L'istituto musicale Gaetano Donizetti* (Bergamo, 1928), pp. 193 ff.

[2] Donati-Pettèni, *L'istituto musicale Gaetano Donizetti*.

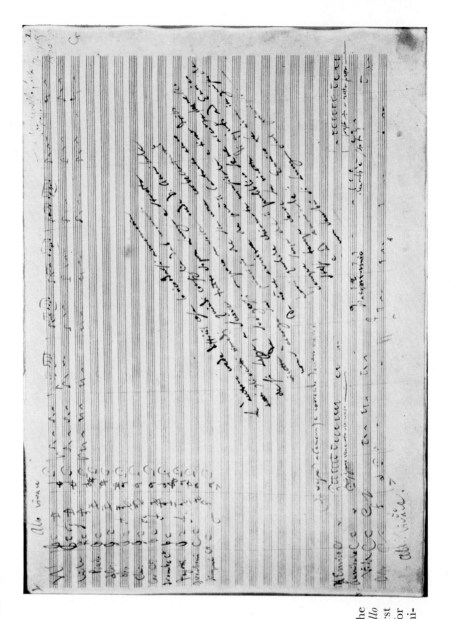

Manuscript page from the score of *Il Campanello* which shows the first page of the duet for Enrico and Don Annibale

Antonio Pourcelot, Donizetti's servant who tended his
master faithfully until the day of the composer's death

Daguerrotype of Donizetti and his nephew Andrea,
taken on 3 August 1847 at the avenue Chateaubriand
No. 6, Paris

Giovannina Rota-Basoni Scotti and her children

The Palazzo Basoni where Donizetti passed the last months of his life

Rosine Stolz and Louis-Gilbert Duprez in Act 4 of *La favorite*

Celestino Salvatori as Belisario

Luigi Lablache as Doge Marino Faliero

Singers in some famous Donizetti premières

Giorgio Ronconi as Cardenio in *Il furioso*

occasion he worked out his ideas laboriously. Yet, it seems fairly clear in the light of Donizetti's prolific output of compositions, and of the unusual speed with which he usually completed them, that he relied heavily on his promptness at conceiving musical ideas implicitly complete; it seems just as clear that if he was dissatisfied with a musical idea for some reason, he usually relied on his *fantasia* to supply another to replace it.

Of the over six hundred compositions by Donizetti that Zavadini lists, five-sixths of the total are vocal music. Besides the operas there are cantatas, religious works, and a wide variety of songs. Thus, when Donizetti spoke of declamation as the origin of melody, in his view he was alluding to his main concern. The majority of Donizetti's instrumental works are juvenilia, composed before he left Bergamo near the close of 1821 to launch his career in earnest.

Although today Donizetti's reputation rests almost exclusively on a handful of his operas, while the rest of his works are ignored, it is worth pausing a minute to glance at a few of his non-operatic works before moving on to details of his characteristic style as it is found in his operatic scores.

Of Donizetti's religious works the most interesting is the *Requiem Mass* written in memory of Bellini. The interest of this work is not limited to the juxtaposition of the names of Donizetti and Bellini. The predominant tone of this score is one of melancholy coupled with a graphically expressed awe in the face of death. The work is composed for five soloists (soprano, contralto,[1] tenor, baritone, and bass) and chorus. Especially in the lyric solos the style of the work seems close to operatic, but this results from Donizetti's responsiveness to the dramatic values of the text.[2] The opening chorus gives an impression of the numbness of grief, and the work builds in intensity up to the dramatic *Dies irae*. While Donizetti's *Requiem* lacks the grandeur of Verdi's, most of the score seems a convincing expression of intimate grief, and its elegiac tone and felicitous instrumentation make this an apt memorial to Bellini.[3]

[1] The soprano and contralto parts are relatively limited in range, suggesting that they were suitable to boys' voices.
[2] Donizetti's *Requiem Mass* for Bellini is divided into these sections: *Introito; Requiem, Te decet hymnus; Kyrie, Dopo l'Epistola; Requiem e graduale; Antifona; Dies Irae; Tuba mirum;* and *Judex ergo.*
[3] There is an interesting description of this Mass in Barblan's *L'opera di Donizetti nell'età romantica*, pp. 223–6, and in the *Rassegna musicale* (July 1948).

Donizetti's string quartets, of which he wrote eighteen, are apt to prove disappointing if they are approached from the viewpoint of the classical Viennese school, for they are peculiarly episodic in character and limited in their development. Donizetti frequently contents himself in his development sections by prolonging a sequence with a few modulations, or by imitating figures among the parts; but of intricate elaboration, especially of exploiting rhythmic variations of his themes, there is little trace. The texture of these quartets is predominantly homophonic; the cello part usually does little more than establish the harmony; and the inner voices frequently provide rhythmic and harmonic support. Instead of looking at Donizetti's string quartets from a Viennese orientation, it is more helpful to view them from the other side of the Alps. In the years of Donizetti's greatest activity in this form (1817–22), chamber music was uncommon in Italy, for the great traditions of the seventeenth and eighteenth century were largely neglected. Considering Donizetti's cultural background and his musical training, it is extraordinary that he should embark upon and persist in writing quartets. These works are noteworthy for their straightforward rhythms and occasionally infectious melodies, but before long they become monotonous because they are wanting in textual interest.

Donizetti's songs tend to fall into three main categories. There are dramatic narratives that seem like scenas in structure as they have passages in recitative style and several changes of tempo and key, like *Il pescatore*, which is set to an Italian translation of a text by Schiller. There are romantic songs, some of them in aria-style and with cabalettas, others simple lyrics which more closely resemble ariettas than lieder. The more operatic songs seem quite dated today because the sentimentality of their texts sometimes borders on the hysterical (as in *La dernière nuit d'un novice*) and in the predictable coloratura passages that burden the melodies. In his more restrained songs Donizetti's good taste and ready sentiment are evident in the broad, but subtly inflected, melodies of such songs as *La sultana*,[1] *Il sospiro*, and *Amore e morto*. These are salon songs, primarily intended for amateurs with highly trained voices, and indeed some of them demand far more of a singer's throat than they do

[1] In this song, the F minor section is the most persuasive even though it suffers from a disconcertingly trivial staccato passage in the fifth phrase.

of his brain. The third category of Donizetti's songs contain those in popular style, many of them set to texts in Neapolitan dialect. These songs, almost always in triple rhythm, have forthright melodies of a prevailing minor colour[1] and idiomatic vigour. One of Donizetti's Neapolitan songs, *Te vojo bene assaje*, is sung today as a folksong.

It is among the songs of this third category that Donizetti makes his strongest impression as a composer of songs. His contact with the idiom of the *canzone popolaresco* contributes to his style a healthy antidote to the vocal elaborations of Rossini's style, as exemplified in *Semiramide*, that Donizetti imitated in such scores as *Alfredo il Grande* and *Elvida*. His instinctive feeling for the popular Neapolitan song came to have, as we shall see, a fortunate effect upon his operatic melodies. The influence of this style can clearly be seen in such an aria as Pierotto's ballata in Act I of *Linda*, where, of course, Donizetti was deliberately trying to reproduce the flavour of a street song.

In Donizetti's operas, the determinant element is melody. As he told the French Academy, 'music is only declamation accented by sounds . . .' a statement that speaks of his central emphasis on vocal line. He tended to use the other elements to surround, to frame, and to set off his vocal melodies.

A simple, well-known example from *Lucia* serves to introduce some characteristics of Donizetti's melody.

Ex. 1

Moderato
(Edgardo)

Tu che a Dio spie-ga-sti l'a- li o bel-
- l'al ma in-na-mo - ra - ta, ti ri- vol- gi a me pla-

---

[1] Even a song in a major key, like *La conocchia*, has a sombre colour at its close.

-ca-ta, te- co a-scenda, te-co a-scenda il tuo fe - del.

The first four phrases of *Tu che a Dio* show a close relationship between the first phrase and the third, a resemblance very frequently encountered in Donizetti's arias; while the second echoes part of the same pattern, but at a different pitch. The expanded fourth phrase serves to complete this unit (half of the first part of the binary form) with a cadence to the mediant. The melodic contours reflect the underlying idea of the text by suggesting the arch of Lucia's spread wings, for here Edgardo conceives of his beloved as an angelic intercessor. In the first phrase this idea is expressed by the progression from F sharp to G, and the expansiveness hinted by the dotted quaver. The influence of the text accounts for the variation in rhythm between the cadence of phrase 1 (♩ ♩) and of phrase 2 (♩ ♩). The scalar progression connecting these phrases adds a sense of unity to the melodic period. The melodic expansion in the fourth phrase results from the repetition of the important words *teco ascenda*, an emphasis strengthened by the beginning of this phrase on a strongly accented second beat. In this passage Donizetti modifies the structure of his melody for the purpose of dramatic expression, but without sacrificing the essential rationale of the form.

This aria serves as the cabaletta of the Tomb Scene in *Lucia*. Instead of the usual complete repetition of a cabaletta, here Donizetti has altered the design for dramatic purposes. Edgardo stabs himself during the episode that separates the two state-ments of the cabaletta. During the repetition, the melody is given to the cello, while the dying Edgardo sings only part of each phrase.[1] In *Tu che a Dio*, then, Donizetti reinforces the romanticism of his subject by modifying conventional form to achieve greater expressiveness.

A more conventional cabaletta, such as Percy's from the second scene of *Anna Bolena*, makes a useful comparison with Edgardo's final aria.

[1] The text of the repetition is changed somewhat to fit the fragmented phrases.

Ex. 2

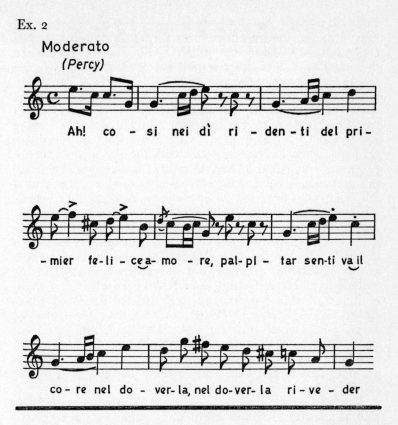

Here the opening phrase is confined almost completely to the notes of the tonic triad. The syncopations in the second phrase form a pattern, a Donizettian cliché which suggests a quickening of the emotions. In the third phrase, detached notes and staccati crudely mirror the 'palpitations' of the text. Donizetti produces a feeling of melodic unity in this passage by the repetition of rhythmic patterns and by his recurrent emphasis on the notes of the dominant. The strong harmonic emphasis in the melody is commonplace not only in Donizetti's cabalettas and strettas, but in those of Rossini and Bellini. In his later operas, Donizetti's melodies, particularly those in slow tempi, rest upon more flexible harmonic bases. For example, the larghetto of the heroine's final aria in *Maria di Rudenz*

375

begins in F major, but at the third phrase it shifts to the parallel minor. Again, the introduction to Fernand's well-known aria in the last act of *La favorite* begins in C major but ends on the dominant of A, and this resultant harmonic ambiguity recurs within the phrases of the aria itself.

One of the most striking aspects of Donizetti's melody is the use of embellishments. In his earlier operas he makes lavish use of highly decorated melodies for all types of voices. During much of the first decade of his active career not only was Donizetti struggling to come to terms with the pervasive influence of Rossini's style, but he had to satisfy the demands of a group of singers whose chief virtue was phenomenal flexibility, and of audiences who expected an opera to be a satisfactory vehicle for that talent. In *Alfredo il Grande* (1823), for instance, even the aria of the comprimaria groans under a burden of extensive gruppetti. Perhaps the most staggering difficulties of execution are to be found in the *rondo d'assieme* from *Elvida* (1826), which is unprepossessing as music but provided a challenge to the technique of Méric-Lalande and Rubini. In his later operas, with the notable exception of those written for Pasta (*Anna Bolena* and *Ugo, conte di Parigi*), and for Persiani (*Rosmunda, Lucia*, and *Pia de' Tolomei*),[1] Donizetti came to place less emphasis on melodic embellishments than on straightforward lyricism. This is not to say, however, that coloratura passages are not found in Donizetti's later scores; they are, but they are relatively less extensive and less frequent.

The most common embellishments in Donizetti's music is the diatonic scale, although chromatic scales and arpeggiated figures are far from uncommon. Most often he writes the more easily sung descending scale, but ascending scales and those combining ascending and descending motion (usually with the latter direction predominant) are also to be found. For example, there is an ascending scale mounting to the top E flat written out in the last variation of the rondo from *Emilia di Liverpool*. The maestoso of Elvida's elaborate entrance aria provides striking examples of scalar figures in combined motion.

[1] Instructive is a comparison between the music of Lucia and that of Linda, the latter written for Eugenia Tadolini. There are fewer vocal embellishments in Linda's part as it appears in the score, although generations of coloraturas from Persiani to Lily Pons elaborated the part in performance. An exceptional passage in the score is the Linda-Pierotto duet at the beginning of Act 2, where Donizetti reverts to his earlier style.

A representative instance of Donizetti's fondness for embellishing a melody with descending scales occurs in *Pia de' Tolomei.*

Ex. 3[1]

Larghetto
(Pia)

O tu che desti il ful-mi — — ne che al

nembo il fren di-scio — — gli al nembo il fren di-

- scio — — — gli, le mie do-len-ti

la-gri - me

This passage provides an illuminating contrast with Donizetti's

[1] Reproduced with kind permission from the autograph score in the Naples Conservatory Library.

earlier florid style. A typical example of this style may be found in Amalia's aria from Act I of *Alfredo il Grande*. This outburst is occasioned by the Queen's relief on her rescue from attempted ambush.

Ex. 4[1]

The passage from *Alfredo il Grande* produces a cruder effect than that from *Pia* because the melody is less closely connected with the text, with the result that the aria seems to express little more than generalized vehemence. The profusion of embellishments turns this into an empty air of parade. The passage becomes ludicrous at the moment of the two-octave leap (entailing a violent shift in vocal register) to describe the effect of 'a serene ray of light'. The passage from *Pia*, on the other hand, produces a more restrained effect. Here the roulades are confined to the

[1] Reproduced with kind permission from the autograph score in the Naples Conservatory Library.

penultimate syllable of each phrase, allowing the text to be projected clearly. The other decorative devices, such as the turns in the second phrase and the brief figure on the word *lagrime*, are intended to reinforce the meaning of the text. Although it could be pointed out that the aria from *Alfredo il Grande* is an effusion of joy while the aria from *Pia* is a lament, they are both examples of vocal rhetoric in which the embellishments are designed to produce emphasis. In the case of the aria from *Alfredo*, Donizetti fails because the emphasis is so exaggerated that the means become the end; he more nearly succeeds with the aria from *Pia* because he subordinates the emphasis to the expressive idea of the aria.

Quite different from Donizetti's elaborate style of vocal melody is a style that might be termed *popolaresco*.[1] This style is related to that of the Neapolitan songs that became internationally popular around the middle of the nineteenth century, largely through the efforts of Donizetti's friend, Guglielmo Cottrau, who published several collections of them. Donizetti's *popolaresco* style has distinctive characteristics. The melodies are practically free of ornament except for an occasional accacciatura. The phrases of the melody are symmetrical and frequently progress sequentially. The melodic rhythms are very regular. In the melodic line there is a great preponderance of conjunct intervals. An example of the *popolaresco* style is found in the Page's mocking song from the one-act farce, *Francesca di Foix* (1831).

Ex. 5[2]

(Paggio)

È u - na gio - va - ne stra - nie - -

---

[1] Here *popolaresco* is not intended in the pejorative sense of 'vulgar', but rather in its stricter meaning: 'of the common people'.
[2] Reproduced with kind permission from the autograph score in the Naples Conservatory Library.

Donizetti's more familiar operas contain other examples of this style. The barcarolle, *Io son ricco, tu sei bella*, from Act 2 of *L'elisir d'amore* and Ernesto's serenade from the last act of *Don Pasquale* both contain the characteristics of the *popolaresco* style. Donizetti makes particularly apt use of it in Gennaro's aria, *Di un pescator ignobile* from the prologue to *Lucrezia Borgia*, in which Gennaro tells how he was brought up by simple Neapolitan fishermen. Many further examples could be mentioned, such as the brindisi from *Il campanello* or the baritone's barcarolle from *Gianni di Calais*.

The style which we might think of as Donizetti's personal idiom develops out of a fusion of the influence of his earlier ornate style with the characteristics of the *popolaresco* idiom. Two characteristics of this combined style are the relative restraint of the vocal ornamentation and the frequently conjunct motion of the melodies.

In his later serious[1] operas he often gave his melodies in this combined style a distinctive colour of romantic melancholy. This colour results in part from Donizetti's ambiguous feeling towards the major and minor modes and in part from his fondness for woodwind timbres.

Although hints of this combined style may be found even earlier, it appears in the opening measures of the soprano's *aria di sortita* from *Il borgomastro di Saardam* (1827).

[1] After *L'elisir*, Donizetti completed twenty-nine operas, but only five of them were comedies: *Il campanello, Betly, La fille du régiment, Rita*, and *Don Pasquale*. And of these, three were in one act.

Ex. 6

Another example occurs in the andante of the soprano-baritone duet, added to the 1828 revision of *Emilia di Liverpool*.

Ex. 7

In both the illustrations the melodies are simple and directly persuasive. Among those operas Donizetti composed before *Anna Bolena*, the long-forgotten *Il paria* (1829) shows his conscious searching towards a personal style. From the point of view of his later development, this score well deserves scrutiny.

In *Il paria* the recitatives are all accompanied, many of them expanding into arioso passages. This tendency is even more marked in *Il paria* than it is in the later *Anna Bolena*. The instrumental melodies accompanying Neala's entrance in the first scene and Idamore's in the second provide expansive moments of musico-dramatic characterization. The suavity typical of Donizetti's combined style is clearly heard in the opening of Neala's aria, *Parea che mentre l'aloe*.

Ex. 8

In the first two phrases the descending motion of the melody moves towards the tonic of G minor. The absence of formal repetition or sequence is consistent with the strange atmosphere of Neala's terrifying dream. In the second verse of this cavatina Donizetti avoids duplicating the melodic patterns of the first. At one point in the cabaletta to the aria there is a striking syncopated passage.

Ex. 9

The first of these phrases hints at a passage sung by Leonora in the *Trovatore* quintet.

Musically and dramatically the climax of the opera is the duet between Neala and Idamore in the second act. Here the warrior reveals that he is a pariah by birth and succeeds in calming the superstitious fears of his beloved Neala. The persuasiveness of Donizetti's combined style, where the melody is unadorned but longer-lined than in the *popolaresco* style, is manifest in Idamore's phrases, which are to be sung *con somma dolcezza*.

Ex. 10

At Neala's reply there is a sudden shift to F minor, and her melody is a faint, uncertain echo of Idamore's. Later, as the tempo quickens to allegro vivace, Donizetti writes a surging chromatic melody which is first heard in F major, but at Idamore's suggestion they escape together, and the melody returns in A flat and again in E flat. For the ardour and urgency of its plaint melodies, this whole duet approaches the intensity of the love duet from *Un ballo in maschera*. Although *Il paria* has moments of unevenness it contains more evidence of Donizetti's search for greater freedom of expressive means than any of its predecessors and some of its successors.[1]

Donizetti's combined style of vocal melody is encountered most frequently in his later works. *Lucia* is full of it, most notably in the music of Edgardo. *Poliuto* contains many instances as well; for example, in the duet for Paolina and Severo, in the massive ensemble in the Temple Scene, and in the famous duet *Il suon dell'arpe angeliche*. The principal melody of the concertante from *Poliuto* was originally composed for the finale to Act 1 of

Ex. 11

Larghetto

Maria di Rudenz. The broadly diatonic, unadorned melody with its clearly marked rhythmic impulse can stand as a summation of Donizetti's combined style. Not the least interesting aspect

---

[1] Donizetti's estimate of the score is given in a letter to Mayr, dated 24 May 1829 (Z. No. 49, p. 268). '(Between ourselves) I would not give one piece of *Il paria* for all of *Il castello di Kenilworth*.' An estimate with which it is easy to agree. *Il paria* does not seem to have survived its first production at San Carlo, 12 January 1829, that date being, it is worth noting, a full seven months before the appearance of *Guillaume Tell* in Paris. Thus, Donizetti's attempt to find his own manner seems more likely to have been stimulated by the recent successes of Bellini rather than by Rossini's French operas.

of this melody is its foreshadowing of an idiom much favoured by Verdi in *Il trovatore*, yet it was composed before Verdi's first opera had been staged. In the sometimes tentative evolution of Donizetti from his earlier obsession with Rossinian embellishments to his more forthright combined style, we can find a necessary link in the main line of nineteenth-century Italian opera.

In his use of rhythms, Donizetti is largely content to follow the general practice of his day. Along with Bellini and the early Verdi, Donizetti is apt to favour triple rhythms for arias in slow tempo and almost invariably prefers duple rhythms for cabalettas. Rhythmic shifts are uncommon in the movements of Donizetti's arias, although he clearly relies on rubato effects in many instances, particularly on phrases that conclude the first section of binary forms. Donizetti frequently introduces syncopation into his vocal melodies, and sometimes reinforces this by instrumental doubling of the vocal line, but he characteristically keeps a regular pattern in his bass line.

Donizetti shows a marked fondness for dotted rhythms. The allegro moderato of the overture to *L'ajo* reveals what almost amounts to an obsession with this pattern. Often he reiterates some such pattern as

in the accompanied recitatives that connect slow arias to their cabalettas. For solemn moments he characteristically employs thudding ostinato figures as in the prelude to *Lucia* or as in the first phrases for the chorus in the Tomb Scene.

Donizetti's clear-cut rhythms often suggest dance movements. Such moments are not limited to his bona-fide dance music, such as the charming Tyrolienne in *La fille du régiment*. Such arias as Lucia's *Spargi d'amaro pianto*, Marie's *Salut à la France*, Linda's *O luce di quest'anima*, and Norina's *So anch'io la virtù magica* are all in dance rhythms.

Donizetti's harmonic practice shows him at least not lagging behind his times, although his scores contain little that could be called advanced. There is a generally close relationship between his treatment of melody and harmony; this results from the chiefly homophonic texture of his music and from the conventional harmonic blocks of the forms he habitually used. Within this framework, however, Donizetti was capable of writing flexible harmonies.

One of Donizetti's trademarks is his frequent use of the augmented fifth in major keys. Since this is the leading note of the relative minor, there is a resultant ambiguity of mode. A familiar passage that clearly illustrates this effect is Lucia's *ti rimprovero tacendo* (Act 2, Scene i). Until the codetta of this passage clearly establishes the major tonality, the colour of E minor predominates. Elsewhere Donizetti produces this ambiguous effect through his use of the French sixth chord, one of his favourite harmonic devices, as, for instance, in the prelude to *Lucia*.

Donizetti's harmonic flexibility is shown in other ways. He makes greater use of modulation in the course of a single number than either Rossini or Bellini. While Donizetti most frequently modulates to the dominant tonality or to keys in third-relationships, he moves, on occasion, to quite distant keys, as when in the Lucia-Edgardo duet he goes from B flat major to C flat. Like most of his contemporaries, Donizetti writes unresolved dissonances at moments of great dramatic tension; he came to write unresolved sevenths as part of the harmonic texture of a scene. An example of this last occurs in the following illustration from the score of *Dom Sébastien*.

Ex. 12

Andante non mosso

The use of altered chords is not unusual in Donizetti's scores, but these are frequently influenced by the chromatic movement of the melodic line and are most commonly found on unstressed beats.

The appositeness of Donizetti's harmonization of a melody can be illustrated by these phrases from Edgardo's *Fra poco a me ricovero*.

Ex. 13

The arch of the melody in these phrases rests upon a harmonic sequence that moves from D major through a hint of D minor to a strong F sharp minor cadence before returning to the original key. The solemn pathos finds expression in a melody moving freely over occasional sustained chords, a procedure more suggestive of an arioso than of formal aria style. In this passage the harmony is clearly ancillary to the melody, while reinforcing the underlying rhythmic impulse as the resolutions occur from weak to strong beats.

The critics of Donizetti's own time, even those who treated his scores most harshly, were almost consistent in their praise of his orchestration. In a period when Italian pit bands were almost uniformly execrable and when the instrumentation of many operas was thin and crude, Donizetti's scores are outstanding for the restraint of his orchestral writing, the sonority of his voicing of instrumental parts, and his sensitivity to colour.

One clear instance of Donizetti's restraint is his avoidance of unnecessary doubling of melody, although he often reinforces a cadence. This practice may be seen in Lucia's cabaletta, *Quando rapito in estasi*, where in the introduction the flutes and clarinets have the melody over harp arpeggios, but the first violins join the top line of the cadences. When the voice enters it carries the melody alone for the first two phrases, except for the addition of the flute and violin at the cadence. The punctuational figures for flute, clarinet, and oboe between the phrases of the vocal melody provide an appropriate ambience for the vocal line, subtly reinforcing and extending it, but never detracting from it nor swamping it. The orchestration of this aria is a model of Donizetti's taste and elegance in this line.

Donizetti understood too, the uses of orchestral colour for dramatic characterization. Not a little of the solemnity of the overture to *Poliuto* comes from the prominent bassoon parts. The oboe phrases that accompany Lucia's first entrance in Act 2 describe her suffering, as does the prominent cello figure at her appearance shortly before the sextet. The jaunty trumpet solo in the final section of Dulcamara's cavatina affords striking contrast with Donizetti's writing for this instrument in the prelude to Act 2 of *Don Pasquale*, where it depicts Ernesto's despair. Further, he appreciated the value of a change in orchestral colour, to heighten contrast. A funereal string figure precedes Lucia's entrance in the Mad Scene, contrasting sharply with the tutti of the coda to Raimondo's aria. She appears to a solemn dirge, scored for strings and brass; in the fifth bar a brief phrase in the low strings lumbers uncertainly towards the dominant and prepares for the famous flute melody.[1] Within the space of a dozen bars Donizetti makes a

[1] As the autograph score shows, Donizetti originally intended the obbligato for this scene to be played not by the flute, but by the *armonico* (the glass harmonica). See pp. 416–17.

transition from Raimondo's aria to the distinctive mood and colour of the Mad Scene.

Donizetti's greatest concern with his scoring is to provide an appropriate frame and support for his vocal lines. He is usually careful to avoid swamping the melodic line. Rarely does he use the brass instruments except for harmonic parts, and thus he avoids the stridency that afflicts too much of the orchestration in Verdi's early works.[1] Although Donizetti's autographs afford evidence of hasty composition, they attest, just as strikingly, to his continuous concern for expressive effect. In elegance and grace of orchestration it might be argued that Donizetti is superior to Rossini, Bellini, and the early Verdi.

Since two of Donizetti's best-known operas are comedies, a glance at his buffo style seems in order. One of the most striking peculiarities of *L'elisir d'amore* and *Don Pasquale* is that some of their most famous moments are not comic at all. One has only to think of Nemorino's aria in Act 2 or his plea, *Adina credimi*, that starts the finale to Act 1, or the pathos of *E' finita, Don Pasquale*. The relief from comedy afforded by these passages is an essential ingredient in Donizetti's comic operas. They remind us that his characters are not merely Ingenuity and Gullibility personified, but the possessors of beating hearts.

In these works Donizetti employs the received conventions of opera buffa as he found them in Rossini. In Donizetti's hands the patter song, the chattering ensemble, and the epigrammatic finale have an air of spontaneity that makes them seem part of a living tradition. Of all the basic ingredients of this tradition the most distinctive is the stylized representation of garrulity. This trait occurs in such patter passages as Dulcamara's *Udite, udite* or the *Cheti, cheti* duet from *Don Pasquale*, where the effect is doubled when Malatesta and Don Pasquale sing a machine-gun burst of syllables in unison. The garrulity of exaggerated sententiousness finds expression in this demanding passage written for the Gran Maresciallo in *Otto mesi in due ore*.

---

[1] Donizetti did not score for the tuba. He usually used the bassoon with the brass instruments, but in his French scores he wrote a part for the ophicleide (as in *La favorite*).

Ex. 14

Gran Maresciallo

ge   –   mo in te   –   –   –   –

–   –   –   tro or – ro   –   –

–   –   –   –   –   –   re

The association of the bass voice with buffo effects goes back at least as far as Pergolesi's *La serva padrona*, but the virtuoso possibilities of the basso buffo have rarely been exploited so thoroughly as by Donizetti. While the Ex. 14 passage from *Otto mesi* demands prowess in coloratura of the basso buffo, the role of Mamm' Agata[1] in *Le convenienze ed inconvenienze teatrali* demands a different sort of virtuosity—a command of the falsetto register.

Ex. 15

Allegro moderato
(Mamm'Agata)

come   balzanel mio   pet   –   –

[1] The part of Mamm' Agata was written for Tamburini, who was famous for his extensive and powerful falsetto, although it was first sung by Gennaro Luzio.

- to   dall' af - fet - to

At this moment, the old harridan, who is the mother of the seconda donna of an itinerant opera troupe, is showing off her own vocal skill. An equally impressive example of Donizetti's vocal demands in male buffo parts occurs in *Il campanello*, in the episode where Enrico comes to the apothecary shop disguised as an ailing opera singer. For the moment of Enrico's 'trying' his voice, Donizetti has peppered his score with high notes and difficult runs and figures. If such exuberant passages as these from *Otto mesi*, *Le convenienze* and *Il campanello* form a contrast to the more traditional patter passages, they are, nevertheless, just one more means of expressing the basic *vis comica* of opera buffa, garrulity.

This trait constitutes an important part of the idiom of the opera buffa heroine. Her traditional role is that of one who finds herself faced with a fixed idea and resorts to her wits to gain her ends. In Donizetti's treatment of the comic heroine, four such characters are memorable: Gilda (in *L'ajo nell'imbarazzo*), Alina the Queen of Golconda, Adina, and Norina. The loquacity of these characters is most frequently found in comic duets and ensembles, but instances also occur occasionally in the heroine's arias, as during the middle section, *Ho testa bizarra*, of Norina's aria. Donizetti's heroines, however, are not merely compacted of ingenuity and an appreciation of the ridiculous; they possess loving hearts.

Mozart reveals Susanna's loving heart in her last-act aria, and this possession becomes the focal point of Zerlina's *Vedrai, carino*. Rossini's comic heroines, on the other hand, only rarely express feelings of a sentimental nature with conviction. In Verdi's *Falstaff*, the traditional traits of the comic heroine are to some extent divided among the women, the loving heart being principally located in Nanetta's bosom. Donizetti understood the importance of giving adequate musical expression to deep feeling in the music of Gilda, Alina, Adina and Norina.

There is a feeling of genuine tenderness in Gilda's cavatina, *Nel fior degl'anni miei*.

Ex. 16[1]

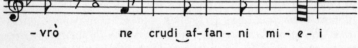

A similar accent of warm sentiment appears in Act 2 of *Alina' regina di Golconda*, in the scene of Alina's reconstruction of her life in rural France with Volmar. Again, romantic sentiment animates Adina's tender *Prendi, per me sei libero*, as it does the *Notturno* from *Don Pasquale*.

Although Donizetti's conception of comic characterization allows some insight into his treatment of buffo style, his manipulation of the comic ensemble is even more noteworthy. Donizetti derived his notions of opera buffa principally from his teacher Mayr[2] and from Rossini, whose comic operas were firmly established by the time Donizetti began his career. In Italy, Donizetti had few opportunities to hear Mozart's comic masterpieces in performance.

[1] On p. 41 of his *Donizetti a Roma*, Cametti speaks of this as a tenor (!) aria, but the non-autograph MS. in the Naples Conservatory Library and the Schoenenberger score both show it as a soprano aria for Gilda.

[2] Today Mayr's comic operas are unknown. Stendhal's jibe that they were the gambollings of an elephant seems unwarranted since some of them were widely performed. His farce *Che originali!* (1798), given in Paris and elsewhere as *Il pazzo per la musica*, was played for half a century. A pasticcio based on the score was played in New York in 1847. The Italian encyclopedia *Spettacolo* gives an interesting insight into Mayr's comic effects, mentioning a scene in *Belle ciarle e tristi fatti* (1807), where a chorus of lawyers is instructed to sing through their noses to the accompaniment of muted trumpets and strings playing pizzicato and *sul scagnadello*.

Donizetti's greatest achievements in comic ensembles are found in the Act 1 finale of *L'elisir* and in Act 2 of *Don Pasquale*. The structure of these scenes is episodic in form and traditionally based on melodic units. The *L'elisir* finale begins with Nemorino's appeal, *Adina credimi*. This melody is developed sequentially and modulated, gaining in intensity but without losing its characteristic shape. Belcore's jaunty complacency and the purling measures of Adina's bemused sympathy are strikingly contrasted with Nemorino's melody. This finale advances by exploiting the conflict of clearly differentiated emotions rather than by introducing new dramatic complications.

The element of dramatic development is certainly not lacking in the second act of *Don Pasquale*. Surprisingly enough the burden of this extended scene is borne by four solo voices without even the support of a chorus, yet Donizetti manages to avoid the impression of thinness or monotony. This is a very different procedure from the deployment of vocal forces used by Mozart and Rossini in their large comic ensembles.

The entrance of the veiled Norina and her supposed 'brother' Malatesta provides the occasion for a trio. Conventionally, Donizetti establishes the tonality of the ensemble by repeating the dominant. Norina's feigned reluctance is depicted by a unison figure with each note repeated a fraction of a beat behind.

Ex. 17

Larghetto

This figure indicates the accompanying action: on the stepwise ascending notes Norina inches forward; on the larger intervals of the descending pattern she withdraws with larger paces. This figure is heard twice before it recurs in the relative minor of C sharp. Norina's principal melody, *Sta a vedere*, accompanied by patter dialogue between Malatesta and Don Pasquale, expresses her barely suppressed hilarity by staccati. As her difficulty in maintaining her composure increases she sings in dotted rhythm and finally dissolves into irrepressible roulades.[1]

At the modulation to G major, Norina's tottering figure (Ex. 17) recurs, but with a counter melody suggesting Don Pasquale's grotesque gallantry. After a repetition of Norina's *Sta a vedere*, Donizetti has written a recitative marked with touches of parody. A languishing violin figure accompanies the bridegroom's simpering over Norina's hand; again, a string tremolando modulating to a major key, accompanies Don Pasquale's rapture at his first glimpse of Norina's face. Both patterns are clichés that are found in many older serious operas.

The quartet begins with the Notary[2] drawing up the marriage contract. The dictation of the terms of the contract is carried against a broad violin melody. The need of a witness for the signatures is met by Ernesto's bursting in, an interruption that introduces the richest parody of the scene. A vigorous A major allegro accompanies this comic counterpart of Edgardo's inopportune appearance at the moment Lucia signs her marriage contract. When Ernesto scornfully addresses his uncle, his idiom is exactly that of a tragic hero.

Ex. 18 (See page 395)
The descending figure, heard alternately in the basses and

[1] The importance of staccato and accent markings to Donizetti's comic characterizations can scarcely be overstressed. Compare, for instance, Malatesta's first-act aria, *Bella siccome un angelo*, with Germont's *Pura siccome un angelo* in Act 2 of *La traviata*. The texts of these passages are roughly analogous, but Germont's purpose is to convince, while Malatesta's is to deceive. The singer who ignores Donizetti's accents and staccati and sings the passage as a smooth cantabile will contravert the comic purpose, for the irony of this aria lies in the discrepancy between the heavily stressed delivery and the apparently sincere words.
[2] In Act 1, Malatesta has revealed that his cousin Carlotto would play the role of Notary in the deception. This brief part is a worthy member of an honourable comic tradition that includes both the stuttering Don Curzio (*Le nozze di Figaro*) and the asthmatic lawyer in Act 1 of *Der Rosenkavalier*.

Allegro

(Ernesto)

Pria   di   par-

-tir,   si - gno - re

violin, depicts his pride and agitation. The broad declamatory style contrasts sharply with the parlando style that has dominated the quartet. On recognizing Norina, he sings brief phrases in recitative punctuated by repeated chords, again in imitation of serious style.

After this moment of serious 'relief', Malatesta restores the comic equilibrium of the scene. His phrases, *Ah, figluol non mi far scene*, consists of voluble roulades, Donizetti's way of expressing barely restrained mirth. Once the contract has been signed and witnessed, Norina abruptly assumes the role of shrew. In this episode (F major, 6/8, moderato), Donizetti places the main melodic sequences in the orchestra, although they are from time to time imitated and even doubled in the voice parts. One important sequence in this passage sets this development in perspective, for it recalls to mind Norina's *Vado, corro*, sung at the moment at the end of Act I when she enthusiastically embraces the plot to deceive Don Pasquale.

Ex. 19

The recurrence of this sequence here shows that Norina is now playing precisely the role she had earlier conceived.

Norina's caprices turn Don Pasquale rigid with amazement. Seeing the old man's condition, Malatesta sings a broad phrase, *E' rimasto là come impietrato*, which is later taken up by the others and sung in unison. The dramatic situation at this moment is strongly reminiscent of the *Freddo ed immobile* episode in the first finale to *Il barbiere*, but Donizetti's treatment is on simpler, broader lines than Rossini's intricate sequential treatment.

Then, as Norina expounds even more extravagant plans, Donizetti employs an accompanying figure that catches the rapidity and sparkle of her scheming.

Ex. 20

This bustling figure plays a large part in Donizetti's success at surrounding the scene with a comic ambience.

The transition to the stretta of the quartet is built upon a protracted modulation to D major. Don Pasquale's *Son tradito* is a patter passage that might come from Leporello. This stretta possesses relatively more rhythmic and melodic variety than Donizetti usually permitted himself in such movements. Particularly striking is a 4-note phrase, first sung by Ernesto directly after Don Pasquale's first outburst. This phrase recurs repeatedly in each of the parts, and the imitation is always real rather than tonal. The coda of the stretta contains the customary sustained and repeated progressions.

For spontaneity and appropriateness of music to the dramatic situation, for richness of comic characterization, the second act of *Don Pasquale* ranks as one of Donizetti's finest achievements and as one of the high-marks of Italian opera buffa.

The elements of parody in the quartet from *Don Pasquale* point towards one of the most individual and distinctive aspects of Donizetti as a composer. A strain of satiric humour was a deeply ingrained part of Donizetti's personality, as many of his letters show. His bent for parody provides much of the humour in such scores as *Il fortunato inganno*, *Le convenienze ed inconvenienze teatrali*, and *Il campanello*. In each of these works the plot is connected at some point with the theatre. Since the librettos of the last two works were written by Donizetti, the implication is clear that he found the pretentiousness and chicanery associated with singers and the opera house a congenial subject for satire.

The plot of *Il fortunato inganno* concerns the members of an operatic company, particularly the prima donna's efforts to make an advantageous marriage for her niece. The milieu is established by the opening scene between the composer Bequadro[1] and the poet Vulcano. At the piano Bequadro sings an aria, *Bella dea*, from his newest opera. The figurations of the melody are, to say the least, fulsome; particularly exaggerated is a rambling sequence (in 3/8, allegretto) on the meaningless expletive, *deh*! Bequadro explains to the poet his plans to orchestrate his aria, giving vocal imitations of the clarinet, oboe, and trombone.[2] Later, the composer asks Vulcano's advice about writing a vocalize on the vowel u; in reply Vulcano declares that while former taste forbade the practice, it is now permissible to sing trills on i, o, and u. Such behind-the-scenes humour is much in the vein of the student productions Donizetti participated in while he attended Mayr's school. While much of the satire is primarily a matter of the libretto (as in the trio of Aurelia, Fulgenzia and Bequadro, where the singers obliquely accuse each other of singing flat and ruining their duet and later round off on the composer for writing unsingable music), yet Donizetti takes advantage of many of the opportunities to illustrate the sense of the words in musical terms.

Le convenienze contains broader and more extensive musical satire than *Il fortunato inganno* because this plot revolves wholly about the fortunes of an itinerant opera company rehearsing a new work. The opera begins with a rehearsal in progress, the

---

[1] Bequadro is the Italian word for the natural sign (♮).

[2] The imitation of sounds for comic effects goes back well into the seventeenth century. A representative example is the imitation of animal cries in Buini's *Il podestà di Colognole* (Bologna, 1673), an effect that Mayr employed in Donizetti's first aria in *Il piccolo compositore di musica* (1811). One of the best-known examples of the imitation of instrumental effects by the voice occurs in a buffo aria from Paër's *Le maître de chapelle* (1821), but this opera had not been given in Italy by the time of the première of *Il fortunato inganno* on 3 September 1823.

Prima Donna singing an aria, *E puoi goder, tiranno.*[1] The moderato section of this aria begins with a purposely banal phrase.

Ex. 21 (See page 400)

In the opening phrase the empty repetitions of F and A indicate Donizetti's intent to parody vacuous music. In the trio of the revised versions, the German tenor, Guglielmo Kol, has pitch problems, and every time he is given the correct pitch, he responds by singing flat. Besides poking fun at emptily pretentious music and at the deficient musicianship of singers,

---

[1] These are the words in the autograph, which is found in the Paris Conservatory Library. The printed score (Schoenenberger) contains at this point a different aria: *Ah! che mi vuoi, che brami?* It seems probable that the Schoenenberger score is closest to the original one-act version of the opera, for the autograph, like that of *Emilia di Liverpool*, records a shortened, revised version. The Paris Conservatory Library also holds a non-autograph MS., which varies considerably from both the Schoenenberger score and the autograph.

A brief comparison of these versions reveals the differences between them.

I. The Schoenenberger score consists of 8 numbers. (1) Introduction. (2) Cavatina for Mamm' Agata. (3) Aria for Proclo. (4) Duet for Prima Donna and Maestro. (5) Duet for Prima Donna and Mamm' Agata. (6) Romanza for Mamm' Agata. (7) Chorus. (8) Finale.

II. The autograph contains only 5 numbers. (1) Introduction. (2) Cavatina for Mamm' Agata. (3) Duet for Prima Donna and Mamm' Agata. (4) Terzetto for Guglielmo, Mamm' Agata and Maestro. (5) Finale nuovo. As an annex to the autograph, there is a 'sestetto nuovo'. This number stands as the finale to Act 1 in the non-autograph MS.

III. The non-autograph score contains all the music from the other versions except two numbers: Nos. 4 and 8 of the Schoenenberger score. Act 1: (1) Introduction. (2) Cavatina for Mamm' Agata. (3) Aria for Proclo. (4) Duet for Prima Donna and Mamm' Agata. (5) Terzetto. (6) Finale primo: sestetto. Act 2: (7) Romanza for Mamm' Agata. (8) Aria for Prima Donna. (9) Finale Nuovo.

The autograph seems to be a revision of an earlier version because on No. 3 (the duet for Prima Donna and Mamm' Agata) the crossed-out No. 5 is plainly legible. Further, in both the autograph version and the Schoenenberger score, the Prima Donna's name is Corilla, but in the non-autograph MS. her name is Daria.

IV. There is still another version of this opera, derived from a score in Milan, presumably a copy of that employed at the production which was sung at the Teatro Canobbiana, Milan, in 1831 for twenty-two performances. It is this version which revived at Milan in September 1963 with good success, Renato Capecchi singing a capital Mamm' Agata. This version is closest to III.

Moderato

(Prima Donna)

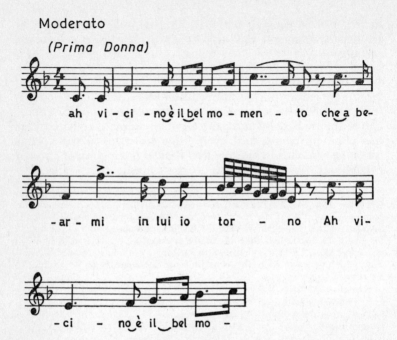

ah vi - ci - no è il bel mo - men - to che a be-

-ar - mi in lui io tor - no Ah vi-

- ci - no è il bel mo -

Donizetti resorts to another form of satire when he causes Mamm' Agata (sung, it will be remembered, by a baritone *en travesti*) to attempt the *Willow Song* from Rossini's *Otello*[1] and add to it a grotesque cabaletta (Ex. 15). In *Le convenienze* the composer goes further than he went in *Il fortunato inganno* to describe and imitate the orchestration of a proposed aria. In her cavatina, Mamm' Agata explains to the maestro just the sort of aria her daughter should be given. First, there should be a cantabile with trills, followed by an allegro with syncopated effects. The accompaniment for this confection is supplied by muted violins playing pizzicato, by an oboe that sounds '*pi-ri-pi*', and by the cellos playing in thirds with the French horns, '*trà, trà, trà*'. Mamm' Agata is a character who deserves

[1] The possibilities of satirizing this aria were apparently irresistible to Donizetti, for he quotes it, again in a humorous context, in *Il campanello*. The parodistic intent of the composer can be seen more clearly in the non-autograph MS. of *Le convenienze* than in the Schoenenberger score, for in the former, the words of the aria begin: *Assisa al piè d'un sacco*.

to be better known than she is, for her nature is solid brass. Donizetti's repeated attention to the score of *Le convenienze*, added to the fact that he chose the subject and wrote his own libretto, proves the enjoyment that he found in parody.

An interesting example of Donizetti's irrepressible sense of humour is found in the autograph of *Gabriella di Vergy*. This is a score that Donizetti wrote without a commission and apparently made no effort to have produced during his lifetime. In Act 1 there is a duet for Gabriella (soprano) and Raoul (contralto); near the end of the cabaletta, *Per te i giorni miei*, he has written this passage for Raoul.

Ex. 22

Over it he has placed the words '*bella cadenza*', an ironic commentary on the violent contrast in timbre such intervals would evoke. It would seem to show, as well, Donizetti's rueful acknowledgement that no matter what cadenza he might write out, each singer would feel free to change it at her whim.

The score of *L'elisir* contains two instances where Donizetti strayed close to the realm of parody. His childhood experiences had given him a keen ear to various types of civic music. In this opera many Italian critics have found touches of rustic flavour indigenous to the region of Bergamo. Viewed in these terms, the fatuous march that accompanies Belcore's entrance could be interpreted as a nod in the direction of brother Giuseppe's background as a bandmaster, while the bumptious band music at the opening of Act 2 could be seen as a little bow in the direction of brother Francesco and his town band.

Donizetti's aptitude for buffo music places him closer to Rossini than to Bellini, who wrote no comic operas, or to Verdi, who, as is well known, wrote only one opera buffa[1] before his final masterpiece, *Falstaff*. To think of Donizetti's

[1] Verdi's *Un giorno di regno ossia Il finto Stanislao* (1840) lasted only one performance at the time of its La Scala première. There are, not surprisingly, many echoes of Donizetti's comic manner in Verdi's score.

operatic style in a larger sense, as it appears in his serious as well as his comic operas, and to compare it with those of Rossini, Bellini and the early Verdi raises problems of discrimination. For one thing, all of them worked within a common tradition that shared notions of genre, of form, and, to a large extent, of musical vocabulary. For another, these composers wrote for a demanding audience that heard new operas with a frequency practically inconceivable today and found the great majority of them expendable. This audience more nearly resembles the fashionable West End or Broadway public of today than the contemporary opera audience that most frequently hears works at least fifty years old. Success for these four composers depended on winning first the support of Italian audiences and later of their counterparts in Paris, Vienna, and London. The general development of operatic style in Italy between 1813, the year of *Tancredi*, and 1848, the year of Donizetti's death, is, in the long view, comparatively slight. And it is slight largely due to the economics of operatic production and to the autocratic power of exigent and only superficially critical audiences.

The fundamental resemblances to be found in these four composers—limiting our view to the period 1813–48—are much more considerable than their individual differences. They may be said to belong to a coherent school. To say this is not at all to deny that each possessed certain characteristics which contribute a sense of his personal style. For instance, the 'harmonic' melody and the patterns of its elaboration in the rondo from *Cenerentola* are readily identifiable as Rossinian. The intricate melodies of *Casta diva* (*Norma*) and *A te, or cara* (*I Puritani*) with their long suspensions seem typically Bellinian. In the same way, Abigaille's propulsive cabaletta from *Nabucco* exemplifies the raw energy that drives through many parts of Verdi's early scores. And so the graceful melancholy of Lucia's *Regnava nel silenzio* or Nemorino's *Una furtiva lagrima* might be characterized as Donizettian.

Yet it is equally true that to encounter a passage from an unfamiliar score by Rossini, Bellini, Donizetti, or the early Verdi, a passage that lacks the more obvious traits of their personal style, and to try to guess the composer would be taxing to the average listener, although he would probably spot the school without much difficulty. One unfamiliar example might illustrate this point.

Ex. 23

A likely first reaction would be to guess this aria comes from one of Bellini's neglected scores. The pattern, the idiom, is strongly reminiscent of Amina's *Ah, non giunge*. But this aria comes from Donizetti's *Pia de' Tolomei*. It is the cabaletta of the contralto's scena in Act 2. It is, of course, easy to accuse Donizetti of being derivative, as *Pia* was composed late in 1836 and *La sonnambula* in the first months of 1831, but at the same time one should not forget the plight of composers who were frequently condemned to write cabalettas to verses in four- and five-syllable units.

To begin to discriminate Donizetti's personal style it might prove helpful, though indirect, to approach the question by considering some passages from his operas which bear obvious resemblances to the idioms of his leading contemporaries.

The maestoso of Argilla's rondo in *La zingara* possesses many traits that might be called Rossinian.

Ex. 24

ciel mi ri - col - mò   È fia ver?   È fia ver?

The short first phrase has an obviously rhetorical, as opposed to a melodic, purpose. This rhetorical purpose is underlined by its harmonic function, as the V—I progression of the accompaniment incontrovertibly asserts the tonality of E major. This pattern can be found in a dozen Rossini scores. The series of triplets, perfectly equal and consistently arpeggiated, are consistent with Rossinian usage. In short, this aria might safely be inserted into an unfamiliar comic opera by Rossini without the casual listener detecting any stylistic deviation. Indeed, at one time a cabaletta by Donizetti was a fixture in Rossini's *L'assedio di Corinto*.

On the other hand, the septet that ends Act 1 of *La zingara* reveals another strand of Donizetti's musical eclecticism of this period (1822). Although he knew that establishing himself with Neapolitan audiences meant mastering the Rossinian idiom, then the expected standard, Donizetti sought to demonstrate his mastery of another vein by writing this septet rather in the manner of his teacher, Mayr. The sectional development and the pattern of key relationships evoke a classical flavour that comes to Donizetti from Mayr. The orchestration is firmly profiled but frequently delicate, especially in the countermelodies for the woodwinds, and this, too, is reminiscent of Mayr. This ensemble contains hints of Donizetti's later style in the fluent melodic lines, particularly the tenor's at the opening, and in the skilful combination of the vocal parts. On the testimony of Florimo,[1] Bellini, while still a student at the Conservatory of S. Pietro a Majella, was enchanted by this ensemble.

The influence of Mayr continued to make its presence felt in Donizetti's scores of the 1830's. It can be identified in some of the preludes and introductions to arias, particularly where there seems to be a sort of Germanic cast to the melody. The introduction to the duet for Giovanna and Enrico in the first act of *Anna Bolena* and the principal theme of the prelude to *L'elisir*

---

[1] Florima, *La scuola musicale di Napoli* (Naples, 1880), vol. IV, p. 274.

are cases in point. This tendency is at its most notable in the splendidly solemn introduction to the Tomb Scene of *Lucia*.

To return to Donizetti's kinship to Rossini, while it is most apparent in the operas Donizetti wrote before *Anna Bolena*, he later came to terms with it and rarely wrote in obviously Rossinian patterns.[1] An interesting contrast can be made between Rosina's *Una voce poco fa* and Norina's *So anch'io la virtù magica*. Both arias are soliloquies in which the young ladies analyse their prowess at practising feminine wiles. Rosina's melody, especially in the andante, is heavily ornamented and accompanied mostly only by an occasional chord; in the moderato scarcely a phrase lacks a run. Norina reads from an old-fashioned romance during the andante of her aria. While her melody is smooth and graceful, it approaches satire at such touches as the extended figure on the word *paradiso*. The allegretto is like a dance tune, clear-cut and rhythmically regular, expanding only at the end of each section into a little flourish. Norina's aria is a portrait of her charm and vivacity; in contrast, Rosina seems rather brittle, with more determination than heart.

The connexion between Bellini's style and Donizetti's is paradoxically closer and more distant than that between Rossini's and Donizetti's. More distant, of course, because Bellini wrote no comic operas nor do his scores contain any comic relief. Bellini stresses solo melody; even such a duet as *Mira, o Norma* is built on a single short melody. Further Bellini's ensembles are apt to be surprisingly homophonic. The quintet in Act 2 of *Beatrice di Tenda* requires the two sopranos to sing in unison, while the men's parts provide little more than snatches of harmonic figures. Again, the bass vocal line during the *Polacca* from *I Puritani* merely reiterates non-melodic rhythmic patterns. There are exceptions to Bellini's deficiencies in texture, such as the quartet from *La sonnambula* or the finale to *Norma*. As a general rule Bellini's ensembles seem thin when compared to the love duet from *Il paria*, the quintet from *Anna Bolena*, the first finale to *Il furioso*, the sextet from *Lucia*, and the unaccompanied quintet in the last act of *Linda*.

The relative closeness between Bellini's and Donizetti's practice can be seen in various melodic patterns they both

[1] The cabaletta to *O mon Fernand* is a striking example of Donizetti relapsing into a style reminiscent of *Semiramide*.

employ. For instance Isoletta's *O tu che sai gli spasimi* from Act I of Bellini's *La straniera* is cut from much the same piece of musical cloth as the tenor's phrase in the love duet from *Il borgomastro di Saardam*. Filippo's passage *Come t'adoro e quanto* from Act I of *Beatrice di Tenda* uses a melodic and rhythmic pattern that Donizetti often wrote for the bass voice. While these resemblances and others are perhaps more readily attributed to their belonging to the same general school, there are certain traits they share. Both were fond of beginning a melody by moving up a fourth from the note of the dominant to the tonic. Both were fond of writing triplets on the unaccented beats of melodies in common time, although Bellini seems to have been proportionately fonder of this effect than Donizetti.

It has become a cliché of criticism to claim that while Bellini is a less versatile composer than Donizetti, he constructed his scores with more care and was a more original melodist. While it is undoubtedly true that *Norma* and *La sonnambula* possess a sense of cumulative drama and mood that Donizetti did not invariably achieve, yet he could muster an intensity of power, even in some of his seriously flawed works like *Il furioso* and *L'assedio di Calais*, that Bellini could match only infrequently. The question of construction might be exemplified by the matter of final scenes. It is difficult to think of any successful opera which has a weak ending. Few of Donizetti's operas written before *Anna Bolena* have effective endings, perhaps because he had little time to spend on them, as in the case of *Chiara e Serafina*, but in the case of such scores as *Anna Bolena*, *Lucia*, and *La favorite*, the final scenes are the musical climaxes.

Bellini's long-lined melodies seem more instrumental than Donizetti's usually shorter-phrased ones. This impression derives in part from Bellini's stress on melody, his apparent ideal of compacting all musical expressiveness into a single fluid line. But Donizetti was capable of writing nearly seamless melodies, as may be seen from Anna Bolena's *Al dolce guidami*, Lucia's *Soffriva nel pianto*, and Fernand's *Ange si pur* (*Spirto gentil*). Perhaps the chief reason that Bellini's melodies seem more instrumental than Donizetti's stems from the fact that they often seem almost independent of the text, except in a general sense. In other words, verbal values characteristically seem the cause of, rather than the occasion for, Donizetti's melodies.

Bellini lacked Donizetti's facility and sought to avoid the

consequences of over-exposure. He fretted to find the best means to exploit his slender resources and schemed for every advantage over his rivals. He wrote fewer than a third of the number of operas that Donizetti turned out in the same period (1825–35); this fact would seem as much an indication of Bellini's knack for avoiding being financially dependent upon the theatre as of his restraint as a composer. Nor does it seem implausible that Bellini's dislike of Donizetti was caused by his fear of Donizetti's greater range, versatility and technical knowledge. Bellini's reputation has been aided by such industrious polemicists as Florimo and by the romantic legend of his untimely death; even today Donizetti suffers in comparison from the scarcity of stout defenders of his reputation and from the aura of scandal surrounding his collapse and death.

The relationship between the later style of Donizetti in his serious operas, and that of the early Verdi can scarcely be overlooked. It is not much of an exaggeration to say that Verdi's first works for the stage stand in almost the same relation to Donizetti's mature operas as do his operas of the '20's to Rossini's style. Even making allowances for the common musical vocabulary of Italian operatic composers during the decade from 1835 to 1845, many echoes of the idiom of Donizetti's 'combined' style of vocal melody appear in Verdi's operas up through *La traviata*. One striking instance may serve as a first support to this contention. In *La fille du régiment*, Marie's aria, *Il faut partir*, begins in F minor and modulates in a series of short, detached phrases to F major, at which point begins a broad descending melody from the F at the top of the stave. A very similar pattern occurs in Violetta's *Ah fors' è lui*. While Verdi may not have consciously imitated Donizetti's progression, there seems a strong likelihood that he was familiar with the score of *La fille du régiment*.[1]

When, in January 1840, *Lucrezia Borgia* was first performed with the revised ending taking the place of the cabaletta

[1] Donizetti's opera received its first Italian production at La Scala, Milan, in October 1840. The opera immediately preceding it in the repertory was the ill-fated *Un giorno di regno*, and Donizetti's opera was still being given when *Oberto* was revived. It would have been strange if Verdi had not been in the theatre while *La fille* was either in rehearsal or in performance, since two of his own operas bracketed it in the repertory. Furthermore, Luigia Abbadia, the first Italian Marie, was in the casts of both Verdi works that season.

written for Méric-Lalande, audiences heard the dying Gennaro
sing a passage that might, out of context, seem almost to have
been written by the Verdi of *Rigoletto* or *Il trovatore*.

Ex. 25

While the first phrase has many Verdian counterparts, the
second contains the Donizetti thumbprint of the augmented
fifth resolved to the adjacent sixth, the tonic of the relative
minor. Other Verdian foreshadowings can be pointed out in
Donizetti's scores. The melody that occurs in both *Maria di
Rudenz* and *Poliuto* (Ex. 11) is a case in point. Again, a phrase
sung by Elisabetta in the Act 2 ensemble of *Maria Stuarda* seems,
as Barblan says,[1] a 'near relative' of Leonora's first phrase in the
Miserere.

Ex. 26

This pattern recurs with much the same insistence with which
Verdi repeats the analogous phrases in *Il trovatore*.

[1] Barblan, *L'opera di Donizetti nell'età romantica*, p. 103.

The most frequent resemblances between Donizetti and Verdi are found in codas and in the strettas of ensembles, but these reflect the most formalized ingredients in nineteenth-century Italian opera. The differences between them, not only in their music, their talents, and their personalities, are of great importance. First of all, it must be recognized that Verdi lived on into a period that was much more favourable to composers than any Donizetti knew. The status of the composer rose sharply, and it must in all fairness be admitted that Verdi was at least partly responsible for such a shift of status. The easing of censorship restrictions in Italy after 1859 was a great boon. During the latter half of the century the rights of composers were increasingly well protected, a change that improved the financial position of popular composers. After 1850 the operatic repertory became more stable: the number of novelties tends to be smaller; the number of revivals greater. Again, this shift of emphasis worked to the financial advantage of popular composers then alive. Much as these advantages helped Verdi, the absence of them provided the limitations within which Donizetti worked.

After this necessarily partial examination of Donizetti's treatment of musical forms, his handling of the elements of music, his buffo style, and his place in the mainstream of Italian operatic history during the first half of the nineteenth century there remains still another important consideration—the impression of the romantic movement upon Donizetti.

In Italy, romanticism took rather different forms than in Germany and England. During the first half of the nineteenth century much of the energy generated by ideas of liberty and individualism found their typical Italian expression in political intrigue and revolutionary activity. The impact of romanticism on Italian opera in Donizetti's day is far less obvious than on German opera, but indications of it are found, even before the mounting excitement over the *risorgimento* produced the demonstrations in the opera houses during the 1840's.

In Italy, and especially in Italian opera, romanticism made little impression upon the received traditions of form. The same sequences of aria and cabaletta, the same general plans for finales, continue to dominate the Italian operatic stage throughout this period. It should be remembered in this connexion that the principal opera houses of Italy were in reactionary hands—those of Naples and Palermo under the Bourbons, those of Rome under the Papacy, those of Milan and Venice under the Hapsburgs. These conditions demanded an external regard for tradition.

Romanticism made its way gradually in the Italian opera house, at first more by a shifting emphasis on choice of subject and effect rather than by a revolution of form. In Donizetti's case, the emergent romantic emphasis can be seen in the contrast between the two versions of the finale to *Lucrezia Borgia*.[1] For the original production Donizetti had written a very conventional cabaletta (in binary form, beginning in E flat minor and ending in the parallel major). For the new ending, Donizetti shifted the emphasis to the dying Gennaro and gave him a brief, eloquent arioso (Ex. 25) rather than a full-scale aria. The second version contains greater romanticism because, instead of the coldly formal pattern of Lucrezia's aria, the focus of interest has moved to the poisoned youth, a victim of his fate and of his loyalty to his friends. The vocal line of his arioso is a simple, unornamented melody, freighted with his tragic despair. His last phrases are sung to a series of unresolved dominant chords in G minor. The whole impression of the '*finale nuovo*' is one of greater freedom of form in comparison to its stereotyped predecessor.

During the first half of the nineteenth century the majority of Italian opera plots were based on French sources; English sources run a poor second, and German a poorer third. The traditional date of the romantic revolution in the French theatre is 25 February 1830, the opening night of Hugo's *Hernani*, but this celebrated evening was rather the culmination of attitudes that had long been gathering force. Subjects of a sort that contributed to the romantic movement had made an impact on Italian operatic stages some time earlier. Such a morbid 'Gothick' plot as du Belloy's *Gabrielle de Vergy* was set successfully by Carafa in 1816. Ten years later this subject so attracted Donizetti that he made a setting of it, even though he

---

[1] My curiosity to hear a first-rate revival of this opera is aroused by a letter by Hans von Bülow to his daughter Daniela (written in 1891), in which he speaks of 'my favourite opera after *Carmen*: Donizetti's *Lucrezia Borgia*. (I admit one has to hear it sung by singers, not screaming dolls, and only in Italy.)' *Letters of Hans von Bülow* (translated by Scott Goddard), p. 431.

had no contract signed for it, and, interestingly enough, it was the first subject with an unhappy ending that he had attempted. Although Rossini's *Otello* (also from 1816) provides music conforming to a pre-romantic tradition for a rather wildly distorted adaptation of Shakespeare's plot, the scene in Desdemona's bed-chamber contains many touches of romanticism.[1] The most representatively romantic setting of Shakespeare, that idol of this movement, was Bellini's *I Capuletti ed i Montecchi* (1830), a superior work to Zingarelli's chillingly formal *Giulietta e Romeo* (1796) or Vaccai's insipid treatment of the same subject (1825).

Donizetti's exploitation of romantic attitudes and situations came about gradually. His early operas were either farces or heroic works with happy endings, late glimmerings of the waning tradition of eighteenth-century opera seria. One of the trademarks of the latter type was a role for an armour-wearing contralto. This now extinct species of role appears in a number of Donizetti's operas: *Enrico di Borgogna* (Enrico), *Zoraide di Granata* (Abenamet), *Alahor di Granata* (Hassem), *Elvida* (Zeidar), *Sancia di Castiglia* (Garzia), *L'assedio di Calais* (Aurelio), and *Pia de' Tolomei* (Rodrigo).[2] Donizetti's adherence to such parts covers a period of nearly twenty years. During the 30's he grew increasingly resentful of the practice, but continued to accede to it if the personnel of a particular company demanded it or if the management insisted upon it. The nature of these roles and the types of music traditionally adapted to them make them inimical to the spirit of romanticism. The catalogue of these anachronistic roles is one way of indicating Donizetti's uneven progress down the road of romanticism.

The prelude to *Emilia di Liverpool* contains one of Donizetti's earliest excursions into romantic effects. Here he attempts with some success to describe a storm and the barren countryside, relying on rumbling timpani, abrupt sforzandi, and unprepared dissonances to make his effects. Donizetti's increasing interest in romantic expressiveness colours such passages in *Il paria* as the unharmonized marriage hymn with its faintly exotic mood,

---

[1] The highly romantic touch of having an off-stage gondolier sing Dante's lines was Rossini's idea not his librettist's.
[2] The contralto-warrior roles belong to a separate, if related, tradition from the contralto-page roles. The former are in the line of such roles as Handel's Ruggiero; the latter in that of Mozart's Cherubino.

and in the tenor's first aria with its fragmented vocal line expressive of the hero's despair.

The final scene of *Anna Bolena* marks Donizetti's first success at sustaining a genuinely romantic effect. Anna's suffering and her escape through madness to her untroubled childhood are the stuff of romantic tragedy. Donizetti's melodies, particularly his quotation of the tune we know as *Home, Sweet Home*, strengthen each nuance of Anna's anguish. After *Anna Bolena* Donizetti's serious operas, with only a few exceptions, become increasingly romantic in spirit. This spirit is present in such scenes as Cardenio's delusion of blindness, where the height of his aberration is depicted by a moment of utter silence. When Azzo hears Parisina mention her lover's name in her sleep, his rage is expressed by violent chromatic melodies. Donizetti's romanticism finds its most characteristic form in *Lucia*. The music surrounds the action with a mournful atmosphere. This is one of the best constructed operas Donizetti ever wrote, building steadily to the romantic catharsis of Edgardo's suicide. Many passages from this score have already been discussed above, but if one passage were to be singled out as summarizing the distinctive qualities of *Lucia*, it might well be the heroine's *Soffriva nel pianto*. The melody develops with unusual freedom, each phrase intensifying the shape of the preceding one until all formal considerations seem to disappear beneath a tide of irrepressible emotion.

Although Donizetti is far from being the sole exponent of the spirit of romanticism in Italian opera, he gave it in *Lucia* its most representative expression. Donizetti understood suffering. His own life was as harrowing as the plot of any romantic melodrama.

CHAPTER 9

Donizetti's Revisions and Self-borrowings

At this date it seems impossible to compile a complete history of Donizetti's revisions and self-borrowings. The wide dispersal of Donizettiana poses great difficulties. The problem is compounded by the easy-going habits of operatic production in his day. Donizetti was under constant pressure to provide singers with new numbers 'expressly written' for them to include in his scores. It was then a common practice to retouch, even to modify drastically, a role to suit the requirements of a particular singer. Sometimes even music by another composer would be included in performances of Donizetti's operas. And just as Verdi was to do on various occasions, Donizetti made *rifacimenti* of some of his works, omitting and adding numbers, sometimes writing whole new acts. All these practices confound at every hand the researcher who tries to decipher the palimpsests of Donizetti's scores.

The following discussion makes no pretence at comprehensiveness; rather its aim is to be representative and to present as clearly as possible examples of the various techniques of revision and occasions of self-borrowing employed by Donizetti. One of the by-products of this examination should be to explode the myth, nurtured by Donizetti himself, of his amazing speed in composing certain parts of his operas. Not that Donizetti wanted facility. But it is clear that he stored up his material more carefully than he liked to admit and that he was not above, on occasion, exaggerating the shortness of time he spent at his work.

There are several kinds of evidence at hand for an examination of his revisions and self-borrowings. By far the most important are the autograph scores. A comparison of printed scores may grant some insight into the revisions, but without some confirmation from Donizetti's letters, the provenance of such revisions must remain dubious. Further, the printed libretti of various productions may reveal changes, but again without some corroboration from the composer, the source of these changes must remain in doubt.

REVISIONS

Three degrees of revision will be discussed. First, such brief alterations as are indicated by passages which Donizetti crossed out or appended to his scores. Second, the addition of new numbers to completed scores. And third, an account of the major reworkings of three of Donizetti's most important scores: the French version of *Lucia*, which he made for the Théâtre de la Renaissance in 1839; the metamorphosis of *Poliuto* into *Les martyrs*, and the curious story of the genesis of *La favorite*, which has never been told before. As an appendix to this section, there will be a brief discussion of *Il duca d'Alba*.

I

None of the autograph scores by Donizetti that I have seen are without revisions which range from a single bar or two to whole pages. As Donizetti often seems to have composed directly on to the full score, and depended on a copyist for a fair copy, these crossings out and changes result from haste and from difficulty in pursuing an idea.

The second act of *Chiara e Serafina*[1] confirms this case. There are many crossings out, and Donizetti's handwriting, never a model of clarity, becomes almost impossible to decipher. A pathetic note at the end of the score, *Così finirà l'opera, o bene o male* (Thus the opera will end for better or worse), reveals Donizetti's lack of confidence in this work.

On another occasion the reworkings were probably caused by

[1] The autograph of *Chiara e Serafina* is in the Ricordi archives.

difficulties of another sort. There are many changes in the autograph of *Ugo, conte di Parigi*.[1] Some result from difficulties with the censors over the text, but there are frequent alterations in the music assigned to Bianca. This role was sung at the *prima* by Giuditta Pasta. This exacting prima donna had only a few months previously persuaded Bellini to make a number of settings of the text of *Casta diva* before she was satisfied with one. The changes in Bianca's part probably indicate that the singer exercised her assumed prerogatives as censor of her music.

In the autograph of *Parisina*[2] there are modifications made to suit the range and technique of particular singers. Donizetti wrote the roles of Parisina and Ugo for Carolina Ungher and Gilbert Duprez. Although he composed Parisina's first cavatina in B flat, he provided a transposition in the recitative which allowed Ungher to sing the aria in what must have been for her the more comfortable key of A. For her aria at the beginning of Act 2 Donizetti discarded two earlier cadenzas for a more elaborate one which touches the top B flat only briefly and provides its most expansive effects in the lower octave of the voice. While most of Donizetti's adjustments for Ungher were to accommodate her mezzo-soprano range, he extended the already high tenor role of Ugo for Duprez. In one phrase near the end of his cabaletta, *Quest'amor doveva in terra*, which was already crowned by a high D flat, Donizetti provided an alternative passage that allowed the tenor to sing (in falsetto, of course) a full tone higher.

Ex. 27[3]

Si me - co in ciel me - co in ciel.

Some of Donizetti's revisions are obviously second thoughts. A representative example occurs in Act 2 of *L'elisir*.[4] In the

[1] The autograph of *Ugo* is in the Naples Conservatory Library.
[2] The autograph of *Parisina* is in the Museo Donizettiano, Bergamo.
[3] Reproduced with kind permission of the Museo Donizettiano.
[4] The autograph of Act 2 of *L'elisir* is in the Museo Donizettiano; that of Act 1 is in the Naples Conservatory Library.

tenor-baritone duet, *Venti scudi*, there are a number of crossings out; sometimes two or three bars are rewritten not once, but twice. Occasionally only a figuration is altered; other times not only the melody but the harmony is changed. The alterations in this duet are explainable only if Donizetti composed the music as he wrote it down on the full score, for the rejected passages are followed in the next measures on the same page by their new versions. One example will illustrate how Donizetti would reject a banal phrase,

Ex. 28[1]

and replace it with a highly characteristic one.

Ex. 29[2]

A very curious example of Donizetti's second thoughts was first brought to light by Maestro Natale Gallini of Milan.[3] For the Mad Scene in *Lucia*, Donizetti conceived the daring notion of using a glass harmonica, the instrument invented by Benjamin Franklin, to add a novel timbre of eerie sweetness to this scene. It is not clear who suggested this notion to Donizetti, whether he knew the compositions for it by Mozart and Beethoven, or even where he had heard the instrument demonstrated, perhaps in Paris, where he had been not long

[1] Reproduced with kind permission of the Museo Donizettiano.
[2] Reproduced with kind permission of the Museo Donizettiano.
[3] Natale Gallini, 'Uno strumento ideato da Franklin: L'armonica a cristalli', *La Scala*, October 1959.

before he started to compose *Lucia*. Neither is it clear why he discarded the idea of using the glass harmonica, whether it was impossible to find a proficient performer, or whether the instrument proved itself impracticable for its intended purpose during rehearsal. In any event, the music originally assigned to the glass harmonica (which Donizetti refers to in his autograph as *armonico*) was later written in for the flute.

The score of *Lucia* contains another revealing after-thought, one that shows Donizetti making a change to obtain a more unified effect. Just before the end of the sextet he excised four bars of routine cadence, replacing them with an ascending phrase for Edgardo, to which, some time later, he joined a phrase for the baritone. Thus, as the sextet began with the tenor and baritone singing together, so it is made to end, thereby giving the ensemble a further sense of balance.[1]

II

More extensive revisions involving the replacing of whole numbers or the addition of new numbers are not uncommon in Donizetti's operas. For easy reference these will be discussed briefly in the order of the opera's original production.

IL FALEGNAME DI LIVONIA I have seen a copy of the libretto of the 1825 production at Verona. This libretto shows the beginning of an altered ending (i.e. different from that in the autograph in the Ricordi archives), but unfortunately the last page(s) of the libretto are missing.[2]

ZORAIDE DI GRANATA Even before this opera was first performed the tragic death of the tenor Sbigoli forced Donizetti to make changes in the score. These involved the omission of three numbers and the alteration of the music of Abenamet from the tenor range to that of the contralto. The autograph score[3] further contains all the later changes that Donizetti made for the *rifacimento* of 1824, a state of affairs that makes it difficult to determine all the alterations necessitated by

[1] The autograph of *Lucia* belongs to a private collector in Milan, but it has been reproduced in facsimile, with an illuminating introductory essay by Zavadini. This facsimile was printed and is available at major libraries.
[2] This libretto belongs to Maestro Raffaele Tenaglia of Milan, who very kindly called my attention to this change.
[3] This autograph is in the Ricordi archives.

Sbigoli's death. A clear instance can be found in the Act I quartet, where Donizetti merely changed the clef and wrote in the new notes on the same stave with the original notes.

The revision of 1824 involved textual changes as well as musical ones. In places Merelli's original lines are crossed out, and Ferretti has written in the new words himself. The principal musical changes involved expanding the finale to Act I, adding a new contralto aria and a tenor-contralto duet, and ending the opera with a new and very elaborate rondo. Donizetti removed the superseded numbers from the score.

L'AJO NELL'IMBARAZZO Since the autograph of this work is apparently lost, it is difficult to speak with absolute assurance about this opera.[1] According to Donizetti's letter to Mayr of 30 May 1826, he added 'several new pieces' to the score when the work was given in Naples under the title of *Don Gregorio*. According to Cametti,[2] these included changing the position of Don Giulio's Act I cavatina, and omitting a duet for Gregorio and Gilda; while in Act 2 a duet for the women was added, and a terzetto replaced by another aria for Don Giulio. Further, for this Neapolitan production Tottola substituted prose for the recitatives and rewrote the buffo role of Don Gregorio in Neapolitan dialect to make the opera conform to the traditions of the Teatro Nuovo. Sometime later the original recitatives were restored, but in a more concise form, and the Tutor's lines restored to standard Italian. In this last metamorphosis *L'ajo* continued to be performed for most of the nineteenth century.

EMILIA DI LIVERPOOL This opera was thoroughly revised in 1828.[3] There were extensive changes both to the music and to the libretto. Giuseppe Checcherini simplified and strengthened the plot, changing the names of some of the characters. From Act I Donizetti dropped the introduction, a tenor-buffo duet, two sections of a quintet, a buffo aria, and the end of the finale; from Act 2, a duet, a trio, and a finaletto. New to the 1828 version are the introduction, a trio, most of the finale to Act I, and a cavatina and rondo at the end of the opera.

OTTO MESI IN DUE ORE The autograph score[4] of this opera

---

[1] There is a non-autograph MS. in the Naples Conservatory Library.
[2] Cametti, *Donizetti a Roma*, pp. 44–5.
[3] This revision is discussed in detail by Jeremy Commons, 'Emilia di Liverpool', *Music and Letters*, 40 (1959), pp. 207–28.
[4] It is in the Naples Conservatory Library.

is in such a state of disorder that it is difficult to determine which are the original numbers of the opera and which were added later. That the score contains parts of at least two versions is evident. The opera was originally produced in 1827, but a note on the first page of the autograph indicates the opera was revised in 1833.[1] The sinfonia is dated 1833, while the brief prelude dates from the original production. The autograph score contains two versions of two numbers, Potoski's benediction and Elisabetta's final rondo, but it is not possible to determine on the testimony of the autograph[2] which of these is the elder version, since the score has been bumblingly gathered—some numbers are out of order, some pages are bound upside-down, and some passages are not autograph. The problem is further complicated by the fact that one version of the benediction uses music from *Gabriella di Vergy* (1826), and one of the rondos first saw service in *Il falegname di Livonia* (1819). As both of these scores were written before the first version of *Otto mesi*, the borrowings could belong to either version of that opera. Since the autograph score includes recitatives with string accompaniment, it is quite possible that these were added to replace the spoken dialogue usual at the Teatro Nuovo during the '20's. The buffo role of the Gran Maresciallo sings a text in standard Italian rather than Neapolitan dialect, and this may be an indication of revision.

Later *Otto mesi* underwent still another revision, but this one occurred after Donizetti's death. At the Théâtre-Lyrique in Paris (31 December 1853) Ugo Fontana added some new music to the first two acts of Donizetti's score and an entirely new last act. This *rifacimento* bore the title *Elisabeth ou La fille du proscrit*; some months later this composite score was sung in Milan in an Italian translation.

LE CONVENIENZE ED INCONVENIENZE TEATRALI Donizetti made at least two revisions of this score.[3] The two-act

---

[1] The note reads: *Poesia di Antonino Alcozer, rapp. al To. Nuovo il 1833*. This information is confirmed in Florimo, *La scuola musicale di Napoli*, vol. IV, pp. 186–7. Since Gilardoni, the original librettist of *Otto mesi*, died in 1831, Alcozer (to whom I have been unable to find any further reference) apparently revised the text in 1833.

[2] The various librettos are no help in the case of Potoski's benediction since the same text was set in each case.

[3] For details of these revisions, see p. 399, n. 1.

version was first produced at the Teatro Canobbiana, Milan, in 1831. *Le convenienze* was successfully revived at the Teatro dei Rinnuovati, Siena, on 20 September 1963, in a composite version by Vito Frazzi, based on the two versions in the Paris Conservatory Library and a third and differing copyist's score in the Library of the Milan Conservatory.[1]

ANNA BOLENA Not Donizetti, but François Henri Joseph (Castil)-Blaze (1784–1857) was responsible for the French version, *Anne de Boulen*, an arrangement that is remarkable not only for its extensive omissions, but for its additions. New to the score are an aria for Henri VIII, *Seymour, ce cœur t'implore*, whose melody is derived from the allegro section of the overture, and an aria for Alfred (Smeton turned into a tenor role) which uses the melody of the barcarolle from *L'elisir*, transposed into A major.

FAUSTA Eleven months after the Neapolitan première *Fausta* was first given at La Scala. For this production Donizetti wrote an expressive sinfonia and added an aria for Fausta to the second scene of Act 1. Instead of writing a new aria for Adelaide Tosi he lifted a cavatina from the last act of *Il castello di Kenilworth*, transposing it up half a tone. The tenor Pedrazzi sang an aria new to the score on this occasion; but the music was not by Donizetti, having been 'expressly' written by Cesare Pugni.

In 1833 *Fausta* was given at the Teatro Fenice in Venice with Pasta and Donzelli. Donizetti personally arranged the role for Pasta and added a new duet for the soprano and tenor in Act 2.

LUCREZIA BORGIA For the La Scala production of 1840 Donizetti replaced the old final cabaletta with a new finale which was sung by Erminia Frezzolini and Napoleone Moriani.

ROSMUNDA D'INGHILTERRA In 1837 Donizetti made a *rifacimento* of the score for Naples changing the title to *Eleonora di Gujenna*. A comparison of the autograph score of *Rosmunda* and the ten numbers from *Eleonora* published by B. Latte of Paris shows that Donizetti provided a new sinfonia, added an aria for Rosmunda to replace *Perchè non ho del vento*, and ended the opera with a new cavatina and cabaletta for Eleonora.[2]

---

[1] For these details I am much obliged to Herbert Weinstock of New York.
[2] Lanari's letter of 31 May 1837 (No. 63718 in the Naples Conservatory Library) confirms the fact that the music at the end of the opera was newly composed. Further, the autograph of *Rosmunda* is not lost as Zavadini states, but is in the Naples Conservatory Library.

BETLY For the Carnival season of 1836–37 in Palermo, Donizetti expanded this work to a two-act version. He added at least two duets to the score.[1]

PIA DE' TOLOMEI This score underwent numerous revisions and presents many puzzles. The most famous of the changes is the new so-called Sinigaglia finale to Act 1, written by Donizetti to fulfil a promise he had made to Lanari when the original Act 1 finale fell flat at the première.[2] Even before Lanari received the new finale he had made some alterations to the score of his own volition: he re-assigned the contralto role of Rodrigo to a second tenor and omitted that role's Act 2 scena. Donizetti could not have liked this change because at the first production at the San Carlo (autumn 1838) the part of Rodrigo was sung by the contralto Buccini.

I know of at least two different versions of the baritone's first aria. One is an autograph in the possession of Maestro Gallini; the other was printed by Ricordi, purporting to be the aria as sung by Ronconi, the original Nello. The melodic structure of these two versions is very similar, but the tessitura in the autograph is lower than in the printed version.[3]

Still a further change was introduced into the score of *Pia* when it was first sung at La Scala in June 1839—a happy ending!

ROBERTO DEVEREUX When this score was first produced in Paris (1838), Donizetti added a sinfonia and a new last-act cavatina for the tenor.

MARIA PADILLA The nature of the changes made by Donizetti in this score may be seen from a letter written to Salvatore

[1] The autograph score of *Betly* in the Naples Conservatory Library is of the original one-act version. I have been unable to see a libretto of the Palermo two-act version.
[2] The text of the Sinigaglia finale is reprinted in *Studi Donizettiani I* (Bergamo, 1962), pp. 146–51. The autograph is among Lanari's papers in the National Library in Florence. I have seen an autograph of a different finale to Act 1 in the collection of Maestro Gallini, but whether this is the original version or a still later one, I do not know.
[3] It is conceivable that the autograph represents the original version written for Celestino Salvatori, who was to have created the role of Nello, but was forced to withdraw from the première because of illness. Ronconi was called in as a last-minute replacement.

Adamo of Naples on 30 June 1842.[1] This letter is worth quoting
because it reveals that Donizetti's concern for his scores did not
cease with the first performance. This letter makes clear both
the lessons he had learned from the Milanese première and his
prudent concern for the capabilities of the San Carlo personnel.

> As I suppose you are still at your post of prompter and
> copyist, I therefore send you my Egyptian hieroglyphics.
> . . . Note that Signora Tadolini will give you her part
> *between which and over which* you will find changes both in
> the vocal parts and in the orchestra. . . .
> . . . Running through the cavatina of Padilla you will see
> that I have made a cut in the coda and need to orchestrate
> two bars with a repeat at the very end. In the duet which
> concludes Act 2 you will find that the adagio is cut in half
> and that the stretta has been newly written as I send it to
> you. And as I do not know what key of horns and trumpets
> there would be in this stretta, you will make the changes
> or you will modify this accompaniment that I have made
> to the key used for the whole duet. The cabaletta, the
> second time, is repeated by both voices in unison, as it is in
> the full score, only the instrumentation is the same as the
> first time in the new version. At the end I believe the
> cadenzas will have to be changed. In Act 2, at the duet for
> the two women, it seems to me that the cadenzas at the
> end are missing; look after it a little. In the finale you see
> there is a new stretta at the beginning and at the end a cut.
> In Act 3 you will see that after the tenor's song from the
> wings there is a little trio for voices alone. Instead of being
> accompanied by the English horn as it stands in the score,
> look in Maria's part where you will find it given to a solo
> violoncello. Further, before the tenor sings from the wings,
> I had put a ritornello for English horn, but you will find
> that I want it given to the flute instead. In the duet
> between the daughter and her father in Act 3, you will see
> that at the end I have changed a piece of the stretta, and
> you will adjust it. . . .

If this letter suggests that Donizetti put great trust in Adamo's
editorial abilities, it also reveals the composer's awareness of
the realities of operatic production: if his score had to be

[1] *Studi Donizettiani I*, pp. 85–6.

tinkered with in his absence, he could at least suggest the general lines of the patching.

CATERINA CORNARO As Maestro Gallini has shown,[1] Donizetti wrote a new ending to this opera. This change primarily involved greater emphasis upon the dying Lusignano rather than upon the grieving Caterina.[2] Further, it dispenses with the distracting figure of the tenor. To compensate Ivanoff for thus shortening his part, Donizetti gave him a cabaletta borrowed from *Roberto Devereux* to be sung earlier in the opera. The new finale of *Caterina Cornaro* was sung at the Teatro Regio, Parma (Carnival 1844–45).

MARIA DI ROHAN For this opera Donizetti made various important changes. He adapted the role of Armando di Gondi, which had been sung at the Vienna première by a tenor, for the contralto Marietta Brambilla when the work was first given in Paris. Later, for the spring season of 1844 at Parma, Donizetti composed a new duet.[3] The new version of this duet at the end of Act 2, first sung at Parma in 1844 by Augusta Boccabadati (Maria) and Fortunio Borioli (Chalais), eliminates the unnecessary figure of the Viscount and provides a more sustained, passionate middle section than the violent short phrases of the original. The ending of the new duet is identical with the original version.

In his *Lettres d'un mélomane* Cottrau relates that when this opera was given in Vienna in 1844 (with Tadolini, Alboni, Ivanoff, and Ronconi), Donizetti made slight changes in the first-act finale, added a new 'duettino' to Act 2, a new cabaletta for the soprano in Act 3, and a new largo to the soprano-tenor duet.

DOM SÉBASTIEN When this opera was produced in German at the Kärnthnerthortheater, 6 February 1845, Donizetti shortened the opera by omitting the preludes, the ballet, and the chorus and made further cuts so the performance would end at the preferred time of 10 p.m.[4] Royer[5] errs when he says that

[1] Gallini, 'Inediti Donizettiani.'
[2] This shift in emphasis parallels that between the old and new finales to *Lucrezia Borgia*.
[3] See Gallini, 'Inediti Donizettiani.'
[4] Letter to Cottrau (Z. No. 616), p. 794.
[5] Royer, *Histoire de l'Opéra*, p. 195.

Donizetti altered the funeral scene, turning it into the corona-
tion of the king's successor, as Donizetti's letters of this period
specifically refer to the scene of the funeral.

III

Donizetti made a drastic revision of *Lucia di Lammermoor* in
1839 when that work was translated by Royer and Vaëz for
production at the Théâtre de la Renaissance. Since these
alterations of this famous work are not widely known today, it is
instructive to examine them for what they reveal of Donizetti's
pragmatism and of the French taste of the time. This French
version of *Lucia* enjoyed a success all over France that all but
equalled its popularity in Italy.[1]

The changes are principally accommodations to the limited
resources, financial as well as artistic, of Antenor Joly's company
at the Renaissance. For example, the character of Alisa is
entirely suppressed. Part of her music is eliminated, and the
rest including her part in the sextet, is taken over by a new
character, Gilbert (who is, in effect, Normanno-*cum*-Alisa). The
two scenes of the first act are combined, an economy that dispenses with a change of scenery. After Henri has been informed
of Lucie's infatuation and goes off hunting with Arthur, Lucie
appears to wait for Edgar, who is obligingly led on by Gilbert.
In Act 3, the expense of another set is saved by bringing Edgar
to Lammermoor Castle, there to challenge Henri to a duel.
This change makes Edgar's second appearance there a dangerous anti-climax to his unexpected arrival during the signing
of the marriage contract. Further, the role of Raimond is much
abbreviated, adapting the role to the capabilities of a singer of
bit parts; his aria before the mad scene is condensed into eight
bars of recitative!

Besides these simplifications and omissions, which include
leaving out the harp solo, the French score of *Lucia* contains
some new material. The recitative before *D'un amour qui brave*
(*Cruda, funesta smania*) is much extended, permitting a clearer
exposition of the feud. Bringing on Arthur after Henri's cabaletta further serves to elucidate the action. The opening chorus
is repeated before the departure of Henri and Arthur. In the

[1] Flaubert in *Madame Bovary* describes a provincial production of this
French version, not a performance of the original Italian score.

printed French score[1] there is no sign of *Regnava nel silenzio* and *Quando rapito in estasi*, not even in an appendix; instead Lucie sings the double aria from *Rosmunda d'Inghilterra*. Further changes include the rewriting of the recitative at the beginning of Act 2 up to Lucie's entrance. The rest of this act is the same except for changes before the sextet and for a very abbreviated stretta in the finale. Act 3 begins with the chorus in the wings singing one verse of *Entourons de nos vœux* (*D'immenso giubilo*) before Edgar arrives to deliver his challenge. After he leaves, the chorus repeats this verse on stage. The Mad Scene is unchanged, but the brief scene immediately following it is omitted. At the end of the Tomb Scene, Henri appears just after Edgar's suicide and expresses his remorse.

Although the French *Lucie* lacks the variety and spaciousness of the Italian original, it is not completely inferior. Particularly, the first scene in the French version explains the background to the plot more clearly than in the Italian. The substitution of the aria from *Rosmunda* weakens the French score, for that aria lacks the harmonic variety and naturalness of declamation which are the particular virtues of *Regnava nel silenzio*. The omission, in the French version, of the interview between Raimondo and Lucia and of the brief recitative for Raimondo and Normanno after the Mad Scene proves that Donizetti did not consider them essential to the score.

Although *Lucie* involved extensive alterations, Donizetti wrote no new music for it except a few passages of recitative.

Donizetti expanded and transformed the Italian three-act *Poliuto* into the French four-act *Les martyrs*. The basic pattern of Donizetti's expansion was to divide the first act into two; further, he added new material elsewhere, deleted some passages, and re-arranged others in new contexts.

In Act 1 of *Les martyrs* the motivation of Pauline's[2] aria is

[1] My own copy of this edition was inscribed by the publisher, Latte, to the soprano Anna Thillon, who sang Lucie in this production at the Renaissance. The copy contains some provocative pencil changes in Lucie's part. Unfortunately these additions were not written in Donizetti's distinctive script, making it impossible to determine whether these were Donizetti's own changes, perhaps written in by Thillon.

[2] To distinguish between the French (Scribe's) version and the Italian (Cammarano's), the appropriate name of the character will be used: Pauline-Paolina; Polyeucte-Poliuto; Sévère-Severo, etc.

altered and the melodic line elaborated; the cabaletta, which follows immediately in the Italian score has been moved to Act 2, and the act closes with a new trio.

Act 2 begins with a new aria for Félix: this role has been changed from tenor to deep bass. At the entrance of the proconsul Sévère, the processional music is expanded to allow for the pageantry possible on the massive stage of the Opéra. The baritone aria, slightly modified, becomes the cue for the new ballet. There are three dances: *Lutte des gladiateurs*, *Pas de deux*, and a *Divertissement général* in several movements.

Act 3, instead of beginning with the brief scene for Callistene, whose part has been reduced to a minor one in the French score, commences with a brief prayer for Pauline. Although Donizetti has retained the accompanying figures for the soprano-baritone duet, he has changed the mode from minor to major and written a new episode to connect the sections of the duet. At Polyeucte's entrance the motivation has been changed; instead of the jealous outburst in the Italian version, he sings a suave cantabile, *Toi, mon trésor*, and a demanding cabaletta that goes up to high F. The changes in the Temple Scene are relatively slight. Berlioz's taunt that *Les martyrs* is a 'credo in four acts' was provoked by the new text to the tenor's aria in this scene.

Donizetti has drastically changed the first scene of Act 4. He has dropped the aria and chorus for the pagan priests and replaced it with a trio derived from the music of Poliuto's jealousy that he had written for Act 2 in the Italian score. In the Prison Scene he has developed the tenor's dream from a perfunctory recitative into an ecstatic vision, *Rêve délicieux*. He has enlarged the chorus of the blood-thirsty spectators in the arena, sharpening the harmony with unresolved dissonances. He has dropped Severo's attempted suicide and ended the opera with a reprise of the duet, *O sainte mélodie* (*Il suon dell'arpe angeliche*).

The French version is both more grandiose and more static than the Italian. The religious conflict has, paradoxically, been heightened by the virtual elimination of the obviously effective music for Callistene and the pagan priests. Because of Scribe's greater emphasis on the characters of Polyeucte and Pauline, his text stands slightly closer to Corneille than Cammarano's, although both are at a considerable distance.

Donizetti's anxiety to give his French declamation an authentic accent is responsible for numerous adjustments in the shape of his phrases. Much of the new music in the score is written to provide for the spectacular effects then *de rigueur* at the Opéra. Since the fundamentally Italian contour and impetus of Donizetti's melodies protrude in the French version, the result is a queasy compromise of disparate styles.

There is a four-act Italian version of *Les martyrs* (Scribe's lines being translated by Callisto Bassi) that bears the title *Paolina e Poliuto*. Shortly after Donizetti's death, Teodoro Ghezzi, to whom Donizetti had presented the autograph of the original *Poliuto*, arranged to have the first version produced at the San Carlo.[1] In this form *Poliuto* held the stage as long as there were tenors like Tamberlik and Tamagno with the stamina and brazen high notes to sing the title role. In Italy today, however, the opera is customarily given in an arrangement by Gino Marinuzzi, a composite edition with the principal characteristic of replacing the act-endings of *Poliuto* with those of *Les martyrs*.

The autograph score[2] of *La favorite* is a strange composite, revealing the tangled origins of the music.

The opening Monastery Scene comes from *L'ange de Nisida* with only a few alterations of the text. The next scene begins in the same fashion, but after *Rayons dorés* (*Bei raggi lucenti*) for Inès and the chorus, Donizetti has crossed out a recitative for Le roi.[3] This deleted passage is followed by a miscellany of material; at the head of it someone, not Donizetti, has written: *Ce manuscrit ne soit pas porté à l'opéra La favorite*. In this mélange of music, there are passages where Italian words have been deleted and French words written in above. The names of Roberto and Il Colonello show that these excerpts come from *Adelaide*, a score begun in 1834 but never completed. This material contains the chorus *Doux zéphirs*, which subsequently found its way into the second scene of *La favorite*. New music,

---

[1] This performance took place on 30 November 1848 with Tadolini (Paolina), Carlo Baucardé (Poliuto); Filippo Colini (Severo), Rossi (Felice), Arati (Callistene) and Domenico Ceci (Nearco).

[2] The autograph is the property of Count Treccani. I am grateful to him for his permission to study a photostat reproduction of it, and to Mr Walter Toscanini for all his help in this matter.

[3] Elsewhere in the *L'ange* material we learn that Le roi is Don Ferdinand d'Aragon. In *La favorite* he becomes Alphonse XI of Castile.

written for *La favorite*, is the recitative at Fernand's entrance, *Gentille messagère*, but some parts of the following duet, *Mon idole*, go all the way back to *Adelaide*.[1] New also is Fernand's martial aria at the close of Act 1.

Act 2 begins with music composed for *La favorite*, but Alphonse's cabaletta, *Léonor, mon amour brave l'univers*, comes from *Adelaide* by way of *L'ange de Nisida*. The music for Léonor's entrance[2] and her duet with Alphonse is also from *L'ange*. Apparently Donizetti had great difficulty in finding a satisfactory transition to the ballet, which is of course newly composed for *La favorite*, as the many excised passages in the autograph score reveal. Besides the passages from *L'ange de Nisida* that have been bound in with the autograph of *La favorite*, there are other manuscript excerpts from *Adelaide* in the Paris Conservatory Library. Among these is a fragment of the music we know now as the finale to Act 2 of *La favorite*.

Most of Act 3, including Alphonse's *Pour tant d'amour* and Léonor's *O mon Fernand* were composed for *La favorite*, for there are no earlier versions of this music among the manuscripts of *Adelaide* and *L'ange*, and the dramatic situation here has no counterpart in the earlier plots. The largo of the finale to Act 3[3] comes from a quintet originally composed for *Adelaide*.

As has already been shown, Act 4 was originally composed for *L'ange de Nisida*,[4] except for Fernand's romance which was adapted from *Le duc d'Albe*, and Léonor's prayer which was written during the rehearsals of *La favorite*. Before the final duet Donizetti had written a new passage of recitative in which

[1] The evolution of this duet is not to be traced through the autograph of *La favorite*, where Donizetti made a fresh copy of the music, but an earlier version is found among the fragments of autograph manuscript of *Adelaide* in the Paris Conservatory Library.
[2] At this point the autograph contains a note, later crossed out, that this scene should be sung half a tone lower, i.e. in E flat. Donizetti wrote the role of Léonor for the high mezzo-soprano of Rosine Stolz, but the role of Sylvie in *L'ange de Nisida* was intended for the English soprano, Anna Thillon, who had made a great success as Lucie at the Renaissance.
[3] Donizetti recopied this ensemble for the score of *La favorite*. The autograph contains two revealing little notes. 'In case these second horns are not in F will M. Leborne have the extreme kindness to arrange the *pistons*?' And in the stretta, where Donizetti has, as was his custom, not copied out the repetitions in the orchestral parts: 'To the end, if you please, M. Leborne—*merci*.' M. Leborne would seem to have been the copyist.
[4] See pp. 244-5.

Léonor explains the failure of Inès to deliver her message, but he later deleted these measures because they retarded the action at a critical point.

Since the score of *La favorite* was derived from several sources, a major puzzle arises. How can a homogeneous plot be patched together out of these disparate origins? I have not found the complete answer, but enough pieces of the puzzle are available to allow a partial solution.

There are three strands of plot. The earliest is that of *Adelaide*, but the extant portions of this score are too jumbled to make identification of source easy. It seems probable that the plot is essentially that of Pacini's *Adelaide e Commingio* (1817).[1] The second strand is the plot of *L'ange de Nisida*, which is derived from Baculard d'Arnaud's Gothic tragedy, *Le comte de Comminges*. The third strand is the story of Leonora de Guzman, mistress of Alfonso XI of Aragon, the subject of *La favorite*.

Now to turn to the interweaving of these strands. The portions of the score of *La favorite* that are most closely related to *L'ange de Nisida* are Acts 1 and 4, the two scenes in the monastery of St. James of Compostella. In the last act of *La favorite*, Balthazar has these words: '*Entre le monde et vous est un tombeau placé!*' This is a clear reference to d'Arnaud's play, which is set in a Trappist monastery and features the gruesome business of the monks digging their own graves. In the last act of the play a young novice dies and is discovered to have been a woman; Comminges recognizes her as his beloved Adelaide.[2] The resemblance of Act 4 of *La favorite* to this incident was recognized by Gautier in his criticism of the first performance.

There still remains the problem of how the subject of *Le comte de Comminges* became entangled with that of the king's mistress. A clue lies in a draft for a libretto that is among the Cammarano papers in the Lucchesi-Palli Library in Naples.

[1] The libretto to this opera is by Rossi and is based, according to Loewenberg (col. 657) 'on a comedy by G. A. Gualzetti'. Oddly enough there is an opera of the same name by Fioravanti, which Clément in the *Dictionnaire des Opéras* (p. 6) says is '*d'une couleur assez sombre*'. Could there be two related subjects, one a comic variant or parody of a tragedy?

[2] The similarity of these names to *Adelaide e Commingio* is obvious. In *L'ange de Nisida*, Royer and Vaëz changed the names to Sylvie and Léon. Could the name Léon have suggested Léonor and the possibility of utilizing the story of Leonora, the mistress of Alfonso?

This draft reveals the nature of the 'Leonora' plot before it becomes entangled with the d'Arnaud material.

This is the substance of Cammarano's outline:

> Alfonso Alvarez, lord of Castille and leader of the Spanish armies, has married Elvira, the daughter of Baldassare Ramirez, a gentleman who lives peacefully on his land with his young son, Gernando.[1]
>
> When Elvira dies, Alfonso plans to make a second marriage to the guardian of his daughter, Leonora di Guzman.
>
> Under that name Alfonso has disguised Zobeide, the daughter of Ismail, the Moorish King of Granada, who had been conquered and slain in battle by Alfonso. Guided by a pious instinct Alfonso had taken Zobeide to live with him and had educated the orphan, seeking to hide from everyone her illustrious origins. Baldassare, however, had come to know this story and with the subtlest arts had created obstacles to the proposed marriage for the purpose of preventing a new mother, who belonged to a hated race, from gaining control over the children of his dear, dead daughter Elvira.
>
> Leonora has had occasion to meet Gernando, the son of Baldassare. She loves him secretly and is loved by him in return, but Gernando knows neither her status nor his father's attitude toward her. He has only learned that she is of noble lineage and to earn favour in her eyes he fights courageously against the Moors and saves Alfonso's life. Alfonso, by the king's orders and because of his own gratitude, has liberally rewarded the man who saved his life.
>
> But Gernando hopes for a sweeter reward—the hand of Leonora. Alfonso is upset by this request, but not wanting to refuse him, agrees. Gernando marries Leonora, but hardly has the ceremony been completed, when the despairing Baldassare, who has learned of the match, arrives, but not in time to prevent the marriage. And

[1] For Neapolitan librettists Gernando had become a traditional avoidance of Fernando, which happened to be the name of the king. For this reason Bellini's *Bianca e Fernando* had been changed by the Neapolitan censors to *Bianca e Gernando*.

because of unconquerable and deep disgust of the Spaniards for African blood, Gernando is scorned by his peers.

Filled with disgust, Gernando flees from Leonora in horror. The unhappy women dies of grief, receiving for her last comfort, her husband's forgiveness.

While many of the details of this plot are incidents that we encounter in *La favorite*, it should be obvious that Cammarano has altered more than the name of Fernando in the original plot to avoid difficulties with the Neapolitan censors. The highly implausible disguising of the historical Leonora as a fictional Moorish princess, a change that causes the Spanish peers to spurn Fernando for marrying an African rather than for marrying the king's cast-off mistress, shows Cammarano's desire to avoid the touchy point of representing royal mistresses on the Neapolitan stage. Demoting Alfonso from king to 'feudatorio' was Cammarano's tactful gesture toward the Bourbons' connexions with Spain.

In Cammarano's plot there is one startling difference from the plot of *La favorite*. Baldassare is the father of Fernando and of Alfonso's first wife; he is not a priest at all. Alfonso's first wife is not dead in the original story; rather he plans to have his marriage with her annulled and marry Leonora, and this is the issue that rouses her father's ire. The pivot, then, that permits the merging of the 'Leonora' plot with the subject of *L'ange de Nisida*, is the identification of Baldassare with the father superior of the *Comminges* story, thereby making Fernando his spiritual son rather than his blood relation.[1] Once the role of Baldassare has been merged with that of Le supérieur in *L'ange*, it becomes possible to frame the central action of the 'Leonora' plot with the beginning and ending of the *Comminges* story.

There still remains the problem of establishing a link between Cammarano's scenario in Naples and Donizetti's revision of *L'ange* into *La favorite* in Paris. Cammarano's draft is neither dated nor is there any indication of the source of the story.

---

[1] Oddly enough, the old Boosey score of *La favorita* makes it clear that Alfonso plans to annul his marriage to Baldassare's *daughter*. In the French libretto there is absolutely no mention of this: Balthazar appears with the Papal Bull against the divorce and threatens the king with excommunication. He is concerned with the king's action is purely on the level of a religious and moral issue not on a personal one.

While it is possible that Donizetti may have heard of the subject from Cammarano or may have known the source, I have not found one shred of evidence to confirm either possibility. But I have found a possible link. On 30 May 1838, some months before Donizetti left Naples for Paris, a work by his pupil, Salvatore Sarmiento, was sung at the San Carlo. The title of the work? *Alfonso d'Aragona*. Donizetti alludes to this occasion in his letter to Toto of 1 June 1838.

> . . . The cantata of the 30th was a fiasco (it was by a pupil) as it was performed and as they do everything. The ballet based on Goethe's *Faust* was so so. It cost a lot and was beautiful to see. . . .[1]

Through Sarmiento's cantata it is clear that Donizetti was familiar with the outlines of the 'Leonora' plot. Therefore it is at least possible that he could have suggested this story to his librettists, Royer and Vaëz, when they were, as much as he, confronted with the problem of salvaging their work on *L'ange de Nisida*, as their contract with the Renaissance was voided by the management's bankruptcy.

The history of *La favorite*, more than any other score Donizetti wrote, is both complex and puzzling.

It is general knowledge that Donizetti left the score of *Le duc d'Albe*[2] incomplete. Donizetti worked on the score in 1839, but for reasons not entirely clear he put it by to work on the revisions of *L'ange* into *La favorite* and other works. The condition of the autograph score shows that Donizetti, after his original spate of work on the project could not have devoted more than a few additional hours to it.

During 1847 and 1848 Duponchel and Roqueplan, who had succeeded Léon Pillet as directors to the Paris Opéra, made repeated efforts to regain possession of the score of *Le duc d'Albe*, believing that the score could be performed and might

---

[1] Z. No. 295, p. 474.
[2] To distinguish between this score as Donizetti left it and its subsequent metamorphoses. I have quite arbitrarily adopted the procedure of using the French title to refer to the incomplete score, and to use the Italian title, *Il duca d'Alba*, since the opera has never been publicly performed to its original French text, to refer to the several 'realizations' of the score performed after Donizetti's death.

prove highly profitable.[1] Near the end of May 1848, Louis
Philippe Dietsch,[2] one of the conductors of the Opéra, came to
Bergamo, where in the company of Donizetti's trustee, Dolci,
he examined the autograph to *Le duc d'Albe* and was dismayed
to find the score so far from complete that it could not be produced without major additions. Dietsch returned to Paris
empty-handed. No further attempt to produce the opera was
made until May 1875, when a committee, including Alborghetti and Galli, the joint biographers of Donizetti, examined
the score to determine whether some part of it might be performed to add lustre to the celebrations in honour of moving
the remains of Mayr and Donizetti to S. Maria Maggiore,
Bergamo. Finding the score less finished than they dared hope,
they gave up the project as impracticable. Next, the score in its
incomplete state was sold in September 1881 to the enterprising
Giuseppina Lucca, who hoped somehow to be able to make
capital of the score in her hard-fought rivalry with Ricordi's.

The widow Lucca obtained the services of a commission
consisting of Antonio Bazzini, Cesare Domincetti, and Amilcare
Ponchielli, all of the faculty of the Milan Conservatory, to
judge whether the opera could possibly be performed. This
commission reported its findings on 14 October 1881.[3] They
concluded that in view of 'the noble line traced by the maestro
and the considerable number of pieces wholly finished or
which could be completed by slight additions, entrusted to a
sure and expert hand, they are persuaded that *Il duca d'Alba*
could be presented to the public as an indubitable work of
Donizetti.' Signora Lucca wasted no time in having Scribe's

[1] In April 1846 Pillet paid a fine of 15,000 francs both to Donizetti as
composer and to Scribe as librettist, on the grounds that the score had been
ready at the date specified in the contract, but that he (Pillet) had refused
to produce it. The reason usually given for Pillet's refusal was Mme.
Stolz's dislike for the role of Hélène (and la Stolz was Pillet's mistress). In
cold fact, of course, Donizetti's score was *not* complete, but he could have
finished it enough so that it could have been rehearsed (thanks to his
famous facility) by completing the missing orchestration and by supplying
the missing music, for which he had made many skeleton sketches in his MS.
[2] Dietsch's place in musical history is secure. He was the man for whom
Pillet bought Wagner's libretto to *Der fliegende Holländer*, and it was he who
set a French translation of it which was launched at the Opéra in November
1842 and promptly sank.
[3] Their report is printed in *Opinione*, 18 October 1881, and is summarized in
Cametti, *Donizetti a Roma*, pp. 260–3.

433

French libretto translated into Italian by Angelo Zanardini and assigning the task of completing the score to the 'sure and expert' hands of Matteo Salvi,[1] whose chief recommendations for the task were that he had been Donizetti's protégé for a few months forty years before and had composed four operas, all unsuccessful. Salvi worked rapidly, for the opera was produced a little more than five months after the committee made its report. The première took place at the Teatro Apollo, Rome, on 22 March 1882, with Abigaille Bruschi-Schiatti (Amelia), Giuliano Gayarré (Marcello di Bruges), Leone Giraldoni (Alba), and Alessandro Silvestri (Daniele). The performance was conducted by Marino Mancinelli.

When Dietsch returned from Bergamo in 1848 and reported on the condition of the autograph of *Le duc d'Albe*, Scribe cannily kept his poem, and when a likely occasion presented itself, he revised and rechristened it. Thus the poem came to be composed under the title of *Les vêpres siciliennes*, by Verdi. In Donizetti's manuscript the lovers are named Hélène and Henri (the counterparts of Verdi's Elena and Arrigo), but it was Zanardini who changed their names to Amelia and Marcello, hoping to disguise the resemblance between *Il duca d'Alba* and Verdi's opera, which had first been given in Italy in 1855.[2]

The autograph of *Le duc d'Albe*, now in Ricordi's archives, clearly shows how far Donizetti had progressed with the score before he put it aside.[3] The prelude[4] is lacking, but otherwise

[1] Salvi's name appears nowhere on the printed score of his version of *Il duca d'Alba*, which Signora Lucca dedicated to the three members of the commission.

[2] Verdi seems to have been unaware of the common ground between his opera and Donizetti's until 1882, when there was considerable talk of it in print. Verdi, in a letter of 16 January 1882 to Piroli, mentions the fact that Toto Vasselli had called his attention to the matter as early as 1859, when Verdi was in Rome for the première of *Un ballo in maschera*. Then, Verdi writes in 1882, he had thought it was only a question of doubt, a notion of Vasselli's.

[3] Besides the autograph score at Ricordi's, there are some thirty pages of sketches for the opera in the library of the Paris Conservatory.

[4] Donizetti gave a clue for the intended key of the prelude and indicated the point at which the curtain was to rise. The prelude in Salvi's version is contrived of the *De profundis* and the principal melody of the Act 3 finale. Cametti (*Donizetti a Roma*, p. 262 n.) records a rumour current in 1882 that the prelude was composed, in fact, by Cesare Domincetti, a member of Signora Lucca's commission.

the first act is complete, save for the dances[1] and the orchestration of two brief choral passages. Act 2 is only slightly less complete; missing are a few passages of recitative, the accompaniment to the drinking chorus and the allegro of the conspirators' oath. Of the last two acts, Donizetti has written little more than the voice parts, the bass lines, and an occasional indication of the entrance for an instrument. Further, there are lacunae of such important passages as the Duke's recitative at the beginning of Act 3 and the tenor aria in Act 4, which was inserted in *La favorite*, and the sailors' chorus in the final scene.

Il duca d'Alba has been twice 'realized'. Once, in 1881–82 by Matteo Salvi who took a comparatively free approach to Donizetti's score; his orchestration is characteristically thicker in texture and less subtle than Donizetti's usual style, and his recitatives and their accompanying figures, where Salvi supplied them, are stylistically at variance with Donizetti's own, suggesting the more chromatic melodies of the latter third of the nineteenth century. Salvi's major contributions to the score were the prelude and a tenor aria in Act 4, taking the place of *Spirto gentil*. Salvi's aria, *Angelo casto e bel*, possesses considerable musical charm and fervour, but it sounds more as though it were written by Ponchielli than by a knowing disciple of Donizetti.

The second 'realization' was made by Thomas Schippers for the Spoleto Festival of 1959. Schippers' version is much more considerate of Donizetti's style and practice than Salvi's. In particular, Schippers has more nearly approximated the texture of Donizetti's orchestration, avoiding the over-thickened sonorities and unnecessary doublings that Salvi fancied. Further, Schippers condensed the score somewhat. He omitted some material, such as an expository recitative in the opening scene, the cabaletta of the tenor-baritone duet at the close of the first scene, the cabaletta of the Duke's aria and that of the soprano-

[1] It has been often asserted that the ballet music for *La favorite* was lifted from *Le duc d'Albe*. The *Favorite* autograph gives no hint the music came from an earlier score. The appearance of the autograph of *Le duc d'Albe* would seem to indicate that Donizetti never got round to writing the ballet for this score. On p. 12 in the autograph, Donizetti has written *Danses*; three blank pages follow; the next page is headed: '*Après la danse*'. If Donizetti had composed these dances in 1839 for *Le duc d'Albe*, why the blank pages? Cametti further suggests there were to have been dances in Act 3, Scene iii, but as then Marcello is arguing with the Duke to save Amelia's life, any interruption for a bit of ballet seems downright preposterous.

tenor duet in the last act. Also, he arranged the first two acts of
the original four-act plan as the two scenes of Act 1. Perhaps
Schippers' happiest thought was to restore the music of *Spirto
gentil* to its original context, thereby eliminating Salvi's *Angelo
casto e bel*. Although Schippers trims the score with a firm hand,
his version strikes the listener as far less hybrid than Salvi's free
adaptation.

SELF-BORROWINGS

On occasion, Donizetti would insert music originally composed for one score into a later work. This practice was frequent
in his day; Rossini's precedent was famous. That Donizetti
engaged in this practice relatively frequently is explained by
the large number of operas he wrote and by the pressure of time
under which he usually worked. In extenuation, it should be
pointed out that Donizetti mined numbers from scores that he
believed to be failures with small prospects of revival.

The following list of Donizetti's self-borrowings is intended
to be representative rather than complete. The instances are
cited in order of their origins.

LE NOZZE IN VILLA A recitative and aria with chorus from
this work was introduced into Scene v of the student production, *I piccioli virtuosi ambulanti*, performed at Mayr's school in
September 1819. The libretto of *I piccioli* acknowledges the
source of the aria.

IL FALEGNAME DI LIVONIA The final rondo, Caterina's *In
quest'estremo amplesso*, was, at various times, added to at least
three of Donizetti's subsequent scores. This aria is printed in
the Schoenenberger score of *La lettera anonima*, but the autograph score of the latter opera ends with the Contessa's
Vendicarmi, io già potrei. The steps by which Schoenenberger
came to use the *Falegname* aria in this score are obscure.[1] This

[1] There would seem to be a direct connexion between the rather surprising
publication of a number of Donizetti's lesser known and hitherto unprinted
scores by Schoenenberger of Paris and the signing of an agreement on 25
April 1855 between Donizetti's brother Giuseppe and the common-law
widow of Francesco Donizetti, Elisabetta Santi Pesenti. By this agreement
Giuseppe acquired most of the rights in return for a sum of money. That he
should want to realize money on these rights by coming to terms with a
publisher seems only natural.

aria shows up again as one of the two alternative final arias
bound in with the autograph score of *Otto mesi*. On the first
page of the MS. Donizetti has crossed out the name Emilia and
written in over it that of Elisabetta, the heroine of *Otto mesi*.
This changing of the name can only suggest that at some time
this rondo was used in *Emilia di Liverpool*.[1]

Donizetti used this rondo

Ex. 30

so frequently because it must have been of proved effectiveness.
As Donizetti's letters show, he believed that one rondo was as
good as another as long as it was adapted to the resources of a
particular singer. On several occasions he urged that a prima
donna be allowed to chose any of his rondos that suited her
fancy.

L'AJO NELL'IMBARAZZO Gilda's rondo, *Donne care*, was
used again in *I pazzi per progetto*.

ALAHOR DI GRANATA Though it might seem strange to cite
an opera whose score is lost as a source for borrowing, the
evidence of the printed libretto for the San Carlo production of
Alahor provides justification, as Jeremy Commons has pointed
out. The final rondo in *Alahor* is identical (except for one word)
with the final aria, *Confusa è l'alma*, included in the 1828 version
of *Emilia di Liverpool* and printed in the Schoenenberger score
of that work.[2]

GABRIELLA DI VERGY This score, composed in 1826, was
not produced in Donizetti's lifetime. He drew upon it on at

---

[1] If this rondo had been used in the original (1827) version of *Otto mesi*, this
copy would indicate that it had been substituted for the original *finaletto* of
the 1824 score of *Emilia*, perhaps at Vienna in 1824.

[2] This rondo has been recorded by Joan Sutherland (Belcantodisc LR 1),
a treasurable memento of her BBC broadcast of *Emilia*. This recording is
with piano accompaniment.

least two future occasions. First, he used the principal melody of the Gabriella-Fayel duet as the foundation of Potoski's *Benedizione* in Act I of *Otto mesi*. A melody in the moderato of the contralto aria recurs, transposed, in the final section of the tenor's scena in *Il paria*.

GIANNI DI CALAIS Gianni's cavatina in Act 2, *Feste? Pompe?* was incorporated into the Italian score of *La fille du régiment*, where it serves as Tonio's entrance air. This music does not appear in the original French score of *La fille*.[1]

IL PARIA At least three excerpts from this score turn up in later works. The B minor theme from the introduction was used for one of the dances in the score of *Il diluvio universale*. Zarete's aria, *Qui pel figlio*, was transferred to the beginning of Act 3 of *Il duca d'Alba*. The final quartet appears in two later manifestations: as a trio in *La romanziera e l'uomo nero* (transposed from A minor to A major) and as the larghetto of the Act I finale to *Tasso*,[2] where it appears in A flat major.

IL CASTELLO DI KENILWORTH Amelia's cavatina from Act 3 was inserted into the La Scala production of *Fausta* (Act I, Scene ii).

ANNA BOLENA The allegro section of the sinfonia is borrowed from the overture to *Alina, regina di Golconda*. Out of the principal theme of this movement, Castil-Blaze evolved a bass aria for his French 'adaptation', *Anne de Boulen*.

GIANNI DI PARIGI Although this score was not performed until 1839, it was composed in 1831. Gianni's second act cavatina, *Tutti qui speri* turns up in almost identical form, but transposed down a fifth, as Don Pasquale's *Un fuoco insolito*.

FAUSTA From the new music Donizetti wrote for the Venice production with Pasta and Donzelli comes a duet which was

---

[1] Tonio's principal aria in the French version, *Pour me rapprocher de Marie* is a Donizetti tenor aria that deserves to be much better known than it is. John McCormack sang it as *Ah, per viver vicino a Maria* when he sang the opera with Tetrazzini.

[2] Cicconetti, *Vita di Gaetano Donizetti* (Rome, 1864), p. 80, tells of being present in the Vassellis' apartment one evening in 1833, when Donizetti, then composing *Tasso*, excused himself from the company and returned half an hour later, announcing that he had finished the first finale. Cicconetti's amazement at this feat might have been tempered had he realized that the music was re-arranged (and for the second time) rather than newly composed.

used again in Act 2 of *Maria Stuarda*. The *Fausta* duet was published by Ricordi. The text of the duet in *Maria Stuarda* begins *Da tutti abbandonata*.

L'ELISIR D'AMORE   One of the least explicable of Donizetti's self-borrowings is his use of the melody of the opening chorus of *L'elisir* in the last act of *Il furioso*.

In 1841 Donizetti wrote for Eugenia Tadolini a cabaletta to incorporate into *L'elisir*. The melody of this cabaletta was inserted into *Don Pasquale* as Norina's *Via, caro sposino*.[1]

ROSMUNDA D'INGHILTERRA   Rosmunda's aria *Perchè non ho del vento*, was used in the French score of *Lucia* to replace *Regnava nel silenzio*. For some time Donizetti had countenanced this substitution in Italian performances.[2] The original sinfonia to *Rosmunda* is shown by Donizetti's letter to Ricordi of 8 March 1834 (*Studi Donizettiani I*, p. 22) to have had a prior existence, but where I have been unable to discover.

MARIA STUARDA   The last-act prayer, *Deh, tu di un umile preghiera*, is one of the most powerful moments in this score. Donizetti thought so well of this passage that he adapted it to two later contexts. First, as the hymn to liberty in Act 2 of *Le duc d'Albe*, where the autograph shows it completely scored, and, second, with the melody slightly changed and the accompaniment much elaborated, as the prayer led by the Prefetto in Act 1 of *Linda di Chamounix*.

IL CAMPANELLO   For the score of *Il campanello*, Donizetti drew on one of his songs rather than borrowing from a previous opera. Enrico's brindisi, *Mesci, mesci*, has all the earmarks of a Neapolitan song, and it was in this form Donizetti originally composed it, even publishing it in the Italian version of a song collection, *Nuits d'été à Pausilippe*, the words by Leopoldo Tarantini.[3] In the scene of Enrico disguised as an opera singer, Donizetti indulges in self-quotation when Enrico sings the opening phrases of the gondolier's off-stage song from *Marino Faliero*. At another point Enrico parodies Desdemona's *Willow*

---

[1] In a letter to Ricordi, 22 October 1842 (Z. No. 448, p. 633), Donizetti wrote out the melody of the first phrases.

[2] Giuseppina Strepponi customarily sang an aria from *Fausta* in place of *Regnava nel silenzio*.

[3] This song appears only in the Italian collection, as No. 12, a *brindisi a due voci*. These songs were published by Ricordi.

Song from Rossini's *Otello*, but here again Donizetti is quoting from his earlier parody of this aria, sung by Mamm' Agata in *Le convenienze.*

MARIA DI RUDENZ Donizetti used the larghetto from the finale to Act 1 in the Temple Scene of *Poliuto.* Corrado's fine aria, *Ah, non avea più lagrime,* was regularly sung by Ronconi in the last act of *Maria di Rohan.*

LE DUC D'ALBE Henri's aria at the beginning of Act 4 was inserted into the last act of *La favorite.* The original MS. of this aria, as it was sketched for *Le duc d'Albe,* is in the Paris Conservatory Library. Donizetti has written out the vocal line, the string bass line, the oboe introduction, and indicated the harp accompaniment. The vocal melody is slightly different from its later, more familiar form.[1]

L'ANGE DE NISIDA Although a large portion of this score went into *La favorite,* one number had a different destination. The duet for the two women in Act 2 of *Maria Padilla,* once a popular concert showpiece, was lifted from the dismembered score of *L'ange de Nisida.*

LINDA DI CHAMOUNIX The overture to *Linda* is largely taken from the first movement of Donizetti's eighteenth string quartet. He prefixed a brief larghetto introduction to the borrowed movement.

DON PASQUALE Although the score of *Don Pasquale* was composed in a surprisingly short time—a little less than a month would seem a more accurate estimate than Donizetti's boast of less than two weeks—not all the music was originally written for this score.

As we have seen, Don Pasquale's *Un fuoco insolito* was originally

---

[1] As the original text is quite unfamiliar and differs significantly from the words sung by Fernand in *La favorite,* I quote it here:

> *Anges des cieux, éloignez-d'elle,*
> *Et le chagrin, et la douleur.*
> *Gardez pour moi, peine cruelle,*
> *Et donnez lui tout mon bonheur,*
> *Ici d'un parjure et d'un traitre,*
> *Hélène, tu purgeais les jours.*
> *Et moi, et moi, je dirai toujours:*
> *Anges des cieux, etc.*

(Quoted with kind permission of the Paris Conservatory Library.)

a tenor aria in *Gianni di Parigi* and Norina's *Via, caro sposino* started out as an added cabaletta for *L'elisir*. There are further instances. According to tradition,[1] the chorus of the servants was first written as an album piece that Donizetti retrieved and transcribed for his opera. In the autograph score,[2] this chorus is written on a separate group of sheets (or *fascicolo*), ending with two blank pages, a fact that suggests that the music following the chorus had already been written when this number was added to the score. The ensemble in the form of a moral that concludes the score was first composed as a song with piano accompaniment, entitled *La bohêmienne*, which Donizetti transcribed for orchestra and supplied with the additional vocal parts. Another tradition[3] has it that Donizetti added Ernesto's serenade, *Com' è gentil*, not long before the first performance. The evidence of the autograph score would not seem to confirm this tradition. The MS. is written on the same type of paper as the rest of the score, and there are revisions of words which would seem to indicate that the music was not composed at the last minute. Even more important, Donizetti's use of this melody in the overture points to his conceiving of this aria as an integral part of the work.

The recitative preceding the buffo duet in the first scene of the last act was not written for the original Paris production, but was added to the opera at the time of its first production in Vienna.[4]

Although the resemblance is not close enough to be described as self-borrowing, there is a strong similarity of melody and rhythmic pattern between the terzetto of *Adelia* and the *Notturno* from the final scene of *Don Pasquale*. The terzetto from *Adelia* is even closer to the duet, *Tu l'amor mio*, from *Caterina Cornaro*.

[1] Florimo is an unreliable source; he tells (*La scuola musicale di Napoli*, vol. III, p. 492) of a '*bellissimo Walzer*' written in the album of Countess de Merlin and later used as the chorus of servants.

[2] In the Ricordi archives. I am indebted to Maestro Tenaglia for these details.

[3] This anecdote is told in Judith Gauthier's *Le roman d'un grand chanteur: Mario de Candia* (Paris, 1912), where it is related as having come from Mario's daughter, Madame Pearse.

[4] Donizetti's letter to Ricordi, 5 January 1843 (Z. No. 465, p. 648) says: '. . . I will make a change in the duet of the two basses. . . .' *Studi Donizettiani I* (pp. 96–7) reprints the recitative as we now know it. The passage is included in a letter to Accursi, dated 26 March 1843.

Few writers about Donizetti have sufficiently stressed the extensiveness of Donizetti's revisions and self-borrowings. Even a representative survey of these activities shows Donizetti as a composer rather more frugal of his material than he was wont to have the public believe.

It is curious that two operas as well regarded as *Don Pasquale* and *La favorite* should reveal themselves on close examination to contain material from many earlier sources. It is no small tribute to Donizetti's consistency as a composer that these disparate elements fuse as well as they do.

CHAPTER 10

The Librettists and Librettos of
Donizetti's Operas

To turn to the librettos of Donizetti's opera might seem, at first glance, an exercise of dubious value. Professor Dent puts it bluntly: 'The first half of the nineteenth century . . . was in fact the most degraded age through which opera ever passed.'[1] Certainly it was a wasteful period for opera, one when composers and librettists worked on short notice, getting short pay and short shrift from impresarios and public. From a long view this period may be seen as a necessary stage of 'growing pains' in the development of opera, a time rich with the seeds of future growth. The great bulk of operas composed during those years have disappeared, but the handful of works by Rossini, Bellini, and Donizetti that do survive form a vital part of our operatic heritage. An examination of the librettos set by Donizetti affords some insight into the taste of the times and the problems then facing a librettist.

Libretto-writing was necessarily part-time work as the pay could not keep a man. Some librettists were literary hacks, turning their hands to any sort of writing assignment; others were attached to a theatre in some capacity, as Giuseppe Checcherini and Salvatore Cammarano worked as stage directors. Some were noblemen who took a dilettante's interest in writing; still others were men like Ferretti, who held a

[1] Dent, 'Donizetti: An Italian Romantic', in *Fanfare for Ernest Newman* (ed. Herbert van Thal), p. 86.

443

sinecure that allowed him leisure for writing. On occasion, Donizetti turned his hand to supply himself with a text. But however a librettist managed to support himself, he had to write for a particular theatre, controlled by a more or less inflexible censorship, and for a conservative public whose taste for novelty was matched only by its fixed preconception of what an opera should be.

Libretto subjects in Donizetti's time were usually drawn from literary sources or from an already existing libretto. Then little stress was given to originality of plot; rather, the choice of subject seemed to depend on the vogue of the day. At the time of the French Revolution there arose a feeling that plots derived from classical mythology, from ancient history, and from Ariosto and Boiardo, had become *passé*. During the Napoleonic era, farces were the most frequently performed type.[1] During the 1820's the proportion of serious operas gradually increased. This restored vogue for serious subjects stemmed, at least in part, from the success of *Tancredi*. The characteristic tone of such works was 'heroic'—that is, they presented a conflict between love and honour or ambition, usually against a military background. Particularly popular became plots dealing with Spanish wars against the Moors.[2] From these 'heroic' plots only a shift of emphasis is required to enter the world of romantic melodrama. From the stereotyped responses and the crude confrontations of opposing forces common to the heroic plot, there is an increasing concern with motivation and with the suffering of an individual trapped by circumstances beyond his control. In heroic plots, no strain on the credulities was thought too severe as long as the ending was a happy one; in romantic melodramas, tragic endings are common and death scenes become protracted. Most often the plots of romantic melodramas are based on pseudo-history, set in other times and other places. The influence of Scott is clear. The vogue for romantic melodrama that Verdi inherited fully developed had been largely fashioned by Donizetti's operas.

[1] At La Scala between 1797 and 1815, the proportion of farces and opere buffe to serious works is approximately three to one. At the same theatre, during the 1850's, of ninety-nine productions staged, only *six* were of opere buffe.

[2] Donizetti wrote four operas in this locale: *Zoraide di Granata*, *Alahor di Granata*, *Elvida*, and *Sancia di Castiglia*. In the last a 'romantic', as opposed to an 'heroic', focus becomes discernible.

The internal ingredients of a libretto written during the first half of the nineteenth century were largely dictated by convention. The action had to be arranged to provide a succession of arias, duets, and ensembles, permitting a suitable variation of personnel and emotional content. For two-part arias, the librettist had to supply a second set of stanzas contrasting in mood and metre with the first set. Usually, each principal character had to be given an *aria di sortita* or entrance aria. Often the entrance of the prima donna was held back until the second scene or even later, and hers had to be a prominent part at the end of the work. Within the cramped quarters of these conventions, the hapless librettist had to work. Small wonder, then, if a librettist at the mercy of the censors, at the beck and call of the composer, impresario and singers, and strait-jacketed by convention, frequently turned out sorry work.

A brief survey of the work of the various librettists that served Donizetti may explain some of the failures and the occasional brilliant exceptions that both plagued and exhilarated the composer. For easy reference, Donizetti's librettists are taken up in alphabetical order.

BARDARI, GIUSEPPE (dates unknown) This obscure figure wrote but one libretto for Donizetti, that of *Maria Stuarda* (produced in its original form, Milan, 1835). When the Queen of Naples objected to the subject, Bardari was either unavailable or unwilling to transform the libretto to its new form, *Buondelmonte*. Bardari's text follows fairly faithfully the outlines of its source, Schiller's *Maria Stuart*, but his verses seldom rise above routine.

BEVILACQUA ALDOVRANDINI, MARCHESE GHERARDO (dates unknown) This Bolognese aristocrat and life-long friend of Rossini supplied Donizetti with the text of *Il falegname di Livonia* (1819). This libretto suffers from a grave structural failing: the problem is practically resolved at the end of the first act, and the second is largely mere 'filler'. Bevilacqua's verse is superior in diction and economy to that of Donizetti's previous librettists—a modest compliment indeed!

BIDERA, (GIOVANNI) EMANUELE (b. Palermo, 1784; d. ?) Not much is known of this Italo-Greek except that he settled in Naples apparently in 1824 and was still living there in 1843.

For Donizetti, Bidera wrote two librettos: *Gemma di Vergy* (1834) and *Marino Faliero* (1835). Donizetti turned to Bidera as he was unable to procure texts from Romani for two important commissions: for the opera to open the La Scala Carnival season of 1834–35 and for his first opera written for Paris. Donizetti never turned to Bidera again.

Gemma di Vergy enjoyed considerable popularity at one time, in spite of its disaffecting plot, derived from Dumas. The characters are repellent: the soprano totters on the brink of hysteria; the tenor is a psychopath; the baritone varies complacency with bullying. *Marino Faliero* is better constructed as the conflict grows out of character rather than from extraneous circumstance as does that of *Gemma*. *Marino* suffers from monotony. There are too many conspiratorial scenes, the romantic interest is almost ignored, and the explanation of how the conspiracy was betrayed is so terse as to be incomprehensible. Bidera uses a larger vocabulary than many of Donizetti's librettists, but his verse is leaden and clumsy.

CAMMARANO, SALVATORE (b. Naples, 19 March 1801; d. Naples, 17 July 1852). One of the most important theatre-poets of his time, Cammarano came from a family long associated with the stage and with painting. In fact, Cammarano was first employed at the San Carlo as a scene-painter and later as a stage manager, before he turned to writing librettos in 1835. Cammarano supplied Donizetti with the texts of *Lucia di Lammermoor* (1835), *Belisario* (1836), *L'assedio di Calais* (1836), *Pia de' Tolomei* (1837), *Roberto Devereux* (1837), *Maria di Rudenz* (1838), *Poliuto* (written in 1838, but not produced until 1848), and *Maria di Rohan* (1843).[1]

Although Cammarano has been severely criticized as a librettist, Donizetti regarded him as second only to Romani as a writer and as his superior as a man to work with. The libretto to *Lucia* is of better quality than its detractors will admit. Although Cammarano omits some of Scott's striking characters and a wealth of incident, he preserves the essential conflict by concentrating on a minimum of essential characters, who seem almost as isolated as the characters in a tale by Poe. Cammarano

[1] Besides those for Donizetti, Cammarano supplied texts to Pacini, Mercadante and others, but especially to Verdi: *Alzira*, *La battaglia di Legnano*, *Luisa Miller*, and *Il trovatore*, this last completed after Cammarano's death by L. E. Bardare.

makes many of his points in short, telling phrases, of the sort Verdi referred to as *parola scenica*. Cammarano's diction is occasionally high-flown but no more so than that of most of his fellows.

The best of Cammarano's librettos are those to *L'assedio di Calais* and *Poliuto*. The former is surprising for its period (Naples, 1836) because it is a stirringly patriotic work and a plea for liberty.[1] The story of the burghers of Calais moved Cammarano to write a libretto that has moments of great dramatic effectiveness, such as the scene in which the men volunteer to die for their city, and approaches real eloquence, as in Eustachio's meditation on the besieged and starving city. The flavour of both text and some of the music makes *L'assedio di Calais* approach the Verdi of *Simon Boccanegra*.

The poem for *Poliuto*, while it obscures the conflicts of Corneille's play, is well constructed and at times achieves a felicitous paraphrasing of Corneille's lines.[2] The rest of Cammarano's texts for Donizetti are of inferior quality. The book of *Belisario* is frequently cold and over-rhetorical; the management of the dénouement and Antonina's repentance is clumsy. *Pia de' Tolomei* contains some powerful individual scenes, especially for the tenor, but the plot lacks clarity of structure, a defect that caused the score to undergo extensive revision. *Roberto Devereux* contains plagiarisms from Romani's earlier libretto, *Il conte d'Essex*; the chief blemish of this text is the wildly overdrawn final scene for Queen Elizabeth. Violent and repulsive melodrama makes *Maria di Rudenz* the poorest libretto Cammarano offered Donizetti. *Maria di Rohan* has many good points, a clear plot line (although it is a little long in getting under way), the conflict is cumulative, but the final scene suffers from exaggerated melodrama.

Cammarano wrote three superior librettos for Donizetti. In

---

[1] Not surprisingly, *L'assedio* ran into censorship troubles, as a comparison of the printed libretto with the text in the autograph score reveals. A single example reveals the character of the changes. In the final scene, the English queen remonstrates with Edward to spare the lives of the burghers of Calais. In the printed libretto, she declares: '*E' di Dio l'immago un Rè*' (A king is the image of God); in the autograph score, she poses at this point what must have seemed to Bourbons a subversive question: '*E' di Dio più grande un Rè?*' (Is a king more powerful than God?).

[2] The tenor Nourrit, a man of unusual culture and an experienced aide in improving librettos, assisted Cammarano with the text to *Poliuto*.

them he demonstrates a strong sense of characterization. His principal weaknesses as a poet for the musical theatre are his frequent difficulties in finding strong, simple resolutions and his weakness for shoddy *coups-de-théâtre*.

CHECCHERINI, GIUSEPPE (b. Florence, 1777; d. Naples, 19 September 1840) This librettist began his career in Rome, where he was connected with the Teatro Valle, and probably in 1807 moved to Naples, where he seems to have spent the rest of his life. His principal connexion in Naples was with the Teatro Nuovo where he acted as stage director as well as supplying occasional librettos. Checcherini's only assignment for Donizetti was the 1828 revision of *Emilia di Liverpool*. Commons describes this revision as using:

> the same chronology as that of 1824, but curtails the length of the opera, especially by employing a much shorter spoken dialogue. Although by no means a fine libretto, this revision sets the confused 1824 libretto in order and is clearly the work of an able man of the theatre.[1]

DONIZETTI, GAETANO The composer supplied himself with books for three of his scores: *Le convenienze ed inconvenienze teatrali* (1827), *Il campanello* (1836), and *Betly* (1836). All of these were originally one-act comedies, but the first and last he later expanded into two acts. Further, Donizetti completed the libretto of *Fausta* (1832), when Gilardoni died leaving his text incomplete. And again, he was so full of suggestions for Ruffini's libretto of *Don Pasquale* that the author preferred not to have his name associated with the work. With Ferretti and Cammarano Donizetti worked closely, and it may be reasonably supposed that he frequently made suggestions to his other librettists.

As a poet, Donizetti commanded a vein of easy, satirical verse. The fugitive lines that occur in many of his letters, such as that of 13 November 1832 which contains the lines beginning, '*Se asmatico è Ferretti*', reveal his knack for well-turned doggerel. It is consistent with Donizetti's understanding of his own inclination that the texts he wrote should be broadly humorous, each of them derived from a viable source.

[1] Jeremy Commons, 'Emilia di Liverpool', *Music and Letters*, 40 (1959), p. 228. Incidentally both Checcherini's wife Francesca, and his daughter, Marianna, sang in the 1828 production of *Emilia*.

In many ways Donizetti's libretto for *Le convenienze* is the most interesting of his efforts. An uninhibited satire of opera companies, the text can still provoke laughter: particularly the aria of the prima donna's father in which he boasts of his daughter's chromatic scales sung while she was still in her mother's womb, and the duet between Mamm' Agata and the prima donna, where the old virago browbeats her daughter's rival by chanting the names of Pasta, Lalande and Fodor.

The text of *Il campanello* is filled with Donizetti's robust sense of humour and of his fondness for the local and topical, as he transports the action to Naples and causes Enrico to remark that he is rehearsing a new opera named *Il campanello*. For *Betly* Donizetti approaches the mood of *L'elisir*; the emphasis rests on the love of a simple-minded youth for a good-hearted but resolutely independent girl.

Donizetti's practical experience in the theatre was a great asset to him. The entrances and exits of the characters are naturally handled and well prepared. His characters are drawn in broad, clear strokes. The conflicts are kept solidly before the audience. Donizetti's chief weakness as a librettist is his failure to let well enough alone. When he expanded *Le convienze* and *Betly* into two acts, the action becomes diffuse and the jokes over-extended. His flair was for one-act farce.

FERRETTI, JACOPO (b. Rome, 16 July 1784; d. Rome, 7 March 1852) Between 1807 and 1846 Ferretti wrote more than sixty librettos. His chief income, however, came from a post with the tobacco monopoly of the Papal States. He was more widely read than most librettists of his day and earned Romani's praise 'as the only one worthy of co-operating with the impulse already given to the Italian musical theatre'.[1] Today Ferretti's name is remembered, if at all, for his words for Rossini's *Cenerentola*; however, he wrote four superior books for Donizetti: *L'ajo nell'imbarazzo* (1824), *Olivo e Pasquale* (1827), *Il furioso all'isola di S. Domingo* (1833) and *Torquato Tasso* (1833), as well as making a *rifacimento* of Merelli's libretto to *Zoraide di Granata*.

---

[1] *Gazzetta ufficiale piemontese*, No. 190 (25 August 1835). At this date Romani had held the editorship of this paper for a year and had retired almost completely from the writing of librettos.

Ferretti wrote the words for Rossini's *Cenerentola* and *Matilde di Shabran*, and many texts for Mayr, Mercadante, Pacini, and Luigi Ricci, among others.

Ferretti's sophistication and sharp sense of the interaction of character permitted him to write texts that were notable for their genuinely sympathetic characters. His text for *L'ajo* shows considerable delicacy in handling a subject that could easily be made to appear gross. Compared with the diction of Ferretti's texts those of Tottola or Gilardoni seem crude and banal. The plot of *Il furioso* turns on implausible coincidence, but this failing is easily overlooked in face of the moving character of Cardenio and of the uncommonly satisfying dénouement. With *Tasso*, Ferretti is less successful. Using Don Gherardo as a 'chorus' character who comments on the action before each act is a dubiously literary practice for a libretto. If the overall effect of this work is dimmed by the essentially passive role played by the great poet, it is at least partially redeemed by the emotional power Ferretti generates in two scenes: that of Tasso's reading a portion of *Gerusalemme Liberata* to Eleonora d'Este and that of the leave-taking between Tasso and Eleonora. *Olivo e Pasquale* is a curiously dated comedy of 'humours', but all the charm of the exposition cannot silence the creakings of the plot. For the most part, Ferretti's texts possess a literacy and a delicacy of effect that are rare in the texts set by Donizetti.

GENOINO, GIULIO (b. Frattamaggiore, 13 May 1778; d. Naples, 8 March 1856) Genoino was a monk, but when his Order was suppressed by the French, he became a military chaplain. For a time he was entrusted with the theatrical censorship; thus Genoino is a rare bird indeed, a censor turned librettist, for he wrote the text of *La lettera anonima* for Donizetti.

This libretto, apparently derived from one of Genoino's own plays, is devoid of suspense in word or action. At one time, Genoino enjoyed some favour as a writer of verse (both in Italian and Neapolitan dialect) and of comedies and dramas, all of his plays being relentlessly didactic.[1]

GILARDONI, DOMENICO (b. ?; d. Naples, 1831) Little information about Gilardoni exists except that he lived in Naples and wrote librettos, of which he provided Donizetti with no fewer than eleven: *Otto mesi in du ore* (1827), *Il borgo-mastro di Saardam* (1827), *L'esule di Roma* (1828), *Gianni di Calais* (1828), *Il giovedì grasso* (1828), *Il paria* (1829), *I pazzi*

---

[1] This Genoino is not to be confused with an earlier Giulio (*c.* 1567–1648), a Neapolitan lawyer and agitator who crossed paths with Masaniello.

per progetto (1830), *Il diluvio universale* (1830), *Francesca di Foix* (1831), *La romanziera e l'uomo nero* (1831), and *Fausta* (1832).

It is clear from a letter Bellini wrote a Neapolitan friend that Gilardoni was pursued by bad luck.[1] The quite surprising unevenness of his librettos seems to suggest that he wrote against time, putting words to paper whether he was interested in his subject or not. Although *Otto mesi* and *Il borgomastro* enjoyed some transitory success, it was not due to any skilful handling on the part of the librettist. *Il diluvio universale, I pazzi per progetto, Francesca di Foix* and *La romanziera* each have moments when they come alive, but for the most part they were still-born texts.

Gianni di Calais and *Fausta*—although the former is a comedy and the latter a tragedy on a grand scale—both possess the merits of clear characterization and consistency of mood. For *Gianni*, Gilardoni's words evoke an aura of romantic humour; while for *Fausta* he achieves something of the nervous energy and tension requisite to convincing tragedy. One of the high points of this work is the Emperor's scene when his son is being tried before the Senate. A comparison of the diction between Gilardoni's poor librettos and his better efforts reveals a striking difference. In such a text as *Francesca di Foix*, his lines are apt to be diffuse and abstract; in *Fausta*, on the other hand, his lines are focused and vivid. Next to *Gianni di Calais*, Gilardoni's best work in the comic vein is found in the one-act farce, *Il giovedì grasso*, a text suffused with unforced high spirits; although it is a little too episodic in its working out, it ends with a felicitously worded ensemble.

Gilardoni's best work is to be found in *L'esule di Roma* and *Il paria*. The former is cleanly constructed, the conflict straightforward, but the total effect is rather frigid. He draws the character of the conscience-ridden Murena with deep insight. *Il paria*, however, contains Gilardoni's most solid work. Using a broad canvas he develops the relations of the characters with convincing detail. The complexity of Neala's feelings for Idamore, her love for him and her superstitious fear of his caste, provide a challenge that Gilardoni overcomes brilliantly. If Gilardoni had been able to work consistently on the level he achieved in *Il paria*, he would rank as an outstanding librettist.

[1] Letter of 16 Jan. 1828, published in Bellini, *Epistolario* (ed. L. Cambi), p. 41.

MARINI, GIROLAMO MARIA (b. Recanati, 4 November 1801; d. 25 July 1867) For Donizetti, Marini performed only the thankless task of supplying a new third act to Romani's old libretto of *Adelia*. Marini's 'happy' ending is anything but happy in its invention.[1]

MERELLI, BARTOLOMEO (b. Bergamo, 19 May 1794; d. Milan, 4 April 1879) Before he became first a theatrical agent and later a famous, even a notorious, impresario, Merelli wrote a number of librettos between 1818 and 1822: two for Mayr, four for Vaccai, and one for Morlacchi. Besides these, he wrote for Donizetti the texts to: *Enrico di Borgogna* (1818), *Una follia* (1818), *Le nozze in villa* (1819), *I piccioli virtuosi ambulanti* (1819), and *Zoraide di Granata* (1822). Merelli's libretto for *Enrico di Borgogna* is pure fustian and the wording is almost unbelievably crude. It would be difficult to argue that Donizetti ever set worse librettos than those provided him by Merelli. The only one of the surviving texts with any glimmer of merit is *Le nozze in villa*. There are several amusing situations, one of them a surprising anticipation of the scene of Beckmesser's serenade.

ROMANI, FELICE (b. Genoa, 31 January 1788; d. Moneglia, 23 January 1865) The most famous librettist of his time, Romani wrote nearly a hundred texts, some of which were set many times. His period of greatest activity as a librettist falls between 1813 and 1834, when he turned to journalism. Although Romani's superiority, both as a poet and as a fashioner of plots, was early acknowledged, he owes his greatest fame to the period of his collaboration with Bellini, starting with *Il pirata* (1827). For Donizetti, Romani wrote nine librettos: *Chiara e Serafina* (1822), *Alina, regina di Golconda* (1828), *Anna Bolena* (1830), *Ugo, conte di Parigi* (1832), *L'elisir d'amore* (1832), *Parisina* (1833), *Lucrezia Borgia* (1833), *Rosmunda d'Inghilterra* (1834), and *Adelia* (1841).[2]

---

[1] An account of Marini's activities as critic for the Roman periodical *Rivista teatrale* and archivist of the Accademia S. Cecilia, may be found in Giuseppe Radiciotti, *Teatro, musica e musicisti in Recanati* (Recanati, 1904), p. 15n.

Of Marini's other librettos, the most important is that to Nicolai's *Il templario* (1840), a setting of *Ivanhoe*. Of some interest to the student of Donizetti is the fact that Marini wrote a *Pia dei Tolomei* for Luigi Orsini.

[2] Actually the libretto to *Adelia* dates back at least to 1817, when it was set by Carafa.

Three of Romani's texts for Donizetti do nothing to justify the librettist's high reputation. Of these, *Chiara e Serafina* and *Adelia* date from the first phase of his career. *Ugo* was so maltreated by the censors that Romani considered withholding his name from the text. The censors cannot be blamed for all the shortcomings of *Ugo*; there is a note of morbidity and a crudeness of rhetoric never found in Romani's best work.

Anna Bolena, *L'elisir*, and *Lucrezia Borgia* have books that would add lustre to any librettist's reputation. The action of *Anna* builds to a moving climax, but the influence of the unhappy queen upon those who come in contact with her endows the drama with a cyclical force as well. Romani handles dramatic situations with ease and power; consider that of the encounter between Anna and Seymour, where each episode increases the tension and poignancy of the situation, and both characters are sympathetic to the audience. Romani's superior grasp of characterization stands out even more clearly in his book to *L'elisir*. Although he is adapting his work from Scribe's book for Auber's *Le philtre*, Romani improves upon the original. Scribe's naïve Guillaume is no more than a pale sketch of Nemorino (literally, 'Little Nobody'). Romani balances farce and romance with innate good taste, especially in the duet between Adina and Dulcamara where the old charlatan admits the superiority of Adina's charms to his elixir. The libretto of *Lucrezia Borgia* is a smooth condensation of Hugo's play and remarkably faithful to it. For it, Romani uses a far larger cast of characters than was then customary. He welds the varied details of the complicated plot into a drama that moves with irresistible momentum.

Romani has written that he tried to be neither a classicist nor a romanticist; he merely pursued the beautiful wherever it might lead him. However that might be, his greatest virtue as a librettist was his ability to reveal a character's innermost feelings, expressing them in words that seem inevitable. Percy's *Vivi tu te ne scongiuro* and Nemorino's *Una furtiva lagrima* are merely the first examples of Romani's achievement in this line that come to mind.

ROSSI, GAETANO (b. Verona, 18 May 1774; d. Verona, 25 January 1855) The most prolific librettist of his time, Rossi wrote more than a hundred texts between 1799 and when he was incapacitated by illness shortly before his death. Although he was at one time associated with the Fenice, his works were brought out at many theatres. He supplied Rossini with two famous texts: *Tancredi* (1813) and *Semiramide* (1823). For Donizetti, he wrote two librettos: *Maria Padilla* (1841) and *Linda di Chamounix* (1842).

Throughout his long career, Rossi laboured to keep abreast of changing fashions in operatic subjects, but his treatment of them was marred by his greater concern for striking situations than for dramatic plausibility or unity of plot. His diction was even more conventionally 'poetic' than Cammarano's.

Maria Padilla is a hotch-potch of melodramatic devices, whose cumulative force is substantially weakened by Rossi's failure to make his heroine even remotely sympathetic. The text to *Linda di Chamounix* is a hotch-potch of another sort. Structurally, the second act is a disaster that piles coincidence on coincidence. Rossi's characters seem more like walking tear-ducts than real people, with the exception of the lecherous old Marchese, whose cynical hedonism blows like a breath of fresh air among the hothouse stereotypes.

ROYER, ALPHONSE (b. Paris, 10 September 1803; d. Paris, 11 April 1875) Before his distinguished career as a director of Parisian theatres (Odéon, 1853–56; Opéra, 1856–62) and his tenure as Inspecteur Général des Beaux-Arts, Royer and his chief collaborator, Gustave Vaëz, served Donizetti in a variety of ways. First, they translated *Lucia* for the Théâtre de la Renaissance. After this success, Joly, the director of the Renaissance, signed a contract on 5 January 1840, with Royer, Vaëz, and Donizetti for *L'ange de Nisida*. This opera was to be completed by 1 February 1840, but some time during the month of January the theatre came to such straits that the production of operas was abandoned. Left with the completed score on their hands, the collaborators re-arranged the work as *La favorite*. It is impossible to tell from Donizetti's autograph how much of the work was written by Royer and how much by Vaëz. Gautier felt this 'poem is rapid, well shaped, and offers two or three fine situations.'[1] It is possible to agree with this

[1] Théophile Gautier, *L'art dramatique en France depuis vingt-cinq ans*, entry for 7 December 1840.

of fifty years. He wrote three texts for Donizetti: the French version of *Poliuto*, *Les martyrs* (1839–40), *Le duc d'Albe* (1839) (with Duveyrier's assistance), and *Dom Sébastien* (1843).

Scribe's verse for *Les martyrs* was damned by a real poet, Gautier, as 'without rhythm, without rhyme, without caesura, without number; in a word, the most anti-musical versification one can imagine.'[1] Although Scribe's lines are heavy and prosaic, they usually define a dramatic situation in clear, if rather impersonal, terms. Scribe's speciality was to write scenes allowing for huge spectacles. The weakest of Scribe's texts for Donizetti is undoubtedly that for *Dom Sébastien*. The action is diffuse and spread among too many half-realized characters. The spectacular element is occasionally in dubious taste (the mock-funeral) or resistant to musical setting (the shooting of Zaïde and Sébastien as they slide down a rope from their prison).

TOTTOLA, ANDREA LEONE (dates unknown) Tottola is often linked with Schmidt as an example of the wretched librettists active in Naples during the early years of the nineteenth century. If to the student of Donizetti, Tottola seems a more inept librettist than Schmidt, it is because Tottola wrote many more texts for Donizetti. These include: *La zingara* (1822), *Alfredo il grande* (1823), *Il fortunato inganno* (1823), *Elisabetta al castello di Kenilworth* (1829), and *Imelda de' Lambertazzi* (1830). On his own, Donizetti set a libretto that Tottola had written for Carafa, *Gabriella di Vergy*.

It is all too easy to point out Tottola's ineptitudes, such as his wild non-history in *Alfredo il Grande* or his butchery of Scott's *Kenilworth*. His texts are full of vacuous lines, such as this lame quatrain from *Alfredo*:

> *Il lasso fianco*
> *Chi vuol posar*
> *Sicuro e franco*
> *Qui può inoltrar.*

(This might be translated: Who hopes to rest/his weary side/with safety blest/may come inside.)

It is an injustice to the poor man not to call attention to the best of his librettos for Donizetti, that of *Il fortunato inganno*.

---

[1] Gautier, *L'art dramatique*, entry for 15 April 1840.

Tottola's best is far from unblemished, and the two long acts need drastic pruning. There are some mildly diverting situations, particularly those that satirize the foibles of opera singers. On the strength of *Il fortunato inganno*, it would seem that farce was Tottola's forte. Certainly, it was not tragedy.

VAËZ, GUSTAVE (pseud. for VAN NIEWENHUYSEN), JEAN NICHOLAS GUSTAVE (1812–62) Besides his collaboration with Royer on the French version of *Lucia* and the libretto of *La favorite*, Vaëz, on his own, wrote the book for the lively farce, *Rita ou Le mari battu*. Vaëz demonstrates an aptitude for rustic humour and laughable situations. The scene in which the two men resort to games of chance and cheat in their anxiety to lose the wife neither of them wants is very funny indeed. *Rita* is a charming, completely unpretentious opéra-comique.

SYNOPSES

IL PIGMALIONE, opera in 1 act.
First performed: Bergamo (Teatro Donizetti), 13 October 1960.
Librettist: Unknown.
Source: Unknown, but follows Ovid's *Metamorphoses*, Book X.
Synopsis:
  Pigmalione, King of Crete (tenor), has renounced women and turned sculptor in order to create his ideal of feminine beauty. He becomes so enamoured of his statue that he can no longer raise his chisel to it for fear of hurting it. In torment, he prays to Venus, through whose intercession Galatea (soprano) is brought to life and reciprocates Pigmalione's love.

OLIMPIADE
  Nothing is known of this work, but one duet which is in the Museo Donizettiano.

L'IRA D'ACHILLE, opera in 1 act.
First performed: No recorded performance.
Librettist: Unknown.[1]
Source: Immediate source unknown, but drawn from *Iliad*, Book I.

[1] A *L'ira d'Achille*, music by Niccolini, text by Romani, was produced at La Scala, 26 December 1814. Another work of the same name, music by Basili, was given at Venice, about 1817.

Synopsis:

As prizes for their valour, Achille (tenor) has been awarded Briseide (soprano), and Agamennone (baritone) has taken Criseide (soprano). When Agamennone is persuaded by Calcante (bass), Criseide's father, to give up his prize, he insists upon Briseide being her replacement. Furious, Achille refuses, but forced to accede to the Greek leader's request, he says farewell to Briseide.[1]

ENRICO DI BORGOGNA, opera semiseria in 2 acts.
First performed: Venice (Teatro S. Luca), 14 November 1818.
Librettist: Bartolomeo Merelli.
Source: Unidentified.
Synopsis:

In exile, Enrico (contralto) learns that his father's murderer has died and that Guido (bass), the usurper's son, has succeeded to the dukedom. Enrico sets off to regain his rights and marry his beloved Elisa (soprano), whom Guido plots to wed. The ceremony is halted by Enrico's timely arrival. Later, he leads a successful assault on the castle and wins Elisa.

UNA FOLLIA, farce in 1 act.
First performed: Venice (Teatro S. Luca), 15 December 1818.
Librettist: Bartolomeo Merelli.
No copy of this work is known.[2]

LE NOZZE IN VILLA, opera buffa in 2 acts.
First performed: Mantua, Carnival 1820–21.
Librettist: Bartolomeo Merelli.
Source: Unidentified.
Synopsis:

The plot turns on the wooing of Sabina (soprano) by two suitors: Claudio (tenor), a wealthy landlord, and Trifoglio (buffo), the village school teacher, whose suit is favoured by her father, Petronio (bass). After many misunderstandings, Trifoglio renounces his claims to Sabina when he learns her dowry

---

[1] The final leaves of the autograph score (in the Paris Conservatory Library) seem to be missing.

[2] Most critics accept Zavadini's assumption that this opera was performed under an alternate title: *Il ritratto parlante*. Manferrari, in his unreliable *Dizionario delle opere Melodrammatiche* (vol. I, pp. 321–55), claims that *Una follia* and *Il ritratto parlante* are two separate works and that the latter was performed in Venice during the spring of 1818. I have seen no evidence to confirm this assertion.

consists of fifty-eight wigs, one aerostatic globe, six dozen pairs of spectacles and no money at all. Claudio wins Sabina's hand when he accepts her without a dowry.

I PICCIOLI VIRTUOSI AMBULANTI, farce in 1 act.
First performed: Bergamo (Lezioni Caritatevoli), September 1819.
Librettist: Bartolomeo Merelli.
Source: Unidentified.
Synopsis:
The plot provides a comic frame for the annual term-end concert of the pupils at Mayr's school.

IL FALEGNAME DI LIVONIA, opera buffa in 2 acts.
First performed: Venice (Teatro S. Samuele), 26 December 1819.
Librettist: Marchese Gherardo Bevilacqua Aldovrandini.
Source: comedy by Alexandre Duval.[1]
Synopsis:
A young carpenter (*falegname*) named Carlo (tenor) loves Annetta (soprano), who is the young friend of Mme Fritz (mezzo), an innkeeper in the province of Livonia. Carlo defends Annetta when a usurer, Firmann (baritone), tries to cheat her out of a bracelet. This altercation is halted by the arrival of two impressive strangers, later revealed to be Czar Pietro (bass) and his wife, Caterina (soprano), who are searching for the Czarina's missing nephew. Pietro questions Carlo about his parentage, but when the youth fails to give satisfactory answers, he is turned over to a bumbling magistrate (buffo). Carlo is about to be led away when Mme Fritz produces an old letter found with the infant Carlo, revealing him to be the son of Carlo Stravonski, the Czarina's brother. Carlo is released, recognized by his aunt, ennobled by his uncle, and granted permission to marry Annetta. The Imperial couple are cheered by the populace for their generosity.

ZORAIDE DI GRANATA, opera seria in 2 acts.
First performed: Rome (Teatro Argentina), 28 January 1822.
Librettist: Bartolomeo Merelli, revisions by Jacopo Ferretti.

[1] It is possible that Bevilacqua adapted a handier source: Romani's libretto for Pacini's *Il falegname di Livonia* (La Scala, 12 April 1819). He had already adapted a Romani libretto the previous year for Rossini, turning *Il califfo e la schiava* into *Adina*.

Source: prose romance by Florian Gonzales.[1]

Synopsis:

Almuzir (tenor) has murdered the King of Granada and usurped his throne; he hopes to secure his position by marrying the late king's daughter Zoraide (soprano), but she loves Abenamet (contralto), leader of the Abencerrages. Almuzir, to rid himself of his rival, makes him leader of the Moorish army, charging him to bring back a banner. Since Almuzir has already arranged for the banner to be seized by the Spaniards, he arrests Abenamet for treason when he returns without it. Zoraide determines to marry Almuzir to save Abenamet's life. Guessing the price of his freedom, Abenamet comes to Zoraide and accuses her of infidelity. When the lovers are found together, Zoraide is arraigned for faithlessness to the king, a capital offence, and she will be executed unless a champion comes forward to defend her. Appearing as an unknown knight, Abenamet wins the combat and forces a confession from Almuzir. Enraged by the usurper's perfidy, the populace turn against him, but Abenamet defends the king, who is so moved by this noble behaviour that he bestows Zoraide's hand upon Abenamet.

LA ZINGARA, opera semiseria in 2 acts.
First performed: Naples (Teatro Nuovo), 12 May 1822.
Librettist: Andrea Leone Tottola.
Source: two-act intermezzo by Rinaldo di Capua (c. 1735).
Synopsis:

The gypsy Argilla (mezzo) is the focal character. She brings the lover Fernando (tenor) and Inès (soprano) together; she foils a plot of Ranuccio (baritone) to assassinate the Duke of Alziras (tenor); she reunites the Duke with his brother Fernando; she secures the freedom of Don Sebastiano (baritone), unjustly imprisoned by Ranuccio; she tricks a foolish servant, Pappacione (buffo), into exploring an old cistern in search of gold; and at the end Argilla turns out to be Don Sebastiano's long-lost daughter.

LA LETTERA ANONIMA, farce in 1 act.
First performed: Naples (Teatro del Fondo), 29 June 1822.
Librettist: Giulio Genoino.

[1] Already used for an opera by Giuseppe Niccolini (text by Romanelli), entitled *Abenamet e Zoraide* (La Scala, 26 December 1805).

Source: probably a farce by Genoino himself.
Synopsis:

Melita (mezzo), writes an anonymous letter to the Countess (soprano), hinting at the Count's infidelity. By chance the letter is read by Rosina (soprano), who interprets it to mean that her fiancé, Filinto (tenor), has been untrue. Before Melita's trouble-making is exposed, a servant, Lauretta (soprano) is accused of having written the letter, but she is exonerated when she proves she can neither read nor write. When Melita finally confesses, Rosina and Filinto are reconciled, and the Countess forgives both Melita and her husband.

CHIARA E SERAFINA, opera semiseria in 2 acts.
First performed: Milan (La Scala), 26 October 1822.
Librettist: Felice Romani.
Source: René Charles Guilbert de Pixérécourt's *La cisterne*.
Synopsis:

Don Alvaro (bass), father of Chiara and Serafina (both sopranos), and Chiara are captured by Algerian pirates. At the Spanish court, Don Fernando (bass), Alvaro's secret enemy, explains this absence as treason, hoping to become Serafina's guardian and to gain control of her wealth. Serafina has fallen in love with Don Ramiro, a Majorcan gallant. In an attempt to dispose of Ramiro's suit, Ferdinando has his rascally servant, Picaro (baritone), pretend to be Alvaro, secretly returned after a ten-years absence and opposed to the match. Meanwhile, Alvaro's faithful friends arrange his release from slavery. En route to Spain, he is driven by a sudden storm to Majorca, where he arrives in time to save Serafina from Fernando's schemes.

ALFREDO IL GRANDE, opera seria in 2 acts.
First performed: Naples (Teatro S. Carlo), 2 July 1823.
Librettist: Andrea Leone Tottola.
Source: Unidentified.
Synopsis:[1]

Queen Amalia (soprano) and the general Edoardo (bass) come in disguise to Somerset in search of Alfredo (tenor).

---

[1] This gallimaufry of English history disregards the famous oatcake. The setting is described as the island of Athelney, 'ringed with pleasant hills overlooking a lake', while 'rustic houses . . . are scattered over the mountain and plain'.

Guglielmo (tenor), a loyal shepherd, offers shelter, unaware the fugitives are being tracked by the Danish general, improbably named Atkins (bass). Amalia is delighted to discover that Guglielmo's hut is Alfredo's hiding-place. In disguise, Atkins informs Alfredo his refuge is known to his enemies. At this news Guglielmo volunteers to lead them to safety. A Danish force surprises the royal refugees,[1] but Guglielmo opportunely arrives with a band of armed shepherds. His foes outnumbered and at his mercy, Alfredo generously offers to meet them in fair fight on open ground. A large force gathers around Alfredo, who urges them on to victory. After the defeat of the Danes, Atkins and a few survivors happen upon the Queen, whom they sieze as hostage. The intrepid Amalia draws a dagger and holds off the Danes until the arrival of the English, who free the Queen. All hail Alfredo as the saviour of England.

IL FORTUNATO INGANNO, opera buffa in 2 acts.
First performed: Naples (Teatro Nuovo), 3 September 1823.
Librettist: Andrea Leone Tottola.
Source: Unidentified.
Synopsis:
  Lattanzio Latrughelli (buffo) manages a troupe of singers, headed by his wife, Aurelia (soprano). She practises a series of deceptions on Colonel Franceschetti (baritone), trying to over-come his scruples against people of the theatre so that he will permit his nephew Edoardo (tenor) to marry Aurelia's niece (soprano), a junior member of the troupe. At length, Aurelia, who has pretended to be a countess, routs the Colonel, who gives his consent to the young couple's wedding.

L'AJO NELL'IMBARAZZO (sometimes given as *Don Gregorio*), opera buffa in 2 acts.
First performed: Rome (Teatro Valle), 4 February 1824.
Librettist: Jacopo Ferretti.
Source: comedy by Giovanni Giraud.[2]
Synopsis:
  The puritanical Don Giulio (baritone) has brought up his

---

[1] At this point the libretto directs Alfredo and Amalia to enter 'on all fours' —surely the most undignified operatic entrance on record!
[2] In the fifteen years before this opera was written, at least four others (with music by Guarnaccia, Pilotti, Celli, and Mosca) had been derived from Giraud's play. Ferretti's text was written for Donizetti.

two sons so strictly that they know nothing of diversions, especially women. This rigorous but limited education has been in the hands of Don Gregorio (buffo), as tutor (*ajo*), but the system soon goes askew. Don Giulio's younger son, the Marchesino Pippetto (bass) falls in love with the only woman he has ever seen, the old housekeeper, Leonarda (mezzo), who is senile and takes him seriously. The elder son, Enrico (tenor), has secretly married a charming young neighbour, Gilda (soprano), and their union is already blessed by an infant son, Bernardino. Through Gilda's skilful manoeuvres, Don Giulio is brought to see the folly of his educational system and blesses the marriage of his heir.

EMILIA DI LIVERPOOL (sometimes given as *L'eremetaggio di Liverpool*), opera semiseria in 2 acts.
First performed: Naples (Teatro Nuovo), 28 July 1824.
Revised version: Naples (Teatro Nuovo), Lent, 1828.
Librettist: Unknown, revised by Giuseppe Checcherini.
Source: Scatizzi's melodrama, *Emilia di Liverpool*.[1]
Synopsis (of the revised version):
    Emilia (soprano) grew up in Naples where she had the bad luck to be seduced, a misfortune that caused her mother's death; now Emilia does penance for her unsavoury past by caring for the poor at a hospice in the mountains near Liverpool. There one day in a furious storm a carriage overturns and a tattered stranger helps the three passengers to safety. The passengers are Don Asdrubale (buffo), a Neapolitan roué searching for his long-missing fiancée, his niece Bettina (soprano), and Colonel Villars (tenor), who later turns out to be Emilia's betrayer, but who now amuses himself by flirting with Bettina. The tattered stranger, lately escaped from the Barbary pirates, is Claudio, who recognizes in Emilia the daughter he has dreamed of punishing for years. When Villars is revealed as Emilia's seducer, Claudio challenges him to a duel. Villars confesses the wrong he has done and resolves to make Emilia an honest woman. Overjoyed, Claudio forgives Emilia.[2]

[1] An earlier opera on the same subject, music by Vittorio Trento, was performed in Naples, 1817.
[2] The original version has substantially the same plot, but is far more prolix. Some characters' names are changed: Villars was Federico; Don Asdrubale, Don Romualdo.

ALAHOR DI GRANATA, opera seria in 2 acts.
First performed: Palermo (Teatro Carolino), 7 January 1826.
Librettist: M.A.[1]
Source: Unidentified, but probably ultimately derived from *Guerras civiles de Grenada* by Ginès Perez de Hita.
Synopsis:

The late chief of the Zegri faction, Aly, has slain all the family of the leader of the rival Abencerrages, but Alahor (baritone) and Zobeida (soprano). Alahor has fled into exile, but Zobeida remains because she loves Muley-Hassem (contralto), who succeeded his brother Aly to the throne. The honourable peace Hassem has arranged with the Spanish foe seems an act of betrayal to the fiercely partisan Zegris. Their leader, Alamor (tenor) conspires to overthrow Hassem. Returned in disguise to avenge his father's murder, Alahor joins the conspiracy and volunteers to slay Hassem. Hassem learns of the plot and forgives Alahor, who defends him against an attack led by Alamor. The attack fails and Alamor is led away. Zobeida rejoices at the reunion of her brother and her beloved Hassem.

IL CASTELLO DEGLI INVALIDI, purported to be a one-act farce.
First performed: Palermo (Teatro Carolino), early 1826?
Librettist: Unknown.
Source: Unidentified.

Definitive evidence that Donizetti wrote this opera or that it was performed has yet to be brought forward. No score or libretto is known to exist.[2]

ELVIDA, opera seria in 1 act.
First performed: Naples (Teatro S. Carlo), 6 July 1826.

[1] These same initials were affixed to the libretto of *Don Pasquale*, as Ruffini refused to put his name to it. It might be possible these initials stand for M(aestro) A(nonimo), or something of the kind, much as N.N. is the traditional sign for an unnamed singer.

[2] For the most plausible arguments against the existence of this opera, see Ottavio Tiby, *Una stagione lirica di 125 anni fa* (Rome, 1951), p. 33. The strongest argument for the existence of this opera rests upon Donizetti's having named it in a list of his operas, included in a letter to Toto, 24 October 1841 (Z. No. 378, p. 558) and specifically identifying it as a farce given at Palermo.

There is at least one other score of the same name. *Il castello degli invalidi* by Giacomo Cordella (1786–1846) was given in Naples (Teatro del Fondo) in 1823.

Librettist: Giovanni Schmidt.

Source: Undetermined.

Synopsis:

Elvida (soprano), a Spanish noblewoman captured by the Moorish chieftain Amur (bass), spurns the suit of Zeidar (contralto), because she is faithful to her fiancé, the Spanish prince Alfonso (tenor). Alfonso knocks down the walls of Amur's stronghold with catapults, causing the chieftain to hide Elvida in a cave. There, Alfonso's sudden arrival provokes Amur to try to stab Elvida, but Zeidar knocks the dagger out of his father's hand. The Spaniards seize Amur and drag him away, followed by Zeidar, who hopes to save his father. Elvida and Alfonso are reunited.

GABRIELLA DI VERGY, opera seria in 2 acts.

First performed: Naples (Teatro S. Carlo), 29 November 1869.[1]

Librettist: Andrea Leone Tottola.[2]

Source: du Belloy's *Gabrielle de Vergy* (1770).

Synopsis:

Gabriella (soprano) has married Fayel, Count of Vermand (tenor), believing her beloved Raoul (contralto) has died on the Crusades. An unknown knight comes to Fayel's castle to announce the arrival of the King of France (bass). Gabriella is overcome to recognize the stranger as Raoul, who reproaches her for her infidelity. When the King appears he proposes to reward Raoul, for having saved his life, by marrying him to Fayel's sister, Almeide (soprano). Raoul's silent shock at this proposal stings Fayel's touchy pride. Gabriella sends secretly for Raoul, but their interview is overheard by Almeide, who summons Fayel. He rushes in to find Raoul kneeling at Gabriella's feet. Furious, he challenges Raoul to a duel and banishes Gabriella to a dungeon. There, Fayel presents her with an urn

---

[1] This was a *rifacimento* by other hands than Donizetti's. Many changes were made, among them recasting the contralto role of Raoul for baritone.

[2] Tottola's text was written for Carafa, whose opera was given in Naples (Teatro del Fondo), 3 July 1816. For his version, Donizetti made a few modifications of Tottola's text. In 1828 a *Gabriella di Vergy* by Mercadante was produced. The text for this work was by Antonio Profumo, who cribbed liberally from Tottola. Later, Mercadante's text was revised by Emanuele Bidera, who had written the books for Donizetti's *Gemma di Vergy* (not to be confused with *Gabriella*) and *Marino Faliero*.

containing the still-warm heart of Raoul. Gabriella dies of grief and horror.

LA BELLA PRIGIONIERA, farce in 1 act (incomplete).
   Nothing is known of this work but two excerpts that survive in manuscript: a soprano-tenor duet and a soprano-bass duet.[1]

OLIVO E PASQUALE, opera buffa in 2 acts.
First performed: Rome (Teatro Valle), 7 January 1827.
Librettist: Jacopo Ferretti.
Source: Sografi's comedy, *Olivo e Pasquale.*[2]
Synopsis:
   Olivo and Pasquale (both basses) are brothers, merchants in Lisbon; the former is rash and intemperate, the latter, easy-going. Olivo's daughter, Isabella (soprano), loves a young apprentice, Camillo (contralto), but her father is anxious she marry a wealthy merchant from Cadiz, Le Bross (tenor). Isabella confesses to Le Bross she loves someone else, but when asked to identify him, she is too shy to tell the truth and says it is Columella (buffo), a vain and foolish old man. Olivo flies into such a rage when he learns that Isabella opposes his wishes that the shocked Le Bross becomes Isabella's active ally and promises to help her marry Camillo. When Olivo refuses to heed the threat that unless he consent to the marriage by five o'clock the lovers will kill themselves, the clock strikes and shots are heard. Pasquale faints, and Olivo declares he would rather Isabella wed Camillo than kill herself. The smiling couple appear at the door to be embraced by the much-relieved Olivo.

OTTO MESI IN DUE ORI (also given as *Gli esiliati in Siberia*), opera romantica in 3 acts.
First performed: Naples (Teatro Nuovo), 13 May 1827.
Librettist: Domenico Gilardoni, revisions by Antonino Alcozer.
Source: de Pixérécourt's play, *La fille de l'exilé ou Huit mois en deux heures*, in turn derived from Sophie Cottin's romance, *Elisabeth ou Les exilés en Sibérie.*

[1] These excerpts, in the Museo Donizettiano, are written out with piano accompaniment. As Donizetti characteristically composed first with a sketch of the orchestral parts, it is possible that he may have intended this farce for private performance, perhaps during one of the periods when the public theatres were closed.
[2] Cametti points out that Ferretti drew the mock-suicide motif from another play by Sografi, *Il più bel giorno della Westfalia.*

Synopsis:

The parents of Elisabetta (soprano) have been unjustly exiled to Siberia. Convinced of her father's innocence, she undergoes all sorts of hardships, including the river Kama in flood and a Tartar horde, before she penetrates the walls of the Kremlin and persuades the Czar that the charges against her father are false.

IL BORGOMASTRO DI SAARDAM, opera buffa in 2 acts.
First performed: Naples (Teatro Nuovo), 19 August 1827.
Librettist: Domenico Gilardoni.
Source: play by Mélesville-Merle-de Boirie (1818).[1]
Synopsis:

Under an assumed name, Czar Pietro (bass) works as a shipwright in the yards at Saardam, where his constant companion is Pietro Flimann (tenor), a deserter from the army turned carpenter. Flimann loves the Mayor's daughter Marietta (soprano), but in his humble position he has small hopes of winning her, even though the disguised Czar has promised his help. The Burgomaster (buffo) has heard a rumour that the Czar works in the shipyard in disguise; he holds an interrogation but succeeds only in getting identical, evasive answers from Pietro and Flimann. Wambert (bass) assumes that Flimann is the true Czar, but after an argument with Pietro, suddenly finds himself with *two* Czars on his hands. The problem is resolved when news of a revolt comes from Russia, making it imperative for the true Czar to resume his throne. Before Pietro leaves Saardam he appoints Flimann to high rank thereby removing the obstacles to his marriage to Marietta.

LE CONVENIENZE ED INCONVENIENZE TEATRALI, farce in 1 act (later expanded to 2).
First performed: Naples (Teatro Nuovo), 21 November 1827.
Librettist: Gaetano Donizetti.
Source: two comedies by Sografi: *Le convenienze teatrali* and *Le inconvenienze teatrali*.[2]
Synopsis (of the original version):

At a rehearsal in a provincial opera house, Luigia, the seconda donna, complains of the insignificance of her role and

---

[1] Lortzing's *Zar und Zimmermann* is the best-known treatment of this subject.
[2] In 1803, Pietro Guglielmo the younger, known as Guglielmini, wrote an opera on this subject.

468

wishes her mother would come to her support. The impresario
(bass) announces that the rehearsal will resume at five; this is
greeted by a storm of excuses as to why the cast cannot attend.
Into this disagreement bursts Mamm' Agata (baritone),[1]
Luigia's mother, ready to do battle to protect her daughter's
interests. She insists Luigia should be given a rondo to sing and
gives the composer explicit instructions how to orchestrate it.
This effrontery is too much for Proclo (bass), the bass of the
company and the prima donna's father, who boasts extrava-
gantly of his daughter's vocal prowess and of her many admirers.
Mamm' Agata now insists that *her* daughter be given a duet to
sing with the prima donna; when Corilla, the prima donna,
protests, Mamm' Agata rudely reminds her that not so long ago
she was a chorus singer in Milan. Soon the singer and the
virago are threatening each other with physical violence. When
Corilla storms out, vowing never to return, Mamm' Agata
assures the impresario that she is perfectly capable of singing
the leading role. She offers a sample of her singing, and when
the composer reproaches her with being off-pitch, she blandly
replies that the prompter threw her off. Now that Mamm'
Agata has joined the cast, a new rehearsal is called. Everyone,
but Agata, foresees a great fiasco.

L'ESULE DI ROMA (also given as *Settimio il proscritto*), opera
   seria in 2 acts.
First performed: Naples (Teatro S. Carlo), 1 January 1828.
Librettist: Domenico Gilardoni.
Source: Unidentified.
Synopsis:
   Settimio (tenor) who has been banished by Tiberius, braves
death by returning secretly to Rome to see his beloved Argelia
(soprano). Her father, Murena (bass), has caused Settimio's
exile by falsely accusing him of treason; Murena's conscience is
troubled by the knowledge that Settimio possesses clear proof
that the charge is false. Though able to spare his own life by
revealing Murena's treachery, Settimio remains silent because
of Argelia. Settimio's noble behaviour plunges Murena into
such depths of remorse that he is driven to confess his guilt.

[1] The idea for this transvestite role may well have been suggested by Tamburini's famous exploit of singing the part of Elisa in Mercadante's *Elisa e
Claudio*. See Sutherland Edwards, *History of the Opera*, vol. 2, p. 272, for an
account of this remarkable *tour de force*.

ALINA, REGINA DI GOLCONDA, opera buffa in 2 acts.
First performed: Genoa (Teatro Carlo Felice), 12 May 1828.
Librettist: Felice Romani.
Source: Chevalier de Bouffler's romance, *La reine de Golconde*.[1]
Synopsis:

Alina (soprano), the Queen of Golconda, is urged by her people to choose a husband, an honour that Seide (tenor), a young prince, hopes to win. He tries to force the issue, but a sound of cannonading announces the arrival of the French ambassador Volmar (baritone) and his aide, Belfiore (buffo), who are in reality the long-lost husbands of Alina and her maid, Fiorina (soprano). The women disguised as slaves visit their husbands, an interview observed by the jealous Seide, who tells the people that Alina plans to betray them to the French. When Volmar comes to arrange an alliance, Seide claims that only a king can sign such a pact and insists that Alina choose one of her subjects. Seide stirs the people to revolt, but the French troops form a protective ring about Alina.

With the help of a sleeping potion, Alina and Fiorina arrange an elaborate fantasy for Volmar and Belfiore. First, Alina appears to her husband in a reconstruction of the Provençal setting where first they met; then Fiorina deceives Belfiore into believing he is back in their French farmhouse. This illusion is interrupted by shouting, as the enraged Seide seizes Alina and drags her to prison. Alina renounces the throne, but Seide forbids this move. Led by Volmar, the French attack the palace and free Alina. After Seide has been taken captive, all hail Alina as their queen.

GIANNI DI CALAIS, opera semiseria in 3 acts.
First performed: Naples (Teatro del Fondo), 2 August 1828.
Librettist: Domenico Gilardoni.
Source: romance by C. V. d'Arlincourt.
Synopsis:

Princess Metilde (soprano) and her young son return to her old home, the port of Seelanda. Some years before she had been captured by pirates and later rescued by the freebooter, Gianni

---

[1] A popular subject, its earliest operatic treatment was by Monsigny (1766) to a libretto by Sedaine; in 1776, F. A. Uttini brought out his *Aline* in Stockholm, to a Swedish adaptation of Sedaine's text; in 1787 J. Schulz set the plot; in 1803 Berton; and in 1804 Boieldieu. A post-Donizettian version is by Gaetano Braga (Naples, 1853).

of Calais (tenor), whom she had married. Metilda is befriended by the Duchess Adelina (soprano), who promises to help her win her father's approval of her marriage. Gianni's ship comes to port, flying a flag with Metilda's portrait on it. Rustano (baritone), a sailor, advises Gianni and accompanies him to the palace, where the King has summoned him to explain the flag with its portrait of the long-missing princess. At the palace, Ruggero (bass) considers Gianni's act an insult, but Ruggero's anger really stems from his long-thwarted design to marry Metilda himself. The King tells Gianni the peers of the realm must give their consent to Metilda's marriage, approval that Ruggero plots to prevent. Rustano exposes Ruggero's treachery, and the King welcomes Gianni, Metilda and their son to his court as his legal heirs.

IL GIOVEDÌ GRASSO (also known as *Il nuovo Pourceaugnac*), farce in 1 act.
First performed: Naples (Teatro del Fondo), autumn 1828.
Librettist: Domenico Gilardoni.
Source: Unidentified.
Synopsis:
    Nina (soprano), the owner of a country estate, loves Teodoro (tenor), but her father (bass) insists she must marry a certain Ernest Roustignac (bass), a gentleman from Paris. M. Piquet (bass) and his wife (soprano) sympathize with Nina's predicament and propose to help her by adapting the plot of Molière's *M. de Pourceaugnac*, in which a city-bred suitor is discomfited by quick-witted country people. When Nina's suitor appears, he is accordingly bamboozled and made to appear the fool until he asks to be released from the match, leaving Nina free to marry Teodoro.

IL PARIA, opera seria in 2 acts.
First performed: Naples (Teatro S. Carlo), 12 January 1829.
Librettist: Domenico Gilardoni.
Source: tragedy by Casimir Delavigne.
Synopsis:
    Neala (soprano) is the daughter of Akebare (bass), the High Priest of the Brahmins; she has fallen in love with Idamore (tenor), but without knowing his true identity. Akebare decrees that his daughter is to marry a military hero. In a sacred grove, Neala and her priestesses encounter an exhausted

471

fugitive, who reveals that he is Zarete (baritone). When Idamore returns victorious from the wars to greet Neala, she tells
him that her father has determined she must marry someone
else. Zarete reveals himself to his son, Idamore, and flies into a
rage when he learns his son loves the daughter of his enemy.
When Idamore next sees Neala, knowing that Akebare has
chosen him as his son-in-law, he tells her he is a pariah's son
and manages to persuade her that the Brahmins' fear and loath-
ing of his caste is only superstition. Hearing the nuptial hymn
for Neala and Idamore, Zarete becomes convinced that his son
has betrayed him by consenting to marry the daughter of the
man who is responsible for the death of Zarete's wife. The
marriage ceremony is interrupted by Zarete. Akebare orders
him killed at once, but Zarete proudly tells him they are born
of the same dust, children of the same god. Both Idamore and
Neala plead the old man's life be spared, but Akebare is
implacable. When Idamore swears he will die with his father,
Akebare orders them both executed; the fanatical priest even
orders the execution of Neala for having loved a pariah. Led to
their fate, the lovers pledge that their love will transcend death.
Zarete dies cursing the Brahmins.

ELISABETTA AL CASTELLO DI KENILWORTH (also given as
Il castello di Kenilworth), opera seria in 3 acts.
First performed: Naples (Teatro S. Carlo), 6 July 1829.
Librettist: Andrea Leone Tottola.
Source: Hugo's *Amy Robsart* (1828) and Scribe's *Leicester ou le
château de Kenilworth*, derived from Scott's *Kenilworth*.
Synopsis:
    The news that Queen Elisabetta[1] will soon come to Kenil-
worth worries Leicester (tenor) because he fears her ire when
she learns he is married to Amelia (soprano). When Warney
(tenor) tries to take advantage of Amelia's ambiguous position,
she spurns him and Warney vows revenge. To Leicester's
relief, Elisabetta arrives without any suspicions of his marriage.
Amelia later confronts Leicester, reproaching him for his shabby
treatment of her and declaring that she would rather die at his
hands than be ignored. Warney enlists Lambourne (bass) to

[1] I have kept the Italian forms of the characters in Donizetti's operas, even
when they refer to figures as well known as Queen Elizabeth I and Henry
VIII because the creatures of Donizetti's librettists often bear little resemblance to the originals.

help him wreak his vengeance on Amelia. Amelia meets Elisabetta unexpectedly in the castle grounds and throws herself at the queen's feet. Elisabetta's suspicions of Leicester's infidelity are confirmed by his obvious agitation at seeing Amelia in her power. After Elisabetta orders Amelia to confinement, she worms from Leicester the confession that he is indeed married to Amelia. Furious, the queen demands revenge; but when Leicester offers himself as her victim, she dismisses him contemptuously. Warney comes to Amelia's cell to administer to her a cup of poison, but Leicester appears in time to save her. When Elisabetta unexpectedly arrives in the cell, she bids Warney and Lambourne be led away and forgives Leicester and Amelia, blessing their marriage. The chorus acclaims Britain's fortune in having such a queen.

I PAZZI PER PROGETTO, farce in i act.
First performed: Naples (Teatro del Fondo), 7 February 1830.
Librettist: Domenico Giraldoni.
Source: Unidentified.
Synopsis:
Cristina (soprano) wins the hand of D'Arlemont (bass) after a variety of misunderstandings revolving around D'Arlemont's distrust of doctors, especially the sententious Don Eustachio (buffo).[1]

IL DILUVIO UNIVERSALE, azione tragica-sacra in 3 acts.
First performed: Naples (Teatro S. Carlo), 28 February 1830.
Librettist: Domenico Giraldoni.
Sources: chiefly Byron's *Heaven and Earth* and Padre Ringhieri's *Il diluvio*.[2]
Synopsis:
For building the ark, Noah (bass) and his sons are persecuted by Cadmo (tenor), even though Sela (soprano), Cadmo's wife, tries to protect them. Ada (soprano), Sela's handmaiden, covets her mistress's place and tells Cadmo his wife is infatuated with Jafet; to Ada's delight, Cadmo casts off his wife and orders the execution of Noah, his sons and Sela, who has taken refuge with them. Noah warns Cadmo; thunder rumbles ominously as Noah describes the coming holocaust. As the marriage of

[1] The chief interest in this dim little work is Don Eustachio, an early study of Dr Dulcamara.
[2] The names of Ada and Sela come from Byron's *Cain*.

Cadmo and Ada is celebrated, Sela bursts in to take farewell of her son. Cadmo offers to take her back if she will renounce Noah's god. Desperate, she renounces Jehovah and falls dead at a great clap of thunder. As a furious storm breaks, all rush out in confusion. In the final tableau of a submerged landscape, a few survivors huddle on the remaining high ground as Noah's ark floats unharmed.

IMELDA DE' LAMBERTAZZI, opera seria in 2 acts.
First performed: Naples (Teatro S. Carlo), 23 August 1830.
Librettist: Andrea Leone Tottola.
Source: Unidentified.
Synopsis:

Although the Lambertazzi and Geremei families of Bologna are feuding,[1] Imelda (soprano) loves Bonifacio Geremei (baritone), but they fall victim to the bad blood between the factions, fomented in large part by Imelda's father, Orlando (tenor), and her brother, Lamberto (tenor). When Bonifacio fails to persuade Imelda to go away with him, he comes to the Lambertazzis' to beg for peace and proposes he marry Imelda to spare the city further bloodshed. Lamberto claims this offer is a dire insult. When Bonifacio tries to see Imelda once more the alarm is roused and Lamberto stabs him. In the midst of the fighting Imelda tries to flee, but she is run through by her dying brother.[2]

ANNA BOLENA, opera seria in 2 acts.
First performed: Milan (Teatro Carcano), 26 December 1830.
Librettist: Felice Romani.
Source: Unidentified, *not* Shakespeare's *Henry VIII*.
Synopsis:

The King's neglect of Anna (soprano) bothers the conscience of Giovanna Seymour (mezzo) for she has yielded to his

[1] In the autograph score, the factions are identified as Guelphs and Ghibellines, but the printed libretto suppresses this identification. This discrepancy proves that Donizetti started to set the text before it was passed by the censors, even though by law a libretto was to be submitted for licensing a full year in advance of its performance.
[2] In his preface to the libretto, Tottola mentions the 'historical truth' of the story and adds the striking detail that Bonifacio was pierced by a poisoned sword, and when Imelda tries to save his life by sucking the venom from the wound, she only succeeds in poisoning herself as well. For all Tottola's lapses as a librettist, he deserves credit for suppressing this scene.

importunities, and his dark hints about Anna's future only increase her distress. Rochefort (bass), Anna's brother, is amazed to see Percy (tenor), Anna's first love, returned from exile, but when the royal hunting party approaches, Percy cannot conceal his agitation at seeing Anna again. The King (bass) plans to use Percy to rid himself of Anna and watches them with grim satisfaction. When Smeton (contralto), Anna's page, tries to return a miniature of Anna, he is forced to hide as Anna hears Percy's confession of love. When Percy draws his sword to kill himself, Smeton rushes forward just as the King appears and orders their arrest. Smeton creates a counter-disturbance and in his flurry, the miniature of Anna falls out of his tunic and lands right at the King's feet. In spite of their protestations of innocence, Anna, Percy, and Smeton are ordered to prison. Giovanna tells Anna that the King will spare her if she will confess. Anna refuses. Hoping to persuade her, Giovanna admits that the King is in love with someone else; but when Anna demands to know the identity of her rival, Giovanna confesses that it is she. Anna's repugnance is overcome by Giovanna's sincere remorse.

At Anna's trial, Smeton lies and admits to being Anna's lover, believing his confession will save her, whereas it seals her fate. When Anna and Percy are summoned before the Council, Giovanna rejects the King's offer of a crown, and pleads for Anna's life. In the Tower, Percy and Rochefort refuse clemency when they learn it does not extend to Anna. In her cell, Anna's mind wanders, recalling her girlhood love for Percy. When cannons announce the King's new marriage, Anna calls on heaven not to curse the new royal couple but to have mercy on them.

GIANNI DI PARIGI, opera comica in 2 acts.
First performed: Milan (La Scala), 10 September 1839.
Librettist: Felice Romani.[1]
Source: Saint-Just's text for Boieldieu's *Jean de Paris* (1812).
Synopsis:

A provincial inn has been rented by the Principessa della Rocca (soprano), daughter of the King of Navarre. To this hostelry comes a page, Oliviero (mezzo-soprano), to arrange a

[1] Romani's libretto was originally written for Morlacchi in 1818. Boieldieu's *Jean de Paris* was sung at Naples in 1816, a time when French operas were uncommon fare on Italian stages.

supper for his master, Gianni of Paris, a rich and honest burgher. The host Pedrigo (bass) explains his establishment is already engaged, but Oliviero insists an inn should be open to all comers. Gianni (tenor) shortly arrives and bids Oliviero not to reveal his true identity nor the purpose of his journey. Gianni is really the Dauphin of France, hoping to discover whether his fiancée, the Principessa, whom he has never seen, is as good and as beautiful as she is reported to be. Gianni secures accommodations by paying Pedrigo double. When the Princess's self-important Seneschal (buffo) arrives, he is outraged by Gianni's presumption. The Principessa drives up and is not at all displeased to find Gianni ensconced in the inn and graciously accepts his invitation to dinner. Later, she reveals to Gianni that she has seen through his ruse and is delighted to marry such an enterprising young man.

FRANCESCA DI FOIX, opera semiseria in 1 act.
First performed: Naples (Teatro S. Carlo), 30 May 1831.
Librettist: Domenico Gilardoni.
Source: a French farce, *Ninette à la cour* by Favert and Saint-Amans.
Synopsis:
The King of France (baritone), the Duke (tenor), and a Page (mezzo) form a conspiracy to teach the jealous Count (bass) a lesson. The Count keeps his lovely young wife in seclusion; afraid to expose her to the temptations of the court, he has spread word that she is too ugly and ill to be seen in public. By a ruse the plotters get the Countess (soprano) to court, where the Count recognizes her, but dares not acknowledge her for fear of being caught out in his lies. But when the King offers the Countess's hand to the victor of a tournament, the Count can control himself no longer. As he confesses his falsehoods, the others moralize on the folly of jealousy.

LA ROMANZIERA E L'UOMO NERO, opera buffa in 1 act.
First performed: Naples (Teatro del Fondo), summer 1831.
Librettist: Domenico Gilardoni.
Source: Unidentified.
Synopsis:
Antonina (soprano), the daughter of the Count (bass) has taken up the fad of extreme romanticism, abetted by the exaggerated Tommaso (bass) and his friends. Finally, Antonina

comes to see the folly of this attitudinizing and swears to her father: *Mai più romanticismo!* (Never again any romanticism!)

FAUSTA, opera seria in 2 acts.
First performed: Naples (Teatro S. Carlo), 12 January 1832.
Librettist: Domenico Gilardoni, completed after his death by Donizetti.
Source: Unidentified.
Synopsis:

Fausta (soprano) is the second wife of the Emperor Costantino (baritone) and loves her stepson, Crispo (tenor). Although she tries to conceal her passion from her husband, she cannot restrain herself from confessing it to Crispo. When Costantino discovers them together, Fausta accuses Crispo, who is speechless, of making advances to her. Costantino orders Crispo into exile. Fausta's father, Massiminiano (bass), leads a conspiracy against Costantino. Crispo overhears their plotting and starts after them sword in hand; suddenly finding himself before his father, he drops his sword. The Emperor's suspicions seem confirmed when Massiminiano hypocritically accuses Crispo oɪ intended parricide. When Crispo is tried before the Senate, Costantino can hardly bring himself to sign the death sentence against his son, although the Senate insists upon it. Massiminiano hurries off to have Crispo executed without delay. When Fausta realizes she is powerless to save Crispo, she drinks poison from her ring. Learning of Massiminiano's conspiracy, Costantino hurries to save his son, but he is too late. Dying, Fausta confesses her guilt to the horrified Emperor.

UGO, CONTE DI PARIGI, opera seria in 2 acts.
First performed: Milan (La Scala), 13 March 1832.
Librettist: Felice Romani.
Source: Unidentified.
Synopsis:

King Louis V (contralto), the last of the Carolingians, has lately ascended the throne. Folco of Anjou (bass) plans to play off the weak king against the powerful soldier, Ugo (tenor),[1] thereby hoping to win the crown for the house of Anjou, but Ugo is loyal to Louis. The King's fiancée, Bianca of Aquitaine (soprano), secretly loves Ugo and despises Louis, but she is stunned to learn that her sister Adelia (soprano) also loves Ugo.

[1] Ugo is better known as Hugues Capet.

Louis sanctions a match between Adelia and Ugo, but this prospect enrages the jealous Bianca, who declares her love for Ugo and insists he confirm it. Horrified, Ugo draws back, but Louis is furious with Ugo's apparent faithlessness and orders his arrest. Bianca comes to Ugo in prison, urging him to lead a revolt against Louis. Ugo refuses, but soon learns his troops have revolted without him. Ugo puts down the rebellion and informs Louis he has no designs on either his throne or his fiancée. Louis returns Ugo's sword and conducts him and Adelia to the chapel. The sounds of the wedding ceremony from the nearby chapel drive Bianca into a frenzy. She drinks poison and dies, bequeathing both her hatred and her love to those about her.

L'ELISIR D'AMORE, opera comica in 2 acts.
First performed: Milan (Teatro Canobbiana), 12 May 1832.
Librettist: Felice Romani.
Source: Scribe's book for Auber's *Le philtre* (1831).
Synopsis:
   Nemorino (tenor) is hopelessly in love with Adina (soprano), but she is put off by his lack of self-assertiveness. The arrival of Sergeant Belcore (baritone) provides a diversion, and the capricious Adina seems in danger of being swept off her feet. Dr Dulcamara (buffo) peddles his cure-all, selling Nemorino a bottle and assuring him he will be irresistible to the ladies— after twenty-four hours. The elixir gives Nemorino a rush of self-confidence, but his spirits are crushed when Adina agrees to marry Belcore that very evening. Thoroughly dejected at the thought that Adina and Belcore will soon be married, Nemorino hopes to buy more elixir, but he is penniless. When Belcore returns chagrined because at the last moment Adina has refused to marry him, Nemorino volunteers for the army, planning to spend the bounty money on elixir. When the village girls hear that Nemorino's rich uncle has died and made him his heir, they crowd around him provocatively, attentions that Nemorino attributes to the elixir he has just drunk. The sight of the girls fawning over Nemorino astonishes Adina, just when she expected to see him downcast. From Dulcamara she learns that Nemorino loves her and has drunk the elixir to win her, but Adina claims she has a more potent art than Dulcamara's to make him hers. Seeing a tear upon her cheek, Nemorino is

moved deeply. After Adina tells him she has bought back his enlistment, she confesses she loves him. The whole village celebrates the happy couple's betrothal.

SANCIA DI CASTIGLIA, opera seria in 2 acts.
First performed: Naples (Teatro S. Carlo), 4 November 1832.
Librettist: Pietro Salatino.
Source: Unidentified.
Synopsis:

Ircano (bass), a Saracen prince, hopes to marry Sancia (soprano), as a reward for his military assistance. The Queen's principal minister, Rodrigo (tenor), is completely opposed to the marriage. Believing her son Garzia (mezzo-soprano) has died in battle, Sancia hopes to quench her grief, in spite of the council's opposition. Garzia returns after a lucky escape from death, and demands the throne. Sancia tells Ircano she wishes only to die, but the Saracen tries to persuade the weak-minded queen to poison her son. Just as Garzia raises the fatal cup prepared by Ircano, Sancia snatches it from his hand and drains it.

IL FURIOSO ALL'ISOLA DI SAN DOMINGO, opera semiseria in 3 acts.
First performed: Rome (Teatro Valle), 2 January 1833.
Librettist: Jacopo Ferretti.
Source: five-act play, *Il furioso nell'isola di San Domingo*.[1]
Synopsis:

Cardenio (baritone), driven mad by his wife's unfaithfulness has come to San Domingo, where he is cared for by Bartolomeo Mergoles (bass) and his daughter, Marcella (soprano). Their servant Kaidamà (buffo) lives in terror of the madman. A tropical hurricane shipwrecks Eleonora (soprano) on the island; for years she has searched for her missing husband. Cardenio tells Kaidamà of his tormenting memories, but Kaidamà, uncomprehending, flees. After the storm, Ferrando (tenor), Cardenio's brother, disembarks; he, too, has long been looking for his brother. Bartolomeo persuades Cardenio to tell of his suffering, but at the climax of his story the madman suddenly sees Eleonora and tries to stab her. Only Ferrando's

---

[1] This play was performed in Rome in 1820 by the Vestris Company, but the subject is ultimately derived from the Cardenio episode in Cervantes' *Don Quixote*, Part I.

swift action prevents a tragedy. Later, Eleonora tries to unburden her conscience to Cardenio, but he is seized with
delusions of blindness. At last he recognizes her and rushes off
to leap into the sea. Ferrando runs after him and saves him.
The shock restores Cardenio's reason, but he believes his
suffering can be resolved only by death. Ferrando brings
Eleonora to him, and she, weeping, confesses her intolerable
guilt. Cardenio hands her a pistol, telling her they will shoot
each other. Eleonora takes the weapon willingly, but when the
others appear carrying torches, in the flickering light Cardenio
sees that Eleonora aims the pistol at her heart. Convinced at
last that Eleonora truly loves him, he welcomes her to his arms.

PARISINA, opera seria in 3 acts.
First performed: Florence (Teatro Pergola), 17 March 1833.
Librettist: Felice Romani.
Source: Byron's *Parisina*, derived from Gibbon's *Antiquities*.
Synopsis:
   Azzo d'Este of Ferrara (baritone) suspects his wife, Parisina
(soprano), who secretly loves Ugo (tenor), his first wife's son.[1]
At one time Parisina and Ugo had planned to marry, but Azzo
had forced her to become his wife instead. When Ugo wins a
tourney, Parisina gives him the victor's crown, and this nearness
to the man she loves troubles her deeply. That night Azzo comes
to her bedchamber, consumed by jealousy, desperately hoping
to have his doubts settled. In her sleep, Parisina murmurs
Ugo's name, and Azzo, enraged, swears vengeance. When Ugo
and Parisina attempt to flee, Azzo intercepts them and orders
Ugo's execution. Parisina dies of grief at the sight of her lover's
corpse.

TORQUATO TASSO, opera seria in 3 acts.
First performed: Rome (Teatro Valle), 9 September 1833.
Librettist: Jacopo Ferretti.
Source: *Tasso* by Giovanni Rosini; for some details, Goethe's
   Tasso.
Synopsis:
   At the court of Ferrara, Tasso (baritone) has two rivals:
Roberto (tenor), who envies his fame; and Don Gherardo

---

[1] Where Byron speaks of Ugo as Azzo's bastard and of Parisina as his wife,
Romani avoids trouble with censors by making Ugo Azzo's son by his late
first wife and by pointedly referring to Parisina as his second wife.

(buffo), who believes Tasso loves Eleonora di Scandiano (mezzo), whom he adores himself. Tasso, however, loves another Eleonora (soprano), the Duke's sister. Don Gherardo steals a poem Tasso has written in praise of Eleonora. Together, the Duchess and Tasso read from his *Gerusalemme*, and she cannot help confessing her love for him. They learn that the Duke has a poem by Tasso that compromises the Duchess. Roberto announces the Duke of Mantua's ambassador is bringing a marriage proposal to the Duchess. The Duke (bass) feigns indifference to these matters and orders them to accompany him to Belriguardo. There, Eleonora, believing Roberto is loyal to Tasso, begs him to arrange a final interview with the poet, but Roberto informs the Duke. When Tasso comes to Eleonora, they are spied on by Gherardo and La Scandiano (herself in love with Tasso) and by Roberto and the Duke. Eleonora begs Tasso to forget her, but he urges they go away together. The Duke comes forward, declaring Tasso has gone mad and orders him confined. After seven years in the madhouse, Tasso has forgotten where he is or why. Courtiers come to announce his freedom and to inform him he is to be crowned poet on the Campidoglio. When Tasso asks for news of the Duchess, he is shocked to learn she died five years before. As his mind wanders and he imagines he sees her again, the courtiers urge him to think of his future glory.

LUCREZIA BORGIA, opera seria in a prologue and 2 acts.[1]
First performed: Milan (La Scala), 26 December 1833.
Librettist: Felice Romani.
Source: Victor Hugo's *Lucrèce Borgia*.
Synopsis:

In Venice, Gennaro (tenor) enjoys the festivities with his friends, especially the loyal Maffio Orsini (contralto). He meets a beautiful woman and is attracted by her tender concern; later he is horrified to learn from Orsini and the others that she is the infamous Lucrezia Borgia (soprano).

In Ferrara, Duke Alfonso (bass), Lucrezia's fourth husband,

---

[1] Also performed as *Alfonso di Ferrara*, *Eustorgia da Romano*, *Giovanna I di Napoli*, *La rinnegata*, *Elisa da Fosco*, *Nizza di Grenata*, and *Dalinda*. These alternative titles were used to avoid the censors' wrath or injuring local sensibilities; usually little more was changed than the names of the characters. The changes in *La rinnegata*, however, were quite extensive; this version was patched together for Paris because of difficulties with Hugo.

hopes to avenge his honour, believing Gennaro to be Lucrezia's lover. Gennaro and his friend have come to Ferrara for adventure, but when he sees Lucrezia's crest, he disfigures the emblem to read ORGIA. Alfonso orders Gennaro seized. In the palazzo Lucrezia demands Alfonso punish the insult. When he produces the culprit, Gennaro, Lucrezia hides her fear and consents to Alfonso's poisoning the young man. When Alfonso leaves, Lucrezia promptly gives Gennaro an antidote and bids him leave Ferrara at once. Before Gennaro can go, Orsini insists he attend a ball at the Princess Negroni's. There, in the midst of the festivities, sinister voices are heard singing of death. Orsini and his friends rush to the doors and find them locked. Lucrezia appears, clad in black, and declares she has had them poisoned for their insults. Horrified to see Gennaro, Lucrezia swears she never meant her vengeance to extend to him. Gennaro refuses her help and recoils when she confesses she is his mother. When he dies, she collapses by his corpse.

ROSMUNDA D'INGHILTERRA (later revised as *Eleonora di Gujenna*), opera seria in 2 acts.
First performed: Florence (Teatro Pergola), 27 February 1834.
Librettist: Felice Romani.[1]
Source: the legend of *Fair Rosamund*.
Synopsis:
Enrico II of England (tenor) has returned from the wars tired of his jealous wife Eleonora (soprano) and longing to see Rosmunda Clifford (soprano), whom he had wooed years before under the alias of Edegardo. When the King confesses the grief caused by his loveless marriage, Clifford (bass) tells him he must not act dishonourably. Rosmunda eagerly awaits a reunion with Edegardo, but when her father tells her the supposed Edegardo is married, Rosmunda is shaken. The jealous Eleonora believes that Rosmunda is her rival and tries to win back Enrico's love by reminding him he owes his power to her. All the King desires is peace. Clifford hopes to get Rosmunda away to safety, but she manages to see Enrico once more to say farewell. When Enrico promises to make her his Queen, Rosmunda is horrified. Eleonora comes to Rosmunda's tower room to have her vevenge, having arranged for

[1] Romani's libretto was not written for Donizetti; it had already been set by Carlo Coccia (Venice, 1829).

Rosmunda to be poisoned. Dying, Rosmunda welcomes the release of death.

MARIA STUARDA, opera seria in 3 acts.

First performed (as *Buondelmonte*), Naples (Teatro S. Carlo), 18 October 1834.[1]

First performed (as *Maria Stuarda*): Milan (La Scala), 30 December 1835.

Librettist: Pietro Salatino (*Buondelmonte*); Giuseppe Bardari (*Maria Stuarda*).

Source: Schiller's *Maria Stuart*.

Synopsis:

Leicester (tenor) and Talbot (baritone) are concerned for the imprisoned Maria. Leicester shows Elisabetta (soprano) a letter he has received from Maria, hoping to arouse sympathy, but the Queen grows jealous and declares she will visit Maria at Fotheringay. Leicester tries to prepare Maria for this interview. The sight of Maria's youth and beauty so infuriate Elisabetta that she insults her. Maria calls Elisabetta her father's bastard and a stain on England's honour. For these words Elisabetta orders her execution. At Westminster, Elisabetta is troubled by her hasty decision, but Cecil (bass) persuades her to sign the death warrant. When Leicester comes to plead for Maria's life, Elisabetta tells him he is too late. Maria receives her sentence without flinching. Wearing a priest's cassock beneath his cloak, Talbot offers her the consolations of her faith and grants her absolution. Maria asks her friends to join her in a prayer of forgiveness for all those who have wronged her. Leicester takes a last farewell of Maria before she is led to the block.

GEMMA DI VERGY, opera seria in 2 acts.

First performed: Milan (La Scala), 26 December 1834.

Librettist: Emanuele Bidera.

Source: Dumas's drama, *Charles VII chez les grands vassaux* (1831).

Synopsis:

When Gemma (soprano) discovers that her husband, Count di Vergy (baritone), plans to divorce her because she has borne

---

[1] *Buondelmonte* was a last-minute revision, patched up when the Queen of Naples objected to the plot of *Maria Stuarda*. Little can be said of this version because the added numbers to the score have been separated: six pieces are in the Museo Donizettiano and three in the Gallini Collection, Milan. These are mostly recitatives.

no children, and to marry again, she is at first stunned with grief and later furious when she learns her successor is already chosen. She refuses to leave without a final interview with the Count. Tamas (tenor), an Arab slave faithful to Gemma, defies the Count. When Gemma complains to the Count about the divorce, she arouses his stubborn contempt. Gemma insults the new Countess, Ida (mezzo), and threatens to stab her. Tamas knocks the dagger from her hand. The Count and Ida go off to their wedding, while Gemma begs Tamas to end her misery. He snatches up the dagger and stabs the Count at the altar, while Gemma, unaware of his action, tries to pray. Tamas confesses his crime, saying he could not bear to see Gemma suffer, and stabs himself. Overwrought, Gemma bemoans her fate, swearing she still loves the Count, and looks forward to the release of death.

MARINO FALIERO, opera seria in 3 acts.
First performed: Paris (Théâtre-Italien), 12 March 1835.
Librettist: Emanuele Bidera.
Sources: Casimir Delavigne's tragedy, *Marino Faliero* (1829), and, secondarily, Byron's tragedy of the same name.
Synopsis:
Ismaele Bertucci (baritone), captain of the Venetian arsenal, is publicly insulted by a young patrician, Michele Steno (bass), who recently aroused the old Doge's ire by impugning the chastity of the young Dogaressa Elena (soprano). Bertucci enlists the support of Doge Marino Faliero (bass) in a conspiracy against the Council. There is, however, some justification for Steno's charge: Elena has fallen in love with the Doge's nephew Fernando (tenor), but she has decided to part with him, giving him her scarf as a token. At a masked ball where the conspirators meet, Elena complains of a masker (Steno) who dogs her steps and insults her. Fernando challenges Steno, setting the square before SS. Giovanni e Paolo as the place. There, Fernando waits, willing to die for Elena's honour. As the conspirators gather, the sound of fighting is heard and Fernando is borne in; dying, he asks that his face be covered with Elena's scarf. The conspirators go off to their appointed tasks, unaware that one of them, Beltrame (bass) has betrayed them. While the Doge tells Elena of Fernando's death, the guards come to arrest him. In the Council chamber, when the Doge is

condemned, he tears off his doge's cap and tramples it. He is granted a final interview with Elena. He shows her the scarf and asks that it be used to cover his face and Fernando's when they are buried in the same tomb. Shaken, Elena confesses her adultery. The Doge rages, but realizing his death is near, he forgives Elena. Elena waits shuddering at the window after the Doge is led away. At the signal for his beheading, she screams and collapses.

LUCIA DI LAMMERMOOR, opera seria in 3 acts.
First performed: Naples (Teatro S. Carlo), 26 September 1835.
Librettist: Salvatore Cammarano.
Source: Scott's *The Bride of Lammermoor*.[1]
Synopsis:

Enrico Ashton (baritone), is outraged to learn from his gillie Normanno (tenor) that Lucia (soprano), his sister, has been secretly meeting Edgardo (tenor), his enemy. Lucia waits with the apprehensive Alisa (mezzo) for a rendezvous with Edgardo, who tells her that he must leave for France, but not before they exchange rings. Some time later Enrico shows Lucia a forged letter, supposedly proving Edgardo's infidelity. Grief-stricken, Lucia consents to a political marriage, arranged by her desperate brother. The wedding guests assemble, and Lucia comes numbly forward to sign the contract. Just then Edgardo bursts in, unexpectedly returned from France, and denounces Lucia's breach of trust. The miserable girl faints. Enrico comes to Edgardo and challenges him to a duel. The presbyter Raimondo (bass) interrupts the wedding festivities with the appalling news that Lucia has gone mad and stabbed her bridegroom. Still carrying the bloody knife, Lucia appears and it is soon apparent that she is unaware of her crime and thinks she will soon marry Edgardo. In his family burying-plot, Edgardo waits for Enrico, thinking bitterly of his fate. When Raimondo brings word of Lucia's death, he stabs himself.

[1] Cammarano and Donizetti were not the first to use this subject. In 1829 Carafa's *Le nozze di Lammermoor* was sung at the Italiens; in 1832 Bredal's *A bruden fra Lammermoor* (text by Hans Christian Andersen) was produced in Copenhagen; on 24 February 1834 Mazzucato's *La fidanzata di Lammermoor* (text by Beltrami) was given at the Teatro Novissimo, Padua. Mazzucato was also a music critic, who frequently dealt harshly with Donizetti's music in the pages of the *Gazzetta musicale di Milano*.

BELISARIO, opera seria in 3 acts.
First performed: Venice (Teatro Fenice), 4 February 1836.
Librettist: Salvatore Cammarano.
Source: Marmontel's *Bélisaire* (1766).
Synopsis:

When Belisario (baritone) returns in triumph to Byzantium, his wife, Antonina (soprano), believing he is responsible for the death of their son, plans to denounce him to the Emperor Giustiniano (bass). Belisario asks freedom for his captives; but one, Alamiro (tenor), elects to stay at his side. Belisario is summoned to the Senate and condemned on forged evidence. Outside Belisario's prison, Alamiro is so enraged to learn that Belisario has been sentenced to exile and blinded that he swears vengeance on Byzantium. Belisario's daughter Irene (mezzo), disguised as a boy, comes to lead her father into exile. Later, Belisario and Irene hide in a cave at the sound of an army and overhear Alamiro and Ottario (bass) plan an assault on Byzantium. Belisario rushes out of hiding and denounces them. Alamiro is overjoyed to see Belisario again; by a cross on the young leader's neck, Irene recognizes him as her long-lost brother. Alamiro goes off with Belisario to prepare the defence of Byzantium. In the resulting victory, Belisario is fatally wounded. Antonina is overcome by remorse and confesses her guilt to her dying husband.

IL CAMPANELLO, farce in 1 act.
First performed: Naples (Teatro Nuovo), 1 June 1836.
Librettist: Gaetano Donizetti.
Source: a vaudeville by Brunswick, Troin and Lhérie, *La sonnette de nuit*.
Synopsis:

Among the guests at the wedding of an aged druggist, Don Annibale Pistacchio (buffo) to Serafina (soprano) is Enrico (baritone). He is a great practical joker and wants revenge on the aged bridegroom because he has toyed with the idea of marrying Serafina himself. According to a Neapolitan statute, any apothecary who does not fill prescriptions in person at any hour is liable to imprisonment. No sooner has Don Annibale got rid of his guests than the nightbell rings. Enrico embarks on a series of disguises and pranks to prevent the old man from getting to his bridal chamber. First he comes disguised as a

French dandy, then as an opera singer out of voice, and last as a rheumatic old man. When Annibale believes he can at last get to his bedroom, he steps on some torpedoes and arouses the household. Enrico and all the wedding guests burst in to speed Annibale on his way, as he has to take an early diligence to Rome to see about an inheritance. Enrico wishes the frustrated bridegroom a whole life as happy as the night he has just passed, a sentiment endorsed by everyone but Don Annibale.

BETLY or *La capanna svizzera*, opera giocosa in 1 act (later expanded to 2).
First performed: Naples (Teatro Nuovo), 24 August 1836.
Librettist: Gaetano Donizetti.
Source: Scribe and Mélesville's text for Adam's *Le chalet*.[1]
Synopsis (of the one-act version):
  Daniel (tenor) arrives at Betly's chalet overjoyed because he has received a letter in which Betly (soprano) accepts his proposal. Since the letter has been written by local pranksters, Betly denies any knowledge of it, stoutly proclaiming she prefers her independence. Betly's brother, Max (baritone), who has been away in the army for years, returns home and decides to keep his identity secret and help Daniel's cause. Max's scheme, involving turning his soldiers loose in Betly's house and even challenging Daniel to a duel, has the desired result of causing Betly to give up her independence and gratefully marry the faithful Daniel.

L'ASSEDIO DI CALAIS, opera seria in 3 acts.
First performed: Naples (Teatro S. Carlo), 19 November 1836.
Librettist: Salvatore Cammarano.
Source: du Belloy's *Le siège de Calais* (1765).
Synopsis:
  Aurelio (mezzo), son of the mayor of beleaguered Calais, narrowly escapes capture on a reconnaissance outside the city's walls. The English king (bass) longs for the day the French capitulate. When Aurelio returns to the city, he tries to enhearten his fellow citizens by reminding them they can still die

---

[1] *Le chalet* is, in turn, derived from Goethe's *singspiel*, *Jery und Bätely* (1780). Goethe's work has frequently been set to music: by Peter von Winter (1790), by Schaum (1795), by J. F. Reichardt (1801), by Conradin Kreutzer (1803), by Bierey (1803), by Frey (1810), and by Julius Rietz (c. 1825).

for Calais. An English spy (bass) bursts into the Hôtel de Ville at the head of a mob, demanding that the mayor, Eustachio (baritone), yield so that his people may avoid certain death. Eustachio exposes the spy and bravely rallies the citizens. An English envoy comes to the audience hall to announce the English king will grant clemency if six citizens of noble blood will die for their city. When Aurelio rejects the offer, Eustachio tells the envoy the victims will be ready at sunset and declares he will be the first to volunteer. Others come forward, but when Aurelio tries to sign the document, his father vainly tries to prevent him. The six doomed men pray for God's guidance, while the citizens mourn. The English soldiers celebrate the arrival of their Queen. The six captives are led in, followed by their weeping wives, who beg for mercy. The Queen is aghast at the King's cruelty and persuades him to pardon the burghers of Calais.

PIA DE' TOLOMEI, opera seria in 2 acts.
First performed: Venice (Teatro Apollo), 18 February 1837.
Librettist: Salvatore Cammarano.
Source: Sestini's *novella* in ottavo rima, ultimately derived from *Purgatorio*, Canto V.
Synopsis:
   Ghino (tenor) lusts after Pia (soprano), the young bride of his uncle Nello of Maremma (baritone). When Pia spurns Ghino, he accuses her of adultery, but her suspected suitor is her brother Rodrigo (contralto), a Guelph and enemy of Nello's party, who has visited her secretly to comfort his unhappy sister. Kneeling to Ghino, Pia confesses her visitor was her brother; her innocence so moves him that he regrets his false accusation. Meanwhile, Nello has given orders Pia is to be poisoned and struggles to convince himself of her guilt. Ghino is fatally wounded in a new assault by Rodrigo's troops, and reveals his treachery before he dies. Nello rushes to Pia's side too late to save her, but in time to receive her forgiveness. When the victorious Rodrigo appears, Pia prays for peace between the warring factions.

ROBERTO DEVEREUX (also known as *Il conte d'Essex*), opera seria in 3 acts.
First performed: Naples (Teatro S. Carlo), 29 October 1837.
Librettist: Salvatore Cammarano.

Source: Ancelot's tragedy, *Elisabeth d'Angleterre*.[1]
Synopsis:

Though Elisabetta is upset that Essex (tenor) has been avoiding her, she resists the efforts of Cecil (bass) and Gualtiero Raleigh (tenor) to charge him with treason. Nottingham (baritone) is suspicious because his wife Sara (soprano) is sad and has tried to hide a blue scarf, suspicions he confides to Essex, who is much in love with Sara. Essex visits Sara to reproach her with marrying Nottingham, while she reproaches him with wearing the Queen's ring. Essex tears off the ring, and Sara gives him the scarf as a memento of their parting. The Council has condemned Essex and informs the Queen he has been arrested. Though Nottingham pleads for his friend, Elisabetta signs the death warrant. When Nottingham recognizes the scarf, he tries to slay Essex on the spot, before he is led away to the Tower. Sara receives a letter from Essex informing her of his fate, but before she can take the ring to the Queen, Nottingham arrives and, refusing to listen to her protestations of innocence, orders her confined. In his cell, Essex wishes he might clear Sara's name before he dies. Just after the signal for Essex's execution, Sara comes to Elisabetta and confesses she is her rival. Convulsed with rage the Queen accuses Sara of holding back the ring until too late, but Nottingham declares he restrained Sara to have his revenge. Elisabetta orders the arrest of the Nottinghams. Oppressed by visions of Essex's ghost and of her approaching death, Elisabetta presses the ring to her lips.

MARIA DI RUDENZ, opera seria in 3 acts.
First performed: Venice (Teatro Fenice), 30 January 1838.
Librettist: Salvatore Cammarano.
Source: Unidentified.
Synopsis:

Corrado di Waldorff (baritone), after a violent youth, hopes to settle down to marriage with Matilde (soprano), heiress of the Count di Rudenz, whose daughter Maria (soprano) is presumed dead. Corrado's brother Enrico (tenor) also loves Matilde and is torn between jealousy and fraternal loyalty.

[1] A comparison of this libretto with Romani's earlier text for Mercadante's *Il conte d'Essex* lends justification to Romani's complaints of Cammarano's plagiarism. (See E. Branca-Romani, *Felice Romani* (Turin, 1882), p. 254.)

Maria returns secretly to Rudenz, intent on vengeance. At the wedding of Corrado and Matilde, Maria suddenly appears and orders the usurping Corrado away and banishes Matilde to a convent. Enrico begs Maria to give Matilde into his protection. Maria hints that Corrado is not his brother. She tells Corrado his father is an assassin, Ugo di Brema; she confesses she loves him and will forgive him everything if he will give up Matilde. When Corrado refuses, Maria shows him a trap-door, saying it opens on Matilde's tomb. Corrado rushes at Maria and stabs her. With what is apparently her last breath, Maria announces she has stabbed herself. Enrico challenges Corrado to a duel and is slain by him. In Corrado's absence, Maria, who has only feigned death, steals into the bridal chamber and stabs Matilde. Maria confesses her crime to Corrado and tells him she has re-opened her wound and is dying in earnest, still loving him and forgiving him. Corrado is left to live with his conscience.

POLIUTO, opera seria in 3 acts: LES MARTYRS, grand opera in 4 acts.

Poliuto first performed: Naples (Teatro S. Carlo), 30 November 1848.[1]

Les martyrs first performed: Paris (Opéra), 10 April 1840.

Librettist: Salvatore Cammarano (*Poliuto*); Eugène Scribe (*Les martyrs*).

Source: Corneille's *Polyeucte*.

Synopsis (of *Poliuto*):[2]

Poliuto (tenor) has resolved to accept Christianity. His wife, Paolina (soprano), suspicious of his secrecy, follows him to the hidden sanctuary and overhears his Baptism. Nearco (bass), the Christian leader, warns her that since Christianity is a proscribed faith Poliuto will die if she reveals what she has learned. Paolina is agitated to learn the proconsul Severo (baritone) has arrived, for once she had loved him, but believing him dead, had married Poliuto. When Felice (tenor), Paolina's father, informs Severo of his daughter's marriage, he is shaken. Callistene (bass), the high priest, observed his emotion and now brings him to an interview with Paolina, having arranged that

---

[1] *Poliuto* was composed in 1838; before the censorship forbade the performance, the work had been rehearsed by Ronzi de Begnis (Paolina), Nourrit (Poliuto), Barroilhet (Severo), and Finocchi (Callistene).

[2] For the differences between these versions, see pp. 425–7.

Poliuto should overhear it. Paolina is profoundly moved by
Severo's declarations, but she begs him to leave her in peace.
Poliuto is filled with jealous rage, but the news that Nearco has
been seized sends him off to try to save him. In the temple of
Jupiter, Nearco is threatened unless he reveals the neophyte's
name. To general astonishment, Poliuto announces that it is he.
When Paolina kneels and begs mercy from Severo, Poliuto
overturns the altar. Both Poliuto and Nearco are seized and
led away. Callistene meets his priests near the temple and tells
them the Christians have chosen martyrdom. With savage joy
he foresees the day when the priestcraft will control the empire.
In his cell, Poliuto dreams of Paolina, who soon comes to him
and begs him to renounce his faith. Hearing his refusal to
renounce his soul, she is moved to embrace his religion and to
share his martyrdom.

IL DUCA D'ALBA, opera seria in 4 acts.
First performed: Rome (Teatro Apollo), 22 March 1882.
Librettist: Scribe-Duveyrier; Italian version by Angelo Zanar-
  dini.[1]
Source: Unidentified.
Synopsis:
   In Brussels, the Flemish seethe under Spanish tyranny. In
an incident, Daniele (bass) is arrested, and Amelia (soprano),
Egmont's daughter, refuses to bow before the Spanish governor.
For her defiance, a Spanish officer asks her to sing a song
praising the Duke; instead she breaks into a patriotic tune that
rouses the Flemish to the point of attacking the soldiers. Only
Alba's arrival prevents bloodshed. Marcello (tenor) comes
from Bruges to tell his beloved Amelia of the unrest there. The
Duke (baritone) approaches Marcello and questions him about
his parentage and childhood. When Marcello rejects the Duke's
offer of pardon, he is led away under guard. Mysteriously,
Marcello is set free and joins Amelia and other conspirators in
Daniele's brewery, where they are surprised by Spanish troops,
who discover a cache of arms. All are arrested but Marcello.
Going to the Duke to plead for his friends' lives, Marcello is
stunned when the Duke claims him as his missing son. Marcello
refuses to acknowledge the relationship, until he realizes that
it is the only way he can save Amelia. Amelia accuses him of

[1] The work was never performed in French; for details, see pp. 432-6.

betrayal and refuses to listen to his protestations of innocence. He goes to Egmont's tomb, hoping to see her again. At first Amelia repulses him; finally she tells him she is resolved to murder the Duke. When Marcello tries to dissuade her, she orders him away. At Antwerp, Amelia comes to the Duke, who is about to embark for Spain, as a suppliant. When she draws a dagger, Marcello throws himself between them and receives the blow. Dying, he begs the Duke to forgive Amelia.

LA FILLE DU RÉGIMENT, opéra-comique in 2 acts.
First performed: Paris (Opéra-Comique), 11 February 1840.
Librettist: Jules Henri Vernoy de Saint-Georges and Jean François Alfred Bayard.
Source: Unidentified.
Synopsis:

Marie (soprano), a young girl found on the battlefield and brought up by the soldiers of the 21st regiment as their 'daughter', confesses to Sergeant Sulpice (buffo) that she is attracted to Tonio (tenor), a young Tyrolean who has saved her life. Tonio has lurked around the camp, hoping for a glimpse of Marie. When he is seized as a spy, Marie claims him as her personal prisoner. Learning that Marie may marry only a member of the 21st, Tonio promptly enlists, but the aged Marquise de Birkenfeld (mezzo) claims that Marie is her long-lost niece and takes her home with her. There, bored with the artificial manners of polite society[1] and longing for her old freedom, Marie is being forced into marriage with a foppish young Duke. The 21st returns to the neighbourhood of the Marquise's château, and Tonio, who has been searching out the facts of Marie's parentage, demands an explanation. The Marquise confesses Marie is really her daughter and, her heart softened by renewed memories of the soldiery, consents to Marie's marriage to the upstanding Tonio.

LA FAVORITE, grand-opéra in 4 acts.
First performed: Paris (Opéra), 2 December 1840.
Librettists: Alphonse Royer and Gustave Vaëz.
Source: Baculard d'Arnaud's *Le comte de Comminges* (1764), plus some unidentified source dealing with Leonora di Guzman.

[1] Among the polite accomplishments, the Marquise includes the singing of a romance by Pierre Jean Garat (1764–1823), who had been Marie Antoinette's favourite singer.

Synopsis:

Fernand (tenor), a novice, confesses to his superior, Balthazar (bass), that a beautiful woman has caused him to lose his religious zeal. Sternly Balthazar orders him away. Fernand is brought blindfolded to an island retreat, where Léonor (mezzo) tells him that although she cannot marry him she will help him advance his career. Fernand receives a military appointment. Later, King Alphonse (baritone) hopes to reward Fernand for saving his life in a battle with the Moors. Léonor, the King's mistress, begs Alphonse to end their relationship. Balthazar informs the King of the Papal Bull issued against this liaison. When the King protests, Balthazar threatens him with excommunication. When Fernand, ignorant of the bond between Léonor and the King, asks for her hand, the King ironically consents. Léonor sends her confidante to inform Fernand of her true status, but Alphonse has the messenger arrested before Fernand learns the truth. After the ceremony, Fernand is stung by the courtiers' contempt. When Balthazar tells him he has married the King's mistress, Fernand defies the King and breaks his sword, before he rushes back to the monastery to resume the life of a religious. There, he is still haunted by memories of Léonor. Disguised as a postulant, she comes to beg his forgiveness. The sight of her finally arouses his old passion, but before they can escape together, the exhausted Léonor sinks at his feet and dies.

ADELIA, opera seria in 3 acts.
First performed: Rome (Teatro Apollo), 11 February 1841.
Librettist: Felice Romani, additions by Girolamo Marini.[1]
Source: A French play, *Adèle de Lusignan ou la fille de l'archer*.
Synopsis:

Arnaldo (bass), captain of the Duke of Burgundy's guards, resolves to kill a man in a red cloak who has been seen climbing out of Adelia's window. When he discovers the man is a noble, Oliviero (tenor), and that a commoner cannot avenge himself against an aristocrat, Arnaldo determines to punish his daughter Adelia (soprano). Arnaldo tries to persuade the Duke (bass) to

---

[1] Romani's libretto had seen much service. Carafa set it in 1817 as *Adele di Lusignano*; in 1819 Ramon Carnicier set the same text. In 1834 Coccia's *La figlia dell'arciere* used the first two acts of Romani's libretto with a new last act by Marchese Domenico Andreotti. In 1845, Pedrotti used the same subject, but whether he employed Romani's text is not clear.

permit a marriage between Oliviero and Adelia, but the Duke claims he would rather see Oliviero dead than married to a commoner and decides to have Oliviero beheaded after the ceremony. Adelia does everything in her power to postpone the marriage, but her father is implacable. Finally the Duke relents and resolves the problem by presenting Arnoldo with a patent of nobility!

RITA *ou Le mari battu*, opéra-comique in 1 act.
First performed: Paris (Opéra-Comique), 7 May 1860.
Librettist: Gustave Vaëz.
Source: Unidentified.
Synopsis:

Rita (soprano) has married a bumpkin, Beppe (tenor), believing her first husband, Gasparo (baritone), has drowned at sea. When Gasparo comes to Rita's inn, Beppe recognizes the name on his passport and sees in the stranger a means of escaping from his shrewish Rita. Checking out a false rumour that Rita has died, Gasparo, who hopes to marry a Canadian girl, cajoles Beppe into playing a game of chance to see which of them wins the wife neither of them wants. When Beppe accuses Gasparo of cheating, they draw straws. Gasparo informs Beppe that a husband should beat his wife to keep her docile. Rita, who has given blows to Beppe and received them from Gasparo, decides that peace and concord make for a happy marriage. On this note, she is re-united with Beppe, as Gasparo sets off for Canada.

MARIA PADILLA, opera seria in 3 acts.
First performed: Milan (La Scala), 26 December 1841.
Librettist: Gaetano Rossi.
Source: Ancelot's play, *Maria Padilla*.
Synopsis:

Maria Padilla (soprano) hopes to become the wife of King Pedro the Cruel of Castille (baritone). By threatening suicide, she extracts his promise that he will marry her, even though reasons of state force him to keep the marriage a secret. They elope, in spite of Maria's certainty that her father, Don Ruiz (tenor) will insist on vengeance. Maria is troubled by the knowledge that a civil war forces Pedro to appear to be negotiating a marriage with Blanche, a Bourbon princess. Don Ruiz comes to court, where his daughter is to all appearances the King's mistress, and challenges the ruler. The old man's mind snaps and he is led home in disgrace. Maria comes to beg his forgiveness and reveal her true status, but her father will not understand her. When Blanche arrives and is hailed as Queen by Pedro's enemies, Maria is terrified by the thought she is rejected. She snatches the crown from Blanche's head and claps it on her own. She dies, as Pedro acknowledges her publicly, of 'a surfeit of joy'.[1]

LINDA DI CHAMOUNIX, opera semiseria in 3 acts.
First performed: Vienna (Kärthnerthortheater), 19 May 1842.
Librettist: Gaetano Rossi.
Source: d'Ennery and Lemoine, *La grâce de Dieu*.
Synopsis:
   Antonio (baritone) and Maddalena (mezzo) become concerned for Linda's virtue, when they learn the Marchese (buffo) intends to seduce their daughter. Linda (soprano) loves Carlo (tenor), whom she believes to be a poor painter, but who is really the Viscount de Sirval. Antonio goes to the Prefetto (bass), who urges him to send Linda, along with the hurdy-gurdy player Pierotto (contralto) and the other silk-workers, to Paris to work in the factories. There, Linda is living in a richly furnished apartment belonging to Carlo, but their relationship is strictly virtuous. She is recognized by the Marchese, but spurns his attentions. Antonio comes to Paris to learn of his daughter's whereabouts and mistakes her for a noblewoman. When he recognizes her as Linda, he misconstrues her circumstances and curses her. Added to this blow, Linda learns from Pierotto that Carlo has apparently married a girl of his own class. Linda loses her reason. The faithful Pierotto leads her back to Chamounix. Here, Carlo, who has refused to go through with the wedding in Paris, is able to restore Linda's wits by offering her his heart and hand.

CATERINA CORNARO, opera seria in a prologue and 2 acts.
First performed: Naples (Teatro S. Carlo), 12 January 1844.
Librettist: Giocamo Sacchero.
Source: Saint-Georges's libretto, *La reine du Chypre*.

---

[1] Originally Maria committed suicide, but the Milanese censors forbade representations of suicide. Much to Donizetti's disgust, this compromise was forced upon him.

Synopsis:

In Venice, the approaching marriage of Caterina (soprano) and a young Frenchman, Gerardo (tenor) is postponed by Mocenigo (bass), who brings word that Lusignano (baritone), the King of Cyprus, wishes to marry her. Andrea (bass) orders Gerardo to forget his daughter, but Gerardo comes to Caterina's room to take her away with him. Having learned from Mocenigo that Gerardo's life is in danger, Caterina tells Gerardo she does not love him, hoping to save his life. Later, when one of Mocenigo's henchmen attempts to assassinate Gerardo, his life is saved by Lusignano. Gerardo, however, has vowed to avenge himself on Caterina's husband, but is thunder-struck to recognize in him the man who had earlier saved his life. Lusignano is being slowly poisoned by Mocenigo, and in his weakened condition he learns that the Venetians are attacking Cyprus. Gerardo, who has joined the Knights of the Cross at Rhodes, comes with his companions to help Lusignano, and Gerardo succeeds in turning the tide of battle. In the fighting, Lusignano receives a mortal wound. As he dies, he confides his people to Caterina's care. Gerardo returns to Rhodes.[1]

DON PASQUALE, opera buffa in 3 acts.
First performed: Paris (Théâtre-Italien), 3 January 1843.
Librettists: Giovanni Ruffini and Gaetano Donizetti.
Source: Anelli's libretto for Pavesi's *Ser Marc'Antonio* (1810).
Synopsis:

The elderly Don Pasquale (buffo) determines to marry a young wife and sire children in order to disinherit his nephew Ernesto (tenor), whose infatuation with Norina (soprano) angers the old man. Don Pasquale consults Dr Malatesta (baritone) and hears of his 'sister', a paragon of demure femininity. Dr Malatesta goes to his cousin Norina and together they concoct the role she must play to bring Don Pasquale back to reason. Don Pasquale is delighted with his naïve 'bride' and signs the mock-marriage contract. Ernesto is dismayed by Norina's apparent infidelity, but when she starts to play the shrew, he begins to see humour in the situation. When Don Pasquale remonstrates with Norina for her extravagant taste and forbids her leaving the house, she boxes his ears

[1] In the revised finale for Parma, Donizetti altered the text of the finale and gets rid of the superfluous figure of Gerardo by having Lusignano inform Caterina that the knight has died in battle.

and orders him to bed. She drops a note, indicating she will have a rendezvous that night in the garden. Outraged, Don Pasquale summons Dr Malatesta, and they plot how they will capture the lovers. Promptly at nine, Ernesto and Norina play a love scene in the garden, as Don Pasquale and Dr Malatesta steal in. When the old man is so discomfited he admits he wishes he was not married, Norina reveals her true identity and gains Don Pasquale's blessing for her marriage to Ernesto.

MARIA DI ROHAN (also given as *Il Conte di Chalais*), opera seria in 3 acts.
First performed: Vienna (Kärthnerthortheater), 5 June 1843.
Librettist: Salvatore Cammarano.
Source: Lockroy's melodrama, *Un duel sous le cardinal de Richelieu*.
Synopsis:
Maria (soprano) is secretly married to the Duke de Chevreuse (baritone), but when her husband kills Richelieu's nephew in a duel, she begs Riccardo, Count de Chalais (tenor), to intercede for Chevreuse. Recognizing Riccardo's noble nature, Maria feels her old love for him re-awaken. Gondi (contralto), a young gallant, makes an insulting reference to Maria, and Riccardo instantly challenges him to a duel. When Chevreuse hears of Riccardo's intercession, he thanks him and insists on being his second. Before the duel, Riccardo sends a farewell note to Maria, which is to be delivered only if he dies. Maria comes secretly to Riccardo to warn him of his enemies, but she is forced to hide when Chevreuse arrives to accompany Riccardo to the duelling ground. When Chevreuse leaves, Maria emerges from her hiding place, having learned of the duel for the first time, and implores Riccardo not to run such danger. A message comes that Chevreuse has taken Riccardo's place in the duel, and Ricccardo hastens away. Later, Riccardo's letter to Maria is discovered by his enemies and delivered to Chevreuse. Confronting Maria, the outraged husband demands to know her lover's name. Suddenly, Riccardo appears through a secret door, an escape route by which he had hoped to lead Maria to safety. Chevreuse thrusts a pistol into his hand and goes off to duel with Riccardo. Chevreuse returns and announces that Riccardo has killed himself. When Maria begs him to kill her, Chevreuse condemns her to a life of disgrace.

DOM SÉBASTIEN DE PORTUGAL, grand-opéra in 5 acts.
First performed: Paris (Opéra), 13 November 1843.
Librettist: Eugène Scribe.
Source: *Memorias . . . o governo del rey D. Sebastião* by Barbosa
  Machado (1736–41).[1]
Synopsis:
  Dom Sébastien (tenor), King of Portugal, is ready to depart
for a crusade against Morocco. During the King's absence, Dom
Juan di Silva (bass), head of the Council, hopes to betray the
country to Philip II of Spain. Camoens (baritone) asks to
accompany the King. When Sébastien sees a Moslem beauty
being led to the stake, he releases her and offers to return her to
her father in Africa. Zaïde (mezzo) throws herself at the King's
feet in gratitude. While the King and his troops sail, Dom Juan
and the Regent pray the expedition will come to disaster. Near
Fez, Zaïde's father, Ben-Selim (bass) tells her he plans to marry
her to the Arab chieftain Abayaldos (baritone), who is preparing to meet the Portuguese army on the plains of Al Kasr
al Kebr. After the battle, Dom Enrique (bass) and one of the
few Portuguese left alive on the field, pretends to be Sébastien
and he is slain by Abayaldos. Though gravely wounded, Sébastien survives and is tended by Zaïde. Begging outside the Lisbon
cathedral, Camoens recognizes Sébastien, whose throne has
been usurped by the Regent. Together they pray the veterans
and common people will remain loyal to their rightful ruler. A
solemn funeral passes, supposedly that of Sébastien. Sébastien
reveals himself to the crowd, but Abayaldos, who has come to
Lisbon with Zaïde, claims he saw the King's corpse on the
battlefield. Sébastien is seized as an imposter and condemned.
Zaïde tries to defend him, but she is accused of treason. Later,
Dom Juan comes to the Tower of Lisbon and tries to force
Zaïde to make Sébastien sign a statement that will legitimize
the Spanish claims to Portugal. When Sébastien sees the document, he refuses to sign it. He and Zaïde agree to die together,
as Camoens appears at the window. With some faithful sailors
he has tried to engineer an escape for the King. As Sébastien,
Zaïde, and Camoens climb down the tower wall on a rope, the
regent observes their escape and orders his soldiers to fire. The
bodies of Zaïde and Sébastien pitch into the harbour below.

[1] Scribe takes considerable liberties with history, he probably worked from
Paul Foucher's drama, *Dom Sébastien*, derived in its turn from Machado.

List of
Donizetti's Compositions

THE FOLLOWING LIST, which is as complete as possible, mentions only the titles of works and some additional identification. Inevitably, it leans very heavily indeed on the monumental compilation of Guido Zavadini, published in his *Donizetti: Vita–Musiche–Epistolario* (Bergamo 1948). Although I have somewhat modified his listing, it is only in the interest of adding some little to his great work. Herbert Weinstock's recent *Donizetti* (1963) contains much useful information; but his listing is primarily a translation of Zavadini's, as is mine.

OPERAS

1	*Il Pigmalione*	Bergamo, 13 October 1960
2	*Olimpiade* (Incomplete)	Unperformed
3	*L'ira d'Achille*	Unperformed
4	*Enrico di Borgogna*	Venice, 14 November 1818
5	*Una follia*	Venice, 15 December 1818
6	*Le nozze in villa*	Mantua, Carnival, 1820–21
7	*I piccioli virtuosi ambulanti*	Bergamo, September 1819
8	*Il falegname di Livonia* (*Pietro il Grande*)	Venice, 26 December 1819
9	*Zoraide di Granata*	Rome, 28 January 1822
10	*La zingara*	Naples, 12 May 1822
11	*La lettera anonima*	Naples, 29 June 1822
12	*Chiara e Serafina*	Milan, 26 October 1822
13	*Alfredo il Grande*	Naples, 2 July 1823
14	*Il fortunato inganno*	Naples, 3 September 1823
15	*L'ajo nell'imbarazzo* (*Don Gregorio*)	Rome, 4 February 1824

499

16	Emilia di Liverpool (L'eremitaggio di Liverpool)	Naples, 28 July 1824
17	Alahor di Granata	Palermo, 7 January 1826
18	Il castello degli invalidi	(No concrete evidence)
19	Elvida	Naples, 6 July 1826
20	Gabriella di Vergy	Naples, 29 November 1869 (a rifacimento)
21	La bella prigioniera (Incomplete)	Unperformed
22	Olivo e Pasquale	Rome, 7 January 1827
23	Otto mesi in due ore (Gli esiliati in Siberia)	Naples, 13 May 1827
24	Il borgomastro di Saardam	Naples, 19 August 1827
25	Le convenienze ed inconvenienze teatrali	Naples, 21 November 1827
26	L'esule di Roma (Settimio il proscritto)	Naples, 1 January 1828
27	Alina, regina di Golconda	Genoa, 12 May 1828
28	Gianni di Calais	Naples, 2 August 1828
29	Il giovedì grasso	Naples, Autumn 1828
30	Il paria	Naples, 12 January 1829
31	Elisabetta al castello di Kenilworth	Naples, 6 July 1829
32	I pazzi per progetto	Naples, 7 February 1830
33	Il diluvio universale	Naples, 28 February 1830
34	Imelda de' Lambertazzi	Naples, 23 August 1830
35	Anna Bolena	Milan, 26 December 1830
36	Gianni di Parigi	Milan, 10 September 1839
37	Francesca di Foix	Naples, 30 May 1831
38	La romanziera e l'uomo nero	Naples, Summer 1831
39	Fausta	Naples, 12 January 1832
40	Ugo, conte di Parigi	Milan, 13 March 1832
41	L'elisir d'amore	Milan, 12 May 1832
42	Sancia di Castiglia	Naples, 4 November 1832
43	Il furioso all'isola di San Domingo	Rome, 2 January 1833
44	Parisina	Florence, 17 March 1833
45	Torquato Tasso (Sordello)	Rome, 9 September 1833
46	Lucrezia Borgia	Milan, 26 December 1833
47	Rosmonda d'Inghilterra (Eleonora di Gujenna)	Florence, 27 February 1834
48	Maria Stuarda (Buondelmonte)	Naples, 18 October 1834
49	Gemma di Vergy	Milan, 26 December 1834

50	*Marino Faliero*	Paris, 12 March 1835
51	*Lucia di Lammermoor*	Naples, 26 September 1835
52	*Belisario*	Venice, 4 February 1836
53	*Il campanello*	Naples, 1 June 1836
54	*Betly*	Naples, 24 August 1836
55	*L'assedio di Calais*	Naples, 19 November 1836
56	*Pia de' Tolomei*	Venice, 18 February 1837
57	*Roberto Devereux*	Naples, 29 October 1837
58	*Maria di Rudenz*	Venice, 30 January 1838
59	*Poliuto (Les martyrs)*	Paris, 10 April 1840
60	*Il duca d'Alba*	Rome, 22 March 1882
61	*La fille du régiment*	Paris, 11 February 1840
62	*La favorite*	Paris, 2 December 1840
63	*Adelia*	Rome, 11 February 1841
64	*Rita*	Paris, 7 May 1860
65	*Maria Padilla*	Milan, 26 December 1841
66	*Linda di Chamounix*	Vienna, 19 May 1842
67	*Caterina Cornaro*	Naples, 12 January 1844
68	*Don Pasquale*	Paris, 3 January 1843
69	*Maria di Rohan*	Vienna, 5 June 1843
70	*Dom Sébastien de Portugal*	Paris, 13 November 1843

OPERAS PROJECTED (either unwritten or left incomplete)

Adelaide Of the approximately 100 MS. pages of this score, many were incorporated into *L'ange de Nisida* and some passages subsequently found their way into *La favorite*

L'ange de Nisida This score was almost completed for production at the Théâtre de la Renaissance in 1840, but when the impresario Antenor Joly went bankrupt Donizetti adapted most of this score to the new libretto of *La favorite*

Circe This subject was probably that of the proposed Donizetti-Romani opera for the English impresario Benjamin Lumley, a work planned for a London production in 1842. Apparently the project never got beyond the stage of preliminary inquiries

La fiancée du Tyrol The tentative title of a proposed re-working of *Il furioso* for the Renaissance in Paris. Donizetti alludes to this project in a letter to Persico, dated 9 October 1839, but apparently the composer never got to it, probably because of the financial straits of the theatre

La fidanzata An aria from this projected one-act farce is in the library of the Paris Conservatory

Gli Illinesi In July 1835 Donizetti corresponded with the Turin impresario Giuseppe Consul about composing an opera to Romani's old libretto, already set by Francesco Basili (La Scala, 1819), and Feliciano Strepponi, the father of Giuseppina (Trieste, 1829). The negotiations between Consul and Donizetti were amicably broken off, the impresario turning to Pier Antonio Coppola, whose *Gli Illinesi* was given in Turin, 26 December 1835. At that time Donizetti was in Milan, rehearsing Malibran in *Maria Stuarda*

Gli Innamorati In Bergamo there exists in Donizetti's hand a scenario for a three-act comic opera, based on Goldoni's play of the same name

Jeanne la folle In 1844 Donizetti briefly considered setting Scribe's text on this subject, which was finally turned into an opera by Clapisson and brought out at the Opéra in 1848

Lara A libretto on this Byronic subject was proposed to Donizetti by a Veronese nobleman, but Donizetti turned it down having little confidence in the plot. Donizetti's protégé, Salvi, set the same subject in 1843, but with no success. A long letter to Donizetti from Pullé, dated 1 March 1837, containing a synopsis and some dialogue from the libretto is printed in *Studi Donizettiani I*, pp. 125–32

Mlle de la Vallière Nothing but the name seems to be known of this projected work

Ne m'oubliez pas Donizetti worked at this three-act comic libretto by Saint-Georges in 1842, completing seven numbers, but leaving the score incomplete. He had signed a contract with Crosnier, manager of the Opéra-Comique, for this opera on 30 September 1842, but the contract was apparently allowed to lapse.

Onore vince amore An opera proposed for the Théâtre-Italien by Donizetti, to be composed to a text by Giovanni Ruffini. Donizetti's failing health prevented this project from passing beyond preliminary discussions

Il pascià di Scutari A libretto to this opera, with an attribution to Donizetti, exists in the library of the Naples Conservatory. It is impossible to tell whether this was really composed by Donizetti or if some of his existing music was spliced together to a new text. The libretto was published in Messina in 1832

Il ritratto parlante This title is usually regarded as an alternative name for the farce *Una follia* (1818)

Ruy Blas After Donizetti halted work on the score that was to become *Caterina Cornaro*, for a time he considered composing an opera to a libretto by Cammarano based on Hugo's drama, but later he returned to *Caterina* and completed it

Sganarello In 1845 Donizetti considered writing a vehicle for Lablache derived from Molière's play, but the deterioration of the composer's health prevented his undertaking the task

Five excerpts, from an unidentifiable work or works. Four of these pieces are in the Museo Donizettiano; one, inscribed to the tenor Moriani and dated 1838, is in the La Scala Museum

ORATORIOS

Oratorio sacro, performed in Acireale, July 1841
Le sette chiese, performed in Rome, 1842

CANTATAS

Il ritorno di primavera, a student work performed at the Liceo, Bologna, in 1818, after Donizetti's departure
Canto accompagnatorio, Bergamo, 1819
Teresa e Gianfaldoni, Mantua, 1821
Angelica e Medoro, composed in Naples, May 1822
L'Assunzione di Maria Vergine, Rome, 1822
Cantata for the birth of Maria Carolina Augusta, daughter of the Prince of Salerno, performed Naples, 6 April 1822
Aristea, performed Naples, 30 May 1823
A Silvio amante, a non-autograph copy of this cantata in the Museo Donizettiano bears the date 1823 but no clue of its performance
La fuga di Tisbe, composed 15 October 1824
I voti dei sudditi, performed Naples, 5 May 1825
La partenza, performed Palermo, 1825.
Cantata, for the birthday of King Francesco I, performed Palermo, 14 August 1825
Licenza, performed Palermo, 1825
Saffo, dedicated to 'Madamigella Virginia Vasselli', and therefore composed before Donizetti's marriage in 1828
Il canto XXXIII della Divina Commedia, composed as a compliment to Lablache during January and February 1828
Il genio dell'armonia, written in collaboration with Costaguti and Capranica. According to Cametti, Donizetti's share of this work was the finale, consisting of a terzetto and the final chorus. The cantata was performed in Rome, 20 December 1829
Il fausto ritorno, performed Naples, during the summer of 1830

Cantata, for the marriage of Ferdinand of Austria, and Maria Anna
Carolina of Savoy; the score is dated 24 January 1831, and the
performance took place in Turin, 27 February 1831

Il fato, performed Rome, 13 June 1833

Cantata, for the name-day of Anna Carnevali, performed Rome, 26
July 1833

Cantata, for the Queen of Naples on the birth of a child, performed
August 1838

Il genio, in honour of Mayr's seventy-eighth birthday, composed in
Paris, May 1841, and performed in Bergamo, 14 June 1841

Cristoforo Colombo, written for the baritone Barroilhet and performed
by him at his benefit, March 1845, in the Paris Opéra

Undated Cantatas

Aci e Galatea

Gloria a Dio dei nostri padri

Niso e Violetta

Per il nome di Francesco I

Uno sguardo, words by Romani and performed at the home of Emilia
Branca (who became Signora Romani) in Milan

HYMNS

Inno reale, performed on the gala opening night of the Teatro Carlo
Felice in Genoa, 7 April 1828

Inno, for the marriage of King Ferdinando II of Naples and Maria
Cristina of Sardinia, performed November 1832

La preghiera di un popolo, performed Naples, 31 August 1837

Inno, for the name-day of Don Pietro Pangrati (undated)

Sacro è il dolore (undated)

RELIGIOUS MUSIC

Asperges me, score dated 8 April 1820

Ave Maria (for soprano, contralto and orchestra), composed Vienna
at the end of January 1844 and performed during the succeeding
Lenten season

Ave Maria (for 2 voices and piano)

Beatus vir (for tenor and small orchestra), dated 1819

Canzoncine sacre, three brief songs (for 2 voices and piano)

Christe eleison (for tenor, 2 violins, clarinet and bass)

Christe (for tenor and orchestra)

Confitebor (soprano, tenor and bass, a cappella)

Credidi (soprano, tenor and bass, a cappella)

Credo (3 voices and orchestra), dated 17 April 1819
Credo (soprano, tenor and bass), dated Almenno, 18 October 1820
Credo (for 4 voices), dated 1824
Credo (for 3 voices and orchestra), undated
Credo (for 4 voices and orchestra), undated
Credo (for 4 voices and orchestra), undated
Credo (*breve*) and *Crucifixus*
Cum Sancto Spiritu, dated Bergamo, 16 July 1817
Cum Sancto Spiritu, inscribed '*per Giuseppe*'
Cum Sancto Spiritu (for 4 voices and orchestra)
Cum Sancto Spiritu (for 3 voices), undated[1]
Cum Sancto Spiritu (for 3 and 4 voices), dated 1819
De Torrente (for soprano and tenor), dated Bergamo, June 1819
Dies irae, MS. incomplete
Dixit (for 3 voices and orchestra), dated 1819
Dixit Dominus (for 3 voices and orchestra), dated 1820
Docebo (for bass solo and small orchestra)
Domine ad adjuvandum (for 3 voices, winds and organ)
Domine ad adjuvandum (for 3 voices and orchestra), dated 1819
Domine Deus (for bass solo, clarinet obbligato, and orchestra), dated
    16 May 1820
Domine Deus (for bass solo)
Domine Deus (for bass solo and small orchestra)
Domine Deus (for 4 voices), undated[2]
Dominus a dextris (for bass solo and orchestra), dated 1819
Dominus a dextris (for tenor solo, violin obbligato and orchestra),
    dated Bergamo, August 1820
Et vitam (a fugue for 4 solo voices)
Gloria in excelsis (for 4 mixed voices and orchestra)
Gloria in excelsis (for 3 voices, violins, horns and organ), dated 1814
Gloria in excelsis (for 3 and 4 voices and orchestra), dated 28 May
    1818
Gloria in excelsis (for 4 voices and orchestra), undated
Gloria in excelsis (for 3 voices and orchestra), dated 16 July 1819,
    Bergamo
Gloria in excelsis (for 3 and 4 voices and orchestra), dated 20 May
    1820
Gloria Patri (for soprano solo, violin obbligato and orchestra), dated
    28 May 1820
Gloria Patri (for 4 voices and orchestra), dated 1843, Paris

---

[1] This composition does not seem to be listed in Zavadini's catalogue
(Z. p. 186), but appears as No. 2 in the catalogue of Donizetti's great-
nephews, Bergamo, 1897.
[2] Not in Zavadini's catalogue (Z. p. 186), but No. 7 in the great-nephews'
catalogue of 1897.

Gloria Patri, undated[1]

Gloria Patri and *Sicut erat* (for 3 voices and orchestra)

Gratias agimus (for soprano solo, flute obbligato and orchestra), dated 6 July 1820

In convertendo (for bass solo and orchestra), undated

In Gloria Dei Patris (4-voice fugue), dated Bologna, 17 September 1816

Inno (a S. Pietro) (for tenor solo and small orchestra)

Iste Confessor (for 3 voices and orchestra), dated Alzano, 6 August 1819

Judica me Deus (Psalm 42) (for 2 boys' voices, with organ or a cappella)

Kyrie (for 4 voices), composed Bologna, 1816

Kyrie (for 4 voices), dated Bolgare, 1 August 1817

Kyrie (for chorus and orchestra), dated Bologna, 7 August 1817, performed at Bologna, St Cecilia's Day (22 November) 1817

Kyrie (for 3 voices), dated Bergamo, 8 August 1818

Kyrie (for 4 voices and orchestra), dated 20 May 1820

Kyrie I (for 4 voices), dated 26 May 1821

Kyrie II (for 4 voices), dated 26 May 1821

Kyrie (for 3 voices and accompaniment of 2 oboes, 2 horns and organ), undated

Kyrie (for same forces as the preceding), undated

Kyrie (for 3 voices and small orchestra), undated

Kyrie (for 4 voices, chorus and orchestra), undated

Kyrie (for 4 voices and orchestra), undated

Kyrie I, Christe, and *Kyrie II* (for voices and orchestra), undated

Kyrie I, Christe, and *Kyrie II* (for 4 voices and orchestra), undated

Laudamus and *Gratias* (for tenor or soprano solo, with oboe or clarinet obbligato, and orchestra), dated 3 July 1819

Laudamus and *Gratias* (chorus and orchestra with clarinet obbligato)

Laudamus and *Gratias* (for 4 voices with orchestra), undated

Laudamus Te (for 4 voices and orchestra), dated Bergamo, 6 July 1820

Laudate pueri (for 4 voices and orchestra), Bergamo, 8 October 1819

Laudate pueri (for 3 voices and orchestra), undated

Libera me de Sanguinibus (for soprano, with violin obbligato and orchestra), dated Almenno, 30 October 1820

Luge qui Leges, 'Marcia funebre' (for chorus), on the words of the *Requiem aeternam*. Composed in Milan, 1842 for Pompeo Marchesi

Magnificat (for 3 voices with orchestra) dated Bergamo, May 1819

Messa di Gloria and *Credo* (for 3 and 4 voices and chorus and large orchestra), performed Naples, 28 November 1837

[1] Not in Zavadini's catalogue (Z., p. 187), but No. 13 in the great-nephews' catalogue of 1897.

Messa da Requiem (for soloists, chorus and orchestra), written in memory of Vincenzo Bellini (1835)

Messa da Requiem, on the death of Zingarelli, May 1837

Messa da Requiem, for the funeral of Abate Fazzini, Naples, 7 November 1837

Miserere (for 4 voices, contraltos, tenors and basses), Venice, January 1820

Miserere (for chorus and 4 separate voices with orchestra). A setting of the first 4 verses, dated 4 April 1820

Miserere (for 4 voices), dated 18 January 1822, Rome

Miserere (for 3 men's voices and string orchestra and organ) offered to Pope Gregory XVI, July 1841

Miserere (a revision of the above), performed in Vienna, December 1842

Miserere (complete for 1st and 2nd tenor, 2 basses and chorus, accompanied by organ, 2 violas, 2 cellos and 2 string basses), undated

Miserere (for 4 voices with orchestra), undated

Mottetto (for tenor with clarinet obbligato and small orchestra), dated 29 March 1820

Ne proicias me (bass solo with horn obbligato and orchestra), dated Almenno, 29 November 1820

Nisi dominus (for tenor with orchestra), undated

Offertorio (*Ave Maria*) (for 5 voices on the Latin text of the Ave Maria accompanied by 2 violins, 2 violas, cello and string bass). Written for the Imperial Chapel in Vienna, 1842

Offertorio, 'Quoniam ad te' (for soprano and small orchestra), 1844

Offertorio, 'Domine, Dominus noster' (for bass solo and orchestra), dated Vienna, 1845

Oro supplex (for bass solo with horn obbligato), written for the funeral of Marchese Giuseppe Terzi, 1819

Pange lingua, a processional

Parafrasi del 'Christus' (for women's voices and string orchestra), composed Naples, 1829, revised Vienna, 1844

Preces me (for tenor solo and 4-part chorus), undated

Qui sedes (for soprano with violin obbligato and small orchestra), undated

Qui sedes and *Quoniam* (for tenor solo, with violin obbligato and orchestra), dated 3 July 1820

Qui sedes and *Quoniam* (for soprano solo, with violin obbligato and orchestra), undated

Qui tollis (for tenor with clarinet obbligato and orchestra), dated 7 September 1814

Qui tollis (for tenor solo, chorus and orchestra), dated 24 May 1820

Qui tollis (for tenor solo with horn obbligato and orchestra), un-
dated
Qui tollis (for 3 voices and orchestra), undated
Qui tollis (for tenor solo and small orchestra), undated
Qui tollis-Miserere (for 3 voices and orchestra), dated 8 July 1819
Requiem (for 3 voices and orchestra), performed for the blessing of
the catafalque of Alfonso della Valle di Casanova, Naples
Salve regina (for tenor solo and orchestra), dated Bergamo, 5 August
1819
Salve regina (for 3 voices with woodwinds and string bass)
Sic transit gloria mundi (for 8 voices and organ), dated Milan, 1844
Sicut erat (for 4 voices and orchestra), undated
Sicut erat (for 3 voices), very short, dated 9 September 1819
Tantum ergo (for 1st and 2nd tenor and bass and orchestra),
dated Bologna, 8 November 1816; performed 22 November
1816
Tantum ergo (for tenor solo and orchestra), undated
Tantum ergo (for soprano and organ), undated
Tantum ergo (for tenor solo, woodwinds and string bass), undated
Tecum principium (for soprano or tenor solo, with oboe or clarinet
obbligato and orchestra), dated 1819
Te Deum (for 2 children's voices, to be sung with or without organ),
undated
Tibi soli peccavi (for soprano solo with bassett horn obbligato and
orchestra), dated 6 April 1820
Tuba mirum (for bass solo and orchestra), dated Bergamo, 5 January
1821
Tunc acceptabis (for 4 voices with full orchestra), dated 6 April
1820

INSTRUMENTAL WORKS FOR ORCHESTRA

Gran Marcia Militare Imperiale, dedicated to Sultan Abdul-Medjid-
Khan, 1840
Introduzione (for string orchestra), dated 1829
Marcia (written for Francesco Donizetti in August 1840)
Preludio (complete for an unpublished or unidentified opera), un-
dated
Rataplan (for orchestra), undated
Sinfonia in C, dated Bologna, 12 June 1816
Sinfonia concertante in C, composed Bologna, 17 September 1816 and
performed there, 9 June 1817
Sinfonia in C, dated Bologna, 24 November 1816
Sinfonia in D, dated 29 March 1817

Sinfonia in G minor (for woodwinds), dedicated to Signor 'Nebbia' Deleide and dated 19 April 1817
Sinfonia originale in D, dated 10 September 1817
Sinfonia 'La partenza', dated Bologna, 25 October 1817
Sinfonia, dated Bergamo, 17 December 1817
Sinfonia in D minor, written to commemorate the death of Antonio Capuzzi, 28 March 1818
Sinfonia 'L'incendio', performed in Bergamo, 19 March 1819
Sinfonia on themes from Bellini's operas, dated 1836
Sinfonia for the Cantata: *In morte di Maria F. Malibran*, performed at La Scala, 17 March 1837
Sinfonia in D, undated
Sinfonia in D, undated; this work contains themes from *Furioso* and *L'elisir*
Sinfonia in 4 tempos; only an *Adagio non troppo* and *Minuetto* survive, undated

CHAMBER MUSIC

Quartets

Quartet for strings in E flat major, dated 26 December 1817
Quartet for strings in A major, undated, but marked *Quartetto II*
Quartet for strings in C minor, undated, but marked *Quartetto III*
Quartet for strings in D major, dated 27 July 1818, marked *Quartetto IV*
Quartet for strings in E minor, undated, but marked *Quartetto V*
Quartet for strings in G minor, undated, but marked *Quartetto VI*
Quartet for strings in F minor, dated 6 May 1819, written on the death of Marchese Terzi and dedicated to Alessandro Bertoli
Quartet for strings in B flat major, dated 26 May 1819, dedicated to Marco Bonesi
Quartet for strings in D minor, dated 22 January 1821
Quartet for strings in G minor, dated 26 January 1821
Quartet for strings in C major, dated 12 March 1821
Quartet for strings in C major, dated 15 March 1821
Quartet for strings in A major, dated 19 April 1821
Quartet for strings in D major, dated 1825
Quartet for strings in C minor, dated 1836

(Zavadini believes the four quartets, undated, listed below, were probably composed 1819–21)

Quartet for strings in D major, undated
Quartet for strings in C major, undated (lacks the final tempo)
Quartet for strings in F major, undated
Quartet for strings in B minor, undated (score contains 122 bars of another quartet in A minor)

Quintets

Quintet (for 2 violins, 2 violas and cello) in C major, undated. One movement
Quintet (for 2 violins, viola, cello and bass viol), undated
Quintet (for 2 violins, viola, cello and guitar), undated. Six movements

Miscellaneous Pieces

Concerto for English horn, dedicated to Giovanni Catolfi, composed 1816; performed Bologna 1817
Concerto with theme and variations, in E flat major, for clarinet and orchestra, undated
Concerto for violin and cello and orchestra, undated
Concerto for unspecified instrument, undated
Fragment of a composition for oboe, incompletely orchestrated, undated
Larghetto for violin and harp in G minor, undated
Larghetto for flute and bassoon with piano accompaniment, undated
Larghetto and *Polonaise* for unaccompanied violin (except the first 26 bars of the polonaise), undated
Largo for cello with piano accompaniment, undated
Scherzo for violin with piano accompaniment. This composition uses 27 themes from operas Donizetti had composed through 1826; dedicated to Virginia Vasselli of Rome
Sestetto for 2 violins, viola, cello, flute and 2 horns. This work is apparently lost; it belonged to Marco Bonesi
Suonata for oboe, dedicated to Severino degli Antonj, undated
Suonata for cello and piano in D major, undated
Suonata for flute and piano, in C minor, dedicated to Signora Marianna Pezzoli-Grattaroli, dated Bergamo, 15 May 1819
Suonata for violin and piano in F minor, dedicated to Signora Pezzoli-Grattaroli, dated Bergamo, 26-7 October 1819
Variazioni, a set of six, for violin and piano, in D flat major, dedicated to Alessandro Zineroni, undated
Variazioni, a set of eighteen, for violin and piano, in D minor and F major, undated
(Work, untitled) in B flat major, for clarinet and small orchestra, undated
(Work, untitled) in B flat major, for woodwinds and organ, undated

PIANO MUSIC

Two hands

Adagio and *Allegro* in G major, undated
Allegro in F minor, undated

LIST OF DONIZETTI'S COMPOSITIONS

Allegro in C major, undated
Allegro vivace in C major, undated
Allegro vivace in G major, undated
Due motivi del celebre Mo. Paër, a sonata, dated Bologna, 7 October 1817
Fuga in G minor, undated
Giuseppina, polka-mazurka (incomplete sketch) in E flat major, undated
Invito, waltz, undated
Larghetto, theme and variations, undated
Larghetto, in C major, dated 30 December 1834
Pastorale in E major, dated 1813
Presto in F Major, undated
La ricordanza, adagio sentimentale in E flat major
Rondo in D major, dedicated to Marchesa Sofia di Marignano, dated Naples, February 1825
Sinfonia in A major, dated Bergamo, 13 October 1813
Sinfonia in C Minor and C major, dated 19 November 1816, Donizetti has written this note: 'Composed in an hour and a quarter by order of Padre Maestro Mattei. . . .'[1]
Sinfonia in D major, undated
Un capriccio in sinfonia in E minor, dated Bologna, 15 August 1817. Donizetti has noted 'written in half an hour between 4:30 and 5'
Valzer, signed '*Donizetti qui vous aime* . . .', undated
Valzer, a set of two, undated
Variazioni on a theme by Mayr, 1815
Variazioni for cembalo in G major, undated
Variazioni in E major, undated
La Vénitienne, waltz, undated

Four Hands

Allegro in C major, undated
Allegro moderato in A major, undated
Il capitan battaglia, sonata in E minor, composed 1819
Il genio di G. D. in G major, dedicated to Signora Pezzoli-Grattaroli, undated
L'inaspettata in E minor, dedicated to Signora Pezzoli-Grattaroli, undated
L . . . (title erased) in C major, dedicated to Signora Pezzoli-Grattaroli, undated
La Lontananza in E minor, undated
Marcia lugubre in F minor, undated

[1] Zavadini has listed this work as an orchestral work No. 231, but the autograph is clearly for piano.

511

Polacca in C major, composed 1819, signed: *Par le fou Donizetti*
Sinfonia IIa in D minor, dedicated to Signora Marianna Pezzoli-
  Grattaroli, dated Almenno, 28 March 1820
La solita suonata in F major, undated
Suonata in C major, dedicated to M. P. G., dated 31 March 1819
Suonata in D major, dedicated to Marianna Pezzoli-Grattaroli,
  dated 12 October 1819
Suonata 'a 4 sanfe', dedicated to Signora Pezzoli-Grattaroli, undated
Suonata in B flat major, *'Per Dolci e Donizetti'*, undated
Suonata in D major, dedicated to M. P. G., undated
Suonata IIIa in F major, undated
Valz, dedicated to the Marchesa Adelaide de Sterlich, dated 1844

All the piano music that bears no date was composed before
Donizetti left Bergamo in 1821. The manuscripts of all these compositions are in the Museo Donizettiano, with the exception of the
waltz subtitled *Donizetti qui vous aime*, which is in the Paris Conservatory Library. Only two of these piano compositions have been
published.

VOCAL COMPOSITIONS
Solo Voice

Addio: 'Partir conviene' No. 3 of *Dernières glânes musicales*
Adieu, tu brise et pour jamais, unpublished
Ah, che miro, o sventurato, unpublished
Ah, non lasciarmi no, bell' Idol mio, unpublished
Ah rammenta, o bella Irene, composed for Signor M. P. de Sevigny
Ah! ingrato m'inganni, published in *Donizetti per camera*
Ah, si tu voulais, toi que j'aime, unpublished
Aimer ma Rose est la sorte de ma vie, No. 6 in *Canzonette e duettini*
Al campo della gloria, No. 1 of *Donizetti per camera*
L'amante spagnuolo: 'Corri destrier', No. 2 in *Soirées d'automne à l'Infrascata*
A mezzanotte: 'Quando notte sarà oscura', No. 3 *Nuits d'été à Pausilippe*
Amiamo: 'Or che l' età ne invita', unpublished
Amis courons chercher la gloire, unpublished
Ammore! Neapolitan song
Amor che a nullo amato, text by Dante, dated 1843 Paris, unpublished
L'amor funesto: 'Più che non m'ama un angelo', written for Metternich,
  1842
Amor marinaro: 'Me voglio fa' na casa', Neapolitan song, No. 4 in
  Soirées d'automne à l'Infrascata
L'amor mio: 'Amo, sì, ma l'amor mio . . .', in *Tre melodie postume*
Amore e morte: 'Odi d'un uom che muore', No. 3 in *Soirées d'automne à
  l'Infrascata*
Amor tiranno: 'Perchè due cori insieme'

Amour jaloux: '*Dans un salon si quelqu'un regarde*', unpublished
Anch'io provai le tenere smanie, unpublished
Antonio Foscarini: '*Quando da te lontano*', text by G. B. Nicolini
A pie' del mesto salice, unpublished
L'attente: '*La mère, ma toute belle . . .*'
Au pied d'un croix: '*Voyez-vous cette femme*', unpublished
Au tic-tac des castagnettes, No. 5 of *Canzonette e duettini*
Il barcaiuolo: '*Voga, voga, il vento tace . . .*', words by L. Tarantini, No. 1 of *Nuits d'été à Pausilippe*
Bedda Eurilla, Sicilian song, No. 11 of *Donizetti per camera*
Bei labbri che amor formò, written in 1822
Berceuse: '*Questo mio figlio*'
La Bohémienne: '*La zingara, sur l'herbe arrosée*'
Cavallo arabo: bolero '*Corridor, più ratto assai . . .*', No. 2 of *Matinées musicales*
Cavatina: '*Ella riposi alcuni istanti almeno . . .*', unpublished
Le chant de l'abeille: '*Sur les fleurs voltige une abeille . . .*', text by H. Lucas, No. 8 of *Dernières glanes musicales*
Che cangi tempra mai più non spero, dedicated to Adele Appiani, unpublished
Combien la nuit est longue: '*Hélas j'entend sonner une heure*', unpublished
Come volgesti rapidi, giorni de' miei primi anni, unpublished
La Conocchia: '*Quann' a lo bello mio vojo parlare . . .*', Neapolitan song, No. 5 of *Nuits d'été à Pausilippe*
La corrispondenza amorosa: '*O dolci righe, pittura del core . . .*', No. 5 of *Matinées musicales*
Le crépuscule: '*L'aube naît et la porte est close . . .*', text by Hugo, No. 6 of *Nuits d'été à Pausilippe*
Il crociato: '*Colle piume sul cimiero . . .*', No. 2 of *Nuits d'été à Pausilippe*
Dell'anno novello, unpublished
Del colle in sul pendio, No. 3 in *Raccolta di canzonette*
Le départ pour la chasse: '*Voici la trace du cerf . . .*', for baritone or bass with horn in F, text by Paul Lacroix
Le départ du croisé: '*Aux champs de la victoire . . .*'
Depuis qu'un autre a su te plaire, dedicated to Marchesina Giovanna de Sterlich, dated 1844, unpublished
Dernier chant du troubadour, unpublished
Doux souvenirs, vivez toujours, text by Émile Barateau
D'un genio che m'accende, No. 2 in *Raccolta di canzonette*
Elle n'existe plus, unpublished
È morta: '*Morta! e ieri ancora . . .*', No. 5 of *Ispirazioni viennesi*
E' più dell'onda instabile, unpublished
Eterno amore e fè ti giuro umil al piè, No. 1 of *Raccolta di canzonette*
L'étrangère, unpublished
La farfalla ed il poeta, unpublished

513

Fausto sempre, aria written by Donizetti for Luiga Boccabadati to sing in *Il barbiere di Siviglia*

Faut-il renfermer mon âme, unpublished

La fiancée du timballier, text by Hugo, written 14 January 1843, unpublished

La folle de sainte Hélène, text by Nourrit

Garde tes moutons: 'Gentille fillette'

Già presso al termine de' suoi martiri, unpublished

Il giglio e la rosa, No. 6 in *Dernières glânes musicales*

Giovanna Gray: 'Io morrò, sonata è l'ora . . .'

Il giuramento: 'Tuo fin che il sol rischiara . . .', No. 7 of *Nuits d'été à Pausilippe*

La gondola: 'Meco in barchetta'

La gondoliera: 'Vieni la barca è pronta', No. 4 of *Matinées musicales*

Le gondolier de l'Adriatique, unpublished

Gran dio mi manca il cor, unpublished

La hart, for bass, *'Non loin de Montfaucon . . .'*

Heureuse qui près de toi, incomplete and unpublished

Il m'aime encore, doux rêve de mon âme, unpublished, with this note: 'Two hours after midnight and you are sleeping'

Il mio ben m'abbandonò, unpublished

Il mio grido getto ai venti, dedicated to Marchesina Caterina de Sterlich, dated 1844, unpublished

Io son pazza capricciosa, arietta

Io te voglio bene assaje, Neopolitan song, words by Raffaele Sacco

J'attends toujours, text by Eugène de Lonlay

Je vais quitter tout ce que j'aime, dedicated to the Escudier brothers

Lamento per la morte di V. Bellini, text by A. Maffei, 1836

Lamento di Cecco di Varlungo, unpublished

Lénor: 'Il faut partir . . .', text by Marie Escudier

La longue douleur, Prayer

La lontananza: 'Or ch'io sono a te rapita', No. 1 of *Soirées d'automne à l'Infrascata*

Malvina: 'Depuis qu'un autre a su te plaire', October 1845

Marie enfin quitte l'ouvrage, unpublished

Mentre del caro lido, unpublished

La Mère et l'enfant, No. 7 in *Dernières glânes musicales*

Le miroir magique, text by Edouard Plouvier

Mon enfant et mon seul espoir, unpublished

La musulmane, text by Maurice Bourges

La negra, No. 6 of *Matinées musicales*

Nice, st'occhiuzzi càlali, unpublished

La ninna nanna, text by A. de Lauzières, No. 2 of *Un hiver à Paris*

Noé, scène du deluge, text by J. de Bouteiller, February 1839

Il nome, No. 5 of *Donizetti per camera*

No, tu non m'hai tradita, for Belluccia and Rosuccia of the Casa
    Vasselli, unpublished
Non amerò che te, text by Vitali
Non amo che te, unpublished
Non giova il sospirar, Venetian song, written in 1822
Non m'ami più, text by Carlo Guaita, No. 4 of *Ispirazioni viennesi*
Non priego mai nè pianto, text by Redaelli, unpublished
Non v'è più barbaro di chi non sente, unpublished
Non v'è nume, non v'è fato, dedicated to Emilia Branca, who married
    Felice Romani
N'ornerà la bruna chioma, written for Lina Cottrau
O anime affanate, venite a noi parlar, text from Canto V of Dante's
    Inferno, unpublished
Occhio nero incendiator, No. 2 of *Canzonette e duettini*
O fille, que l'ennui chagrine, unpublished
Oh Cloe, delizia di questo core, unpublished
Oh, je rêve d'une étrangère plus douce que l'enfant qui dort, unpublished
On vous a peint l'amour, unpublished
L'ora del ritorno, No. 3 of *Ispirazioni viennesi*
Or che la notte invita, dedicated to Teresina Spadaro, unpublished
Oui, je sais votre indifférence, unpublished
Oui, ton Dieu est le mien, text by M. Michonne, unpublished
Ov'è la voce magica, dedicated to Marchesina Caterina de Sterlich for
    her name-day, 25 November 1844
Pas d'autre amour que toi, text by Émile Barateau
Le pauvre exilé, text by de Leuven
Il pegno, unpublished
Perchè due cori, unpublished
Perchè mai nigella amata, unpublished
Perchè se mia tu sei, dedicated to Countess Ludolf, unpublished
Il pescatore, text by Schiller, translated; No. 1 of *Un hiver à Paris*
Le petit joueur de la harpe, text by Paul Lacroix, unpublished
Le petit montagnard, text by Mme X
Philis plus avare que tendre, unpublished
Plus ne m'est rien, unpublished
Pourquoi me dire qu'il vous aime, unpublished
La preghiera, No. 3 of *Matinées musicales*
La prière, text by B. Jacob, unpublished
Quand un soupçon mortel, unpublished
Quand je vis que j'étais trahie, religious scena with accompaniment of
    piano and organ, unpublished
Quando da te lontano, No. 10 of *Donizetti per camera*
Quando il mio ben io rivedrò, unpublished
Quando morte coll'orrido artiglio, unpublished
Quando verrà sul colle, No. 4 of *Donizetti per camera*

Quando mio ben t'adoro, unpublished
Questi capelli bruni, No. 9 of *Donizetti per camera*
Qui sospirò, là rise, unpublished
Rendimi il core, o barbara, written in 1822
Le renégat, dedicated to Levasseur
Les revenants, unpublished
Il ritorno del trovatore da Gerusalemme, unpublished
Il ritratto, text by Romani, improvised at the Casa Branca, unpublished
Rose che un dì spiegaste, unpublished[1]
La savoiarda, in *Tre melodie postume*
Se talor più nol rammento, written for Pasta
Seul sur la terre en vain j'espère, unpublished
Si o no, No. 1 of *Dernières glânes musicales*
Si tanto sospiri, ti lagni d'amore, unpublished
Si tu m'as fait à ton image, unpublished
Sorgesti alfin aurora desiata, unpublished
Il sorriso è il primo vezzo, No. 4 in *Raccolta di canzonette*
Sospiri, aneliti che m'opprimete, unpublished
Il sospiro, text by Carlo Guaita, No. 4 of *Ispirazioni viennesi*
Il sospiro del gondoliere, unpublished
Sovra il canto della vita, dedicated to Caterina de Sterlich, unpublished
La speranza
Spunta il dì, l'ombra sparì, romanza for tenor, unpublished
Su l'onda tremula ride la luna, No. 5 of *Raccolta di canzonette*
La sultana, written for Giulia Grisi, No. 4 of *Un hiver à Paris*
Su questi allori, unpublished
Taci invan mia cara Jole, dedicated to De Martino, 1835, unpublished
T'aspetto ancor!, No. 5 of *Dernières glânes musicales*
Te dire adieu, text by Gustave Vaëz
Tengo no n'namurato, faccia d'empiso, No. 3 of *Canzonette e duettini*
La torre di Biasone, No. 4 of *Nuits d'été à Pausilippe*
Lu trademiento, Neopolitan song, No. 4 of *Canzonette e duettini*
Troppo vezzosa è la ninfa bella, unpublished
Trova un sol mia bella Clori, unpublished, Donizetti set this text twice to different music
Il trovatore, dedicated to Mme Therese Spadaro, unpublished
Il trovatore in caricatura, No. 3 in *Un hiver à Paris*
Tu, mi chiedi se t'adoro, dedicated to Madame de Coussy, 1840, unpublished
Il tuo pensiero è il mio, No. 1 of *Matinées musicales*
L'ultima notte di un novizio, text by Nourrit, No. 5 of *Un hiver à Paris*
L'ultimo dì, published in *I dodici album*
Una tortora innocente, dedicated to Virginia Vasselli, unpublished

[1] This is the same text as Zoraide's cavatina in Act 2 of *Zoraide di Granata*.

Una vergine donzella per amore sospirò, unpublished
Un bacio di speranza
Un cœur pour abri, text by Auguste Richomme
Un detto di Speranza, No. 2 of *Dernières glânes musicales*
Uno sguardo, text by Felice Romani, improvised at the Casa Branca, unpublished
V'era un dì che il cor beato, unpublished
Vien ti conforta, o misera, unpublished
Le violon de Crémone, text by Hoffman, unpublished
Vision, text by Édouard Plouvier
Voix d'Espoir, text by M. Cimbal
Viva il matrimonio, cavatina buffo, text by Leopoldo Tarantini
Les yeux noirs et les yeux bleus, text by Étienne Monnier
La zingara, text by Carlo Guaita, No. 1 of *Ispirazioni viennesi*

Two Voices

L'addio, text by Felice Romani, No. 6 of *Rêveries napolitaines*
L'addio, text by Émile Deschamps, No. 7 of *Matinées musicales*
Ah, non lasciarmi, no, unpublished
L'Alito di Bice, text by F. Puoti, No. 9 of *Nuits d'été à Pausilippe*
Amor voce del cielo, text by L. Tarantini, No. 10 of *Nuits d'été à Pausilippe*
Armida e Rinaldo, text by Tasso, unpublished
L'aurora, text by Tarantini, No. 8 of *Nuits d'étés à Pausilippe*
I bevitori, 'Mesci, mesci e sperda il vento', No. 12 of *Nuits d'été à Pausilippe*[1]
Canzónetta con l'eco, written at Bologna, 27 August 1817, unpublished
C'est le printemps, waltz, text by Édouard Plouvier
Che bel mar, che bel sereno, No. 9 of *Dernières glânes musicales*
Che cangi tempra mai più non spero, unpublished
Che vuoi di più, text by Carlo Guaita, No. 7 of *Ispirazioni viennesi*
Da me che vuoi, che brami? in *Donizetti per camera*
I due carcerati, duet for soprano and bass, unpublished
Duettino for 2 sopranos, unpublished
Duetto for 2 sopranos, dedicated to the Marchesa Medici, unpublished
Duetto, written for Clementina Carnevali and Nicola Cartoni, 19 December 1822, unpublished
Il fiore, No. 5 of *Soirées d'automne à l'Infrascata*
La gelosia, scherzo for soprano and bass, No. 8 of *Matinées musicales*
Il giuramento, text by Palazzolo, No. 7 of *Nuits d'été à Pausilippe*
Godi filetta ingrata nell'ingannarmi tu, unpublished
Ha negli occhi un tale incanto, No. 7 of *Raccolta di canzonette*

---

[1] This song was included in the score of *Il campanello*.

Héloise et Abelard, text by Crevel de Charlemagne
Ho perduto il mio tesoro, No. 8 of *Raccolta di canzonette*
L'incostanza di Irene, dedicated to Virginia Vasselli. '*Donizetti nel-
l'anniversario suo D. D. D. -Sono 29. 30 Nov. 1826*'
Io d'amor o Dio mi moro, No. 6 of *Raccolta di canzonette* and No. 12 of
Donizetti per camera
Lumi bei del mio martire, unpublished
Les Napolitains, text by Crevel de Charlemagne
Non mi sprezzar licori, unpublished
O crudel che il mio pianto non vedi, No. 8 of *Canzonette e duettini*
Predestinazione, text by Carlo Guaita, No. 6 of *Ispirazioni viennesi*
Quegli sguardi e quegli accenti, unpublished
Se mai turbo il tuo riposo, unpublished
Sempre più t'amo mio bel tesoro, unpublished
Sempre sarò costante, dedicated to the Countess Ravizza-Botti
Se tu non vedi tutto il mio cor, unpublished
Si soffre una tiranna, unpublished
Sta negli occhi un tale incanto (version for 2 voices), unpublished
Sull'onda cheta e bruna, Barcarola, unpublished
T'intendo sì mio cor, duet for soprano and tenor, in *Donizetti per
camera*
Ti sento, sospiri, in *Donizetti per camera*
L'ultimo rimprovero, No. 10 of *Dernières glânes musicales*
Uno sguardo ed una voce, No. 1 of *Nuits d'été à Pausilippe*
Vedi là sulla collina, unpublished

Three or more Voices
Ah che il destino, for 3 voices, 2 sopranos and tenor, unpublished
La campana, little quartet for 2 tenors and 2 basses, No. 9 of *Matinées
musicales*
Cedè la mia costanza, Irene, al tuo rigor, for soprano, contralto, tenor
and bass, unpublished
Clori infedel (for soprano, contralto and bass), unpublished
Finchè fedele tu mi sei stata, canzonetta for 4 voices, dated Bologna,
5 May 1817
Io morrò, sonata e l'ora, trio, unpublished
Madrigale for 2 sopranos and 2 basses, dated Bologna, 12 June
1817
Qui sta il male, terzetto, unpublished
Rataplan, quartet for 2 tenors and 2 basses, No. 19 of *Matinées
musicales*
Se schiudi il labbro, o Filide, for 5 voices, No. 9 of *Raccolta di can-
zonette*
Strofe di Byron, set for 4 voices (a) '*Sien l'onde placide*' (b) '*Per noi la
vita* (c) '*Ma poi passati stragi e orror*,' unpublished

MISCELLANY

L'amor materno, dedicated to Countess Amélie Taaffe, 1844, unpublished

Sestetto: '*Ah! qui Guglielmo, qual sorpresa, o ciel che miro* . . .', dated in 1812, but Donizetti has added '*Fatto prima degli studi di Bologna seguiti nel 1816–17.*' For 2 sopranos, 2 tenors, 2 basses, and orchestra, unpublished

Aria: '*Ognun dice che le donne*' for bass and orchestra. An autograph note indicates Donizetti wrote this aria for his own use on 20 March 1815

Anacreontica: '*Guarda che bianca luna* . . .', Donizetti wrote this for Gian Battista Capitanio on 30 March 1815

Aria: '*Amor mio nume, eccomi a' piedi tuoi*', for soprano and orchestra. Written in 1816, Bologna.

Duetto: '*Perchè quell'alma ingrata*', for soprano, tenor, and small orchestra, dated 28 September 1816

Aria: '*Ti sovvenga amato bene, che fedel ti serbo il cor*', dated 10 May 1817

Terzetto: Isabella ormai mi rende, dated 1818, for 2 tenors and bass

Aria for soprano and English horn obbligato and orchestra. Written for Carolina Magni for her benefit night at the Teatro Riccardi of Bergamo, 11 September 1820

Cabaletta: '*Pietosa all'amor mio*' written for Tosi and Tamburini to insert into Rossini's *L'assedio di Corinto*, Genoa, May 1828

Duetto, Lisetta e Proclo: '*Se bramate che vi sposi*, unpublished

Duetto for 2 sopranos, '*Taci, tu cerchi invano*' for orchestra

Recitativo and *duetto* for soprano and bass. '*Sposo, lo so, lo so*'

Recitativo and *romanza* for tenor and small orchestra, '*Che avvenne, che fu*'

Grande offertorio for organ or piano, published by L. Bertuzzi

Studi di contrappunto e fuga, this is the lesson book used by Donizetti while he studied with Padre Mattei at Bologna. From 22 November 1815 through 1816, he worked 22 studies in counterpoint and 40 fugues for 2, 3, and 4 voices

Fughe, this book contains 11 studies of fugues for 4, 5, and 6 voices made by Donizetti at Bologna in 1817

Fuga for 4 separate voices, unpublished; in Naples

Fuga for 4 voices, orchestrated

Fughe, three for 4 voices, juvenilia

Studio for clarinet in B flat major, dedicated to 'my friend Benigni, 1821'

Solfeggi for mezzo-soprano, written in Paris by Donizetti and copied by his nephew Andrea

Vocalizzi (or *Gorgheggi*), used by Donizetti in his singing lessons

Besides these works there are many sketches, drafts, and miscellaneous sheets of manuscript in the Naples Conservatory Library and in the Paris Conservatory Library.

519

Bibliography

Abbiati, Franco, *Giuseppe Verdi*, 4 Vols., Milan, 1959
—— 'La musica in Turchia con Giuseppe Donizetti pascià', in *Bergomum*, Vol. 22, Nov. 1928
Acton, Harold, *The Last Bourbons of Naples (1825–61)*, London, 1961
Adam, Adolphe, *Derniers souvenirs d'un musicien*, Paris, 1859
Ademollo, Alessandro, *Bibliografia della cronistoria teatrale italiana*, Milan, 1881
Alborghetti, Fedorico, and Galli, Michelangelo, *Gaetano Donizetti e G. Simone Mayr, Notizie e documenti*, Bergamo, 1875
Amore, Antonino, *Vincenzo Bellini: Vita, studi e ricerche*, Catania, 1894
Anon., 'Account of "Duca d'Alba": The posthumous opera of Donizetti', in *Monthly Musical Record*, Vol. 11, pp. 230–1, London, 1881
—— Accursi, M., *'Donizetti e il "Don Pasquale"'*, Milan, n.d.
—— *Cenni biografici di G. Donizetti raccolti da un vecchio dilettante di buona memoria*, Milan, 1874
Antonini, D. G., 'Un episodio emotivo di Gaetano Donizetti', in *Rivista musicale italiana*, Vol. VII, pp. 518–35, Turin, 1900
Apeelius, Elda, 'Il Centenario dell' "Elisir d'amore" ', in *Rivista di Bergamo*, Vol. 11, pp. 195–201, 1932
Apel, Willi, *Harvard Dictionary of Music*, Cambridge, Mass., 1962
Armstrong, W. G., *A Record of the opera in Philadelphia*, Philadelphia, 1884
Baccaro, M., *'Lucia di Lammermoor' prima at S. Carlo di Napoli*, Naples, 1948
Ballini, Marcello, *Guido Zavadini*, Bergamo, 1960
—— 'Ritorno dell' "Anna Bolena" ', in *La Scala*, No. 89, pp. 17–22, April 1957
Barbiera, Raffaello, *Un amico sconosciuto di Verdi*, Milan, 1903
—— *Arte ed amori; profili lombardi*, Milan, 1888
—— *Figure e figurine del secolo che muore*, Milan, 1899
—— *Grandi e piccole memorie; pagine di letteratura, d'arte e di storia*, Florence, 1900

Barbiera, Raffaello, *Ideali e caratteri dell'ottocento*, Milan, 1926
—— *Immortali e dimenticati*, Milan, 1901
—— *Nella gloria e nell'ombra, immagini dell'ottocento*, Milan, 1926
—— *Passioni del risorgimento*, Milan, 1903
—— *Polvere di palcoscenico, note drammatiche*, 2 Vols., Catania, 1908
—— *La principessa Belgioioso, i suoi amici e nemici: il suo tempo*, Milan, n.d.
—— *Salotto della Contessa Maffei e la società Milanese, 1834–1886*, Milan, 1895
—— *Silvio Pellico*, Milan, 1926
—— *Vite ardenti nel teatro (1700–1900)*, Milan, 1931
—— *Voci e volti del passato (1800–1900) da archivi segreti di stato e da altre fonti*, Milan, 1920
Barblan, Guglielmo, 'Donizetti nel passato e nel presente', in *Rivista musicale italiana*, pp. 284–9, July–December 1948
—— 'La "Messa di Requiem" di Gaetano Donizetti', in *Rassegna musicale*, pp. 192–8, July, 1948
—— *L'opera di Donizetti nell'età romantica*, Bergamo, 1948
Beccherini, Bianca, 'Il Don Sebastiano di Donizetti al XVIII maggio musico fiorentino', in *Revue belge musicologie*, No. 9, pp. 143–53, 1955
Bellini, Vincenzo, *Epistolario* (ed. Luisa Cambi), Milan, 1943
Berlioz, Hector, *'La fille du Régiment'*, Paris, 1840
—— *La grotesque dans la musique*, Paris, 1871
—— *Memoirs* (ed. Ernest Newman), New York, 1932
—— *Les musiciens et la musique*, Paris, 1903
Berri, Pietro, 'Il Librettista del Don Pasquale: Leggende, ingiustizie, plagi', in *La Scala: Rivista dell'opera*, No. 110, January 1959
Bettòli, Parmenio, 'Le opera di Donizetti: Errori e lacune', in *Numero unico*, Bergamo [1897]. (*Numero unico* (edited by Bettòli), is filled with articles commemorating the centenary of Donizetti's birth.)
Biedenfeld, Ferdinand Freiherr von, *Die komische Oper der Italiener, der Franzosen und der Deutschen*, Leipzig, 1848
Bienenfeld, Elsa, 'Donizetti und Verdi', in *Musik*, Vol. 22, pp. 801–6, 1930
Bignami, Luigi, *Cronologia di tutti gli spettacoli, rappresentati al Teatro Communale di Bologna dalla su Apertura 14 Maggio 1763 a tutto l'Autunno 1881, compilata da Luigi Bignami*, Bologna, 1882
Blasis, Carlo, *Della musica drammatica italiana in Francia*, Milan, 1841
Bonaventura, Arnaldo, *L'opera italiana*, Florence, 1928
—— *Saggio storico sul teatro italiano*, Leghorn, 1913
Bonesi, Marco, *Note biografiche su Donizetti* (MS. in Biblioteca Civica, Bergamo)
Bonetti, G., *G. Donizetti*, Naples, 1926

Bossi, Lea, *Donizetti*, Brescia, 1956

Bottura, Giuseppe Carlo, *Storia aneddotica documentata del Teatro Communale di Trieste*, Trieste, 1885

Branca-Romani, Emilia, *Felice Romani ed i più riputati maestri di musica del suo tempo*, Turin, 1882

Breggi, Paolo, *Serie degli spettacoli rappresentati al teatro Regio di Torino (1688–1872)*, Turin, 1872

Brown, James D., and Stratton, Stephen, *British Musical Biography*, London, 1897

Bülow, Hans von, *Letters* (edited Scott Goddard), London, 1931

Bustico, Guido, 'Gli spettacoli musicali al Teatro Novo' di Novara (1779–1873)', *Rivista musicale italiana*, Vol. XXV, pp. 84–103, 204–48, 1918; Vol. XXVI, pp. 615–52, 1919

Calvi, Gerolamo, *Gio. Simone Mayr*, Milan, 1847

Calzado, Adolfo, *Donizetti e l'opera italiana in Spagna*, Paris, 1897

Cambiasi, Pompeo, *La Scala (1778–1889): Note storiche e statistiche*, 4th edition, Milan, 1889

Cametti, Alberto, *Bellini a Roma*, Rome, 1900

—— *Donizetti a Roma*, Turin, 1907

—— *La musica teatrale a Roma cento anni fa: 'Olive e Pasquale' di Donizetti*, Rome, 1927

—— *La musica teatrale a Roma cento anni fa: 'Il Corsaro' di Pacini, il 'Furioso' e 'Torquato Tasso' di Donizetti, 'La sonnambula' di Bellini, la 'Norma' di Bellini*, in *Reggia accademia di Santa Cecilia, Roma, Annuario*, 1930–31, pp. 445–89, 1933–34, pp. 365–421

—— *Un poeta melodrammatico romano: Appunti e notizie in gran parte inedite sopra Jacopo Ferretti e i musicisti del suo tempo*, Milan, 1898l

—— *Il Teatro di Tordinona, poi di Apollo*, 2 Vols., Tivoli, 1938

Capeli, Dr G., 'La Calotta cramica di Donizetti', in *Archivio italiano per le malattie nervose e più particolarmente per le alienazioni mentali, Organo della Società freniatrica italiana*, 1887

Capri, Antonio, 'Linda di Chamounix', in *La Scala*, pp. 46–50, May 1952

Carducci, Edgardo, 'The Tenor Voice in Europe', in *Music and Letters*, Vol. XL, pp. 318–23, 1930

Castil-Blaze, *L'opéra-Italien: de 1548 à 1856*, Paris, 1856

Cattini, Umberto, 'Note sul Roberto Devereux', in *Ricordiana*, Milan, November 1957

Caversazzi, Ciro, *Gaetano Donizetti (discorso), a cura della Congregazione di carità*, Bergamo, 1926

—— *Gaetano Donizetti la casa dove nacque*, Bergamo, 1924

Chilesotti, Oscar, *I nostri maestri del passato*, Milan, 1883

Chocquet, Gustave, *Histoire de la musique dramatique en France*, Paris, 1873

Chorley, Henry F., *Thirty Years' Musical Recollections* (ed. E. Newman), New York, 1926

Cicconetti, Filippo, *Vita di Gaetano Donizetti*, Rome, 1864

Clément and Larousse, *Dictionnaire des Opéras* (new ed.). Paris, n.d.

Codignola, Arturo, *I fratelli Ruffini: Lettere di G. e A. Ruffini alle madre dall'esilio francese e svizzero*, Genoa, 1925

Colombani, Alfredo, *L'opera italiana nel secolo XIX*, Milan, 1900

Commons, Jeremy, 'Emilia di Liverpool', in *Music and Letters*, Vol. 40, pp. 207-28, 1959

—— 'An introduction to "Il duca d'Alba" ', in *Opera*, Vol. 10, pp. 421-6, July 1959

Cottrau, Guillaume Louis, *Lettres d'un mélomane*, Naples, 1885

Croce, Benedetto, *I Teatri di Napoli*, Bari, 1947

Curzon, Henri de, 'L'Opéra en 1843; mémoire du directeur Léon Pillet', in *Revue de Musique*, Vol. II, pp. 223-33, 1920-21

Dal Fabbro, B., 'Donizetti e l'opera buffa', *I bidelli del Valhalla*, Florence, 1954

Damerini, A., 'Vita tragica di Donizetti', in *Melodramma*, Vol. 1-2, 1954

D'Arcais, Francesco, 'Il duca d'Alba, opera inedita di Donizetti', in *Nuova Antologia* (Secondo Serie), Vol. XXXI, p. 149, 1 January 1882

Dassari, Carlo, *Opere e operisti (dizionario lirico) 1541-1902*, Genoa, 1903

Daub-Mohr, Marie, 'Ein Meister der italischen Oper: zum 100 Todestag von Donizetti', in *Neue Musikzeitschrift*, pp. 209-10, July 1948

Davison, J. W., *From Mendelssohn to Wagner*, London, 1912

De Angelis, Alberto, 'Cantanti italiani del secolo XIX: Erminia e Giuseppe Frezzolini', in *Rivista musicale italiana*, Vol. XXXII, pp. 438-54, 1925

de Boigne, C., *Petits mémoires de l'Opéra*, Paris, 1857

Delessert, Gabriel Abraham Margueritte, *Articolo estratto del giornale l'Univers*, pp. 12-13, June 1848 (in Widener Library, Harvard University)

Della Corte, Andrea, *Canto e bel canto (Tosi e Mancini)*, Turin, 1933

—— 'Un secolo di critica per l'opera di Donizetti', in *Melodramma*, Vol. 1-2, 1954

—— *Tre secoli di opera italiana*, Turin, 1938

Dent, Edward, 'Donizetti: An Italian Romantic', in *Fanfare for Ernest Newman* (ed. Herbert van Thal), London, 1955

Desarbres, Nérée, *Deux siècles à l'Opéra (1669-1868)*, Paris, 1868

Donati-Pettèni, Giuliano, *L'arte della musica in Bergamo*, Bergamo, 1930

—— 'Attraverso le biografie donizettiane', in *Rivista di Bergamo*, Vol. 8, pp. 389-406, 1929

Donati-Pettèni, Giuliano, *Donizetti*, Milan, 1930
—— *L'istituto musicale Gaetano Donizetti*, Bergamo, 1928
—— *Studi e documenti donizettiani*, Bergamo, 1929
—— 'Una visita al museo donizettiano di Bergamo', in *Emporium*, Vol. 65, No. 2, pp. 17–33, Bergamo, 1927
Donizetti, Gaetano, *Alcune lettere di Gaetano Donizetti pubblicata per la auspicatissime nozze S. Scotti*, Bergamo, 1875
—— 'Lettere inedite', in *Bollettino bibliografico musicale*, Vol. 5, pp. 5–51, Milan, July–September 1930
—— 'Lettres inédites de Donizetti' (ed. Paul Nettl), in *Revue musicale*, Vol. 7, pp. 24–32, Paris, July 1926
—— 'Per il carteggio di Gaetano Donizetti (lettere inedite, a cura di Vicenzo Epifanio)', in *Bollettino della civica biblioteca di Bergamo*, Vol. 9, pp. 49–69, April–June 1915
—— *Studi Donizettiani I: Contributo all'Epistolario di Gaetano Donizetti* (ed. G. Barblan and F. Walker), Bergamo, 1962
—— *Tre lettere inedite di Gaetano Donizetti*, Florence, 1891
Donizetti, Giuseppe, *Ricordi di Gaetano Donizetti esposti nella mostra centenaria tenutasi in Bergamo nell'agosto-settembre 1897, raccolti da Gius. e Gaet. Donizetti, collezione di proprietà dei fratelli Gius. e Gaet. Donizetti*, Bergamo, 1897
Duhamel, Raoul, 'Quelques maîtres de l'opéra-comique au XIXᵉ siècle', in *Revue Musicale*, Vol. XIV, pp. 291–302, November 1933
Duprez, Gilbert, *Souvenirs d'un chanteur*, Paris, 1880
Edwards, Henry Sutherland, *History of the Opera from Monteverdi to Donizetti*, 2 Vols., London, 1862
—— *The Lyrical Drama*, London, 1881
—— *The Prima Donna*, London, 1888
—— *Rossini and His School*, New York, 1881
Eisner-Eisenhof, Angelo de, *Lettere di Gaetano Donizetti*, Bergamo, 1897
Enzinger, Moriz, *Die Entwicklung des Wiener Theater vom 16. zum 19. Jahrhundert*, 2 Vols., Berlin, 1918–19
Escudier, Léon, *Etudes biographiques sur les chanteurs contemporains, précédées d'un esquisse sur l'art du chant*, Paris, 1840
—— *Mes souvenirs*, Paris, 1863
—— *Les pirates de la littérature et de la musique; questions de propriété, par L. E.*, Paris, 1862
Escudier, Marie Pierre Yves, *Vie et aventures des cantatrices célèbres, précédées des Musiciens de l'Empire et suivie de la vie anécdotique de Paganini*, Paris, 1856
Fantoni, Gabriele, *Storia universale del canto*, 2 Vols., Milan, 1873
Farga, Franz, *Die Wiener Oper von ihren Anfängen bis 1938*, Vienna, 1947
Ferrari, A. Rodigino, *Le convenienze teatrali: analisi della condizione presente del teatro italiano*, Milan, 1843

Ferrari, Vittorio P. E., *Spettacoli drammatici, musicali e coreografici in Parma dal 1628 al 1883*, Parma, 1884

Ferris, George Titus, *The great Italian and French composers*, New York, 1888

Filippi, Filippo, *Musica e musicisti*, Milan, 1876

Finazzi, Giovanni, *Memorie di G. S. Mayr*, Bergamo, 1853

Florimo, Francesco, *Cenno storico sulla scuola musicale di Napoli*, 2 Vols., Naples, 1869–71; 4 Vols., Naples, 1880–84

Fraccarali, Arnaldo, *Donizetti*, Milan, 1945

Gabriele, Annibale, 'Le case di Donizetti a Napoli', in *Fanfulla della Domenica*, Vol. XV, December 1893

—— *Gaetano Donizetti*, Rome, 1904

—— *Lettere inedite di Gaetano Donizetti*, Rome, 1892

—— 'Le lettere inedite di Gaetano Donizetti', in *Fanfulla della Domenico*, Vol. XIV, January 1892

Galli, Antenore, *La musica ed i musicisti, ovvero biografie d'illustri maestri*, Milan, 1871

Gallini, Natale, 'Inediti Donizettiani', in *Rivista musicale italiana*, Vol. LV, pp. 257–75, July–September 1953

—— 'Uno strumento ideato da Franklin', in *La Scala*, October 1959

Gara, Eugenio, '*Interpreti di 119 anni fa*', in *Melodramma*, Vol. 1–2, 1954

Gatti, G. M., *50 Years of Opera and Ballet in Italy*, Rome, 1956

Gauthier, Judith, *Le roman d'un grand chanteur: Mario de Candia*, Paris, 1912

Gautier, Théophile, *L'art dramatique en France depuis vingt-cinq ans*, Paris, n.d.

—— *Les beautés de l'opéra*, Paris, 1845

Gavazzeni, Gianandrea, 'Donizetti e l'Elisir d'Amore', in *Rassegna Musicale*, Vol. VI, pp. 44–50, 1933

—— *Gaetano Donizetti*, Milan, 1937

—— *La morte dell'opera*, Milan, 1954

—— *Il suono è stanco: saggi e divertimenti*, Bergamo, 1950

—— *Trent'anni di musica*, Milan, 1958

Geddo, Angelo, *Bergamo e la musica: sintesi storica biografica e critica*, Bergamo, 1958

—— *Donizetti, l'uomo, le musiche*, Bergamo, 1956

—— 'Ordine fra i suoi quartetti', in *La Scala*, Vol. 77, pp. 63–6, 111–14, April 1956

Genest, Émile, *L'Opéra-comique connu et inconnu*, Paris, 1925

Ghezzi, Teodoro, 'Ricordi su Donizetti', in *Omnibus*, Naples, 7 March 1860

Giocamo, Salvatore di, *Il conservatorio dei poveri di Gesù Cristo e quello di S. M. di Loreto*, Palermo, 1928

Giovagnoli, *Il duca d'Alba*, Rome, 1887

Giulini, Maria Ferranti, *Giuditta Pasta e i suoi tempi*, Milan, 1935
Gravier, Leopold, 'Musique et procédure', in *Chronique musicale*, Vol. 8, pp. 241–51, Paris, 1875
Grout, Donald J., *A Short History of Opera*, 2 Vols., New York, 1947
Halévy, Jacques Fromental, *Souvenirs et portraits, études sur les beaux arts*, Paris, 1861
—— *Derniers souvenirs et portraits*, Paris, 1863
Harman, Alec and Mellers, Wilfrid, *Man and His Music*, London, 1962
Henriot, Angus, *The Castrati in Opera*, London, 1956
Hogarth, George, *Memoirs of the Musical Drama*, 2 Vols., London, 1838
—— *Memories of the opera in Italy*, etc., 2 Vols., London, 1851
Hughes, Spike, *Great Opera Houses*, New York, 1959
Iarro (Giulio Piccini) *see* Piccini
Istel, Edgar, *Die komische Oper*, Stuttgart, 1906
Jean-Aubry, G., 'A Romantic Dilettante: Émile Deschamps (1791–1871)', in *Music and Letters*, Vol. XX, pp. 250–65, 1939
Kapp, Julius, *Geschichte der Staatsoper Berlin*, Berlin, 1937, 2nd ed., 1942
Kleefeld, Wilhelm Joseph, *Don Pasquale von Gaetano Donizetti*, Leipzig, 1901
Klein, John W., 'Gaetano Donizetti, 1797–1848, a centennial tribute', in *Musical Opinion*, pp. 205–6, March 1958
—— 'Verdi's Italian Contempories and Successors', in *Music and Letters*, Vol. XV, pp. 37–45, 1934
Labat, Jean Baptiste, *Oeuvres littéraires—musicales*, 2 Vols., Paris, n.d. (See Vol. 2, pp. 357–76)
Lajarte, Théodore de, *Bibliothèque musicale du théâtre de l'Opéra*, 2 Vols, Paris, 1878
—— *Curiosités de l'opéra*, Paris, 1883
Lasalle, Albert de, *Mémorial du Théâtre-Lyrique*, Paris, 1877
Laserre, Pierre, *L'esprit de la musique française*, Paris, 1917
Lazzari, Alfonso, 'Giovanni Ruffini, Gaetano Donizetti e il Don Pasquale', in *Rassegna Nazionale*, Florence, 16 October 1915
Leo, Sophie Augustine, 'Musical Life in Paris (1817–1848)', in *Musical Quarterly*, Vol. XVII, pp. 259–403, 1931
Lesimple, August, *Erlebnisse und erinnerungen aus dem Musiker-Leben von August Lesimple*, Dresden, 1886
Lespes, Léo, *Les mystères du grand-opéra*, Paris, 1843
Liberatore, R., *Nicolò Zingarelli*, Naples, 1837
Loewenberg, Alfred, *Annals of Opera*, 2 Vols. 2nd ed., Geneva, 1955
Lui, Ernesto, *I cento anni del Teatro Sociale di Mantova (1822–1922)*, Mantua, 1922
Lumley, Benjamin, *Reminiscences of the opera*, London, 1864

Malherbe, Charles Théodore, *Centenaire de Gaetano Donizetti*, Paris, 1897

Manferrari, Umberto, *Dizionario delle opere melodrammatiche* (Vol. I, pp. 321–55 for Donizetti), Florence, n.d.

Marangoni, Guido and Vanvianchi, Carlo, '*La Scala* studie e ricerche, note storiche e statistiche (*1906–20*), Bergamo, 1922.

Marchetti, Parisotti, and Cecchi, *Lettere inedite di Gaetano Donizetti*, Rome, 1892

Marcello, Benedetto, *It teatro alla moda* (ed. Andrea d'Angeli), Milan, 1956

Mariotti, Filippo, *Dante e la statistica delle lingue da Filippo Mariotti; con la raccolta dei versi della Div. Comm. messi in musica da G. Rossini, G. Donizetti, F. Marchetti e R. Schumann*, Florence, 1880

Martens, Federick H., *A Thousand and One Nights of Opera*, New York, 1942

Martin, George, *The Opera Companion*, London, 1962

Masutto, Giovanni, *I maestri di musica italiani del Secolo XIX*, 3rd ed.

Mazzini, Giuseppe, *Scritti letterari*, Lugano, 1897. (See Vol. II, p. 313)

Mérimée, Prosper, *Lettres de Mérimée à la famille Delessert*, Paris, 1931

Micca, Cesare Botto, 'Giovanni Ruffini e il libretto del Don Pasquale, in *Rivista di Bergamo*, Vol. 10, pp. 537–41, 1931

Miragoli, Lina, *Il melodramma italiana nell'ottocento*, Rome, 1924

Monaldi, Gino, *Gaetano Donizetti*, Turin, 1938

—— 'Pel centenario di Gaetano Donizetti', in *Rivista d'Italia*, Vol. VI, pp. 361–71, suppl. 1898

—— *I teatri di Roma negli ultimi tre secoli*, Rome, 1928

Monnet, Jean, *Mémoires*, Paris, 1884

Moore, Lillian, *Artists of the Dance*, New York, 1938

Morazzoni, G., *Lettere inedite di Gaetano Donizetti, seguite da un saggio di iconografia donizettiana*, Milan, 1930

Morini, Ugo, *La Re Accademia degli Immobili ed il suo teatro 'la Pergola' (*1649–1925*), Pisa, 1926

Moynet, M. J., *L'Envers du théâtre: machines et décorations*, Paris, 1875

Musical Opinion, June, July and August 1948, 'Letters concerning Donizetti'

Nani-Mocenigo, Mario Filippo, *Il Teatro la Fenice*, Venice, 1926

Nerval, Gerard de, *Notes d'un amateur de musique*, Paris, 1926

Northcott, Richard, *Donizetti*, Private printing, London, 1915

—— *Opera Chatter*, London, 1921

Oliario, T., 'La Malattia ed i Medici di Gaetano Donizetti', in *Minerva Medici*, Vol. XXIX, 1938

Ortigue, Jos. Louis D'., *Du théâtre-italien et de son influence sur le goût musical français*, Paris, 1840

Pacini, Giovanni, *Le mie memorie artistiche*, Florence, 1875

Pannain, Guido, 'Saggio sulla musica a Napoli nel XIX', in *Rivista musicale italiana*, Vol. XXV, pp. 198–268, 331–42, 1928; Vol. XXVI, pp. 197–210, 1929; Vol. XXVII, pp. 231–42, 1930; Vol. XXXVIII, pp. 193–206, 1931ᵉ Vol. XXXIX, pp. 51–72, 1932

Pardo Pimentel, Nicolas, *La ópera italiana*, Madrid, 1841

Pavin, Giuseppe, *Teatri musicali veneziani*, Venice, 1916

Piccini, Giulio (pseud. Iarro), *Memorie d'un impresario fiorentino*, Florence, 1892

Pinetti, Gian Battista, *La stagione d'opera alla Fiera di Agosto (1784–1936)*, *Teatro Donizetti (già Riccardi)*, Bergamo, 1937

Pironti, Alberto, 'Duca d'Alba', in *La Scala*, No. 34, pp. 38–41, September 1952

Pizzetti, Ildebrando, *La musica italiana dell'ottocento*, Turin, 1947

—— *Vincenzo Bellini*, Milan, 1936

Polver, 'Le vicende della calotta cranica di Donizetti', in *Gazzetta del popolo della Domenica*, Nos. 2 and 3, 1895

Pougin, Arthur, *Adolphe Adam*, Paris, 1877

Prod'Homme, Jacques G., *L'opéra (1669–1925)*, Paris, 1925

Prout, Ebenezer, 'Auber's "Le Philtre" and Donizetti's "L'Elisir"', a comparison', in *Monthly Musical Record*, Vol. 30, pp. 25–7; pp. 49–53; pp. 73–6, 1900

Radiciotti, Giuseppe, *Gioacchino Rossini: vita documentata*, 3 Vols., Tivoli, 1927–29

—— *Teatro, musica e musicisti in Recanati*, Recanati, 1904

—— *Teatro, musica e musicisti in Sinigaglia*, Milan, 1893

—— *Teatro e musica in Roma (1825–1850)*, Rome, 1905

Regli, Francesco, *Dizionario biografico dei più celebri poeti ed artisti melodrammatici . . . in Italia dal 1800 al 1860*, Turin, 1860

Riehl, Wilhelm Heinrich, *Musikalische characterköpfe*, 2 Vols., Stuttgart, 1899

—— *Zur Geschichte der romantischen Oper*, Berlin, 1928

Rinaldi, Mario, 'Antonio e Pasquale', in *La Scala*, July 1950

Rius, José, *Opera espãnola*, Barcelona, 1840

Riva, Ubaldo, 'Un bergamasco (Gius. Donizetti pascià), riformatore della musica in Turchia', in *Rivista di Bergamo*, Vol. 1, pp. 349–53, 1922

Rizzi, Aldo, . . . *Gaetano Donizetti nel primo centenario della morte*, Bergamo, n.d.

Roberti, Giuseppe, 'Donizettiana', in *Rivista musicale italiana*, 1895

Rogers, Francis, 'Adolphe Nourrit', in *Musical Quarterly*, Vol. XXV, pp. 11–25, 1939

Romani, Felice, *Gazzetta ufficiale piemontese*, No. 190, 25 August 1835

Romani, Luigi, *Teatro alla Scala—Cronologia*, Milan, 1862

Roncaglia, Gino, 'Il centuario di "Lucia" ', in *Rivista musicale italiana*, 1936
—— 'Ricuperato anche "Il furioso all'isola di S. Domingo" ', in *La Scala*, No. 115, pp. 34–9, 69–75, June 1959
Rossato, Arturo, 'Donizetti', in *Commedia* (a play in 4 acts), Vol. 70, 1929
Rossi-Scotti, G. B., *Della vita e delle opere di Francesco Morlacchi*, Perugia, 1861
Rovani, Giuseppe, *Cento anni; romanzo ciclico*, 2 Vols., Milan, 1868–69
—— 'Gaetano Donizetti', in *Storie delle lettere e delle arti in Italia*, Vol. IV, p. 619, Milan, 1858
Royer, Alphonse, *Histoire de l'Opéra*, Paris, 1875
—— *Histoire du théâtre contemporain en France et à l'étranger 1800–1875*. Paris, 1878
Sacchi, F., 'Sensazzionale tragedia in Scozia', in *Melodramma*, Vol. 1–2, 1954
Sacerdote, Giacomo, *Teatro regio di Torino*, Turin, 1892
—— *Saggio bibliografico relativo ai melodrammi di Felice Romani (per) Luigi Lianvosani (pseud.)*, Milan, 1878
Salvioli, Giovanni, *La Fenice, Serie degli spettacoli dal 1792 al 1876*, Milan, 1878
—— *I melodrammi di F. Romani*, Milan, 1877
Sartori, C., *Il R. Conservatorio di musica G. B. Martini di Bologna*, Florence, 1942
—— *Dizionario degli editori musicali italiani, tipografi, incisori, librai, editori*, Florence, 1958
—— *Dizionario Ricordi della musica e dei musicisti*, Milan, 1959
Schletterer, Hans Michael, 'Die Opernhäuser Neapals', in *Monatschefte für Musikgeschichte*, Vol. XIV, pp. 175–81, 1882; Vol. XV, pp. 12–19, 1883
Schlitzer, Franco, 'Curiosità epistolari inedite nella vita teatrale di Gaetano Donizetti', in *Rivista musicale italiana*, July–December, pp. 273–83, Milan, 1948
—— *Donizetti, G.—Episodi e testimonianze F. Fiorentino*, Naples, 1954
—— *L'eredità di Donizetti; da carteggi e documenti dell'archivio dell'Acc. chigiana (Quaderni dell'Accademia chigiana No. 30)*, Siena, 1954
—— *Mondo teatrale dell'ottocento*, Naples, 1954
—— *L'ultima pagina della vita di Gaetano Donizetti, da un carteggio inedito dell'Accademia chigiana (Quaderni dell'Accademia chigiana, No. 28)*, Siena, 1953
Scotti, Baronessa Ginevra Rota-Basoni 'Le memorie donizettiane della Baronessa Basoni Scotti', in *Rivista di Bergamo*, 1928
Scudo, Paul, *Critique et littérature musicales*, 'Donizetti et l'école italienne depuis Rossini', pp. 75–100, Paris, 1850

Second, Albéric, *Les petits mystères de l'opéra*, Paris, 1844
Serie cronologica delle opere teatrali, cantate ed oratori del maestro Giovanni Comm. Pacini, Milan, 1875
Settembrini, Luigi, *Ricordanze della mia vita*, Bari, 1934
Simone, Giuseppe de, *Della musica melodrammatica ragionamento dell'avv. Gius. de Simone*, Naples, 1859
Soubies, Albert, *Histoire de l'opéra-comique, la seconde salle Favart*, (*1840–1887*), 2 Vols., Paris, 1892–93
—— *Histoire du Théâtre-Lyrique 1851–1870*, Paris, 1899
—— *Le Théâtre-Italien de 1801 à 1913*, Paris, 1913
Spiro, F., 'Le lettere di Donizetti', in *Fanfulla della Domenica*, Vol. XIV, No. 48, 1892
Stendhal, *Correspondance Inédite*, Paris, 1855
—— *Life of Rossini* (trl. Richard N. Coe), London, 1956
—— *Rome, Naples and Florence* (trl. Richard N. Coe), London, 1959
Stierlin, Leonhard, *Biographie von Gaetano Donizetti*, Zurich, 1852
Streatfield, R. A., *Masters of Italian Music* (Masters of Contemporary Music Series), London, 1895
[Teatro di San Carlo] *Cento Anni di Vita (1848–1948)*, Naples, n.d.
Tebaldini, Giovanni, 'Giuseppe Persiani e Fanny Tacchinardi; memorie ed appunti', in *Rivista musicale italiana*, Vol. XII, pp. 579–91, 1905
Teneo, Martial, 'Le Chevalier de Malte ou la reine de Chypre', in *Zeitschrift der internationalen Musikgesellschaft*, Vol. VIII, pp. 352–4, 1906–07
Thurner, Auguste, *Les transformations de l'Opéra-Comique*, Paris, 1865
Tiby, Ottavio, *Gaetano Donizetti a Palermo, estratto dall'Annuario dell'Accademia di Santa Cecilia, 1949–51*, Rome, 1951
—— *Il Real Teatro Carolino e l'ottocento musicale palermitano*, Florence, 1957
Tintori, Giampiero, *L'opera napoletana*, Milan, 1958
Tonelli, Luigi, *Il teatro italiano dalle origini ai giorni nostri*, Milan, 1924
Touchard La Fosse, G., *Chroniques secrètes et galantes de l'opéra depuis 1667 jusqu'au 1845*, 4 Vols., Paris, 1846
Toye, Francis, *Giuseppe Verdi: His Life and Works*, London, 1931
—— 'The New Interest in Italian Nineteenth-Century Opera', in *Fanfare for Ernest Newman* (ed. Herbert van Thal), London, 1955
—— *Rossini, A Study in Tragicomedy*, Heinemann, 1934
Trebbi, Oreste, 'Lo Stabat di Rossini', in *Le grandi esecuzioni musicali a Bologna*, Bologna, 1918
Tripier Le Franc, J., *M. Gabriel Delessert*, Paris, 1859
Vallebona, G. B., *Il teatro Carlo Felice: Cronisteria di un secolo 1828–1928*, Genoa, 1928
Verdi, Giuseppe, *Copialettere* (ed. Alessandro Luzio)

Verzino, Edoardo Clemente, *Contributo ad una biografia di Gaetano Donizetti*, Bergamo, 1896
—— *Le opere di Gaetano Donizetti*, Bergamo, 1897
Viani, Adelio G., *Towards music*, Tralee, 1945
Villarosa, Marchese di, *Memorie dei compositori di musica nel Regno di Napoli*, Naples, 1840
Walker, Frank, 'Donizetti, Verdi and Mme. Appiani', in *Music and Letters*, Vol. 32, pp. 19–34, January 1951
—— 'Giuditta Turina and Bellini', in *Music and Letters*, Vol. 40, pp. 19–34, 1959
—— 'The Librettist of Don Pasquale', in *Monthly Musical Record*, Vol. 88, No. 990, pp. 219–23, November–December 1958
—— 'Mercadante and Verdi', in *Music and Letters*, Vol. 33, pp. 311–21, 1952, also 'Verdi and Mercadante', in *Music and Letters*, Vol. 34, pp. 33–8, 1953
—— *The Man Verdi*, London, 1962
Weinstock, Herbert, *Donizetti and the World of Opera in Italy, Paris and Vienna in the First Half of the Nineteenth Century*, London, 1964
Wolff, Stéphanie, *Un demi-siècle d'Opéra-Comique, 1900–1950*, Paris 1953
Wyndham, Henry Saxe, *The Annals of Covent Garden Theatre from 1732–1897*, 2 Vols., London, 1906
Zavadini, Guido (ed.), *Bergamo, museo donizettiano*, Bergamo, 1938
—— *Donizetti l'uomo*, Bergamo, 1958
—— *Donizetti: Vita–Musiche–Epistolario*, Bergamo, 1948
—— *G. Simone Mayr*, Bergamo, 1957

Index

Index

(Principal entries appear in bold-face type. Works (operas, plays, etc.), appear under the composer's, dramatist's name.)

Abbadia, Luigia, 236, 257, 407 n.
Abdul Medjid, Sultan of Turkey, 252, 508
Abenamet e Zoraide; *see* Niccolini, Giuseppe
Académie (Royale) des Beaux-Arts (*Paris*), 273, 275, 370, 373
Académie (Royale) de Médecine (*Paris*), 318
Académie (Royale) de Musique; *see* Opéra (*Paris*)
Accademia Carrara (*Bergamo*), 17, 18
Accademia di Santa Cecilia (*Rome*), 57, 452 n.
Accademia filarmonica romana (*Rome*), 56, 136
Accursi, Elisa, 294, 324
Accursi, Michele, 28 n., 160, 215, 216, **217–18**, 219, 248, 249, 256, 263, 271, **294–8**, 303, 306–7, 313, 319, 324, 325, 332, 333, 336, 441 n., 455; quoted: 217–18, 294–6
Acton, Harold, quoted: 171 n., 345
Adam, Adolphe Charles, 160, 161, 189, 190, 222, 223, 234, 235, 242, 487
  Brasseur de Preston, Le, 223
  Chalet, Le, 161, 190, 223, 234, 235, 487
  Giselle, 246
  Marquise, La, 223
  Postillon du Longjumeau, Le, 223
Adamo, Salvatore, 422
Adelaide; *see* Donizetti
Adelaide e Comingio; *see* (1) Fioravanti, V., (2) Pacini, G.
Adelasia ed Aleramo; *see* Mayr
Adèle de Lusignan ou la fille de l'archer, 493
Adele di Lusignano; *see* (1) Carafa, (2) Carnicier

Adele e Emerico; *see* Mercadante
Adelia; *see* Donizetti
Adelson e Salvini; *see* Bellini
Adina; *see* Rossini
Adoratori del fuoco, Gli, 99
Agazzi, Paolo, 83, 106, 107
Agnese di Fitz-Henry, *see* Paër
Agnesi, 69
Aiblinger, Johann Caspar, 281–2, 283
Aïda; *see* Verdi
Ajo nell'imbarazzo, L'; *see* Donizetti
Alahor di Granata; *see* Donizetti
Albano, 204
Albertazzi, Emma Howson, 226, 260
Alborghetti, Federico, 15, 26, 141 n., 317, 433
Alboni, Marietta, 261, 423
Alcide al Bivio; *see* Mayr
Alcozer, Antonino, 419 n., 467
Alessandria (*Piedmont*), 91
Alfonso XI, King of Aragon, 429
Alfonso d' Aragona; *see* Sarmiento
Alfredo d'Inghilterra; *see* Mercadante
Alfredo il grande; *see* (1) Donizetti, (2) Mayr
Alina, la regina di Golconda; *see* Donizetti
Almenno, 9, 32, 95 n.
Alzira; *see* Verdi
Amadeo, Giovanni Battista, 7
Amati, Caterina, 41
Amazzoni di Boemia, Le, 53
Ambrogi, 175
Ambrosini, Paolo, 108, 110, 111, 112, 122
Amiens, 340
Amy Robsart; *see* Hugo
Ancelot, François
  Elisabeth d'Angleterre, 210, 489
  Maria Padilla (1838), 256, 494

535

Ancona, 30–1
Andersen, Hans Christian, 485n.
Andral, Gabriel, 291, 292, 293, 337
Andreotti, Marchese Domenico, 493n.
Anelli, Angelo, 455, 496
Ange de Nisida, L'; see Donizetti
Angelini, Emilio, 250
Anna, Empress of Austria, etc. (Maria Anna Carolina of Savoy), 119, 264, 266, 504
Anna Bolena; see Donizetti
Anton(y), 281, 310, 311
Antonioli, Doro, 28
Antonj, degli, 27
Antonj, Clementina degli, 261
Antonj, Severino degli, 510
Appiani, Adele, 513
Appiani, Giuseppina Strigelli, 259, 268, 290, 334
Appony, Count Rudolfo, 160, 312, 318, 319, 337, 338, 339
Appony, Countess Rudolf, 160, 312, 339
Arati, Marco, 239, 280, 427n.
Archivio Visconti, 141n.
Ariosto, Lodovico, 444
Aristodemo; see Pavesi
Arlincourt, Charles Victor Prévôt d', 470
Arrigotti, Arturo, 105, 111
Arrivabene, Ferdinando, 37
Assedio di Calais, L'; see Donizetti
Assedio di Corinto, L'; see Rossini
Aspa, Mario, 85
Astino, 347
Atalia; see Mayr
Athelney, 462n.
Attila, 6
Auber, Daniel François, 108, 126, 160, 217
  Domino noir, Le, 223
  Lac des fées, Le, 227
  Philtre, Le, 126, 127, 453, 478
Audiences, 42, **49–50**, 54, 62, 65, 67, 68, 77, 83, 84, 88, 150, 402, 444
Aureliano in Palmiro; see Rossini
Autopsy, Donizetti's, **346–7**
Avaro, L', 53
Aversa, 350

Baculard d'Arnaud, François Thomas, 429, 492
  Comte de Comminges, Le, 246, 429, 431
Baden-Baden, 256, 294, 296, 297
Badessi, 182

Baillou-Hillaret, Felicità, 126, 153
Baizzini, Abbate Giovanni Battista, 20, 21, 22
Baldovino; see Cammarano, Salvatore
Balestracci, Achille, 152
Balestrieri, 170
Ballo in maschera, Un; see Verdi
Balocchino, Carlo, 262
Balzac, Honoré de, 178n.
Barateau, Émile, 513, 515
Barattini, Timoleone, 210
Barbaja, Domenico, 9, 36n., 57, 58, 60, **87**, 88, 94n., 97, 101n., 104, 108, 109, 113, 123, 124, 162, 164, 166, 167, 169, 174, 184, 190, 197, 220, 262
Barbiera, Raffaello, 290
Barbiere di Siviglia, Il, 136
Barbiere di Siviglia, Il; see Rossini
Barblan, Guglielmo, 408
Bardare, Leone Emmanuele, 446
Bardari, Giuseppe, 151, **445**, 456, 483
Barili, Caterina, 153, 192
Barone di Dolsheim, Il; see Pacini, G.
Baroni, Clementina, 250
Barrielle, 255
Barroilhet, Paul, 192, 195, 210, 211, 245, 286, 295, 330n., 490n., 504
Basadonna, Giovanni, 112, 125, 132, 195, 210, 258
Basel, 340
Basili (Basilj), Francesco, 164, 458n., 502
  Illinesi, Gli, 164
  Ira d'Achille, L', 458n.
Basoni; see Rota-Basoni
Bassi, Antonio, 180, 181, 184
Bassi, Calisto, 175n., 236, 427
Battaglia di Legnano, La; see Verdi
Baucardé, Carlo, 239, 427n.
Bayard, Jean François Alfred, 236, 456, 492
Bazzini, Antonio, 433
Beatrice di Tenda; see Bellini
Beauharnais, Eugène, 25
Beaumarchais, Pierre Augustin Caron de, 58n.
Beethoven, Ludwig van, 12, 13, 72n., 94n., 267n., 274, 277, 416
  Fidelio, 274
  Mount of Olives (Christus am Oelberge), 274
  Septet, 274
  Symphony IX (1824), 94n.
Begnis, Giuseppe de 32 *and* n., 132n.

Begnis, Giuseppina Ronzi de; *see* Ronzi de Begnis, Giuseppina
Béhier, Louis Jules, 319, 329, 330, 331, 332, 338, 339
Belgioioso, Count Pompeo, 261
Bélisaire; see Marmontel
Belisario; see Donizetti
Bella prigioniera, La; see Donizetti
Belle ciarle e tristi fatti; see Mayr
Bellini, Vincenzo, 9, 49, 50, 63, 76n., 83, 94 *and* n., 97, 98, **99–100**, **116–18**, 119, 124, 135, 137, 138, 149, 150, **154–60**, 161, **171–3**, 196, 209, 325, 355–6, 359, 365, 366, 369, 371, 384n., 385, 386, 389, 401, 402, 403, 404, **405–7**, 415, 443, 451, 452, 507, 509; quoted: 94, 97, 100, 149–50, 154, 155, 156, 157–8, 159
Adelson e Salvini, 83, 356n.
Beatrice di Tenda, 138, 154, 257n., 356, 405, 406
Bianca e Gernando (later *Bianca e Fernando*), 83, 99, 100, 430n.
Capuletti ed i Montecchi, I, 118, 165n., 356n., 411
Ernani, 117
Norma, 9, 124, 126, 133, 135, 155, 157, 165, 188, 402, 405, 406, 415
Pirata, Il, 97, 118, 452
Puritani (di Scozia), I, 138, **154–6**, 178, 402, 405
Sonnambula, La, **117–18**, 119, 157, 356, 403, 405, 406
Straniera, La, 94n., 136n., 356, 406
Zaira, 356n.
Belloc-Giorgi, Teresa, 63n.
Belloy, Dormant du (*pseud.* for Pierre Laurent Buirette), 85, 410, 466, 487
Gabrielle de Vergy, 410, 466
Siège de Calais, Le, 487
Beltrami, Pietro, 174, 212, 485n.
Ghismonda di Mendrizio set by de Paolis (1843) and Badia (1846), 212
Benedetti, Giuseppe, 67, 192, 210
Benedetti, Michele, 105, 112
Benedict, Sir Julius, 190
Beneventano, Giuseppe (Baron della Piana), 279
Benevento, Aniello, 197, 207, 208, 212, 269, 292, 300, 314
Benigni, 519
Benvenuto Cellini; see Berlioz
Bergamo, 3, 4, **6–10**, 11, 12, 14, 18n., 28, 29, 31, 33, 34, 35, 37, 39, 41,

45, 52, 66, 70n., 72, 82, 83, 90, 91, 93, 95n., **97**, 101, 103, 106, **108**, 111, 112, **113**, 127, 128, 132, 134, 135, 139, 153, 172, 176, 177, 178, 180, 184, 185, 186, 194, 213, **240–1**, 251, 253, 267, **268**, 281, **289**, 292, 301, 302, 307, 311, 313, 317, **318–19**, 322, 323, 324, 327, 333, 335, 337, **339–40**, 341, 342, 345, **346**, 371, 401, 433, 434, 452, 458, 460, 502, 512, 519
Bergamo Civic Band, 5, 93, 401
Bergamo Civic Library, xii, 11, 13n., 18n.
Bériot, Charles Auguste de, 178n.
Berlioz, Hector, 95, 217, 222, 224, 234, 235, 238, 299, 426; quoted: 95, 234–5
Benvenuto Cellini, 222
Bernardis, Raffaela de, 61
Berryer, Antoine, 339
Berti, Count, 187–9, 212, 213
Bertoli, Alessandro, 13, 31, 42, 509
Bertolucci, Andrea, 72
Berton, Henri Montan, 470n.
Bertuzzi, L., 519
Betley; see Donizetti
Bevilacqua, Aldovrandini, Marchese Gherardo, 41, **445**, 460 *and* n.
Bezzi, Antonio de, 72
Bianca e Gernando; see Bellini
Biblioteca Civica; *see* Bergamo Civic Library
Biblioteca nazionale, 421n.
Bibliothèque de l'Opéra, 242n.
Bibliothèque du Conservatoire de Paris; *see* Paris Conservatory Library
Bidera, Giovanni Emanuele, 152, 153, 169, **445–6**, 456, 466n., 483, 484
Biery, Gottlob Benedikt, 487n.
Biondi, Lorenzo, 115
Bishop, Anna Rivière, 279
Bizet, Georges
Carmen, 410n.
Blanchard, 233
Blassis, Virginia, 163
Blaze, François Henri Joseph (Castil-), 420, 438
Boccabadati, Augusta, 423
Boccabadati-Gazzuoli, Luigia, 70, 107, 108, 110, 111, 122, 163, 514
Bochsa, Robert Nicholas Charles, 118
Messicani, I, 118
Boiardo, Matteo Maria, 444

Boieldieu, Adrien Louis Victor, 223
  Marguerite, 223
Boieldieu, François Adrien, 121, 470 n.,
  475
  Jean de Paris, 121, 475 *and* n.
Bologna, 9, 13, 22, 23, 24, **25–9**, 38,
  41 *and* n., 45, 112, 120, 145, 196,
  260–2, 263, 264, 268, 269, 357 n.,
  445, 503, 519
Bologna, University of, 27
Bonesi, Marco, 13, 16, 31, 32, 39, 42,
  97, 340, 509, 510; quoted: 31,
  32, 42
Bonfigli, Lorenzo, 122
Bonini, Emilia, 87–8
Bonneau, 319
Bonzi, Antonio Mauro, 3
Boosey & Co., 431 n.
Bordogni, Giulio Marco, **9**, 160, 302;
  quoted: 302
Borghese, Princess Pauline (Bona-
  parte), 54, 71, 133
Borgomastro di Saardam, Il; *see* Donizetti
Borioli, Fortunio, 423
Bosio, Angiolina, 191
Bosio, Antonio, 15, 16
Botticelli, Vincenzo, 41, 67
Boufflers, Stanislas Jean, Chevalier de,
  470
  Reine de Golconde, La, 470
Boulanger, Lilli, 233 n.
Boulanger, Marie Julienne, 233 *and* n.
Boulanger, Nadia, 233 n.
Bourgeois (Borghèse), Juliette Eu-
  phrosyne, 231, 233
Bourges, Maurice, 514
Boutellier, J. de, 514
Bozzi, Gambattista, Cavaliere, 318–19
Braga, Gaetano, 470 n.
Brambilla, Marietta, 144, 182, 264,
  265, 283, 423
Branca, Emilia; *see* Romani, Emilia
  Branca
Branciforti, Duke Giuseppe, 76, 79
Brasseur de Preston, Le; *see* Adam
Bravo, Il, 229
Bredal, Ivar Frederik, 485 n.
  Bruden fra Lammermoor, A, 485 n.
Brémond, Hippolyte, 286
Brescia, 14
Bride of Lammermoor, The; *see* Scott
British Broadcasting Company, 75
Bruden fra Lammermoor; *see* Bredal
Brunswick, Léon Lévy, 486
  Sonnette de nuit, La, 189, 486
Bruschi-Schiatti, Abigaille, 434

Brussels, 127, 178 n., 340
Buccini, 195, 421
Budapest, 94
Bülow, Hans von; quoted: 410 n.
Buini, S. M., 398 n.
  Podestà di Colognole, Il, 398 n.
Bunn, Alfred, 179
Bulwer-Lytton, Edward; *see* Lytton
Burgravi, I; *see* Salvi, Matteo
Byron, George Gordon, 6th Baron, 110,
  152, 473, 480, 484, 502, 518, *Cain*
  473 n., *Heaven and Earth*, 473,
  Marino Faliero, 484, *Parisina*, 480

Cabarrus, C., 318
Cain; *see* Byron
Califfo e la schiava, Il; *see* Romani
Calmeil, Juste Louis, 308, 320, 337
Calvarola, 61
Calvetti, Luigi, 341, 346
Cametti, Alberto, 51 n., 56 n., 68,
  103 n., 110, 112, 392 n., 418,
  434 n., 435 n., 467 n., 503
Cammarano, Filippo, 168 *and* n.
  Comico inglese, Il, 169
Cammarano, Giuseppe, 168 n.
Cammarano, Salvatore, 46, 48, 131,
  167, **168–9**, 174, 187, 188, 195 n.,
  209, 210, 213, 218, 276, 425 n.,
  426, **429–31**, 432, 443, **446–8**,
  454, 456, 485, 486, 487, 488,
  489 n., 490, 497; quoted: 131,
  430–1
  Baldovino, 169
  Leonora di Guzman; quoted: 430–1
Cammarano, Vincenzo, 168
Camoens, Luis de, 282
Campagnoli, Giovanni Battista, 96,
  105, 106, 122, 125
Campagnoli, 233
Campanello di notte, Il; *see* Donizetti
Candia, Marchese Giovanni di; *see*
  Mario
Canonici, Giacinta, 60, 72
Canova, Antonio, 54
Cantiran de Boirie, Eugène, 468
Capecchi, Renato, 399 n.
Capacelatro, 170
Capet, Hugues, 477 n.
Capitanio, Gian Battista, 519
Capranica, 96, 105
Capranica, Marchese Domenico, 110,
  503
Capricciosa e il soldato, La; *see* Carafa
Capuletti ed i Montecchi, I; *see* Bellini

Capuzzi, Antonio, 14, 31, 32, 33, 509
Carafa, Michele Enrico, Prince di Colobrano, 53, 59, 64, 85, 410, 452n., 457, 466n., 493n.
  Adele di Luisignano, 493n.
  Capricciosa e il soldato, 53, 59
  Gabriella di Vergy, 64n., 85
  Nozze di Lammermoor, Le, 485n.
Carbonari, 27
Carchen, Gerolamo, 347
Carish, 29
Carlo Alberto, King of Sardinia and Piedmont, 346
Carlo Felice, King of Sardinia and Piedmont, 101
Carmen; *see* Bizet
Carnevali, Anna (*of Rome*), 56–7, 60, 66, 86, 504
Carnevali, Clementina; *see* Mongardi, Clementina Carnevali
Carnevali, Paolo, 57
Carnicier, Ramon, 493n.
  Adele di Lusignano, 493n.
Carraro, Maria, 105, 110, 111
Carocci, Angelina, 140
Carretto, Marshal Marchese Francesco Saverio del, 171
Cartagenova, Orazio, 136, 153
Cartoni, Nicola, 66, 517
Casaccia, Carlo, 60, 68, 72, 73 *and* n., 94, 190
Cassaccia, Raffaele, 68, 94
Cascini, 169
Casino de' Carobagni, 250
Cassago, Adelaide, 36
Cassis, Giovanni, 341, 342, 343, 346
Castagna, Bruna, xi
Castellan, Jeanne Anaïs, 72n., 258, 296
Castello degli invalidi, Il; *see* (1) Cordella, (2) Donizetti
Castil-Blaze; *see* Blaze, François Henri Joseph (Castil-)
Catalani, Adele (Adelina), 35
Catalani, Angelica, 35, 54
Caterina Cornaro; *see* Donizetti
Caterina Howard; *see* Salvi, Matteo
Catolfi, Giovanni, 509
Cavalcanti, Marchesa, 336
Caversazzi, Ciro, 4, 5
Cecconi, Teresa, 67
Ceci, Domenico, 239, 280, 427n.
Celli, Abbate, 54–5 *and* n.; quoted: 55
Celli, Filippo, 463n.
Cenerentola, La; *see* Rossini

Cenni biografici di Donizetti e Mayr raccolti dalle memorie di un vecchio ottuagenario dilettante di musica, 33, 36n., 37, 40, 41; quoted: 34, 40
Censorship, 44, **47–8**, 53, 59, 62, 68, 83n., 96, 97, 112, 117, 125, 133, 139, **143-4**, 145, 166, 167, 175, 179n., 219–20, 247, 257 *and* n., 279, 280, 409, 415, 430n., 431, 444, **447n.**, 450, 453, 474n., 480n., 481n., 490n., 495n.
Cento Anni di Vita di San Carlo: 1848–1948, 168n.
Cerere, La, 77, 78; quoted: 78
Cerri, Giovanni, 171
Cerrito, Fanny, 165n.
Cervantes Saavedra, Miguel de, 479n.
  Don Quixote de la Mancha (1605–15), 479n.
Cesare in Egitto; *see* Pacini, G.
Charles VII chez les grands vassaux; *see* Dumas
Chalet, Le; *see* Adam
Chalet, Le; *see* Scribe
Chambéry, 92, 328
Chaste Suzanne, La; *see* Monpou
Che originali!; *see* Mayr
Checcherini, Francesca, 68, 72, 73, 74, 448
Checcherini, Giuseppe, 46, **74**, 443, **448**, 464
Checcherini, Marianna, 75, 448n.
Checchetelli, 327, 328, 331
Chiara e Serafina; *see* Donizetti
Chizzola, Gaetano, 67, 81, 84, 94, 96, 105, 106, 111
Cholera, 123, 175, 180, 181, 192–3, **197–9**, 200, 201, 202, **203–6**, 208, 209, 211, 229
Chomel, 337
Chorley, Henry Fothergill, 72, 88, 118, 123, 136n., 142, 159; quoted: 72, 88, 118–19, 123, 159
Cicconetti, Filippo, 28, 139, 141n., 242n., 438n.
Cicimarra, Giuseppe, 58
Cimarosa, Domenico, 8, 9, 12, 77, 196
  Matrimonio segreto, Il, 77
Cimbal, M., 517
Cimino, Ferdinando, 192
Circe; *see* Donizetti
Cisalpine Republic, 3, 6
Cisterne, La; *see* Pixérécourt
Civitavecchia, 252, 268
Clapisson, Antoine Louis, 223, 502
  Figurante, La, 223

Clément, Félix, 429
Cobianchi, Gaetano, 170
Coccia, Carlo, 26, 147, 247, 482n., 493n.
Figlia dell'arciere, La, 493n.
Colbran, Isabella; *see* Rossini, Isabella Colbran
Coletti, Filippo, 187, 258, 279, 280
Colini, Filippo, 239, 265, 427n.
Colleoni Chapel, 7
Colleoni-Corti, Benedetta, 250
Colombo; see Morlacchi
Colonna armonica, La, 27
Comico inglese, Il; see Cammarano, Filippo
Comelli-Rubini, Adelaide [Mlle Chaumel], 101, 105
Commercio, Il, 138
Commons, Jeremy, 418n., 437
Como, 113, 117, 340
Comte Ory, Le; see Rossini
Congregazione di Carità (Bergamo), 12, 14, 15, 16, 17, 20, 21, 23, 24, 39, 40
Conservatorio di musica (Milan); *see* Milan Conservatory
Conservatorio di S. Pietro a Majella (Naples); *see* Naples Conservatory
Constantinople, 4, 91, 92, 149, 225, 289, 302, 304, 305, 322, 324, 327, 330, 342
Consul, Giuseppe, 164-5, 169, 174, 502; quoted: 165-6
Consultations, Medical *on D.,* 294, 308-10, 317, 318, 319-22, 337-8, 339, 341
Conte d'Essex, Il; see (1) Donizetti, (2) Mercadante
Conte d'Essex, Il; see Romani
Contini, Carolina, 41n.
Convenienze ed inconvenienze teatrali, Le; see Donizetti
Convenienze teatrali, Le; see Sografi
Copenhagen, 485n.
Coppola, Pier Antonio, 195, 502
Illinesi, Gli, 502
Cordella, Giacomo, 465
Castello degli invalidi, Il, 465
Corelli, Leone, 284
Corini, 43, 44
Corini, Angela Donizetti, 4
Corini, Gaetana, 53
Corini, Giacomo, 4, 90
Corneille, Pierre, 426, 447, 490
Polyeucte, 219, 490
Corradi-Pantanelli, Clorinda, 125

Corradino; see Morlacchi
Corrado d'Altamura; see Ricci, F.
Corricolo, Le; see Dumas
Cortesi, Letizia, 99, 100
Così fan tutte; see Mozart
Cosselli, Domenico, 87, 138, 150, 170, 171
Cossotto, Fiorenza, 247
Costaguti, Marchese Vincenzo, 110, 503
Cottin, Sophie, 467
Elisabeth ou les exilés en Sibérie, 467
Cottrau, Félix, 178n.
Cottrau, Guillaume Louis, 122, 123, 148, 170, 178n., 189, 191, 197, 220, 299, 315, 379, 423; quoted: 132n., 178n., 189-90, 191, 220-1, 315
Cottrau, Jenny, 160, 170, 178n.
Cottrau, Lina, 160, 515
Coussy, Auguste de, 160, 185, 186, 215, 247, **294-8**, 306, 325, 329, 332, 335, 336; quoted: 248, 296
Coussy, Zélie de, 160, 185, 215, 248, 273, **294-8**, 304, 306, 307, 312, 328, 329, 330, 332, 333, **335-7**, **339**, 516
Coussy, Mlle de, 335
Creation, The; see Haydn
Crémieux, Adolphe, 339
Crespi, Federico, 110, 152
Crevel de Charlemagne, Louis Ernest, 518
Crippa, Antonio, 115
Criticism, 36, 41, 55, 60, 61, 65, 72, 73, 78, 81, 88, 96, 97, 101, 127-8, 136, 138, 234-5, 237-8, 240, 245-6, 265, 272-3, 287
Crosnier, Louis François, 502
Curioni, Alberico, 88

Dabadie, Henri Bernard, **126 *and* n.**, 127
Danaidi, Le; see Mayr
Danao, re d'Argo; see Persiani, G.
Danini, Ambrogio, 192
Dante Alighieri, 102, 188, 411n., 488, 503, 512, 515
Da Ponte, Lorenzo, 59n.
Dardanelli, Girolama, 58, 72
David, Giacomo, **8-9**, 18n.
David, Giovanni, 9, 99, 100, 107, 108, 133
Delavigne, Casimir, 106, 152, 471, 484
Marino Faliero, 484

Delegazione di Bergamo, 93
Deleide, Luigi 'Nebbia', 509
Delessert, Gabriel Abraham Margueritte, **319**, 320, 328, 329, 330, 331, 332, 335, 337, 338, 339
Dell'Oro, 182
Del Serre, Anna, 148, **151**, 152
Demetrio; *see* Mayr
Dent, Edward; quoted: 443
Dérivis, Prosper, 237, 264
Deschamps, Émile, 517
Dietsch, Louis Philippe, 433, 434
Diluvio universale, Il; *see* Donizetti
Diluvio universale, Il; *see* Ringhieri
Dolci, Antonio, 18 *and* n., 43, 93, 101, 113, 127, 149, 153, 158, 176, 177, 178, 179, 180, 181, 183, 185, 186, 192, 193, 194, 217, 225, 226, 229, 240, 241, 251, 252, 253, 254, 264, 266, 267, 268, 269, 270, 276, 277, 290, 292, 293, **301-2 and n.**, 304, 305, 313, 314, 315, 317, 318-19, 322, 323, 324, 325, 329, 330, 331, 332, 340, **341-2**, 345, 349, 350, 433, 512; quoted: 315, 322, 345, **350**
Dom Sébastien; *see* Donizetti
Domincetti, Cesare, 433, 434n.
Dominicis, Luigi de, 71
Domino noir, Le; *see* Auber
Don Giovanni; *see* Mozart
Don Pasquale; *see* Donizetti
Don Quixote de la Mancha; *see* Cervantes
Donati-Pettèni, Giuliano, 21 n., 38, 39
Donizetti, Ambrogio, 4
Donizetti, Andrea, **3-6**, 15, 17, 22, 29, 33, 89, 90, 91, 92, 93, 94, 98, 102, 103, 104, 105, 106, 107, 108, 109, 110, 114, 119, 121, 127, 128, 134, 136, 145, 149, **176-7**, 178, 323
Donizetti, Andrea, 91, 106, 127, 128, **145-6**, 305, 306, 307, 308, 310, 313, 314, 316, 317, 318, 319, 320, 322, 323, 324, **327-37**, 338, 339, 342, 345, **349-50**, 519; quoted: 329, 330-3, 335
Donizetti, Angela; *see* Corini, Angela Donizetti
Donizetti, Angela Tondi, 91, 225
Donizetti, Domenica Nava, 3, 4, 5, 90, 96, 104, 105, 107, 108, 145, 177, 179, 180, 181, **183**
Donizetti, Elisabetta Santi-; *see* Santi-Pesenti, Elisabetta
Donizetti, Filippo Francesco, **108-10**
Donizetti, Francesco, 4, 18n., 22, **92-3**, 95, 104, 176, 177, **181**, 183-4, 186, 213, 225, 240, 241, 277, 302, 305, 318-19, 322, 323, 331, 335, 339, 342, **349**, 401, 436n., 508
Donizetti, (Domenico) Gaetano (1797-1848), *see* also entries for Autopsy; Consultations, medical; Criticism, Fees, etc.)

COMPOSITIONS
OPERAS
(dates refer to first performance, unless otherwise indicated)

Adelaide, 218, 242, 427, 428, 429, 501; *see* also *Ange de Nisida, L'* and *favorite, La*
Adelia (1841), 147, 240, 247, **250-1**, 252, 441, 452, 453; synopsis: 493-4
Ajo nell'imbarazzo, L' (1824), 71-3, 78, 81, 84, 97, 250, 281, 385, 391, 392, **418**, **437**, 449, 450; example: 392; synopsis, 463-4
Alahor di Granata (1826), 74n., **81-2**, 83, 84, 86, 411, **437**, 444n.; synopsis: 465
Alfonso, duca di Ferrara; *see Lucrezia Borgia*
Alfredo il grande (1823), **67**, 357n., 373, 376, 378-9, 457; example: 377; synopsis: 462-3
Alina, la regina di Golconda (1828), 99, **100-2**, 110, 111, 153, 278, 391, 392, 438, 452; synopsis: 470
Ange de Nisida, L' (*comp.* 1839), 231, 232, 235, 240, 241, **242-5**, 427, 428, 429 *and* n., 431, 432, 440, 454, 501; *see* also *favorite, La*
Anna Bolena (1830), 10, 51, 105, 107, 113, **114-19**, 123, 128, 132, 136, 137, 150, 157, 159, 219, 234, 281, 331, 358, 361n., 365, 375-6, 381, 404, 405, 406, 412, **420**, **438**, 452, 453; example: 375; synopsis: 474-5
Anna de Boulen, 420, 438; *see* also *Anna Bolena*
Assedio di Calais, L' (1836), 47, **192-3**, 214, 215, 355, 357, 406, 411, 446, 447; synopsis: 487-8
Belisario (1836), 169, 174-5, 176, **180-2**, 183, 186, 187, 188, 195, 281, 283, 284, 345, 446, 447; synopsis: 486

Bella prigioniera, La (*incomplete,* c. 1826?), 86, 467

Betly (1836), 36 n., **190–2**, 209, 235, 353, 380 n., 421; synopsis: 487

Bianca d'Aquatania; see Ugo, conte di Parigi

Borgomastro di Saardam, Il (1827), **93–4**, 97, 98, 357, 380, 406, 450, 451; example: 381; synopsis: 468

Buondelmonte (1834), 152, 175, 446, 456, 483; *see* also *Maria Stuarda*

Campanello di notte, Il (1836), 184 n., **189–90**, 191, 192, 380, 380 n., 390, 391, 398, 400 n., **439–40**, 448, 449; synopsis: 486–7

Capanna svizzera, La; see Betly

Castello degli invalidi, Il (*questionable,* 1826?), 82, 465

Castello di Kenilworth, Il; see Elisabetta al castello di Kenilworth

Caterina Cornaro (1844), 270–1, 276, 278, **279–80**, 288, **423**, 441, 455, 503; synopsis: 495–6

Chiara e Serafina (1822), **63–6**, 135, 406, 414, 452, 453; synopsis: 462

Circe (*projected*), 501

Conte d'Essex, Il; see Roberto Devereux

Conte di Chalais, Il; see Maria di Rohan

Convenienze ed inconvenienze teatrali, Le (1827), **95–6**, 390, 391, **398–401**, **419–20**, 440, 448, 449; examples: 391, 400; synopsis: 468–9

Daila; see favorite, La

Dalinda; see Lucrezia Borgia

Diluvio universale, Il (1830), 110, **111**, 353 n., 438, 451; synopsis: 473–4

Dom Sébastien (1843), 276, 282, **283–6**, 287, 289, 357, 386, **423–4**, 455, 457; example: 386; synopsis: 498

Don Gregorio (1826), 72, 73, 83, 93, 463; *see* also *Ajo nell'imbarazzo L'*

Don Pasquale (1843), 6, 19 n., 32, 270, **271–3**, 275, 277, 287, 356, 358, 359, 360, 363–4, 365, 366, 379, 380 n., 385, 388, 389, 391, 392, **393–7**, 405, 438, 439, **440–2**, 448, 455, 465; examples: 393, 395, 396, 397; synopsis: 496–7

Duc d'Albe, Le, xi n., 228, 229, 233, 235, 241, 242, 243, 253, 270, 276, 277, 323, 428, **432–5**, 439, **440**, 457

Duca d'Alba, Il (1882), xi n., xii, 267, 357 n., 414, **433–6**, 438; synopsis: 491–2

Duello sotto Richelieu, Un; see Maria di Rohan

Elda; see favorite, La

Eleonora di Gujenna, 420; *see* also *Rosmunda d'Inghilterra*

Elisa Fosco; see Lucrezia Borgia

Elisabeth ou la fille du proscrit, 89, 419; *see* also *Otto mesi in due ore*

Elisabetta al castello di Kenilworth (1829), 107, **108**, 281, 384 n., 420, 438, 457; synopsis: 472–3

Elisir d'amore, L' (1832), **126–8**, 139, 167, 175, 189, 217, 225, 227, 257 n., 353 n., 355, 360, 361, 369, 379, 380 n., 388, 389, 391, 392, 393, 401, 402, 404, 415–16, 420, **439**, 441, 449, 452, 453, 473 n., 509; synopsis: 478–9

Elvida (1826), **84**, 93, 142, 355, 362 n., 373, 376, 377, 411, 444 n., 456; synopsis: 465–6

Emilia di Liverpool (1824), 72 n., **73–5**, 362, 377, 399 n., 411, **418**, 437; *rifacimento* (1828), 74, 81, **418**, 437, 448 *and* n.; synopsis: 464

Enrico di Borgogna (1818), **34–6**, 37, 39, 68 n., 358, 411, 452; synopsis: 459

Eremitaggio di Liverpool, L'; see Emilia di Liverpool

Esiliati in Siberia, Gli; see Otto mesi in due ore

Esule di Roma, L' (1828), **96–7**, 102, 240–1, 251, 252, 450, 451; synopsis: 469

Eustorgia da Romano; see Lucrezia Borgia

Falegname di Livonia, Il (1819), 38, **41**, 42, 74 n., **417**, 419, **436–7**, 445; synopsis: 460

Fausta (1832), 124, **125**, 129, 130, 132, 137, 146, 169, 196, 281, 357, 420, **438–9**, 448, 451; synopsis: 477

Favorita, La; see favorite, La

Favorite, La (1840), xi, xii, 47, 224, 232, 240, **241–7**, 249, 253, 295, 324, 358, 359, 360, 362, 363, 366, 376, 405 n., 406, 414, **427–32**, 435, 440, 442, 454, 458, 501; synopsis: 492–3

Fiancée du Tyrol, La, 231, 232, 501; *see* also *Furioso*

Fidanzata, La, 501

Figlia del reggimento, La; see fille du régiment, La

Fille du régiment, La (1840), xi n., 123, 232, **233–6**, 353 n., 358, 359, 361, 364, 380 n., 385, **407**, 438; synopsis: 492

Follia, Una (1818), 36n., 37, 39, 452, 459, 502

Fortunato inganno, Il (1823), **68**, **398**, 400, 457–8; synopsis: 463

Francesca da Foix (1831), 47, **122**, 379, 451; example: 380; synopsis: 476

Furioso all'isola di S. Domingo, Il (1833), **128–31**, 133, **135–6**, 137, 139, 231, 232, 281, 331, 358, 406, 412, 439, 449, 450, 501, 509; synopsis: 479–80

Gabriella di Vergy (*comp.* 1826), 64n., 85, 153n., 401, 419, **437–8**, 457; example: 401; synopsis: 466-7

Gemma di Vergy (1834), **153–4**, 164, 166, 299, 345, 446, 466n.; synopsis: 483–4

Gianni di Calais (1828), **104–5**, 121, 380, **438**, 450, 451; synopsis: 470–1

Gianni di Parigi, 121, **122**, 139, 240n., 353n., **438**, 441; synopsis: 475–6

Giovanna I di Napoli; see Lucrezia Borgia

Giovedì grasso, Il (1828), **105**, 355, 450, 451; synopsis: 471

Illinesi, Gli, **164–6**, 174, 502

Imelda de' Lambertazzi (1830), 47, **112**, 457; synopsis: 474

Innamorati, Gli, 502

Ira d'Achille, L', 28; synopsis: 458–9

Jeanne la folle, 502

Lara, 502

Lettera anonima, La (1822), **61**, 436, 450; synopsis: 461–2

Leonora di Guzman; see favorite, La

Linda di Chamounix (1842), 119, 185, 259, **264–6**, 267, 270, 271, 277, 278, 353, 358, 359, 360, 362, 363, 364, 365, 373, 376n., 385, 405, 439, **440**, 454; synopsis: 495

Lucia di Lammermoor (1835), 6, 9, 148, 161, **166–71**, 172, 173, 182, 188, 196, 214, **215**, 220, 223, 224, 231, 234, 254, 281, 296, 325, 342, 354, 355, 356, 360–1, 362, 363, 363n., 364, 365, 366–7, 373–4, 376, 384, 385, 386, 387, 388, 402, 405, 406, 412, 414, **416–17**, 424, 446; French version (1839): **230**, 231, 235, **424–5**, 428n., 439, 454, 458; examples: 373, 387; synopsis: 485

Lucrezia Borgia (1833), **141–5**, 146, 147, 167, 255, 257n., 354, 355, 360, 361, 361n., 363, 365, 379, 407–8, 410, **420**, 423n., 452, 453; example: 408; synopsis: 481–2

Mlle de la Vallière (*projected*), 502

Maria di Rohan (1843), 209, 275, 276, 277, **278**, 283, 284, 285, 287, 358, 359, 366, **423**, 440, 447, 455; synopsis: 497

Maria di Rudenz (1838), **212–13**, 219, 281, 376, 384, 408, **440**, 447; synopsis: 489–90

Maria Padilla (1841), 243, **255–8**, 259, 269, 270, 280, **421–3**, 440, 454; synopsis: 494–5

Maria Stuarda (1835), **151–2**, 155, 171, **175–9**, 281, 408, **439**, 445, 456, 502; synopsis: 483

Marino Faliero (1835), 152–3, **155–60**, 187, 188, 250, 270, 281, 439, 446, 455, 466n.; synopsis: 484–5

Martyrs, Les (1840), xin., 224, **227–8**, 229, 231, 232, 233, 234, 235, **236–9**, 244, 276, 281, 414, **425–7**, 457, 490; *see also Poliuto*

Ne m'oubliez pas (*incomplete*), 253, 502

Nizza de Grenade; see Lucrezia Borgia

Nozze in villa, Le (1820–21?), **40–1**, **436**; synopsis: 459–60

Nuovo Pourceaugnac, Il; see Giovedì grasso, Il

Olimpiade (*comp.* 1817), 28, **458**

Olivo e Pasquale (1827), **86–8**, 133, 281, 449, 450; synopsis: 467

Onore vince amore (*projected*), 455, 502

Otto mesi in due ore (1827), **88–9**, 353n., 389, 390, **418–19**, 437, 438, 450, 451; example: 390; synopsis: 467

Paolina e Poliuto, 427; *see also Martyrs, Les*

Paria, Il (1829), 105, **106–7**, 108, 139, 281, 366, **381–4**, 405, 411–12, **438**, 450, 451; examples: 381, 382, 383; synopsis: 471–2

Parisina (1833), **138**, 139, 140, 150, 167, 168, 213, 215, 357n., 412, 415, 452; synopsis: 480

Pazzi per progretto, I (1830), **110**, 111, 281, 437, 451; synopsis: 473

Pia de' Tolomei (1837), 68n., 188, 189, 190, 193, **194–5**, 281, 376, **377–9**, 403, 411, **421**, 446, 447; examples: 377, 403; synopsis: 488

Pascià di Scutari, Il, 502

Piccioli virtuosi ambulanti, I (1819), 40, 436, 452, **460**

Pietro il grande, czar delle Russie; see Falegname di Livonia, Il

Pigmalione, Il (*comp.* 1816), **28**; synopsis: 458

Pirati, I; see Chiara e Serafina
Poliuto (*comp.* 1838), xin., **218-20**, 225, **227-8**, 233, **239**, 244, 359, 384, 388, 408, 414, **425-7**, 440, 446, 447, 457, 490n.; example: 384; synopsis: 490-1; *see also Martyrs, Les*
Proscritto, Il; see Esule di Roma L'
Provinciali, I; see Nozze in villa, Le
Regina di Cipro, La; see Caterina Cornaro
Rinnegata, La; see Lucrezia Borgia
Ritratto parlante, Il (1818?), **36n.**, 459n., 502; *see also Follia, Una*
Rita ou le mari battu (*comp.* 1841), **254-5**, 323, 380n., 458; synopsis: 494
Roberto Devereux (1837), 131n., 206, 209, **210**, 211, 217, 225, 226-7, 233, 281, 357, **421**, 423, 446, 447; synopsis: 488-9
Romanziera e l'uomo nero, La (1831), **122**, 355, 435, 451; synopsis: 476-7
Rosmunda d'Inghilterra (1834), 141n., **147-8**, 196, 357n., 376, **420**, 425, **439**, 452; synopsis: 482-3
Ruy Blas (*projected*), 275, 276, 503
Sancia di Castiglia (1832), **131-2**, 411, 444n., 456; synopsis: 479
Settimio il proscritto; see Esule di Roma L'
Sganarello (*projected*) 503
Torquato Tasso (1833), 133, 138, **140-1**, 189, 219, 438 *and* n., 449, 450; synopsis: 480-1
Ugo, conte di Parigi (1832), **125-6**, 157, 165, 281, 357n., 376, 415, 452, 453; synopsis: 477-8
Zingara, La (1822), **59-60**, 67, 172, 403, 404, 457; example: 403; synopsis: 461
Zoraide di Granata (1822), 9, 42, 43-5, 46, **53-5**, 57, 67, 71, 133, 308, 411, **417-18**, 444n., 452, 516n.; *rifacimento* (1824), 66, **68-71**, **417-18**, **449**; synopsis: 460-1

CANTATAS
Aristea, 67
Cantata (for the marriage of Ferdinand of Austria), 119
Cantata (for Mayr's 78th birthday), 253-4
Canto XXXIII della Divina Commedia, Il, 102
Genio dell'armonia, Il, 110
Partenza, La, 77
Ritorna di primavera, Il, 33
Voti dei sudditi, I, 75

HYMNS
Inno reale (for To. Carlo Felice, Genoa, 1828), 99

RELIGIOUS MUSIC
Ave Maria (ded. to Empress Anna), 266
Kyrie, 29
Miserere (for the Vatican choir), 258
Requiem Mass (for V. Bellini), 173, 371
Requiem Mass (for Ab. Fazzini), 210-11
Requiem Mass (for N. Zingarelli), 196, 197

INSTRUMENTAL WORKS FOR ORCHESTRA
Gran Marcia Militare Imperiale, 252
Sinfonia concertata, 29
Sinfonia (in mem. of Bellini), 173
Sinfonia (in mem. of Capuzzi), 33
Sinfonia ('*In morte di Maria F. Malibran*'), 195
Sinfonia ('*L'incendio*'), 37

CHAMBER MUSIC
Scherzo for violin and piano, 86
String quartets, 13, 31, 33, 42, 185, 372

PIANO MUSIC
Two Hands
Juvenilia, 43, 229
Sinfonia (dated 19 Nov. 1816), 357n.
Waltz (in *Il piccolo compositore di musica*), 19

VOCAL COMPOSITIONS
Solo Voice
Amore e morto, 372
Bohêmienne, La, 441
Conocchia, La, 373n.
Dernière nuit d'un novice (*Ultima notte di un novizio*), 372
È morta, 208 *and* n.
Fiancée du timballier, La, 275
Lamento per la morte di V. Bellini, 173
Matinées musicales (collection) 253
Nuits d'été à Pausilippe, Les (collection), 439
Pescatore, Il, 372
Sospiro, Il, 372
Sultana, La, 372
(*Io*) *te vojo bene assaje*, 373
Two Voices
Bevitori, I, 439n.
Duetto (for C. Carnevali & N. Cartoni), 66
Duetto (for 2 sopranos, ded. to Va. Vasselli), 87

INDEX

MISCELLANY
Cabaletta: Pietoso all' amor mio, 102
Sextet (1812), 24
Studies in counterpoint, 26

LIBRETTOS
Betly, 95, 161, 190, 447, 448, 487
Campanello di notte, Il, 95, 190, 447, 448, 486
Convenienze ed inconvenienze teatrale, Le, 95, 447, 448, 468–9
D., as librettist, 95, 124, 271, 444, **448–9,** 477, 496

MUSIC (general)
Forms (aria, cabaletta, cavatina, duet, ensemble, prelude, romanza, sinfonia), **353–67**
Style, general discussion, **368–412;** also 12, 32, 42, 71, 96, 274, 275

Donizetti, Gaetano, 350
Donizetti, Giovanni, 4
Donizetti, Giuseppe, **4,** 5, 22, 54n., **90–2,** 98, 104, 106, 107, 127, 149, **153,** 176, 177, 181, 183, 184, 186, 208, 225, 278, 289, 302, 304–5, 322, 325, 327, 332, 337, 342, 349, 401, 436n., 505
Donizetti, Giuseppe (great nephew), 350
Donizetti, Giuseppina Gabuzzi, 350
Donizetti, Maria Antonia; *see* Tironi, Maria Antonia Donizetti
Donizetti, Maria Rachele, 5
Donizetti, Maria Rosalinda, 4
Donizetti, Virginia Vasselli, 56, **86–7,** 89, 90, 93, 97, 98, **103,** 108, 112, 114, 119, 120, 121, 125, 128, 133, 147, 148, 149, 153, 161, 162, 170, **176,** 182, **183,** 184, 186, **193,** 196, **197,** 198, **199,** 202, 203, 209, 211, 255, 280, 293, 315, 317, 349, 503, 510, 517; quoted: 104, 114
Donna del lago, La; see Rossini
Dorus-Gras, Julie, 237
Donzelli, Domenico, **9,** 53, 54, 55, 59, 63n., 69, 70, 71, 97, 125, 126, 135, **164–5,** 241, 257, 263, 420, 438
Double échelle, La; see Thomas
Drapier, Le; see Halévy
Dresden, 99n.
Duc d'Albe, Le; see Donizetti
Duca d'Alba, Il; see Donizetti
Dumas père, Alexandre, 218
Charles VII chez les grands vassaux, 153n., 483

Dumas père, *Corricolo, Le,* 218
Duponchel, Charles, 214–15, 217, 239, 432
Duprez, Alexandrine, 138, 141
Duprez, Gilbert Louis, 138, 141, 148, 170, 171, 214, 215, 217, 220, 232, 233, 237, 239, 245, 246, 286, 288, 325, 330n., 415
Duval, Alexandre, 460
Duveyrier, Charles, 457, 491

Eckerlin, Fanny, 35, **36n.,** 40
Eco, L', 116, 136; quoted: 116
Eden, 108, 125
Edinburgh, 455
Edwards, Henry Sutherland, 469n.
Elba, 91
Elian, 245
Elisa; see Mayr
Elisa e Claudio; see Mercadante
Elisabeth, Empress of Austria, etc., 262
Elisabeth d'Angleterre; see Ancelot
Elisabeth ou les exilés en Sibérie; see Cottin
Elisabetta al castello di Kenilworth; see Donizetti
Elisabetta, regina d'Inghilterra; see Rossini
Elisir d'amore, L'; see Donizetti
Elizabeth I, Queen of England, 175, 472n.
Elvida; see Donizetti
Emilia di Liverpaut; see Trento
Emilia di Liverpool; see Donizetti
Emilia di Liverpool; see Scatizzi
Ennery, Adolphe Philippe d', 259n., 495
Grâce de Dieu, La, 259n., 495
Enrico di Borgogna; see Donizetti
Ernani; see (1) Bellini, (2) Verdi
Escudier, Marie, 514
Escudier & Cie, 297, 514
Esquirrol, Jean Étienne Dominique, 308
Esule di Roma, L'; see Donizetti

Fabbrica-Montrésor, Isabella, 64, 64n., 65
Fabbrici, Natale, 174–5, 187, 188
Fabré, Giuseppina, 58, 61
'Fair Rosamund' 147, 482
Falegname di Livonia, Il; see (1) Donizetti, (2) Pacini, G.
Falstaff; see Verdi
Faust; see Goethe
Fausta; see Donizetti

545

Favart, Charles Simon, 476
  Ninette à la cour, 476
Favere, Marchese Ugo delle, 77
Favorite, La; *see* Donizetti
Fazzini, Abbate, 210–11, 507
Fedra; *see* Mary
Fedrighini, Camillo, 266
Fees, 44, 47–8, 49, 62–3, 66, 69, 73, 75, 76, 79, 83, 87, 92, 93, 97, 128, 131, 139, 152, 153, 163, 166, 174, 178, 187–8, 193–4, 219, 263, 268, 269, 272, 279, 310
Fenice; *see* Teatro la Fenice (*Venice*)
Ferdinand I, Emperor of Austria, etc., 119, 268, 269, 504
Ferdinando I, King of the Two Sicilies, 61, 75, 83n.
Ferdinando II, King of the Two Sicilies, 83n., 122, 170, 193, 198, 205, 208, 209, **213–14**, 219, 226, 231, 504
Ferlito, Vincenzo, 155
Ferrara, 145, 194, 212, 261
Ferretti, Cristina, 66
Ferretti, Emilia 'Teta' Terziani, 51, 66
Ferretti, Jacopo, 45, 46, **51–2**, 53, 55n., 59, 66, 67, 68–9, 71, 86, 128, **129–30**, 131, 132, 133, 139, 151, 162, 170, 192, 418, 443–4, 448, **449–50**, 460, 463, 467, 479, 480
Ferris, George T., **5–6**; quoted: 5
Ferron, Elisabetta, **67**, 76, 77, 80, 81
Festa, 111
Festa in villaggio, La; *see* Puccita
Fétis, François Joseph, 25
Fiancée du timballier, La; *see* Hugo
Fiancée du Tyrol, La; *see* Donizetti
Fidanzata, La; *see* Donizetti
Fidanzata di Lammermoor, La; *see* Mazzacuto
Fidelio; *see* Beethoven
Figlia dell'arciere, La; *see* Coccia
Figurante, La; *see* Clapisson
Filarmonici romani; *see* Accademia filarmonica romana
Fille du régiment, La; *see* Donizetti
Finocchi, 490n.
Finzi, Orianna Santunioni, 28
Fioravanti, Giuseppe, 36, 60, 68, 73, 74, 88, 191
Fioravanti, Valentino, 429n.
  Adelaide e Comingio, 429n.
Fiorini, Girolamo, 18n.
Fischer, Annetta; *see* Venier, Annetta Fischer

Fischer, Lugwig, 74n.
Flaubert, Gustave, 230, 424n.
  Madame Bovary, 424n.
Flauto, Vincenzo, 279, 280
Fliegende Holländer, Der; *see* Wagner
Florence, 94n., 128, 135, **136–8**, 140, 145, **147–8**, 160, 186, 187, 188, 212, 448, 480, 482
Florimo, Francesco, 94, 97, 99, 100, 125, 137, 149, 154, 155, 156, 161, 172, 196, 239, 325, 336, 404, 407, 419n., 441n.
Fodor-Mainvielle, Josephine, 122, 449
Folie, Une; *see* Méhul
Foligno, 138
Follia, Una; *see* Donizetti
Fontana, Ugo, 89, 419
Fornasari, Luciano, 72n., 284
Fortunato inganno, Il; *see* Donizetti
Fosconi, Giuseppe, 35
Fossati, Giovanni Antonio, 335, 337
Fosso, Luigi, 250
Foucher, Paul, 498n.
Fouquier, Pierre Eloi, 318
Fovis, 317
Fraccalini, Vincenzo, 44n.
Fraccaroli, Arnaldo, 39, 117
France musicale, La, 255, 328, 332
Francesca di Foix; *see* Donizetti
Franceschini, Marianna, 135
Francesco I, King of the Two Sicilies, 75, 503
Franchetti, 62, 63
Franchi, de, 61
Franci, 208
Franklin, Benjamin, 416
Franz Josef, 262
Fraschini, Gaetano, 279, 280
Frattamaggiore, 450
Frazzi, Vito, 420
Freni, 192
Frey, 487n.
Frezzolini, Erminia, 127, 145, 257, 420
Frezzolini, Giuseppe, 87, 100, 101, 105, 127, 257n.
Furioso all'isola di S. Domingo, Il; *see* Donizetti
Furioso nell' isola di S. Domingo, 479

Gabrielle de Vergy; *see* Belloy
Gabriella di Vergy; *see* (1) Donizetti, (2) Carafa, (3) Mercadante
Gabriella di Vergy, 64
Gabrielle, Annibale, 290; quoted: 290–1

Galassi, Giacomo, 70
Galli, Filippo, 115, 116
Galli, Michelangelo, 15, 26, 141 n.,
    317, 433
Galli, Vincenzo, 88
Galli-Marié, Célestine, 233
Gallini, Natale, xii, 416, 421, 423,
    483 n.
Galzerani, Antonietta, 112
Galzerani, Giovanni, 99
Garat, Pierre Jean, 492 n.
Garcia Sr., Manuel, 142
Gardoni, Italo, 265
Garofolini, 333
Garofolo, Luigi, 87
Gaspari, 29 n.
Gasperini, Pietro, 250
Gastillon, Stefano, 99
Gatti, Armando, 28
Gatti, Isidoro, 80 n.
Gautier, Théophile, 237, 245, 246,
    265, 272–3, 429, 454; quoted:
    237–8, 245–6, 272, 454, 457
Gavazzeni, Gianandrea, 369
Gayarré, Giuliano, 434
Gazza ladra, La; see Rossini
Gazzetta di Genova; quoted: 101
Gazzetta musicale di Milano, 485 n.
Gazzetta (priveligiata) di Milano, 65, 97,
    115, 116, 126, 127, 128, 328;
    quoted: 65, 97, 115–16, 126, 127–8
Gazzetta priveligiata di Torino, 328
Gazzetta priveligiata di Venezia, 36, 41;
    quoted: 36
Gazzetta ufficiale piemontese (Turin), 147,
    449 n.
Gemma di Vergy; see Donizetti
Generali, Pietro, 83
Genero, Giambattista, 127
Genoa, 41, 88, 92, **98–102**, 127, 128,
    145, 146, 153, 154, 175 n., 176,
    180, 183, 186, 193, 194, 213, 268,
    270, 289, 455, 470, 519
Genoa, Royal College of, 106, 145
Genoino, Giulio, 450 n.
Genoino, Giulio, 61, **450**, 461, 462
Gentili, Pietro, 110
Gerusalemme librata; see Tasso
Ghezzi, Teodoro, 108, 111, 199, 203,
    207, 208, 212, 268, 279, 292, 300,
    314, 315, 316, 317, 324, 332, 349,
    427
Gianni di Calais; see Donizetti
Gianni di Parigi; see (1) Donizetti, (2)
    Morlacchi
Gianni, Pietro, 192

Giarrattelli, Gennaro, 239
Gibbon, Edward, 480
Gibert, 230
Gilardoni, Domenico, 48, 93, 96, 106,
    109, 110, 124, 169, 419, 448,
    450–1, 467, 468, 469, 470, 471,
    473, 476, 477
Ginevra di Scozia; see Mayr
Gioia, Gaetano, 64
Gioia, Maria; *see* Tamburini, Maria
    Gioia
Giomo, 14
Giorgi, de, 182
Giornale del Regno delle due Sicilie, 60, 67;
    quoted: 60, 67, 73
Giovanna d'Arco; see Verdi
Giovanna I di Napoli; see Marsuzi
Giovedì grasso, Il; see Donizetti
Gioventù di Enrico V, La; see Mercadante
Giraldoni, Leone, 434
Girard, B., 122, 148
Giraud, Count Giovanni, 463
Giselle; see Adam
Giulietta e Romeo; see (1) Vaccai, (2)
    Zingarelli
Giusti, Carolina, 237
Glossop, Joseph, 67 n.
God Save the Queen, 226, 359
Godard d'Aucour de Saint-Just,
    Claude, 475
Goethe, Johann Wolfgang von
    Faust, 432
    Jery und Bätely, 487 n.
    Tasso, 480
Goldberg, Fanny, 279–80
Goldoni, Carlo, 169, 502
Gonzales, Antonio, 14
Gonzales, Florian, 461
Gottardi, Teodoro, 141, 142
Goudenone, 333
Gounod, Charles, 271
Grâce de Dieu, La; see Ennery d'
Granchi, Almerinda, 210, 233
Grappallo, Marchese, 91
Grecis, Nicola de, 64
Gregory XVI, 119, 204, 247, 507
Grétry, André Ernest, 36 n.
    Tableau parlant, Le, 36 n.
Grey, Lady Jane, 152
Gris, Paolo de, 176, 332
Grisi, Carlotta, 242 n., 246
Grisi, Giuditta, 164–5, 246 n.
Grisi, Giulia, 36 n., 119, 125, 154, 159,
    164, 191, 215, 217, 223, 226,
    246 n., 260, 271, 272, 284, 296,
    299, 516

Grossi, Rosalinda, 105
Guaita, Carlo, 515, 516, 517, 518
Guaita, Ismaele, 144
Gualzetti, G. A. 'Eriso', 429n.
Guarnaccia, E., 463n.
Guasco, Carlo, 278
Guglielmi, Pasquale, 109
Guglielmi, Pietro Carlo, 52, 468n.
Guillaume, Édouard, 269
Guillaume Tell; *see* Rossini
Guzman, Leonora de, 429, 492

Habeneck, François Antoine, 215, 232, 245
Halévy, Jacques Fromental, 219, 227, 232, 270
  Drapier, Le, 227, 232
  Juive, La, 160–1, 219, 222
Handel, George Frederick, 411n.
Harris, Sir Augustus, 67n.
Havana, 61
Haydn, Franz Josef, 12, 13, 277
  Creation, The, 12
Haymarket Theatre (*London*); *see* King's Theatre
Heaven and Earth; *see* Byron
Heinefetter, Maria; *see* Stöckl-Heinefetter, Maria
Heinefetter, Kathinka, 127n.
Heinefetter, Sabine, 127
Henri (*pseud.* for Deshayes), 233
Henry II, King of England, 147
Henry VIII, King of England, 472n.
Hernani; *see* Hugo
Herz, Leo(n), 284, 289, 299, 328
Hiller, Ferdinand, 25
Hoche, Lazare, 5, 6
Hoffman, Ernst Theodor Amadeus, 517
Home, sweet home, 412
Homer
  Iliad, 458
Hugo, Victor, 142, 145, 255, 453, 472, 481n., 503, 513, 514; *Amy Robsart*, 472; *Fiancée du timballier, La*, 275; *Hernani*, 117, 410; *Lucrèce Borgia*, 142, 255, 481; *Ruy Blas*, 503
Huguenots, Les; *see* Meyerbeer
Hughes, Spike, 131n., 168n.
Hunter, John, 292
Hurteaux, 230

Ifianassa a Melampo; *see* Legrenzi
Illinesi, Gli; *see* (1) Basili, (2) Coppola, (3) Donizetti, (4) Strepponi

Illinesi, Gli; *see* Romani
Imelda de' Lambertazzi; *see* Donizetti
Imperial Theatre (*St Petersburg*), 193n.
In morte di Beethoven; *see* Mayr
In morte di Maria F. Malibran, 195
Inconvenienze teatrali, Le; *see* Sografi
Ines de Castro; *see* Persiani
Infrascata, 170
Ingolstadt, 10
Inganno felice, L'; *see* Rossini
Innamorati, Gli; *see* Donizetti
Ira d'Achille, L'; *see* (1) Basili, (2) Donizetti, (3) Niccolini
Istituto musicale Gaetano Donizetti; *see* Lezioni caritatevoli
Italiana in Algeri, L'; *see* Rossini
Italiens; *see* Théâtre-Italien (*Paris*)
Ivanhoe; *see* Scott
Ivanoff, Nicolai, 128, 159, 191, 217, 227, 261, 423
Ivry, 308, 311, 312, 313, 314, 315, 316, 317, 318, 319, 323, 324, 325, 326, 327, 328, 329, 330, 331, 332, 333, 335, 339
Izett, Donald, 5

Jacovacci, Vincenzo, 240, 247, 251
Javille, 317
Jean de Paris; *see* Boieldieu, F. A.
Jeanne la folle; *see* Donizetti
Jeanne la folle; *see* Scribe
Jery und Bätely; *see* Goethe
Joly, Antenor, 232, 242 *and* n., 424, 454, 501
Journal des débats, 234, 299
Juive, La; *see* Halévy

Kärthnerthortheater (*Vienna*), 57, 87, 262, 267n., 276, 278, 290, 423, 495, 497
Kelm, J., 230
Kenilworth; *see* Scott
King's Theatre, 59n., 132n.
Kock, Paul de, 178n.
Kozeluch, Leopold, 267
Kreutzer, Conradin, 487n.
Krommer, Fritz, 267

Lablache, Federico, 72n., 192
Lablache, Luigi, 53, 63, 72, 74, 81, 84, 96, 102n., 105, 106, 110, 111, 118, 119, 128, 130, 132, 154, 156, 158, 159, 191, 192, 217, 218, 220, 223, 227, 265, 271, **272**, 273, 503

Labocetta, Domenico, 290
Lac des fées, Le; see Auber
Lachner, Franz, 271
Lacoste, 296
Lacroix, Paul, 513, 515
La Hoche; *see* Hoche, Lazare
Lalande, Henriette; *see* Méric-Lalande, Henriette (Enrichetta)
Lampieri, Alessandro, 164, 166
Lanari, Alessandro, 17, 126, 128, **137-40**, 141, 147, 164, 168, 184, **186-9**, 195, 196, 200, 212, 420n., 421 *and* n.; quoted: 187, 196-7, 213
Lanassa; see Mayr
Landini, Antonio, 53n.
Lange, Aloysa, 94n.
Lannoy, Baron Eduard von, 325, **339, 341**; quoted: 325-7; *Emmy Teels,* 325n.
Lara; see (1) Donizetti, (2) Ruolz, de (3) Salvi, Matteo
Laroche, Enrichetta, 115
La Scala; *see* Teatro alla Scala (*Milan*)
La Scala Museum; *see* Museo teatrale alla Scala
Latte, Bernard, 160, 420, 425n.
Launer, 191, 235
Lauretti, Ferdinando, 135, 140
Lauzières (de Thémines), Achille de, 514
Lazzari, Alfonso, 271
Leborne, 428
Lefebvre (-Faure), Caroline, 255
Leghorn, 161, 176, 183, 186, 189, 193, 247, 270
Legion of Honour, 156, 183, 185, 318
Legrenzi, Giovanni, 39; *Ifianassa a Melampo,* 39n.; *Nino il giusto,* 39n.; *Totila,* 39n.
Leicester ou le château de Kenilworth; see Scribe
Lemoine, Gustave, 259n., 495
Lenzi, Carlo, 10
Leo XII, 68, 70, 82
Léon, 233
Lesser, Count von, 326
Lettera anonima, La; see Donizetti
Leuven (de Ribbling), Count Adolphe de, 515
Levasseur, Nicholas Prosper, 215, 245, 246, 286, 516
Lewis, 157
Lezeret, 331
Lezione stravagante, Una, 295
Lezioni caritatevoli di musica, 7, 11,

13, **14-22**, 25, 39, 40, 80n., 91, 106n., 153, 254, 340, 398, 436, 460
Lhérie, Victor, 486
Librettos, 46-8, 65, **443-98**
Liceo Filarmonico (Musicale) Communale (*Bologna*), xii, **25-9**, 33, 112, 260, 367n., 503
Lind, Jenny, 148, 236
Linda di Chamounix; see Donizetti
Linz, 275
Lipparini, Caterina, 78, 76, 88
Lisbon, 71, 85n.
Liverpool, 75
Locatelli, Giovanni, 346
Lochis, Count Guglielmo, 340
Lockroy (*pseud.* of Simon, Joseph Philippe), 209, 497
Duel sous le Cardinal de Richelieu, Un, 209, 276, 497
Lodi, Angelo, 210
Lodoïska; see Mayr
Löwe, Sofia (*soprano*), 257, 354
Loewenberg, Alfred, 72n., 94n., 189, 193n., 429n.
Lowenstein (-Wertheim-Freudenberg), Countess Sophie von, 304, 313, 315-17, 328, 329
Loira, Giuseppe, 88
Lombardi alla prima crociata, I; see Verdi
Lombardia, La, 350
London, 9, 11, 72, 88, 118, 121, 122, 125, 139, 142, 148, 159, 175, 228, 303, 501
Lonlay, Eugène de, 514
Lorenzani, Brigida, 81, 84, 100
Lotti, Antonio, 39n.
Lortzing, Gustav Albert, 93, 468n.
Zar und Zimmermann, 93, 468n.
Louis-Philippe, King of the French, 185, 346, 456
Lovere, 289, 318
Loyselet, Agnese, 71, 87, 110
Luca, Signor de, 336
Lucas, Hippolyte, 191, 258, 270, 513
Lucca, Francesco, 246
Lucca, Giuseppina, 433, 434n.
Lucchesi-Palli Library (*Naples*), 131n., 429
Lucia di Lammermoor; see Donizetti
Lucrèce Borgia; see Hugo
Lucrezia Borgia; see Donizetti
Ludolf, Countess, 515
Luisa Miller; see Verdi
Lumley (Levi), Benjamin, 501
Lupo d'Ostenda, Il; see Vaccai

Luzio, Gennaro, 74, 88, 95, 110, 122
Lyons, 145, 328
Lytton, Edward George Earle Lytton Bulwer-, first Baron Lytton, 209
  Rienzi, the Last of the Tribunes, 209

Machado, Barbosa, 498
  Memorias . . . o governo del rey D. Sebastião, 498
Madama Butterfly; see Puccini
Madame Bovary; see Flaubert
Mlle de la Vallière; see Donizetti
Madrid, 136n.
Maffei, Andrea, 173, 514
Magni, Carolina, 519
Mahmud II, Sultan of Turkey, 91
Maironi, Federico, 346
Maironi da Ponte, 34
Maître de chapelle, Le; see Paër
Malherbe Collection, 35
Malibran, Maria Felicita Garcia, 129, 130, 132, 138, 152, 164, **175-9**, 195, 502, 509
Malvezzi Ranuzzi, Ottavio, 29
Mancinelli, Marino, 434
Manferrari, Umberto, 193n., 459n., Manfredonia, 198
Manghenoni, Giuseppe, 18, 20, 39, 304
Mantua, 39, 40-1, 52, 459
Manzocchi, Almerinda, 84, 94, 192
Maometto II; see Rossini
Marchesi, Pomepo, 506
Marchesi, Tommaso, 25, 29, 30
Marconi, Napoleone, 144
Marguerite; see Boieldieu, Adrien
Mari de circonstance, Le; see Plantade
Maria II, Queen of Portugal, 286
Maria Anna Carolina of Savoy; see Anna, Empress of Austria
Maria Carolina Augusta, Princess; see Orléans, Marie Caroline Auguste
Maria Cristina, Queen of the Two Sicilies, 152, 445, 483, 504
Maria di Rohan; see Donizetti
Maria di Rudenz; see Donizetti
Maria Isabella, Queen of the Two Sicilies, 77, 84
Maria Padilla; see Ancelot
Maria Padilla; see Donizetti
Maria Stuarda; see Donizetti
Maria Stuart; see Schiller
Maria Theresa, Queen of the Two Sicilies, 504

Mariani, Luciano, 118, 144
Mariani, Rosa, 88
Marie Amélie, Queen of the French, 237
Marie Antoinette, Queen of France, 492n.
Marié, 339
Marié de l'Isle, Mécène, 233
Marieni, 177
Marignano, Marchesa Sofia di, 511
Marini, Girolamo Maria, 247, **452**, 493
Marini, Ignazio, 97, 122, 153, 179, 187, 240, 241, 250, 251
Marino Faliero; see Donizetti
Marino Faliero; see (1) Byron, (2) Delavigne
Marinuzzi, Gino, 427
Mario (Marchese Giovanni di Candia), 72n., 119, 125, 216, 232n., 260, 265, 271, 272, 295, 296, 297, 299, 441n.
Marmontel, Jean François, 486
  Bélisaire, 486
Maroncelli, Piero, **27**
  Laudamus, 27
Marotta, Madama, 301
Marquise, La; see Adam
Marseilles, 154, 247, 252, 292
Marsuzi, 152
  Giovanna I di Napoli, 152
Martin y Soler, Vincente, 59n.
  Scuola de' maritati (also given as *La cappricciosa coretta*), 59n.
Martinelli, Luigi, 41
Martini, Padre Giovanni Battista, 25
Martino, de, 516
Martyrs, Les; see Donizetti
Mary Stuart, Queen of Scots, 175
Masaniello, 450n.
Massimi, Princess, 208
Massol, Eugène Etienne August, 237, 286
Matilde de Shabran; see Rossini
Matrimonio segreto, Il; see Cimarosa
Mattei, Padre Stanislao, 13, 22, 23, **25-6**, 41, 45, 99, 122, 357n., 511, 519
Mayr, Angela Venturali, 105n.
Mayr, Giovanni Simone (Johann Simon), 4, 7, 8, **10-13**, 14, 15, 16, 17, 18, 19, 20, 22, 23, 24, 26, 29, 30, 31, 32, 33, 34, 35, 39, 40, 43, 44, 45, 51, 52, 55, 57, 58, 59, 61, 62, 64, 67, 72, 78, 79, 80-1, 82, 83, 84, 85, 86, 89, 90, 95 and n., 96, 97,

98, 101, 102, 104, 105, 108, 111,
113, 116, 121, 128, 132, 148, 150,
171, 176, 177, 181, 184, 194, 197,
210, 213, 225, 227, 228, 240,
253-4, 255, 256, 268, 281, 282,
283, 284, **302**, 304, 334, 339n.,
347, 368, 384n., **392 and n.**,
398n., **404**, 418, 433, 449n., 452,
460, 504, 511; quoted: 23-4, 39
Adelasia ed Aleramo, 20
Alcide al Bivio, 15
Alfredo il grande, 34n.
Atalia, 57-8
Belle ciarle e tristi fatti, 392n.
Che originali!, 20, 78, 257, 392n.
Danaidi, Le, 35
Demetrio, 11
Elisa, 54n., 91
Fedra, 43
Ginevra di Scozia, 11, 70n., 358
In morte di Beethoven, 12
Lanassa, 34n.
Lodoiska, 11
Medea in Corinto, 102
Piccolo compositore di musica, Il, **18-20**,
368, 398n.
Saffo, 10
Sisara, 15
Voto di Jefte, Il, 52n.
Mayr, Lucrezia Venturali, 11, 105n.
Mayr's School; *see* Lezioni caritatevoli
Mayseder, Josef, 13
Mazzanti, 53
Mazzarelli, Rosina, **187-9**, 194
Mazzini, Giuseppe, 119, 120, 455
Mazzotti, Eugenio, 192
Mazzucato, Alberto, 485n.; *Fidanzata
di Lammermoor, La*, 485n.
McCormack, John, 438n.
Medea in Corinto; *see* Mayr
Medici, Marchesa, 517
Medonte, re di Epiro; *see* Sarti
Méhul, Etienne Nicholas, 36n.
Folie, Une, 36n.
Melas, Teresina, 68, 73
Mélesville, Anne Honore Joseph, 468,
487
Melzi, Count Gaetano, 123, 124, 128,
133
Mendelssohn-Bartholdy, Felix, 122-3
Mendorf, 10, 282
Mercadante, Saverio, 59, 62, 63, 64
and n., 69, 72, 73, 74n., 80, 85n.,
141n., 142-3, 149, 195, 231, 446n.,
449n., 466n., 469n.
Adele e Emerico, 59n., 63, 64

Alfredo d'Inghilterra, 59
Conte d'Essex, Il, 489n.
Elisa e Claudio, 63, 80, 469n.
Gabriella di Vergy, 64n., 85n., 466n.
Gioventù di Enrico V, La, 143n.
Normanni a Parigi, I, 137
Merciaiuolo in angustie, Il, 65
Merelli, Bartolomeo, 33n., **34**, 36n., 37,
40, 41, 43, 67, 145, 256, 262, 264,
290, 418, **452**, 459, 460
Viaggio a Vienna, Un, 262
Méric, Josephine de, 88
Méric-Lalande, Henriette (Enrichetta),
81, 84, 88n., 96, **142**, **144**, 354,
362n., 376, 408, 449
Merimée, Prosper, 319
Merle, Jean Toussaint, 468
Merlin, Countess de, 178n., 441n.
Merola, Giuseppina, **137-8**, 148
Messager, Le, 158
Messicani, I; *see* Bochsa
Messina, 85, 166, 198, 456, 502
Metternich, Prince Clemens, 263, 318,
346, 512
Metz, 255
Meyerbeer, Giacomo, 218, 234, 271, 276
Huguenots, Les, 218, 222
Robert le diable, 222
Michonne, M., 515
Milan, 9, 43, 44, 47, 55, **62-6**, 72, 94,
96, 97, 98, 99, 112, 113, 115, 116,
117, 119, 124, 125, 133, 135, **141-
5**, 149, 150, **153**, 154, 163, 166,
171, 172, 175, 176, 177, 180, 182,
192, 194, 213, 240, 241, 243, 252,
256, 258, 261, 262, 266, 268, 289,
305, 318, 323, 327, 335, 399n.,
410, 419, 445, 452, 455, 462, 474,
475, 477, 478, 481, 483, 494, 502
Milan Conservatory, 25, 64, 433
Milan Conservatory Library, 420
Mitvié, Jean, 308, 320, 330, 331, 333,
337, 338, 339
Modena, 88
Moïse; *see* Rossini
Moja, Teresa, 179
Molière (Jean Baptiste Poquelin), 471,
503; *Monsieur de Pourceaugnac*, 471;
Sganarelle, 503
Mombelli, Maria Ester, 53, 55, 71
Monastero delle Vergini, 56
Moncada, Carlo, 60, 68
Monelli, Savino, 64, 71, 72
Mongardi, Clementina Carnevali, 57,
66, 86, 517
Mongardi, Natale, 86

Moniteur universel, Le, 235
Monnier, Etienne, 517
Monpou, Hippolyte, 242 n.
Chaste Suzanne, La, 242 n.
Monsieur de Pourceaugnac; see Molière
Monsigny, Pierre Alexandre, 470 n.
Monteleone, Andrea, 76
Monterasi, Lorenzo, 302, 304; quoted: 302–4
Monteraso, 204
Monticelli, Caterina, 60
Morabito, Don Francesco, 75, 78, 79
Morandi, Rosa, 64, 65
Moreau de Tours, Jean Jacques, 311, 316, 318, 319, 320, 326, 328, 329, 331, 333
Morelli, Bortolo, 215
Moretti, 350
Moriani, Napoleone, 145, 196, 213, 217, 264, 265, 420
Moriggia, 82
Morlacchi, Francesco, **99**, 121, 452, 475 n.; *Colombo,* 99; *Corradino,* 111; *Gianni di Parigi,* 121; *Tebaldo ed Isolina* 99 n.
Mosca, Giuseppe, 463 n.
Mosè; see Rossini
Mount-Edgcumbe, Richard Edgcumbe, 2nd Earl of, 8
Mozart, Wolfgang Amadeus, 12, 13, 74 n., 267, 268, 274, 277, 391, 392, 411, 416
Così fan tutte, 94 n.
Don Giovanni, 274, 391
Nozze di Figaro, Le, 391, 394 n., 411 n.
Requiem, **12**
Munich, 71, 275, 281–2, 283
Museo Donizettiano (Bergamo), xi, 26, 27 n., 85 n., 108, 146 n., 166 n., 195 n., 197 n., 215 n., 281, 327, 341 n., 347, 357 n., 415 n., 416 n., 458, 467, 483 n., 503, 512
Museo Rubini (Romano), 9 n.
Museo Teatrale alla Scala (Milan), 503
Musikfreunde, Gesellschaft der (Vienna), 267

Nabucco; see Verdi
Naples, 9, 44, 47, 48, 55, **57–61**, 62, 66, 68, 73, 75, 76, 77, 79, 82, 84, 85, 87, 88, 89, 90, 93, 94 n., 97, 98, 101 n., 102, 103, 105, 107, 108, 109, 112, 120, 121, 122, **123–5**, 128, 130, 131, 133, 137, 139, 145, **148–52**, 153, 158, 160, 161, 162,

168, 171, 172, 175, 176, 178 n., 182, 183, 184, 185, 187, 190, 193, 194, 197, 198, 202, 204, 205, 208, 213, 216, **220**, 225, 229, 231–2, 233, 237, 248, 258, 266, **268–70**, 275, 276, 277, 278, 279–80, 288, 289, 291, 292, 293, 300, 301, 303, 305, 314, 315, 316, 317, 324, 349, 357 n., 410, 418, 420, 429, 431, 432, 445, 446, 448, 449, 450, 461, 462, 463, 464, 465, 466, 467, 468, 469, 470, 471, 472, 473, 474, 475 n., 476, 477, 479, 483, 485, 486, 487, 488, 490, 495
Naples Conservatory (Royal College of Music *or* Conservatorio di S. Pietro a Majella), 25, 83, 94 n., 110, 124, 148, 149, 172, 185, 196, 197, 198, 202, 206, 208, 214, 217, **219**, 220, 225, 231, 239, 241, 404
Naples Conservatory Library, xii, 40, 68 n., 74 n., 94 n., 146 n., 165, 166 n., 186, 195 n., 197 n., 295 n., 296, 298 n., 377 n., 378 n., 392 n., 415 n., 418 n., 420 n., 421 n., 502, 519
Nasolini, Sebastiano, 19
Nau, Maria Dolores Josefina, 330 n.
Nava, Domenica; *see* Donizetti, Domenica Nava
Navarino, Battle of, 92 n.
Ne m'oubliez pas; see Donizetti
Negrini, Vincenzo, 126
New York City, 27 138, 392 n.
New York Public Library, 242
Niccolini, Antonio, 169
Niccolini, Giuseppe, 458 n., 461 n.
Abenamet e Zoraide, 461 n.
Ira d'Achille, L', 458 n.
Nice, 304, 310, 313, 316
Nicolai, Otto, 452 n.
Templario, Il, 452 n.
Nicolini, Giambattista, 513
Nino il giusto; see Legrenzi
Niobe; see Pacini
Noah, 110
Noblet, Aubert, 99
Norma; see Bellini
Normanni a Parigi, I; see Mercadante
Notizie del giorno, 54, 71, 88; quoted: 55, 71
Nourrit, Adolphe, 215, 217, 218, **220–1**, 447 n., 490 n., 514, 516
Nourrit, Madame Adolphe, 220–1, 230
Novara, 143

Novelli, Pietro, 179
Novello, Clara, 261
Nozzari, Andrea, **9**, 10, 67, 75, 106
Nozze di Figaro, Le; *see* Mozart
Nozze di Lammermoor, Le; *see* Carafa
Nozze in villa, Le; *see* Donizetti
Nuovo Figaro, Il; *see* Ricci, Luigi

Oberto, conte di S. Bonifacio; *see* Verdi
Octave, 286
Olimpiade; *see* Donizetti
Olivo e Pasquale; *see* Doniazetti
Olivo e Pasquale; *see* Sografi
Onore vince amore; *see* Donizetti
Opéra (Académie Royale du Musique,
    Paris), 126, 160, 191, 193, 214,
    215, **216**, 217, **222**, 223, 224, 225,
    226, 227, 228, 229, 230, 231, 232,
    233, 234, 237–8, 239, 241, 244,
    245, 246, 270, 276, 279, 286, 287,
    288, 304, 426, 427, 432, 433,
    433 n., 454, 490, 498, 502, 504
Opéra-Comique (*Paris*), 161, **223**, 224,
    231, 233 *and* n., 234, 235, 236,
    253, 255, 275, 276, 330, 492, 494
Orlandi, Elisa, 105, 115, 116, 135, 136
Orlandini, Antonio, 67
Orléans, Marie Caroline Auguste,
    Princess, 59, 503
Orobii, 6
Orsini, Luigi, 452 n.
    Pia dei Tolomei, 452 n.
Otello; *see* (1) Rossini, (2) Verdi
Otto mesi in due ore; *see* Donizetti
Ottojano, Prince (*of Naples*), 166
Ovid (Publius Ovidius Naso), 458
    Metamorphoses, 458

Pace, Giovanni, 61, 72, 94, 105
Pacini, Antonio, 160, 182
Pacini, Giovanni, 41, 49, 52, 53, 54,
    71, 72, 76, 87, 94 n., 99, 109, 133,
    150, 154, 195, 429, 446 n., 449 n.,
    456, 460 n.; quoted: 87, 456;
    Adelaide e Comingio, 429; *Barone di
    Dolsheim, Il*, 76; *Cesare in Egitto*
    53 *and* n.; *Falegname di Livonia, Il*,
    41, 460 n.; *Niobe*, 94 n.
Pacini, Luigi, 99
Padua, 41, 261, 277
Paër, Ferdinando, 32, 398 n., 511
    Agnese di Fitz-Henry, 32
    Maître de chapelle, Le, 398 n.
Paganini, Angelo, 38
Paganini, Giuditta, 38–9

Palazzo della Misericordia, 13
Palazzolo, 517
Palermo, 47, 72, **75–82**, 83, 84, 96, 110,
    122, 171 n., 191, 199, 410, 421,
    445, 465
Palermo Conservatory, 80
Palezzesi, Matilde, 196
Pallade, 327 n.
Pangrati, Don Pietro, 504
Paria, Il; *see* Donizetti
Paris, 11, 27, 36 n., 47, 102 n., 105, 118,
    121, 122, 127 n., 139, 140, 142,
    145, 149, 150, 152, **154–61**, 170,
    185, 191, 214–15, 216–18, 219,
    220, **222–5**, 229, 230, 232, 233,
    235, 241, 247, 251, 252, 253, 256,
    258, 260, 263, 264, 266, 270, 275,
    277, 282, 283, 287, 290, 291, 292,
    293, 294, 298, 300, 301, 302, 303,
    305, 307, 310, 315, 318, 319, 322,
    323, 324, 325, 326, 328, 333, 334,
    335, 337, 339, 357, 384 n., 392 n.,
    416, 431, 432, 433, 441, 446, 454,
    455, 456, 484, 490, 492, 494, 496,
    498
Paris Conservatory, 9, 101 n., 160, 302,
    324
Paris Conservatory Library, 28, 245,
    399 n., 420, 428, 434 n., 440,
    459 n., 501, 512, 519
Parisina; *see* Byron
Parisina; *see* Donizetti
Parma, 102 n., 327, 423, 496 n.
Pascià di Scutari, Il; *see* Donizetti
Pasini, Ignazio, 83, 175, 182, 183
Passaro, A. 236
Pasta, Giuditta Negri, 101, 113, 115,
    116, 117, 118, 119, 125, 135, 164,
    376, 415, 420, 438, 449, 516
Paterni, Giovanni, 43–4, 44 n., **52**, 66,
    67, 68, 128
Patria, 219
Patriossi (or Patriozzi), Domenico,
    69, 70
Patti, Adelina, 78, 154, 236
Patti, Salvatore, 78, 81, 153
Paul, la, 99
Pavesi, Stefano, 19, 271, 455, 496;
    Aristodemo, 20; *Ser Marc'Antonio*,
    271, 272, 455, 496
Pavia, 136 n.
Pazzi per progetto, I; *see* Donizetti
Pearse, Mme, 441 n.
Pedrazzi, Francesco, 125, 144, 152, 182,
    195, 420
Pedroni, Giovanni, 305

Pedrotti, Carlo, 493 n.
Pellegrini, Felice, 72
Pellico, Silvio, 27
Pepoli, Count Carlo, 154
Perez de Hita, Ginés, 465; *Guerras civiles de Grenada*, 465
Pergolesi, Giovanni Battista, 389; *Serva padrona, La*, 389
Perruqier de la régence, Le; see Thomas
Persiani, Fanny Tacchinardi-, **147**, 148, 170, 171, 186, 187, 188, 194, 215, 217, 227, 258, 265, 278, 376 and n.
Persiani, Giuseppe, 147, 169, 188
Danao, re d'Argo, 188
Ines de Castro, 169
Persico, Leopoldo, 231
Persico, Tommaso, 197, 199, 204, 207, 230, 231, 232, 233, 236, 239, 248, 261, 262, 263, 269, 279, 280, 290, 292, 300–1, 501
Perucchini, Giovanni Battista, 117, 118
Petrali, 35
Petrarch, 207
Petrazzoli, Francesco, 144
Pezzi, Francesco, 65, 97; quoted: 65, 97
Pezzoli family (*of Bergamo*), 347
Pezzoli-Grattaroli, Marianna (*of Bergamo*), 43, 229, 510, 511, 512
Philtre, Le; see Auber
Philtre, Le; see Scribe
Pia de(i) Tolomei; see (1) Donizetti, (2) Orsini
Piatti, Alfredo, 254
Piatti, Monsignor, 59
Piccinni, Nicola, 12, 14
Piccioli virtuosi ambulanti, I; see Donizetti
Piccolo compositore di musica, Il; see Mayr
Pigmalione, Il; see Donizetti
Pillet, Léon, 239, 241, 253, 270, 276, 432
Pilotti, Giuseppe, 463 n.
Pio Istituto Musicale (*Bergamo*), 12
Pio Luogo della Misericordia Maggiore (*Bergamo*), 7
Piracy of author's rights, 50, 136, 139, 167, 409
Pirata, Il; see Bellini
Piroli, Giuseppe, 434 n.
Pisaroni-Carrara, (Benedetta) Rosamunda, 69, **70**, 71
Pistoni, Aniceto, 85
Più bel giorno della Westfalia, Il; see Sografi

Pius VII, 55, 67
Pius VIII, 110
Pixérécourt, René Charles Guilbert de, 65, 462, 467
Cisterne, La, 65, 462
Fille de l'exilé ou Huit mois en deux heures, 467
Pizzochero, Carlo, 41 n., 64
Plainati, 233
Plantade, Charles Henri, 223
Mari de circonstance, Le, 223
Plouvier, Edouard, 514, 517
Pochini, Ranieri, 144
Podestà di Colognole, Il; see Buini
Poe, Edgar Allan, 446
Poggi, Antonio, 140, 175, 178, 187, 188, 194, 195, 257 n.
Poggioli, Carlo, 64
Poliuto; see Donizetti
Polyeucte; see Corneille
Ponchielli, Amilcare, 433, 435
Pons, Lily, 376 n.
Pontiroli, Giuseppe, **18**, 43, 149, 184
Portici, 76
Porto, Carlo Ortolini, 138, 148, 152, 170, 171
Portoferraio, 91
Postillon du Longjumeau, Le; see Adam
Pourcelot, Antonio (Antoine), 316, 324, 328, 334, 335, 339, 341, 342, 343
Prelli, 304
Presse, La, 237, 245
Prévot, Ferdinand, 286
Previdali, Luigi, 174
Prima donna, La; see Salvi, Matteo
Prò, Stanislao, 87
Profumo, Antonio, 466 n.
Public; *see* Audience
Puca, Dr Annibale, 350 n.
Puccini, Giacomo, 6, 46
Madama Butterfly, 6
Turandot, 6
Puccita, Vincenzo, 54
Festa in villaggio, La, 54
Puglieschi, Giovanni, 71
Pugni, Cesare, 125, 420
Pullé, Count Giulio, 502
Puoti, F., 517
Puritani, I; see Bellini
Puteaux, 171
Puzzi-Toso, Giacinta, 178

Quarenghi, Antonio, 32, 95, 180

Rachel (Elisabeth Félix), 330
Raineri-Marini, Antonietta, 122
Rambaldi, Gaetano, 53
Ravizza-Boti, Countess, 518
Recanati, 452
Redaelli, 515
Redoutensaal (Vienna), 262, 266
Reicha, Anton, 13
Reichardt, Johann Friedrich, 487n.
Reina, Domenico, 153, 179
Reine de Chypre, La; see Vernoy de
    Saint-Georges
Reine de Golconde, La; see Boufflers
Rendu, 339, 340, 341
Revalden, 125, 192
Reviews; see Criticism
Ricci, 105
Ricci, Corrado; quoted: 26
Ricci, Edvige, 96, 106, 125
Ricci, Federico, 445
    Corrado d'Altamura, 455
Ricci, Luigi, 189, 449n.
    Nuovo Figaro, Il, 189
Ricciardi, Achille, 230
Richomme, Auguste, 517
Ricord, Philippe, 291, 292, 308, 309,
    310, 320
Ricordi, Casa, xii, 24, 25, 189, 305,
    349, 414n., 417, 417n., 421, 433,
    434, 439, 441n., 455
Ricordi, Giovanni, 24, 133, 136, 139,
    152, 160, 162, 163, 170, 172, 173,
    175, 179, 181, 188, 192, 210, 240
    and n., 265, 273, 276, 283, 334,
    439, 441n.
Rienzi, the Last of the Tribunes; see
    Lytton
Rietz, Julius, 487n.
Rigoletto; see Verdi
Rillosi, 344
Rinaldi, Antonio, 140
Rinaldo di Capua, 461
Ringhieri, Padre Francesco, 473;
    Diluvio universale, Il, 473
Rio de Janeiro, 138
Riofreddo, 56
Riquier, 233
Rita ou le mari battu; see Donizetti
Ritratto parlante, Il; see Donizetti
Rivista teatrale, 452n.
Rizzi, Giovanni, 182
Robert, Édouard, 140, 160, 217, 223
Robert le diable; see Meyerbeer
Roberto Devereux; see Donizetti
Roche, 318
Rolla, Monsignor, 96

Romanelli, Luigi 461n.
Romani, Emilia Branca, 116–17, 504,
    515
Romani, Felice, 41, 62, 63-4, 98, 113,
    115, 117, 121, 125, 126-7, 128,
    131, 134, 135, 137, 138 and n.,
    140, 142-4, 147, 152, 154, 155,
    164-6, 167, 247, 328, 446, 447,
    449, 452-3, 456, 458n., 460n.,
    461, 470, 474, 475, 477, 478, 480,
    481, 482, 489n., 493, 501, 502,
    515, 516, 517; quoted: 449
    Califfo e la schiava, Il, 460n.
    Conte d'Essex, Il, 447, 489n.
    Illinesi, Gli, 164-5
    Saffo, 142-3
Romano, 9n., 342
Romanticism, 51, 85, 165, 171, 224,
    375, 392, 409-12, 444, 476-7
Romanziera e l'uomo nero, La; see Doni-
    zetti
Ronconi, Giorgio, 135-6, 139, 140-1,
    189, 190, 194, 195, 213, 257, 258,
    278, 307, 364n., 421, 423, 440
Ronzi de Begnis, Giuseppina, 32, 125,
    128, 129, 130, 132 and n., 150,
    151, 152, 153, 164, 195, 210,
    490n.
Rome, 43, 47, 51-7, 59, 60, 62, 66, 67,
    68-71, 75, 85-8, 89, 97, 98, 102,
    103, 108, 110, 114, 119-20, 123,
    125, 128, 131, 133-6, 137, 139-
    41, 145, 148, 153, 183, 203-6,
    211, 212, 240, 241, 247, 249, 251,
    252, 289, 291, 301, 303, 307, 313,
    314, 324, 410, 434, 434n., 448,
    449, 460, 463, 467, 479, 480, 491,
    493
Roqueplan, Louis Victor Nestor, 432
Rosa, Antonio de, 78
Rosini, Giovanni, 480
    Tasso, 480
Rosmunda d'Inghilterra; see Donizetti
Rossi, Gaetano (bass), 257
Rossi, Gaetano (librettist), 34n., 255-6,
    259, 429n., 453-4, 494, 495
Rossi, Giuseppe, 304
Rossi, Teofilo, 170 210, 281, 427n.
Rossini, Gioacchino Antonio, 8, 9, 11,
    12, 13, 25-6, 36n., 51, 52, 54,
    57-9, 70n., 72, 76, 79, 85, 94n.,
    96, 98, 99, 100, 102 and n., 118,
    134, 147n., 149, 150, 154-5, 156,
    157-8, 159, 160, 185, 186, 190,
    196, 218, 221, 223, 225, 231, 236,
    256, 260-2, 263, 266, 273, 274,

275, 354, 355–6, 358, 358n., 359, 360, 366, 373, 376, 384n., 386, 389, 391, 392, 396, 401, 402, **403-4**, 405, 407, 411 *and* n., 436, 443, 460n.; quoted: 25, 94n., 102n.

Adina, 460n.; *Assedio di Corinto, L'*, 102, 181, 404, 519; *Aureliano in Palmira*, 77; *Barbiere di Siviglia, Il*, 52, 77, 100, 175, 273, 278, 360, 396, 405, 514; *Cenerentola, La*, 32, 52, 132, 278, 402, 449; *Comte Ory, Le*, 126n.; *Donna del Lago, La*, 70n.; *Elisabetta, regina d'Inghilterra*, 57; *Gazza ladra, La*, 40, 132; *Guillaume Tell*, 126n., 214, 222, 274, 384n.; *Inganno felice, L'*, 79; *Italiana in Algeri, L'*, 36, 76; *Maometto II*, 102n.; *Matilde di Shabran*, 36n., 52; *Moïse (Mosè)*, 126n., 250, 251; *Otello*, 100, 101, 129, 132, 175, 179, 400 *and* n., 411, 440; *Scala di seta, La*, 356; *Semiramide*, 36n., 256, 358n., 373, 405n., 454; *Siège de Corinth, Le; see Assedio di Corinto, L'; Signor Bruschino, Il*, 356; *Soirées musicales*, 190; *Stabat Mater* (1842), **260-2**, 266; *Tancredi*, 8, 81, 256, 402, 444, 454; *Zelmira*, 57

Rossini, Isabella Colbran, 57, 58, 60, 354

Rossini, Olympe Pelissier, 157 *and* n.

Rostand, Louis Léon, 294, 337

Rota-Basoni, Giovannina; *see* Scotti, Maria Giovanna Ginevra, Baroness

Rota-Basoni, Baroness Rosa (*of Bergamo*), 153, 184, 194, 268, 304, 315, 318–19, 323, 324, 334, 340, 341, 343

Rothschild's Bank (*of London*), 248

Rovere, Agostino, 122, 264, 266

Royer, Alphonse, 141n., 230, 242n., 243, 244, 293, 324, 423, 424, 429n., 432, **454-5**, 458, 492; quoted: 243

Rubini, Adelaide Comelli; *see* Comelli-Rubini, Adelaide

Rubini, Giovanni Battista, **9**, 10, 61, 73n., 84, 96, 101n., 105, 106, 115, 116, 118, 119, **121-2**, 128, 139, 154, 156, 158, 159, 191, 215, 217, 223, 226, 331, 342, 362n., 376

Ruffini, Agostino, 28n., 455

Ruffini, Giovanni, 28n., 271, 286, 319, 448, **455**, 496, 502

Ruffini, Iacopo, 455

Ruolz, Viscount Henri Catherine Camille de, 217, **218**; *Lara*, 218

Rusponi, Countess Virginia, 108

Ruy Blas; see Donizetti

Ruy Blas; see Hugo

Sacchero, Giacomo, 270, **455**, 495

Sacchi, Marietta, 138

Sacco, Raffaele, 514

Saffo; see Mayr

Saffo; see Romani

Saint-Amans; *see* Favart

Saint-Cloud, 334

Saint-Georges; *see* Vernoy de Saint-Georges, Jules Henri

Saint-Germain, Fair of, 223

St James of Compostella, 429

Saint-Just; *see* Godard d'Aucour de Saint-Just

Saint-Laurent, Fair of, 223

St Mark's (*Venice*); *see* San Marco (*Venice*)

St Peter's (Rome), *see* San Pietro (*Rome*)

St Petersburg, 11, 193n.

Salari, Francesco, 14, 18n.

Salatino, Pietro, 131, **456**, 479, 483

Salerno, Leopoldo, Prince of, 59, 145, 149, 171, 503

Salle des Nouveautés (*Paris*), 223; *see* also Opéra-Comique

Salle Favart (*Paris*), 223, 242n.; *see* also Théâtre-Italien

Salle Herz (*Paris*), 229

Salle Ventadour (*Paris*), 223, 260; *see* also Théâtre-Italien

Salvatori, Celestino, 94, 182, 194, 421n.

Salvetti Manzi, 280

Salvi, Lorenzo, 111, 122, 135, 191, 236, 250

Salvi, Matteo, **266-7**, 277, 281, 282, 357n., **434**, **435**, 436, 502; *Burgravi, I*, 267n.; *Caterina Howard*, 267n.; *Lara*, 267n.; *Prima donna, La*, 267n.

Samayloff, Countess Giulia, 49, 133, 195

Sampieri, Marchese Francesco, 24

San Carlo; *see* Teatro San Carlo (*Naples*)

San Ferdinando (*Naples*), 197

San Gennaro, Novena of, 59, 163

San Giacomo (*Bologna*), 29

San Giacomo (*Rome*), 206
San Marco (*Venice*), 39n.
San Petronio (*Bologna*), 25, 26, 262, 263
San Pietro (*Rome*), 204
San Silvestro, Order of (*Pontifical*), 258
San Vigilio (*Bergamo*), 4
Sancia di Castiglia; see Donizetti
Sandrini, Giuseppe (?), (*of Milan*), 259
Santa Grata inter Vites (*Bergamo*), 3
Santa Maria delle Grazie (*Naples*), 199
Santa Maria in Via (*Rome*), 103
Santa Maria Maggiore (*Bergamo*), 7, 8, 10, 11, 14, 16, 18n., 21, 33n., 347, 433
Santi-Pesenti (Santi-Donizetti), Elisabetta, 349–50, 436n.
Santini, 159
Santolini, Diomilla, 128, 132
Santorelli, Antonio (*of Naples*), 166, 170
Sappho, 142
Saragossa, Siege of, 91
Sarmiento, Salvatore (*cantata*, 1838), 432
  Alfonso d'Aragona, 432
Sarti, Giuseppe, 8; *Medonte, re di Epiro*, 8
Sbigoli, Americo, **53-4**, 417
Scala di seta, La; see Rossini
Scalese, Raffaele, 88, 236
Scandrini, 331
Scatizzi, Stefano, 73n., 464
  Emilia di Liverpool, 73n., 464
Schaum, Johann Otto Heinrich, 487n.
Schayet, 330, 331
Schiller, Friedrich, 151, 372, 515
  Maria Stuart, 445, 483
Schippers, Thomas, xii, **435-6**
Schlesinger, Léon, 224
Schmidt, Giovanni Federico, 67, 75, 84, **456**, 457, 466
Schneider, Amalie, 27
Schober (Schoberlechner), Giovanni, 164
Schoberlechner, Sofia (del'Oca), 176, 178, 195
Schoenerberger's, 399n., 400n., 436, 437
Schubert, Franz, 31, 267n.
Schulz, Johann Abraham Peter, 470n.
Schütz-Oldosi, Amalia, 190
Scott, Sir Walter, 108, 167, 444, 446, 485
  Bride of Lammermoor, The, 167, 485
  Kenilworth, 472
  Ivanhoe, 452n.

Scotti, Maria Giovanni Ginevra Rota-Basoni, Baroness (*of Bergamo*), 184, 318, **323-4**, 340, 341, 342, **343**; quoted: 343–5
Scribe, Eugène, 126, 190, 215, 217, 227, 232, **237**, 253, 283–4, 285, 425n., 426, 427, 433, 433n., 453, **456-7**, 472, 478, 487, 490, 491, 498, 502; *Chalet, Le*, 190, 487; *Jeanne la folle*, 502; *Leicester ou le château de Kenilworth*, 108, 472; *Philtre, Le*, 126, 478
Scudellari-Cosselli, 87
Scuola de' maritati, La; see Martin y Soler
Sebastião I, King of Portugal, 282
Secci-Corsi, Irene, 191
Sechter, Simon, 267
Sedaine, Jean Michel, 470n.
Semiramide; see Rossini
Ser Marc'Antonio; see Pavesi
Serda, 237
Seriate, 22, 134
Serradifalco, Domenico La Faso Pietrasanta, Duke di, 76, 77, 78
Serva padrona, La; see Pergolesi
Sestini, Bartolomeo, 188, 488
Severini, Carlo, 140, 160, 185, 223
Sevigny, Signora M. P. de, 512
Sganarelle; see Molière
Sganarello; see Donizetti
Shakespeare, William, 411
Siège de Calais, Le; see Belloy
Siena, 138, 420
Signor Bruschino, Il; see Rossini
Silvestri, Alessandro, 434
Simionato, Giulietta, 247
Sinigaglia, 195, 421
Sisara; see Mayr
Società d'Industria e Belle Arti (*Naples*), 162, 163–4, 167, 168, 169, 170, 184
Sografi, Antonio Simone, 86, 95, 467, 468; *Convenienze teatrali, Le*, 468; *Inconvenienze teatrali, Le*, 468; *Olivo e Pasquale*, 467; *Più bel giorno delal Westfalia, Il*, 467n.
Soirées musicales; see Rossini
Sonnambula, La; see Bellini
Sonnette de nuit, La; see Brunswick
Sontag, Henriette, 236
Spada, Filippo, 110
Spadaro del Bosch, Count Luigi (*of Messina*), 166, 170, 192, 198, 200, 456n.

Spadaro del Bosch, Countess Teresina, 515, 516
Spaur und Thurn und Taxis, Count Karl, 318–19, 327
Spech, Adelina, 140
Spech, Giuseppe, 35
Spettacolo, 35 n., 392 n.
Spiaggi, Domenico, 96, 144, 153
Spielberg, 27
Spoleto, 41, 435
Spontini, Gasparo, 79, 81
  Vestale, La, 80, 81
Stabat Mater; see Rossini
Stendhal (Marie Henri Beyle), 11, 71, 132 n., 392 n.; quoted: 11, 71, 132 n.
Sterlich, Marchesa Adelaide de, 512
Sterlich, Marchesina Caterina de, 514, 515, 516
Sterlich, Marchesina Giovanna de, 513
Stignani, Ebe, 247
Stockholm, 470 n.
Stöckl-Heinefetter, Maria, 127 n.
Stolz (Stoltz), Rosine, 239, 241, 243, 245, 246, 276, 285 n., 288, 428 n., 433 n.
Straniera, La; see Bellini
Strassburg, 275
Strauss, Richard
  Der Rosenkavalier, 394 n.
Strepponi, Feliciano, 164 *and* n., 165, 502
  Illinesi, Gli, 165
Strepponi, Giuseppina; see Verdi, Giuseppina Strepponi
Studi Donizettiani I (1962), 147 n., 169, 195 n., 421 n., 502
Stürmer, Count von, 337
Sutherland, Joan, 75, 148 n., 437 n.

Taafe, Countess Amélie, 519
Tacchinardi, Nicola, 147
Tacchinardi-Persiani, Fanny; see Persiani, Fanny Tacchinardi
Tacci, Nicola, 71, 78
Tadolini, Eugenia, 97, 136, 182, 212, 239, 241, 258, 264, **265**, 267 n., 278, 279, 376 n., 422, 423, 427 n., 439
Talma, François Joseph, 142
Tamagno, Francesco, 239, 427
Tamberlik, Enrico, 239, 427
Tamburini, Antonio, 64, 71, 76, 77, 78, 81, 83, 99, 100, 101, 102, 105, 112, 122, 125, 136, 154, 159, 191, 215,

217, 223, 226, 227, 260, 265, 271, 272, 469, 519
Tamburini, Maria Gioia, 64, 76, 81, 122
Tancredi; see Rossini
Tarantini, Leopoldo, 439, 513, 517
Tartini, Giuseppe, 14
Tasso; see (1) Goethe, (2) Rossini
Tasso, Torquato, 139, 517
  Gersualemme liberata (1576–93), 450
Tati, Federico, 105
Tavecchi, Antonio, 18, 19, 304
Teatro alla novità, 28
Teatro alla Scala (*Milan*), 36 n., 40, 41, 52, 59 n., 62, 63, 65 n., 66, 72, 87, 88, 94, 95, 96, 97, 118, 122, 124, 125, 127 n., 134, 136, **141-4**, 145, 146, 150, 152, 165 n., 175, 175 n., 177, 182, 195, 236, 240, 240 n., 247, 255, 256, 258, 262, 265, 267 n., 271, 357, 401 n., 407 n., 420, 421, 438, 444 n., 446, 458 n., 460 n., 461 n., 462, 475, 477, 481, 483, 494, 502, 509
Teatro Apollo (*Rome*), 51, 52, 53, 54, 136, 137, 240, 247, 250, 331, 349, 434, 491, 493
Teatro Apollo (*Venice*), 194, 488
Teatro Argentina (*Rome*), 43, 44, 45, 52, 53, 70, 460
Teatro Argentino (*Buenos Aires*), 239 n.
Teatro Canobbiana (*Milan*), 95, 126, 127, 258, 399 n., 420, 478
Teatro Carcano (*Milan*), 105, 112, 115, 117, 118, 157, 331, 474
Teatro Carlo Felice (*Genoa*), **98-9**, 470, 504
Teatro Carolino (*Palermo*), **75-82**, 83, 122, 171 n., 191, 465
Teatro dei Rinnuovati (*Siena*), 420
Teatro del Fondo (*Naples*), 61, 93, 95, 105, 122, 163, 184, 190, 209, 461, 465 n., 466, 470, 471, 473, 476
Teatro della Pergola (*Florence*), 128, 147, 480, 482
Teatro di Società (*Bergamo*), 8, 21, 32, 34, 37
Teatro Donizetti (*formerly Teatro Riccardi*) (*Bergamo*), 8, 9, 23, 28, 38, 91, 240, 458, 519
Teatro Ducale (*Mantua*), 40
Teatro Fiorentino (*Naples*), 73 n., 168
Teatro Italiano; see Théâtre-Italien
Teatro la Fenice (*Venice*), 34 n., 125, 134, 173, 181–2, 186, 187, 190, **193**, 194, 196, 213, 420, 454, 489

Teatro Novissimo (*Padua*), 485 n.
Teatro Nuovo (*Naples*), 60, 66, 72, 73, 74, 74n., 87, 88, 89, 93, 95, 184, 189, 190, 191, 236, 418, 419, 448, 461, 463, 464, 467, 468, 486, 487
Teatro Nuovo-Nazionale (*Naples*), 75
Teatro Regio (*Parma*), 423
Teatro Regio (*Turin*), 164n.
Teatro Riccardi (*Bergamo*); see Teatro Donizetti
Teatro San Benedetto (*Venice*), 34n.
Teatro San Carlino (*Naples*), 169
Teatro San Carlo (*Naples*), 52, 66, 67, 71, 74, 76, 79, 81, 84, 85n., 87, 96, 106, 107, 108, 121, 122, 128, 132, 134, 148, **162-3**, 165, 167, 169, 170, 184, 190, 192, 195, 196, 210, 213, 215, 239, 269, 384n., 422, 432, 437, 446, 462, 465, 466, 469, 471, 472, 473, 474, 476, 477, 479, 483, 485, 487, 488, 490, 495
Teatro San Luca (*Venice*), 34, 35, 36, 37, 40, 459
Teatro San Mosè (*Venice*), 40, 41
Teatro San Samuele (*Venice*), 41, 460
Teatro Sociale (*Bergamo*); see Teatro di Società
Teatro Tordinona (*Rome*); see Teatro Apollo (*Rome*)
Teatro Valle (*Rome*), 43, 52, 52n., 66, 71, 73, 78, 86, 87, 88, 110, 134, 135, 139, 140, 250, 448, 463, 467, 479, 480
Teatro Victoria (*Buenos Aires*), 239n.
Tebaldini, Giovanni, 39n.
Tebaldo ed Isolina; see Morlacchi
Templario, Il; see Nicolai
Tenaglia, Raffaele, xii, 41n., 417n., 441n.
Terracina, 120, 123-4, 133
Terzi, Marchese Giuseppe (*of Bergamo*), 507, 509
Terziani, Pietro, 66
Tetrazzini, Luisa, 438n.
Théâtre de la Bourse; see Opéra-Comique
Théâtre-Italian (des Italiens) (*Paris*), 9, 36n., 94n., 105, 121, 127n., 128, 140, 150, 154, 156, 159, 160, 191, 214, 215, 217, 218, **222-3**, 224, 226, 227, 228, 229, 270, 271, 272, 283, 284, 287, 299, 357, 455, 484, 485n., 496, 502
Théâtre de la Renaissance (*Paris*), 224, 230, 231, 232, 235, 240,

242n., 414, 424, 425n., 428n., 432, 454, 501
Théâtre de l'Odéon (*Paris*), 454
Théâtre Français (Comédie-Française), 330
Théâtre-Lyrique (*Paris*), 419
Thiers, Louis Adolphe, 185
Thillon (Sophie) Anna (Hunt), 148, 230, 242n., 425n., 428n.
Thomas, Ambroise, 223; *Double échelle, La*, 223; *Perruquier de la régence, Le*, 223
Thourat, Order of (*Turkish*), 252
Tiby, Ottavio, 76n., 82, 171n., 465n.
Tiepolo, Giovanni Battista, 7
Tironi, Beppina, 90, 146 *and* n., 184, 186
Tironi, Giovanni Battista, 5, 186
Tironi, Maria Antonia Donizetti, 5, 90, 146n., 186
Tivoli, 204
Toldi, Adelaide, 128, 191
Tomaselli, Carlotta, 78
Torella, Giuseppe Caraccioli, Prince of (*of Naples*), 170
Torquato Tasso; see Donizetti
Torre di Gombito (*Bergamo*), 7
Torresani Lanzfeld, Carlo Giusto de, Baron di Camponero, 63
Torri, Alberto, 53
Tortoli, Francesco, 73
Toscanini, Arturo, 66n.
Toscanini, Walter, xii, 242n., 427n.
Tosi, Adelaide, 75, 96, 99-100, 102, 106, 107, 108, 420, 519
Totila; see Legrenzi
Toto; see Vaselli, Antonio
Tottola, Andrea Leone, 48, 59n., **60**, 67, 68, 85, 108, 112, 418, 450, **457-8**, 461, 462, 463, 466 *and* n., 472, 474
Toulon, 247
Traviata, La; see Verdi
Treccani degli Alfieri, Count Luigi (*of Milan*), xii, 242, 427n.
Trélat, Ulisse, 319
Trento, Vittorio, 73n., 464n.
Emilia di Liverpaut, 73n.
Trieste, 144, 327, 502
Trionfo della musica, Il, 77, 78n.
Troin, Matthieu Barthélmy, 486
Troupenas, 160
Tucci, Nicola, 192
Turandot; see Puccini
Turin, 11, 119, 146, 147, 164, 165n., 166, 171, 328, 502
Turina, Giuditta Cantù, 49, 117, 135

Ugo, conte di Parigi; see Donizetti
Ungher (Unger), Carolina, **94**, 138,
    150, 165, 182, 183, 212, 213, 415
Unione filarmonico (*Bergamo*), 82
Uttini, Francesco Antonio, 470n.

Vaccai, Nicola, 34n., 41, 195, 411, 452
    Giulietta e Romeo, 175, 411
    Lupo d'Ostenda, Il, 34n.
Vaëz (van Nieuwenhuysen), Gustave,
    230, 242n., 243, 245n., 254, 324,
    424, 429n., 432, 454, 458, 492,
    494, 516
Valadier, Giuseppe, 52
Vaque Moulin, Elisa, 99
Valentini, Carlo, 51
Valentini, Filippo, 135, 250
Valle di Casanova, Alfonso della (*of
    Naples*), 508
Valtesse (*Bergamasc cemetery*), 346
Varesi (Varese), Felice, 264, 290,
    364n.
Vaschetti, Giuseppe, 144
Vasselli, Antonio 'Toto', 56, 59, 68,
    80, 82, 86, 103, 108, 139, 162, 195,
    199, **200-10**, **211-12**, 213, 217,
    218, 219, 250, 251, 252, 255, 256,
    257, 258, 259, 260, 263, 265, 268,
    269, 271, 273, 275, 278, **280-1**,
    284, 290, 291, 292, 294, 300, 302,
    304, 305, 306, 313, 314, 324, 331,
    332, 339, **349**, 432, 434, 438n.,
    465n.; quoted: 200-1, 201-2, 203,
    306-7, 313, 314
Vasselli, Francesco, 56
Vasselli, Gaetano, 56, 200
Vasselli, Irene, 200
Vasselli, Luigi, **55-6**, 87, 88, 103, 104,
    125
    *Formulario di tutti gli procedura analoga-
    mente al Codice pubblicando con Notu
    proprio del 22 novembre 1817 (codex,
    1818)*, 55n.
Vasselli, Rosa Costanti, 56, 199, 200,
    201, 203, 515
Vasselli, Serafina, 56
Vasselli, Virginia; *see* Donizetti, Vir-
    ginia Vasselli
Vasselli, Virginia (Toto's daughter), 281
Vatel, 297
Vendemmiatore, 327
Venice, 6, 10, 14, 18n., **34-7**, 39 and
    39n., 41, 44, 47, 52, 137, 140,
    165n., 173-4, 175, 179, **180-2**,
    187, 189, **194**, 195, 196, 206, 208,

209, 210, 211, **212-13**, 410, 438,
    458n., 459, 460, 482n., 486, 488,
    489
Venice Conservatory, 25
Venier, Annetta Fischer, 74, 83, 88,
    110
Venier, Marco, 60, 68, **74**n.
Venturali, Lucrezia; *see* Mayr, Luc-
    rezia Venturali
Venturali, Signora, 105
Vêpres siciliennes, Les; see Verdi
Verdi, Giuseppe, 28n., 46, 50, 120,
    125, 236, 258, 259n., 260n., 261,
    276, 334, 345, 349, 354, 356,
    364n., 369, 385, 389, 401, 402,
    407-9, 413, 434, 444, 446n.,
    447; quoted: 334
    Aïda, 356
    Alzira, 446n.
    Ballo in maschera, Un, 47, 343, 384,
        434n.
    Battaglia di Legnano, La, 446n.
    Ernani, 276, 354
    Falstaff, 273, 356, 391, 401
    Forza del destino, La, 356
    Giorno di regno, Un (Il finto Stanislao),
        236, 401n., 407n.
    Giovanna d'Arco, 257n.
    *Jérusalem; see Lombardi alla prima
        crociata, I*
    Lombardi alla prima crociata, I, 257n.,
        334 and n.
    Luisa Miller, 356, 446n.
    Manzoni Requiem (1874), 371
    Nabucco (Nabucodonosor), 258, 260n.,
        261, 276, 402
    Oberto, conte di S. Bonifacio, 407n.
    Otello, 356
    Rigoletto, 47, 349, 356, 408
    Simon Boccanegra, 447
    Traviata La, 394n., 407
    Trovatore, Il, 169, 356, 383, 385,
        408, 446n.
    Vêpres siciliennes, Les, 356, 434
Verdi, Giuseppina Strepponi, 164n.,
    196, **250**, 251, 439n., 502
Verger, Giovanni Battista, 41, 41n.,
    87, 99, 100, 101
Verni, Andrea, 35, 41n.
Vernoy de Saint-Georges, Jules Henri,
    236, 270, **456**, 492, 495, 502
    Reine de Chypre, La, 270, 495
Verona, 33, 41 and n., 255, 417, 453,
    502
Verzino, Edoardo Clemente, 88, 93,
    141n., 175n., 293, 323

Vestale, La; see Spontini
Vestris Company, 479n.
Viaggio a Vienna, Un; see Merelli
Vial, Antonietta, 181, 182, 183
Viardot, Pauline Garcia, 277–8
Vicenza, 261, 262
Victor Emmanuel I, King of Sardinia, 119
Victoria, Queen of England, 253
Vienna, 9, 36n., 57, 72, 73–4, 94n., 99, 127n., 145, 252, 259, 260, 261, 262, **263**, 264, 266, 268, 270, 271, 272, 275, 276, 279, 280, 281, 289, 290, 293, 299, 300, 303, 304, 305, 310, 311, 325, 349, 357, 423, 441, 495, 497
Viganoni, Domenico, **9**, 32
Vincenti, de, 101
Visanetti, Giuseppe, 144
Visconte di Modrone, Duke Carlo, 141–4, 146–7, 150, 152–3, 167, 175, 177
Vitali, G. 515
Viviani, Vittorio, 168n.
Voisin, Félix, 317
Voto di Jefte, Il; see Mayr

Wagner, Richard, 99n., 209, 224, 433n.; *Fliegende Holländer, Der,* 433n.; *Rienzi,* 224
Walker, Frank, 35n., 259n.
Walsh, Madame (*of Paris*), 249

Warot, 255
Wartel, Pierre François, 237, 245
Weber, Carl Maria von, 99n.
Weinstock, Herbert, xii, 65n., 420n., 499
Westminster Abbey, 175
Winter, Berardo Calvari, 76, 78, 81, 83–4, 94, 96, 107, 108, 111, 112, 136
Winter, Peter von, 172, 487n.

Zaira; see Bellini
Zampi, Giovanni Battista, 103
Zanardini, Angelo, 434, 491
Zancla, Paolo, 34, 35, 36, 37, 40
Zanica, Domenico Iraina, 3
Zappucci, Teresa, 170
Zar und Zimmermann; see Lortzing
Zavadini, Guido, xi, 36n., 38, 42, 68n., 112, 114, 146n., 165, 169, 311, 347, 357n., 371, 417n., 459n., 499, 505n., 509, 511n.
Zelger, 230
Zelmira; see Rossini
Zendrini, Bernardino, 11n.
Zilioli, Domenico, 73
Zineroni, Alessandro, 510
Zingara, La; see Donizetti
Zingarelli, Nicola, 52, 149, **196**, 197, 507; *Giulietta e Romeo,* 411
Zingaro, Le, 242n.; *Zoraide di Granata; see* Donizetti